11th Edition

Real Estate Finance

By J. Keith Baker

Real Estate Finance, Eleventh Edition

J. Keith Baker

Executive Editor: Sara Glassmeyer

Project Manager: Elizabeth King, KnowledgeWorks Global Ltd.

Cover Designer: Brian Brogaard

Cover Image: choness/iStock/Getty Images

Chapter Opener Image Credits:
© DoveLee

Copyright © 2021 Mbition LLC

ALL RIGHTS RESERVED. No part of this work covered by the copyright herein may be reproduced, transmitted, stored, or used in any form or by any means graphic, electronic, or mechanical, including but not limited to photocopying, recording, scanning, digitizing, taping, web distribution, information networks, or information storage and retrieval systems, except as permitted under Section 107 or 108 of the 1976 United States Copyright Act, without the prior written permission

> For product information and technology assistance, contact us at
> **Mbition Customer Support, 800-532-7649.**
>
> For permission to use material from this text or product, please contact **publishingsupport@mbitiontolearn.com.**

Library of Congress Control Number: 2018965761
ISBN-13: 978-1-62980-230-5
ISBN-10: 1-62980-230-1

Mbition, LLC
18500 W Corporate Drive, Suite 250
Brookfield, WI 53045
USA

Visit us at **www.mbitiontolearn.com**

Printed in the United States of America
1 2 3 4 5 23 22 21 20 19

BRIEF CONTENTS

	Preface	xxi
1	The Nature and Cycle of Real Estate Finance	1
2	Money and the Monetary System	43
3	Additional Government Influence	89
4	The Secondary Mortgage Market	159
5	Sources of Funds	195
6	Instruments of Real Estate Finance	237
7	Loan Types, Terms, and Issues	275
8	Government Loans	339
9	Lender Loan Processes	393
10	Defaults and Foreclosures	469
11	Property Analysis	493
12	Commercial Loans: Construction and Land Loans	537
13	Commercial Building and Farm Loans	565
14	Environmental Issues	593
15	Technology Advances in Mortgage Lending	635
	Answer Key for Multiple Choice Questions	661
	Appendix	665
	Glossary	737
	Index	765

CONTENTS

Preface	*xxi*
1 The Nature and Cycle of Real Estate Finance	**1**
Key Terms and Phrases	1
Learning Objectives	2
The Nature of Real Estate Finance	2
Introduction	*2*
Landownership	*3*
Background of Financing	*4*
Mortgage Lending Activities	5
Home Builder Commitments	*5*
Loan-to-Value Ratio (LTV)	*7*
Dollar Amount of Loan	*9*
Land Leases	*12*
Financing Development on Leased Land	*12*
Sale of Equity Interests	*17*
Like-Kind Exchanges—Internal Revenue Code 1031	*19*
SEC Regulations for Real Estate Transactions	*19*
Supplier Financing	*20*
Seller-Financed Home Mortgages	*21*
Foreclosure	*22*
Obligations Involved with Default Insurance: Indemnity	*23*
Real Estate Cycles	25
Home Buyer Education Programs	*25*
The Real Estate Cycle	25
Impact of the Economy	29
Financing Real Property Loans	*30*
The Mortgage Loan Market	*31*
Financial Market Instruments	*32*
A Look at the Future	*33*
The Mortgage Crisis Development	*35*
Questions for Discussion	40
Multiple Choice Questions for Review	41
Information Resources	42

2 Money and the Monetary System — 43

- Key Terms and Phrases — 43
- Learning Objectives — 44
- What is Money and the Federal Reserve System? — 44
  - Introduction — 44
  - Federal Reserve Bank System — 45
  - Compliance Role — 55
- Instruments of Credit Policy — 57
  - Financial Evaluation of the Borrower — 57
  - Ability to Pay — 58
  - Willingness to Pay — 64
  - Credit Reports — 65
- The U.S. Treasury and U.S. Mint — 69
  - The United States Treasury — 69
- The Federal Deposit Insurance Corp (FDIC) — 74
  - Deposit Insurance — 74
  - The Federal Deposit Insurance Corp (FDIC) — 74
  - Reorganization of Deposit Insurance Funds — 75
  - How We Got to this Point — 76
  - The Great Recession Era Reforms — 76
  - Analysis of Mortgage Debt — 78
  - Analysis of Loan Sources — 78
  - Savings Association Regulatory Authorities — 79
  - Savings Banks — 80
  - Reserve Requirements for Depository Institutions — 81
- The Federal Home Loan Bank (FHLB) System — 82
  - Regulated Lenders — 82
  - Savings Institutions — 83
  - Savings Associations — 83
  - Mortgage Partnership Finance Program® (MPF®) — 85
- Questions for Discussion — 86
- Multiple Choice Questions for Review — 87
- Information Resources — 88

3 Additional Government Influence — 89

- Key Terms and Phrases — 89
- Learning Objectives — 90
- U.S. Department of Housing and Urban Development (HUD) — 90
- Significant Federal Legislation (CRA, TILA, RESPA, SAFE, APA, Dodd-Frank) — 90
  - Community Reinvestment Act (CRA) — 90
  - CRA Amended by FIRREA — 91
  - Truth-in-Lending Act — 93
  - What is RESPA? — 96

Contents vii

      The Secure and Fair Enforcement for Mortgage
      Licensing Act of 2008 (SAFE Act)   100
      The Administrative Procedures Act (APA)   101
      Wall Street Reform and Consumer Protection Act
      (The Dodd-Frank Act)   103
      Additional Federal Regulation of Home Mortgage Lending   106
      Mortgage Lending   108
  State and Local Programs (including TDHCA)   110
      State and Local Government Programs   110
      Affordable Housing Loans   111
  Agricultural Lending   115
      Government Loan Programs   115
      Farm Credit System   116
      U.S. Department of Agricultural Development   117
  Review of the Loan Estimate (Formerly Known
  as Good Faith Estimate)   118
      Preliminary Information   120
      Loan Status Report   120
      Preliminary Title Report   120
      RESPA Requirements   121
  Review of Closing Statement or Settlement Statement (A.K.A. HUD-1)   127
      Standardizing Loan Documentation   127
      Disclosure of Settlement Costs   128
      Borrower's Right to Disclosure of Costs Prior to Closing   134
      Prohibited Practices   134
      Settlement Practices and Costs   135
  Final Closing Instructions   147
      Mortgagee's Closing Instructions   147
      Setting the Closing   152
  Disbursement of Funds   153
  Questions for Discussion   154
  Multiple Choice Questions for Review   154
  Information Resources   156

4   The Secondary Mortgage Market   **159**
  Key Terms and Phrases   159
  Learning Objectives   159
  Introduction   160
      Expansion of the Secondary Market   160
      Introduction of Uniform Documentation   161
  Selling Mortgage Loans   161
      Procedures Used in Secondary Markets   162
      Loan Purchasers   166
  Major Participants in the Secondary Market   171

Federal Underwriting of Mortgage Pools   171
The Government-Sponsored Enterprises
(GSEs including FNMA, FHLMC, GNMA, FHLB, Farmer Mac)   172
    Government National Mortgage Association (Ginnie Mae)   172
    Federal Home Loan Mortgage Corporation (Freddie Mac)   174
    Federal National Mortgage Association (Fannie Mae)   176
    Federal Agricultural Mortgage Corporation (Farmer Mac)   179
Loan Pools   182
    Assembling a Loan Pool   183
Tax-Exempt Bonds   184
Mortgage-Backed Securities (MBS)   185
    Mortgage Pass-Through   186
    Collateralized Mortgage Obligations   187
    Differences between CMOs and Mortgage Pass-Throughs   187
    Structure of a CMO   188
Real Estate Mortgage Investment Conduits (REMICs)   190
Questions for Discussion   192
Multiple Choice Questions for Review   192
Information Resources   194

5   Sources of Funds   195

Key Terms and Phrases   195
Learning Objectives   196
Commercial Banks   196
    Limits on Real Estate Loans   197
    Lending Policies   197
    Regulation of Commercial Banks   199
Life Insurance Companies   199
    Investment Policies   200
    Regulation of Life Insurance Companies   201
Pension and Retirement Programs   201
    Introduction   201
Credit Unions   202
    The Mortgage Credit Market   202
    Credit Unions   202
    Regulation of Credit Unions   203
Mortgage Brokers and Bankers   204
    Mortgage Brokers   204
    Mortgage Bankers   207
    Qualifications of a Mortgage Lender   208
    Licensing of Mortgage Loan Officers   209
    Mortgage Company Operations   213
    How a Mortgage Company Funds Loans   214

	Mortgage Company Income	216
	Loan Servicing Disclosure Notice	219
	Automated Loan Underwriting	220
	Real Estate Trusts (REIT, REMT)	221
	Real Estate Investment Trusts (REITs)	221
	Real Estate Bonds	224
	Stock Certificates	224
	Bonds	224
	The Securities Market	226
	Commercial Paper	227
	Competitive Market	228
	Private Lenders	228
	Individuals	228
	Miscellaneous Other Sources	229
	Title Companies	229
	Endowment Funds Managed by Universities, Colleges, and Hospitals	229
	Foundations	230
	Fraternal, Benevolent, and Religious Associations	230
	Foreign Lenders	230
	Recent Trends	231
	Questions for Discussion	232
	Multiple Choice Questions for Review	233
	Information Resources	235
6	**Instruments of Real Estate Finance**	**237**
	Key Terms and Phrases	237
	Learning Objectives	238
	Introduction	238
	History and Development	238
	State Laws Control Property Rights	239
	The Mortgage as a Grant of Title	239
	Encumbrances and Liens	240
	The Mortgage as a Lien	240
	The Note and Deed of Trust	241
	Mortgage Variations	241
	Regular Mortgage	241
	Deed of Trust	241
	The Note and Mortgage	242
	Mortgage Instrument	243
	Parties Involved	243
	Identification of Property	243
	Principal Amount Due	244
	Estoppel	244
	Contract for Deed	245

Subordinate Finance Instruments	246
Open-End Mortgage	246
Construction Loan	247
Interim Loan	247
Mortgage with Release Clauses	248
Junior Mortgage	248
Purchase Money Mortgage	249
Chattel Mortgage	250
Package Mortgage	250
Blanket Mortgage	250
"Subject To" Mortgage	250
Special Provisions in Mortgage Lending Instruments	252
Prepayment Penalty	252
Acceleration Clause	254
Right to Sell/Due-On-Sale Clause—Assumption	254
Review of Promissory Note Form	256
The Promissory Note	256
Conforming Loans	257
Review of Trust Form	259
Property Insurance	260
Flood Insurance	261
Property Taxes	263
Federal Tax Claims	264
Mortgage Procedures	265
Recording	266
Subordination	267
GSE-Conforming Loans as a Catalyst for Uniform Loan Documentation	268
Questions for Discussion	270
Multiple Choice Questions for Review	270
Information Resources	272
7 Loan Types, Terms, and Issues	**275**
Key Terms and Phrases	275
Learning Objectives	276
Introduction	276
Interest	278
Interest Rate Indicators	281
Usury	285
Fixed-Interest, Constant-Level Plan	286
Adjustable-Rate Mortgage (ARM)	287
Types of Loans	288

Other Primary Market Lenders	288
Private Mortgage Insurance	290
Refinancing Existing Conventional Loans	291
Where to Refinance	292
Rate Reduction	292
Refinancing Costs	293
Effect of Tax Law	293
Restructuring the Loan	293
Appraisal Problems	293
Subprime and Predatory Lending	294
Participation Agreement	296
Large Residential Loans	296
Tax Impacts in Mortgage Lending	298
Property Taxes	298
Interest Expense and Real Estate Tax Deductions for Home Residence Loans	299
Fair Housing Requirements	300
Tax Deductions	301
Review of Fixed-/Adjustable-Rate Note	302
Borrower Protection	302
Up-Front Information Required	302
Subsequent Disclosure Requirements	303
Use of an Index	303
Historical Record of Indexes	304
Application of an Index	304
Limitations on Changes (Caps)	307
Continued Evolution of ARM Product Offerings	309
Graduated-Payment Mortgage (GPM)	311
Buydown Mortgage	312
Pledged-Account Mortgage	314
Balloon Payment Note	315
Balloon Due to Amortization	315
Balloon Allowing an Adjusted Rate	316
Straight Note (More Popularly Advertised as an Interest-Only Mortgage)	316
The Piggyback Loan	318
The Advantages and Disadvantages of Piggyback Loans	318
Mortgages that Can Reduce Total Interest Cost	320
Home Equity Revolving Loans	323
Other Alternative Plans	324
Mortgage Fraud	328
The Closing Disclosure and Red Flags	328
PITI Workshop–Conventional	330

Defining "Principal, Interest, Taxes, Insurance (PITI)"   330
VA Income Ratio Method of Qualification   331
Conventional/Conforming Loan Qualification   332
Other Conventional Loan Qualifications   335
Questions for Discussion   335
Multiple Choice Questions for Review   336
Information Resources   337

8 Government Loans   339

Key Terms and Phrases   339
Learning Objectives   339
Introduction   340
Federal Housing Administration   342
  First-Time Home Buyer with HUD-Approved Prepurchase Counseling   342
  Home Equity Conversion Mortgage (HECM) Loans   342
  Assumption of an FHA Loan   343
  Investor Mortgagors Eliminated   346
  Exceptions to Restrictions on Investor Financing   347
  FHA Loan Limits   347
  Secondary Financing with HUD/FHA-Insured Commitments   349
  Analyzing the Loan Application   349
FHA Insured Loan Program   352
  HUD/FHA Terminology and Basic Procedures   352
  Acquisition Cost   352
  Calculation of Down Payment   352
  Prepaid Items   353
FHA Mortgage Insurance Premiums   355
  Programs Not Affected by the Premium Changes   356
  Up-front Premiums and Annual Premiums   357
  Practice Exercise: UFMIP and Annual MIP Calculation   357
Underwriting Guidelines   359
Most Frequently Used FHA Loans   360
  HUD/FHA Program Details   360
  Section 203(b)—Home Mortgage Insurance   360
  Section 203(k)—Rehabilitation Home Mortgage Insurance   362
  Section 245—Graduated-Payment Mortgage (GPM)   363
  Title 1—Home Improvement Loan Insurance   367
Direct Endorsement   369
  HUD/FHA Qualification Procedures   369
FHA Contributions to Real Estate Finance   370
  Early History   370
VA Loan Guaranty Program   371
  Department of Veterans Affairs (VA)   371
  Eligibility of a Veteran   372

Active Duty Service Personnel	372
Selected Reserves or National Guard and Other Qualifying Military or Service Personnel	372
Owner-Occupied	374
Eligibility of Spouses of Otherwise Qualifying Veterans	374
Sliding Scale Guaranty	374
Tier 1 or Partial Entitlements	376
Restoration of Entitlement	377
Release of Liability	379
Loan Default and Foreclosure	380
Funding Fee	380
Negotiated Interest Rate and Discount	382
Adjustable-Rate Mortgage (ARM)	382
Interest Rate Reduction Refinancing Loans (IRRRLs)	382
Other VA Requirements and Procedures	383
Manufactured Home Loans	384
Analyzing the Loan Application	385
Additional VA Loan Programs	386
The Loan Guaranty Entitlement	386
Assumption of a VA Loan	386
FHA Case Study/Workshop	388
Suggested Solution to FHA Case Study	388
VA Case Study/Workshop	389
Suggested Solution for VA Case Study	390
Questions for Discussion	390
Multiple Choice Questions for Review	391
Information Resources	392

9 Lender Loan Processes — 393

Key Terms and Phrases	393
Learning Objectives	393
Introduction	394
Equal Credit Opportunity Act	396
The Loan Application	397
Commercial Loan	397
Qualifying the Borrower	398
HUD/FHA Borrower Income Qualification	398
Percentage Guideline Method	399
Recent Additional Credit Score Requirements for HUD/FHA	402
FHA Institutes Minimum Credit Scores and Loan-to-Value Ratios	402
VA Borrower Qualification	403
Residual Method of Income Qualification	403
Qualifying the Collateral	406

Qualifying the Property	406
Scope of Appraisal	408
Qualifying the Property	408
Commercial Loans	409
Commercial Loan Application	410
Private Mortgage Insurance	412
History of Private Mortgage Insurance	413
Private Mortgage Insurance Companies	414
Qualifying Information Required	414
Amount of Coverage Offered	414
Premiums Charged	415
Cancellation of PMI Coverage	416
Review of Sample Credit Report	418
Credit Scoring	418
Review of Uniform Residential Loan Application	420
Review of Request for Verification of Deposit	439
Review of Request for Verification of Employment	443
Review of Uniform Residential Appraisal Report	446
Three Value Methodologies	447
How Are Automated Underwriter System Findings Indicative of Property Values?	449
Required Lender Notices	457
Qualifying the Title	459
Title Protection	459
Attorney's Opinion Based on Abstract	459
Title Insurance	461
Who Pays for Title Insurance?	462
Torrens System	462
Review of the Title Commitment	463
Lender Closing Costs	464
Credit Score Case Study/Workshop	465
Questions for Discussion	466
Multiple Choice Questions for Review	466
Additional Online Resources	468
10 Defaults and Foreclosures	**469**
Key Terms and Phrases	469
Learning Objectives	469
Defaults	470
Loan Default and Foreclosure	470
How Delinquency and Defaults Impact Lenders	470
Reporting Defaults and Foreclosures	471
Adjustments and Modifications	473
Temporary "Making Home Affordable" Programs	473

	Comparison of Qualification Guidelines	477
	Types of Foreclosures	478
	Judicial Foreclosure	478
	Nonjudicial Foreclosure	479
	Strict Foreclosure	480
	Mortgagor Redemption Rights in Foreclosure	480
	Deficiency Judgments	484
	Tax Impacts of Foreclosure	486
	Relief of Debt	486
	Dealing with Foreclosure Capital Gains and Losses	487
	Questions for Discussion	488
	Multiple Choice Questions for Review	489
	Information Resources	491
11	**Property Analysis**	**493**
	Key Terms and Phrases	493
	Learning Objectives	493
	Introduction	494
	Property Appraisal	495
	Federal/State Certification	496
	Standards for Appraisers	497
	Standards for Appraisers and FHA Mortgages	498
	Appraiser Selection in FHA Connection	499
	Standards for Appraisals	500
	New Quality Mortgage (QM) Appraisal Issues	501
	Appraisal Associations	502
	Principles of Appraising	503
	Types of Appraisals	504
	Appraisal Report	506
	Three Approaches to Property Value	508
	Property Value as Estimated by Cost Approach	508
	Property Value as Estimated by Sales Comparison Analysis	510
	Property Value as Estimated by Income Approach	514
	Property Characteristics	517
	Location of Property	519
	Age of Property	521
	Usage of Property	522
	Condominiums	524
	Commercial Condominiums	526
	Cooperative Apartments	527
	Manufactured Housing/Mobile Homes	528
	Conversion of Manufactured Homes to Real Property	529
	Use of Broker Price Opinion (BPO)	529
	Surveys	530

	Legal Descriptions	531
	Lot and Block	531
	Metes and Bounds	532
	U.S. Geodetic or Government Survey	532
	Questions for Discussion	534
	Multiple Choice Questions for Review	534
	Information Resources	536
12	**Commercial Loans: Construction and Land Loans**	**537**
	Key Terms and Phrases	537
	Learning Objectives	537
	Introduction	538
	Information Sources	539
	The Loan Application	539
	Information Required for a Commercial Loan Application	540
	Permits Obtained or Zoning Requirements Met	546
	Preparation of Financial Statements	547
	Property Evaluation	548
	Appraisal	548
	Feasibility Study	549
	Land Purchase Loans	551
	Land Development Loans	552
	Release Clause	553
	Office of Interstate Land Sales	553
	Construction Loans	555
	Definition	556
	Construction Loans for Residential Properties	558
	Construction Loans for Income Properties	560
	Loan Syndications or Participations	561
	Questions for Discussion	562
	Multiple Choice Questions for Review	562
	Information Resources	564
13	**Commercial Building and Farm Loans**	**565**
	Key Terms and Phrases	565
	Learning Objectives	565
	Introduction	566
	Special-Purpose Buildings	567
	Earnings Record of Applicant	568
	Endorsement	568
	Future Purchase Contract	568
	Apartment Buildings	569
	Location	569
	Physical Facilities	569

	Management	570
	Analysis of Income and Expenses	571
	Term Leases	572
	Retail Store Buildings	573
	Analysis of Income and Expenses	573
	Net Lease	574
	Shopping Centers	574
	Anchor Tenant	574
	Classification of Centers	575
	Income and Expenses	576
	Percentage Leases	577
	Financing of Shopping Centers	578
	Office Buildings	580
	Business Owner-Occupied Buildings	580
	Office Buildings for Lease to Others	581
	Warehouse Buildings	583
	General Warehouse	584
	Net Lease	585
	Office/Warehouses	585
	Mini Warehouses	585
	Farm and Ranch Loans	586
	Family-Resident Farm Loans	586
	Agricorporate Farm Loans	587
	Ranch Loans	587
	Religious Facility Financing	588
	Questions for Discussion	590
	Multiple Choice Questions for Review	590
	Information Resources	592
14	**Environmental Issues**	**593**
	Key Terms and Phrases	593
	Learning Objectives	594
	Introduction	594
	Environmental Assessments for Home Loans	594
	Environmental Assessments for Commercial Loans	596
	Environmental Requirements of the Secondary Market	597
	Loan Documents	598
	Principal Environmental Problems	598
	Other Environmental Issues	599
	Toxic Waste Sites	599
	Discovery of the Problem	599
	First Federal Action on Toxic Waste Sites	600
	Environmental Protection Agency (EPA)	600
	Liability for Cleanup Costs	601

Innocent Landowner Defense	604
Environmental Consultants	610
Private Insurance for Superfund Liabilities	611
Brownfields Program	611
Indoor Air Pollution	614
Formaldehyde Gas	614
Asbestos as Used in Building Materials	615
Radon Gas	616
Lead Poisoning	617
Sources of Lead Poisoning	618
How Lead Affects Property Value	619
Lead-Based Paint Rule	619
Handling Lead When Found	619
Wetlands Protection	620
Break for Small Landowner	622
Effect of Wetlands on Financing	622
Endangered Species	622
The Endangered Species Act's Net Effect on Loans	623
Recent Rulings Mitigating the Act	624
Private Property Rights	625
Underground Storage Tanks	626
UST Effect on Loans	627
Electromagnetic Forces	628
Waste Producers and Their Toxic Impact	629
Energy-Efficient Buildings	630
Conclusions	631
Questions for Discussion	632
Multiple Choice Questions for Review	632
Information Resources	634

15	**Technology Advances in Mortgage Lending**	**635**
	Key Terms and Phrases	635
	Learning Objectives	635
	Introduction	636
	Computerized Loan Origination (CLO)	636
	Loan Origination Systems (LOS)	640
	Automated Underwriting Systems	641
	Freddie Mac's Loan Prospector®	642
	Fannie Mae's Desktop Underwriter®	646
	Mortgages on the Internet	648

Online Real Estate Service	651
Using Computerized Information in the Future	655
Questions for Discussion	656
Multiple Choice Questions for Review	657
Additional Online Resources	658

Answer Key for Multiple Choice Questions   661

Appendix   665

Glossary   737

Index   765

ILLUSTRATIONS

Figure 2-1	Flow Chart of Federal Reserve Structure and Operations	46
Figure 2-2	History of How Federal Reserve Changes in Federal Discount Rate Influences Short-Term Borrowing and CD Rates	53
Figure 3-1	TILA-RESPA Integrated Disclosure known as the Loan Estimate Form	124
Figure 3-2	Closing Disclosure Settlement Statement for residential loans	129
Figure 3-3	Mortgagee's Closing Instructions	148
Figure 5-1	Real Estate Investment Trusts	222
Figure 11-1	Section of Township Divided into Quarters	533
Figure 15-1	Smart doc® Framework	647

PREFACE

Real estate finance comprises nearly three-fourths of total mortgage lending. Residential mortgage debt increased at an astounding 9.875% per year—from $5.7 trillion in 1999 to $14.6 trillion at the end of 2008, the end of the first year of the "Great Recession." At the end of the second quarter of 2018, this declined to $10.7 trillion. The mortgage finance industry entered a new era during which over 90% of all residential mortgages made are marketed through a secondary market controlled by federal government agencies such as Ginnie Mae, Fannie Mae, and Freddie Mac (the last two Government-Sponsored Enterprises ("GSEs") are still in conservatorship). This will likely continue until government leadership decides on the fate of the GSEs or there is sufficient recovery in the private mortgage-backed securities market.

Between 1999 and 2009, nominal house prices rose by 61%, a 4.875% annual compounded rate increase, according to the Federal Housing and Finance Agency. After a nationwide decline in prices, recent quarters show steady average increases in home prices. A January 2015 Corelogic report indicates that average home prices were up 5.7% between January 2014 and January 2015. However, this good news belies the other data indicating house prices in 27 states and the District of Columbia are still within 10% of the 2005 peak prices. Still, many homeowners who purchased homes between 2001 and 2005 are more likely to be able to sell without a loss or refinance without the aid of government programs, thanks to the economic upturn.

The median of residential real estate mortgages with a loan-to-value (LTV) of over 95% moved from an approximate 6% low in 2004 to a high of over 25% in 2011 to below 15% in 2013. With the economic recovery allowing more homeowners better employment opportunities, the problems of underwater home mortgages may be a diminishing trend for some. The effects of the financial crisis upon house value and underwater mortgages have had a more profound effect upon lower-income and younger homeowners. This is thought to be one of the causes of the

Millennial Generation's not participating in home ownership as soon as the baby boomers.

The Millennial Generation is now the largest cohort coming of age for their first and second home purchase. They differ from previous generations due to being more ethnically and racially diverse. The Millennials' desires for a broader range of housing options, including easy walking access to shopping, dining and recreation, a preference for walking to work or the grocer, and using Uber will have a profound impact on growth patterns of urban and suburban population centers. It appears that suburban areas may become less desirable and, as evidence of this, some low-end suburban subdivisions are terribly deteriorated today. One example of the "Millennials" influence on housing trends is the "Urban Reserve" community in Dallas, Texas—a modern, sustainable community with alternative energy sources and within easy walking distance to trains, shopping and more. These types of housing communities may become more in demand. Mortgage lenders will have to adapt to a new type of lending, much as the lenders in London and Stockholm did when many old warehouses and industrial areas were turned into urban residential communities of townhouses and co-op type properties.

During the period from 2004 to 2013, the share of single-family homes purchased by business investors has risen from 0.08% to over 6.4%. There appears to be a high correlation between the price paid to rent ratio. High investor ownership of single-family homes is found in Atlanta, Phoenix and Las Vegas. As these markets begin to share in the nationwide improvement in home prices, the opportunities for the financing of these homes for owner occupants will be dramatic. Many of the investments in homes came from pools of capital that normally have cash-out period expectations of 7 to 10 years. This trend continues to build momentum. An example is Invitation Homes, a Blackstone Company, which started investing in single-family homes in 2012 and with an initial investment of nearly $10 billion on a portfolio of 48,000 homes. Invitation Homes went public at the beginning of 2017, now has 80,000 properties, and is the third largest single-family investor REIT in the United States.

The changes that the past few years have wrought are driving changes to real estate financing. Governmental intervention and market forces are contributing to the creation of a new model of residential mortgage financing that has more risk sharing by loan originators over the life of loans made under the Ability to Repay and Qualified Mortgage Standards required by the Dodd-Frank Wall Street Reform and Consumer

Protection Act that went into effect in January of 2014. Real estate professionals of all stripes need a sound understanding of the specialized financing procedures used by lenders today, as well as a sense of the changes that are likely to occur in future lending. The real estate market has a cyclical nature; it will flourish at times and then languish for a while. Such ups and downs are part of the normal workings of the free market system. There is no central government planning authority empowered to set limits on the number of housing units that can be built in any given market area. However, state and federal governments and the policies of various departments and agencies can influence naturally evolving market trends. The control of market demand is evident in what the United States has experienced between 2007 and the present based on the actions of the Federal Reserve Bank and U.S. Treasury Department. These actions, taken to mitigate the tightening of credit markets for residential mortgage finance due to the recent financial crisis, linger on. Federal Reserve Bank intervention in the mortgage bond market has finally abated. The Federal Reserve Bank raised the federal discount rate for the first time in a decade in December of 2015 and has continued to raise it about 300 basis points since. As this is being written, the Federal Reserve is expected to raise the discount rate again in December of 2018.

The eleventh edition of this text covering real estate finance has continued with its emphasis on residential financing due to its more clearly structured set of uniform practices that exist within that segment of real estate finance than in commercial real estate finance. The text has been updated to follow the guidelines for those pursuing a real estate license to initially cover materials cogent to their examination for licensing. While the general organization of the book has changed, each chapter lists useful links to additional resources to aid student in keeping current or researching additional materials have been fully updated and enriched. Students and readers of this text will find that it has an improved flow of the materials covered to allow a more thorough presentation of real estate finance needed by lenders, real estate agents, appraisers, investors and regulators. The new structure of the text is as follows:

- **Chapter 1—The Nature and Cycle of Real Estate Finance**
  Includes discussion of changes in downpayment requirements for first-time homebuyers, including a line of 97% LTV option mortgage loans reintroduced by Fannie Mae in 2014, as well as the HomeReady® update from 2017.

- **Chapter 2—Money and the Monetary System**

  A discussion of how the Federal Reserve Bank has lowered its reserve requirements for the first time in 12 years in January 2018 with the main beneficiaries being community banks. There is an expanded description of the U.S. Treasury and U.S. Mint that covers their role in the United States economy. Included is a complete update on the role of the Federal Deposit Insurance Corporation as a regulator and the shift of some responsibilities for consumer compliance to the Consumer Financial Protection Bureau.

- **Chapter 3—Additional Government Influence**

  The Truth in Lending Act and Real Estate Settlements Procedures Act coverage has been expanded, covering the new coordination between the Loan Estimate and the Closing Disclosure that has replaced the HUD-1 Settlement Statement in all cases except for FHA Reverse Mortgages. The impact of the Administrative Procedure Act has been added to this chapter and the 11th edition. There is a discussion with examples of how Fannie Mae is partnering with state Realtor® associations to provide product education for agents and consumers. Changes in the Uniform Residential Loan Application effective February 2019 and its redesign is covered.

- **Chapter 4—The Secondary Mortgage Market**

  A short status on Fannie Mae and its capital position compared to major banking institutions. Updates on the product volume and current market share position of the main Government Sponsored Enterprises.

- **Chapter 5—Sources of Funds**

  Update on the recovery and growth in mortgage lending and the number of licensed mortgage originators. Discussed that despite the low interest rate market, mortgage REIT's continued to grow in size and diversity.

- **Chapter 6—Instruments of Real Estate Finance**

  A detailed outline of the main provisions of a Deed of Trust. Commentary on common property tax errors made at closing is now part of the ad valorem tax section. Added is a full discussion of what and how Federal Tax Claims work that a Realtor® should know. New tables with the increases in conforming loan limits.

- **Chapter 7—Loan Types, Terms, and Issues**

    Updates on how to calculate payments for conventional mortgages with an added Workshop for classroom or online instructional use. Introduction to the tax impacts for residential real estate of the Tax Cuts and Jobs Act of 2017.

- **Chapter 8 – Government Loans**

    Updates to loan programs and loan limits. Addition of Case Studies for Federal Housing Administration and Veterans Administration sponsored mortgage loans. Current FHA maximum loan limits.

- **Chapter 9—Lender Loan Processes**

    An expanded discussion of the credit report in the lending process. A detailed discussion of the new Fannie Mae and Freddie Mac Form 1003 that will be used starting February 2019. This is the first change in the form in 9 years. An expanded section on qualifying the title on real estate pledged to secure loans. A more detailed explanation of state real property filing systems with an expanded explanation of the use of the Torrens system.

- **Chapter 10—Defaults & Foreclosures**

    A new section on "How Delinquency and Defaults Impact Lenders" and dealing with "VA Default and Foreclosure." Includes information on other "Major Changes to Loan Terms" such as an expanded look at a Loan Modification Agreement. More detail about the redemption process and how it varies by state and a discussion of a judicial foreclosure state with redemption rights and how the formal foreclosure process would take place. How and why settlement of a federal lien depends on the debtor's circumstances and is handled on a case-by-case basis. Generally, the obligation can be mitigated only in cases of proven hardship. A discussion of how capital gains or losses are handled when there is a debt extinguishment and the changes due to the recent Tax Cuts and Jobs Act of 2017.

- **Chapter 11—Property Analysis**

    Includes discussion of the most recent updates to the education requirements recently adopted by the Appraisal Foundation that includes not requiring a college degree for entry level professionals.

- **Chapter 12—Commercial, Construction and Land Loans**

    Comparing and contrasting the "Profit and Loss Statement" and the "Operating Statement." The difference between an appraisal and feasibility study is reviewed. How a standby commitment in commercial mortgage lending differs from a residential mortgage rate lock or pre-approval.

- **Chapter 13—Commercial Building and Farm Loans**

  Unique features of lending for religious facilities is expanded.

- **Chapter 14—Environmental Issues**

  Covers recent trends in the conversion of former industrial sites for mixed-use retail facing looming environmental risks. The expansion of marijuana growing operations causing extensive damage to walls, ceiling and floors is covered, along with dealing with tenant hazards from illegal drug operations. Dealing with natural disaster and climate change risks to property that must be addressed to meet some lending standards.

- **Chapter 15—Technology Advances in Real Estate Finance**

  Updates discussing the current dominant loan origination systems in use by the residential real estate finance industry. Examples of disruptive technology in use by leading-edge loan originators.

INSTRUCTIONAL SUPPORT

Instructors who adopt this book receive access to an online Instructor's Manual. Each chapter is supported with chapter overview and objectives, an outline of each chapter with teaching tips, multiple choice questions, and suggested answers to the discussion questions found at the end of each chapter in the text. Plus, there is a 180-question final exam with answer key and four 60-question exams made up from the questions in the final. Finally, 5-question topic quizzes are provided for each chapter.

Classroom PowerPoint presentation slides also support each chapter, outlining learning objectives, emphasizing key concepts, and highlighting real-world applications to help further engage learners and generate classroom discussion.

These instructional support materials are available online only to adopters of the text at the companion website, www.mbitiontolearn.com.

ACKNOWLEDGMENTS

I would like to thank Sara Glassmeyer, Executive Editor at Mbition LLC, for confidence in me. I also want to express my appreciation for the support of the numerous other educators and real estate practitioners like Jason Glater, MS, Theda Redwine, MBA, and Joe Goeters, MBA, of the Texas Real Estate Educators Association, and a special thanks to Dr. Pamela Smith Baker for her contributions to Chapter 2 of the text, as well as Tony Ettinger of Credit Based Capital LLC for his insights on leading-edge new product concepts and industry innovation. I thank my family for their support and their patience with me during the many months that I worked on this text.

I also want to thank Abby Franklin, copyeditor, as well as Charlie Alfortish, Delgado Community College; Edward J. Stankunas, CMB, CREI, North Lake College; and Shawn D. Wagner, Grand View University, for carefully reviewing this revision and giving worthwhile suggestions and discerning observations.

ABOUT THE AUTHOR

J. Keith Baker is an accomplished author, noted speaker, and knowledge leader in the fields of real estate finance and mortgage banking. Mr. Baker began his work in real estate finance performing inspections for construction loan draws with Peoples Bank & Trust and later was a team member that helped start a mortgage loan department. Mr. Baker then worked as an investment officer for Texas Commerce Bank, dealing with financing of state residential mortgage bonds and underwriting multifamily project note financing. After finishing post-baccalaureate work, he started to work for Kenneth Leventhal and Co., then the global CPA firm leader in real estate accounting and finance (now a division of Ernst and Young). At Leventhal, Mr. Baker performed due diligence for bond issues and housing bonds and worked on audits of home builders, mortgage companies, and savings and loans. He was recruited by the Mutual of New York (MONY), where he served as Vice President of Management Resources; President of MONY CS, Inc., a troubled asset management company in Houston; Interim CFO of MONY Subsidiary North American Mortgage Company; member of the Board of Directors for MONY Bank & Trust – Grand Cayman, and was a standing member of the Investment Committee for MONY.

Mr. Baker was later a Senior Vice President for Enhance Financial Services Group, Inc., serving as CFO of Credit Based Business; a member of the New Products & Ventures Team; a member of the Board of Managers for Credit Based Asset Securitization & Servicing, LLC and Sherman Financial, LLC; and a member of the Board of Directors of SBF Security and Guarantee SA. He was on the business development team, forming a mortgage financing subsidiary in Brazil and a mortgage servicing software development firm in Peru.

He is a Certified Financial Planner, a Certified Public Accountant, a Certified Real Estate Instructor, and holds both an MBA and an MS in Financial Services. He is CEO of Baker Capital Consultants, providing consulting services for hedge funds and private wealth management firms, performing pre-offer due diligence reviews, and developing models for mortgage origination and mortgage servicing operations. He is the Program Coordinator for the Mortgage Banking Program at North Lake College. He serves on the Board of Directors for the Sustainability Management Association and the Mortgage Lending Institute, both non-profit organizations.

Chapter 1

THE NATURE AND CYCLE OF REAL ESTATE FINANCE

KEY TERMS AND PHRASES

- allodial
- build-to-suit
- collateral
- commercial paper
- discount
- dollar limitations
- feudal
- foreclosure
- hypothecation
- land leases
- like-kind exchange
- limited partnerships
- loan originator
- loan-to-value ratio
- mortgage
- negotiable instruments
- points
- primary market
- promissory note
- realty funds
- sale-leaseback
- SEC requirements
- secondary market
- security interest
- subordinated lease agreement
- supplier financing
- syndication
- takeout commitment
- yield

CHAPTER 1 The Nature and Cycle of Real Estate Finance

LEARNING OBJECTIVES

At the conclusion of this chapter, students will be able to:
- Describe the nature and origins of real estate finance and landownership.
- Understand the development of and compensation for financing called mortgage lending.
- Understand how loan-to-value ratios tie into the residential real estate finance process.
- Describe the various types of leases involved in real estate and how they can serve to conserve cash, increase flexibility, and reduce liquidity risk.
- Explain the basics of the mortgage loan market.
- Describe the future of mortgage financing.
- Differentiate between syndications and realty funds.
- Understand the real estate cycle.
- Describe the process of foreclosure.

THE NATURE OF REAL ESTATE FINANCE

Introduction

The history of real estate financing presents a fascinating record of civilizations learning to live with, and enjoying the benefits of, the land upon which they live. Sir Leonard Woolley, excavating the Mesopotamian city of Ur, found cuneiform texts in the financial district that dated from the early years of the reign of King Rim-Sin (1822–1763 BCE), who ruled from the capital city of Larsa, a few miles north of Ur, shortly before Hammurabi's time.[1] Woolley's excavations reveal that ancient residents of Ur buried their personal financial records, along with their ancestors, in the floors of their houses for safekeeping. Marc Van De Mieroop, a professor of history at Columbia University, used Woolley's careful excavation notes to describe the "mortgage" lending activities of one businessman, Dumuzi-gamil, whose ancient cuneiform business and accounting records show deeds and security instruments, and a sale of these notes to two other ancient investors, Nur-ilishu and Sin-ashared. Indeed, these are likely the first documented secondary-market participants for mortgage loans. While the private ownership of land can be traced back to civilizations existing over 3,800 years ago,[2] only in

---

[1] Marc Van De Mieroop, *Society and Enterprise in Old Babylonian Ur* (Berlin: Dietrich Reimer, 1992).
[2] Matthew W. Stolper, *Entrepreneurs and Empire* (Leiden: Nederlands Instituut voor het Nabije Oosen, 1985).

ILLUSTRATION OF ACCOUNTING RECORDS OF
SECURITY TRANSACTION FROM 2900 BC
UNDER REIGN OF JEMDET NASR

the last several hundred years has it become possible for the average person to own land. Nevertheless, many of the practices used in modern real estate financing trace their origins to earlier civilizations.

The underlying principle of real estate finance has changed very little over the centuries, and remains rather simple. It involves the pledging of land as collateral to secure a loan. **Collateral**, in this case meaning something of value, is conveyed by a limited pledge as protection for a lender to assure repayment of a loan. Over time, the rights to land that can be pledged have undergone some changes; however, the availability of money that can be borrowed continues to reflect an earlier record of restricted practices and very limited pools of money. The development of private landownership has required stable legal systems for the enforcement of that ownership and the right of the lender (a.k.a. mortgagee) to take and enforce a **security interest**—normally a mortgage or deed of trust recorded to perfect the lender's collateral.[3]

Landownership

The pledging of land as collateral has long been a normal protection for the lender. The way in which land is pledged has to do with how it is

---

[3]Rajkumar R., "History Mystery: The First Written Word Part. I," *Elixir of Knowledge* (blog), January 14, 2011, https://www.elixirofknowledge.com/2011/01/history-mystery-first-written-word.html

owned. The concept of ownership has developed along two paths: the **allodial** concept of ownership and the **feudal** right of ownership. In Roman times, the allodial system applied. The ownership of land by individuals was absolute. The landowner had few limitations or restrictions on the right to use or dispose of it.

The feudal system came into existence as continental Europe developed. In medieval times, as Roman authority disintegrated, marauding tribes became more common. In return for protection from these marauders, small groups of people would grant a form of landownership to a leader. Occupants of the land held rights to their parcels as tenants and paid fees consisting of produce from the land and personal services due to the "landlord." Thus, the feudal system primarily granted the right to occupy and use land owned by a social superior. English land law developed as a modified feudal system dating from the Norman Conquest in 1066.

While both these systems have shaped the ownership of property in the United States, the allodial concept dominates. Ownership of real property in the United States is considered free and absolute, subject only to governmental and voluntary restrictions. As the country grew, states developed a variety of laws governing landownership and how property rights could be conveyed. The early colonies on the East Coast preserved much of English law, including its concept of male dominance in marriage, in its laws relating to property rights. The southwestern states were more influenced by Spanish law and its concept of family protection, which is the source of community property laws in marriage and homestead protection in those states. Louisiana is unique in its adherence to the Napoleonic Code. The result has been a mix of real property laws that require different mortgage documents for each state.

Background of Financing

In earlier civilizations, landownership was restricted and the availability of borrowed money was limited. There were no insurance companies or depository institutions with cash to loan. In Roman society, landowners were joined in the *curia* with tax gatherers who made funds available for loans. In medieval Europe, only a few wealthy individuals were capable of loaning money. Access to this money was limited to elite classes that, by definition, were the landowners. Thus, land became a fairly standard form of collateral.

Historically, the growth of widespread landownership parallels the increase in pools of money available for long-term loans. With the advent of the Industrial Revolution in the eighteenth century, more individuals became capable of producing wealth with their ideas and their machinery. People began to find that other options were open to them; the life of a serf grubbing an existence from the land owned by the nobility was no longer the only way to sustain a living. With more widespread wealth came the demand for ways to make better use of accumulated money, and the seeds of our publicly owned savings institutions began to grow.

The economics of the development of housing are important for many reasons. Estimates from a 2011 study performed by the National Association of REALTORS® indicate that the median sale price of a new home contributes $58,792 to the economy. Home ownership rose from about 40% in 1940 to a peak of 68% in 2005, and has dropped to 64.3% at the end of the second quarter of 2018.[4]

MORTGAGE LENDING ACTIVITIES

Introduction

While practices in the real estate finance business do vary across the country, a number of conditions, terms, and procedures are commonly used. This chapter explains many of these practices.

Home Builder Commitments

When a new home is purchased directly from a builder, the builder may already hold a **takeout commitment** for mortgage money that can be used to provide permanent financing to the home buyer and take out (pay off) the construction lender or builder if the lender or builder is using their own sources of funding. We will discuss some of the ways these commitments are handled in the sections that follow.

Competitive Method

Small- to medium-sized builders may have their construction money secured without any commitment for the permanent loans. For example, a commercial bank carrying construction financing may not be interested in making a permanent loan to a buyer. If there is no commitment, the purchaser is free to seek whatever source of mortgage money may be found.

---

[4]U.S. Census Bureau, "Homeownership Rates by Region," chart, Current Population Survey/Housing Vacancy Survey, Release Number: CB18-107, accessed September 11, 2017 https://www.census.gov/housing/hvs/files/currenthvspress.pdf

Commitment Method: Construction

When any builder obtains construction money, the lender may request a first-refusal right to all permanent loans on the project. The construction lender thus ties up a good source of loans for the future, which is one of the incentives to make the construction loan in the first place. To enforce this right, the lender may include in the construction loan agreement the bank's right to add a penalty provision that would provide for an extra .5% or 1% of the construction loan to be paid for a release of the construction mortgage if the loan is not handled through the same lender.

A purchaser cannot be required to borrow money from a particular lender, but it can be a bit more costly to go elsewhere. This type of arrangement is more common in commercial construction loans than in residential construction.

Commitment Method: Purchase

Some of the larger builders who can qualify for the lowest rates on their construction money, or use their own funds for this purpose, may purchase a future commitment for money directly from a savings association or other major source to protect future customers needing loans. The builder will pay at least 1% of the total commitment amount to hold the money, or may pay additional fees to ensure future home buyers receive a lower, more competitive interest rate. This expense, which is, in effect, a prepayment of interest by the builder for the benefit of the buyer, is charged back to the cost of the house. This is how builders can advertise lower-than-market interest rates and obtain a competitive advantage in the housing market.

Associated Companies

Most of the larger builders that are basically national in scope own affiliated mortgage companies or money sources to provide permanent loans. The tie-in is generally competitive with market rates for money and, in many instances, provides an additional source of income and competitive advantage for the builder. Associated companies are subject to a 1992 Department of Housing and Urban Development (HUD) rule that requires full disclosure of ownership in related companies. The rule applies to any affiliation with service providers within the real estate industry. These companies are not permitted to require the use of an affiliate's service as a condition for closing a transaction, nor are they allowed to pay

> Under Texas Finance Code Chapter 156, there is a *de minimis* exemption from licensure for an owner of real property who, in any 12-consecutive-month period, makes no more than five mortgage loans. The primary Texas regulator for residential mortgage lending is the Texas Department of Savings and Mortgage Lending. This entity's literature states that "where a seller financer exceeds the number of transactions exempt under the act, the seller financer must either become licensed as a residential mortgage loan originator or must engage a licensed residential mortgage loan originator to conduct all loan origination activities that require a license, including taking applications and/or negotiating the terms of a loan."[5] All state regulators are required to adopt this requirement under Section 1007.101(c)(2) of the SAFE Act.
>
> [5]"Texas SAFE Act and Seller Financing Questions," Texas Department of Savings and Mortgage Lending, accessed January 31, 2015, http://www.sml.texas.gov/tdsml_faq_mb_texas_SAFE_Act_seller_financing.html

each other fees for referrals. However, they carry a competitive edge by being available at the proper time and place to consummate a deal.

The SAFE Act of 2008 covers "associated companies" of homebuilders. The homebuilder or any other person or entity involved in seller financing of residential real estate must be licensed under the SAFE Act with both the National Mortgage Licensing System (NMLS) and the state mortgage lending regulator. The SAFE Act allows states to determine certain *de minimis* exemptions from licensure when there are few transactions or a family member is involved in the transaction.

Loan-to-Value Ratio (LTV)

The **loan-to-value ratio** is the amount of a loan as a percentage of the property's value. For this purpose, the property value is the lesser of the appraised value or the sales price. An exception is the VA, which accepts only its own appraised value for property offered as collateral, called the certificate of reasonable value (CRV). Of course, if a sale is not involved, such as in refinancing, the appraised value would be the proper measure.

The LTV ratio is an important standard for mortgage lenders. It is used by the industry in the following ways:

1. **as a standard for pricing a loan** (The higher the ratio, the greater the risk; the greater the risk, the higher the price required. A borrower offering 5% down has a lesser stake in the property than one offering 20% down. Lender experience indicates that those with greater equities are less likely to allow a default to occur. Thus, a 95% LTV loan requires the highest interest rate and the greater number of discount points.

Generally, the price distinction levels out at an 80% LTV. A buyer offering more than 20% down achieves only marginally better pricing.);

2. **as a standard for default mortgage insurance (also called private mortgage insurance or PMI)** (Federal rules require that residential loans greater than 90%[6] LTV must be insured against default. Most lenders apply their own rules, and may require such insurance on loans greater than 80% LTV. Buyers making down payments of more than 20% can usually obtain loans with no default insurance required. Also, the price of mortgage insurance varies with the LTV.); and

3. **as a standard for quality of loan.** (The role of an LTV in setting standards for most conventional residential loans had, for a short period from 1999 to 2008, been diminished by the growth of no-down-payment loans and even home loans made at 125% of the value of the house. Nevertheless, prudent lenders still class a 95% LTV conventional loan as a high-risk loan. In 1998, the Federal Reserve issued a warning to banks under its authority to tighten credit standards. During the same time period, in the spring of 1998, the number of subprime lenders grew from less than 10 to more than 50, and 10 of the 25 largest subprime lenders were affiliated with federally chartered bank holding companies. This was not the response one might have expected, and yet federal bank regulators remained unconcerned. In 2000, Edward Gramlich, a Federal Reserve governor, proposed to then-Federal Reserve Board Chairman Alan Greenspan that the Federal Reserve use its discretionary authority to send bank examiners to the offices of such lenders. However, Greenspan opposed the idea, and Gramlich never brought his concerns to the full Federal Reserve Board.)[7]

While commercial banks do not make many home loans with their deposit assets, the warning was a caution to all lenders. Many did not heed the warning, creating one of the factors that led to the recent mortgage crisis. Federal bank examiners still use the LTV ratio as one standard of loan quality. On August 21, 2017, the Office of the Comptroller of the Currency issued Bulletin 2017-28. That has cracked open a small niche for making high-LTV loans that in the past would have not passed

---

[6]Office of Thrift Supervision, *Interagency Guidance on High LTV Residential Real Estate Lending* (Washington, DC: U.S. Department of the Treasury, 2011), Examination Handbook Section 212C.1.
[7]Timothy A. Canova, "The Legacy of the Clinton Bubble," *Dissent Magazine*, Summer 2008.

the risk test used by the regulator of our nation's banks. Bulletin 2017-28 allows banks to originate high-LTV loans in "distressed communities," including loans with LTVs of 100% or more. These should be permanent first-lien mortgages that finance owner-occupied residences with original loan balances of $200,000 or less.

Dollar Amount of Loan

There are some **dollar limitations** on the amount of residential loans. HUD/FHA and VA set their own limits, as described in Chapter 8. For conventional loans, the various regulatory agencies can set limits. Most of these involve a limitation on the amount of any single loan as a percentage of the lender's total assets and limits on the amount that can be loaned to any one individual. In years past, states have set limits on dollar amounts for single-family residential loans, but most of these have since been eliminated.

Fannie Mae/Freddie Mac Limits

A widely used standard for loan limits is employed by secondary-market investors Fannie Mae and Freddie Mac. Each November, the two federal underwriting agencies adjust the limit on the dollar amount of loans they can purchase (or allow into a mortgage pool) in accordance with federally mandated guidelines to become effective on January 1 of the following year. The limit is adjusted based on the amount of change in the average purchase price of a single-family house financed by a conventional mortgage, as determined by the Federal Housing Finance Board. The change is based on the 12-month period prior to the end of October each year.

The limit becomes the conforming/conventional loan limit. Furthermore, the limit on FHA loans is calculated each year as a percentage of the conforming loan limit. An increase is not mandatory, but cannot exceed the calculated limit.

The Fannie Mae/Freddie Mac single-family loan limit for 2018 was $453,100. The 2018 conforming loan limit for the number of dwelling units was as follows.

Fannie Mae High-Cost Area Loan Limits for 2018

Loans originated between July 1, 2007, and September 30, 2011, are subject to previously announced limits determined under those laws. The applicable loan limits for such seasoned loans are as high as $729,750 for one-unit properties in 2017, for loans originated in the contiguous United States. In 2017, high-cost area loan limits have increased for 46 counties due to a high-cost area adjustment or the county being newly assigned to a high-cost area. The maximum limits allowed are guided by the provisions of the Housing and Economic Recovery Act of 2008. The specific high-cost area loan limits are established for each county (or equivalent) by the Federal Housing Finance Agency (FHFA). Lenders are responsible for ensuring that the original loan amount of each mortgage loan does not exceed the applicable maximum loan limit for the specific area in which the property is located. Loans originated on or after January 1, 2018, will use the "permanent" high-cost area loan limits established by the FHFA under a formula of 115% of the 2017 median home price, up to a maximum of $679,650 for a one-unit property in the continental United States. Data for specific county-by-county limits, including high-cost area loan limits are available at https://www.fanniemae.com/singlefamily/loan-limits.

Number of Family Units	Contiguous States, District of Columbia, and Puerto Rico	Alaska, Guam, Hawaii, and the U.S. Virgin Islands
	Loan Limit	Loan Limit
1	$453,100	$679,650
2	$580,150	$870,225
3	$701,250	$1,051,875
4	$871,450	$1,307,175

Minimum Loan Limits

There are no regulatory minimums for mortgage loans, but there are some practical limits. Compare, for instance, the fee for servicing a $100,000 loan with the fee for a loan of $20,000. Normally, the servicing fee amounts to one-fourth of a percentage point; thus, for a $100,000 loan, the servicer would make $250 per year, or $20.83 per month. For a $20,000 loan, the quarter-point earns $50 per year, or $4.16 per month. Because the cost of servicing can exceed the fees earned on a smaller loan, any sale of the loan requires substantial discounting. For these reasons, some conventional lenders set minimum dollar amounts for loans they will make, at the risk of being charged with discrimination. HUD/FHA has never allowed its approved mortgagees to set minimum amounts for acceptable loans.

The problem arises from the fact that smaller loans are most likely to be needed by lower-income families. If a mortgage lender sets minimum limits on acceptable loans, the practice could be discriminatory. In fact, in 1993, several conventional mortgage lenders were charged with violation of the Fair Housing Act because they had refused to make loans of less than $50,000. In September 2010, HUD stated that the FHA has no minimum loan amount, only maximum mortgage amounts, but lenders may impose their own minimum loan amounts.[8] Recent regulations issued by the Consumer Financial Protection Bureau (CFPB) that took effect in January of 2014 referred to as the Qualified Mortgage rules meant to protect borrowers from taking loans they cannot afford. These basic rules listed below will prohibit the government-sponsored enterprises (GSEs) from purchasing any loans if they are subject to the ability-to-repay requirements and are either:

- loans that are not fully amortizing (e.g., no negative amortization or interest-only loans);
- loans with terms in excess of 30 years (e.g., no 40-year terms); or
- loans with points and fees in excess of 3% of the total loan amount or such other limits for low-balance loans as set forth in the ability-to-repay final rule.

The last point becomes the real problem with smaller FHA mortgage loans made by many lending institutions. In an attempt to encourage smaller-balance loans to be made, the CFPB issued additional guidance for lenders making Qualified Mortgages as follows.[9]

- For a loan of $100,000 or more: points and fees must be 3% of the total loan amount or less.
- For a loan of $60,000 to $100,000: points and fees must be $3,000 or less.
- For a loan of $20,000 to $60,000: points and fees must be 5% of the total loan amount or less.
- For a loan of $12,500 to $20,000: points and fees must be $1,000 or less.
- For a loan of $12,500 or less: points and fees must be 8% of the total loan amount or less.

---

[8]Department of Housing and Urban Development, FHA Updates Presentation, 2010.
[9]"My lender says it can't lend to me because of a limit on points and fees on loans. Is this true?" Consumer Financial Protection Bureau, updated February 22, 2017, http://www.consumerfinance.gov/askcfpb/1795/my-lender-says-it-cant-lend-me-because-limit-points-and-fees-loans-true.html

Many lenders have complained that on a loan of $30,000 the $1,500 limitation on fees isn't enough to offset their underwriting costs, let alone other costs of originating this type of loan.

Land Leases

While most developments are built on land owned by the developer or builder, there is a growing use of **land leases** for development purposes. There are several reasons for leasing land instead of buying it outright, as outlined below:

- **The land is not for sale.** In some areas of the country—such as Hawaii, Orange County, California, and certain high-density downtown areas—land is simply not available for purchase. Landownership in these areas may be limited to large holders who see greater value in leasing than in converting the land asset into cash that is subject to capital gains tax.

- **Leasing may cost less.** It is quite possible to negotiate a multiyear lease on land at a lower cost than financing the purchase price. Lease payments are tax-deductible (provided the land is used for business purposes), while land is nondepreciable as an asset.

- **You can separate ownership.** Another purpose for a land lease might be to separate the ownership of improvements from the land ownership. The separation allows either one to be sold without capital gains tax being assessed on the other. And a sale of either one, rather than both, could reduce the financing requirements.

Financing Development on Leased Land

When a lease on land is consummated between a landowner and a builder/developer, the contract is generally known and referred to as a *ground lease*. The landowner's interest is termed the *underlying fee*, and the lessee's (builder's) interest is known as the *leasehold*. Ground leases are usually net leases that create a tenancy for years, typically with terms of 55, 75, or 99 years. The 99-year limit derives from some early state laws that held that leases of 100 years or longer were transfers of title rather than leases.

Financing construction on land that is leased has some limitations, as the builder can pledge only the leasehold interest, not the underlying fee, as collateral. This can cause a problem for lenders accustomed to working with mortgages that include a pledge of the land itself. While the legal terminology varies a bit, there are two basic ways to handle loans involving property where the land is leased: an unsubordinated ground lease and a **subordinated agreement lease**.

Unsubordinated Ground Lease

Under this procedure, the landowner does not subordinate the ownership (fee title) to the leasehold interest. This means that if the ground rent is not paid, the landowner can foreclose and terminate the leasehold rights. In such a case, improvements could be claimed by the landowner, thus defeating any claim by a lender holding only a pledge of the leasehold interest. To minimize such a consequence, with this kind of lease the lender would normally require the borrower to pay the ground rent in escrow to the lender as a part of each mortgage payment. The lender would then pass the ground rent on to the landowner when it becomes due, or even advance the ground rent, if necessary, to protect the lender's collateral position. Handling of the ground rent as part of a mortgage payment may be likened to the handling of property taxes; usually one-twelfth of the annual tax assessment is paid into escrow for future timely remittance by the lender.

Subordinated Agreement Lease

With a subordinated agreement lease, the landowner grants the lease and then encumbers the fee title with a subordination agreement. This means that the landowner subordinates the ownership of the land in favor of the mortgage holder. With this kind of lease, the developer, with only a leasehold interest, can pledge title to the land itself as part of the collateral to secure a development loan. The reason is that the subordination agreement signed by the landowner grants a priority claim to the lender, which is similar in effect to granting a first lien with a mortgage instrument.

The concept is often used in the development of motel properties and some fast-food operations. It is true that the landowner places valuable property at risk with a subordination agreement, but would be encouraged to do so if a greater return can be realized than simply holding unimproved land. If the mortgage loan for the development is not paid, the mortgagee has the right to take both the land and improvements in a foreclosure action. To protect the landowner against such a consequence, the subordination agreement would normally require timely notification to the landowner of any act in default on the mortgage loan. If such an act should occur, the landowner would then have the right to step into the position of tenant/borrower, with rights to the property's cash flow and the obligation to pay the balance due on the mortgage note.

Build-to-Lease

A popular investment with lesser risk to the investor is for the lessor to agree to construct a building to certain tenant specifications in return for a lease commitment from the prospective tenant. The procedure is also called **build-to-suit** or *build-to-let*. The builder/investor has an assured tenant upon completion of the building and an immediate cash flow. The advantage for the tenant is obtaining a specially designed building that meets its needs more precisely. Examples of how this procedure is used would be freestanding store buildings for a tenant such as Safeway Corporation (grocers) and service stations built for major oil companies. This method is also used by the U.S. Post Office for outlying facilities. The Post Office leases buildings built to its specifications based on open bidding of projected rental rates.

Sale and Leaseback

Another financing technique that involves lease procedures occurs when an owner/occupant sells his or her property to an investor and simultaneously leases it back for continued occupancy. For the owner/seller, the advantage is the cash realized from the sale that can be used for further expansion of a company. The continued occupancy of the facilities allows an uninterrupted operation. And the lease payments are tax-deductible if they are for a business purpose. The investor/buyer obtains a sound real estate property with an immediate cash flow presumably calculated to yield a fair return.

While the procedure is most commonly used with commercial properties, it also has an application for a homeowner. A homeowner, perhaps a parent, might sell his or her house to a son or daughter and lease the premises for continued occupancy. While the lease payments are not tax-deductible for the tenant (it classifies as property used for personal purposes), the son or daughter would own the property as an income-producing asset subject to all deductions available for rental property, including depreciation. But it is critical to remember that any transaction between family members must be at fair market value or the tax treatment may be disallowed.

The Secure and Fair Enforcement for Mortgage Licensing Act of 2008 has been interpreted to mean that those involved in seller financing might have to have a mortgage broker's license and make all the standard disclosures discussed in Chapter 16 to prospective borrowers/buyers. At the time of the publication of this text, Congress was only willing to grant a narrow exemption for sellers providing certain types of seller financing for no more than three properties in any 12-month period. The new regulations went into effect on July 21, 2011. Suggest that this sentence may need to be revised, as the current acting director of the CFPB appears to be pulling back from any oversight or enforcement.

The **sale-and-leaseback** technique is also used in certain instances of company acquisition. To reduce the amount of cash needed up front to acquire a company, a buyer may arrange a sale and leaseback of property owned by the company to be acquired. Simultaneously, with the closing of the acquisition, the buildings are sold to an investor and the cash is applied to the purchase of the company. At the same time, the buildings are leased back to the acquired company with no interruption in its operation.

Companies and investors increasingly use sale-leasebacks in Internal Revenue Code Section 1031 exchanges, as well as to trigger gains to utilize expiring net operating losses.

Discounted Sale-Leasebacks

When market conditions are such that a residential or commercial property cannot be sold at its full appraised value, the property owner may decide to sell at a decreased price under what's known as a discounted sale and leaseback (DSL). This strategy is often used by property owners who have been unsuccessful in attempting to refinance. The property owner might have an existing home, commercial building, or factory, and a DSL can allow him/her to sell the real estate and hold the right to buy it back at a later time while still retaining possession and use of it through a leaseback of the real estate sold.

Within the residential mortgage market, when a property is "underwater"—that is, when more money is owed on the property than it would normally sell for, given the current market conditions—then a DSL can be the perfect solution for a stressed owner who cannot refinance due to appraisal problems. As long as the property owner has good credit, he/she could lower their monthly outlay through a discounted sale (*short sale*) that a lender agrees to, and then lease the property back with the right to purchase it again later at a higher price.

Where Are We Now?

How a Land-Sale-Leaseback Works

Let's develop one square foot of office space; we want to start small.

	Costs (all numbers are per square foot)
Land	$100
Hard Costs	190
Soft Costs	30
Total Costs	$320
Pro Forma	
Gross Schedule Income	$50
Less Vacancy and Credit Loss (10%)	-5
Adjusted Gross Income	45
Expenses	-15
Net Operating Income (NOI)	30
Debt Service on $240 (75%LTV) @7%; 30 yrs.	19.20
Net Cash Flow	10.80
With Sale of Land Back to Lender	
Yields $100 back to us, so we actually have no money in the project; in fact we now have	$20
Land Lease Payment (@8%)	8
Net Cash Flow after Lease Payment	2.8
Return on Equity with No Lease 10.80/80 =	13.5%
Return on Equity with Lease 2.8/0 =	∞

Within the commercial property market, a stressed property owner might find themselves with a loss due the one of the following common conditions:

- The current property owner may have purchased the property at a comparatively high price at the end of the last economic boom and it appears that there is a low possibility for a gain in the long term.

- The current property owner has too high a debt load on the property and their creditor may be insisting that the owner sell due to debt covenant breaches or other issues.
- The appeal of the area has diminished or is diminishing, putting the current property owner with rather limited upside potential when thinking of a sale in the future.

In these situations, you should take great care in the structure of the transaction and seek advice from tax professional, as the current property owner might incur a tax loss on the sale of the property involved in a DSL. Tax regulations may prohibit recognition of a tax loss to a property owner that is not considered a dealer when the sale is followed by an immediate acquisition of leasehold of 30 years or more for real estate. In many cases, this type of transaction would likely be considered by the IRS as a nontaxable exchange of like-kind property.

Sale of Equity Interests

Two types of equity investment have become popular as methods for financing real estate: syndications and realty funds.

Syndication

Syndication is a term that describes land or property acquisition and ownership by a group of participants. A syndicate is not a type of business organization; rather, it is a name applied to any group set up to pursue a limited objective in business. The participants may be individuals, partnerships, or corporations. While a number of different types of business organization may be used to form a syndicate, the most popular is the **limited partnership**. As a form of business organization, the limited partnership is recognized in all states. Essentially, it provides for one or more general partners who are responsible for the management and are personally liable for the partnership's obligations. Another class of partner is also recognized; these are limited partners, who are not permitted to participate in management decisions and whose liability is limited to the amount of their invested capital. A limited partnership must file its chartering agreement with the state in accordance with the applicable laws.

Real estate syndicates operate by two basic methods:

1. **sale of interests in existing properties** (Under this method, the property is identified for the participants. For example, a builder

or developer (usually called a *syndicator*) owns or controls (by option or contract of sale) a suitable investment property. The syndicator then sells participating interests to raise the money to develop the land, or possibly to complete the acquisition of an existing building.); and

2. **sale of interests in property to be acquired.** A syndicator sells interests to raise money for the acquisition of property to be determined later by the syndicator. This procedure is also referred to, quite accurately, as a *blind pool*. Because it allows so much freedom to the syndicator in the use of other people's money, many states forbid its use.

Since a participating interest in a syndicate can be classed as an investment in securities, most states place limits on the number of people who can be offered participating interests, or the amount of capital that can be raised without a complete registration under the state's security laws. If sales are made across state lines, or the number to whom participations are offered exceeds 35, a registration must be made with the federal Securities and Exchange Commission. Failure to comply with the law can result in felony action against the syndicator for the sale of unregistered securities.

Realty Funds

Whenever a larger group (generally more than 35 persons or companies) is formed to participate in a real estate venture, registration with federal and state regulatory agencies is necessary. The participation can be in the form of "units" purchased in a realty fund, which is usually organized as a limited partnership. If choosing this route of funding, make sure that the fund is in compliance with Regulation D.

Realty funds are organized by persons or companies wishing to raise equity money for real estate projects, such as the purchase of raw land, a construction project, or the purchase of existing income properties. The interests are sold in the form of participation certificates at a fixed price per unit. A unit generally costs anywhere from $100 to $5,000, depending on the plan of organization, and represents a certain percentage of interest in the total fund. Federal and most state laws classify the sale of such participating interests as a sale of securities; they must be registered and approved before any sale can be made.

The participant is actually a limited partner and may share in the tax losses and depreciation as well as in the profits generated through the fund's investments. The organizer of the fund is usually the general partner, or a company controlled by the general partner is so designated, and also serves as managing agent for the fund's properties.

Like-Kind Exchanges—Internal Revenue Code 1031

What is the purpose of a **like-kind exchange** that is available under Section 1031 of the U.S. IRS Code? Basically, it is a swap of one business or investment asset for another. Even though most exchanges are taxed as sales, if done correctly the transaction will fall under the parameters of Internal Revenue Code 1031, and an owner will have little or no tax payable at the time of the exchange. The IRS in essence allows the change in form of an investment without cashing out and recognizing a capital gain. This allows the investment in commercial real estate to maintain and grow on a tax-deferred basis. Theoretically, there is no limit to the number of like-kind exchanges that can be performed using the Section 1031 in rolling over the gain from one real estate investment into another. Section 1031 like-kind exchanges allow property owners not to pay capital gains taxes until the final exchanged property is sold for cash (years later), and then only a one-time, long-term federal capital gains tax is charged. At the beginning of 2018, this rate was between 15% and 20%. There is a scenario in the new tax law where, for those with incomes of $36,800 or less, the long-term capital gains rate is 0%.

Any firm or individual considering using a Section 1031 like-kind exchange should consult with a tax professional to make sure that they have followed all the procedures and rules associated with a successful transaction—particularly with regards to timing. As an example, Section 1031 requires that when exchanging a property, the new property must be closed on within 180 days of the sale of the old property. That means that should you identify a replacement property 40 days after the sale of the old property, then there are only 140 days left to close on the replacement property.

If for some reason the exchange, when finalized, results in the commercial property owner receiving cash, that cash—known as "boot"—will be taxed as partial sales proceeds from the sale of the property, generally as a capital gain.

SEC Regulations for Real Estate Transactions

The Securities and Exchange Commission (SEC) was created during the Depression years of the 1930s. It is charged with correcting possible abuses in the sale of securities to the general public, as well as overseeing market activities. There are several ways that real estate transactions can become involved with **SEC requirements**.

Sale of Mortgage Bonds

Large, well-known corporations have access to a method of raising money that is not generally available to an individual. This consists of borrowing in the financial markets through the sale of bonds. If the purpose of the money is to build a commercial or industrial building, the builder might sell mortgage bonds. Such an issue of bonds would be secured by a pledge of the real estate being developed. If such an issue is sold to the general public, it is subject to registration with the SEC. SEC examination of any proposed security issue is directed toward ensuring accuracy of the information distributed for the protection of the general public. It does not, however, assess the risk of any issue.

Advance Payments on Real Estate

There are many ways of offering real estate for sale, but only a few present any possible problems with the SEC. In general, the SEC considers suspect any transactions designed to raise money from the general public through the sale of "paper" that may evidence receipt of cash, rather than through delivery of a contract giving a clear right of title to property. Under certain circumstances, the paper could be construed as a security and consequently subject to SEC registration requirements. The sale of securities in violation of SEC regulations is a felony offense.

Real estate transactions that may be subject to SEC registration include the sale of predevelopment certificates for lots; the sale of condominium units in a building yet to be constructed for which a down payment is required; and the sale of limited partnership interests, if offered publicly. In these instances, where the line between selling real estate and selling a security is difficult to draw, it is best to consult with competent legal counsel.

Supplier Financing

Under certain conditions, it is possible for a builder/developer to obtain **supplier financing** assistance. This is a tool sometimes used by a supplier to gain an advantage in a competitive market. Such assistance may be obtained in two ways: (1) extended terms that allow later payment, or (2) a direct loan by the supplier.

Extended Terms

Most companies selling a service or product need their accounts receivable paid promptly and often offer cash discounts for timely payments. A few companies utilize credit terms as an incentive to do business with these firms and, in so doing, provide additional financing for the customer. For instance, in building an apartment, an office building, or even a house, a major supplier—such as a lumber dealer, cement company, or electrical or plumbing contractor—may agree to extend payment terms for 60 or 90 days or, in some cases, until the project is finished and sold.

This method does conserve cash for the builder/developer, but usually comes at a higher price—an increase in the product or service price plus interest. And the supplier may be exposed to a payment delay that could mean forfeiture of lien rights, which limits a supplier's willingness to use the procedure. The extended terms method of auxiliary finance should not be confused with slow payment or nonpayment of material suppliers' bills; both are very poor procedures. Building supply companies are fully aware of the 90- to 120-day time limits within which to file liens for nonpayment and, without a specific agreement allowing delay in payment, they normally make sure their interests are protected.

Supplier Loans

In recent years, some of the major appliance companies and, in a few cases, utility companies, have given larger builder/developer financial assistance with outright loans secured by second mortgages. The ulterior motive in supplier financing is always to ensure the use of the lender's products. This could be heating and air conditioning equipment or a full range of kitchen equipment, or it could be a utility company seeking a competitive advantage.

Seller-Financed Home Mortgages

Market conditions, with adequate money at reasonable interest rates, have diminished the need for seller financing. Nevertheless, **seller-financed mortgages** should be examined as a possible sales tool. While a large majority of property sellers want the cash generated by a sale to use for other purposes, there is a growing group who may think otherwise. These are mostly older people whose financial obligations have dwindled, and to whom sound investments are important. An assured source of income could be more important than a top-dollar sales price. In spite of some publicity to the contrary, home mortgages carry very high ratings as creditworthy investments. On average, at any given time, less than 5% of home mortgages are delinquent and less than 1% suffers default. For those selling houses to seek smaller accommodations, accepting all or part of the sales price in the form of a secured note can be a wise investment.

Because structuring a mortgage loan and qualifying applicants require specialized knowledge of the business, consideration should be given to using a reputable mortgage company to handle a seller-financed transaction. Mortgage companies are familiar with the documentation needed, can provide private mortgage insurance where necessary, and have access to secondary-market purchasers should it be necessary for the seller to convert the loan into cash. If a seller-financed loan is handled by an approved seller/servicer with uniform documentation, Fannie Mae is able to purchase the loan should an emergency need for cash arise. Any discount at the time of loan purchase would be only what it takes to match the seller-financed interest rate with current market yield requirements. However, no premium would be paid should the seller-financed interest rate exceed market yield requirements.

Foreclosure

Foreclosure is a legal procedure by which property pledged as collateral is sold to satisfy the debt thereby secured. A mortgage grants a lender the right to foreclose in the event of default. While default most often occurs because of nonpayment, there are other reasons that can trigger such action. For instance, the debtor must maintain the property in good condition, keep it free of liens, and comply with all local laws that affect the property. If an act in default occurs, the lender may take such action as is authorized by applicable state laws to protect its interests. In the foreclosure process, title passes at an auction to the highest bidder. This is usually the holder of the mortgage note (the lender), but it could be to a third party who may purchase it at the foreclosure auction sale. If the price paid at foreclosure is more than the debt to the lender, the lender is entitled only to the money due on the note. In the unlikely event of any surplus money, those funds are paid to the foreclosed owner.

Foreclosure is a step that lenders want to avoid if at all possible. There are seldom any winners in this action. For the lender, it is costly, time-consuming, and may require additional funds to be advanced for payment of various foreclosure costs. If the property is vacated, there is danger of vandalism. Also, foreclosure brings up the additional problem of future disposition of the property.

Foreclosure for the borrower results in the loss of property, possibly the homestead. It is a traumatic experience and will result in a negative report on one's credit record. For a borrower facing default, the first step should be to discuss the problem with the lender. Most lenders recognize the fact that various personal and business problems beyond the control of a borrower can cause default. While the lender is not always able to modify a repayment agreement, it is possible that a moratorium on payments could be granted for a limited period of time, or the release of some tax escrow funds could provide temporary assistance to the debtor.

Lenders do not normally seek out borrowers to offer assistance, as their responsibility is to the holder of the note and to pursue timely repayment of the loan. So it falls to the borrower to initiate any move to delay payments or to rework the mortgage obligation. The earlier a repayment problem can be called to the attention of a lender, the more likely it is to be resolved with forbearance for the borrower.

Obligations Involved with Default Insurance: Indemnity

When a foreclosure occurs and losses are sustained, who bears the cost? The party holding the secured note undertakes foreclosure action if there is a default, and bears the initial cost. But if the loan is insured against default, the note holder can claim reimbursement for the loss. Exactly how the claim is handled depends on the type of default coverage. This can be private mortgage insurance, a HUD/FHA-insured commitment, or a VA guaranty.

Where Are We Now?

Why Is Debt Relief Considered Income?

If George gives Tom $100, Tom will have to consider the $100 as income for tax purposes.

However, if George lends Tom $100, there will be no tax consequence. (Another example: When a lender funds a loan, the borrower does not have to pay taxes on that money since it is a loan.)

If a year after George makes the loan he tells Tom that Tom does not have to pay the $100 back, then in that year, Tom has to show the $100 as income for tax purposes.

The same would be true in a deed in lieu of foreclosure proceeding. The lender is basically converting the loan to a taxable gift. This "debt forgiveness" was temporarily modified by the Mortgage Debt Relief Act 2007 that excluded as income any debt discharge up to $2 million for a primary home. The Act has been extended again to cover debt forgiven within the calendar years of 2007 to 2017 and includes debt discharged in 2018, provided that there was a written agreement entered into in 2017[10].

A qualified tax advisor should be consulted when negotiations occur between a borrower and a lender concerning debt relief. There must be a determination of the value of the property received by the lender as compared to the amount of debt relief.

Regardless of the type of default protection, all kinds insure the lender against loss, not the borrower. This is true even though it is the borrower who pays the insurance premiums. It is often misunderstood since, unlike other kinds of insurance, the party paying for the coverage is not the one insured. What the borrower is paying for is an assurance to the lender that the loan will be paid should the borrower suffer a default. The benefit to a borrower is in obtaining a loan that might otherwise not be available.

There is another major difference between this coverage and other kinds of insurance. As a qualification requirement for coverage, the borrower must indemnify the insurance company against loss. This means that if the insurance company must reimburse a lender for a loss, the insuring company (or federal agency) has a right to demand reimbursement from the defaulted borrower. This right applies to all three major types of coverage: private mortgage insurance, HUD/FHA, and VA.

---

[10]"Extension of the Exclusion of Forgiven Mortgage Debt and Certain Energy Credits," Internal Revenue Service, last modified March 1, 2018 "Home Foreclosure and Debt Cancellation," Internal Revenue Service, updated January 5, 2015, https://www.irs.gov/newsroom/home-foreclosure-and-debt-cancellation.

REAL ESTATE CYCLES
Home Buyer Education Programs

A corollary to the need to improve mortgage lending to existing and other markets is recognition that many people are simply not familiar with normal real estate acquisition and lending procedures.

Successful home ownership depends on a prospective homeowner having basic knowledge of how to acquire a home, how to assure proper title, how the acquisition might be financed, and how to care for a home. To some, home ownership is an impossible dream. The addition of pre-purchase home buyer education programs to the requirements for loan qualification is of benefit to many. Benefits include finding more people who are eligible for home ownership. Education programs also make borrowers more aware of their responsibilities to lenders, resulting in sound loans with fewer defaults. Initial implementation of these programs has already proven their value to home buyers and lenders. A further gain is the fact that restoring the market acceptance of mortgage-backed securities will increase the market for homes, thus creating many new jobs. Home building has historically led the United States out of recessions, but the lack of housing demand due to the nature of the recent financial crisis was a continued drag on economic recovery well into 2012. Single-family housing starts dropped to a low of 445,000 in 2009, and by 2011, had continued to decline to 431,000. By the end of 2017, starts increased to over 893,000 according to National Association of Home Builders Chief Economist Robert Dietz[11]. Since new home and commercial construction has been as high as 8.9% of the U.S. gross domestic product (GDP), this reduced level caused a slower-than-normal recovery from the recent low point in the residential real estate cycle.

THE REAL ESTATE CYCLE

Business cycles can be thought of as when and how the direction of economic activity changes or peaks from an expansion in the economy

---

[11] Elizabeth Thompson, "Economic Panel Predicts Housing Will Continue to Gain Ground in 2018," National Association of Home Builders, January 9, 2018, https://www.nahb.org/en/news-and-publications/press-releases/2018/01/economic-panel-predicts-housing-will-continue-to-gain-ground-in-2018.aspx

and the time that a contraction/recession ends.[12] A business cycle peak represents the last month before several key economic indicators—such as gross domestic output, employment, housing starts, and retail sales—start to decline. The low point of a business cycle represents the last month before the economic indicators mentioned above begin to go up. Since the differing economic indicators frequently change directions at somewhat differing points in time, there can be some differences between industries' declines and recoveries.

According to the National Bureau of Economic Research, the average duration of a business cycle from 1945–2009 was 68.5 months from peak to peak. Real estate cycles, however, are about cyclical fluctuations of quantities and prices of construction, sales, permits, and inventories of real estate. Many times, the real estate cycle starts down before a recession is officially recognized and recovers before the rest of the economy—which was often the case between 1945 and 2009, when real estate related spending led the economy out of recession. One of the reasons that the recent "Great Recession" was the worst downturn since the Great Depression is that the real estate bubble and other factors discussed earlier in this chapter caused the residential real estate industry *not* to be the first mover in economic recovery. At its peak in 2006, real estate construction contributed $1.195 trillion, or 8.9%, to the nation's economic output as measured by GDP. By 2013, this had only recovered to $925 billion, a dramatic decrease to only 5.8% of GDP. This dramatic decline in housing construction was a large contributor to the recent "Great Recession's" high unemployment rate. Real estate cycles do not always follow the same pattern as business cycles, and within the same marketplace, office, retail, single-family residential, multifamily, and industrial properties may be at different phases of a cycle and of differing durations.

For office, retail, and multifamily properties, the real estate cycle can be summed up in four general phases: the growth phase, the excess supply phase, the downturn phase, and the recovery phase. The growth phase generally has good absorption of new space, decreasing vacancy rates, and a higher rate of rental income growth. This will in turn lead to increases in the level of new construction and planned new construction,

---

[12]"Single Family Housing Starts Jump in Final Month 2015," StrucSure, last modified January 23, 2015, accessed July 10, 2015, https://www.strucsure.com/News/Home_Building/Articles/Single_family_housing_starts_jump_in_final_month_of_2014

yielding higher employment growth in the construction trades. The excess supply phase shows sustained high periods of new construction, with construction cranes dotting the horizon. New space absorption rates drop, and oftentimes turns negative, triggering a downward spiral in rental rates as firms move out of older buildings into newer, better spaces for lower rents. The excess supply phase causes lower employment growth, thus slowing the need for new space. The downturn phase usually shows escalating vacancy rates due to low absorption rates for existing buildings and new buildings coming online from the excess supply phase. Often this is caused by an increase in unemployment and lower-to-negative rental rates. The recovery phase shows very little new construction activity, increased space absorption (as unemployment decreases), employment growth, and little-to-no rental rate growth.

Residential real estate tends to peak just before business cycles do and, thus, the demand for new housing (thus housing starts) is at a euphoric state beyond what can be absorbed by new household creations. To illustrate this effect, the data presented in table 1-1 shows how the residential real estate markets have historically peaked shortly before subsequent recessions.

TABLE 1-1

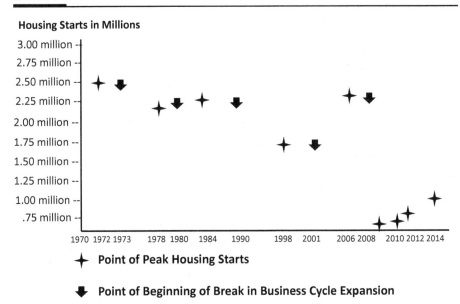

Source: © 2021 Mbition LLC

The time lag between the peak in the residential sector and the next recession is just one indicator and must be balanced from a predictive tool, considering the rate of inflation, the interest rate yield curve, whether there are continuing productivity improvements, industry capacity utilization rates, the unemployment rate, the stock and securities market levels, and liquidity.

At any point in time, one market segment or region of the country may be in a period of decline, while another is in expansion. Moreover, a period of decline in one area might push another area into a decline. In the early 1990s, a commercial real estate decline started in the northeastern United States, and there was a rolling commercial real estate decline that went through the Midwest and ended with a mild decline in California. Similarly, there was a decline in residential real estate made worse by the "Oil Belt" recession and the savings and loan crisis of the mid-1980s. Oil Belt states like Colorado, Louisiana, Oklahoma, and Texas were hit particularly hard. There is a difference between the commercial real estate cycle on occasion and that of residential real estate. An example was that in 2008 when the S&P 500 hit a bottom, down 54% from its peak the prior year, commercial real estate was only off by 30% and it recovered much more quickly[13].

In the recent mortgage crisis, cities like San Bernardino, California, saw home prices plummet by 30% in 2007, not hitting rock bottom until recently. As a result, cities heavily dependent on real estate taxes to support the municipal budget, such as San Bernardino, have declared bankruptcy, causing the layoffs of many municipal workers and school teachers. The layoffs further negatively affected the economy of the area. If this were to hold for over a period of more than a year, the plans for drilling many new oil wells may not go forward, as these plans were made based on a higher price of oil. Many injection wells will be closed down, and the investors and workers dependent on these could find themselves in a regional decline. South Dakota, Louisiana, and Wyoming could be hit particularly hard. In Louisiana, state services were cut in 2016 after Louisiana depleted its rainy-day funds on university spending. Louisiana cut 30,000 employees and furloughed others[14]. Contrast this with the significant differences regionally and locally in the remainder of the real

---

[13] Albert Haworth, "Real Estate in Present and Future Tense," *Real Assets Adviser* 5, no. 5 (May 2018).
[14] Chico Harlan, "Battered by Drop in Oil Prices and Jindal's Fiscal Policies, Louisiana Falls into Budget Crisis," *The Washington Post*, March 4, 2016.

estate market and an obvious upswing in the real estate cycle in areas like Denver and San Francisco had recovered to 98% and 99% of prerecession levels by the middle of 2017 and Dallas and Ft. Worth had also recovered to 93% and 94% of prerecession levels[15].

In the most recent residential real estate market cycle that started around 2000 and peaked in 2007, the market in most of the United States declined through 2011 with some modest recovery in values after that. Most areas of the United States had recovered to 1% higher than the peak in 2007 by the end of 2017, according to a March report issued by CoreLogic[16].

IMPACT OF THE ECONOMY

The national economic health does have a bearing on the real estate investment and financing industries. As an example, in 2017 real estate construction contributed $1.34 trillion to the United States GDP or about 7 percent, most of that was commercial real estate at $935.1 billion[17]. That level is above the previous peak of $1.19 trillion that occurred just before the recent "Great Recession" that represented 8.9 percent of GDP. While the definition of the investment space including a bull or bear market, a stock market correction or recession or recovery are fairly consistent, the same cannot be said of the housing or commercial real estate markets. When any economic conditions cause homeowners or commercial real estate investors to believe they are losing equity in their investment, then various types of market collapses occur. This can be due to commercial real estate developers producing more commercial space that the market can absorb or what can happen if inflation takes hold and the Federal Reserve (discussed in Chapter 2) raises interest rates. So when individuals or investors have a positive view to the future and the economic indicators are good for real estate, then they will use real estate as collateral for borrowing funds they need in excess of their cash capital on hand. A brief description of how this is accomplished follows with some detail of other market functions

---

[15] Ralph McLaughlin, "The U.S. Housing Recovery that Wasn't," Trulia, last modified May 3, 2017, https://www.trulia.com/research/home-value-recovery-2017/

[16] "Evaluating the Housing Market Since the Great Recession," CoreLogic, March 1, 2018, http://www.corelogic.com

[17] Zander, Andrea, 2018, Commercial Real Estate Contributes 935b to U.S. GDP in 2017. Institutional real Estate, Inc. Research report dated February 28, 2018. Accessed at: https://irei.com/news/commercial-real-estate-contributes-935b-u-s-gdp-2017/

that are appropriate to understanding market economics and mechanics. Finally, a review follows of more recent impacts of the economy that have been caused either within the real estate industry or from outside factors.

Financing Real Property Loans

Real property financing is the pledging of land as collateral to borrow money. The pledge as protection for a lender is called **hypothecation**, which comes from the Latin word *hypotheca*,[18] a term signifying taking a security interest similar to the security interests used in the lending laws of the Roman Empire; the borrower remains in possession of the property while also offering security for the loan. It is only by defaulting on the loan agreement that a borrower can forfeit possession of and title to the property. **Default** is nonperformance of an obligation that is part of a contract. Failure to repay a loan is the most common act in default, which can activate rights that allow a lender to claim title to the pledged property.

The loan itself is evidenced by a **promissory note**, which is an unconditional written promise of a person (or persons) to pay a certain sum to another party. The "loan agreement" is commonly identified as a **mortgage**. A mortgage pledges property (collateral) as security for the note. Further details on the instruments of real estate finance will be covered in detail in Chapter 6. The mortgage and the promissory note are interlinked documents, and if the note is not paid or another form of default occurs, the terms of the mortgage instrument can trigger an action allowing the lender to take title to the property. Such action is called **foreclosure**, which means that the property offered as collateral for the loan is sold to satisfy the debt. The instruments and steps just discussed will be more fully explained in later chapters, but the underlying procedure remains the same: land is pledged as security for a loan by a conveyance that limits the lender to claiming title only if a default occurs.

Compensation for Borrowed Money

Even in earlier societies, pledging rights to landownership as security for a loan meant some kind of compensation was due to the lender. This fact

---

[18] Henry John Roby, *Roman Private Law in the Times of Cicero and of the Antonines* (Cambridge: Cambridge University Press, 1902).

created a problem because charging interest for the use of one's money was considered a sin by many religious groups, including Christians, until the Middle Ages. Acceptable income was essentially only that earned by one's labor. Even today, in many parts of the world, some societies do not permit interest to be paid for the use of another's money. To bypass the religious constraint, a common practice developed: charging for the use of money "up front"—that is, deducting the cost of the borrowed money from the amount loaned and calling it something other than interest. Just call it a discount.

A **discount** is a portion of the loan amount taken by a lender as a cost for borrowed money. It is measured today in **points**; one point is 1% of the loan amount. In financial markets today, some borrowed money is paid for with interest only, some with discount only, and some by a combination of the two. Discounts collected tend to increase the yield on the amount loaned. Real property loans are most often paid for through a combination of interest and discounts.

The Mortgage Loan Market

The mortgage loan market functions at two different levels: the **primary market**, which is loan origination, and the **secondary market**, which consists of investors who purchase loans made by others.

The loan origination market is composed of borrowers and lenders. Negotiation for a loan at this level involves a discussion of the interest rate and discount. How the requirements for loan qualification are determined depends on who the lender is and whether or not the loan will be sold to secondary-market investors. Regulated lenders must adhere to the rules set by their regulatory authority. Unregulated lenders are not as restricted. If a loan is intended for sale rather than to be held by the lender as its own investment (held "in portfolio"), the loan must meet the secondary-market purchaser's requirements.

First, let us examine the nature of the lenders who deal one-on-one with borrowers—the loan originators. A person or company seeking mortgage loan contracts or customers is called a loan originator. The **loan originator** may be a bank, an insurance company, a mortgage company, or other entity. The negotiation involves the loan amount, interest rate and discount to be charged, the collateral, qualification of the borrower, and the terms for repayment of the loan. Each of these important items will be discussed in later chapters.

Once a loan has been finalized, the promissory note and its security instrument become salable to others. Almost every mortgage note is written as a **negotiable instrument**, which means that the holder of the note has the right to sell it. Even so, the originator may opt to retain the loan in its own investment portfolio to earn the interest and discount it produces. If the originator makes the decision to sell the loan, a secondary-market investor is contacted to purchase the loan. The purchaser is most interested in two aspects of the loan: (1) its quality, meaning its level of risk, and (2) its yield.

Secondary-market purchasers consider interest relatively unimportant; it is the yield that matters, as that is the return that will be received. **Yield** is a combination of the interest plus the discount. If the interest is too low, the discount must be increased to make up any difference necessary to meet the secondary-market yield requirement.

The secondary market for mortgages can be affected by changes in both the economy and the demand for money. Changes in the real estate cycle, covered later in the chapter, can be made more or less extreme by changes in the economy and the demand for money.

Financial Market Instruments

An increasing portion of the money flowing into residential loans comes from the sale of various kinds of securities in the financial markets, rather than from savings deposits. The sale of securities is the business of investment bankers and stockbrokers. It is the method by which corporations raise equity money and one way they borrow money. Because of the importance of this market, students of real estate finance should understand terminology that applies to securities and the purpose for which securities are issued.

Corporations can be financed through the sale of securities, paper certificates that represent some kind of an investment in the corporate structure. There are two major classes of securities: (1) stock certificates, representing an ownership, or equity, interest in the corporation; and (2) bonds, representing a loan to the corporation. Stock evidences ownership; bonds evidence indebtedness.

Where Are We Now?

Lenders' Willingness to Loan Money Coupled with the Availability of Lendable Funds

During the Great Depression of the late 1920s and the early 1930s, the federal government took steps to encourage lenders to make mortgage loans. It accomplished this aim by creating the Federal Housing Administration (FHA), which insured loans against default. However, there was little money available to lend. Deposits in banks and savings institutions, historically used to make loans, were virtually depleted. So the federal government created the Federal National Mortgage Association, which was authorized to purchase loans insured by the FHA. This practice allowed lenders to make loans without depleting their deposits. As a result, lenders had a new source of mortgage money. When Fannie Mae was privatized in 1968, its function as the principal purchaser of FHA mortgages was assumed by the Government National Mortgage Association. The mortgage crisis that erupted in 2008 raised the importance of the FHA; its market share of the number of new home loans increased from 5% in 2006 to nearly 50% by June of 2010. That created an anchor to support the fragile new home construction market until the conventional mortgage market recovered. A fall 2017 survey performed by the Mortgage Bankers Association indicates that the FHA still has 11.3% of all loan applications.

A Look at the Future

The function of a mortgage-backed security is to convert a mortgage loan into a financial instrument that can be more easily sold to investors. By opening the financial markets as a source of money to fund mortgage loans, adequate money at a competitive cost for sound loans has become more available.

The fuel that has expanded this market is federal agency underwriting. Federal agency underwriting accounts for more than half the funding of all residential loans. Four federal agencies are involved, of which Fannie Mae and Freddie Mac are the largest. These two agencies fall under the oversight authority of the Federal Housing Finance Agency.

The Federal Housing Administration (FHA) falls under the Department of Housing and Urban Development, or HUD. Ginnie Mae is limited to underwriting FHA and VA loans, and is also a part of HUD. The fourth agency, the Federal Agricultural Mortgage Corporation, or "Farmer Mac," was formed in the mid-1980s. Farmer Mac was deemed to have too many restraints and was not very active. Therefore, in 1996, Congress gave Farmer Mac similar powers to Fannie Mae and Freddie Mac, although Farmer Mac is limited to underwriting agricultural loans and rural home loans outside incorporated areas. These government-sponsored enterprises (GSEs) are now under the oversight of the Federal Housing Finance Agency (FHFA), which was created on July 30, 2008, when President George W. Bush signed into law the Housing and Economic Recovery Act of 2008. The Act created a regulator with the authority necessary to oversee vital components of the nation's secondary mortgage markets: Fannie Mae, Freddie Mac, and the federal home loan banks. In addition, this law combined the staffs of the Office of Federal Housing Enterprise Oversight (OFHEO), the Federal Housing Finance Board (FHFB), and the GSE mission office at HUD. With financial crisis facing the world, strengthening the regulatory and supervisory oversight of the 14 housing-related GSEs seemed imperative. The hope is that the establishment of FHFA will promote a stronger, safer U.S. housing finance system. In December 2009, the combined debt and obligations of these GSEs totaled $5.5 trillion—around half of the $11.7 trillion in U.S. residential mortgage debt. Since Fannie Mae and Freddie Mac were placed into government conservatorship in 2008, the Federal Reserve Bank has been the primary purchaser of both of these GSE's mortgage-backed securities. The Federal Reserve Bank thus served as the purchaser of last resort for over $1.47 trillion of Fannie Mae and Freddie Mac MBS through November 2009,[19] keeping the mortgage lending markets open. Representatives of the Federal Reserve Bank announced that the Bank would pull out of this market in the first quarter of 2010; however, officials later discovered that such a change would have too great a negative impact on the mortgage market and mortgage rates. The Fed was still making purchases in July 2010 that at the time totaled $2.31 trillion.[20] The Federal Reserve Bank has maintained that the

---

[19]Federal Reserve Bank, "FMOC Statement," press release, December 16, 2009, https://www.federalreserve.gov/newsevents/pressreleases/monetary20091216a.htm
[20]"Agency Mortgage-Backed Securities (MBS) Purchase Program," Federal Reserve Bank, last modified February 12, 2016, https://www.federalreserve.gov/regreform/reform-mbs.htm

purchases made between March and July 2010 were intended only to "stabilize" the market, and most purchases made after March 2010 appear to have been sold by the Fed to commercial banks and others in the aftermarket. Since August 2014, the Fed continues to purchase mortgage-backed securities as part of its extended support of the housing industry. The Federal Open Market Committee (FOMC) directed the Open Market Trading Desk (the Desk) at the Federal Reserve Bank of New York to purchase additional MBS and longer-term Treasury securities. Moreover, the FOMC directed the Desk to maintain its existing policies of reinvesting principal payments from the Federal Reserve's holdings of agency debt and agency MBS and of rolling over maturing Treasury securities at auction. The FOMC noted that these actions should put downward pressure on longer-term interest rates, supporting mortgage markets.[21] Considering the impact of these GSEs on the U.S. economy and mortgage market, it is critical that we intensify our focus on the oversight and restructuring of Fannie Mae, Freddie Mac, and the federal home loan banks.

Constraints increasingly imposed on underwriters' loan purchase policies have put a virtual halt to the subprime mortgage market. As a result, pressure has been applied by HUD to direct activities into more diverse areas of lending. Four results are probable: (1) an increase in home loans available to minority groups, immigrants, and those in underserved urban areas; (2) a growth in the offerings and market share of Federal Housing Administration (FHA) mortgage loans; (3) the rehabilitation of Fannie Mae and Freddie Mac from government conservatorship and the market acceptance without Federal Reserve Bank market intervention of their issues of MBS; and (4) the emergence of private mortgage-backed securities that have a retained loss interest by the mortgage loans' original lenders as a market discipline to diminish the moral hazard that was created by the recent originate-to-distribute model, which has been blamed for the recent mortgage crisis.

The Mortgage Crisis Development

Up to this point, most responses to the mortgage crisis have focused on efforts to stem the negative effects on homeowners, financial institutions, mortgage markets, and investors. However, it is important to understand

---

[21]"Why is the Desk Purchasing Agency MBS?" Federal Reserve Bank of New York, accessed December 12, 2014, http://www.newyorkfed.org/markets/ambs/ambs_faq.html

how we as a society got into this position. There are no simple answers, but what follows are some of the generally agreed-upon causes of the crisis.

A low interest rate environment was created by two destabilizing events:

1. the technology stock bubble burst; and
2. terrorists attacked the United States.

In response, the Federal Reserve lowered interest rates to help calm financial markets, lowering its Fed Funds target rate from 6.5% at the end of 2000 to 1.75% at the end of 2001. The Fed continued to make other rate cuts until the target rate reached 1.0% in June 2003, and did not begin to raise rates until mid-2004. This long period of low interest rates has been confirmed by economists, regulators, and capital markets experts as a contributor to the housing bubble, as it inordinately stimulated demand for mortgage debt and housing price inflation. At the same time, white collar crime units were shifted to Homeland Security efforts; these units were not replaced between 2001 and 2007, allowing fraudsters to instigate problems with greater impunity. Even in 2012, the FBI white collar crime units had not reached even 20% of their former investigative staffing levels.

A renewed refinance boom occurred at a level unequaled in history. This boom caused lenders to expand their operations to meet additional demand along with the already increased demand for housing allowed by the low interest rate environment. When the eventual satiation of refinance demand occurred, many lenders, accustomed to easy and plentiful profits, began to offer more innovative loan products to bring new borrowers to the market. These included not only subprime products with lower credit and asset requirements of borrowers, but also novel payment plans such as interest-only and option ARM mortgages that allowed some borrowers to qualify for larger homes and others to enter the housing market for the first time.

The passage of the Housing and Community Development Act of 1992 amended the charter of Fannie Mae and Freddie Mac to reflect Congress's view that these GSEs "have an affirmative obligation to facilitate the financing of affordable housing for low-income and moderate-income families."[22] Fannie Mae and Freddie Mac were required to meet the "affordable housing goals" set by the Department of Housing and

---

[22]U.S. Code, Title 12§4501. Cornell University Law School, Legal Information Institute at point (7), accessed August 11, 2011, https://www.law.cornell.edu/uscode/text/12/4501

Urban Development. In 1999, the Clinton administration placed pressure on Fannie Mae and Freddie Mac to expand mortgage loans to low- and moderate-income borrowers by increasing the ratios of their loan portfolios in distressed inner city areas designated in the CRA of 1977. These two policy decisions allowed Fannie Mae and Freddie Mac to promote the widespread use of high LTV ratios. Fannie Mae began offering a 97% LTV program in 1994. Industry experts issued strong objections to this decision, citing Fannie Mae's early 1980s experiment allowing 5%-down loans in Texas—a decision that proved disastrous, with one in four borrowers defaulting. Ongoing competitive pressure and the lure of high profits pulled Fannie Mae and Freddie Mac into the subprime market, leading to the introduction of first-time home buyer programs with up to 105% LTV. Thus, the stage was set for the demise of these organizations. By 2001, Fannie Mae and Freddie Mac controlled the subprime market, "having . . . absorbed the largest and best parts of the 'old' subprime world that developed over the 1990s using risk-based pricing. They continued to make mortgage loans to borrowers with FICO scores of around 540,"[23] and made up to 105% LTV loans as late as the first quarter of 2007. Fannie Mae reintroduced a line of 97% LTV option mortgage loans in 2014. The latest product updates made in February 2017 included the HomeReady®; Fannie Mae standard mortgages allow for LTV up to 105% if the subordinate lien is an eligible Community Seconds® loan.

The profitability of mortgage securitization and the moral hazard facing many lenders with larger operations and falling demand from borrowers caused lenders to further reduce underwriting standards or simply ignore them. This increased loan production that was facilitated by the development of automated underwriting by the GSEs. In 1996, Freddie Mac indicated that up to 35% of borrowers who obtained mortgages from the subprime market could have qualified for a conventional loan through Loan Prospector, its automated underwriting system.[24]

Other traditional lenders and secondary market players, including Fannie Mae and Freddie Mac, began to feel further market pressure to accept an increasingly substandard product. These GSEs were government-chartered, which gave them access to cheap capital based on the

---

[23]Tom LaMalfa, Mortgage Corner column, *Holm Mortgage Finance Report*, January 19, 2001.
[24]Office of the Comptroller of Currency, "Economic Issues in Predatory Lending," working paper, accessed July 10, 2015, http://www.selegal.org/occ_workpaper0730.pdf

assumption by investors that they would be bailed out in a crisis. The federal government is not legally required to cover these entities' liabilities, but the belief to the contrary was a good assumption nonetheless. The GSEs had actually been privately owned since the late 1960s and early 1970s, which drove them to maximize profits. Therefore, Fannie Mae and Freddie Mac had both the incentive and the capacity to take on excessive risk, and they did so with vigor. Many industry experts, regulators, and elected government officials—liberals, conservatives, and progressives alike—attempted to rein in these excesses as the possible consequences were well known, but their efforts were stymied by some of the most well-funded lobbying campaigns in history. (Fannie Mae and Freddie Mac spent some $164 million on lobbying from 1999 through 2008.)[25]

Events that occurred during the summer of 2007 in the structured investment vehicles (SIV) financing market began to expose the flaws in agency ratings methodologies—flaws that did not become fully apparent until housing prices stopped appreciating. The general market's acceptance of the high ratings on mortgage-backed securities and collateralized debt obligations belied the liquidity risk contained in the fact of these substandard products backing commercial paper issued by many major banks. **Commercial paper** is a simple promise to pay that is unsecured (a corporate IOU). The first banking regulators to see the danger to financial institutions in time to avert major damage were the Canadian banking regulators. This revelation had a ripple effect, leading to a spike in interest rate spreads and collateral values, causing many firms to incur losses not thought possible just a year earlier in the United States and Europe. (No Canadian banks went out of business during the Great Depression or during the recent financial crisis;[26] there may be some lessons to be learned from our neighbors to the north.)

---

[25]Phil Angelides, "Fannie, Freddie and the Financial Crisis," op-ed, *Bloomberg*, August 3, 2011.
[26]Mark J. Perry, "Due North: Canada's Marvelous Mortgage and Banking System," *The Journal of the American Enterprise Institute* (2010), accessed August 11, 2011, http://www.aei.org/publication/due-north-canadas-marvelous-mortgage-and-banking-system/

Where Are We Now?

What the Future Holds

Since the creation of the Federal Housing Administration, the number of loans insured in any given year has varied dramatically. When conventional lenders were making high loan-to-value (LTV) loans and those loans were being readily purchased by the secondary market, the demand for FHA-insured loans virtually disappeared. However, when FNMA, FHLMC, and other players in the secondary market became insolvent and unable to provide money for the purchase of mortgage loans, FHA became very popular again. Just as government agencies were essential to the recovery after the Great Depression, their role will be equally important in recoveries from current and future depressions and recessions. If anything has been learned from the disasters of 2007 through 2011, it is that proper oversight is critical. Private sector lending will always be the most important aspect of mortgage lending, but it must work in tandem with well-structured, well-monitored, and well-controlled government programs. One of the reasons for this government involvement is that since 1995 loan origination has become more dependent on automated loan analysis, which involves a computer program using artificial intelligence to help analyze a loan application (more fully described in Chapter 9). This practice actually began in the secondary market with the large purchasers of loans such as Fannie Mae and Freddie Mac as a method of expediting their own loan analyses. With advances in technology, it is now possible for an individual to negotiate a mortgage loan over the internet. Prior to the passage of the Wall Street Reform and Consumer Financial Protection Act of 2010 ("Dodd-Frank Act"), regulated lenders handled about 75% of the mortgage loans. Since the passage of Dodd-Frank, nearly any entity involved in mortgage lending—whether a depository or nondepository institution—falls into the category of regulated lenders.

> Oddly enough, as of the beginning of 2017, no real decisions have been made about how to bring FNMA or FHLMC out of government conservatorship. Current profits made by these entities are funding federal government operations, and members of the House of Representatives would have to either raise taxes to replace this new source of revenue or reduce federal spending. Investors, seeing recovered profits going to the U.S. Treasury instead of the investors themselves, filed suit to try and recover, but recently lost their bid to remove FNMA and FHLMC from full government control.[27]
>
> ---
>
> [27] Jody Shenn, Margaret Cronin Fisk, and Clea Benson, "Fannie Mae, Freddie Mac Plunge after Court Ruling on Profit," Bloomberg News, October 1, 2014, accessed December 11, 2014, https://www.bloomberg.com/news/articles/2014-10-01/fannie-freddie-plunge-after-court-ruling-on-profits-correct-

Questions for Discussion

1. Define "security interest" and explain how it has been used in real estate finance since the Industrial Revolution.
2. What is meant by the term "collateral"? By "hypothecation"?
3. What is the purpose of a promissory note? Of a mortgage?
4. Describe the origin of a loan discount.
5. Distinguish between the functions of the primary and secondary mortgage markets.
6. How can prepurchase home-buyer education programs affect the mortgage market?
7. How is loan-to-value ratio used in lending practices?
8. Who benefits from a sale-and-leaseback deal, and how?
9. What is the risk involved in an unsubordinated leasehold mortgage, and how might protection from this risk be obtained?
10. What is syndication? What is a realty fund?

Multiple Choice Questions for Review

1. Security interest gives the _____ the right to bring about sale of a loan if there is default.
   a. mortgagor
   b. interest
   c. collateral
   d. none of the above

2. Compensation for borrowed money is called:
   a. hypothecation
   b. borrower
   c. mortgagee
   d. grantee

3. Which of the following is normally executed contemporaneously with a mortgage and creates the obligation of repayment?
   a. promissory note
   b. payment insurance
   c. charges and liens
   d. deed covenants

4. The allodial system of landownership that forms the basis of ownership in the United States is best described as the:
   a. right to occupy and use land owned by a superior
   b. right of a democratic government to control how land is used
   c. ownership of land is free and absolute, subject only to governmental and voluntary restrictions
   d. origin and development of community property laws

5. Which of the following is a charge that is itemized separately from loan fees as a primary purpose to raise the yield?
   a. statutory costs
   b. loan closing costs
   c. effective interest
   d. discount points

6. Residential real estate tends to peak:
   a. after a recession has begun
   b. at the trough of a business cycle
   c. just before business cycles do
   d. at the peak of commercial real estate cycles

7. Which of the following best describes a good reason for a firm to sell an existing building that it owns and lease it back?
   a. the tax advantage of a capital gain upon sale
   b. as a way to raise cash without borrowing money
   c. interest on commercial mortgage is not tax deductible and lease payments are
   d. none of the above

8. Which of the following is the chief risk involved in an unsubordinated leasehold mortgage?
   a. The title to the land is retained by lessor and impairs the claims of the lender financing the building.
   b. The taxes and insurance on the ground lease are paid by the lessee.
   c. Interim construction finance is often not available.
   d. If the ground lease is not paid in a timely manner, the collateral position of the mortgage holder on the improvements can be impaired.

9. Which one of the following is an untrue statement about syndications?
   a. Syndications are formed to acquire, develop, manage, operate, or market real estate.
   b. Syndicators put up the lion's share of the investment in the proposed deal.
   c. Syndications allow smaller investors to participate in ventures that would otherwise be beyond their individual financial ability.
   d. Syndications are sometimes referred to as limited partnerships.

10. How much should the loan-to-value ratio be for the average mortgage in order to avoid the requirement to pay a mortgage insurance premium?
    a. 95%
    b. 90%
    c. 85%
    d. 80%

Information Resources

http://www.islandtime.com/re-intro/re-weblk.htm
   The Real Estate Professional – Internet Guide provides information for most real estate professionals as well as a listing of real estate software and other real estate professional tools.

http://www.hud.gov/
   The Department of Housing and Urban Development is an excellent source of information about FHA mortgage lending, which made 43% of mortgage loans made in 2010, according to a study by the National Association of REALTORS®.

http://www.nber.org/cycles/cyclesmain.html
   The National Bureau of Economic Research provides excellent information about business cycles in the past from several viewpoints.

http://www.ired.com
   A thorough real estate directory and good source of information on subjects such as commercial real estate, international real estate, and professional real estate services.

http://www.corelogic.com
   Extensive data and reports are available that can allow you to walk through the residential real estate downturn and recovery. An excellent recent report dated March 1, 2018, is recommended reading, titled: "Evaluating the Housing Market Since the Great Recession."

Chapter 2

MONEY AND THE MONETARY SYSTEM

KEY TERMS AND PHRASES

- assets
- assured income
- comptroller of the currency
- credit markets
- credit report
- credit scoring
- discount rate of interest
- eCommitting™
- Fair and Accurate Credit Transactions Act (FACT)
- Fair Credit Reporting Act (FCRA)
- Federal Deposit Insurance Corporation (FDIC)
- federal funds rate
- Federal Reserve Bank
- Federal Trade Commission's Privacy Rule
- Financial Institutions Reform, Recovery, & Enforcement Act
- liabilities
- LIBOR
- monetary system
- money
- mortgage pools
- Office of Thrift Supervision (OTS)
- open market operations
- prime rate
- production-related income
- regulated lenders
- Resolution Trust Corporation
- savings banks
- time deposit
- willingness to pay

> **LEARNING OBJECTIVES**
>
> At the conclusion of this chapter, students will be able to:
> - Understand the development of the monetary system in the United States.
> - Explain the importance of the Federal Reserve Bank, including its role in establishing monetary policy within the monetary system of the United States.
> - Understand the general workings of the U.S. Treasury and the economic effects of borrowing by the government versus those of other sectors of credit users.

WHAT IS MONEY AND THE FEDERAL RESERVE SYSTEM?

Introduction

When you need a shirt and the only thing you have of value to trade is a goat, you have a problem. The system of barter allows someone with one skill or trade good to purchase by exchanging another good or service; it does not always work very well. Historically, this system dampened the growth of trade and economies in general. **Money**—symbols of value—succeeded the barter system.

No commodity is more widely used and less understood than money. Most of us know very well what money can do; its value lies primarily in our confidence that other people will accept it in exchange for goods and services. Money has been a part of all known civilizations, functioning as a means to improve on the barter system of trading goods and services among people. Commodities of high intrinsic value, such as precious metals, gemstones, furs, and even salt and spices, have long been used to facilitate trade. In fact, in many areas of the world, people still use such standards for trade. Our modern incarnation of business, however, is supported by the intangible qualities of trust and confidence—the trust and confidence that individuals and nations place in currency and credit lines extended for bonds or other promissory certificates issued under a recognized government's authority. Of course, the confidence placed in a government and its international trading power is indicated by the relative value placed on a nation's money in the realm of international trade.

The **monetary system** used in the United States was molded over many years of practical experience generated by trial and error. The U.S. Constitution contains no provisions to control its development. Monetary policy has been powerfully shaped by political debates taking place during the Civil War, the Great Depression years of the 1930s, and the present Great Recession (also called the Financial Crisis of 2007). In the early years of this country's growth, lacking constitutional guidance, the control of money was considered a right belonging to each state, and the political battles between state's rightists and Federalists were clearly reflected in the development of the monetary system. Two early efforts to create a central national bank failed, and it was not until the Civil War that the federal government actually took over the issuance and control of currency. Prior to that time, individual states authorized their state-chartered banks to perform this function.

Federal Reserve Bank System

The step that firmly established federal control over the nation's money supply was the creation of the **Federal Reserve Bank**, or "the Fed," in 1913. The Fed became the nation's bank and was given responsibility for handling the country's monetary policies. Its seven-member board of governors is appointed by the U.S. president; members serve terms of 14 years, thus shielding them from politics—at least in theory.

The chairman of the Federal Reserve Bank Board, chosen from among its members by the nation's president, serves a four-year term, but one that is not concurrent with the presidency. While the chair has only one vote on the board, the authority to influence the selection of the 12 Federal Reserve District presidents adds to the power of that office. The chair also influences the selection of which of the five out of 12 district presidents will sit on the powerful Open Market Committee. (See figure 2-1 for an illustration of the structure of the Federal Reserve Operations.)

The board is responsible for many other functions, such as overseeing the Truth-in-Lending Act, monitoring the Equal Credit Opportunity Act, and implementing other national credit policies. But it is the Fed's monetary policies that most influence the cost and availability of mortgage money. The Federal Reserve Bank Board and its policy of low interest rates from 2001 to 2004 helped fuel the housing bubble by promoting adjustable-rate mortgages and other new alternative mortgage financing, such as option ARMS and interest-only loans. These products were popular until interest rates rose in 2005. The prevalence of these types of loans helped drive up delinquencies, as those who borrowed at 2% eventually had to adjust to a rate of 4%, and saw their mortgage payments double. The Federal

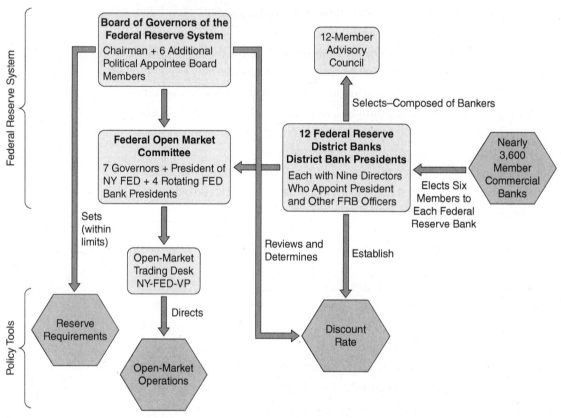

FIGURE 2-1 Flow Chart of Federal Reserve Structure and Operations
Source: © 2021 Mbition LLC

Reserve Board has used its monetary policy powers to keep interest rates on mortgages historically low from February 2010 to early 2016. Since the Federal Reserve started increasing the Federal Discount rate in December of 2015, interest rates on mortgages have begun to rise to levels not seen in six years by the end of 2018.

Monetary Policies

What is it that the Fed controls when deciding the nation's monetary policies? The Fed's underlying mission in setting policies is to maintain a stable and prosperous economy that provides jobs and better living conditions. However, the nation's monetary policies now affect a global economy, and the monetary policies of other nations directly affect those of the United States. So the Fed must function within global constraints.

The Fed uses four basic tools to influence the economy through the nation's monetary system:

1. controlling the amount of money in circulation in the country, called the *money supply;*
2. adjusting the amount of funds available within the commercial banking network as manipulated through its "open market operations";
3. signaling interest rate movements through changes in its discount rate of interest or in the federal funds rate, which is a short-term (sometimes just overnight) rate that banks charge each other for loans; and
4. setting cash reserve requirements for depository institutions.

Further explanation of each of these four tools follows, beginning with the most important: decisions about the nation's money supply.

Money Supply

The difficult task faced by the Fed is to create equilibrium so that growth in the nation's money supply is commensurate with growth in its population and productivity. Too much money in circulation can cause destructive inflation, and too little growth in the available money supply can create damaging recessions or even deflation in the price of assets. But true measures of the amount of money in this country are difficult to determine, which in turn makes sound decisions difficult.

The size of our total money supply—and the enormous economy it serves—makes the problem appear almost beyond comprehension. For clarification, we will use a simplified example. First, remember that the value of money used today is represented by the amount of goods and services that it can buy (or be traded for).

> ### Example
>
> If we have an economy with exactly 10,000 units of goods and services and an amount of money available to purchase these products totaling $1 million, each unit of goods and services is worth $100. By increasing workforce productivity over several years, the economy would have more units of goods and services. Therefore, assume that the growth has created 20,000 units of goods and services for sale, but no increase has been made in the available money. With twice as much to buy for the same amount of money, the price of each unit of goods and services would drop to $50. Stated another way, the value of the dollar would double; it would take only 50 cents to buy what a dollar bought before.

> If a different policy were used so that over the same period of time our increased workforce productivity supplied 20,000 units of goods and services, and the money supply was increased to $3 million, then each unit would be worth $150. With so much more money available, the dollar becomes less valuable. It would take $1.50 to buy what formerly cost $1.00—which amounts to a debasement of the value of the currency, a major component of inflation.
>
> To support a stable pricing structure, a careful balance must be maintained between the nation's money supply and increases in workforce productivity. Failure to do so can result in inflation or recession.

Definition of Money

To better understand how decisions are made on whether or not to increase the available money supply, it is first necessary to define the term "money." The broad definition used by the Fed is that money consists of those assets that have immediate purchasing power. In this definition, bank deposits are a key factor. A problem arises in that recent banking laws and regulations have altered the way bank accounts can be used. The line between "time deposits" and "demand deposits" is no longer so clear-cut, and some banks allow a savings account to be automatically drawn on to replenish an overdrawn checking account. In a "zero balance" checking account offered to businesses, the checking account is automatically fed daily from the savings account by the amount of checks cleared. The savings account pays interest to the depositor.

Another challenge to the Fed's handling of the money supply in this country is the declining role of commercial banks as the keepers of monetary assets. Today, the assets of all mutual funds have increased to the point where they exceed the total time and savings deposits in the banking system. The measure of money that the Fed uses in making its decisions excludes some money market funds, all individual retirement balances in IRA and Keogh accounts, deposits with nonbank institutions, and some dollar deposits held overseas. Nonbank companies, such as Raymond James, hold customers' deposits and have money market accounts that are not subject to banking regulations, nor are the deposits insured.

Thus, decisions on money supply must be made using only a partial measure of the total market. Nevertheless, the Fed considers "money supply" to be currency in circulation plus both demand and time deposits within the banking system. To distinguish between some of the differences in the nature of money and to provide a basis for its measurement, the Fed identifies four categories of money, using the letter "M" to signify money, as follows:

M1 includes currency in circulation, nonbank travelers' checks, demand deposits in commercial banks, and other checkable deposits at commercial banks and thrift institutions, including credit union share drafts accounts. As of April 2018, M1 totaled $3,859 billion, an increase from $1,091 billion at the end of 2000.

M2 is the total of M1 plus savings and small-denomination time deposits at all commercial banks and thrift institutions, retail money funds, and institutional money funds (a.k.a. general-purpose money market mutual funds). As of April 2018, M2 totaled $13,952 billion, an increase from $4,896 billion at the end of 2000.

M3 is the total of M2 plus large-denomination ($100,000 and over) time deposits at all depository institutions, term Eurodollars held by U.S. residents at foreign and U.S. banks, term repurchase agreements at commercial banks and savings associations, and balances of institutional money market mutual funds. As of November 2014, M3 totaled $16,470 billion[1], an increase from $7,343 billion at the end of 2000. On March 23, 2006, the Federal Reserve Bank stopped calculating M3. In a press release, the Federal Reserve Bank stated that M3 did not appear to convey any additional information about economic activity that was not already embodied in M2, and that it had not played a role in the monetary policy process for many years. Consequently, the board judged that the costs of collecting the underlying data and publishing M3 outweighed the benefits. It took M3 six years to grow by $2,647 billion from 2000 to early 2006; it grew $4,231 billion over the next two years leading up to the financial crisis. Some analysts believe that the repurchase

---

[1] Though M3 is no longer tracked by the Federal Reserve Bank, there are still estimates produced by various private institutions. The starting figure came from the Federal Reserve Bank; the ending figure was obtained at http://www.explistats.com, accessed December 19, 2014.

agreements and other derivative instruments might have set off an alarm earlier if they had been followed and regulatory action taken in response. Others speculate that the increases in what the Fed would have reported as M3 might expose the escalation of the United States trade deficit and massive Eurodollar holdings.

MZM is the total of M3 plus other liquid assets such as all other money market funds that can be redeemable at par on demand. As of December 8, 2014, MZM totaled $12,887 billion, an increase from $4,659 billion at the end of 2000. MZM is not an official weekly release by the Federal Reserve System as are M1 and M2, but rather a tracking measure developed and reported by the Federal Reserve Bank of St. Louis.

A cursory analysis of the growth in money supply between 2000 and 2014, as indicated in the preceding figures, shows a 161% increase in M1 but a 177% increase in MZM. Overall, the Fed maintained a fairly stable rein on the money supply until 2001, but then allowed it to increase at a fairly fast pace, with the largest increases coming in 2008 and continuing through August 2014 to offset the effects of the recent financial crisis, including the high levels of deficit spending.

Management of the Money Supply

The amount of money available in the United States is controlled by the Federal Reserve Bank Board. It operates through a system of 12 districts, each with some branch Federal Reserve Banks to facilitate local operations. The system works with the approximately 8,800 commercial banks that handle most of the cash transfers in the country. The Fed's Open Market Committee, comprising seven governors and five of the 12 Federal Reserve District presidents, meets each month. At these meetings, the committee reviews monetary aggregates, examines the influence of current interest rates, and considers the state of the economy. Then it makes a decision on whether or not an increase in the available money supply is justified.

To increase the supply of money, the Fed simply creates additional money and uses it to purchase U.S. Treasury securities on the open market. In a sense, the Fed writes "hot checks" to buy government securities. Of course, the checks are not actually "hot" because the Fed clears them through its own bank. And in fact, no actual checks are written; the Fed grants a credit to the U.S. Treasury bank account in exchange for Treasury securities. This authority to create money, backed only by government promises, gives the Fed tremendous influence in financial markets. Obviously, an influx of new money creates an increase in the money supply, which is expected to lower interest rates and thus give the economy a lift—although in practice, this strategy does not always work.

Open Market Operations

Another tool the Fed can use to influence the economy is called **open market operations**. Because it has access to a large supply of both government bonds and cash, the Fed can move these assets in and out of the banking system at any time it deems desirable. If the Fed decides the economy needs slowing down, it can issue an order—through a limited group of approved investment bankers who must be qualified and capable—to sell some of the Fed's supply of government bonds. These bonds are purchased by investors throughout the country, and the money to buy them is withdrawn from various banks, sent to the Fed in payment for the bonds, and locked away in the Federal Reserve. Therefore, the cash is no longer available for banks to use in making further loans. Alternatively, if the Fed decides it is necessary to speed up the economy, it can buy government bonds, thus increasing the cash available to banks. The increased cash is meant to enhance banks' ability to make more loans, thus improving business activity.

Open market operations can be used to influence interest rates in the short term. For example, it takes about $1 billion in bond purchases on the New York market to lower effective interest rates about one-quarter of a percentage point. However, many other factors influence interest rates over the long term, such as supply and demand for money, foreign money markets, government taxing and spending policies, and investors' perceptions of the general health of the economy. By keeping interest rates low during the recent financial crisis, the Fed caused many adjustable-rate mortgage holders' payments to go down instead of up.

Discount Rate of Interest

A third tool that the Fed can use is changing its **discount rate of interest**. Commonly called the "discount rate," it is that rate charged by the Fed to depository institutions that are eligible to borrow from it. This tool is probably the Fed's most widely publicized means of economic influence because it is the easiest for the general public to recognize and understand.

Yet in practice, it is the least effective, as a change in the discount rate is not a critical factor in the banking industry because it does not represent a cost of funds. Even though an institution is eligible to borrow from the Fed, this money cannot be used as a source of capital. The purpose of such loans to depository institutions is to provide a cushion when unanticipated needs for cash arise. Thus the Fed's discount rate of interest is more of a signal to the banking community than a true cost of funds.

By increasing the discount rate, the Fed signals to all lenders that an increase in rates is in order. The immediate effect of such an increase is almost always an increase in most institutions' **prime rate** of interest—the rate on which a bank bases its charges to borrowers. Conversely, a reduction in rates signals a lowering of all interest rates. In practice, the signal may or may not be heeded by lenders, who remain free to adjust their rates as they see fit.

As indicated earlier in this chapter, more recently the Fed has been acting to change the **federal funds rate** rather than to change the discount rate of interest. While any such change is widely reported in the media as an increase, or decrease, in interest rates, it is not a mandatory change. The federal funds rate is a constantly changing rate, different in all parts of the country, as it is what banks charge each other for short-term loans that enable a bank to meet its liquidity requirements under federal rules. Thus, it has picked up the name of "federal funds rate." Between banks, it is a negotiated rate. The rate that the Fed targets is the one involving the big New York banks. The Fed moves this rate by injecting or withdrawing cash from its large deposits with New York banks.

Prior to January 2003, discount window lending consisted of adjustment credit, extended credit, and seasonal credit programs. Under unusual and exigent circumstances, the Federal Reserve Bank had legal authority to advance credit to individuals, partnerships, and corporations that were not depository institutions, following consultation with the Board of Governors of the Federal Reserve System. To advance this credit, the Federal Reserve Bank had to determine that credit was not available from other sources and that failure to provide credit would adversely affect the economy. Emergency credit, authorized under section 13(3) of the Federal Reserve Act, had not been used since the 1930s, but it was initiated again in response to the recent financial crisis, and several special emergency credit facilities were created in 2008 and 2009. By keeping the federal discount rate at historically low levels since 2009, the Fed has kept the cost of mortgage funding low. This allows those with fixed-rate or adjustable-rate mortgages who experienced upward rate adjustments in 2007 and 2008 to refinance or see their rate adjustments decline over time.

The Dodd-Frank Act changed the Federal Reserve's authority to lend under unusual and exigent circumstances. Federal Reserve Banks now can no longer extend credit to an individual, partnership, or corporation other than through a "program with broad-based eligibility." Such emergency facilities can only be created with prior approval of the Treasury Secretary, and must be used for the purposes of providing liquidity to the financial system and not to aid a failing financial institution.

Figure 2-2 is an example of how an adjustment of the discount rate of interest by the Federal Reserve Bank can impact short-term credit costs for prime borrowers and the cost of short-term deposits—another key cost that drives financial institutions' profits.

Reserve Requirements

The fourth tool available to the Fed is control of the reserves that must be set aside (unavailable for loans) by all federally insured depository

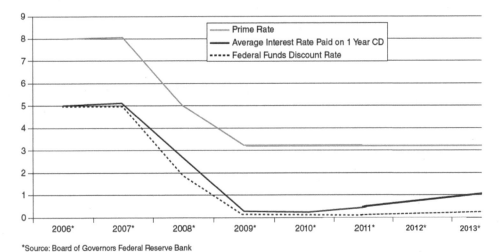

*Source: Board of Governors Federal Reserve Bank

FIGURE 2-2 History of How Federal Reserve Changes in Federal Discount Rate Influences Short-Term Borrowing and CD Rates

institutions. These institutions must maintain certain cash reserves on deposit with the Fed—reserves that pay no interest. This practice allows the banking system to borrow its own non-interest-bearing deposits from the Fed at the discount rate of interest. The Federal Reserve can be a very profitable operation for the government. In October 2006, the Financial Services Regulatory Relief Act was passed, allowing the Fed to pay interest on bank reserves held. The law went into effect in 2008 and was fully implemented in late 2011. Recent developments include the Federal Open Market Committee Policy Normalization Principles and Plans, created on September 17, 2014. During monetary policy normalization, the Federal Reserve has begun to move the federal funds rate into the target range set by the FOMC, primarily by adjusting the interest rate it pays on excess reserve balances. The reserve held by the Fed represents a cushion, a backup for the banking system to use on short-term loans that allows an eligible institution greater flexibility in meeting unexpected demands for funding. All such loans must be fully collateralized by the borrowing institutions.

The Garn–St. Germain Act of 1982 exempted the first $2 million of reservable liabilities from reserve requirements. Today, these liabilities are established by the Monetary Control Act and the Garn–St. Germain Act, and must be based on the following criteria:

- Total transaction accounts consist of demand deposits, automatic transfer service (ATS) accounts, NOW accounts, share draft accounts, telephone or preauthorized transfer accounts, ineligible bankers' acceptances, and obligations issued by affiliates maturing in seven days or less.
- Net transaction accounts are total transaction accounts less amounts due from other depository institutions and less cash items in the process of collection. These are referred to as "liabilities" since they are owed by the depository institution to their depositors.

The reserve requirement in place as of January 17, 2019, for those defined financial depository institutions is 0% for a liabilities balance below $16.3 million, 3% for those with $16 million up to $124.2 million, and 10% for those with liabilities in excess of $124.2 million. The Fed made no change in the reserve requirement for 12 years running; then on April 2, 1992, it lowered the rate on over-$25 million demand deposits from 12% to 10% during the recession. The decrease in the reserve requirement brought a release of $8 to $9 billion in additional cash into the banking system with the expectation that it would spur the economy with minimal effect on inflation. When the economy recovered, the reserve requirement—the easing of which had allowed an increase in the money supply multiplier effect—was not increased to its previous levels; this decision was made as a way to control the growth of credit as the economy picked up in the late 1990s. In October 2008, the Federal Reserve Board established the interest rates on required reserve balances and excess balances.

Compliance Role

The Federal Reserve Bank is tasked with supervising (i.e., examining, monitoring and inspecting) certain financial institutions to make certain they conform to rules and regulations required by law. They are also tasked with assuring that banks operate in a safe and sound manner. The form of supervision of financial institutions is customized based on the size and complexity of the financial organization for which they have oversight.

The dominant consumer compliance laws for which the Federal Reserve Bank is responsible are:

- Regulation B - Equal Credit Opportunity that prohibits lenders from discriminating against credit applicants, establishes guidelines for gathering and evaluating credit information, and requires written notification when credit is denied.
- Regulation G - Disclosure and Reporting of CRA-Related Agreements by use of the implementation provisions of the Gramm-Leach-Bliley Act that require reporting and public disclosure of written agreements between insured depository institutions or their affiliates and nongovernmental entities or persons, made in connection with fulfillment of Community Reinvestment Act requirements.
- Regulation M - Consumer Leasing that requires the implementation of the consumer leasing provisions of the Truth in Lending Act by requiring meaningful disclosure of leasing terms.
- Regulation Z - Truth in Lending that prescribes uniform methods for computing the cost of credit, for disclosing credit terms, and for resolving errors on certain types of credit accounts.
- Regulation BB – Assures the compliance with the Community Reinvestment Act that encourages banks to help meet the credit needs of their communities.

The Federal Reserve Bank is also responsible for the compliance by all state member banks with the Fair Housing Act, the National Flood Insurance Act, the Servicemembers Civil Relief Act, along with prohibitions on unfair or deceptive acts or practices under the Federal Trade Commission Act, and certain other federal consumer financial protection laws not specifically under the Consumer Financial Protection Bureau's authority discussed in more detail in Chapter 3.

Where Are We Now?

The Federal Reserve Bank is in charge of the Uniform Interagency Consumer Compliance Rating System. Recently the Federal Financial Institutions Examination Council (FFIEC) announced the issuance of an updated Uniform Interagency Consumer Compliance Rating System (CC Rating System) in November 2016[2]. FFIEC member agencies' examiners are using the CC Rating System to evaluate financial institutions' adherence to consumer compliance laws and regulations. Beginning on or after March 31, 2017, the updated rating system will apply to consumer compliance examinations.

Updates in July 2015 to the Military Lending Act (MLA) as enacted in 2006 with the goal of protecting active duty military personnel, as well as their spouses and other dependents, engaged in consumer credit transactions. Its biggest protection was that the MLA limited the cost of covered transactions, which are subject to a Military Annual Percentage Rate (MAPR) cap of 36 percent. The Department of Defense amendments to the MLA's regulation were that it was extended to apply to most types of traditional consumer credit covered under the Truth in Lending Act and Regulation Z. Some examples would be:

- credit cards,
- deposit advance products,
- overdraft lines of credit,
- certain installment loans.

---

[2]FFIEC, 2017, FFIEC Issues Uniform Interagency Consumer Compliance Rating System, Accessed on September 11, 2019 at: https://www.ffiec.gov/press/pr110716.htm

Consumer compliance protection policies of the Federal Reserve Bank and other Federal and State regulators are meant to ensure that consumers are fairly treated and the dominant factors in decisions to extend credit are related to the financial evaluation of a borrower's ability to repay based on a common review of transparent instruments used in the execution of credit policy by lenders.

INSTRUMENTS OF CREDIT POLICY

Financial Evaluation of the Borrower

The high loan-to-value ratios (LTVRs) often found in residential loans place a premium on an accurate examination of the borrower's repayment ability. In the event of default, the conventional lender, or the private mortgage insurance company covering only a portion of the loan, would be hard pressed to make full recovery from disposition of the collateral in case of an early foreclosure. Proper analysis of the borrower to determine total available income, any claim against that income, and the borrower's credit record are important for a home loan.

A borrower's other assets are helpful as additional security for a loan and can result in a lower rate of interest, but other assets cannot always be counted on for use in repayment. The lender knows that in many cases of actual default in payments, the borrower has met with financial problems that were beyond his or her control. Accidents, job layoffs, or a serious illness in the family can deplete most of a family's financial assets, leaving the lender with few means of recourse beyond the house that has been pledged as loan collateral.

No two borrowers ever present the same credit picture. Even so, analysis of a borrower can be handled two different ways: (1) by a human underwriter, called *manual underwriting*, or (2) by a computer, called *automatic underwriting*. Software programs have been developed for computers that can reference a variety of information and give loan approval when it is justified. However, the machine does not provide a rejection of the applicant. Any questions that should be answered are referred back to the lender's underwriter for further work.

Because a computer is more number-oriented, it also uses **credit scoring**, which is a method of giving a default probability number based on an individual's credit record. The method has been available for nearly

50 years but has received publicity recently because of its wider use. A more detailed explanation of the procedure appears in Chapter 14 as a part of the discussion on automated underwriting.

There are some guidelines and general rules, mainly based on common sense, that are helpful in determining whether or not a borrower should be able to make a loan repayment. One popular rule is to always follow the "three Cs" of good underwriting:

1. **c**apability—evaluating a borrower's capacity to make the required payments;
2. **c**redit—assessing the borrower's credit reputation (willingness to pay); and
3. **c**ollateral—determining that the property is adequate collateral for the mortgage loan.

Thus, to make a sound prediction, the underwriter must consider the three basic questions: (1) What is the applicant's ability to pay? (2) What is the applicant's willingness to pay? (3) Does the property provide enough collateral?

We will examine the issue of collateral in the next chapter.

Ability to Pay

More than for any other type of loan, the residential lender looks to a family's income as the basic resource for repayment. Assets are important, but are used in part to determine the spending or saving patterns practiced in the use of that income. Therefore, a careful review of the employment record, present income, and future potential is important. The following are some of the income elements considered by a lender, with commentary on each.

Types of Income

Lenders make a broad distinction between **production-related income** and **assured income**. Production-related income means commissions, bonuses, and in some cases, piecework pay. It does not have the certainty of assured income such as wages or a salary and normally requires a longer record of earnings to qualify. The major types of income, along with comments on their acceptability, are:

1. **salary** (A salary, particularly from a major company or institution, is highly acceptable for loan qualification. It can be easily verified from IRS W-2 reports.);
2. **bonus** (A bonus should not be counted on unless a regular pattern can be established for several successive years.);
3. **commission** (A straight commission job can be very lucrative, or it can be a complete bust. Only a past record of income culled from several years of tax returns can be accepted as factual.);
4. **hourly wages** (An hourly wage is a solid basis for continuing income and one that can usually be confirmed by an employer.);
5. **overtime wages** (This is an uncertain basis for making a long-term loan, as most employers try to avoid overtime, using it only for an emergency situation or as a temporary practice. Again, a consistent pattern of overtime payments for several years would make this an acceptable addition to an applicant's gross income.);
6. **second job** (Many people today hold more than one job on a full- or part-time basis. Teachers, police officers, and skilled hourly workers all can have other capabilities and may spend extra hours augmenting their income. If the second job has been held over a period of several years on a regular basis, it provides a substantial lift to the regular income.);
7. **unreported income** (A few people accept extra work, or even become involved full-time, in jobs that pay in cash and on which income is not reported for tax purposes. Such income, if not reported, is illegal and cannot be used under any condition to justify a loan. This "borrower" could lose this income abruptly and spend some time in prison.);
8. **co-borrower's income** (Prior to enactment of the Federal Equal Credit Opportunity Act, it was a fairly common practice to reduce the effective income that could be accepted from a working wife. The reasoning then was that young married couples were also interested in raising families, and earlier customs generally assigned more of the problems concerned with family emergencies, sickness, and childcare to the wife. The new laws recognize changing customs, and a lender is now required to apply the same qualification standards to each borrower without questioning marital status or gender.);

9. **income from children** (While many young men and women living with their parents earn substantial money at full- or part-time jobs, these earnings are not generally a recognized addition to the family income for loan purposes. The obligation on the part of children to contribute to family finances for support of the home is not a continuing one. Normally, children will leave home to set up their own households within a few years. Therefore, temporary income supplied by grown children lends no real weight to most loan requests. There is another qualification pattern that considers children's income differently. Many state and local housing authorities offer loan assistance programs using lower cost "bond money" that limit eligible income. Generally, for qualification, eligible "family income" is the combined income of all persons who will live in the house to be financed. Similar provisions apply to the more recently designated category of affordable housing loans.);

10. **pension and trust income** (In years past, not many have enjoyed pensions, retirement funds, or other work benefits at a sufficiently early age to apply them toward a home purchase. However, this pattern is changing. For instance, many veterans of military, government, and corporate services have completed 20 or 30 years of employment before the age of 50 and are eligible for further lifetime benefits. These benefits are one of the most reliable forms of income.);

11. **child support and alimony** (Some states do not permit alimony in divorce actions but provide child support as a matter of court decree. Other states permit both alimony and child support. Such payments can be considered as regular income for a divorced spouse or remarried person, depending on the court ruling. However, the record of payment must show dependability over a period of time before it would constitute an acceptable addition to total income. ECOA restricts information that must be provided on this source of income if it is not to be counted as income for repayment of the loan.);

12. **self-employed persons** (Many people operate their own businesses or work as self-employed individuals in professional capacities. This type of income is one of the more difficult to evaluate because of the flexibility in accounting procedures that define such income.

Some small business owners are able to pay certain living expenses from their business (car expenses, entertainment, travel, etc.), but weight can only be given to the individual's income that is reported as taxable. Without an employer to verify income, lenders must rely on several years of federal income tax returns. Certified copies of these returns can be obtained from the Internal Revenue Service for a small fee upon application by the taxpayer only.);

13. **interest and dividends** (This type of income derives from investments that may or may not provide an ongoing source of funds. If the assets can be held as an investment, they represent stable income. However, losses can occur and the assets might be sold, which would eliminate that particular source of income. Again, the past record would give some indication of how investment assets have been managed.); and

14. **part-time employment** (In the past, income derived from part-time work was not accepted at full value toward a person's income applicable to repayment of a mortgage loan. The concern was about the future stability of this source of income. ECOA requirements now permit no discounting of income from part-time employment. However, the lender may still require that an applicant show evidence of stability and reasonable assurance that part-time work will continue.)

Stability of Income

Along with the size of an applicant's income, the assurance that it will be continued must be investigated. Two measures are most commonly used: (1) time on the job and (2) type of work performed.

Length of Time on Job

While standards vary, some length of time on the same job is a measure of stability. The changing nature of job tenure has brought a reduction in the former three-year standard to a more common one-year requirement. There is a basis for this restriction in that any new job may or may not work out due to personality factors, lack of accomplishment, or dissatisfaction with the work.

With the more rapid changes in jobs today, tenure may be more fairly judged from the individual's job history. Has the applicant made a record of "job-hopping" without noticeable improvement in income? Is the present job one of greater responsibility and growth potential than the previous job? Has the applicant maintained a record of employment in a chosen field of work, or is the present job an entirely new type of work? The lack of standards makes this question a judgment call for an underwriter.

Type of Work

While a person with a long record of steady employment provides a very good answer to the question of income stability, many seeking loans cannot provide such a record. Thus an additional standard is helpful in analysis of an applicant: the type of work.

Persons with salaried jobs employed by major companies or institutions rate very well. So do professional people with job tenure of various kinds. Hourly workers, some with the protection of union contracts, can be more stable (and often more highly paid) than lower-level management and clerical staff workers. Government employees carry good security, as do teachers, police officers, and other service workers.

On the lower side of the scale, new sales representatives enticed by stories of high commissions, entertainers, and seasonal workers give poor evidence of continued stable income. To some lenders, socially unacceptable types of work carry unduly low ratings. It might be noted that laws do not protect persons against credit discrimination due to type of work.

Liabilities

For residential loan qualification, fixed liabilities must be reported on the application. If **liabilities** are excessive, an applicant can be rejected (a judgment call). The standard measure applied is a conversion of liabilities to a per-month basis. Not all liabilities are included or measured in this manner—only those that are required by the lender to be listed. The key determinant is whether or not the required monthly payments could prevent making a mortgage payment. However, that determinant is limited. For instance, cost of food, clothing, transportation, and income taxes need not be listed, even though they are all essential.

To qualify an applicant's income, certain monthly obligations should not exceed guideline percentages of the applicant's income. The obligations that fall under this criterion are housing costs, as reflected in the monthly mortgage payment, plus other fixed obligations such as installment payments and revolving account payments. In general, more than half of an applicant's income is open to use for unlisted obligations. Each of the major categories of loans (FHA, VA, and RHS, conforming/conventional, and other conventional) apply slightly different guideline standards for listing liabilities. These will be more fully explained later in this chapter.

While there are some differences between lenders and types of loans as to which monthly obligations must be listed, caution should be taken before incurring additional debt prior to qualifying for a mortgage loan. A recent study indicates that a major cause of loan rejection is not the housing payment itself; rather, it is heavy monthly installment obligations for other items such as cars, computers, video equipment, and similar purchases that might well be postponed.

Assets

Unlike applicants for commercial loans, residential applicants need not show substantial **assets** to qualify. Many home buyers are younger people who have had little time to accumulate much in other assets yet still qualify for suitable home loans. However, there is an advantage if assets other than a home are held by an applicant. Ownership of stocks, bonds, real estate, savings funds, and other such assets does indicate an ability to live prudently and conserve a portion of one's income. If this is the case, the applicant should find qualification of income much easier, as the percentage guidelines that limit the amount of obligations will most likely be relaxed a bit.

As a commentary on how lenders might look at other assets, life insurance is viewed as both an asset (due to its cash value and protection features) and a liability (due to its cost). Cars and boats represent some trade-in value, but are usually discounted. Furniture and personal property are often overvalued in an applicant's statement of assets because of the owner's personal attachment to these items, and these values are not given much weight by lenders. Employee trust and pension funds can represent value if the interest is a vested one—that is, if employees can take the funds with them should they leave the job. An interest in one's own business is best determined by an audited financial statement of that business. Accounts and notes receivable should be detailed for proper valuation.

Willingness to Pay

The element of **willingness to pay**, sometimes called *credit character*, is the most difficult to analyze and judge. Yet this factor alone can be the cause of loan rejection. An underwriter's judgment is crucial in making this decision because it can involve questions of credit discrimination.

Creditworthiness is judged from an applicant's previous record of meeting obligations. The most common source of information to make this determination comes from credit reports as issued by credit bureaus. Information for mortgage loans is also obtained from public records covering litigation, judgments, or criminal actions. Conversations with persons involved in the house sale transaction can sometimes bring to light information on the applicant's manner of living, personal attitudes, and activities that might give cause for a more detailed investigation.

Some lenders prefer to take loan applications at the borrower's place of residence because a person's manner of living can be helpful in judging credit character. There is a question as to when personal inquiry becomes an invasion of one's privacy. But lenders are obligated to exercise prudent judgment, and need information to make sound decisions. The true picture can be just as advantageous for the borrower as for the lender and is mandatory in making proper judgment on any loan. Individuals asking to borrow someone else's money should be willing to provide complete and accurate information about themselves within the requirements of the Equal Credit Opportunity Act.

Under the category of willingness to pay, lenders have always tried to assess an applicant's motivation for owning a home. Lenders in the past have felt that the strongest incentive for owning a home came from a family unit committed to the rearing of children. But lifestyles have changed, and many persons today are not interested in having a family, but do want houses. Even prior to the enactment of the Equal Credit Opportunity Act, lenders were enlarging qualification standards and making loans to single persons, both men and women, and nonfamily units where there was reasonable assurance of continuity of interest in owning a house. ECOA has eliminated gender and marital status as a basis for loan rejection, but it has not foreclosed the lender's right to exercise judgment as to the continuing need to repay a mortgage loan. This is an area that does not lend itself to clear-cut definitions and thus can present problems for a responsible loan officer.

Credit Reports

Most adults in this country have **credit reports** compiled by the more than 1,100 credit bureaus, whether or not they are aware of it. Information is routinely submitted to local credit bureaus by their members, who normally are those extending credit within the community. Credit bureau members consist of local merchants, financial institutions, gasoline retailers, providers of medical services, taxing authorities, and possibly utility companies. (Many utility companies do not submit credit information because they have very effective constraints if payment becomes delinquent.)

Records of credit card accounts are generally kept separately in huge computer data banks, not in local credit bureaus. Information in credit files is classed as proprietary, available only to approved credit bureau members and to individuals seeking information on their own records. Those who pay bills only in cash are not likely to have credit records anywhere, which can create some problems when seeking a mortgage loan. However, to properly handle such persons wanting to obtain credit, the fairly new credit criteria allowed under "affordable housing loans" recognizes insufficient credit records and accepts timely cash payments as proof of sound payment practices.

Keepers of Credit Records

Before applying for any loan, it is wise for an individual to review any credit information that he or she may have on file. The Fair Credit Reporting Act grants individuals the right to do this. Errors can be corrected, and this is best handled before a loan officer examines the record. The place to begin is with the local credit bureau, which is listed under "Credit Reporting Agencies" in the Yellow Pages. Large cities have multiple bureaus and usually one will dominate mortgage loan information—the one commonly used by FHA, VA, and mortgage companies. Individual credit reports generally cost about $20 and may take several days for delivery; they are free if a bad report is the reason for denial of credit.

Three major national credit data companies (also called national repositories) hold credit information on individuals and may be contacted directly. Most mortgage lenders now require reports from at least two of the three, in addition to the local credit bureau report, as part of the loan documentation. The three do not share credit information, and their reports can differ. Contacts are as follows:

EQUIFAX
Box 740241
Atlanta, GA 30374-0241
Phone: 1-888-202-4025 Business Service for Lenders; 1-800-685-1111 for Consumers

EXPERIAN
475 Anton Blvd.
Costa Mesa, CA 92626
Phone: 1-888-243-6951

TRANSUNION
2 Baldwin Place
P.O. Box 1000
Chester, PA 19022
Phone: 866-922-2100 Business Service for Lenders; 800-916-8800 for Consumers

Credit Information

Credit bureaus provide records of credit accounts and payment histories of those accounts. Each creditor makes the decision as to whether or not to grant credit. The information contained in a report covers the past seven years (10 years for bankruptcy filings). If an individual files a complaint against a credit reporting company, the law requires that an answer be provided within 30 days. Disputed information may be removed from the credit record while an investigation is made into the original creditor. If the information is accurate, it is returned to the record. If it is inaccurate, the information must be deleted and the individual can instruct the credit bureau to send a correction to all creditors who reviewed the file in the previous six months. If unfavorable credit information is on the record and there are mitigating circumstances (such as a serious injury causing delay in making payments), an individual can file a statement with the credit bureau of up to 100 words in explanation.

Responsible Federal Agency

The basis for the preceding information on consumers' rights stems from the **Fair Credit Reporting Act (FCRA)**, passed in 1970. The FCRA is administered by the Federal Trade Commission, which is headquartered in Washington, DC, with regional offices in major cities. In 2003, the **Fair and Accurate Credit Transactions Act (FACT)** was passed, which significantly amended the Fair Credit Reporting Act. The FACT sought to protect consumers from inaccurate credit information that might be reported by credit reporting agencies. In addition to protecting consumers' privacy rights when reporting their credit, the FCRA included consumers' right to inspect their credit reports for accuracy. Consumers can also contest possible errors and attach explanations regarding derogatory listings.

When notifying prospective borrowers that their mortgage loan application was denied based on information in their credit report, lenders must also meet the requirement of the Equal Credit Opportunity Act for disclosure of detailed reasons for the loan denial. To comply with both FACT and ECOA requirements, these notifications must include statements of the reasons for the denial and/or a counteroffer notice. For approvals, notifications must include consent for credit disclosure along with disclosure of any lock agreements. Approvals, denials, and counteroffers all must come with privacy policy disclosures to consumers stating how they meet the requirements of FCRA and FACT. The necessity for compliance with these privacy policy rules (which we will cover more fully below) stems from the new Red Flag Rules issued by the Federal Trade Commission (the primary regulatory oversight and enforcement agency for FACT) that became effective on November 1, 2008. These Red Flag Rules, also adopted by the banking and credit union regulators, require financial institutions and creditors to have developed and implemented written identity theft prevention programs as part of their compliance with FACT. The Red Flag Rules cast a wide net, covering almost all credit extension that falls under the two broad categories below:

1. creditors—a category that includes mortgage companies, mortgage brokers, banks, credit unions, and any other entity that regularly grants credit; or
2. covered accounts—in which credit is extended with multiple payments; these include mortgages, credit cards, checking or savings accounts, and public utilities.

Almost everyone taking a mortgage loan application is covered by these Red Flag Rules, and compliance officers must have in place staff training programs that explain the role of each person involved in the mortgage loan origination process. Each employee must be alert to the following requirements:

- *identify:* Each covered entity must identify and incorporate relevant patterns, practices, and specific forms of activity that constitute "red flags" signaling possible identity theft.
- *detect:* Once a covered entity identifies its red flags, it must then develop policies and procedures to detect these red flags when they occur.
- *respond:* Each covered entity must develop appropriate policies and procedures to respond to any detected red flags in order to prevent and mitigate identity theft.
- *update:* Each covered entity must update its program periodically to identify new red flags or adjust to changes in risks of identity theft.

FTC Privacy Rule

All the information collected from borrowers to be able to qualify them for the various loan programs comes under the **Federal Trade Commission's Privacy Rule**, issued in 2003. This ruling established that mortgage brokers are financial institutions because brokering loans is a financial activity, as referenced in section 4(k)(4)(F) of the Bank Holding Company Act and listed in 12 C.F.R. § 225.28(b)(1) (see 15 U.S.C. § 6809[3]; 16 C.F.R. § 313.3[k][2][xi]). Mortgage brokers are subject to the FTC's enforcement authority, its Privacy Rule, and its Safeguards Rule. The Privacy Rule requires that mortgage brokers, as well as depository institutions, provide an initial privacy notice as soon as the customer relationship is established. Under 16 C.F.R. § 313.4(a), such a customer relationship is considered to be established as soon as an individual provides personally identifiable financial information to a lender in an effort to obtain a mortgage loan. Depository institutions or mortgage brokers involved in taking mortgage loan applications must deliver a privacy notice before or at the same time as any individual borrower provides this information in person. In 2003, the federal government passed the Identity Theft Deterrence Act (ITDA) and worked closely with the Federal Trade Commission to find ways to protect consumers from lenders who might make use of consumer credit to commit loan fraud, mortgage fraud, credit fraud, credit card fraud, and commodities and services frauds. The IDTA made the possession of any means of identification for the purpose of knowingly transferring or using it without lawful authority a federal crime. This applies to any persons or institutions collecting information required under the Patriot Act as well.

Credit Reporting Problems

Almost all credit information is now maintained in computerized systems. Large creditors send data to their own bureau on computer tapes, minimizing the possibility of errors. Nevertheless, problems remain in the confusion of persons with similar names and changes of married names, and just plain errors in the recording of data. Confusion over names is not always simplified by the use of Social Security numbers because creditors are prohibited from demanding a Social Security number when considering granting credit. The Social Security Act itself classifies an individual's number as private. However, depository institutions must record a depositor's number in order to report any payment of interest to the IRS. But the refusal to disclose a Social Security number to a creditor cannot be used as a basis for denial of credit.

Credit Scoring

The increased use of computer analysis has brought greater use of credit scoring to mortgage lending. Credit scoring is the assignment of a numerical rating to consumers based on their credit history. Credit scores continue to have a rising influence by residential mortgage lenders, auto lenders, credit card issuers, and other extenders of credit. Credit scoring is calculated by credit bureaus using information from one or more of the three major credit repositories: Equifax, Experian, and TransUnion. Therefore, they can report different ratings.

A number of other factors enter into judging a person's creditworthiness; scoring is just one. Further information on this subject may be found in Chapter 14, "Technology Advances in Mortgage Lending." For a detailed walk-through of a typical credit report, with explanations from the issuer, browse to http://www.experian.com/credit_report_basics/pdf/samplecreditreport.pdf and go through the sample. Each page begins with a description of what you will see. There is also a sample three-party credit report included in the appendices of this text.

THE U.S. TREASURY AND U.S. MINT

The United States Treasury

While the Federal Reserve Bank Board holds responsibility for the amount of money circulating in the country, the United States Treasury is responsible for raising the cash to pay the government's bills. How the

Treasury decides to handle this requirement can easily upset the Fed's best-laid plans.

At the end of 2017 the Department of the Treasury employed over 125,000 people and is structured into two main business sections. These are the Treasury Department offices that are responsible for formulation of policy and management of the Department of the Treasury and the operating bureaus that discharge the specific operations related to the Department. The basic operations of the Treasury include:

- government accounting, cash and debt management;
- production of coin and currency;
- assessment and collection of internal revenue;
- promulgation and enforcement of tax and tariff laws;
- economic, international economic, and fiscal policy; and
- supervision of national banks and thrifts.

In the simplest terms, the money to pay the government's obligations comes from three sources: tax revenues, borrowed funds, and printing money. If the government lives within its income, tax revenues are sufficient to pay all obligations. When it spends more money than it raises in taxes, however, the additional money must either be borrowed or printed. This crucial decision whether to borrow rather than print more money rests primarily with the Treasury. However, to pay for overspending by printing additional money is a choice that requires the consent of the Federal Reserve's Board of Governors. The reason is that the Fed, with its "open-ended checking account," is the only entity with the power to create money by purchasing government securities issued by the Treasury. It is this authority to create money based solely on Treasury securities that gives the Fed its tremendous aura of power. Currently, the power to actually print currency and mint coins rests with two departments of the Treasury: the Bureau of Engraving and Printing (BEP) prints currency, and the U.S. Mint produces coins. While relegated to minting coins like the pennies, nickels, dimes, and quarters we use every day, the U.S Mint was one of the first and more important agencies of the U.S. government, demonstrated by the fact that the first U.S. Mint building was the first federal building erected by the U.S. government under the Constitution. The BEP develops and produces U.S. currency notes referred to as Federal Reserve notes. The BEP is also involved in advanced counterfeit deterrence and, in addition to currency, the BEP produces many different kinds of identification cards, forms, and other special security documents for a variety of government agencies.

However, if the Treasury opts to borrow money rather than printing it to pay for deficit spending, it can do so without the Fed's approval. Treasury borrowing is accomplished through periodic sales of government bonds, notes, and bills to the general public at open auctions. Since both procedures—printing and borrowing money—require the issuance of government bonds, the only limit is the national debt ceiling established by Congress. In practice, this is little hindrance, as the debt ceiling is raised periodically to accommodate such overspending as Congress deems necessary.

The politically less obvious method of covering deficit spending is for the Fed to agree to an increase in the money supply. By printing more money to cover the deficit (a practice known as *monetizing* the debt), the need to borrow money from the general public is reduced. When government securities are sold to the Fed for the purpose of increasing the money supply, the Fed holds the securities off the market in reserve. The downside to this practice is that an increase in the money supply in excess of the country's growth rate is certain to cause an increase in the rate of inflation because excessive increases in the money supply debase the value of the currency. But an increase in inflation is not an immediate result of printing more money, and it is much less obvious to the average citizen; in a period of negative economic growth, printing money may be a good idea as long as when growth resumes, excess money is slowly withdrawn from the economy to reduce its inflationary effects.

Politicians generally prefer that the Fed be more accommodating with its approval of money aggregate increases, particularly in election years. The popular political call to the Fed to "lower interest rates" (translation: to create more money) is really a call for an increase in the money supply with little mention of the fact that such an action can debase the nation's currency. In the late 1990s, the government seemed to be running a surplus, which had substantially reduced the amount of borrowing necessary to lower competitive demand for longer-term money and fuel lower mortgage rates. Many felt the search for high-quality yields propelled the demand for highly rated mortgage securities, and that the subsequent formation of new, creative mortgage-backed securities, collateralized debt obligations, and financial derivatives, combined with lax and poorly funded regulatory oversight, led to the recent financial market meltdown.

From the viewpoint of the real estate industry, borrowing by the government to pay its obligations competes directly with the demand for mortgage money. Any increase in demand can easily increase the cost of money. In this sense, increasing the money supply rather than borrowing money may hold interest costs lower for mortgages, but always at the risk of a growing rate of inflation and higher rates later on. It is not an easy trade-off. Some industries, including real estate, have found that short-term benefits can be derived from an inflationary trend.

The Treasury Department commenced the Making Home Affordable® Program (MHA) to help struggling homeowners avoid foreclosure in 2009. The main feature of the MHA was to provide to eligible homeowners the opportunity to reduce their mortgage loan payments to be more affordable. It was aimed to aid the unemployed, those borrowers that owed more on their homes than its market value or those with a crippling second lien. The MHA program included options to allow a transparent forbearance agreement for someone unemployed, a modification or refinance of their mortgage, or a conversion of homeownership through a deed-in-lieu of foreclosure or the use of a short sale.

During the life of the program that was extended several times through the end of 2016, the pool of eligible borrowers was expanded. The consumers that took advantage of the MHA programs still have protections and features of the programs that are supervised by the Treasury Department and the Department of Housing and Urban Development.

One of the more visible bureaus within the Treasury Department is the Alcohol and Tobacco Tax and Trade Bureau (TTB) that collects federal excise taxes on alcohol, tobacco and firearms. The TTB is also tasked with enforcement of laws that regulate alcohol and tobacco production and manufacturing and importation. The TTB is involved with regulatory compliance for the permitting of labeling and marketing of alcohol and tobacco products to protect consumer interest.

The Treasury Department is involved in domestic and international economic affairs through their involvement with the International Monetary Fund (IMF), where the Secretary of the Treasury serves as the U.S. Governor to the IMF and selects the U.S. Executive Director of the IMF who exercises voting rights over the strategic direction of the institution. The Treasury Department is also the coordinator of U. S. participation in the G7 and G20 summits, which meet regularly to address the global financial issues facing the member countries of these groups.

Recent policy discussions have brought one of the more important functions of the Department of the Treasury to the forefront: that is, its responsibilities coordinated through its Office of Tax Policy. One of the Office of Tax Policy duties is determining policy standards shown in regulations and rulings and managing their formulation with the Internal Revenue Service; negotiating tax treaties for the United States and representing the United States in meetings and work of multilateral organizations dealing with tax policy matters; and providing economic and legal policy analysis for domestic and international tax policy decisions.

The Financial Crimes Enforcement Network (FinCEN) is a bureau of the United States Department of the Treasury that gathers and evaluates information about financial transactions in order to fight domestic and international financing of terrorists, money laundering, and other financial crimes.

Unfortunately the real estate market transactions have particular traits that allow them to be susceptible to individuals or governments seeking to launder criminal proceeds. For example, many real estate transactions comprise high-value assets, impervious entities using procedures that can inhibit transparency because of their convoluted structure and variety (high-value residential, commercial and development properties). A high-profile case illustrating money laundering risks in the real estate sector involves:

> "1Malaysia Development Berhad (1MDB), a Malaysian sovereign wealth fund. In 2016, the U.S. Department of Justice sought forfeiture of over $1 billion in assets—including luxury real estate—associated with funds stolen by corrupt foreign officials from 1MDB. This included a hotel, two homes, and a mansion in Beverly Hills, CA; a home in Los Angeles, CA; a condominium, two apartments, and a penthouse in New York, NY; and a townhouse in London, England; all with a collected value estimated at approximately $315 million."[3]

Regrettably the real estate market continues as an appealing medium for laundering illegal profits since it screens huge amounts of money in typically

---

[3]FinCEN, "Advisory to Financial Institutions and Real Estate Firms and Professionals," United States Department of the Treasury advisory, August 22, 2017, https://www.fincen.gov/sites/default/files/advisory/2017-08-22/Risk%20in%20Real%20Estate%20Advisory_FINAL%20508%20Tuesday%20%28002%29.pdf

individual transactions. These types of transactions have been structured to protect illicit profits from market and exchange rates because of the manner in which they appreciate in value, "clean" large sums of money in a single transaction, and shield ill-gotten gains from market and exchange-rate instability. So criminals of all stripes have found the use of real estate to hide the existence and sources of their ill-gotten gains a favored vehicle.

Regulation and oversight of national banks comes under the purview of the Office of the Comptroller of the Currency (covered in detail later in this chapter), another agency that falls under the Treasury Department. Further information about how the Treasury Department has oversight of the Federal Deposit Insurance Corporation will be covered later in this chapter.

THE FEDERAL DEPOSIT INSURANCE CORP (FDIC)

Deposit Insurance

Savings associations, savings banks, commercial banks, and credit unions are all classified as depository institutions, meaning that they are specifically authorized by their charters to hold deposits for their customers. Governments treat this activity as a special kind of trust. When the Great Depression of the 1930s caused the collapse of about half of these institutions, savings were lost and depositor confidence was destroyed. To help restore that trust, the federal government created a deposit insurance system.

The Federal Deposit Insurance Corp (FDIC)

In 1934, Congress established the Federal Deposit Insurance Corporation (FDIC) to insure deposits to commercial banks and savings banks. At the same time, the government created the Federal Savings and Loan Insurance Corporation (FSLIC) to insure deposits in savings associations. Later, the National Credit Union Share Insurance Fund was set up to insure credit union deposits. Life insurance companies are not considered depository institutions and are not federally insured. However, a few states opted to establish their own deposit insurance funds for state-chartered institutions, and a few permitted private insurance companies to underwrite the risk. Several failures of state insurance funds occurred in the early 1980s; federal protection has proved to be more effective.

The FDIC was created by the 1933 Banking Act, enacted during the Great Depression to restore trust in the American banking system. More than one-third of banks failed in the years before the FDIC's creation, and bank runs were common. The insurance limit was initially $2,500 per ownership category, and this was increased several times over the years. Since the passage of the Dodd-Frank Wall Street Reform and Consumer Protection Act in 2011, the FDIC insures deposits in member banks up to $250,000 per ownership category.

It is worth noting that no public funds are used for the FDIC's reserves. The FDIC reserves are funded by member bank's dues and if needed the FDIC has a $100 billion line of credit with the Treasury Department.

The FDIC remains under the Treasury Department and now has authority to manage both the bank deposit insurance fund and the savings association insurance fund. Before the enactment of FIRREA in 1989, the savings associations' insurance fund was managed by the Federal Savings and Loan Insurance Corporation (FSLIC). It was this fund that became insolvent, not the bank's FDIC fund, necessitating a taxpayer bailout of the system. The FSLIC was dissolved by FIRREA.

Reorganization of Deposit Insurance Funds

The 1989 Financial Institutions Reform, Recovery, and Enforcement Act dissolved the FSLIC and reorganized the deposit insurance system. A new Deposit Insurance Fund (DIF) was created, administered by the FDIC. Under the DIF, there are two separate insurance funds. One is the Savings Association Insurance Fund (SAIF), which replaced the insolvent FSLIC. The other is the Bank Insurance Fund, which is simply the old FDIC fund under a new name. Effective in 1994, Congress prohibited the FDIC from reimbursing depositors for accounts in excess of the $100,000 limit, an option that had been used in previous years to avoid further collapsing an already weakened banking system. The recent financial crisis once again brought to the fore the need to stabilize the depositor base in the U.S. banking system. On October 3, 2008, President George W. Bush signed the Emergency Economic Stabilization Act of 2008, temporarily raising the basic limit on federal deposit insurance coverage from $100,000 to $250,000 per depositor. This legislation provided that the basic deposit insurance limit would return to $100,000 after December 31, 2009; however, the passage of the Dodd-Frank Act in 2010 permanently raised the limit to $250,000[4].

---

[4]FDIC, "Basic FDIC Insurance Coverage Permanently Increased to $250,000 Per Depositor," press release, July 21, 2010, https://www.fdic.gov/news/news/press/2010/pr10161.html

Congress passed legislation that phased in the merging of the separate insurance funds (the BIF and the SAIF), retaining the FDIC as administrator. In addition, the legislation called for rechartering savings associations as banks. This provision simplified some of the regulatory confusion and overlap that had existed in the banking system.

The term "noninterest-bearing transaction account" includes a traditional checking account or demand deposit account on which the insured depository institution pays no interest. It also includes Interest on Lawyers' Trust Accounts ("IOLTAs"). It does not include other accounts, such as traditional checking or demand deposit accounts that may earn interest, NOW accounts, or money-market deposit accounts.

How We Got to this Point

Resolution Trust Corporation (RTC)

The Resolution Trust Corporation filled an important role in handling the liquidation of failed savings associations in the late 1980s and into the mid-1990s. Created by FIRREA in 1989, the RTC was given the authority to take the necessary steps to sell or liquidate failing thrifts.

The RTC was a receiver, not a regulator, and was responsible for those assets assigned to it by either the OTS or the FDIC. The RTC could close and liquidate a failed institution or it could take over its management under a conservatorship. The RTC inherited some overvalued loan collateral and quite a bit of inadequate loan documentation in its takeover of insolvent associations. These problems made fast resolution difficult. Since the core of the RTC's personnel initially consisted of FDIC employees, its remaining functions and personnel were transferred back to the FDIC. The remaining problems of this agency were transferred to the FDIC in July 1995 and the RTC was dissolved.

The Great Recession Era Reforms

The Emergency Economic Stabilization Act of 2008, enacted on October 3, 2008, is commonly referred to as a bailout of the U.S. financial system. This law was enacted in response to the subprime mortgage crisis, and authorized the United States Secretary of the Treasury to spend up to $700 billion to purchase distressed assets, especially mortgage-backed securities (MBS), and make capital injections into banks.

However, the plan to purchase distressed assets, known as the Troubled Asset Relief Program (TARP), has since been abandoned. Both foreign and domestic banks are included in the program. The original proposal was submitted to the United States House of Representatives with the purpose of purchasing bad assets, reducing uncertainty regarding the worth of the remaining assets, and restoring confidence in the credit markets.

Supporters of the plan argued that the market intervention called for by the plan was vital to prevent further erosion of confidence in the U.S. credit markets and that failure to act could lead to an economic depression. Opponents objected to the plan's cost and rapidity, pointing to polls that showed little support among the public for "bailing out" Wall Street investment banks, and claiming that better alternatives had not been considered and that the Senate had forced passage of the unpopular version through the House by "sweetening" the bailout package.

"This plan can be described as a risky investment, as opposed to an expense. The MBS within the scope of the purchase program have rights to the cash flows from the underlying mortgages. As such, the initial outflow of government funds to purchase the MBS would be offset by ongoing cash inflows represented by the monthly mortgage payments. Further, the government eventually may be able to sell the assets, though whether at a gain or loss will remain to be seen." Thompson, Mark. 7 Questions About the $700 Billion Bailout", Time, September 24, 2008.). A key challenge lay in valuing the purchase price of the MBS, which is a complex exercise subject to a multitude of variables related to the housing market and the credit quality of the underlying mortgages. The ability of the government to offset the purchase price (through mortgage collections over the long run) would depend on the valuation assigned to the MBS at the time of purchase. It turned out that most of the TARP funds were used to purchase nonvoting blocks of equity in many of the nation's troubled financial institutions to shore up their capital positions, rather than to buy up toxic mortgage assets.

The bailout option finally used was primarily aimed at shoring up the capital positions of financial institutions through investments made by the U.S. Treasury Department in purchasing the preferred stock of banks. A vast majority of this investment has been paid back by the institutions. The U.S. Treasury Department sold its investments in three banks in November 2014. At that time, 39 banks still owed TARP funds; many of these were past due in their TARP dividend payments on the funding they received under the Capital Purchase Program. These financial institutions that are past due represent about $381.2 million or about 0.2% of the $204.9 billion initially given to 707 banks and financial institutions, less than a typical seller would expect to be uncollectible[5]. The FDIC as part of the U.S. Treasury Department is carefully coordinating the takeover and liquidation of the banks that ultimately cannot recover.

Analysis of Mortgage Debt

The term *mortgage debt* includes all kinds of loans secured by mortgages and all types of lenders handling these loans. Mortgage debt includes long-term residential loans, short-term construction loans, and warehouse lines of credit used by mortgage companies. To better clarify how this debt is distributed, table 2-1 identifies the four major categories of mortgage debt by type of loan. Clearly, residential loans dominate the market with more than three-fourths of the total debt outstanding—a percentage that has held steady for two decades. Farm loans continue to decline in both dollar amount and as a percentage of the total debt.

Analysis of Loan Sources

The mortgage loan analyst must distinguish between those making mortgage loans and those holding mortgage loans; they are not necessarily the same. Loan originators make the loans. Some originators hold these loans

TABLE 2-1 Major Categories of Mortgage Debt 1998 & 2017 (in billions of dollars)

	1998		2017	
	Amount	Percentage	Amount	Percentage
Total mortgage debt	$5,782	100%	$14,904	100%
Residential (one- to four-family)	4,376	76	10,616	71
Apartments (multifamily)	362	06	1,311	9
Commercial	949	16	2,741	18
Farm	95	02	236	02

Source: © 2021 Mbition LLC

---

[5] Michael Krantz, "40 Banks Late on their TARP Bailout Payments," *USA Today*, April 20, 2014.

in portfolio—meaning as their own investments in income-producing assets. From 2000 to 2008, most originators sold their loans within a few months to secondary market investors dominated by private mortgage conduits and Ginnie Mae securities.[6]

Table 2-2 shows the percentage of mortgage loans held by the principal lender sources. It compares the percentages held in 1998 with those at the end of the fourth quarter of 2017 to illustrate how the market has shifted. The migration of mortgage lending away from savings associations began over 30 years ago. Now the major source for residential loans has shifted from **mortgage pools**, which serve as collateral for the issuance of mortgage-backed securities issued by federal and related funding sources such as the government-sponsored enterprises, primarily Fannie Mae and Freddie Mac.

Savings Association Regulatory Authorities

Office of Thrift Supervision (OTS)—Now Merged into the Office of the Comptroller of the Currency

Until the rechartering of savings associations as banks, federal regulatory authority for savings associations was held by the **Office of Thrift Supervision (OTS)**. Section 312 of the Dodd-Frank Act mandated the merger of OTS with the **Office of the Comptroller of the Currency (OCC)**, the Federal Deposit Insurance Corp. (FDIC), the Federal

TABLE 2-2 Mortgage Debt as Held by Class of Lender

A Comparison from 1998 to 2017 (in billions of dollars)

Lender Source	1998		2017	
	Amount	Percentage	Amount	Percentage
All holders	$5,782	100%	$14,904	100%
Depository institutions	$1,981	34%	$4,801	32%
Life and P&C insurance companies	$212	4%	$507	3%
Federal and related	$292	5%	$5,315	36%
Mortgage pools	$2,632	46%	$2,952	20%
Finance companies, REITs, and others	$665	11%	$1,329	9%

Source: © 2021 Mbition LLC

---

[6]*Mortgage Debt Outstanding 3rd Quarter 2014 Report* (Washington, DC: Federal Reserve Bank, 2017), accessed June 6, 2018, https://www.federalreserve.gov/data/mortoutstand/current.htm

Reserve Board, and the Consumer Financial Protection Bureau (CFPB) as of July 21, 2011. The OTS ceased to exist on October 19, 2011. An arm of the Treasury Department under the OCC, the OTS at one time replaced the FHLBB as regulator for the associations. Its authority extended to both federal- and state-chartered institutions that carried federal deposit insurance.

Federal Housing Finance Board (FHFB)

The OTS was not given all the authority formerly held by the FHLBB. The new Federal Housing Finance Board (FHFB) was assigned as overseer of mortgage lending for the 12 regional Federal Home Loan Banks. In addition, the FHFB is responsible for handling statistical data for the housing industry.

Savings Banks

Savings banks originated during the early years of the United States when most people traded in cash and needed a place to deposit their surplus for safekeeping. Our modern-day "check society" was still a long way off; there was little need for checking accounts.

For many years thereafter, savings banks (formerly called "mutual savings banks" because most were owned by their depositors) operated with good success in the northeastern part of the country. They were located particularly in New York and Massachusetts, with a few in the far northwest. Originally, these institutions were all state-chartered.

Because of the emphasis on savings account deposits over demand deposits, savings banks looked with favor on longer-term mortgage loans. As a result of their location in generally cash-rich areas of the country and the conservative nature of their investment policies, many savings banks favored FHA and VA loans. There was no restriction on making this kind of loan out of state, and savings banks purchased these loans from originators all over the country. In recent years, however, lending policies shifted away from individual mortgage loans to investing in federally underwritten mortgage-backed securities.

The Federal Home Loan Bank Board has full authority over federally chartered, stockholder-owned savings banks. When the FSLIC was faced with major problems disposing of failed savings associations in the mid- to late 1980s, it undertook a new policy. Instead of dissolving troubled savings associations, it would selectively merge four or five such institutions into one and recharter the operation as a "federal savings bank," or FSB. There were some advantages to this procedure. It postponed the need for bailout cash in the hope that the reorganized entity might resolve its own problems. Moreover, it took direct regulation away from state banking commissions that may have been in some conflict with federal deposit insurance policies. Furthermore, the cost of deposit insurance was much less at that time for a savings bank than for a savings association, which gave the newly reorganized groups lower operating costs. In the late 1980s, commercial banks and savings banks, both insured by the FDIC, were paying an 8.33 cents premium per $100 of insured deposit[7], while savings associations were paying nearly double that amount, with further increases expected.

The 1980 Depository Institutions Deregulation Act altered the way the banking system could serve the public. One of the changes was formal approval for savings associations and savings banks to offer checking accounts. In addition, the door was opened for these institutions to make other kinds of loans. The result of these changes was that savings banks and savings associations could offer services very similar to those of commercial banks.

Reserve Requirements for Depository Institutions

Institutions handling deposits are required to hold a certain percentage of their deposit assets in a reserve account, making these funds unavailable for lending purposes and thus providing a backup source of emergency money should one be needed. In the past, state-chartered institutions operated under their respective state laws governing reserve requirements, while national charters adhered to federal requirements. These regulations often differed as to the amount of reserves required and whether or not the reserves could earn interest. Furthermore, the Federal Reserve Bank Board had authority to alter reserve requirements for its own member banks, but not for nonmember state charters. Changing reserve requirements gave the Federal Reserve Bank one more

---

[7]The Federal Deposit Insurance System, "Committee on Banking, Housing, and Urban Affairs, United States Senate, One Hundred Eighth Congress," First session on The condition of the FDIC system and to consider reforms which would make it more effective, February 26, 2003. Accessed on September 11, 2018 at: https://www.gpo.gov/fdsys/pkg/CHRG-108shrg92305/html/CHRG-108shrg92305.htm

tool with which to stabilize the national economy; however, it also created some inequities within the banking system, as the application of reserve requirements was not uniform.

Any institution holding reserves on deposit with the Fed has the right to borrow from the Fed at the discount rate of interest. The Fed's "discount window" is open for emergency use, but the money cannot be used as additional capital for ordinary lending purposes. Many exceptions to this last guideline have been made as a result of the recent financial crisis.

THE FEDERAL HOME LOAN BANK (FHLB) SYSTEM
Regulated Lenders

Regulated lenders are those depository institutions and life insurance companies that are subject to various government regulatory agencies. This class of lender is limited in many ways: in the kind of loans the entity is allowed to make, by the percentage of total assets that can be held in certain types of loans, in the kind of mortgage repayment plans the entity can offer, and by the qualifications for borrowers and for property that is pledged as collateral. Because a number of different regulatory authorities are involved, including separate state and federal chartering systems, there is an overlap of authority and no countrywide uniform standards can be clearly defined.

For many years, regulated lenders dominated the mortgage market, particularly the market for home loans. About 75% of the money for residential mortgage lending came from savings accounts held by institutional, or regulated, lenders. This source of money began to disappear, however, as an escalation of interest rates and alternative investments such as money market mutual funds began siphoning cash out of lower interest-bearing savings association deposits. With their depositors' money invested in long-term mortgage loans, depository institutions were caught in a serious cash shortage dilemma. The late 1980s saw the collapse of many savings associations, and this particular source began withdrawing from originating long-term, fixed-rate mortgages in order to maintain their portfolios held on their balance sheets.

Although regulated lenders have reduced their investments in the mortgage market (that is, holding loans in portfolio), they are still major players in the primary market. Some still hold loans as sound portfolio investments, while others originate loans that are sold to investors. Most regulated lenders retain the loan servicing function on their loan originations; it involves collection of monthly payments and proper disposition of the money. During the past five years, there has been a consolidation of mortgage loan servicing, and the field is no longer dominated by nondepository institutions, but rather by depository institutions, the largest of which are Bank of America, Citigroup, JPMorgan Chase, and Wells Fargo N.A. However, now some sell this function to specialized servicing companies like American Home Mortgage Servicing, Inc., or outsource to firms like ClearSpring Loan Services.

Savings Institutions

The term *savings institutions* describes both savings associations and mutual savings banks (now called simply *savings banks*). Because both these institutions were initially limited to holding only time deposits (savings accounts), they also acquired the combined name *thrift institutions*, or *thrifts*.

A **time deposit** is one that does not permit withdrawal on demand, but instead usually requires a waiting period of 14 to 30 days depending on which regulatory authority is in control. In addition to the obvious time factor in savings certificates and certificates of deposit that give a withdrawal date or time period on their face, all passbook savings accounts are classed as time deposits. Even though the withdrawal limit on time deposits exists, few institutions attempt to use it under normal conditions. To delay a withdrawal would most likely discourage further deposits by customers. Nevertheless, it is this access to the more-stable time deposits that has provided justification for the practice of savings institutions to make long-term mortgage loans.

Savings Associations

The original purpose of savings associations was to provide a source of money for home loans. As a result, in their earlier years, some were called *building societies*. Congress established the Federal Home Loan Bank Board (FHLBB) in 1934, giving it the authority to charter new federal savings associations. The Board required all federal charters to keep at least 80% of their deposit assets in residential loans (including multi-family housing loans).

As recently as 40 years ago, savings associations were limited by law to paying an interest rate of 5.50% on passbook savings accounts (according to Federal Reserve Regulation Q), which was well below market rates at that time. To help overcome this problem, new savings certificates were introduced that allowed payment of higher rates for longer-term deposits. The result of this and other factors was a rapid increase in the cost of funds. Indeed, the national average cost of funds for FSLIC-insured savings associations rose from 7.87% at the end of 1979 to 11.58% at the end of 1981. At that time, savings associations held most of their mortgage loans in portfolio, and the fixed income generated by low-interest, long-term mortgage loans failed to keep pace with the rising cost of funds.

In 1980, Congress passed the Depository Institutions Deregulation and Monetary Control Act, which substantially altered many rules that had formerly distinguished the various kinds of depository institutions from each other. No longer were savings associations firmly committed to making mostly residential loans. New rules allowed them to expand their investment portfolios to many new kinds of loans, including higher-risk investments. In addition, they could now offer their customers checking account services, credit card accounts, and the advice of trust departments—services formerly restricted to commercial banks. While the intention of Congress was to help savings associations recover from the dilemma created by escalating interest rates, they overlooked the role played by federal deposit insurance.

To cope with massive losses on insured deposits, Congress enacted legislation, signed by the first President Bush on August 9, 1989, in the form of the **Financial Institutions Reform, Recovery, and Enforcement Act (FIRREA)**, which created an overhaul of banking practices with the primary goal of restructuring the savings and loan association system. The 900-plus-page document touched many aspects of mortgage lending, including federal and state licensing of appraisers, setting minimum capital requirements, and providing more stringent enforcement of banking regulations.

In 1996, Congress passed legislation that set the stage for the eventual elimination of savings institutions, which would be rechartered as banks.

The two separate deposit insurance funds (SAIF for savings associations and BIF for commercial banks and savings banks) were merged into one fund under FDIC management. To facilitate this merger, savings associations and a few banks agreed to pay $4.7 billion into the SAIF fund, which had been the weaker of the two funds. Two reasons for the weakness of the savings association fund were the declining number of S&Ls (below 1,200 in 2014) and the annual $780 million paid by this fund on government bonds issued to help bail out troubled associations.

With the additional cash added mostly by savings associations, the deposit insurance funds had reached the legal protection requirement ($1.25 for each $100 of insured deposits), and therefore most insured institutions were no longer required to pay an assessment to the fund except for the $2,000 per year membership fee.

Mortgage Partnership Finance Program® (MPF®)

In 1997, the Federal Home Loan Bank System started the Mortgage Partnership Finance program to fund mortgage loans through the Chicago FHL Bank to its member institutions in Illinois and Wisconsin. Within its first 12 months, the MPF® program had funded $195 million in MPF® loans. The program was well-received, and in 1999, the Federal Housing Finance Board, which oversees the FHL Banks, authorized an expansion of the program to all six FHL Banks and raised the funding limit from $750 million to $9 billion system-wide.

At that time, $9 billion represented only about 1% of the annual mortgage market in this country, the initial expansion coming from a huge financial resource. However, within the first six months of 2010, the MPF® program funded 1,291,650 loans totaling $182.9 billion, and funding limits for this program have continued to expand. In March 2018 the MPF® Program and Ginnie Mae announced that they had exceeded $1 billion in MBS issued since the inception of the program.

Congress created the FHLB System during the Depression years to help banks finance housing, in one effort to restore the nation's economy. In the 1930s, banks were not particularly interested in making more mortgage loans, as they had experienced substantial defaults. The FHL Banks found other kinds of investments and grew in manifold ways during subsequent years of operation. Today, in net assets, the FHLB System ranks second only to Fannie Mae.

The MPF® represents an important incentive to regulated lenders to expand their efforts in the mortgage loan origination market. Over a number of years, mortgage companies have expanded their market share of the residential mortgage market to well over 50%, dealing primarily through nonbank lenders and the sale of mortgages to federal agencies and private lenders to be securitized.

The MPF® program allows the FHL Bank to purchase mortgages from, or fund them through, its participating member institutions. The program is limited to fixed-rate mortgages on one- to four-family residences originated by these member institutions. The size of eligible loans is limited to conforming loan limits, generally up to $453,100 as of 2018.

The program is an alternative to selling these loans to a secondary-market agency and paying a guarantee fee. The FHL Bank manages the funding, interest rate, liquidity, and prepayment risks associated with the loans. Participating lenders eliminate the interest rate risk of their fixed-rate loans while fully maintaining their customer relationships.

Questions for Discussion

1. Outline the monetary system used in this country.
2. How does the Federal Reserve increase the money supply?
3. How does the Treasury raise money when it has to borrow?
4. Explain the major factors that influence interest rates and describe the effects interest rate factors have on the residential mortgage market.
5. Explain the meaning of the terms "fiscal policies" and "monetary policies."
6. Define a "time deposit" and contrast with a "demand deposit."
7. Identify the four major areas of demand for money.
8. How does a change in interest rates affect business borrowing?
9. Discuss the effects of the new loan commitment software applications on residential mortgage lending.
10. Suggest ways to improve our banking system.

Multiple Choice Questions for Review

1. Long before coin or currency came into use:
   a. humans began to use base metal pieces as coins
   b. bartering was the only method of exchange
   c. trade didn't exist
   d. none of the above

2. The major source of money funding residential mortgage loans today is:
   a. money market funds
   b. commercial bank time deposits
   c. the federal government
   d. the sale of mortgage-backed securities

3. In the United States, monetary policy is carried out by:
   a. the president
   b. Congress
   c. the Federal Reserve System
   d. Congress and the Treasury Department

4. The Federal Reserve System measures monetary aggregates each week to keep track of the growth or decline in the:
   a. national monetary liquidity
   b. national loan demand
   c. money supply
   d. national debt

5. When the Federal Reserve sells a government bond on the open market:
   a. reserves in the banking system increase and the economy will speed up
   b. reserves in the banking system decline and the economy will slow down
   c. Federal Reserve liabilities remain unchanged
   d. both A and B occur

6. Which of the following statements is true about M3?
   a. Its total value is smaller than that of M2.
   b. Apart from those assets also included in M1, it includes no assets that offer check-writing features.
   c. Its total value is more than four times as large as M2.
   d. It includes large-denomination time deposits.

7. Four major classes of regulated lenders are:
   a. commercial banks, life insurance companies, credit card companies, savings institutions
   b. savings institutions, commercial banks, stocks and bonds, credit unions
   c. savings institutions, commercial banks, credit unions, life insurance companies
   d. savings institutions, commercial banks, credit unions, credit card companies

8. Categories of demand for money are all of the following EXCEPT:
   a. government requirements
   b. consumer loans
   c. mortgage loans
   d. deposits in saving associations

9. Of the following, which can be the best indicator of mortgage interest rates?
   a. the discount rate of interest
   b. Fannie Mae/Freddie Mac–administered yield requirements
   c. the results of weekly Treasury bill offerings
   d. reports made by the Farm Credit System

10. Which of these does a lender NOT look at when determining a borrower's "ability to repay"?
    a. commissions
    b. pension
    c. part time employment
    d. life insurance

Information Resources

http://www.bankrate.com/calculators.aspx
When you want indications of interest rates for various financial products such as residential mortgage loans, websites like the one above offer a good source of information.

https://www.fanniemae.com/singlefamily/ecommitone
In 2004, Fannie Mae introduced new technology to allow its approved mortgage lenders to gain access to its loan commitment system, allowing lenders to lock rates with their borrowers in advance of closings. A free webinar series on one of these systems, ecommitONE™, is available from Fannie Mae at the URL above.

http://www.federalreserve.gov/releases/h6/current/
The Federal Reserve Bank still gives the changes in M1 and M2 every week, and its report is carefully reviewed by financial analysts and bankers. Easy access to this information is available at the URL above.

https://www.fincen.gov/resources/advisories-bulletinsfact-sheets/advisories
This website provides access to FinCEN advisory bulletins that cover issues with real estate that include good examples of real world cases that FinCEN has pursued.

https://www5.fdic.gov/edie/
FDIC's Electronic Deposit Insurance Estimator can be used by consumers and bankers to allow them to calculate the way FDIC insurance rules apply to their deposits at any individual bank and if any of those deposits exceeds the coverage limits for that bank.

https://www.annualcreditreport.com/cra/index.jsp
In accordance with the Fair and accurate Credit Transactions Act (FACT Act), three nationwide consumer credit reporting companies (Equifax, Experian, and TransUnion) formed AnnualCreditReport.com, which provides consumers with the secure means to request and obtain a free credit report once every 12 months.

CHAPTER 3

ADDITIONAL GOVERNMENT INFLUENCE

KEY TERMS AND PHRASES

affordable housing loans
annual percentage rate
Closing Disclosure
closing instructions
Community Reinvestment
 Act (CRA)
Consumer Financial Protection
 Bureau (CFPB)
disbursement procedures
down payment assistance programs
escrow closing
Farm Credit Administration (FCA)
Farm Credit System (FCS)

finance charge
kickback
Loan Estimate
loan status report
preliminary title report
Real Estate Settlement Procedures
 Act (RESPA)
right of rescission
Rural Housing Service (RHS)
settlement agent
Truth-in-Lending Act (TILA)
Wall Street Reform and Consumer
 Protection Act

> **LEARNING OBJECTIVES**
>
> At the conclusion of this chapter, students will be able to:
> - Understand the key provisions of the Real Estate Settlement Procedures Act.
> - Describe how the Loan Estimate is used and delivered in the settlement process.
> - Explain the Truth-in-Lending Act disclosures both prior to loan application and during advertising.
> - Explain the unique disclosure requirements of the Truth-in-Lending Act, including the right of rescission.
> - Describe the reasons for many of the closing costs listed on the HUD-1 and Closing Disclosure.

U.S. DEPARTMENT OF HOUSING AND URBAN DEVELOPMENT (HUD)

HUD was formed as a cabinet-level agency in 1965 with the passage of the Department of Housing and Urban Development Act of 1965. However the Federal Housing Administration (FHA) that evolved out of the National Housing Act of 1934 to provide strong, sustainable, quality, and affordable housing had been in existence for many years and is within HUD's umbrella today. To understand the impact on home ownership in the U.S. and on HUD, one must understand the early years of the FHA and its evolution from a Depression-era New Deal program aimed at restoring stability to the U.S. housing markets, providing jobs, and restoring home building by easing mortgage credit. This was accomplished by a visionary idea to create low down payment loans that had mortgage insurance that protects lenders from the risk of default. All the mortgage insurance premiums were paid into a fund (the Mutual Mortgage Insurance Fund) to cover the costs of loan defaults. The FHA mortgage insurance program was designed to be self-sustaining.

SIGNIFICANT FEDERAL LEGISLATION (CRA, TILA, RESPA, SAFE, APA, DODD-FRANK)

Community Reinvestment Act (CRA)

The **Community Reinvestment Act**, passed in the late 1970s, has gone through many changes, but its original purpose—to ensure that regulated depository institutions serve the needs of their communities—remains. It requires regulated institutions to publicize their lending services in their own communities and encourage participation in local lending assistance programs. Enforcement of these requirements is handled by the particular federal supervisory agency regulating the institution. There are four: (1) the Comptroller of the Currency, (2) the Federal Reserve Bank, (3) the FDIC, and (4) the Office of Thrift Supervision. Thus the Act covers most of the nation's financial institutions. The penalty for failure to comply is a limitation on any approval that may be required from federal authorities by the offending institution.

The Act requires that each institution undertake four procedures, as follows:

1. *Define the lender's community.* Each lender must prepare a map of the area it serves, which is the neighborhood from which it draws its deposits and into which it makes loans.
2. *List the types of credit offered.* A list of credit services available from the institution must be submitted to the regulators and made available to the public; the emphasis is on publicizing methods of borrowing rather than saving money.
3. *Post public notice and public comments.* Each relevant institution must post a notice in its place of business stating that the institution's credit performance is being evaluated by federal regulators. Furthermore, the notice should state that the public has the right to comment on the institution's performance and to appear at open hearings on any request for expansion.
4. *Report on efforts to meet community needs.* A periodic report must be made available to the public on the efforts of the institution to ascertain the credit needs of its community and the ways it is attempting to meet those needs.

CRA Amended by FIRREA

The 1989 Financial Institutions Reform, Recovery, and Reinforcement Act (FIRREA) amended the Community Reinvestment Act, sharpening the performance ratings for regulated institutions and requiring public disclosure of what each is doing to meet local needs. FIRREA also amended the 1975 Home Mortgage Disclosure Act, expanding its reporting requirements to include all mortgage lenders—both regulated and, for the first time, unregulated lenders. The purpose of these changes is to encourage greater participation in home buyer assistance programs through increased publicity of lenders' actual performance.

CRA Grading of Regulated Lenders

FIRREA requires that CRA ratings be made public for each institution, evaluating how well the entity:

1. knows the credit needs of its community;
2. involves its board of directors in setting up and monitoring CRA programs;
3. informs the community about its credit services;
4. offers a range of residential mortgages, housing rehabilitation, and small business loans;
5. participates in government-insured, -guaranteed, or -subsidized loans;
6. distributes credit applications, approvals, and rejections across geographic areas; and
7. avoids discrimination in its lending practices.

The CRA grading consists of four categories: (1) outstanding, (2) satisfactory, (3) needs to improve, and (4) substandard compliance. Each institution's grade is publicized periodically, a practice that has proven to be a substantial incentive for compliance with CRA requirements. Furthermore, a satisfactory or better CRA rating is necessary to obtain regulatory approval of an institution's request for such activities as mergers, acquisitions, expansions, and siting new branches. Previously, third parties could petition regulatory agencies to deny approval of these activities for an institution with a poor CRA record. However, in January 1997, the Office of the Comptroller of the Currency issued a rule change that cut out such community groups, announcing that the OCC would send in its own team to review a bank's lending record and render a verdict.

In 1999, President Clinton signed into law the Gramm-Leach-Bliley Act, also known as the "Financial Services Modernization Act." This law extended the provisions of the CRA to those institutions wishing to use a bank holding company as the vehicle for entering into the commercial banking business to the other lending practices within the banking holding company.

With the passage of the Higher Education Opportunity Act, Pub. L. 110-315, on August 14, 2008, each appropriate federal financial supervisory agency shall now consider, as a factor in assessing the record of a financial institution's CRA compliance, any and all low-cost education loans provided by the financial institution to low-income borrowers.

In October 2017 the Office of the Comptroller of the Currency (OCC) issued Policies and Procedures Manual (PPM) 5000-43, which set the OCC's policy and framework for determining the effect of evidence of discriminatory or other illegal credit practices on the Community Reinvestment Act (CRA) rating of a national bank, federal savings association, federal branch, or community bank.

The incentive generated by the recent CRA requirements has spawned a new loan qualification pattern that will be examined under the umbrella term *affordable housing* as another kind of borrower-qualification standard.

Truth-in-Lending Act

The **Truth-in-Lending Act (TILA)** is a federal law that became effective in July 1969 as a part of the Consumer Credit Protection Act. It is implemented by the Federal Reserve Board's Regulation Z. The purpose of the law is to require lenders to give meaningful information to borrowers on the cost of consumer credit, which includes credit extended in real estate transactions. The credit covered must involve a finance charge or be payable in more than four installments. Credit extended for business purposes, which includes dwelling units containing more than four families, are not covered by this law. No maximum or minimum interest rates or charges for credit are set by the law, whose purpose is primarily one of disclosure.

While TILA contains a limited right allowing the borrower to rescind or cancel the credit transaction, and covers in considerable detail all types of advertising to promote the extension of consumer credit, the principal features discussed here are the disclosure of the finance charge and the annual percentage rate (APR).

When dealing with a Truth-in-Lending disclosure now called the Loan Estimate that has replaced the Good Faith Estimate as the new integrated disclosure for a residential mortgage, creditors must re-disclose and make new disclosures if the annual percentage rate at consummation differs from the estimate originally disclosed by more than one-eighth of one percentage point in regular transactions (a fixed-rate mortgage) or by more than one-fourth of one percentage point in irregular transactions (an adjustable-rate mortgage), as defined in footnote 46 of § 226.22(a) (3). Should a re-disclosure be required, then the 3/7/3 waiting period is reset. This reset and re-disclosure may have been eliminated or modified under the recent Economic Growth, Regulatory Relief, and Consumer Protection Act as discussed earlier.

Where Are We Now?

The Federal Truth-in-Lending Act—Regulation Z

Details can be found by visiting the Consumer Financial Protection Bureau website at http://files.consumerfinance.gov/f/201311_cfpb_tila-narrative-exam-procedures.pdf

Purpose

The purpose of this regulation is to promote the informed use of consumer credit by requiring disclosures about its terms and cost. The regulation also gives consumers the right to cancel certain credit transactions that involve a lien on a consumer's principal dwelling, regulates certain credit card practices, and provides a means for fair and timely resolution of credit billing disputes. The regulation does not generally govern charges for consumer credit, except that several provisions in Subpart G set forth special rules addressing certain charges applicable to credit card accounts under an open-end (not home-secured) consumer credit plan.

The regulation requires a maximum interest rate to be stated in variable-rate contracts secured by the consumer's dwelling. It also imposes limitations on home equity plans that are subject to the requirements of § 226.5b and mortgages that are subject to the requirements of § 226.32. The regulation prohibits certain acts or practices in connection with credit secured by a consumer's principal dwelling. The regulation also limits certain practices of creditors who extend private education loans as defined in § 226.46(b) (5).

Coverage

In general, this regulation applies to each individual or business that offers or extends credit when four conditions are met:

1. the credit is offered or extended to consumers;
2. the offering or extension of credit is done regularly;
3. the credit is subject to a finance charge or is payable by a written agreement in more than four installments; and
4. the credit is primarily for personal, family, or household purposes.

Finance Charge

The **finance charge** is the total of all costs that the consumer must pay for obtaining credit. These costs include interest, the loan fee, a loan-finder's fee, time-price differentials, discount points, and the cost of credit life insurance if it is a condition for granting credit. In a real estate transaction, purchase costs that would be paid regardless of whether or not credit is extended are not included in the finance charge, provided these charges are reasonable, bona fide, and not included to circumvent the law. Among these excluded purchase costs are legal fees, taxes not included in the cash price, recording fees, title insurance premiums, and credit report charges. However, such charges must be itemized and disclosed to the customer. In the case of first mortgages intended to purchase residential dwellings, the total dollar finance charge need not be stated, although the annual percentage rate must be disclosed.

Annual Percentage Rate (APR)

The **annual percentage rate** as determined under Regulation Z is not an "interest rate." Interest is one of the costs included in the finance charge. The APR is the relationship of the total finance charge to the total amount to be financed and must be computed to the nearest one-quarter percentage point.

Right of Rescission

It is worth noting that TILA provides that for certain transactions secured by a consumer's principal dwelling, the consumer has three business days after becoming obligated on the debt to rescind the transaction. The **right of rescission** allows the consumer time to reexamine the credit agreement and cost disclosures and to reconsider whether he or she wants to place his or her home at risk by offering it as security for the credit. Transactions exempt from the right of rescission include residential mortgage transactions, such as purchase money transactions under Section 226.2(a)(24), and refinancing or consolidations with the original creditor when no "new money" is advanced.

If a transaction is rescindable, a consumer must be given a notice explaining that the creditor has a security interest in the consumer's home, that the consumer may rescind, how the consumer may rescind, the effects of rescission, and the date the rescission period expires.

To rescind a transaction, the consumer must notify the creditor in writing by midnight of the third business day after the latest of three events: (1) consummation of the transaction, (2) delivery of material TILA disclosures, or (3) receipt of the required notice of the right to rescind. For purposes of rescission, "business day" means every calendar day except Sundays and legal public holidays.

What is RESPA?

RESPA is an acronym for "Real Estate Settlement Procedures Act," a federal consumer protection statute, originally enacted in 1974 (updated several times since). RESPA is enforced by the Consumer Financial Protection Bureau coordinating with Department of Housing and Urban Development (HUD), the Federal Reserve Bank, and the Federal Deposit Insurance Corporation.

What is the purpose of RESPA?

As defined by HUD, its purposes are:

- "to help consumers become better shoppers for settlement services"; and
- "to eliminate 'kickbacks' and referral fees that unnecessarily increase the costs of certain settlement services."

Key Details of the Real Estate Settlements Procedures Act

Some of the key details of RESPA are as follows:

- It requires that borrowers receive disclosure at various times in the transaction (detailing costs, outlining lender servicing and escrow account practices, and describing business relationships).
- RESPA requires a lender to deliver or place in the mail, no later than three business days after, not including the day the application is received, a copy of CFPB or HUD's current Home Loan Toolkit special information booklet.

Effective on mortgage applications taken October 3, 2015 and later, lenders are required to use two new disclosures created by the CFPB. The Loan Estimate, which replaces the 2010 Good Faith Estimate and the law referred to as Regulation Z or Truth in Lending; and the Closing Disclosure, which replaces the HUD-1 Settlement Statement.

These new disclosures, the Loan Estimate and the Closing Disclosure, have "wait periods" that restrict how soon a real estate transaction with a mortgage can close. The Loan Estimate is issued once a lender has received an application (the six points of information that create an application per the CFPB) within three business days. There is a 7-day waiting period that takes place once the Loan Estimate has been delivered, before the borrower can sign their final loan documents (also referred to as "consummation").

If the lender needs to re-issue the Loan Estimate due to a bona fide "changed circumstance" (such as locking in a rate after the initial Loan Estimate was issued), the re-issued Loan Estimate triggers a 4-day waiting period before consummation/signing can occur.

Borrowers must receive the Closing Disclosure at least three days prior to signing their final loan documents. If corrections are required to a Closing Disclosure that has been issued, an additional 3-day waiting period may be triggered.

A Loan Estimate cannot be issued on the same day as the Closing Disclosure and a lender cannot issue a revised Loan Estimate after the Closing Disclosure has been provided to the borrower. However, a lender can issue the Closing Disclosure the day after the final Loan Estimate has been issued and those waiting periods may run at the same time.

The waiting periods are based on when the borrower receives the disclosures versus when the lender delivers the documents. In most cases, the lender needs proof that the documents have been received by the borrower. Different methods of delivery may have different waiting periods. For example, if a lender meets with the borrower and receives signed documentation, the waiting period may start that day. If the lender sends the documents electronically, the date the borrower acknowledges the documents will start the waiting period. If the lender opts to send the documents via mail, it is assumed the borrower received the documents in seven days.

The 3-day waiting period associated with the Closing Disclosure is NOT a right of rescission. Borrowers still may have contractual obligations to the purchase under a sales agreement. However, if a borrower is refinancing a home, they will enjoy the 3-day waiting period after they receive their Closing Disclosure before they can sign their loan documents. Later when it's time for the borrower to sign their loan documents, the borrower will have a 3-day wait with the right of rescission before their loan can fund/close.

It's more critical than ever for borrowers to make sure they communicate with their lender. Make sure that your borrower lets you as their loan originator know if there are any changes to the contract (sometimes real estate brokers forget to forward addendums to the contract) including changes to the closing date, seller credits, or the sales price. A loan originator or mortgage broker needs to counsel their borrower to inform them of any vacations that they have planned during the mortgage process, as the waiting periods cannot be waived. It's also important to quickly review, acknowledge, and return the disclosures as, in most cases, the date a borrower acknowledges the document will start the clock ticking for the borrower's waiting period.

Section 109 of the Economic Growth, Regulatory Relief and Consumer Protection Act of 2018 removes the three-day wait period required for the combined TILA/RESPA mortgage disclosure if a creditor extends to a consumer a second offer of credit with a lower annual percentage rate.

TABLE 3-1

TRID TOLERANCE BUCKETS

UNLIMITED / NO TOLERANCE (AMOUNTS CAN INCREASE WITHOUT REDISCLOSURE)	10% TOLERANCE (CUMULATIVE INCREASES WITHIN EACH CATEGORY OF CLOSING COSTS)	ZERO TOLERANCE (AMOUNTS CANNOT INCREASE WITHOUT REDISCLOSURE)
REQUIRED SERVICES/THAT CAN BE SHOPPED FOR/OR NOT ON WRITTEN LIST	UNAFFILIATED THIRD PARTY FEES/MAY SHOP FOR/AND ON WRITTEN LIST	REQUIRED SERVICES/ PAID TO CREDITOR, BROKER, AFFTILIATE INCLUDING ORIGINATION CHARGES
SERVICES NOT REQUIRED	RECORDING FEES	TRANSFER TAX
PREPAID INTEREST		REQUIRED SERVICES PAID TO UNAFFILIATED THIRD PARTY/NO SHOPPING
PROPERTY INSURANCE PREMIUMS		

TRID, Truth in Lending/Real Estate Settlements Procedure Integrated Disclosure.
Source: © 2021 Mbition LLC

Mortgage Servicing Disclosure Statement

RESPA also requires the disclosure and note of transfer of mortgage servicing. This disclosure is a two-part process. The first part is a servicing disclosures statement at the time of loan application. This form should disclose the servicing activities of the lender and the odds of the applicant's loan being sold. The second is when the borrower's loan is sold, a second disclosure is sent to the borrower, detailing who is the new owner of their mortgage. The second disclosure must be sent no fewer than 15 days prior to the loan sale or transfer. These notices must contain certain information. They must contain the effective date of the transfer of the servicing to the new servicer and the name, address, and toll-free or collect-call phone number of the new servicer. Also, these notices must contain the toll-free or collect-call number of the person or department for both the present servicer and the new servicer who will answer questions about this transfer. Finally, the regulation specified that during the 60 days following this transfer, a mortgage payment received prior to the due date by the old servicer couldn't be considered late by the new servicer.

RESPA prohibits such practices as:

- giving or accepting any "thing of value" for referrals of settlement service business; and/or
- giving or accepting any part of a charge for services not actually performed.

RESPA restrictions do not apply to brokerage commissions splits among real estate agents or to referral fees paid by one real estate agent to another, including a licensed relocation management company. It is not a violation for a service provider to use a marketing program involving giveaways to all real estate agents in a particular area, trade organization, group, etc.

RESPA covers loans secured with mortgages placed on one- to four-family residential properties, along with most purchase loans, assumptions, refinances, property improvement loans, and equity lines of credit.

Violations of RESPA are subject to criminal and civil penalties:

- Criminal penalties include: fines up to $10,000 and imprisonment for up to one year.
- Civil penalties include: being held liable for an amount equal to three times the amount paid for the service.

Interestingly enough, RESPA gives the mortgage applicant the right to request of the lender that they be provided a copy of the appraisal performed and used in their loan package. It must be a formal request in writing and the lender must then comply. However, the appraiser will not be allowed to discuss an appraisal with the applicant; the appraiser can only review the appraisal with the client—the lender. Simply because an applicant paid for the appraisal does not give the applicant(s) the ownership of the appraisal.

The Secure and Fair Enforcement for Mortgage Licensing Act of 2008 (SAFE Act)

In response to the most recent credit crisis:

- The Secure and Fair Enforcement for Mortgage Licensing Act of 2008 (SAFE Act) was passed on July 30, 2008. The new federal law gave states one year to pass legislation requiring the licensure of mortgage loan originators according to national standards and the participation of state agencies on the Nationwide Mortgage Licensing System and Registry (NMLS). The SAFE Act was designed to enhance consumer protection and reduce fraud through setting minimum standards for the licensing and registration of state-licensed mortgage loans. Mortgage loan originators who work for an insured depository (or its owned or controlled subsidiary that is regulated by a federal banking agency), or for an institution regulated by the Farm Credit Administration, are registered. All other mortgage loan originators are licensed by the states. The SAFE Act requires state-licensed mortgage brokers or loan officers to pass a written qualified test, to complete pre-licensure education courses, and to take annual continuing education courses. The SAFE Act also requires all mortgage brokers or loan officers to submit fingerprints to the Nationwide Mortgage Licensing System (NMLS) for submission to the FBI for a criminal background check; and state-licensed mortgage brokers or loan officers to provide authorization for NMLS to obtain an independent credit report.
- The SAFE Act requires more expanded disclosures for estimates of closing costs in 2009 along with expanded definitions of predatory credit practices and consumer liability for providing inaccurate or misleading information to obtain credit.

Additional discussion of specific mortgage broker/loan originator licensing processes is covered later in this textbook.

The Administrative Procedures Act (APA)

The Administrative Procedures Act (APA) was passed in 1946 to establish how federal government agencies will propose and establish regulations and the way that federal courts are to review any agency decisions. Later the Model State Administrative Procedure Act was passed as a measure to create similar oversight for state agencies. Even though the Model State Act was endorsed and initially drafted by the National Conference of Commissioners on Uniform State Laws, most (but not all) states have adopted the Model State Law by the end of 2015. The only real difference between the Model State Act and the federal APA is that the Model State Act suggests that that there be an orderly management of regulations prior to their adoption.

An example of one such Model State Act was instituted in Texas and is called the Texas Administrative Procedures Act (TAPA) and can be found in Title 10, chapter 2001 of Texas Government Code. According to the Texas Administrative Law Handbook, the purposes of the TAPA are to:
- provide general legal requirements that agencies must adhere to when adopting rules or conducting contested cases;
- incorporate the Texas Open Meetings Act that requires that all governmental bodies deliberate in public meetings, unless a closed or executive session is expressly authorized; and
- incorporate the Public Information Act, which specifies that documents or records of a state agency are open, unless an express exception to disclosure applies to a particular record.

Some of the more salient provisions of the TAPA, and how they might affect the actions of state regulators such as the Texas Real Estate Commission (TREC), are discussed below:
- Texas Government Code § 2001.004 requires the state's agencies to adopt rules of practice stating the nature and requirements of all available formal and informal procedures; and make available for public inspection all rules and other written statements of policy or interpretations that are prepared, adopted, or used by the agency in discharging its functions; and provide an index that is cross-indexed to any statute, and make available for public inspection all final orders, decisions, and opinions.
- Texas Government Code § 2001.007 requires that state agencies shall make generally available access to text of its rules; any material, such as a letter, opinion, or compliance manual, that explains or interprets one or more of its rules and that the agency has issued for general distribution to persons affected by one or more of its rules be made available through the internet.
- Texas Government Code § 2001.021 provides that interested persons may petition a state agency to request the adoption of a rule. It requires any such rule adoption request to be responded to within 60 days after its submission. Generally the requesting party, defined as an interested person,

must be: (1) a Texas resident, and (2) a business located in the state of Texas or a governmental subdivision located in Texas.
- Texas Government Code § 2001.022 requires that a state agency shall determine whether a rule may affect a local economy before proposing the rule for adoption. If a state agency determines that a proposed rule may affect a local economy, the agency shall prepare a local employment impact statement for the proposed rule. The impact statement must describe in detail the probable effect of the rule on employment in each geographic area affected by the rule for each year of the first five years that the rule will be in effect and may include other factors at the agency's discretion.
- Texas Government Code § 2001.029 requires that before adopting a rule, a state agency shall give all interested persons a reasonable opportunity to submit data, views, or arguments, orally or in writing. It will do this by granting an opportunity for a public hearing before it adopts a substantive rule if a public hearing is requested by: (1) at least 25 persons; (2) a governmental subdivision or agency; or (3) an association having at least 25 members. Any state agency shall consider fully all written and oral submissions about a proposed rule.
- Texas Government Code § 2001.030 says that upon adoption of a rule, any Texas state agency, if requested to do so by an interested person either before adoption or not later than the 30th day after the date of adoption, shall issue a concise statement of the principal reasons for and against its adoption. The agency shall include in the statement its reasons for overruling the considerations urged against adoption.
- Texas Government Code § 2001.031 says a state agency may use an informal conference or consultation to obtain the opinions and advice of interested persons about contemplated rulemaking. A Texas state agency may appoint committees of experts or interested persons or representatives of the public to advise the agency about contemplated rulemaking; however, the power of a committee appointed under this section is advisory only.
- Texas Government Code § 2001.032 says the Texas State legislature has the right to review the rulings of agencies and each house of the legislature by rule shall establish a process under which the presiding officer of each house refers each proposed state agency rule to the appropriate standing committee for review before the rule is adopted. The procedure to execute this legislative review is when a written request is received from the lieutenant governor, a member of the legislature, or a legislative agency, the secretary of state shall provide the requestor with electronic notification of rulemaking filings by a state agency under Section 2001.023.
- Texas Government Code § 2001.038 grants that the validity or applicability of a rule, including an emergency rule adopted under Section 2001.034, may be determined in an action for declaratory judgment if it is alleged that the rule or its threatened application interferes with or impairs, or threatens to interfere with or impair, a legal right or privilege of the plaintiff.
- Texas Government Code § 2001.051 grants the opportunity for a hearing and the participation of all parties. Should there be a contested case; each party is entitled to an opportunity for: (1) a hearing after reasonable notice of not less than 10 days; and (2) the right to respond and to present evidence and argument on each issue involved in the case.
- Texas Government Code § 2001.053 says that should a contested case (as defined in Section 2001.051) occur, each party to a contested case is entitled to the assistance of counsel before a state agency, and each party may expressly waive the right to assistance of counsel.
- Texas Government Code § 2001.054 contains provisions concerning contested cases that apply to the grant, denial, or renewal of a license that is required to be preceded by notice and opportunity for hearing. It allows that, for a license holder who makes timely and sufficient application for the renewal of a license or for a new license for an activity of a continuing nature, the existing license does not expire until the application has been finally determined by the state agency. If the application is denied or the terms of the new license are limited, the existing license does not expire until the last day for seeking review of the agency order or a later date fixed by order of the reviewing court.

Any revocation, suspension, annulment, or withdrawal of a license is not effective unless, before institution of state agency proceeding the agency must give notice by personal service or by registered or certified mail to the license holder of facts or conduct alleged to warrant the intended action; and the license holder is given an opportunity to show compliance with all requirements of law for the retention of the license.

- Texas Government Code § 2001.087 provides that, in a contested case, a party may conduct cross-examination required for a full and true disclosure of the facts.
- Texas Government Code § 2001.141 says that a decision or order of a state agency that may become final that is adverse to any party in a contested case must be in writing and signed by a person authorized by the agency to sign the agency decision or order.
- Texas Government Code § 2001.171 says that a person who has exhausted all administrative remedies available within a state agency and who is aggrieved by a final decision in a contested case is entitled to judicial review under this chapter.
- Texas Government Code § 2001.176 allows a party to a contested case to petition the final decision for judicial review. Any such review must be initiated not later than 30 days after the date the decision or order that is the subject of complaint is final and appealable. In a contested case in which a motion for rehearing is a prerequisite for seeking judicial review, a prematurely filed petition is effective to initiate judicial review.
- Texas Government Code § 2001.901 says a party may appeal a final district court judgment in the manner provided for civil actions generally.

A good reference guide is available online at: https://www.texasattorneygeneral.gov/files/og/adminlawhb.pdf. It is the 2014 Administrative Law Handbook of Texas provided by the Texas Attorney General's Office. Some of the more interesting points in this handbook are that:

- A governmental body may conduct a closed session to discuss real estate, if deliberation in an open meeting would have a detrimental effect on the governmental body's negotiating position.
- The Act requires written notice of all meetings. A governmental body must give the public advance notice of the subjects it will consider in an open meeting or a closed session. Notice is usually sufficient if it alerts the public that some action will be taken on a topic. The word "consideration" alone is sufficient to put the general public on notice that the Commission might act during the meeting.
- The Open Records Policy of the TREC is covered by the TAPA.
- TREC Standards & Enforcement Services Division (TREC SES) deals with signed written complaints from the public and license holders concerning alleged violations. Should any of those complaints have evidence that suggests a violation has occurred, attempts will first be made to resolve the complaint through alternative dispute resolution (ADR) methods, such as informal settlement discussions or mediation. When ADR is not effective or appropriate, TREC SES pursues formal disciplinary action and a hearing may be set at the State Office of Administrative Hearings. These hearings are covered by the TAPA.

Wall Street Reform and Consumer Protection Act (The Dodd-Frank Act)

The financial crisis and resultant mortgage crisis brought about unparalleled foreclosures on home mortgages not seen since the Great Depression. Congress passed several pieces of legislation as a result of the crisis, including the Housing and Economic Recovery Act of 2008 and the Secure and Fair Enforcement for Mortgage Licensing Act of 2008. These laws are intended to provide consumer protection against unethical mortgage practices. Sustained deterioration from the mortgage crisis of 2007 brought about continuous debate in Congress about the need for wide-ranging financial institution regulatory reform. Under strong public pressure, Congress passed the **Wall Street Reform and Consumer Protection Act** in 2010, also known as the "Dodd-Frank Act." Dodd-Frank ushered in some of the most momentous changes to financial regulation in the United States since the regulatory reform that followed the Great Depression. It made changes in the American financial regulatory environment of all federal financial regulatory agencies and virtually every segment of the financial services industry. The Dodd-Frank Act was intended to focus on the systemic risk that existed in the financial industry that seemed more obvious after the 2007 financial crisis. Prior to 2010, many consumer protection and mortgage banking regulations were enforced by one agency or another, and many were enforced and monitored by several different agencies covered. However, the problem existed due to the fact that noncompliance of one regulation can influence or jeopardize the performance of other requirements.

The mortgage banking industry today is large and varied, including a wide range of financial service firms. The volume of interrelated regulatory laws and governmental agencies has made mortgage banking one of the most highly regulated industries in history. With the passage of the Dodd-Frank Act, rulemaking authority was transferred to a new independent Bureau of the Federal Reserve System under the Treasury Department called the **Consumer Financial Protection Bureau** (CFPB) by seven different agencies for more than a dozen federal consumer financial protection laws. While many have been intimidated by these laws, remember that mortgage regulation compliance is crucial to sustainable home ownership and the need to correct the policy and systemic structural issues that gave rise to the mortgage crisis.

Dodd-Frank was passed to:

1. *address regulatory gaps* (The Dodd-Frank Act grants power to a single regulator and charges it with the responsibility to mitigate the systemic risks within the system.);
2. *address structural concerns* (Dodd-Frank deals with additional structural issues that are now obvious. Large depositories and other non-bank financial institutions could be just as vulnerable to liquidity issues and bank runs not seen since the Great Depression.);

3. *address liquidity issues* (The Act emphasizes the need to focus on liquidity concerns for large financial institutions caused by the inordinate amount of leverage used by those firms and increased concern over the regulation of "nonbank" activities, including payment, clearing, and settlement systems.); and

4. *establish the CFPB.* (One of the purposes of the Dodd-Frank Act was to create the CFPB with a high level of autonomy over all consumer protection with little appeal from its decisions. Therefore, it takes full Congressional action to change any part of the Dodd-Frank Act; its funding comes from the Federal Reserve System (not Congress) and it is therefore more independent from lobbying by Congressional representatives forum-shopping for their constituents and lobbying from industry within Congress. The responsibilities of the CFPB were anticipated to include:

    a. conducting rule-making, supervision, and enforcement for federal consumer financial protection laws;
    b. restricting unfair, deceptive, or abusive acts or practices;
    c. taking consumer complaints;
    d. promoting financial education;
    e. researching consumer behavior;
    f. monitoring financial markets for new risks to consumers; and
    g. enforcing laws that outlaw discrimination and other unfair treatment in consumer finance.

The CFPB has the power to enforce many of the consumer compliance and protection laws passed over the past five decades for consumer and mortgage credit. While the CFPB's regulatory authority extends to a wider span than just mortgage lending, this text covers only how the CFPB's actions affect mortgage lending. In May 2018 Congress passed the Economic Growth, Regulatory Relief, and Consumer Protection Act that relaxed some of the capital requirements for financial institutions and removed some consumer protection provisions of the Dodd-Frank Act, most notably:

- Section 108 expanded an exemption that allows lenders to avoid escrowing taxes and insurance for many higher-cost, higher-risk loans, making it less likely that borrowers will be able to meet recurring costs of homeownership; and

- Section 109 eliminates the requirement of a 3-day waiting period on mortgage disclosures in cases where the lender offers a new interest rate, giving borrowers less time to examine whether other loan terms have also been changed in the process.

Further sources of information about the pros and cons of this Act are at the Information Resources section at the end of this chapter.

Additional Federal Regulation of Home Mortgage Lending

The Home Mortgage Disclosure Act

Public concern over credit shortages in urban neighborhoods led to the passage of the Home Mortgage Disclosure Act (HMDA) in 1975. Congress believed that some financial institutions contributed to the decline of some geographic areas by their failure to provide adequate home financing to qualified applicants on reasonable terms and conditions. HMDA was passed to provide the public with data used to:

- help determine whether financial institutions are serving the housing needs of their communities;
- assist public officials in distributing public-sector investments so as to attract private investment to areas where it is needed; and
- assist in identifying possible discriminatory lending patterns and enforcing antidiscrimination statutes.

Federal legislation passed in 1975 that was initially directed only toward regulated lenders has since been expanded to include independent mortgage companies. HMDA requires most financial institutions to disclose the number of mortgage loans they make and the dollar amount of these loans by geographic area. The intent was to generate a statistical basis for judging if and where discrimination was prevalent in lending practices.

In 1989, FIRREA expanded its reporting requirements to include all home loan originators and information relating to the income level, racial characteristics, and gender of mortgagors and mortgage applicants. This requirement covers both loans originated and applications rejected. In addition, disclosure is required regarding to whom the loans are sold. The intent is to determine what loan originators are doing with the loans they make. For this purpose, each of the federal underwriters of mortgage pools (Ginnie Mae, Fannie Mae, Freddie Mac, and Farmer Mac) is classified separately.

Information generated through HMDA is enabling Congress to take steps toward further restructuring of the home loan market. In the 1992 Federal Housing Enterprises, Financial Safety, and Soundness Act, a goal was set for federal secondary-market agencies to purchase at least 30% of their mortgages on housing units located in central city areas.

The Housing and Economic Recovery Act (HERA), enacted in July 2008, specifically addressed the subprime mortgage crisis. It authorized the Federal Housing Administration to guarantee up to $300 billion in new, 30-year, fixed-rate mortgages for subprime borrowers if lenders write-down (reduce) principal loan balances to 90% of current appraisal value. It also gave states the authority to refinance subprime loans using mortgage revenue bonds. HERA was passed with the intention of restoring confidence in Fannie Mae and Freddie Mac by strengthening regulations and injecting capital into the two large U.S. suppliers of mortgage funding. HERA did not achieve this aim, but it did establish the Federal Housing Finance Agency (FHFA) out of the Federal Housing Finance Board (FHFB), as well as the Office of Federal Housing Enterprise Oversight (OFHEO). The FHFA still has the oversight of Fannie Mae and Freddie Mac it gained when these institutions were put into conservatorship later in 2008. These two institutions remain in that status at this time.

Many primary market lenders must deal with the various risks associated with a business in which the ability to sell the mortgage loan you originate to an investor—without having to buy it back later if it fails to perform as underwritten—is commonplace. There are many moving parts to this process. Events leading up to the financial crisis and subsequent mortgage meltdown share an interesting common theme: the lack of loan-level underwriting quality control. Recent Federal Housing Administration and enhanced GSE requirements for underwriting and quality control standards, as well as third-party business partner oversight, can no longer take a backseat to other regulatory matters. Legacy primary market originators need to break free of the daily struggle to find creative ways to source and fund loans in the secondary markets. They have become entangled in the legal battles that ensue from new court rulings almost daily as a result of lax quality control standards and lack of assurance that third-party originators are in compliance with underwriting standards and investor documentation requirements.

Mortgage Lending

Most mortgage financing comes from regulated lenders, and the evolution of regulation has shaped the way they operate. Historically, regulated lenders dominated the mortgage industry because savings deposits were necessary to making long-term loans and federal laws encouraged such use of deposit assets. As financial institutions suffered through changes in the 1980s, secondary-market funding of mortgage loans grew, creating loan pools and selling securities backed by these pools. These new security packages opened the door to many newcomers entering the loan origination business, especially mortgage companies that specialized in subprime mortgages. Many of these have been forced to shutter operations over the past few years. Mortgage-backed securities were more easily sold to investors than mortgages until the financial crisis that began in late 2007. By 2011, the residential mortgage-backed securities market had been slow to recover, as without an implied or direct guarantee from the government to protect investors in the event of default, there was no demand for this investment product. While the private, mortgage-backed securities market is nowhere near recovery, one of several firms at the forefront of the toxic mortgage crisis—Goldman Sachs—issued its first post-crisis prime jumbo residential mortgage-backed securitization in November 2014.[1]

Let's examine the mortgage companies that serve as intermediaries between lenders and borrowers. The term "mortgage companies" covers both mortgage bankers and mortgage brokers, some operating in the wholesale market and some in retail brokerage. Mortgage companies were a dominant source of total residential mortgages originated from the late 1980s to 2007, when they handled close to half of all loan originations each year. One effect of the recent financial crisis has been the consolidation of the mortgage banking industry and the increasingly important role of commercial banks as residential mortgage originators in the market today. At the end of 2013, commercial banks originated 54% of residential mortgage loans.[2] Agricultural real estate finance encompasses a smaller segment of the loan market, and its primary federal regulatory

---

[1] Ben Lane, "Goldman Sachs Launches First Jumbo Mortgage Bond Since Crisis," *Housing Wire*, November 26, 2014, accessed December 27, 2014, http://www.housingwire.com/articles/32191-goldman-sachs-launches-first-jumbo-mortgage-bond-since-crisis

[2] Author calculated from data from the American Bankers Association and "Credit Market Borrowing, All Sectors, by Instrument," Table F.4 from the December 11, 2014 Federal Reserve Statistical Release.

has remained the same, but the structure and sources of its funding have seen extensive changes in the past 20 years. Other types of direct loans by federal and state government agencies will be reviewed later. Another portion of the loan origination market involves individuals and others who, for various reasons, participate in making mortgage loans.

Mortgage Companies

From its origin as a brokerage-type service that arranged loans, the mortgage banking industry has grown into a major business, handling over one-quarter of the conventional loans and half of all HUD/FHA and VA loans in this country.

In the early years of the twentieth century, mortgage companies arranged for the sale of their own bonds and used these funds to make small home and farm loans. Because of the thrift-conscious nature of farmers and homeowners, mortgage loans were amazingly free of defaults and provided a steady return for the holders of mortgage bonds. Mortgage companies achieved such a good record of repayments that the small-denomination bonds they sold to the general public for mortgage financing became known as *gold bonds*.

The 1920s brought further expansion of mortgage companies' financing from home loans to include loans on income properties such as office buildings, apartments, and hotels. With little regulation and a "let the buyer beware" attitude, some projects were overfinanced as speculators moved into these lucrative markets. The Depression years, beginning in 1929, revealed many basic weaknesses in the mortgage loan system. Most mortgage companies that had issued bonds, as well as those that guaranteed bonds for other development companies, were faced with massive foreclosures. Unable to meet their obligations, many were forced into bankruptcy.

Unlike regulated depository institutions, mortgage companies without depositors were not a concern for the government. The money that mortgage companies used to make their loans was derived from the sale of bonds, which was considered a business transaction, not a savings account deposit procedure. Therefore, mortgage companies were granted no help in recovery after the Depression years. One method that mortgage companies used to reestablish their business was the promotion of FHA and, later, VA loans, which had been widely rejected by regulated lenders. Mortgage companies such as Franklin American Mortgage Company are still the main originators of FHA and VA loans.

Mortgage companies share the mortgage market with regulated lenders; each has a market share of about half of all loan originations. A major difference between mortgage companies and regulated lenders, however, is that mortgage companies do not hold depositors' cash for the purpose of funding their loans. Nor do they normally have investment cash with which to hold loans. To fund loans at closing, most mortgage companies rely on commercial banks that grant them "warehouse" lines of credit. The loans are short-term, collateralized by the mortgage notes they fund, and normally repaid through the sale of these notes to secondary-market investors. Warehouse lines of credit will be discussed more fully in subsequent chapters.

Even within the industry, mortgage companies may operate in substantially different ways. Some, including mortgage bankers, offer a full-service facility including loan origination, funding, and servicing. Others, including mortgage brokers, specialize in serving as agents for large lenders. A number of individuals and companies serve as correspondents or agents representing specific investors.

STATE AND LOCAL PROGRAMS (INCLUDING TDHCA)

State and Local Government Programs

This book does not attempt to cover all the specific unique state housing agencies, such as the Texas Veterans Land Board, or state-specific residential mortgage lending. Because of the opportunity to assist home buyers, and perhaps some political advantage for the officials involved, many state and local housing agencies have developed since the mid-1970s. Some offer direct loans to qualified buyers. It is worth pointing out, however, that over the past 10 years, states have universally adopted **down payment assistance programs**. It is theorized that with an in-depth understanding of the needs of local housing markets, housing agencies are uniquely situated to sensibly underwrite mortgages. This local understanding is key in programs that offer down payment assistance for low-income, first-time home buyers and finance the development of multifamily, affordable rental housing. State-designated entities are often called agencies, authorities, or development corporations. These programs are funded by state bond programs backed by mortgages. Many analysts considered these housing finance agencies' loans to be of higher quality than many low down payment loans, since buyers must take classes in home finance in order to obtain these loans. Since the financial crisis, some state housing finance agencies have experienced trouble issuing the bonds they have used in the past to help home buyers with down payment assistance and mortgages. States including West Virginia, Ohio, Wisconsin, and California have suspended all or part of their mortgage and down payment assistance programs financed through bond issues.

Many consumers and real estate professionals are not as familiar with the various programs that are available. A good source for state-by-state levels of housing agency funding can be found at the website of the First Home Advisor organization, http://www.firsthomeadvisor.com/index.php/first-time-home-buyer-loan-mortgage/state-bond/. Real estate professionals should not look at this link as a complete picture of all the funding available, as it doesn't have all the city- or county-specific programs that recently have targeted redevelopment and rehabilitation.

Affordable Housing Loans

The Financial Institutions Reform, Recovery, and Enforcement Act (FIRREA) passed in 1989 expanded the 1977 Community Reinvestment Act to target both regulated and nonregulated lenders. FIRREA sharpened the performance ratings for regulated institutions and required disclosure of what each is doing to meet local credit needs.

Grades ranging from "outstanding" to "substandard compliance" are issued periodically by an institution's regulatory authority and publicized locally. Satisfactory ratings are a prerequisite for regulatory approval of activities including mergers, acquisitions, expansions, and the establishment of new branches.

While satisfactory compliance involves a number of activities, one is to offer a range of residential mortgage, housing rehabilitation, and small business loans. One result of the application of FIRREA is the creation of a new category of conventional loan that targets low- and moderate-income people. The generally accepted definition of *low income* is 80% of the local area's median income and 115% for *moderate income*. Loans are limited to low- and moderate-income families. Some programs limit the maximum purchase price of the house and all include an education course for home buyers. The education course is usually six hours of instruction covering the functions of brokers, appraisers, title companies, and mortgage lenders. The course also explains the responsibilities of owning a home.

Fannie Mae and Freddie Mac, as well as private mortgage insurers such as Radian Group, Inc. and Mortgage Guaranty Insurance Corporation, have shown strong support for **affordable housing loans**. All four of these organizations sell their services to regulated lenders and are interested in assisting them in this particular activity. All have developed special programs for this purpose. Fannie Mae, for example, has a variety of community-oriented programs, such as the following:

- My Community Mortgage®
- HomeStyle® Renovation Mortgage
- Making Home Affordable™
- MH Advantage™
- HomeReady®

Freddie Mac's affordable housing and mortgage relief programs go by the following names:

- Freddie Mac Relief Refinance Mortgage™
- Home Possible®
- Home Possible® Advantage™
- Neighborhood Solution®

The purpose is not to make risky loans to unworthy borrowers, but rather to recognize that many people simply follow different living practices. Studies have indicated that lower-income families normally pay a higher percentage of their income for housing than others do. Some (but not all) affordable housing programs will allow a higher ratio of income applied to housing, such as 33% of gross income instead of the 28% or 31% found with other kinds of loans. These families do not normally commit to an overload of other debt, so total fixed obligations are limited to 38% of income—somewhat less than the 43% and 41% found in FHA and VA qualification, respectively.

Many lower-income people prefer to pay bills with cash instead of using checking accounts. To accommodate this practice, these programs accept timely payment of rent and utility bills as evidence of creditworthiness. Cash requirements for closing, a special problem when income is low, can be reduced by allowing some borrowing or acceptance of grants from others. A number of housing agencies and local communities offer support programs that include cash grants.

What has become evident from this particular program in its few years of existence is that the credit experience has been excellent. Low income does not mean poor payment. The higher default rates seen in the recent financial crisis seem to stem from higher-income borrowers, those with poor credit scores, and those who were underwritten using nontraditional credit reviews that are no longer allowed under current affordable housing programs.

Texas Loan Programs

Texas has made its own loan programs available for veterans and low- to middle-income borrowers. All of them have had a very beneficial impact on the Texas housing industry and deserve more detailed discussion.

Texas Veterans Land Fund

The Texas Veterans Land Board has made a program available by which an eligible veteran may buy land from the Veterans Land Board (VLB) by a contract of sale, installment land contract, or contract for deed at very favorable interest rates determined by the Texas Veterans Land Board.

The contract cannot exceed 30 years, and the purchase price of the property cannot exceed the least of the following options:

- $80,000;
- 95% of the final agreed purchase price; or
- 95% of the appraised value of the land.

There must be a minimum down payment of 5%. The land must be at least 1 acre.

The veteran may either purchase land owned by the Board, or designate certain land that the Board may purchase on his/her behalf and then sell it to him/her under the installment land contract.

Veterans Housing Assistance Program

Another program that the Texas Veterans Land Board has made available is the Veterans Housing Assistance Program (VHAP).

- The program is available to eligible veterans purchasing a new or existing home.
- The home must be the veteran's primary residence for at least three years.
- The VHAP loan is used in conjunction with any other type of financing, and allows the veteran to borrow up to $45,000 as a first or second lien mortgage. For single mortgage loans of less than $45,000, the Veterans Land Board will be the only note holder.
- If more than $45,000 will be borrowed, the Veterans Land Board and the first lien lender will share the first lien position, and the first lien lender will service and originate the loan.

All VLB-originated loans are subject to an 85% loan-to-value ratio. The VLB will lend only 85% of the home's appraised value up to $45,000. The VHAP does not guarantee an interest rate on any loan. The interest rate on the VHAP loan is determined at the time the lender secures a rate lock.

Additional information on both of these Veterans Land Board approved loans can be obtained by calling the Texas Veterans Land Board at their toll-free number: 1 (800) 252-VETS, or by visiting their website: www.texasveterans.com.

Veterans Home Improvement Program

For eligible Texas veterans, the Veterans Home Improvement Program (VHIP) will provide up to $25,000, on a fixed rate note, for making substantial repairs to the veteran's existing primary residence.

The loans can be for as long as 20 years; no down payment is required. However, if the loan is less than

$10,000, the maximum term of the loan will be 10 years. The loan is funded when the improvements have been completed and a Veterans Land Board Representative has conducted an inspection. There is also an emergency loan program for eligible Texas veterans who, for self-help or safety reasons, need immediate home repairs. This "rapid response home improvement loan" can be approved the same day, with final approval for a loan up to $25,000 the following day.

Texas Department of Housing and Community Affairs (TDHCA)

By periodically selling tax-exempt mortgage revenue bonds (MRBs), the Texas Department of Housing and Community Affairs (TDHCA) raises money in financial markets at the lower interest rates available to state and municipal bonds. (The interest paid on such bonds is exempt from federal income tax.)

By passing the lower rates on to home buyers, mortgage loans can be made for less than conventional market rates.

There are also the Texas governmental agencies administrating several significant programs under the American Recovery and Reinvestment Act of 2009. They oversee roughly 17 housing programs, including the First-Time Homebuyer Program, the "Bootstrap" Homebuilder Loan Program, the Down Payment Assistance Program, and the HOME Investment Partnerships Program (HOME).

To qualify for the First-Time Homebuyer Program, the applicant must:

- not have owned a principal residence in the past three years;
- have an annual income in the low to moderate range;
- be considered creditworthy; and
- agree to buy a residence within the state of Texas.

Income limits vary, depending on the area, the number of people in the family, and whether or not the property is within a targeted or nontargeted area. (Targeted areas are federally designated regions defined as being economically depressed. Some program restrictions are waived or reduced to encourage development and housing in these areas).

"Bootstrap" Homebuilder Loan Program

The "Bootstrap" Homebuilder Loan Program provides up to $30,000 in low-interest home mortgage loans to low-income Texas families agreeing to help build their own homes. Two-thirds of the funds are used to help residents of impoverished border colonies and communities build new and better homes. The remaining one-third of the funds is available statewide to low-income families. Funds for the initiative come from the housing trust fund and other sources. The Bootstrap program is administered through TDHCA's Colonia Self-help Centers and other nonprofit organizations across the state.

HOME Investment Partnerships Program

The HOME Investment Partnerships Program (HOME) provides grants and loans to help local governments, nonprofit agencies, for-profit entities, and public housing agencies provide safe, decent, affordable housing to extremely low-, very low-, and low-income families.

HOME allocates funds through four basic activities:

1. homebuyer assistance;
2. rental housing development;
3. owner-occupied housing assistance; and
4. tenant-based rental assistance.

HOME has a 15% "set-aside" for community housing development organizations, and a 10% set-aside for special needs, including the homeless, the elderly, persons with disabilities, and persons with AIDS. HOME reserves funds for people at or below 80% of average medium family income (AMFI) for an area.

TDHCA receives a statewide block grant of home funds for participating jurisdictions made on an annual basis according to a formula based on several HUD criteria. The home regulations allow for a variety of housing activities, all aimed at providing safe, affordable housing to low-income families. These programs change from time to time.

For more information about TDHCA programs, visit their website at http://www.tdhca.state.tx.us

Housing Finance Corporation

Texas also provides a mechanism whereby a local governmental unit can authorize the creation of a

Housing Finance Corporation within that governmental unit. This is a nonprofit corporation that can sell bonds and use other methods of incurring income to provide financing to local lending institutions for low- and middle-income housing, similar to a state-sponsored program administered by the Texas Department of Housing and Community Affairs.

There are also similar criteria for providing housing for the elderly. These corporations can be enabled only by a local governing body, such as a city council. The determination must be made from town to town as to whether or not a housing financing corporation is available as a source for these types of funds.

Fannie Mae REALTOR® Programs

Fannie Mae partnered with the Texas Association of REALTORS® (TAR) to create the "Borrow With Confidence" program, teaching agents how to use Fannie Mae products.

A similar program was created with the Texas Department of Housing and Community Affairs (TDHCA), termed "United Texas: Housing Initiatives That Work," which is offered around the state through the local Associations of REALTORS®.

For more information about this and other Texas home programs, visit TAR's website at: http://www.texasrealtors.com, and click on the "Affordable Housing" link.

Texas State Affordable Housing Corporation

The Texas State Affordable Housing Corporation (TSAHC) provides home ownership opportunities to Texans who may not qualify for financing through conventional channels.

TSAHC works with Texas REALTORS® and participating lenders to provide affordable loans and assistance with down payment and closing costs for:

- firefighters;
- police and corrections officers;
- veterans;
- teachers; and
- low- and moderate-income homebuyers.

More information is available at TSAHC's website: http://www.tsahc.org

AGRICULTURAL LENDING

Government Loan Programs

While most government programs involved with mortgage financing are designed to encourage private lenders to make loans, there are some programs that handle direct loans to borrowers—that is, the agencies work in the primary market. However, to avoid the appearance of direct competition with private business, many such programs require that the loan applicant first attempt to borrow the money from private sources. This is true of the Small Business Administration and the Rural Housing Service, or "RHS" (formerly known as Farmers Home Administration, or "FmHA"), an agency of the U.S. Department of Agriculture (USDA) that offers a wide range of programs under the USDA's Rural Mission. The Rural Housing Service has taken over the loan programs formerly offered by the Farmers Home Administration. In 2009, the American Recovery and Reinvestment Act was passed, further expanding the role and mission of the USDA's Rural Development agency.

Direct mortgage loan programs offered by the federal government are almost all farm-related. State- and municipal-sponsored loan programs are mostly housing-related and are usually handled by one or more local housing authorities. Because of its earlier importance in the mortgage credit structure of the country, we will first consider the federal Farm Credit System.

Farm Credit System

The **Farm Credit System (FCS)** dates back to 1916 at the time of the passage of the Federal Farm Loan Act. Since that time, other federal agencies have become involved with farm credit and are now under the supervision of one agency. Today, the Farm Credit System is an elaborate cooperative (or borrower-owned) network of farm lending banks under the supervision, examination, and coordination of the **Farm Credit Administration (FCA),** an independent federal agency. Administratively, the FCS is composed of five regional farm credit districts (reduced to four in 2011) owned by over a million American farmers and 5,000 of their marketing and business services cooperatives. The system makes long-term mortgage loans and short-term production or crop loans through different organizations.

The FCS funds its loans and other assets primarily through the sale of system-wide consolidated securities. Most of the financing is handled through the sale of 6- to 9-month securities, and some with 2- to 5-year coupon notes. The interest rates charged to borrowers are determined periodically based on the FCS's average cost of system funds.

Three different FCS organizations were originally involved in making direct loans to the farming community: federal land banks, federal intermediate credit banks, and banks for cooperatives. Their functions have been absorbed, consolidated, or replaced by the five cooperative credit organizations owned by local member/borrowers that make long-term machinery and livestock loans. The local associations assist members in need of loans, screen and approve acceptable loan applications, and forward the applications to one of the banks listed below for funding. Approved loans are guaranteed by the local associations, a practice that makes all members liable and encourages peer pressure and assistance in loan repayments. The federal land banks, federal intermediate credit banks, and banks for the cooperatives have merged and are now known as:

1. AgriBank, FCB, 30 E. 7th St., Suite 1600, St. Paul, MN 55101
2. Farm Credit Bank of Texas, P.O. Box 202590, Austin, TX 78720
3. AgFirst Farm Credit Bank, P.O. Box 1499, Columbia, SC 29202
4. CoBank, ACB, 5500 S. Quebec St., Greenwood Village, CO 80111

Generally, loans are limited to 85% of the appraised value of the property, with a term of not less than five years and not more than 40 years. Interest rates for most loans apply a variable-rate plan, allowing interest to be adjusted periodically. Rates are based on the FCS cost of funds.

U.S. Department of Agricultural Development

The Farm Credit System holds $199 billion in farm debt. The **Rural Development Housing and Community Facilities Programs**, also known as the **Rural Housing Service (RHS)**, holds another $181 billion of the debt owed by farmers. The Farmers Home Administration (FmHA) was established in 1946 as part of the Department of Agriculture for the purpose of making and insuring loans to farmers and ranchers. In 1995, FmHA was eliminated and its essential programs were transferred to the Rural Development Service, also under the Department of Agriculture. The scope of RHS activities extended well beyond farm and home loans into financing for parks, camping facilities, hunting preserves, access roads, and waste disposal systems, as well as to making loans in designated disaster areas.

Rural Development provides loan guarantees to help local lenders extend credit needed for the growth and preservation of jobs. It has expanded its traditional lending base to include towns of up to 50,000 but gives priority to towns of less than 25,000. Suburbs and urbanizing areas that surround towns of over 50,000 citizens are not eligible. Eligibility for loan assistance requires that the loan be used for the purpose of saving existing jobs, expanding existing business, and new plant location or business start-up. There is no minimum loan size, and the maximum size is based on existing program priorities from year to year.

Home Ownership Loans

The Rural Development Service's home loan program is limited to rural areas and to low- and moderate-income families who are unable to qualify for home financing in the private market. The USDA Rural Development's Section 501 Direct Loan Program can be made for up to 100% of the appraised value of a house for a maximum term of 33 years (38 years for those with incomes below 60% of AMI and who cannot afford 33-year terms). The term is 30 years for manufactured homes. Eligibility is limited to those with very low income, defined as below 50% of the area median income (AMI); low income is between 50% and 80% of AMI; moderate income is 80% to 100% of AMI. One can visit http://www.rd.usda.gov/files/RD-DirectLimitMap.pdf and scroll through the list of states to find the Metropolitan Statistical Area, or "MSA," nearest one's location to learn current income limits listed by family size. Alternately, the Rural Development county supervisor can determine an applicant's eligibility.

Adjusted income limits vary in different sections of the country based on the difference in cost of living in different areas. A typical limit for a single person might be $19,250. For a family of four, it could be $27,500, with higher limits for larger families. Calculation of the qualifying income follows HUD standards generally, with certain additional limitations.

Evaluation of the 10-page loan application (Form RD 410-4) is handled in a manner similar to that of other lending agencies and requires a complete financial statement, a history of family income, and a credit report. Each loan is reviewed periodically to determine if the borrower's financial condition has improved to the extent that the loan could be handled by a private lending institution.

For single-family housing, Rural Development will make loans on new or existing structures. However, there are maximum allowable amounts listed by county and income limits that can be found at http://www.rd.usda.gov/files/RD-GRHLimitMap.pdf. The final maximum amount of a loan permitted is determined by the applicant's ability to repay the loan.

For RHS-guaranteed loan programs, applicants may have an income of up to 115% of the median income for the area. These limits can be found at http://www.rd.usda.gov/files/RD-GRHLimitMap.pdf. Families must be without adequate housing but be able to afford the mortgage payments, including property taxes and homeowner insurance. In addition, applicants must have reasonable credit histories. Loans can be made in amounts up to 100% of the value of the home for up to 30 years and are subject to the same loan limits as described in the section above on the RHS direct loan program.

REVIEW OF THE LOAN ESTIMATE (FORMERLY KNOWN AS GOOD FAITH ESTIMATE)

Since property laws involving ownership and conveyance of land are essentially determined by each state, differences are reflected in the methods used to close, or settle, real estate transactions. Customs and practices have developed in every region of the country that best suit its unique business and legal requirements. The person or company selected to bring together the instruments of conveyance, mortgages, promissory notes, and, of course, the monetary consideration to be exchanged between the buyer and seller of real estate is most generally known as the **settlement agent**. The agent can be a lender, a real estate broker, a title company, an attorney, or a company specializing in these procedures, called an *escrow company*. In most parts of the country, the settlement agent arranges for the principals involved in the transaction to meet at a location where all the documents needed to transfer title and to secure and fund a loan can be reviewed and executed. At the conclusion of this process, if all documents are in order, the instruments and the money are then distributed to the various parties entitled to receive them.

Another procedure, called **escrow closing**, is commonly used in some states. In this procedure, however, the parties involved do not meet around a table to sign instruments or exchange cash or documents. Rather, at the time of entering a contract of sale, the parties sign an escrow agreement. The agreement requires the deposit of certain documents and funds with the escrow agent within an agreed-upon time. The agent is responsible for meeting the requirements of the escrow agreement, which usually include the adjustment of taxes, insurance, and rentals, if any, between the buyer and seller. The agreement also includes the payoff of any existing loan, if required, arrangements for hazard insurance coverage, the computing of interest, and any other requirements for a new loan. If all papers and monies are deposited within the agreed-upon time limit, the escrow is considered closed. The appropriate documents are then recorded and delivered to the proper parties along with the money that each is entitled to receive.

It was this area of diverse procedures that Congress focused on and began to regulate in 1974. The purpose of the proposed legislation, by Congress's own findings, was to protect consumers from "unnecessarily high settlement charges caused by certain abusive practices that have developed in some areas of the country." The result of these efforts was the **Real Estate Settlement Procedures Act (RESPA)**. A subsequent amendment in 1976 resolved some of the problems that had developed from the initial Act. Implementation was assigned to HUD, which makes periodic changes in the rules to accommodate new requirements. RESPA does not change any local practices and sets no prices for settlement services. It is primarily directed toward providing better information on the settlement process so that a home buyer can make informed decisions.

Preliminary Information

Two pieces of information are closely associated with the settlement of a real estate transaction: an existing loan status report and a preliminary title report. We will discuss them separately because of their special usefulness in any property disposition. Many good real estate brokers arrange for both pieces of information at the time a property is listed for sale. In this way, any problems with either an existing loan or legal title to the property are discovered early on, allowing more time for resolution before the seller is faced with an impending closing date. It is very important that the seller or agent have accurate information on these two subjects because they are of critical interest to any prospective buyer.

Loan Status Report

Several different names are used within the industry to describe the information contained in an existing mortgage **loan status report**. Some call it a *mortgagor's information letter*, some a *mortgagee's report*, and others the *prequalification form*. Adding to the confusion, in some areas of the country a *mortgagee's information letter* means a preliminary title report on the land. For our purposes, a loan status report is a report on the current status of an existing loan prepared by the mortgagee for the mortgagor. It is a statement, usually in letter form, citing the remaining balance due on the loan, the monthly payments required, the reserve held in the escrow account, and the requirements and cost of a loan payoff.

A request for this information must come from the mortgagor, although brokers often use form letters for the request that require only the mortgagor's signature. While this information is very helpful in providing accurate financial information, it is not normally used by the settlement agent in closing a real estate transaction. The agent must call for a current report immediately prior to closing so that it reflects the loan status as of the date of settlement.

Preliminary Title Report

When an earnest money contract has been signed, it is a good idea to "open title" with whatever title insurance company has been selected to handle the closing. Under RESPA rules, the seller may not require that title insurance be purchased from a particular title company as a condition of the sale. However, the mortgage lender has a right to accept or reject a proposed title company, as the insurance coverage must be adequate for the lender. To facilitate selection, lending institutions are required to submit a statement to the borrower listing acceptable title companies and attorneys, along with the charges the borrower might expect. Also, any business relationship between the lender and a settlement service provider must be disclosed. In practice, the title company selected is normally located in the same county as the property being sold.

A **preliminary title report** is normally furnished by the title company to both the real estate agent and the mortgage company. The information contained is a confirmation of the correct legal description, and it also includes the names of the owners of the property as filed in the county records, any restrictions or liens on the property, any judgments against the owners of record, and a listing of any requirements the title company may have to perfect title before issuance of a title insurance policy. The report is for information only; it is not to be confused with a *title binder*, which legally obligates the title company for specific insurance. Title companies normally make no charge for the preliminary report, as it is part of their service in anticipation of writing the title insurance policy at closing.

RESPA Requirements

As amended in 1976, RESPA applies to residential mortgage loans only. Commercial loans are not included in the provisions of the Act. Residential mortgage loans are defined as those used to finance the purchase of one- to four-family housing, a condominium, a cooperative apartment unit, a lot with a mobile home, or a lot on which a house is to be built or a mobile home located. RESPA requirements can be divided into two general categories: (1) information requirements, and (2) prohibited practices.

Information Requirements

Lenders are required to furnish certain specific information to each loan applicant and additional information to the borrower prior to closing a loan, as follows.

Special Information Booklet

At the time of a loan application, or not more than three business days later, the lender must give the applicant a copy of the 1997 revised HUD-prepared booklet titled **"Your home loan toolkit: A step-by-step guide."** The booklet is prepared by the Consumer Financial Protection

Bureau in conjunction with the Office of Consumer Affairs and Regulatory Functions of the U.S. Department of Housing and Urban Development.

Part 1 of this booklet describes the settlement process and the nature of the charges that are incurred. It suggests questions for the home buyer to ask that might help clarify charges and procedures. It also lists unfair and illegal practices and gives information on the rights and remedies available to home buyers should they encounter a wrongful practice.

Part 2 is an item-by-item explanation of settlement services and costs. Sample forms and worksheets are included to help guide home buyers in making cost comparisons.

Loan Estimate (Formerly Known as Good Faith Estimate)

Within three business days of accepting a loan application, a lender is required to submit a **Loan Estimate** (formerly known as the **Good Faith Estimate**) of settlement costs to the loan applicant. Settlement charges are estimated for each item anticipated, except for prepaid hazard insurance and cash reserves deposited with the lender. (Reserves are subject to RESPA restrictions, which are detailed later.) The estimate may be stated as a dollar amount, and the information must be furnished in a clear and concise manner using the Loan Estimate promulgated form. The Loan Estimate form uses the terminology, but no longer the account numbers, from Section L of the mandatory Settlement Statement.

Servicing Disclosure Statement

Servicing Disclosure Statement is required under the same 3-day disclosure rule where the lender must disclose whether or not the servicing of the loan may be assigned, sold, or transferred to any other person at any time while the loan is outstanding. The disclosure is delivered to the applicant usually by the processor, loan originator of a insured financial institution, or mortgage broker.

The lender or broker is required to deliver the disclosure that is required under the Consumer Finance Protection Board (CFPB) Regulation X 12 CFR 1024. Regulation X, as described as the Federal Reserve Regulation that covers the initial implementation of RESPA, has in its appendix MS-1 a sample template that specifies the content requirements of the template with some leeway as to additional information that clears up or improves the model language and best explains the specific situation. A sample of a Servicing Disclosure Statement is in the appendix.

> ## Where Are We Now?
>
> **RESPA, the Real Estate Settlement Procedures Act**
>
> As of July 21, 2011, the Real Estate Settlement Procedures Act (RESPA) is administered and enforced by the Consumer Financial Protection Bureau (CFPB).
>
> Consumers with questions or complaints related to their mortgage or mortgage servicer can contact the CFPB's Consumer Response team at 855-411-2372 (855-729-2372 TTY/ TDD) or can visit their website at: http://www.consumerfinance.gov/
>
> Settlement service providers with questions about RESPA can email the CFPB at CFPB_RESPAInquiries@cfpb.gov.
>
> The Real Estate Settlement Procedures Act ensures that consumers throughout the nation are provided with more helpful information about the cost of the mortgage settlement and protected from unnecessarily high settlement charges caused by certain abusive practices.
>
> The most recent RESPA Rule makes obtaining mortgage financing clearer and, ultimately, cheaper for consumers.[3]

RESPA Roundup

In following up on the guidance given to the new CFPB, and after several years of the use of the GFE introduced in 2010, a new combined GFE and Truth-in-Lending Disclosure form, now known as the TILA-RESPA Integrated Disclosure, or the **Loan Estimate** was introduced in October 3, 2015 (see figure 3-1).

Designated Service Providers

If a lender designates settlement service providers—who perform such tasks as legal services, title examination, title insurance, or the conduct of the settlement—the normal charges for these specific providers must be incorporated into the Loan Estimate. Furthermore, when such a designation occurs, the lender must provide, as part of the Loan Estimate, the name, address, and telephone number of each designated provider. Any business relationship between the lender and an affiliated service provider

---

[3]"Real Estate Settlements Procedures Act," Department of Housing and Urban Development, https://www.hud.gov/hudprograms/respa

Additional Information About This Loan

LENDER	ABC Mortgage Company	**MORTGAGE BROKER**	
NMLS/__ LICENSE ID		**NMLS/__ LICENSE ID**	
LOAN OFFICER	Joe Smith	**LOAN OFFICER**	
NMLS/__ LICENSE ID	12345	**NMLS/__ LICENSE ID**	
EMAIL	Joesmith@ABCMortgageCo.com	**EMAIL**	
PHONE	123-456-7890	**PHONE**	

Comparisons
Use these measures to compare this loan with other loans.

In 5 Years	$56,582	Total you will have paid in principal, interest, mortgage insurance, and loan costs.
	$15,773	Principal you will have paid off.
Annual Percentage Rate (APR)	4.274%	Your costs over the loan term expressed as a rate. This is not your interest rate.
Total Interest Percentage (TIP)	69.45%	The total amount of interest that you will pay over the loan term as a percentage of your loan amount.

Other Considerations

Appraisal	We may order an appraisal to determine the property's value and charge you for this appraisal. We will promptly give you a copy of any appraisal, even if your loan does not close. You can pay for an additional appraisal for your own use at your own cost.
Assumption	If you sell or transfer this property to another person, we ☐ will allow, under certain conditions, this person to assume this loan on the original terms. ☒ will not allow assumption of this loan on the original terms.
Homeowner's Insurance	This loan requires homeowner's insurance on the property, which you may obtain from a company of your choice that we find acceptable.
Late Payment	If your payment is more than *15* days late, we will charge a late fee of *5% of the monthly principal and interest payment.*
Refinance	Refinancing this loan will depend on your future financial situation, the property value, and market conditions. You may not be able to refinance this loan.
Servicing	We intend ☐ to service your loan. If so, you will make your payments to us. ☒ to transfer servicing of your loan.

Confirm Receipt

By signing, you are only confirming that you have received this form. You do not have to accept this loan because you have signed or received this form.

Joe Borrower 10/3/16
Applicant Signature   Date   Co-Applicant Signature   Date

LOAN ESTIMATE

FIGURE 3-1 TILA-RESPA Integrated Disclosure known as the Loan Estimate Form

Source: www.consumerfinance.gov/mortgage-estimate

Closing Cost Details

Loan Costs

A. Origination Charges		$1,802
.25 % of Loan Amount (Points)		$405
Application Fee		$300
Underwriting Fee		$1,097

B. Services You Cannot Shop For		$672
Appraisal Fee		$405
Credit Report Fee		$30
Flood Determination Fee		$20
Flood Monitoring Fee		$32
Tax Monitoring Fee		$75
Tax Status Research Fee		$110

C. Services You Can Shop For		$3,198
Pest Inspection Fee		$135
Survey Fee		$65
Title – Insurance Binder		$700
Title – Lender's Title Policy		$535
Title – Settlement Agent Fee		$502
Title – Title Search		$1,261

D. TOTAL LOAN COSTS (A + B + C)	$5,672

Other Costs

E. Taxes and Other Government Fees		$85
Recording Fees and Other Taxes		$85
Transfer Taxes		

F. Prepaids		$867
Homeowner's Insurance Premium (6 months)		$605
Mortgage Insurance Premium (months)		
Prepaid Interest ($17.44 per day for 15 days @ 3.875%)		$262
Property Taxes (months)		

G. Initial Escrow Payment at Closing		$413
Homeowner's Insurance	$100.83 per month for 2 mo.	$202
Mortgage Insurance	per month for mo.	
Property Taxes	$105.30 per month for 2 mo.	$211

H. Other		$1,017
Title – Owner's Title Policy (optional)		$1,017

I. TOTAL OTHER COSTS (E + F + G + H)	$2,382

J. TOTAL CLOSING COSTS	$8,054
D + I	$8,054
Lender Credits	

Calculating Cash to Close

Total Closing Costs (J)	$8,054
Closing Costs Financed (Paid from your Loan Amount)	$0
Down Payment/Funds from Borrower	$18,000
Deposit	– $10,000
Funds for Borrower	$0
Seller Credits	$0
Adjustments and Other Credits	$0
Estimated Cash to Close	**$16,054**

FIGURE 3-1 (*Continued*)

Additional Information About This Loan

LENDER	ABC Mortgage Company	**MORTGAGE BROKER**	
NMLS/__ LICENSE ID		**NMLS/__ LICENSE ID**	
LOAN OFFICER	Joe Smith	**LOAN OFFICER**	
NMLS/__ LICENSE ID	12345	**NMLS/__ LICENSE ID**	
EMAIL	Joesmith@ABCMortgageCo.com	**EMAIL**	
PHONE	123-456-7890	**PHONE**	

Comparisons
Use these measures to compare this loan with other loans.

In 5 Years	$56,582	Total you will have paid in principal, interest, mortgage insurance, and loan costs.
	$15,773	Principal you will have paid off.
Annual Percentage Rate (APR)	4.274%	Your costs over the loan term expressed as a rate. This is not your interest rate.
Total Interest Percentage (TIP)	69.45%	The total amount of interest that you will pay over the loan term as a percentage of your loan amount.

Other Considerations

Appraisal	We may order an appraisal to determine the property's value and charge you for this appraisal. We will promptly give you a copy of any appraisal, even if your loan does not close. You can pay for an additional appraisal for your own use at your own cost.
Assumption	If you sell or transfer this property to another person, we ☐ will allow, under certain conditions, this person to assume this loan on the original terms. ☒ will not allow assumption of this loan on the original terms.
Homeowner's Insurance	This loan requires homeowner's insurance on the property, which you may obtain from a company of your choice that we find acceptable.
Late Payment	If your payment is more than *15* days late, we will charge a late fee of *5% of the monthly principal and interest payment.*
Refinance	Refinancing this loan will depend on your future financial situation, the property value, and market conditions. You may not be able to refinance this loan.
Servicing	We intend ☐ to service your loan. If so, you will make your payments to us. ☒ to transfer servicing of your loan.

Confirm Receipt

By signing, you are only confirming that you have received this form. You do not have to accept this loan because you have signed or received this form.

Joe Borrower   10/3/16

Applicant Signature   Date   Co-Applicant Signature   Date

LOAN ESTIMATE

FIGURE 3-1 (*Continued*)

must be fully disclosed, including an ownership interest of 1% or more. A rule issued by HUD in December 1992 prohibits any fee paid between affiliated companies for a referral, and there can be no condition requiring use of an affiliated company in consummation of the transaction.

REVIEW OF CLOSING STATEMENT OR SETTLEMENT STATEMENT (A.K.A. HUD-1)

Standardizing Loan Documentation

Documentation for residential loans has become more uniform throughout the country. Both regulators and the industry have worked to promote standard procedures. Uniform methods make it easier for consumers to better understand the process and enable more accurate comparisons between lenders. Standardization has become a necessity for loan pools in which individual loans are assigned as collateral for securities and the cash flow from each must be accounted for. However, commercial loans are still mostly one-of-a-kind types of transactions and are not subject to the regulations imposed on residential loans.

Three standardized instruments are now required for residential loan transactions. All three are mentioned here and will be examined in later chapters. The relevant forms are reproduced in the appendix of this text.

Uniform Residential Loan Application

The Equal Credit Opportunity Act imposed certain nondiscriminatory requirements that must be incorporated in all residential loan applications. The form used to implement the requirements is a modified version of Fannie Mae's Form 1003 and Freddie Mac's Form 65. It has undergone several revisions, with the most recent one made mandatory for use as of July 2010. On September 26, 2017, Fannie Mae announced the implementation timeline for the redesigned Uniform Residential Loan Application (URLA) and related automated underwriting system specifications. Fannie Mae is allowing lenders to begin using the redesigned URLA starting July 1, 2019, and requiring its use beginning in February 2020 for all new loan applications[4]. An example of the current form appears in the

---

[4] "Implementation Timeline Announced for the Redesigned Uniform Residential Loan Application (URLA)," The Federal Home Loan Banks' Mortgage Partnership Finance Program, January 4, 2018, https://www.fhlbmpf.com/about-us/news/details/2018/01/04/implementation-timeline-announced-for-the-redesigned-uniform-residential-loan-application-(urla)

appendix. There is a URL for the new form in the Additional Online Resources section of this chapter.

Uniform Residential Appraisal Report (URAR)

FIRREA established standards for appraisals that apply to federally regulated lenders. The requirements resulted in a revision of the Uniform Residential Appraisal Report (URAR) form made mandatory for use with certain loans after March 1, 2005, for basis URAR (Form 1004) and Market Conditions Addendum (Form 1004MC). Effective April 1, 2009, this form replaced the old Statement of Limiting Conditions and Appraiser's Certification (Form 1004B). The form is required for all loans involving Fannie Mae, Freddie Mac, VA, HUD/FHA, and RHS. An example appears in the appendix. While all residential loans are not included in this mandate, it is a document used in more than 90% of all residential mortgage loans and represents another step toward standardization.

HUD-1 Settlement Statement

RESPA sets standards for closing all residential loans, and one of its requirements is the use of a HUD-1 Settlement Statement that is still used only in residential closings for FHA Reverse Mortgage Loans. The purpose is proper disclosure of information to a consumer/borrower. It is an itemized listing of the consideration tendered in closing a transaction and how the money is distributed to the various parties to the transaction.

The HUD-1 settlement statement form was replaced by the Closing Disclosure form seen in figure 3-2 for a fixed-rate mortgage. This new Closing Disclosure form went into effect on October 3, 2015.

Disclosure of Settlement Costs

As a part of the RESPA requirements, the newly required disclosure designed by the Consumer Financial Protection Bureau called the Closing Disclosure (figure 3-2), a uniform settlement statement, is mandatory for residential loan closings. Account numbers and terminology are standardized on the form, and it is expected that settlement charges, however designated in various parts of the country, fit into this form. A copy of the completed form must be delivered by the settlement agent to both the buyer and the seller at or before the closing. Since some of the information needed to complete the form may not be available until the

Closing Disclosure

This form is a statement of final loan terms and closing costs. Compare this document with your Loan Estimate.

Closing Information
- **Date Issued** October 3rd, 2016
- **Closing Date** October 15th, 2016
- **Disbursement Date** October 19th, 2016
- **Settlement Agent** The Great Title Company, USA
- **File #** 1234567
- **Property** 777 Gadzooks Drive, Anytown, USA 00000
  Lot 7 Block 11, Small Mountain Subdivision
- **Sale Price** $180,000

Transaction Information
- **Borrower** Joe Borrower
  123 Front Street
  Anytown, USA 000000
- **Seller** Hellen Seller
  321 Front Street
  Anytown, USA 000000
- **Lender** ABC Mortgage Co
  456 Front Street
  Anytown, USA 000000

Loan Information
- **Loan Term** 30 years
- **Purpose** Purchase
- **Product** Fixed Rate
- **Loan Type** ☒ Conventional ☐ FHA ☐ VA ☐ _____
- **Loan ID #** 123456789
- **MIC #** 000654321

Loan Terms

		Can this amount increase after closing?
Loan Amount	$162,000	NO
Interest Rate	3.875%	NO
Monthly Principal & Interest See Projected Payments below for your Estimated Total Monthly Payment	$761.78	NO

		Does the loan have these features?
Prepayment Penalty		YES • As high as **$3,240** if you pay off the loan during the first 2 years
Balloon Payment		NO

Projected Payments

Payment Calculation	Years 1-7	Years 8-30
Principal & Interest	$761.78	$761.78
Mortgage Insurance	+ 82.35	+ —
Estimated Escrow *Amount can increase over time*	+ 206.13	+ 206.13
Estimated Total Monthly Payment	**$1,050.26**	**$967.91**

Estimated Taxes, Insurance & Assessments *Amount can increase over time* *See page 4 for details*	$356.13 a month	This estimate includes ☒ Property Taxes ☒ Homeowner's Insurance ☒ Other: Homeowner's Association Dues	In escrow? YES YES NO

See Escrow Account on page 4 for details. You must pay for other property costs separately.

Costs at Closing

Closing Costs	$9,712.10	Includes $4,694.05 in Loan Costs + $5,018.05 in Other Costs – $0 in Lender Credits. See page 2 for details.
Cash to Close	$14,147.26	Includes Closing Costs. See Calculating Cash to Close on page 3 for details.

CLOSING DISCLOSURE   PAGE 1 OF 5 • LOAN ID # 123456789

FIGURE 3-2 Closing Disclosure Settlement Statement for residential loans

Source: www.consumerfinance.gov

Closing Cost Details

Loan Costs		Borrower-Paid		Seller-Paid		Paid by Others
		At Closing	Before Closing	At Closing	Before Closing	
A. Origination Charges		**$1,802.00**				
01 0.25 % of Loan Amount (Points)		$405.00				
02 Application Fee		$300.00				
03 Underwriting Fee		$1,097.00				
04						
05						
06						
07						
08						
B. Services Borrower Did Not Shop For		**$236.55**				
01 Appraisal Fee	to John Smith Appraisers Inc.					$405.00
02 Credit Report Fee	to Information Inc.		$29.80			
03 Flood Determination Fee	to Info Co.	$20.00				
04 Flood Monitoring Fee	to Info Co.	$31.75				
05 Tax Monitoring Fee	to Info Co.	$75.00				
06 Tax Status Research Fee	to Info Co.	$80.00				
07						
08						
09						
10						
C. Services Borrower Did Shop For		**$2,655.50**				
01 Pest Inspection Fee	to Pests Co.	$120.50				
02 Survey Fee	to Surveys Co.	$85.00				
03 Title – Insurance Binder	to The Great Title Company, USA	$650.00				
04 Title – Lender's Title Insurance	to The Great Title Company, USA	$500.00				
05 Title – Settlement Agent Fee	to The Great Title Company, USA	$500.00				
06 Title – Title Search	to The Great Title Company, USA	$800.00				
07						
08						
D. TOTAL LOAN COSTS (Borrower-Paid)		**$4,694.05**				
Loan Costs Subtotals (A + B + C)		$4,664.25	$29.80			

Other Costs						
E. Taxes and Other Government Fees		**$85.00**				
01 Recording Fees	Deed: $40.00 Mortgage: $45.00	$85.00				
02 Transfer Tax	to Any State			$950.00		
F. Prepaids		**$2,120.80**				
01 Homeowner's Insurance Premium (12 mo.) to Insurance Co.		$1,209.96				
02 Mortgage Insurance Premium (mo.)						
03 Prepaid Interest ($17.44 per day from 10/15/16 to 11/1/16)		$279.04				
04 Property Taxes (6 mo.) to Any County USA		$631.80				
05						
G. Initial Escrow Payment at Closing		**$412.25**				
01 Homeowner's Insurance $100.83 per month for 2 mo.		$201.66				
02 Mortgage Insurance per month for mo.						
03 Property Taxes $105.30 per month for 2 mo.		$210.60				
04						
05						
06						
07						
08 Aggregate Adjustment		− 0.01				
H. Other		**$2,400.00**				
01 HOA Capital Contribution	to HOA Acre Inc.	$500.00				
02 HOA Processing Fee	to HOA Acre Inc.	$150.00				
03 Home Inspection Fee	to Engineers Inc.	$750.00			$750.00	
04 Home Warranty Fee	to XYZ Warranty Inc.			$450.00		
05 Real Estate Commission	to Alpha Real Estate Broker			$5,700.00		
06 Real Estate Commission	to Omega Real Estate Broker			$5,700.00		
07 Title – Owner's Title Insurance (optional) The Great Title Company, USA		$1,000.00				
08						
I. TOTAL OTHER COSTS (Borrower-Paid)		**$5,018.05**				
Other Costs Subtotals (E + F + G + H)		$5,018.05				

J. TOTAL CLOSING COSTS (Borrower-Paid)		**$9,712.10**				
Closing Costs Subtotals (D + I)		$9,682.30	$29.80	$12,800.00	$750.00	$405.00
Lender Credits						

FIGURE 3-2 (Continued)

Review of Closing Statement or Settlement Statement (A.K.A. HUD-1)

Calculating Cash to Close

Use this table to see what has changed from your Loan Estimate.

	Loan Estimate	Final	Did this change?	
Total Closing Costs (J)	$8,054.00	$9,712.10	YES	• See Total Loan Costs (D) and Total Other Costs (I)
Closing Costs Paid Before Closing	$0	− $29.80	YES	• You paid these Closing Costs before closing
Closing Costs Financed (Paid from your Loan Amount)	$0	$0	NO	
Down Payment/Funds from Borrower	$18,000.00	$18,000.00	NO	
Deposit	− $10,000.00	− $10,000.00	NO	
Funds for Borrower	$0	$0	NO	
Seller Credits	$0	− $2,500.00	YES	• See Seller Credits in Section L
Adjustments and Other Credits	$0	− $1,035.04	YES	• See details in Sections K and L
Cash to Close	**$16,054.00**	**$14,147.26**		

Summaries of Transactions

Use this table to see a summary of your transaction.

BORROWER'S TRANSACTION		SELLER'S TRANSACTION	
K. Due from Borrower at Closing	**$189,762.30**	**M. Due to Seller at Closing**	**$180,080.00**
01 Sale Price of Property	$180,000.00	01 Sale Price of Property	$180,000.00
02 Sale Price of Any Personal Property Included in Sale		02 Sale Price of Any Personal Property Included in Sale	
03 Closing Costs Paid at Closing (J)	$9,682.30	03	
04		04	
Adjustments		05	
05		06	
06		07	
07		08	
Adjustments for Items Paid by Seller in Advance		**Adjustments for Items Paid by Seller in Advance**	
08 City/Town Taxes to		09 City/Town Taxes to	
09 County Taxes to		10 County Taxes to	
10 Assessments to		11 Assessments to	
11 HOA Dues 10/15/16 to 10/31/16	$80.00	12 HOA Dues 10/15/16 to 10/31/16	$80.00
12		13	
13		14	
14		15	
15		16	
L. Paid Already by or on Behalf of Borrower at Closing	**$175,615.04**	**N. Due from Seller at Closing**	**$115,665.04**
01 Deposit	$10,000.00	01 Excess Deposit	
02 Loan Amount	$162,000.00	02 Closing Costs Paid at Closing (J)	$12,800.00
03 Existing Loan(s) Assumed or Taken Subject to		03 Existing Loan(s) Assumed or Taken Subject to	
04		04 Payoff of First Mortgage Loan	$100,000.00
05 Seller Credit	$2,500.00	05 Payoff of Second Mortgage Loan	
Other Credits		06	
06 Rebate from The Great Title Company, USA	$750.00	07	
07		08 Seller Credit	$2,500.00
Adjustments		09	
08		10	
09		11	
10		12	
11		13	
Adjustments for Items Unpaid by Seller		**Adjustments for Items Unpaid by Seller**	
12 City/Town Taxes 1/5/16 to 10/15/16	$365.04	14 City/Town Taxes 1/5/16 to 10/15/16	$365.04
13 County Taxes to		15 County Taxes to	
14 Assessments to		16 Assessments to	
15		17	
16		18	
17		19	
CALCULATION		**CALCULATION**	
Total Due from Borrower at Closing (K)	$189,762.30	Total Due to Seller at Closing (M)	$180,080.00
Total Paid Already by or on Behalf of Borrower at Closing (L)	− $175,615.04	Total Due from Seller at Closing (N)	− $115,665.04
Cash to Close ☒ From ☐ To Borrower	**$14,147.26**	**Cash** ☐ From ☒ To Seller	**$64,414.96**

FIGURE 3-2 (Continued)

Additional Information About This Loan

Loan Disclosures

Assumption
If you sell or transfer this property to another person, your lender
☐ will allow, under certain conditions, this person to assume this loan on the original terms.
☒ will not allow assumption of this loan on the original terms.

Demand Feature
Your loan
☐ has a demand feature, which permits your lender to require early repayment of the loan. You should review your note for details.
☒ does not have a demand feature.

Late Payment
If your payment is more than 15 days late, your lender will charge a late fee of 5% of the monthly principal and interest payment.

Negative Amortization (Increase in Loan Amount)
Under your loan terms, you
☐ are scheduled to make monthly payments that do not pay all of the interest due that month. As a result, your loan amount will increase (negatively amortize), and your loan amount will likely become larger than your original loan amount. Increases in your loan amount lower the equity you have in this property.
☐ may have monthly payments that do not pay all of the interest due that month. If you do, your loan amount will increase (negatively amortize), and, as a result, your loan amount may become larger than your original loan amount. Increases in your loan amount lower the equity you have in this property.
☒ do not have a negative amortization feature.

Partial Payments
Your lender
☒ may accept payments that are less than the full amount due (partial payments) and apply them to your loan.
☐ may hold them in a separate account until you pay the rest of the payment, and then apply the full payment to your loan.
☐ does not accept any partial payments.
If this loan is sold, your new lender may have a different policy.

Security Interest
You are granting a security interest in

777 Gadzooks Drive, Anytown, USA 00000
Lot 7 Block 11, Small Mountain Subdivision

You may lose this property if you do not make your payments or satisfy other obligations for this loan.

Escrow Account
For now, your loan
☒ will have an escrow account (also called an "impound" or "trust" account) to pay the property costs listed below. Without an escrow account, you would pay them directly, possibly in one or two large payments a year. Your lender may be liable for penalties and interest for failing to make a payment.

Escrow		
Escrowed Property Costs over Year 1	$2,473.56	Estimated total amount over year 1 for your escrowed property costs: *Homeowner's Insurance Property Taxes*
Non-Escrowed Property Costs over Year 1	$1,800.00	Estimated total amount over year 1 for your non-escrowed property costs: *Homeowner's Association Dues* You may have other property costs.
Initial Escrow Payment	$412.25	A cushion for the escrow account you pay at closing. See Section G on page 2.
Monthly Escrow Payment	$206.13	The amount included in your total monthly payment.

☐ will not have an escrow account because ☐ you declined it ☐ your lender does not offer one. You must directly pay your property costs, such as taxes and homeowner's insurance. Contact your lender to ask if your loan can have an escrow account.

No Escrow		
Estimated Property Costs over Year 1		Estimated total amount over year 1. You must pay these costs directly, possibly in one or two large payments a year.
Escrow Waiver Fee		

In the future,
Your property costs may change and, as a result, your escrow payment may change. You may be able to cancel your escrow account, but if you do, you must pay your property costs directly. If you fail to pay your property taxes, your state or local government may (1) impose fines and penalties or (2) place a tax lien on this property. If you fail to pay any of your property costs, your lender may (1) add the amounts to your loan balance, (2) add an escrow account to your loan, or (3) require you to pay for property insurance that the lender buys on your behalf, which likely would cost more and provide fewer benefits than what you could buy on your own.

FIGURE 3-2 (*Continued*)

Loan Calculations

Total of Payments. Total you will have paid after you make all payments of principal, interest, mortgage insurance, and loan costs, as scheduled.	$285,803.36
Finance Charge. The dollar amount the loan will cost you.	$118,830.27
Amount Financed. The loan amount available after paying your upfront finance charge.	$162,000.00
Annual Percentage Rate (APR). Your costs over the loan term expressed as a rate. This is not your interest rate.	4.174%
Total Interest Percentage (TIP). The total amount of interest that you will pay over the loan term as a percentage of your loan amount.	69.46%

Questions? If you have questions about the loan terms or costs on this form, use the contact information below. To get more information or make a complaint, contact the Consumer Financial Protection Bureau at www.consumerfinance.gov/mortgage-closing

Other Disclosures

Appraisal
If the property was appraised for your loan, your lender is required to give you a copy at no additional cost at least 3 days before closing. If you have not yet received it, please contact your lender at the information listed below.

Contract Details
See your note and security instrument for information about
- what happens if you fail to make your payments,
- what is a default on the loan,
- situations in which your lender can require early repayment of the loan, and
- the rules for making payments before they are due.

Liability after Foreclosure
If your lender forecloses on this property and the foreclosure does not cover the amount of unpaid balance on this loan,
- [X] state law may protect you from liability for the unpaid balance. If you refinance or take on any additional debt on this property, you may lose this protection and have to pay any debt remaining even after foreclosure. You may want to consult a lawyer for more information.
- [ ] state law does not protect you from liability for the unpaid balance.

Refinance
Refinancing this loan will depend on your future financial situation, the property value, and market conditions. You may not be able to refinance this loan.

Tax Deductions
If you borrow more than this property is worth, the interest on the loan amount above this property's fair market value is not deductible from your federal income taxes. You should consult a tax advisor for more information.

Contact Information

	Lender	Mortgage Broker	Real Estate Broker (B)	Real Estate Broker (S)	Settlement Agent
Name	ABC Mortgage Co		Omega Real Estate Broker Inc.	Alpha Real Estate Broker Co.	The Great Title Company, USA
Address	456 Front Street Anytown, USA 000000		789 Local Lane Sometown, ST 12345	987 Suburb Ct. Someplace, ST 12340	123 Commerce Pl. Somecity, ST 12344
NMLS ID					
ST License ID			Z765416	Z61456	Z61616
Contact	Joe Smith		Samuel Green	Joseph Cain	Sarah Arnold
Contact NMLS ID	12345				
Contact ST License ID			P16415	P51461	PT1234
Email	Joesmith@ABCMortgageCo.com		sam@omegare.biz	joe@alphare.biz	Sarah@Greattitleco.com
Phone	123-456-7890		123-555-1717	321-555-7171	987-555-4321

Confirm Receipt

By signing, you are only confirming that you have received this form. You do not have to accept this loan because you have signed or received this form.

Joe Bonower   10/3/16
Applicant Signature   Date   Co-Applicant Signature   Date

CLOSING DISCLOSURE

FIGURE 3-2 (*Continued*)

time of actual closing, the borrower may waive the right of delivery at closing. However, in such a case, the completed settlement statement must be mailed at the earliest practical date.

Borrower's Right to Disclosure of Costs Prior to Closing

A borrower has the right under RESPA to request an inspection of the Closing Disclosure three business days prior to closing. The form is completed by the person who will conduct the settlement procedures. If a buyer wishes to make such a request, it would be wise to do so several days prior to the closing date. Preparation of the information takes time, and a late request may simply force a delay in the closing date. The Act does recognize that all costs may not be available three days prior to closing, but there is an obligation to show the borrower what is available, if requested. The variance rule governing the GFE in use in early 2011 would also be in effect. With the passage of the Mortgage Disclosure Improvement Act of 2008 (MDIA), the 3/7/3 Rule mandates a 7-business-day waiting period once the initial disclosure is provided before closing a home loan. Therefore, before a borrower can close on a transaction, he or she must have received the initial Loan Estimate statement disclosing the final annual percentage rate (APR) seven days prior to the scheduled closing.

Prohibited Practices

The vast majority of settlement procedures have always been conducted in an ethical manner by qualified professionals. However, abuses do occur occasionally, and it is one of the purposes of RESPA to expose unfair practices and make them illegal. Two such practices are described next.

Kickbacks

The law specifically prohibits any arrangement in which a fee is charged, or accepted, when no services have actually been performed—an arrangement known as a **kickback**. The prohibition does not prevent agents for the lender, attorneys, or others from actually performing a service in connection with the mortgage loan or settlement procedure. Nor does it prohibit cooperative brokerage arrangements such as are normally found in multiple listing services or referral arrangements between real estate agents and brokers. The target for the prohibition is the arrangement wherein one party returns a part of the fee to obtain business from the referring party. The abuse involved here, of course, is that such an arrangement can result in a higher settlement fee for the consumer/borrower with no increase in the services rendered.

Title Companies

A seller is not permitted to require the use of a specified title insurance company as a condition of sale. The buyer has the right to compare the services and charges of competing title companies. In many states, the rates for title insurance fall under the regulatory authority of the state and are therefore uniform. In such cases, competition would be in the quality of services offered. Also, lenders retain the right to reject title insurance companies that do not meet their minimum requirements of financial strength.

Settlement Practices and Costs

As noted earlier in this chapter, settlement practices vary considerably in different sections of the country. There is no federal requirement to change any basic practices for residential loans except where it is necessary to add some disclosure procedures and to eliminate any prohibited practices. RESPA set limitations on the amount of reserve, or escrow, accounts that may be held by lenders, and there is one mandatory form to be used in the settlement of residential loans.

The mandatory uniform settlement statement is illustrated in figure 3-2 and will be used as the basis for the following discussion of the various services involved with a loan closing. While the emphasis is on residential loan practices, the procedures used in closing commercial loans involve most of the same services.

Settlement Statement

The design of the **Closing Disclosure** Form (formerly known as the HUD-1 settlement statement) places all the costs chargeable to the buyer, or the seller, on the first page, and a detailed accounting of these costs on the second page. The first section, A through I, contains information concerning the loan and the parties involved.

Section J lists the amounts due from, or paid by, the borrower, and Section I details the same for the seller. The bottom line in each column indicates the cash due by the borrower/buyer on the left-hand side, and that due by the seller on the right-hand side. Whatever money must change hands is the result of the two figures. Section L on the second page of the form lists various settlement services that can be involved in a closing, with some blank lines for any separate entries not otherwise clearly identified. The HUD-1 settlement statement is still used, however, for reverse mortgages.

This particular form must be completed for the settlement meeting by the person conducting the settlement procedures. A copy of the completed form is either given to both the buyer and seller at the meeting or mailed as soon as practical after the meeting. If there is no actual meeting of the parties involved for settlement, the agent must still mail the completed forms after the closing has been finalized. This is the same form that a borrower has the right to inspect one business day prior to closing. It is not required that all information be filled in one day prior to closing, but the settlement agent must disclose whatever is available if requested to do so by the borrower.

A settlement costs worksheet is also available and is intended for use by the prospective borrower as a handy guide for making comparisons of the charges quoted by the various service providers.

Sales/Broker's Commission

The sales commission is usually paid by the seller and is listed on the settlement in the total dollar amount, then divided between participating brokers as the sales agreement may provide. The amount is negotiable and may be a flat fee for the sale or a percentage of the sales amount.

Items Payable in Connection with Loan

As identified by RESPA, the costs of the loan are the fees charged by the lenders to process, approve, and make the mortgage loan.

Loan origination fee is the fee charged by the primary lender to assemble information necessary to evaluate a loan application, to determine its acceptability, and to prepare the completed loan package. The charge is negotiable and varies from 1% to 1.5% of the loan amount. (The stated amount should match the Closing Disclosure section titled "Loan Costs Section A – Origination Charges.")

> ### Example
>
> Compute the interest charges for 15 days (June 16 through June 30) on a $45,000 loan at 10% interest, as follows:
>
> $45,000 × .10   = $4,500 (annual interest cost)
> $4,500 ÷ 360   = $12.50 (daily interest cost)
> $12.50 × 15 days   = $187.50 (prepaid interest due)
>
> The prepaid interest amount of $187.50 would be due at closing and the full monthly payment on a 30-year loan amounting to $394.91 would begin on August 1.

A **loan discount** is not truly a fee, in that it is not considered payment for services rendered. Rather, it is another cost of borrowed money similar to interest. The discount is expressed as a percentage of the loan amount, normally measured in *points*; one point is 1% of the loan amount. The purpose of a discount is to adjust the yield on a fixed interest rate certificate to a level of return that is commensurate with the current market rate for money loaned. By charging a discount for a loan, the lender increases the return, or yield. Six to eight points of discount give the lender about the same return on a loan as increasing the interest rate by 1%. The value of the discount depends on the rate of interest: the higher the market rate, the greater the value of a point of discount. As a cost of borrowed money paid at the time of loan settlement, a loan discount becomes one of the items payable for obtaining a loan. (The stated amount should match the Closing Disclosure form section titled "Loan Costs Section A - Origination Charges.")

An **appraisal fee** is charged because an appraisal of the property is necessary to establish the value basis for a mortgage loan. Depending on the size of the loan, regulated lenders may be required to use a state-certified appraiser. Otherwise, a qualified member of the lender's staff or an independent fee appraiser may be used to provide factual data on the value of the property offered as loan collateral. Since an appraisal is of value to both the buyer and seller of property, it may be paid for by either. Often, the cost of an appraisal is included as part of the initial application fee. (The stated amount should match the Closing Disclosure form section titled "Loan Costs Section B – Services You Cannot Shop For.")

A **credit report fee** is charged because applicants for mortgage loans are required to submit **credit reports**, usually from both a local credit bureau and a national repository of credit data. The information is normally obtained by the loan processor from local credit bureaus (a sample credit report can be viewed in the appendices of this text). This report is a necessary verification of information submitted in the loan application plus statistical data on the bill-paying record of the applicant. A credit report is one source of information that a lender uses to determine if the applicant is an acceptable credit risk. Payment for the report is most often made by the borrower. (The stated amount should match the Closing Disclosure form section titled "Loan Costs Section B – Services You Cannot Shop For.")

The lender is permitted to assess a **lender's inspection fee** for an inspection of the property offered as collateral. The inspection can be made by the lender's personnel or by an independent inspector. The purpose is to examine the physical facilities and any mechanical equipment and possibly to report on environmental problems. This inspection is not to be confused with pest inspections, which we will discuss later. It is used primarily on construction loans. (The stated amount should match the Closing Disclosure form section titled "Loan Costs Section B – Services You Cannot Shop For.")

Private mortgage insurance companies charge **mortgage insurance application fees** for the processing of a loan application. This fee sometimes covers both an appraisal fee and an application fee. (The stated amount should match the Closing Disclosure form section titled "Loan Costs Section B – Services You Cannot Shop For.")

An assumption fee is essentially a paper-processing fee charged in transactions in which the buyer takes title to the property and assumes liability for payments on a prior obligation of the seller. (The stated amount should match the Closing Disclosure form section titled "Loan Costs Section B – Services You Cannot Shop For.")

The **document preparation** charge for preparing legal documents may be listed separately or may be included with other service fees, most likely as a part of the attorney's fee. (The stated amount should match the Closing Disclosure form section titled "Loan Costs Section B – Services You Cannot Shop For.")

Instruments that are to be recorded in the public records usually require that all signatures be acknowledged by a notary public or properly witnessed, which incurs a **notary fee**. Settlement agents are often licensed for this purpose and may ask a separate charge for their official services. (The stated amount should match the Closing Disclosure form section titled "Loan Costs Section B – Services You Cannot Shop For.")

Few lenders will permit a loan to be closed without the assurance of a qualified attorney that all instruments have been properly prepared and executed. In any real estate transaction, the buyer and the seller may each be represented by their own attorney and, in such a case, each may pay the attorney outside the closing procedure. In the handling of residential loans, the title company or settlement agent involved may employ an attorney to handle the legal requirements and, if both parties agree, the **attorney's fees** are allocated equally between buyer and seller. (The stated amount should match the Closing Disclosure form section titled "Loan Costs Section B – Services You Cannot Shop For.")

Items Required by Lender to Be Paid in Advance

There are certain items that must be prepaid in advance at the closing of a loan, as follows.

Since mortgage loans extend for long terms, it is a common practice to adjust the monthly payment to a convenient date each month, most often the first of each month. The normal monthly payment on a mortgage loan includes a charge for interest paid at the end of the month—that is, after the borrower has had the use of the money loaned. So, to adjust the monthly payment to a date other than that of loan closing, the **interest** charge is computed for the time period from the date of closing to the beginning of the period covered by the first monthly payment. For example, if the settlement takes place on June 16, a prepayment of charges is needed through June 30. The period covered by the regular monthly payment begins on July 1, and the first regular payment is due on August 1. (The stated amount should match the Closing Disclosure form section titled "Other Costs Section F – Prepaids.")

Almost all lenders now require private mortgage insurance on loans in excess of 80% of the property value. And the FHA has its annual **mortgage insurance premium** payable as a part of each monthly payment. The protection for the lender is against a borrower default in the payment of the loan. It enables a lender to make higher ratio loans (up to 95% for a conventional loan) than would otherwise be possible, and thus allows lower down payments for the borrower. The first premium charge for a conventional loan is always higher than the continuing annual payments, as it includes an issuing fee and is payable in full at the loan closing. This type of mortgage insurance should not be confused with mortgage life, credit life, or disability insurance, all of which are designed to pay off a mortgage in the event of the physical disability or death of the borrower. None of these types of insurance are a standard requirement for a mortgage loan. (The stated amount should match the Closing Disclosure form section titled "Other Costs Section F – Prepaids.")

Hazard Insurance protects both the lender and the borrower against loss to a building by fire, windstorm, or other natural hazard. Such coverage is a requirement for mortgage loans that include any buildings as part of the collateral. In addition, loans in certain areas of the country with development land in designated flood plain zones require flood insurance. It is customary to name the lender as a loss payee in addition to the homeowner.

The normal lender requirement is for insurance coverage in an amount not less than the loan amount. This standard does not necessarily recognize coinsurance clauses found in most states' insurance codes. Coinsurance requirements set a minimum insurance coverage amount (usually 80% of the building value at the time of loss) to assure the property owner full recovery of partial losses. So while the lender may set a minimum requirement to cover the loan amount, on a low-ratio loan the coverage could be insufficient to fully protect the property owner.

Most lenders require a full first year's premium of hazard insurance paid at the time of closing. Often, the paid-up policy is delivered at the closing table as proof of insurance. In addition to the first year's premium, lenders may require a reserve of up to two months' worth of annual premiums deposited with them at closing. (The stated amount should match the Closing Disclosure form section titled "Other Costs Section F – Prepaids.")

Reserves Deposited with Lenders

Almost all residential loans require cash deposited with the lender at the time of loan closing to be used for future payment of recurring annual charges such as taxes, insurance, and maintenance assessments. The identification of these accounts differs, as they may be referred to as **reserves**, escrow accounts, impound accounts, or reserve accruals. The purpose of the initial deposits is to assure the lender enough cash to make the first annual payment that comes due after the closing date. Because real estate practices differ throughout the country, RESPA allows some variations in how deposits are handled. In some parts of the country, taxes are paid a year in advance; in others, they are paid at the end of the tax year. The same is true of maintenance assessments.

Initial Deposit for the Escrow Account

RESPA places a limit on the deposits that may be required to meet the first year's payments on residential loans. The amount cannot exceed a sum sufficient to pay taxes, insurance premiums, or other charges that would have been paid under normal lending practices up to the due date of the first full monthly installment payment. In addition, the lender is permitted to require a cushion of up to one-sixth of the annual charges for the escrowed expenses. Then, each monthly installment payment can include one-twelfth of the annual charges on a continuing basis. RESPA rules restrict the lender to collecting no more than one-twelfth of the annual taxes and other charges each month, unless a larger payment is necessary to make up a deficit in the reserve account. A deficit in the account may be caused, for example, by increases in the taxes and insurance premiums during the loan payment year. (The stated amount should the Closing Disclosure form section titled "Other Costs Section G – Initial Escrow Payment at Closing.")

Most home buyers elect to purchase new insurance policies to fit their own needs. To do this, the normal lender requirement, approved as being in compliance with RESPA restrictions, is for a one-year premium paid in advance, plus a deposit to a reserve account in an amount not exceeding two months' worth of the annual premium. A buyer may purchase **hazard insurance** from whatever company he or she chooses, so long as the company meets the lender's minimum standards for financial responsibility. If the buyer opts to continue an existing insurance policy, an adjustment would be necessary to reimburse the seller for any portion of the premium not used by date of closing plus a reimbursement of the two-month premium cushion. (The stated amount should match the Closing Disclosure form section titled "Other Costs Section G – Initial Escrow Payment at Closing.")

The premium reserve requirement for **mortgage insurance** is negotiable with the lender. It may be required that a part of the total annual premium be placed in a reserve account, but no more than one-sixth of the annual premium may be held as a cushion by the lender. (The stated amount should match the Closing Disclosure form section titled "Other Costs Section G – Initial Escrow Payment at Closing.")

A reserve is required so as to have sufficient cash on hand to make timely payment of **city/county property taxes** when they come due. The reserve is determined by the time between the date of closing a transaction and the date the next payment of taxes becomes due. An example of this calculation follows. (The stated amount should match the Closing Disclosure form section titled "Other Costs Section G – Initial Escrow Payment at Closing.")

> ### Example
>
> Initial Tax Reserve Requirement for a Settlement Date of June 30
>   First monthly payment due August 1
>   Taxes for prior calendar year due December 1
>   Annual taxes: $900 ($75 each month)
>
>   Initial reserve from previous December 1 to July 30
>   8 months × $75   = $600
>   Plus 2 months cushion: 2 months × $75   = $150
>   Escrow deposit required at closing   = $750

In considering this example, keep in mind that taxes due for the months prior to actual closing are the financial responsibility of the seller. This would mean that seven of the eight months' requirement, amounting to $525, would be paid by the seller. One month's worth (from June 30 to July 31) plus the two-month cushion, amounting to $225, is the responsibility of the buyer. So the settlement statement would reflect the proration of the tax liability.

If the house is newly constructed, the tax assessment during the construction period would most likely be a lesser amount than that for the finished house. In areas where taxes are paid at the beginning of each tax year, the deposit requirement to meet the coming year's taxes would fall to the buyer. One of the most common errors made in loan closings is failing to calculate the real estate taxes that must be escrowed to assure that taxes can be paid from the account by the time the next tax remittance is due. Often lenders and closers reduce loan amounts by prorated amounts collected from sellers instead of making sure this is addressed in closing. In high real estate tax states like California, New York, and Texas, borrowers may experience hardship if payments must be adjusted upward to pay for not only the shortage advanced by the lender, but on some occasions sales involving a senior citizen seller with a real estate tax exemption. This makes taxes due for the new owner considerably higher. Some borrowers' payments double to make up for under-withholding for the initial escrow alongside having to pay back lender advances on their behalf, but also for the increased tax due, as the new owner does not qualify for over-age-65 tax reductions.

The reserve that may be required for **annual assessments** covers such charges as a homeowners association fee, a condominium maintenance charge, or a municipal improvement assessment. The same previously described RESPA reserve limitations apply to all forms of reserves. (The stated amount should match the Closing Disclosure form section titled "Other Costs Section G – Initial Escrow Payment at Closing.")

Title Charges

In the uniform settlement statement, the term *title charges* designates a variety of services performed to conclude a real estate transaction properly. These include searching records, preparing documents, and acquiring insurance against title failure. While practices and terminology differ in some areas, the services referenced are basically the same.

Title Services and Lender's Title Insurance

Title services and lender's title insurance are the sum of all title charges less the owner's premium and endorsements and attorney representation for the borrower. This line item includes all administrative and processing charges related to title insurance (for example, search and exam fees). This line item does not include premium charges for any owner's title insurance that will be provided; it does include the charge for lender's title insurance (including the charge for any lender-only endorsements). It also includes settlement charges under the heading of "Title Services." (The stated amount should match the Closing Disclosure form section titled "Loan Costs Section C – Services You Can Shop For.")

Settlement or closing fees are the charges made by the person or company for the service of handling the settlement procedures. Payment of the fee is negotiable between buyer and seller and is often divided equally between them. (The stated amount should match the Closing Disclosure form section entitled "Loan Costs Section C – Services You Can Shop For.")

In a real estate transaction, it is reasonable to expect a seller to offer some solid proof of his or her right to convey the property with good title to the buyer. This proof can be obtained through a search of all the recorded documents affecting the land title (an abstract of title), incurring **abstract or title search, title examination, or title insurance binder fees.** In some cases, an attorney will review the abstract and issue a title opinion. Buyers can accept the opinion if it proves good title and proceed with the transaction, although such an opinion provides no insurance against future adverse claims. More commonly, proof of title is handled through a title insurance company, which continuously searches the records and, if justified, insures the title against adverse claims for a specified period of time.

In some areas of the country, the obligation to prove that good title is being conveyed places the cost burden on the seller. However, in other areas the fact that title insurance protects the buyer against future claims indicates the cost should be borne by the buyer. A *title insurance binder* is a preliminary assurance by a title company that the title is valid and that a title insurance policy will be issued at a later date. (The stated amount should match the Closing Disclosure form section titled "Loan Costs Section C – Services You Can Shop For.")

The **Lender's Title Policy** runs with the mortgage. Its value declines as the mortgage is paid down and it transfers to whomever holds the mortgage note. Furthermore, a payoff of the loan automatically cancels the lender's insurance coverage. The lender's title policy is paid for as a single premium at closing. In many areas, it is issued simultaneously with an owner's policy, since the same basic risk is covered. Local practice varies as to whether the lender's or the owner's policy must pay the major share of premium cost. If the lender's policy carries the major cost, the owner's policy is usually issued for a nominal amount. Payment for a lender's policy is most likely to be made by the buyer, as it is clearly part of the cost of obtaining a loan. (The stated amount should match the Closing Disclosure form section titled "Loan Costs Section C – Services You Can Shop For.")

Title insurance offers protection to the policyholder/landowner against adverse claims to ownership rights. Contrary to popular belief, it is not a guarantee of title, but instead offers a legal defense should an adverse claim arise. If title does prove defective, a prior owner may assert ownership, and the policyholder may recover the value of the insurance coverage.

In most states, title insurance is classed as another type of insurance and falls under the regulatory authority of the state's insurance commission. Premiums can be set uniformly by the state, limiting competition to the kind of service that different companies may offer. Title insurance is available in two separate types: (1) an owner's policy, which protects the landowner, and (2) a mortgagee's policy, which protects the lender. (On the Closing Disclosure form, this section is titled "Other Costs Section H – Other.")

An **owner's title insurance** policy protects against adverse claims up to a specified amount and for a given number of years, usually 20 or 25 years. It cannot be transferred to another owner. The owner's policy is purchased at closing with a one-time premium charge. The time period for title insurance coverage is determined by each state's limitation statutes. Even though an owner may hold actual title to property for only a short period, say a year or so, liability may continue after disposition of the property because the warranty deed normally used to convey title leaves the seller with responsibility. The deed states that the seller "will warrant and defend generally the title to the property against all claims and demands." Thus the owner's title policy protects the owner not only while he or she is in possession of the insured premises, but also for the time period after it is sold, as the seller is still liable for possible adverse claims.

Customs vary regionally as to whether or not the buyer or seller pays for owner's title insurance. Since the issuance of such a policy represents good proof of the validity of the seller's title to the land to be conveyed, in some areas the cost is paid by the seller. In other areas, if the seller can prove good title to the property through an attorney's opinion based on the abstract of title or by the issuance of a title binder by a title company, then payment for the attorney's opinion or for the owner's policy falls to the buyer as the party who carries the future benefit. (On the Closing Disclosure form, this section is titled "Other Costs Section H – Other.")

Government Recording and Transfer Charges

Recording fees and transfer fees are those charged by city, county, or state governments for recording services, or as a tax on the transaction. The fees may be based on the amount of the mortgage loan or on the value of the property being transferred. Payment of these charges is negotiable between buyer and seller, but they are usually paid by the buyer. (On the

Closing Disclosure form, this section is titled "Other Costs Section E – Taxes and other Government Fees.")

Additional Settlement Charges

Charges that are not easily classified within previous categories of costs appear in this section. Mostly, they include costs of a survey and inspections that may be required to determine adequacy of the structure and its equipment.

Almost all lenders require that a **survey** of the property offered as collateral be included in the loan package. An acceptable survey, which can only be prepared by a registered surveyor, gives a description of the land with an outline of its perimeter boundaries. It should show the precise location of buildings as well as any easements or rights-of-way that may cross the land. The survey can disclose any encroachments on the land that may create a cloud on the ownership rights. It is not unusual for an attorney to require a survey before preparing a deed or mortgage instrument to make sure of the land and the rights being conveyed. Payment for the survey is negotiable; the seller has an obligation to prove exactly what land is to be conveyed, while the buyer needs the survey to complete the loan requirements. (On the Closing Disclosure form, this section is titled "Loan Costs Section C – Services You Can Shop For.")

In certain areas of the country where termites or other insects infest buildings and can create damage, it is normal to require a separate **pest inspection**. In such areas, sales agreements may call for the property to be delivered free of infestation. The pest inspection—plus treatment if necessary, along with a certified letter of proof of treatment—is the seller's method of fulfilling this requirement. Even though the buyer and seller do not address this question, the lender may require a pest inspection to assure that the property offered as collateral is free of pest-caused structural damage. In such a case, the cost may be paid by the buyer as part of the requirements for obtaining a mortgage loan. (In the Closing Disclosure form, this section is titled "Loan Costs Section C – Services You Can Shop For.")

Total Settlement Charges

At the bottom of the page listing the various settlement charges, the totals for the borrower's and seller's charges are listed and transferred to the summary section of the first page.

FINAL CLOSING INSTRUCTIONS

How the proceeds of a loan are disbursed is of prime importance to the lender. General instructions are often kept on file with closing agents by major lenders to expedite handling. Another kind of instruction preparatory to closing is normally provided by the agents representing the principals in the transaction. We will consider these instructions below.

Mortgagee's Closing Instructions

Once a loan has been approved, the mortgage company prepares a sheet of instructions for delivery to the settlement agent handling closing procedures. The **closing instructions** shown in figure 3-3 detail such items as the correct legal name for the mortgage instruments, the name of the trustee if a deed of trust is involved, and the terms of the mortgage note. Any special requirements to be included in the mortgage or deed of trust (that is, if the mortgage company is not submitting its own forms, or standardized documents, for a note and mortgage) are itemized. The lender will ask that specific instructions on monthly payments be given to the borrower, along with details of the escrow requirements and details of **disbursement procedures**. Along with the instructions, the mortgage company will send the buyer and seller affidavits as may be required, which certify the actual down payment (cash and/or property exchanged) and the use of the loan proceeds, which must be acknowledged by the notarized signatures of all buyers and sellers. Also, a truth-in-lending statement is prepared for the purchaser/borrower's signature at closing. Some mortgage companies require certifications of occupancy for purposes of homestead information. The instruments may vary between companies according to how their legal counsels interpret state laws.

The instructions of a mortgage company invariably call for a certain amount of work on the part of the settlement agent closing the loan, if only as a means of clarifying the loan requirements. This is in addition to other details of closing that a settlement agent must handle, such as assembling the title information, preparing or reviewing the note and mortgage, verifying tax requirements, and determining the insurance payments needed.

It is advisable to allow the settlement agent a reasonable amount of time for his/her work in preparing for a closing. A forced deadline can induce errors and omissions. Figure 3-3 gives an example of typical mortgagee's closing instructions.

CHAPTER 3 Additional Government Influence

Specific Closing Instructions v.2.2

SPECIFIC CLOSING INSTRUCTIONS

These Specific Closing Instructions are to be read in conjunction with the General Closing Instructions, which are incorporated by reference and may be found at www.mbaa.org/gci.htm. If any provisions in these Specific Closing Instructions conflict with the provisions in the General Closing Instructions, the Specific Closing Instructions shall control.

FILE/CASE NUMBER: DATE & TIME:

SETTLEMENT AGENT CONTACT INFORMATION

Settlement Agent Name: Phone Number:

Company Name: Fax Number:

Mailing Address: Email:

LENDER CONTACT INFORMATION

Instructions: If settlement is not completed within __ hours after receipt of funds, Settlement Agent must notify the Lender's Contact Person immediately and return Lender's funds and Closing Documents to Lender immediately unless otherwise indicated.

Contact Name: Phone Number:

Lender Name: Fax Number:

Mailing Address: Email:

MORTGAGE BROKER CONTACT INFORMATION

Contact Name: Phone Number:

Mortgage Broker Name: Fax Number:

Mailing Address: Email:

BORROWER INFORMATION

Borrower Name: Phone Number:

Borrower Type: Fax Number:

Mailing Address: Email:

Power of Attorney Information:

Borrower Name: Phone Number:

Borrower Type: Fax Number:

Mailing Address: Email:

Power of Attorney Information:

SELLER INFORMATION

Seller Name: Phone Number:

Mailing Address: Fax Number:

                                                                Email:

PROPERTY INFORMATION

Property Address: Property County:

Property Type: Sales Price: Down Payment:

Appraised Value: LTV:

FIGURE 3-3 Mortgagee's Closing Instructions

Source: www.mbaa.org/gci.htm

Final Closing Instructions

Specific Closing Instructions v.2.2

CLOSING DOCUMENT INFORMATION

Closing Document Expiration Date: Interest Rate Expiration Date:

Other Document Specific Information:

LOAN INFORMATION

Loan Purpose: Closing Date:

Vesting to Read:

Loan Number:	MERS Number:	Loan Amount:
Loan Type:	Anticipated Disbursement Date:	Funding/Settlement Date:
APR:	Initial Payment Amount:	Term/Amortization:
First Payment Date:	Last Payment Date:	Maturity Date:
Index:	Margin:	Interest Change Date:
Lifetime Rate Cap:	Lifetime Rate Floor:	Periodic Rate Cap:

REQUIRED DOCUMENTATION

Instructions: The following documents are necessary to complete the above-referenced loan transaction. Within [__] hours after settlement, Settlement Agent must return to Lender the following documents, other than those to be presented for recording. [Settlement Agent must [use the enclosed envelope or label provided, and] send package to Lender by: [Regular Mail/Overnight/Expedite Delivery [If Lender is to pay for overnight delivery bill to [Carrier][Account Number]]]. Settlement Agent must submit for recording, immediately upon obtaining signatures and receiving funds, the original Mortgage/Deed of Trust, Riders and/or Assignments.

Deed of Trust Legal Exhibit A Hazard Insurance Requirements 4506	Borrower's Certification Initial Escrow Acct. Disc. Statement Notice of Right to Cancel	Credit Agreement Fair Lending Notice Patriot Act
	This list should be populated based on the loan package. Additional information may appear such as an annotation of who signs which document and references to the General Closing Instructions may be added, ex. Instructions for Notice of Right to Cancel.	*Overflow to appear on Attachment*

TITLE INSURANCE

Instructions: Settlement Agent shall not disburse Lender's funds until the following conditions are met:
1) Mortgagee's title insurance policy must insure that Lender's security instrument constitutes a valid [1st/2nd] lien on the borrower's estate or interest identified in the title insurance commitment, title report or binder, dated [date], subject to the following exceptions:
2) The following endorsements must be incorporated into the final title insurance policy:
3) Insured Lender must appear as: [Insured Lender]
4) Secondary Financing in the amount of [amount] has been approved:
5) Title Policy Coverage Amount:
6) Survey Required: [Yes/No]
7) Other Conditions:

HAZARD INSURANCE

Loss payee/mortgagee clause to read:

Flood: Deductible:
Hazard: Deductible:
Other: Deductible:

FIGURE 3-3 (*Continued*)

CHAPTER 3 Additional Government Influence

Specific Closing Instructions v.2.2

LOAN FEES, CHARGES, RESERVES & PAYOFFS

Instructions: The final HUD Settlement Statement must be completed at settlement and must accurately reflect all receipts and disbursements indicated in these closing instructions and any amended closing instructions subsequent hereto. If any changes to fees occur, Settlement Agent may not fund loan without Lender's prior written approval. Fax a certified copy of the final HUD-1 Settlement Statement to [_____], Attention: [___].
(may be laid out without lines for programming concerns – also add column/mark to indicate fees deducted from wire)

HUD #	Fee/Charge	POC	POC By	Bal. Due	Paid By	Paid To
	Blank Page With No Data					

B = Borrower, R = Broker, L = Lender, I = Investor, S = Service Provider, T = Title Company, O = Other
D = Deducted from Wire

FIGURE 3-3 *(Continued)*

Final Closing Instructions

Specific Closing Instructions v.2.2

LOAN FEES, CHARGES, RESERVES & PAYOFFS

Instructions: The final HUD Settlement Statement must be completed at settlement and must accurately reflect all receipts and disbursements indicated in these closing instructions and any amended closing instructions subsequent hereto. If any changes to fees occur, Settlement Agent may not fund loan without Lender's prior written approval. Fax a certified copy of the final HUD-1 Settlement Statement to [_____], Attention: [_____].

This is A REPEAT OF PAGE 3 with SAMPLE DATA – organized by fee type rather than line number – from copy of HUD.

HUD #	Fee/Charge	POC	POC By	Bal. Due	Paid By	Paid To
	Lender Fees					
801.	Loan Origination Fee			$605.00	B	L
802.	Loan Discount 1 %			$720.00	S	L
809.	Document Prep Fee			$150.00	S	L
	Total			$1,475.0		
	Broker Fees					
810.	Yield Spread Premium - 1.625%	$1,170.00	L			
815.	Automated Underwriting			$45.00	B	R
	Total			$45.00		
	Service Provider Fees					
804.	Credit Report Fee to Credit Report Service			$9.50	B	S
804.	Credit Report Fee to Credit Report Service			$25.00	R	S
814.	Courier Fee to Quick Courier			$40.00	B	S
	Total			$74.50		
900.	**Items Required By Lender To Be Paid In Advance**					
901.	Interest from 12/25/11 to 01/01/12 @ $13.06851/day			$91.48	B	L
903.	Hazard Insurance to Good Insurance Co.			$580.00	B	L
	Total			$671.48		
1000.	**Reserves Deposited with Lender**					
1001.	Hazard Insurance 3 months @ $48.33 per month			$144.99	B	L
1004.	County Property - Taxes 4 mos. @ $101.77 per			$407.08	B	L
1009.	Aggregate Adjustment			$48.33	B	L
	Total			$503.74		
1100.	**Title Charges**					
1101.	Settlement or Closing fee to Jane's Title Company			$255.00	S	T
1102.	Title Search			$140.00	S	T
1108.	Title Insurance			$600.00	B	T
	Total			$995.00		
1200.	**Government Recording and Transfer Charges**					
1201.	Recording Fees – Harris County			$86.00	B	O
1203.	State Tax Stamps			$56.35	B	O
	Total			$142.35		
	Payoffs					
	Lien Payoff #1			$1,777.77	S	O
	Lien Payoff #2			$585.00	S	O
	Total			$2,362.77		

B = Borrower, R= Broker, L = Lender, I = Investor, S = Service Provider, T = Title Company, O = Other
D = Deducted from Wire

FIGURE 3-3 (*Continued*)

Specific Closing Instructions v.2.2

CONDITIONS TO BE SATISFIED PRIOR TO DISBURSEMENT OF LOAN PROCEEDS

Settlement Agent must obtain satisfactory evidence that all taxes are paid through settlement or Settlement Agent must otherwise notify Lender of procedures to assure timely payment. [Lender is to be at no expense in this transaction.]

Additional Funding Instructions:

Attachments: The following documents are attached:
__Attachment to Specific Closing Instructions (Overflow Page)
__Construction Addendum (outside scope of closing instruction project)
__Government Loan Addendum (outside scope of closing instruction project)
__Texas Loan Addendum (outside scope of closing instruction project)

FIGURE 3-3 (*Continued*)

Setting the Closing

When the mortgage company has approved the loan and prepared its closing instructions, it is usually the responsibility of the real estate agent, or agents, involved to arrange a mutually agreeable closing time. Practices vary in different parts of the country: in some areas all parties meet for the settlement procedures; in other parts, no actual meeting is required, and escrow agents are authorized to request that the necessary instruments be delivered to them for release after all escrow requirements have been met.

Whenever the local practices require a meeting of the parties involved, it is usually held in the offices of the company or person designated to handle the settlement procedures. This may be a title company, an attorney, a real estate agent, an escrow agent, or the lender itself. Whoever handles the loan closing must have the approval of the lender, as it is the lender's money that is generally most involved.

Closings can be accomplished with separate meetings—the buyer at one time and the seller at another—leaving the settlement agent to escrow the instruments and consideration until the procedure is completed and distribution can be made. It is easier for the agents involved, and provides greater clarity for both buyer and seller, to arrange for a single meeting. Although a closing is no place for negotiations, if a misunderstanding crops up, it can be more readily resolved if all parties are immediately available for decision making.

DISBURSEMENT OF FUNDS

In many parts of the country, a closing is just that. Instruments are signed and funds are disbursed before anyone leaves the closing table. In some areas, it is more common to execute and acknowledge the instruments at the closing but delay disbursement of funds until later. The purpose for any delay in releasing funds is twofold. First, it gives the lender an opportunity to make a second review of all instruments and to verify proper signatures and acknowledgments; second, it allows the settlement agent time to clear any checks that may have been submitted by the parties involved before releasing its own disbursement checks. Because any delay in the delivery of executed documents and funds can create problems, there is growing pressure not to call for the parties to meet until all loose ends have been resolved and good money is available for distribution at the closing table.

The actual disbursement of funds at or following the settlement procedures is usually made to several different individuals and companies. One of the reasons an escrow agent is employed in the closing process is to make sure that all parties with claims in the settlement are paid. Commercial banks use the Federal Reserve Fed Wire system to electronically submit good funds for loan payoffs and other closing costs. The mortgage lender wants to be certain that taxes are paid, that the insurance coverage is in force and has been paid for, and that no subsequent claims can be filed that might cloud its right to a valid lien securing the loan. Sales agents, inspectors, attorneys, and service agents all normally expect to receive their fees from the closing agent. After all required payments have been made, the necessary instruments are filed in the county records, the balance due to the seller is disbursed, and the transaction is considered closed.

Questions for Discussion

1. Discuss the purpose of the Real Estate Settlement Procedures Act (RESPA) and its key provisions.
2. Why should a listing agent obtain a preliminary title report on the listed property?
3. Discuss the importance of a survey in the settlement procedure.
4. Describe the essential elements of the Closing Disclosure.
5. What is the reason for a prepayment of interest at the time of settlement procedures?
6. What information is normally furnished to the settlement agent (closer) by the mortgage lender just prior to closing?
7. Describe at least three RESPA requirements that call for disclosure of information to a borrower.
8. Discuss the requirements of the Truth-in-Lending Act related to finance charges for mortgage loans.
9. What is the general policy of life insurance companies toward mortgage lending?
10. How does the Farm Credit System structure the various agencies that handle oversight of the farm mortgage lending function?

Multiple Choice Questions for Review

1. What is the purpose of RESPA?
   a. to protect lenders from unqualified borrowers
   b. to protect borrowers from improper lending practices
   c. to make it easier to lend money
   d. to keep lenders from having relationships with service providers

2. A title report does not include information on:
   a. property description
   b. tax rate
   c. property history
   d. liens

3. What is the primary importance of the survey in the closing process?
   a. Its performance is required by state law in cases of property transfers.
   b. It will disclose any possible discrepancies in size or whether any new improvements have been made within or over the property boundaries.
   c. It will disclose where utility easements are located.
   d. It is required by most title insurance policies for issuance.

4. Which of the following documents itemizes all settlement costs, including lender charges?
   a. form 1003
   b. agreement of sale
   c. the Closing Disclosure or HUD-1 form
   d. forbearance agreement

5. What is the daily interest for a 30-day month, calculating per diem interest using a $125,000 loan at 5.15%?
   a. $17.31
   b. $17.88
   c. $207.66
   d. $17.46

6. RESPA allows for the borrower to inspect the Closing Disclosure form how many days prior to the actual settlement?
   a. 1 day
   b. 2 days
   c. 3 days
   d. 7 days

7. Which of the following is not one of the four procedures that financial institutions covered by the CRA must implement?
   a. List types of credit offered by the institution.
   b. Issue to the public a report on efforts to meet community needs.
   c. List loan policies with lower credit criteria to help lower-income areas.
   d. Define the area they serve, which is the neighborhood from which they draw their deposits and into which they make loans.

8. What three RESPA federally required disclosures must be provided within three days of receipt of the loan application for a purchase money loan?
   a. Loan Estimate, CHARM Booklet, and HUD-1
   b. Loan Estimate, Mortgage Disclosure Servicing Statement, and a Special Information Booklet, which contains consumer information regarding various real estate settlement services
   c. Loan Estimate, Affiliate Business Arrangement, and Mortgage Disclosure Servicing Statement
   d. Loan Estimate, HUD-1, and the truth-in-lending disclosures

9. Which of the following are not included in the finance charge?
   a. interest
   b. fee for preparation of mortgage loan documents
   c. loan origination fee
   d. discount points

10. If a loan includes an escrow account, the lender is allowed to require a cushion of up to two months according to what law?

   a. ECOA
   b. HOEPA
   c. RESPA
   d. TILA

Information Resources

https://www.consumerfinance.gov/policy-compliance/rulemaking/final-rules/2013-real-estate-settlement-procedures-act-regulation-x-and-truth-lending-act-regulation-z-mortgage-servicing-final-rules/
> A source of current updates to the recent new RESPA reform measures available from the Consumer Financial Protection Bureau and the Department of Housing and Urban Development.

https://www.fdic.gov/regulations/compliance/manual/5/v-3.1.pdf
> The FDIC provides this link to banks to assure that they are in compliance with RESPA.

https://www.bankersonline.com/regulations/12-1026-000
> A good source of information on mortgage compliance such as Regulation Z or the Truth-in-Lending Act is maintained by Bankers Online.

https://www.easysoft-usa.com/loan-estimate-form-software/
> EasySoft Real Estate Closing Solutions keeps all aspects of the real estate closing process, including the Loan Estimate form.

http://www.complianceease.com/mainsite/
> ComplianceEase® is a suite of new loan documents closing solutions that is fully leveraged with recent technological advancements in the form of secure e-delivery, automatic MERS registrations, multilevel compliance testing, data exchanges between numerous LOS and Enterprise Systems, and adoption of document bar codes for imaging and document storage.

https://civilrights.org/oppose-s-2155-economic-growth-regulatory-relief-consumer-protection-act-2/
> Read this web page to better understand an argument against the final Economic Growth, Regulatory Relief, and Consumer Protection Act of 2018.

https://www.govtrack.us/congress/bills/115/s2155/summary
> Read this web page to better understand a good summary review of the positives about the Economic Growth, Regulatory Relief and Consumer Protection Act of 2018.

https://www.fanniemae.com/singlefamily/uniform-residential-loan-application

The government-sponsored entities Fannie Mae and Freddie Mac have redesigned the Uniform Residential Loan Application (Form 1003). This was done so that the application would correspond to the Uniform Loan Application Dataset (ULAD) that was created with new Desktop Underwriter Specifications. This URL takes you to the current version of the redesigned Form 1003/65 document that aims to better support changes in mortgage industry credit, underwriting, eligibility policies, and regulatory requirements.

Chapter 4

THE SECONDARY MORTGAGE MARKET

KEY TERMS AND PHRASES

annual return
basis point
collateralized debt
 obligations (CDOs)
collateralized mortgage
 obligation (CMO)
discount
mortgage-backed securities
mortgage loan pool
net yield

originate-to-distribute model
pass-through
point
price
private mortgage conduits
Real Estate Mortgage Investment
 Conduit
secondary market
tax-exempt bonds
yield

LEARNING OBJECTIVES

At the conclusion of this chapter, students will be able to:
- Describe the changes that caused most primary lenders to cease to be permanent investors in residential mortgage loans.
- Describe how the development of uniform loan origination documents and expansion of the private mortgage insurance market impacted the growth of the secondary mortgage market.

- Understand how yield on mortgages and market yield requirements affect the pricing of mortgages and mortgage securities.
- Explain the basic differences between mortgages purchased for portfolio purposes and those purchased for underwriting.
- Describe the concept of federal underwriting.
- Understand the specific details of the major federal loan programs.
- Describe the evolution of loan pooling and its importance to the other primary sources of securitization in facilitating real estate mortgage financing.

INTRODUCTION

The previous two chapters focused on the primary market—the loan origination market. Prior to the mid-1970s, the loan origination market was dominated by regulated depository institutions. This group of lenders held the major source of deposit assets that could be used to fund long-term loans. Unless a lender had money on deposit to fund loans, there was little opportunity to enter the business except in a loan brokerage capacity. Mortgage companies handled the brokerage function.

Using deposits to fund mortgage loans worked fairly well for about four decades following the Great Depression of the 1930s. During this time, there was a federal limit on interest rates that never exceeded 5.5% paid to depositors (as per the Federal Reserve's Regulation Q). This restriction allowed lenders to make long-term mortgage loans at not more than 7% to 8% with reasonable protection for the lender of a stable cost of funds. Access by home buyers to this huge, low-cost source of funds began to unravel as interest rates started to escalate in the late 1970s, with 30-year, fixed-rate Freddie Mac mortgages hitting an all-time high interest rate of 16.63% in 1981.

While the real growth of the secondary market began in the early 1970s, its participants throughout that decade were generally limited to loan purchasers who normally invested in mortgage loans. These included large savings associations and savings banks, plus Fannie Mae and Freddie Mac, because the purchase of a mortgage loan by a secondary-market investor generally involved certain responsibilities for managing the loan itself. It was not until the development of the mortgage-backed security concept, which converted mortgage loans into a more acceptable type of security, that the secondary market was opened to investors throughout the international financial markets.

Expansion of the Secondary Market

Besides the earlier constraints of interest rates, there were other problems limiting the mortgage market prior to the 1970s. It was difficult to sell mortgage loans for two important reasons: First, the documents used for conventional loans were not uniform; second, there was no acceptable insurance protection against loan default. Only the FHA and VA were able to overcome these problems. Both of these agencies offered uniform documentation that enabled an investor anywhere in the country to know in advance exactly how a note and mortgage instrument would be worded, and both offered a very acceptable underwriting guarantee (the VA terminology) or an insured commitment (the FHA term).

It was not until 1972 that steps were taken to create a class of conventional loans offering similar advantages to the FHA/VA loans. The move was undertaken by the Federal National Mortgage Association (FNMA, better known as Fannie Mae) in an effort to increase its market. Prior to that time, only FHA and VA loans could be purchased by Fannie Mae, and these amounted to only about 20% of the total residential mortgage market.

Introduction of Uniform Documentation

In 1968, Fannie Mae was partitioned by Congress; one part became the Government National Mortgage Association (Ginnie Mae), and the other remained as Fannie Mae but converted to a federally chartered private corporation, no longer a government-owned entity. Obviously, with 80% of the market, conventional loans offered a big opportunity for expansion for a private corporation. Thus Fannie Mae, joined by Freddie Mac (the Federal Home Loan Mortgage Corporation that was created in 1970), began a several-year process of devising uniform documents acceptable for conventional loans. Together, these three government-sponsored enterprises (GSEs) dominated market leadership in the introduction of new uniform documentation as regulatory rules and market pressures evolved. The result has been the *conforming loan*, a loan written with uniform documents and loan qualification parameters that is readily marketable throughout the country.

SELLING MORTGAGE LOANS

So what is the **secondary market**? In essence, the secondary market is the market wherein loan originators are able to sell loans, thus recovering their cash for the purpose of originating more loans. But the secondary market uses a different terminology because its function differs from the market in which loans originate. Secondary market investors do not "lend" money; they "purchase" mortgage notes as investments to earn a return. The return is also called *yield* and it represents the money earned on an investment. In the mortgage market, yield is the combination of interest earned over the life of the loan plus the discount taken at loan origination. These are combined and expressed as an **annual return**. The following section explains this process more fully.

Procedures Used in Secondary Markets

Note the difference in terminology at this point. The originator of a loan speaks to customers/borrowers in terms of loaning money, and expresses the cost of the borrowed money as interest plus points of discount and fees. Once the originator closes the loan to the borrower, the note and mortgage instrument become marketable paper that can be assigned—and the terminology changes. The mortgage note is now a salable commodity and is negotiated as such. The originator of the loan becomes a seller, and the large investing institutions that deal in the secondary market for mortgage loans are called purchasers. Thus, when a mortgage loan is offered for sale, the potential purchaser is interested in only one factor for loans of similar type, size, and quality, and that is the **net yield**.

Pricing Loans to Adjust Yields

Since the interest rate on the loan or loans held by the originator has already been established, the only way a seller can change the yield to a purchaser is to adjust the **price** of the loan. For example, if the mortgage note is for $10,000 at 7% interest, the yield would be 7%. If the seller must offer a yield higher than 7% to attract a purchaser, the loan must be sold for less than $10,000; that is, the face value is discounted to increase the yield. By selling the $10,000 loan for, say, $9,500, the purchaser is putting up less cash but still collects the originally agreed interest and principal payment applicable to the $10,000 loan at 7%. The result is a greater return, or yield, for the $9,500.

The principal balance due on an existing mortgage loan normally changes each month as installments are paid, making it difficult to quote a price in dollars as is commonly done in the bond market. (Unlike the mortgage note, for a bond with a fixed denomination of, say, $1,000, the principal is normally not paid until the bond matures.) For this reason, the price on a mortgage note is quoted as a percentage figure. The price is that percentage of the loan balance for which the loan is sold. One hundred is, of course, par. If we were quoting the $10,000 loan just mentioned to sell for $9,500, the price would simply be "95." This indicates a 5% reduction in whatever the principal balance due on the mortgage note may be, or a five-point discount. (One point is 1% of the loan amount.)

In times of falling interest rates, a loan calling for a higher-than-current market interest can sell for a premium[1] of as high as 102%, or even 104%, of its face value. Examples of prices and yields are shown in table 4-1 to illustrate their relationship.

A simple reading of the table shows that the length of time a loan is outstanding has a direct effect on the yield for that loan. Since loans vary considerably in the time to payoff, it is necessary to use some standard payoff time in order to compare yields when a loan is originated. The reason is that the discount is a lump-sum amount paid at closing and must be spread over the life of the loan to calculate an expected annual yield.

Yield and Discount

Yield can be defined as the return to the investor expressed in a percentage of the price paid for the note. **Discount** is the difference between the face value of the note and the price the investor paid for the note. Yield includes both the interest earned and the discount taken. So to express the discount as a part of the yield, it must be converted to an annual percentage rate. The discount is a one-time charge, a lump sum taken at the time the loan is funded. To determine how much it adds to each year's earnings, or yield, the discount must be

TABLE 4-1 Price/Yield Table Calculated at 7% Interest for Term of 30 Years

Price	Discount	Yield if Prepaid 8 Years	Yield if Prepaid 10 Years	Yield if Prepaid 12 Years	To Maturity
102	+2 (premium)	6.66	6.71	6.74	6.81
100	0	7.00	7.00	7.00	7.00
96	4	7.70	7.61	7.54	7.41
92	8	8.44	8.24	8.12	7.85

Source: © 2021 Mbition LLC

[1] Paying a premium for higher-than-market interest rate debt instruments is a common practice in the bond market. However, many investors in mortgage loans refuse to pay any premium because of the ease with which mortgage loans can be refinanced at lower rates when the market declines.

converted to an annual amount spread over the life of the loan. But what is the life of the mortgage loan? While most residential loans, including FHA- and VA-supported loans, are granted for a term of 30 years, the realistic life of a loan is approximately 10 to 12 years; that is, within 10 to 12 years the average loan is paid off, usually by resale or refinancing. Fannie Mae and Freddie Mac use a time span of 12 years to determine the yield value of a discount. In round figures, this means that one-twelfth of the discount amount would be considered as earned each year.

The purchase requirements for Fannie Mae to buy a loan are expressed in terms of a net yield, usually carried to two decimal places. The accepted yield can be converted to a discount mathematically or more easily by means of a standard conversion table. Table 4-2 shows several typical yield figures. The sequence of steps in the table shows the fixed interest rate for the note, the price that is used to achieve the yield, and the discount needed to achieve the price.

The mortgage banking industry is able to use both Fannie Mae's and Freddie Mac's daily posting of required yields as solid criteria on which to base its own handling of individual mortgage loans. For example, assume a mortgage company is making mortgage loans at 9.5%, which is competitive in its current market, and must meet a yield of 9.80% to sell the loans. Using table 4-2, we determine that the price must be 97.45, which requires a discount of 2.55 points to achieve. The mortgage lender would probably quote a discount of 2.75 points as a rounded-out figure if the market is strong. Added to the quoted discount is the origination fee of about 1% for a total of 3.75 points taken at closing.

Consider the 9.5% interest rate just quoted as a *net basis rate*—the rate applied to dealing with a secondary-market purchaser. The *gross rate*—that applied to the borrower—must include two additional charges: One is a servicing fee of about 0.25%, and the other is for private mortgage insurance, if applicable—say, another 0.25%. Thus, the market rate paid by a borrower in this transaction would amount to 10% interest plus 3.75 points.

TABLE 4-2 Example: Conversion of Yield to Price

For a Yield Amount	At Interest Rate	Price Must Be	Points to Achieve
9.500	9.500	100	0
9.800	9.500	97.45	2.55
10.600	9.500	91.12	8.88

Source: © 2021 Mbition LLC

Loan originators using Fannie Mae/Freddie Mac yields as a guide to trends would be watching for an upward or downward movement to further influence decisions as to what interest rate and discount might be needed to make loans that could be profitably sold.

Points

A **point** is 1% of the loan amount. In the jargon of mortgage lending, discounts are sometimes identified as "points." This is accurate insofar as a discount is usually measured in points. But the two words, point and discount, are not synonymous. A point as a unit of measure is frequently used to identify other costs such as mortgage insurance premiums, an origination fee, a finance charge, and various other charges. Yet it is not uncommon to lump all the costs of financing—even attorney's fees and title insurance—into one lump sum and call it "points." This practice can be confusing to the borrower/consumer and is not a compliant disclosure methodology under the Real Estate Settlement Procedures Act as amended by the Dodd-Frank Act.

From a practical standpoint, the borrower should demand that each cost be identified. Such insistence on disclosure may help to uncover an error or possibly an overcharge. Former tax law distinguished between points taken as discount—which was considered a deductible cost of borrowed money the same as interest—and fees charged—which were considered nondeductible expenses. However, the difference in the makeup of points taken at closing is no longer a tax question. Recent rulings by the IRS (involving several revisions) allow a home buyer to take a tax deduction on all discount points paid as these are considered financing costs in the tax year incurred, regardless of the purpose involved, whether paid by buyer or seller. (Commercial loans and refinanced home loans must amortize point deductions over the life of the loan.)

Basis Points

To identify fractions of a point, the financial markets use a finer measure. A **basis point** is one one-hundredth of 1% (not of the loan amount, as is a point). This unit of measure has long been used to report the small daily fluctuations in Treasury bill rates and is now moving into the mortgage language. For example, a servicing fee of, say, 0.25% can also be called "25 basis points."

Loan Purchasers

As noted earlier, the secondary market is where loan originators can sell their loans—where they can convert their loans back into cash in order to originate more loans. Loan purchasers operate in two different ways:

1. **purchase for portfolio** (Purchasers of loans may acquire them as a sound investment for the purpose of earning interest. This would include some savings institutions, insurance companies, pension funds, housing agencies, Fannie Mae, and, to a lesser degree, Freddie Mac.); and

2. **acquisition for underwriting.** Some loan purchasers do so with the intention of creating mortgage pools that can be used as collateral for the issuance of mortgage-backed securities. These purchasers, as well as some loan originators, use their own funds to create the mortgage pools, and then recover their cash through the sale of securities. Among those active in this field are large investment bankers such as Morgan Stanley and Goldman Sachs, large commercial banks such as Bank of America and JPMorgan Chase, and Fannie Mae and Freddie Mac.

Purchase for Portfolio

The secondary market originated with the idea of purchasing mortgage loans to be held in portfolio. It began when Congress created the Federal National Mortgage Association (Fannie Mae) as part of the Act that also created the Federal Housing Administration in 1934. The original purpose was a simple one—to provide a market for FHA loans. As an agency of the federal government, Fannie Mae was able to sell debenture bonds (unsecured promises to pay) that paid a fairly low rate of interest, such as 4% to 5%. The money derived from the sale of bonds was then used to buy FHA mortgage loans that paid 6% to 6.5% interest. That gave Fannie Mae a margin of 1% to 2% over its cost of funds. In 1968, Fannie Mae held $7 billion in such loans.

The risk to Fannie Mae lay in maintaining that margin. If its cost of funds increased, there was no way it could increase the interest earned on its investment in fixed-interest, long-term loans. To finance its mortgage loan purchases, Fannie Mae sold short-term debenture bonds (with 3- to 5-year maturities) because the interest paid to short-term investors is customarily lower than that paid for long-term money. For many years, the system worked very well. In industry jargon, Fannie Mae was borrowing money on the short term and lending it on the long term. It was not until market interest rates began to escalate between 1979 and 1981 that the cost of funds exceeded the interest earned. Losses ensued for all holders of mortgage loans, not just Fannie Mae.

During this same time period, savings institutions made up the largest group of loan purchasers holding mortgage loans. Their cost of funds had been protected by the federal limitation on interest rates paid to their savings account depositors. While the federal limit was not removed until March 1986, it was substantially undermined in the late 1970s by the introduction of a variety of savings certificates that paid higher interest rates. To hold deposits, savings associations had to pay higher rates to their depositors, as they could not call in their long-term mortgage loans. The result was devastating losses for savings institutions and a general dissatisfaction with the "portfolio approach" to mortgage loans. (Remember our earlier discussion of the RTC in chapter 3.)

Nevertheless, there remains a substantial market for mortgage loans purchased by those who hold them as investments. Some of the risk of fluctuating interest rates has been reduced by the introduction of adjustable-rate mortgage designs. Also, mortgage rates that were once held low by an artificial restraint on lenders' cost of funds are now free to fluctuate in a competitive market that has produced a near-steady decline from earlier peaks. Indeed, in 1982, home loan rates reached in excess of 16%. In 2018, 30-year, fixed-rate, conventional mortgage interest rates fluctuated between 4.03% and 4.94% below the long-term average of 8.04% (1976-2018).[2]

Purchase for Underwriting

"Purchase for underwriting" is actually an overly abbreviated title for this section. It is meant to explain the process through which loans are purchased, or otherwise acquired, for the express purpose of creating **mortgage loan pools**. A mortgage pool is a collection of loans, or a block of loans. The pool can be made up of a particular kind of mortgage loan distinguished by its collateral, such as all condominium loans. It can be a geographically diversified block of residential loans, as is most commonly

---

[2]"US 30 Year Mortgage Rate Chart," YCharts, 2018, accessed November 28, 2018, http://ycharts.com/indicators/30_year_mortgage_rate

found in the Freddie Mac offerings. It can be exclusively FHA/VA, as is required for a Ginnie Mae-type pool, or it can be a block of commercial loans.

Participants in this type of secondary-market activity are mostly investment bankers, commercial banks, Fannie Mae, Freddie Mac, hedge fund managers, and foreign sovereign wealth funds. These companies have the cash to acquire huge blocks of loans and establish the specific mortgage pools with identification of the individual mortgages assigned to them, and then issue a series of securities that are backed by the mortgage pool. The securities are then sold to various investors.

All pools are organized in a manner that collects and accounts for the payments received on the individual loans, then passes this "cash flow" on through to the investors who have bought the securities. The intricacies involved in the proper handling of these huge cash flows could not be managed without the recent advances in computer technology. Just how the cash flow is handled as it passes through to the security holders differs in a number of ways. It is these differences that distinguish one kind of mortgage-backed security from another, as will be explained later in this chapter.

How do the participants in the creation of mortgage pools make money? It is easier to understand if you think of the process as selling the cash flows rather than selling the mortgages. In fact, the mortgages remain locked up in the care of a trustee. The trustee may be a bank's trust department, or it could be the creator of a pool if properly authorized to hold the mortgages in trust. (The pooler is the company that issues the securities backed by the mortgages.) The point is that the mortgages themselves are not "delivered" to the purchaser of a mortgage-backed security; just the cash flows generated by those mortgages are passed through to the purchaser/investors.

There must be a margin between what the mortgages deliver in cash flows to the pool and what is passed on to the holders of the securities, or there would be no benefit to loan poolers. That margin is generated by **three factors**:

1. Investors in high-grade securities accept lower interest rates than those produced by the mortgages because of lower risk for the investments. In spite of some adverse publicity about foreclosures, home loans are classed as a low-risk investment, and when converted to a security, they can command lower interest rates than more risky investments.

2. Larger investments are usually made for lesser rates than are small ones, so long as the risk justifies it. Mortgage-backed securities are generally offered in large denominations.
3. By segmenting the cash flows to the security holders, issuers can attract even lower cost money from the short-term money market. This is the purpose of the "collateralized mortgage obligation," which is explained later.

The handling of cash flows differs, and the margins between what mortgages pay and what is delivered to the security holders vary slightly with almost every issue. The following example illustrates a hypothetical profit margin for an issuer of a mortgage-backed security.

Example

Assume a residential mortgage pool of $1 million with each of the mortgages in the pool paying 10% interest. The result is a cash flow of $100,000 in interest plus whatever is repaid on principal each year. Say the issuer of the security backed by this block of mortgages offers to pay 9% interest to the security holder. A logical purchaser of such a security could be a pension fund. Say the pension fund pays $1 million for the security and accepts $90,000 a year in interest. The $10,000 difference between what is paid into the pool by home buyers in interest and what is paid to the security holder/pension fund must be shared. The loan servicer (usually the loan originator) will earn between one-quarter and three-eighths of that 1% differential; if a trustee is involved, it would earn perhaps 20 basis points (one-fifth of 1%), and the rest, perhaps 45 to 55 basis points, would belong to the security issuer.

This example is deliberately reduced in size to $1 million for easier comprehension. In practice, the amount of $1 million would be much too small to attract any issuer of securities. Loan pools range from $250 million up to more than $1 billion. With those kinds of numbers, the margins become far more interesting. To attract investors, interests in the huge pools are sold through a series of securities in smaller denominations, such as $100,000 units. Mutual funds may offer much smaller denominations for individual investors.

A key point in this kind of transaction is that the risk of interest rate fluctuation passes to the holder of the mortgage-backed security. In the past, those who held mortgages in portfolio were exposed to the risk of rising interest rates, meaning that their cost of funds might increase to an amount greater than the earnings on the loan portfolio. While this fact has not changed—those who hold mortgage loans in portfolio are still exposed—there is now another option. By converting mortgage loans to securities, the risk is passed on to the security holder.

To explain the meaning of this "passing of the risk," let us take another look at the example of the $1 million block of loans, and say it is converted to a single $1 million denomination security. Assume that security was sold to a pension fund. What the pension fund now holds as an asset is a $1 million security (call it a mortgage-backed bond) that pays 6% each year on the principal balance. What happens if the market interest rate now moves from 6% to 8%? This shift would reduce the pension fund's $1 million asset value by about a 12-point discount, to an asset value of approximately $880,000. If the pension fund has to sell that mortgage-backed bond for some reason, it would take a $120,000 loss. However, unlike savings associations, pension funds and similar investors do not face depositors who can withdraw their cash whenever they want, so it is very unlikely that such an investor would be forced to accept such a loss. If held to maturity, the underlying mortgage pool would eventually repay the full $1 million in principal plus interest, and all parties would recover precisely what they expected when the investment was made.

In fact, the attraction of mortgage-backed securities has encouraged savings institutions to exchange their portfolios of mortgages for securities. This was the cause of the massive "swaps" that boosted pool underwriting between 1982 and 1984. A swap occurs when an institution trades its own portfolio of mortgages to, say, Freddie Mac, in return for a series of mortgage-backed securities. This may appear to be an unrealistic exchange. After all, does the savings institution not still carry the risk of interest rate fluctuation if it holds a security tied to the mortgages? The answer to this question has to be "yes," in that the principal value of a mortgage-backed security may rise or fall depending on the fluctuation of market interest rates as described in the previous paragraph.

But there are two differences that account for the attraction of mortgage-backed securities over holding mortgages themselves: First, a security is more easily sold than a mortgage loan, thus providing greater liquidity should cash be needed. Second, the security can carry an additional protection against loss that was not available for the individual mortgage loan. The additional protection is an underwriting guarantee of the mortgage-backed security by a federal agency. About half of the mortgage-backed securities backed by residential mortgage loans have this protection. This kind of underwriting is the subject of the next section.

MAJOR PARTICIPANTS IN THE SECONDARY MARKET

Federal Underwriting of Mortgage Pools

The concept of a block of loans serving as collateral for the issuance of a security is not new. And it is not limited only to mortgage loans. It is used in other areas of supplying credit, such as with car loans, student loans, and even for credit cards. In market jargon, it is called an "asset-backed" security (ABS). Those who issue securities backed by blocks of loans can range from banks to homebuilders, from investment bankers to finance companies, and from retail merchants to real estate brokers.

A trend that has substantially enhanced the wide acceptance of **mortgage-backed securities** has been the rapid growth of federal agency underwriting. Remember that the issuers of mortgage-backed securities earn a margin between what the individual mortgages pay each month and what the issuers have to pay the holders of the securities. Therefore, the larger the margin, the greater the profit; and the lower the risk, the lower the rate that has to be paid security investors. What federal underwriting has added is an element of reduction in the risk for holders of mortgage-backed securities.

Since reducing the risk for the investor encourages lower interest rates, the long-range results are not only slightly higher margins for the issuers, but also lower interest rates for home buyers. In fact, the reduction in risk was quantified by the Federal Reserve Bank Board with a ruling effective in 1989. That rule increased banks' capital requirements from 6 to 8%, tied to the risk level of their assets (meaning loans outstanding). For most kinds of commercial loans held in portfolio by a bank, capital required is 100% of the 8% requirement, or $8 for every $100 of loans outstanding. For approved residential mortgage loans, the risk-based capital requirement is reduced to 50%, or $4 for every $100 of such loans. If the investment is made in mortgage-backed securities that are federal agency insured, the risk drops to 20%, or $1.60 for every $100, and to zero for federal government-guaranteed loans (which includes government bonds and Ginnie Mae mortgage-backed securities).

So who are the federal underwriters offering these benefits? There are four involved with mortgage loans: Ginnie Mae, Freddie Mac, Fannie Mae, and Farmer Mac, the newest entrant in the field as of July 1989. None of these agencies is limited in its activities solely to underwriting mortgage loan pools. The following section describes the origin, ownership, underwriting requirements, and other functions of each agency.

THE GOVERNMENT-SPONSORED ENTERPRISES (GSES INCLUDING FNMA, FHLMC, GNMA, FHLB, FARMER MAC)

Government National Mortgage Association (Ginnie Mae)

Ginnie Mae was created by partitioning the Federal National Mortgage Association in 1968. As a result, Fannie Mae became a federally chartered public corporation (listed on the New York Stock Exchange) and Ginnie Mae was assigned to the Department of Housing and Urban Development (HUD). Of the four federal underwriting agencies, Ginnie Mae is the only one that belongs to the government and thus carries unique powers.

Ginnie Mae was assigned two of the three functions formerly handled by Fannie Mae: (1) to implement special assistance for housing as may be required by Congress or the president, and (2) to manage the portfolio of loans assigned to it by the partition from Fannie Mae. (The third function—stabilizing the mortgage market through the purchase of loans—remained with Fannie Mae.) To minimize duplication of facilities, some of Ginnie Mae's operations are handled by agreement through the offices of Fannie Mae.

What has overwhelmed the original intent in creating Ginnie Mae is the success it has had with "managing" its loan portfolio. To liquidate some of the loans acquired in its partition from Fannie Mae, Ginnie Mae created pools of these loans and issued a guarantee certificate backed by the pools as a type of security. The pool guarantee concept became the mechanism by which mortgage loans are converted into more salable securities. Ginnie Mae pools today are limited to FHA, VA, and certain

USDA Rural Development Agency loans. (The Farmers Home Administration, FmHA, was eliminated in 1996 and the name has changed to USDA Rural Development at this time. It remains under the administration of the Department of Agriculture.)

However, Ginnie Mae does not purchase mortgage loans to create its pools. It approves "loan poolers," usually investment bankers such as Deutsche Bank and JPMorgan Chase, who purchase mortgage loans from loan originators across the country. These loans must comply with Ginnie Mae requirements. Then Ginnie Mae issues its guarantee certificates, which are backed by specific loan pools. The loan poolers then sell the Ginnie Mae certificates. As the individual mortgage loans produce monthly payments, the cash passes through the servicing agent, to the loan pooler, and on to the holders of the Ginnie Mae certificates. Ginnie Mae guarantees the payment to holders of the certificates but not the individual mortgage loans.

Of the four underwriting agencies, Ginnie Mae is the only one authorized to issue a "government guarantee," a commitment backed by the full faith and credit of the United States. For this commitment, Ginnie Mae charges a fee amounting to 6 basis points (six one-hundredths of 1% of the commitment amount). A pooler who owns the right to service each individual mortgage in the pool is limited to a servicing fee of 44 basis points on Ginnie Mae I MBS and the same commitment fee of 6 basis points, and from as little as 25 basis points to as high as 75 basis points for servicing fees on Ginnie Mae II MBS. Application fees for the commitment guarantee are $500 on the first $1.5 million of mortgage pool purchase commitment and an additional $200 on each additional increment of $1 million.

A Ginnie Mae certificate, called a "Ginnie Mae" in financial markets, offers a powerful incentive for an investor. It carries the zero-risk equivalent of a government bond and offers up to one percentage point higher return than the bonds. While the smallest denomination of a Ginnie Mae is $25,000, a number of mutual funds offer participation in much smaller denominations.

In the first quarter of 2018, Ginnie Mae's MBS outstanding amounted to $1.924 trillion, or 21.66% of the $8.88 trillion of residential mortgage debt in this country.

It has become more difficult in the last five years to meet Ginnie Mae's eligibility requirements to be an issuer of MBS or HMBS. The requirements language below was taken directly from the Ginnie Mae website.

Ginnie Mae requires its issuers to meet the following minimum criteria:

- Issuers must be approved FHA mortgages in good standing. A mortgagee approved only as an FHA loan correspondent is not eligible to be a Ginnie Mae issuer.
- Issuers must possess demonstrated experience and management capacity in the underwriting, origination, and servicing of mortgage loans. Issuers may utilize a Ginnie Mae-approved sub-servicer; however, the issuer must have an individual on its staff to oversee the sub-servicer's performance. This individual must possess at least three years of broad servicing experience.
- Issuers must have fidelity bond and a "mortgagee errors and omissions" policy in effect.
- Issuers must have a quality control plan in place for underwriting, originating, and servicing mortgage loans as well as for secondary marketing.
- Net worth requirement: For the single-family program, issuers must have a minimum net worth of $2,500,000. For the HMBS programs, issuers must have a minimum net worth of $5,000,000. For the multifamily program, issuers must have a minimum net worth of $1,000,000. For the manufactured housing program, issuers must have a minimum net worth of $10,000,000.
- *Liquidity requirement: For the single-family, multifamily, and HMBS programs, issuers must also have liquid assets totaling 20% of its Ginnie Mae net worth requirement.*
- Institution-wide capital requirement: Depository institutions must meet the regulatory definition of well-capitalized. Nondepository institutions, including credit unions, must hold equity capital of 6% of the institution's total assets.[3]

Federal Home Loan Mortgage Corporation (Freddie Mac)

With a bit of imagination added, the acronym FHLMC becomes "Freddie Mac." Freddie Mac is a federally chartered corporation owned primarily by the savings association industry. It functions in a similar manner to

---

[3] "Eligibility Requirements," Ginnie Mae, accessed December 29, 2014, http://www.ginniemae.gov/doing_business_with_ginniemae/issuer_resources/how_to_become_an_issuer/Pages/eligibility_requirements.aspx

Fannie Mae with an 18-member board of directors and is subject to an oversight committee under HUD. HUD sets target goals for both Freddie and Fannie, including loan purchase requirements in central city areas and for low- and moderate-income families, which both agencies report meeting.

Prior to its being put into conservatorship by the federal government, Freddie Mac's only remaining ties to the federal government existed around the fact that five of its directors were appointed by the president of the United States and it carried a $2.25 billion line of credit with the U.S. Treasury. Congress sets limits from time to time on the maximum loan amount that all federal agencies may purchase. In late 2008, the Treasury agreed to fund up to $810 billion in loans investments to shore up both Fannie Mae and Freddie Mac. At the time, it was announced that the huge combined portfolio of $1.5 trillion was to be reduced by 10% a year. Neither Fannie Mae nor Freddie Mac has more than $250 billion. (Note, this was later changed to a 15% annual reduction rate in 2012.)

From its creation as a part of the savings association system in 1970 for the purpose of purchasing mortgage loans, Freddie Mac has favored securitizing loans. Rather than purchasing loans for its portfolio, a practice initially followed by Fannie Mae, Freddie Mac elected to raise its money through the sale of mortgage participation certificates. These certificates, called "PCs" in the financial market, are backed by multimillion-dollar blocks of geographically diversified single-family (one- to four-family) loans that serve as collateral. The certificates are unconditionally guaranteed by Freddie Mac. This is an "agency" guarantee, which falls short of a federal government guarantee. What is meant by an agency guarantee is that, while the agency is not legally a part of the government, its ties are close enough that investors assume the government will not allow it to default on an obligation. But there is no legal obligation for the government to do so. Warning signs that an implicit guarantee was developing, along with the possibility of a housing finance crisis, were being openly discussed in 2003, and John Corzine (D-NJ) proposed legislation to put Fannie Mae and Freddie Mac under the supervision of the U.S. Treasury department as part of a new agency, to be responsive to direction from the Secretary of the Treasury—an agency that would be authorized and directed to regulate and supervise Fannie and Freddie as though they were insured banks. This would have included raising their capital requirements to levels currently deemed adequate for insured banks, and limiting their activities outside the secondary mortgage market. Unfortunately, Senate Bill 1508, written for the creation of a "Federal Enterprise Regulatory Reform Act of 2003," failed to gain enough support to pass. Ironically, it was opposed by Congressman Barney Frank, the ranking member of the Financial Services Committee, who described Fannie Mae and Freddie Mac as "not facing any kind of financial crisis."[4] A similar bill of the same name was introduced by Senator Chuck Hagel (R-NE) in 2005 with the support of such powerful co-sponsors as Senators Elizabeth Dole, John McCain, and John Sununu, but it too failed to pass.

Freddie Mac acquires its loans through purchases from its approved seller/servicers. While these have been mostly savings associations, the right to do business with Freddie Mac is open to any loan originator meeting its qualifications. However, as a part of the savings association system, its policies are more suitable for loan originators who hold deposit assets. Most of its purchases are conventional loans that must carry private mortgage insurance unless there is a 20% or more down payment. Freddie Mac may also acquire FHA and VA loans, but almost all of these loans are now handled through Ginnie Mae.

Even though Freddie Mac earns most of its money from fees charged for underwriting blocks of mortgage loans, it still holds a relatively small amount of mortgage loans in its own portfolio earning interest. On September 30, 2010, its loan portfolio amounted to a little over $302 billion, while its mortgage-backed securities programs amounted to $2.192 trillion, totaling a market share of 21% of all residential mortgage loans. This figure represents an increase from a 12% and 16% market share in 1989 and 1998, respectively.

Federal National Mortgage Association (Fannie Mae)

The oldest participant in the secondary mortgage loan market is Fannie Mae. Fannie Mae began its life in 1938 as a government agency responsible for purchasing only FHA loans. At that time, Congress correctly anticipated a rejection of the newly formed FHA-insured loan program by regulated lenders. The solution was to create another method of

---

[4]Stephen Labaton, "New Agency Proposed to Oversee Freddie Mac and Fannie Mae," *The New York Times*, September 11, 2003.

funding loans through their sale to secondary-market investors. Since this market was close to nonexistent in those days, Fannie Mae was established as a part of the original Act creating the FHA for the purpose of purchasing FHA loans. Later, Fannie Mae was authorized to also buy VA loans.

In those early days, the loan originators willing to work with FHA loans were mostly mortgage companies. They were able to fund these loans through sale to Fannie Mae, thus bypassing depository institutions. Ever since, Fannie Mae has worked closely with mortgage companies by providing forward loan commitments that give good assurance of funding.

In 1968, Fannie Mae was converted from a government agency to a federally chartered private corporation with its stock listed on the New York Stock Exchange. However, through its federal charter, it retains close ties to the United States government. For example, five of its 18 directors are appointed by the president of the United States, and it can borrow up to $225 billion from the U.S. Treasury. Fannie Mae is subject to an oversight committee under HUD, as is Freddie Mac, and its policies must conform to government requirements. After becoming a private corporation in 1968, Fannie Mae expanded its loan purchases from FHA and VA loans to include the much larger market for conventional loans.

Fannie Mae has long followed the policy of selling short-term securities, mostly debenture bonds, and using the proceeds to buy loans for its own portfolio. Its profits have come from the difference between what it paid its bondholders and what it earned on its mortgage loan portfolio. When this margin began to dry up in the early 1980s, Fannie Mae shifted to selling services for fees. In 1982, it undertook the guarantee of mortgage-backed securities for its seller/servicers. The guarantee is an "agency" guarantee, like Freddie Mac's. In addition, Fannie Mae began assembling its own blocks of mortgage loans to use as collateral for other mortgage-backed securities.

As of 1992, Fannie Mae was overseen by the Office of Federal Housing Enterprise Oversight (OFHEO), and the Federal Housing Enterprises Financial Safety and Soundness Act of 1992 (FHEFSSA). These entities were created to reduce the risk of failure of government-sponsored enterprises (GSEs) like Ginnie Mae, Fannie Mae, and Freddie Mac. The OFHEO used to issue regulations necessary to carrying out its function and purpose, examine and set risk-based capital levels for the GSEs, and initiate administrative and enforcement actions. These agencies proved to be less than effective, however,[5] and the Federal Housing Finance Agency (FHFA) was created on July 30, 2008, when President George W. Bush signed into law the Housing and Economic Recovery Act of 2008. The Act created a regulator with the authority necessary to oversee vital components of the United States secondary mortgage markets: Fannie Mae, Freddie Mac, and the federal home loan banks. In addition, this law combined the staffs of the Office of Federal Housing Enterprise Oversight (OFHEO), the Federal Housing Finance Board (FHFB), and the GSE mission office at the Department of Housing and Urban Development (HUD). With the very turbulent market facing the world, strengthening the regulatory and supervisory oversight of the 14 housing-related GSEs seemed imperative. The establishment of FHFA will hopefully promote a stronger, safer U.S. housing finance system. Fannie Mae is currently in conservatorship and under the oversight of the Federal Housing Finance Agency, and consequently not able to fully function independently, meaning it cannot fund loans or issue securities without intervention and support from the Federal Reserve Bank. In a very few years, Fannie Mae's MBS programs had exceeded its portfolio of loans. As of the 3rd quarter 2014, its loan portfolio and mortgage-backed securities programs amounted to $2.86 trillion, totaling a market share of 29% of all residential mortgage loans. This figure represents an increase from a 17% and 4% market share in 2000 and 2010, respectively. Considering the importance of these GSEs on the U.S. economy and mortgage market, it is clear that an intensified focus must be placed on the oversight of Fannie Mae, Freddie Mac, and the federal home loan banks.

As of early 2015, there was still no final resolution of the conservatorship. Fannie Mae is still under the oversight of the FHFA, and how Fannie Mae might emerge from conservatorship has yet to be determined. This situation is still no closer to resolution than it was five years ago. Fannie Mae continues to be highly leveraged with a Leverage Ratio MRQ in March 2018 of 853.34[6] compared to JP Morgan Chase's Leverage Ratio

---

[5] Edward Paisley, "The McCain Blame Game Misfires," ThinkProgress.org, September 19, 2008, accessed December 28, 2014, http://thinkprogress.org/economy/2008/09/19/172363/mccain-blame-game/

[6] "Federal National Mortgage Association Fannie Mae's Leverage Ratio," CSI Market, 2018, https://csimarket.com/stocks/singleFinancialStrength.php?code=fnma&Le=1&image.x=11&image.y=15&image=go

MRQ on the same date of 9.19, which means that Fannie Mae most likely will not survive a market to market test in a rising interest rate market nor in any future slight downturn in the residential real estate market. This reality, and the recent setbacks to shareholder claims to recent "profits" being struck down in the U.S. Supreme Court, has more firmly left Fannie Mae in a limbo status of a federal ward of the state.

Federal Agricultural Mortgage Corporation (Farmer Mac)

To expand the source of funds for farm lenders, Congress passed the Agricultural Credit Act of 1987, creating the Federal Agricultural Mortgage Corporation under the supervision of the Farm Credit Administration. Farmer Mac was created by Congress to improve the ability of agricultural lenders to provide credit to America's farmers and ranchers as well as rural homeowners, businesses, and communities. Its initial capitalization was through a $20 million subscription sale of common stock sold primarily to financial institutions that deal in agricultural loans. Farmer Mac, as it has become known, was originally patterned after Ginnie Mae as an underwriting agency for pools of farm loans. Farmer Mac could not purchase loans; rather, it granted approval for loan poolers and the loans that were permitted in its pools.

Farmer Mac originally had other restrictions. For instance, it could provide only a 90% guarantee for the timely repayment of its mortgage-backed securities. The other agencies could guarantee 100%. Furthermore, its securities had to pass requirements of the Securities and Exchange Commission, which the other agencies did not, and poolers were required to establish a 10% reserve for each pool. These restrictions impeded the credit enhancement for agricultural loans. Another factor that hampered its growth was a substantially improving farm economy in the late 1980s, which did not need as much help with credit.

Limitations on Farmer Mac changed with Public Law 104-105, signed by President Clinton on February 10, 1996. Farmer Mac was thereby granted about the same powers as Fannie Mae and Freddie Mac. It can now purchase agricultural loans directly from originators and can issue its own 100% guaranteed, mortgage-backed securities based on its loan pools.

A *qualified agricultural real estate loan* is defined as one secured by land or structures that are used for the production of one or more agricultural commodities. In general, individual loans may not exceed

$2.5 million—a measure intended to preserve smaller, family-run farms. Loan pools may also consist of *rural housing loans*. Such loans are defined as those made to finance single-family residential dwellings in rural areas and communities with populations of no more than 2,500.

Farmer Mac did not issue its first guarantee certificates until 1992. These took the form of a $233 million package of securities collateralized by agricultural loans that was originated by Travelers Insurance Company. Since the law passed in 1996, Farmer Mac has become America's secondary market for first-mortgage agricultural real estate loans, primarily by purchasing qualified loans from lenders, thereby replenishing its source of funds to make new loans. Farmer Mac funds its loan purchases by issuing debt or securities backed by pools of loans and selling them into the capital markets. In so doing, Farmer Mac facilitates the flow of lendable money from Wall Street to rural America, thus providing a stable supply of mortgage credit to lenders and borrowers. It has used three secondary funding programs to accomplish its mission. These are as follows:

- **The Farmer Mac I Program,** whereby Farmer Mac purchases qualified loans from lenders who are approved sellers, replenishing its source of funds to make new loans. Farmer Mac meets lenders' unique needs through structures that shift the credit risk to Farmer Mac, while leaving the loans with the originating institution.

- **The Farmer Mac II Program,** whereby Farmer Mac provides secondary-market funding to support USDA-guaranteed loans. Through Farmer Mac II, lenders sell the guaranteed portions of USDA loans directly to Farmer Mac. Farmer Mac buys the guaranteed portions at attractive rates, allowing agricultural lenders to increase profits and provide better services to their borrowers and communities.

- **The Farmer Mac III Program,** which offers the option of combining both Farmer Mac I and II by purchasing first-lien mortgage loans that are senior to loans guaranteed via state or federal programs. Farmer Mac's greater powers granted in 2008 have not had sufficient time for analysts to be able to judge whether Farmer Mac III's new limits impact the farm credit markets.

By December 31, 2017, Farmer Mac held $6.9 billion in securitizations as investments and over $19.7 billion in outstanding securitizations.

Where Are We Now?

What You Should Know About GSEs

A government-sponsored enterprise (GSE) is:

- a financial services corporation created by the United States Congress;

- used to enhance the flow of credit to targeted sectors of the economy and make those segments of the capital market more efficient and transparent; and

- used to enhance the availability and reduce the cost of credit to the targeted borrowing sectors (agriculture, home finance, and education).

The following are the major GSEs:

- Federal Farm Credit Banks (FCBanks) (1916)

- the 12 Federal Home Loan Banks (FHLBanks) (1932)

- Federal National Mortgage Association (Fannie Mae) (1938–2008*)

- Government National Mortgage Association (Ginnie Mae) (1968)

- Federal Home Loan Mortgage Corporation (Freddie Mac) (1970–2008*)

- Student Loan Marketing Association (Sallie Mae) (1972–2004**)

- Federal Agricultural Mortgage Corporation (Farmer Mac) (1987)

- Financing Corporation (FICO) (1987)

- Resolution Funding Corporation (REFCORP) (1989)

- National Veteran Business Development Corporation (1999)

*Taken over by the federal government in 2008.
**Privatized in 2004; no longer a GSE.

LOAN POOLS

Assembling a block of loans into a loan pool can be arranged by a number of different types of companies: investment bankers, commercial banks, finance companies, large real estate brokerages, Fannie Mae, Freddie Mac, and even homebuilders. Loan pools serve as the collateral for a class of securities generally identified as mortgage-backed securities. Three of the federal underwriters—Fannie Mae, Freddie Mac, and Farmer Mac—serve a dual function. They may form their own pools and issue guarantee certificates for themselves, or they may approve pools assembled by others and issue guarantees covering other pools. Either way, the guarantee enables those who pool loans to sell the securities more readily and at slightly lower interest rates. The guarantee, of course, provides credit enhancement that reduces the risk of the security.

However, not all loan pools are guaranteed by a federal agency, nor are all mortgage loans assigned to pools. Many mortgage loans are held by individual investors and by institutions as part of their portfolios. Some pools that are not federally underwritten are assembled by large financial institutions that issue their own mortgage-backed securities collateralized by their pools. This is particularly true of jumbo residential loans (those that exceed conforming loan limits), nonconforming residential mortgages referred to as Alternate A or *subprime mortgages*, and some limited types of commercial loans. Such securities are sold on the strength of the issuing institution and are generally not guaranteed. These securities have often been issued by **private mortgage conduits** that have emerged in a new loan origination model referred to as the **originate-to-distribute model**. In the originate-to-distribute model, the originator of the loan often does not have the incentive to act fully in the interest of the ultimate holder of the loan (in most cases, a REMIC, CMO, RMBS, or CDO). Often the banks, mortgage companies, and other financial firms embraced the originate-to-distribute model when the development of securities products allowed them to escape any significant retained exposure to losses for loans they originated; it had the added bonus of allowing them to eliminate the expense of keeping the employees specialized in loan workouts who could properly deal with creditor discussions with mortgagees. As a result, nearly all delinquent mortgage workout responsibilities went to those firms specializing in mortgage loan servicing. Since there was insufficient staffing of mortgage workout specialists when the mortgage crisis broke, there was a lack of sufficiently trained mortgage workout specialists available to deal with the sheer volume of delinquencies. Studies by the Federal Reserve, mortgage trade groups, and academics have shown that it takes not months but years to adequately train a mortgage workout specialist. This fact alone explains a great deal about the recent problems that financial institutions are encountering as they attempt to deal with the volume of delinquent mortgages. Loan originators had every incentive to maintain origination volume because that would allow them to earn substantial fees while not retaining any ownership interests in the mortgage itself. Once these types of loans were accepted by the market, many originators had to face the moral hazard of no or weak incentives to maintain loan underwriting quality. The sheer volume of these issues in 2005 and 2006—$1.2 trillion of subprime alone[7]—and the importance of the profits that they created not only for the originate-to-distribute lenders but for the investment banking firms, led to an overheated expansion of the subprime mortgage market. Later in this chapter, we will discuss the structure of CMOs and CDOs, and the moral hazards of the originate-to-distribute model will become clearer.

Assembling a Loan Pool

A pool can be assembled by two different methods: One is to acquire the loans first; the other is to first sell the securities that provide cash for the purchase of loans. If the chosen method is to acquire the loans first, this may be accomplished through either outright purchase or by internal origination of the loans. For example, the purchasing of loans from loan originators throughout the country may be handled by an investment banker, such as Credit Suisse Securities LLC. Alternatively, a commercial bank such as Bank of America or JPMorgan Chase may generate its own block of loans through its retail branch offices.

The other method of assembling a loan pool is to first sell securities, and then use the proceeds of the sale to purchase those mortgage loans that meet the requirements of the issuer of the securities. This method is most commonly implemented through the sale of tax-exempt bonds. It is often used by states and municipalities to fund various housing agency programs for low- and moderate-income families.

---

[7]Joint Economic Committee, *The 2007 Mortgage Market Statistical Annual* (Bethesda, MD: Inside Mortgage Finance Publications, 2007).

If the origin of the pool is not by one of the federal underwriters but is to be so underwritten if the originator would want to later sell or securitize them, the assembled loans must comply with that federal underwriter's requirements. Once underwriting approval is obtained, a fee is paid to the federal agency underwriter for the guarantee certificate. With the underwritten loan pool serving as collateral, a series of securities can be issued and sold to investors throughout the world, thus recovering the initial investment made in acquiring the loans.

Following is a more detailed explanation of the two methods. First, we will examine the tax-exempt bond procedure that raises money before the loans are acquired. Then we will review the alternative method, which consists of assembling a pool of loans first and then issuing mortgage-backed securities. Finally, we will cover some of the variations in mortgage-backed securities.

TAX-EXEMPT BONDS

The most effective way of bringing lower-cost money into the mortgage market has been through the sale of **tax-exempt bonds**. A tax-exempt bond is a type of security sold by states and municipalities paying interest that is not subject to federal income taxes. The federal government does not tax states or municipalities. Whether or not this freedom from taxation should extend to funds used to assist an individual purchasing a house, or for entrepreneurial industrial development, has been a question debated for many years. However, the procedure has proven beneficial to home buyers and other community development projects, so it carries substantial political support.

Approval by Congress allowing the tax exemption for private use of municipal bonds was made permanent on August 10, 1993. However, since any claim of tax exemption falls under the scrutiny of the U.S. Treasury and its IRS arm, some qualifying requirements have been issued. For instance, properties financed with tax-exempt bond money may be subject to a recapture tax if sold during the early years of ownership. Almost every year, changes have been made in what states and municipalities may do in qualifying tax-exempt issues when the proceeds are used to make mortgage loans. Generally, the total of such issues is limited by an allocation of dollar amounts to each state.

"Bond money" is available to consumers at lower cost because the associated tax savings are generally passed on to the borrower. People in upper tax brackets are generally the ones attracted to tax-exempt bonds because they can benefit from a lower interest rate not subject to income taxes. For example, a corporate bond paying a 10% rate subject to tax would yield only about a 6.1% return to a taxpayer if he or she is in the 39.6% tax bracket.[8] Thus, a tax-exempt bond yielding an investor 6.1% would be roughly an equivalent return to the investor and of substantial benefit to the home buyer.

Almost all states and many municipalities have entered this market to raise lower-cost money through the sale of various kinds of securities. In some cases, the money raised from the sale is used to buy mortgage loans from approved lenders within the state or community. Thus, tax-exempt bond money becomes another source of secondary-market funding. In some cases, however, housing authorities use this money to make direct loans to qualified borrowers. Almost always, there is an upper-income limitation for home buyers so as to direct the money primarily to lower- and middle-income families.

Another use of tax-exempt bonds is in financing industrial development projects. Sometimes a single developer may be the beneficiary of the low-cost money, or the money may be used to finance a project open to any qualified commercial development. The basic purpose of these bond issues is to attract business to a community or state, thus increasing available jobs and the tax base.

MORTGAGE-BACKED SECURITIES (MBS)

The growth of the secondary market indicates the success that lenders and investors have had in developing practical procedures and uniform instruments for mortgage loans. Yet, as investments, mortgage loans carry certain problems, such as the need for long-term supervision of each individual loan and an uncertain return caused by unpredictable prepayments. Furthermore, most major investors are more comfortable dealing in securities, a type of investment that can be bought and sold with greater ease than mortgage loans. By packaging a block of mortgage loans to be held as collateral for an issue of securities, mortgage loans are in effect converted to securities and become more acceptable to investors.

---

[8]A simple formula to determine comparative yields for investors is as follows: Divide the municipal bond rate offered by the result of 100% less the taxpayer's tax bracket. The result is the yield equivalent for an investment subject to tax. For example, consider a municipal bond offering 7% for a taxpayer in the 39.6% tax bracket. Seven divided by .6040 equals 11.59%, the equivalent taxable yield.

While both Freddie Mac and Ginnie Mae have offered mortgage-backed securities since the early 1970s, it has only been since the early 1980s that other institutions and companies began entering this field. One reason for the surge of activity in mortgage-backed securities was the losses sustained by traditional mortgage lenders beginning in the late 1970s as interest rates escalated. Holding long-term, fixed-rate investments inevitably lost some of its appeal. Another reason was the climb in mortgage interest rates to levels of or above other long-term investments, particularly government bonds. The higher rates proved attractive to investors and allowed those packaging the blocks of mortgages a profitable margin for their work. Securities are a far more attractive investment vehicle than mortgage loans in the big financial markets. The new originate-to-distribute model discussed earlier allowed the shift of risk to the investor in a way not available in earlier periods of the development of more sophisticated mortgage-backed securities products. In 2001, subprime mortgage originations represented only 8.6% of total mortgage originations, and only 50% of that volume ended in securitized debt obligations with full risk transfer to the investor. By 2006, however, subprime mortgage origination had grown to 20.1% of total mortgage originations, with over 80% of that volume ending up in full transference of risk through subprime mortgage securitization. The shift to the securities market to raise mortgage money proved to be a more than adequate replacement for the loss of passbook savings money, but at a somewhat initial higher cost. As the market expanded, competition reduced the interest rates charged so that it became a cost-saving method for home buyers. In the growth of securities as a source of funding, a number of variations have developed. Two of the most popular types are mortgage pass-throughs and collateralized mortgage obligations (CMOs), as described in the following section.

Mortgage Pass-Through

The original concept of a mortgage-backed security was to assemble a diversified block of mortgage loans—generally identified as a "pool" of loans—and then issue a series of securities collateralized by that block of loans. The issuer of the securities may or may not guarantee them. If the securities are issued by a private institution or company, they are seldom guaranteed, and they are more difficult to sell. As the popularity of a government agency underwriter dominated the market, the guarantee certificate became the security that is sold.

At first, the purpose behind this strategy was to simply pass on the risk of a fluctuating interest rate to other investors more familiar with the risks involved. The income derived from the underlying block of loans in pro rata shares was simply passed on to the security holders. If a loan was paid off prematurely, the additional principal was passed through to the security holder, thus repaying a portion of the principal itself. If interest rates increased, the payments on the underlying block of loans remained unaffected. In such an instance, security holders would suffer a loss of value in the security, but that was a risk they understood.

The **pass-through** type of payment created some uncertainty in its cash flows and thus in the true yield on the investment itself. To overcome this inherent problem, the financial market issuers of these securities developed an alternative method of handling cash flows to investors. This method was the collateralized mortgage obligation.

Collateralized Mortgage Obligations

Another variation on the mortgage-backed security is the **collateralized mortgage obligation (CMO)**. The first CMO was issued by the Federal Home Loan Mortgage Corporation in June 1983. It has several advantages over the mortgage pass-throughs that are attractive to traditional investors in corporate-type bonds. By early 1986, securities dealers (investment bankers), home builders, mortgage bankers, thrift institutions, commercial banks, and insurance companies had also begun issuing CMOs.

Differences between CMOs and Mortgage Pass-Throughs

The innovation of the CMO structure lies in its segmentation of the mortgage cash flows. The older pass-through type of mortgage-backed security offers its holders an irregular cash flow since it includes the repayment of principal whenever a home buyer prepays a loan or refinances to achieve a lower interest rate. This happens because holders of mortgage pass-throughs own undivided interest in a pool of mortgages. Whatever the particular pool of mortgages produces in principal payments and interest is then passed directly through to the security holders.

In contrast to this procedure, the CMO investor owns bonds that are collateralized by a pool of mortgages or by a portfolio of mortgage-backed securities. The variability and unpredictability of the underlying cash flows remain, but since the CMO substitutes a sequential

STRUCTURE OF COLLATERALIZED DEBT OBLIGATION

Source: © 2021 Mbition LLC

distribution process instead of the pass-through's pro rata distribution of these cash flows, the stream of payments received by the CMO bondholder differs dramatically from that of the holder of a pass-through security.

Structure of a CMO

The CMO structure creates a series of bonds with varying maturities that appeal to a wider range of investors than do mortgage pass-throughs. While all CMOs follow the same basic structure, significant variations have developed in how their segmentation is set up. Both CMOs and **collateralized debt obligations (CDOs)**, which may have other asset classes beyond single-family residential mortgages (such as credit card receivables, automobile loans, and second mortgages), have followed the basic pattern outlined below in order to attract different investors who have varying risk, liquidity, and interest earning objectives.

1. Several classes of bonds are issued against a pool of mortgage collateral or other collateral in the case of a CDO. The most common CMO structure contains four classes of bonds. The first three pay

interest at their stated rates from date of issue; the final one is usually an accrual-class bond.

2. The cash flows from the underlying mortgages or other collateral in the case of a CDO are applied first to pay interest and then to retire bonds.

3. The classes of bonds are retired sequentially. All principal payments are directed first to the shortest-maturity Class A bonds. When these bonds are completely retired, all principal payments are then directed to the next shortest-maturity bonds—the B class. This process continues until all the classes of bonds have been paid off.

One of the attractions of CMOs for investors is that some of the bonds offer shorter maturities. Many investors prefer to make short-term investments. For the issuers of the securities, tapping the short-term money market means they can pay a lower interest rate for the money used to buy mortgage loans, thus increasing the margin that can be earned in such a transaction. Short-term money almost always receives lower interest rates than long-term money.

The first-priority Class A bonds may offer maturities as short as two years. Class B and C bonds may offer maturities from four to 10 years. The interest rate offered on these bonds is usually measured against U.S. Treasury securities of similar maturities, only at a slightly higher rate to attract investors. Following is a general description of the basic bond classes.[9]

Class A Bonds

The shortest-maturity class of bonds receives all principal payments and any prepayments from the entire pool of mortgage collateral until the entire Class A issue is paid off. Holders of Class A bonds begin to receive significant principal payments from the first payment date.

Class B and C Bonds

The intermediate classes receive only interest payments until each of the prior bond classes has been retired. The interest payment is a known, fixed amount, but the principal repayment will depend on how quickly the mortgage collateral—or other collateral in the case of a CDO—pays down.

---

[9] In the financial community, these bond classes are also identified as "tranches," as in first tranche, second tranche, and so on. *Tranche* is the French world for "slice."

Class Z Bonds

Class Z bondholders receive no principal or interest payments until all earlier classes have been retired. However, the interest earned by the Class Z bond is added to the principal balance (compounded), accruing additional interest. During this accrual period, the cash that would otherwise be used to pay interest on the Z bonds is used to accelerate the retirement of the shorter maturity classes. When all the earlier classes are retired, the accrual period ends, and principal and interest payments to Z bondholders commence.

The purpose of CMOs was to broaden the market for mortgage-backed securities and thus assure a sufficient flow of capital into the mortgage market. They attract investors by offering higher returns than Treasury securities of similar maturities, albeit with a greater risk. This kind of financing—that is, a variety of mortgage-backed securities deriving income from huge, multimillion-dollar pools of loans—became practical with the advent of high-grade computer technology. The process simply would not be possible without recent advances in investor accounting software, telecommunications, and other computer capabilities.

REAL ESTATE MORTGAGE INVESTMENT CONDUITS (REMICs)

Tax liabilities of the various handlers and holders of mortgage-backed securities created some confusion. For instance, does the issuer of a mortgage-backed security owe income taxes on the interest income that is passed through to a security holder? To clarify the situation and avoid double taxation that might diminish the availability of mortgage money, Congress approved the **Real Estate Mortgage Investment Conduit** concept in 1986. A REMIC is a tax device that allows cash flows from an underlying block of mortgages to be passed through to security holders without being subject to income taxes at that level. Thus, the interest income is taxed only to the security holder, not to the trustee or agent handling the pass-through of cash. Various requirements must be met to establish a REMIC, and reports on its activities, which are handled by the issuer of the security involved, must be made to the IRS. As a result, most residential mortgage-backed securities adopt either the pass-through or REMIC status, and by default most CMOs are generally structured for tax purposes as REMICs. Effective January 1, 2005, Sections 860A and 860O of the IRS regulations allow REMICs to buy interest in reverse mortgages as well.

Where Are We Now?

Commercial Mortgage-Backed Securities

Commercial mortgage-backed securities (CMBS) are a type of mortgage-backed security that is secured by the loan on a commercial property. CMBS can provide liquidity to real estate investors and to commercial lenders. As with other types of MBS, the increased use of CMBS can be attributable to the rapid rise in real estate prices over the years.

CMBS are usually issued in tranches where several classes of bonds are issued against a pool of commercial mortgage collateral. The most common CMBS structure contains multiple classes of bonds. The first classes will pay interest at their stated rates from date of issue; the final one is often an accrual-class bond. The cash flows from the underlying commercial real estate mortgages that serve as collateral are applied first to pay interest and then to retire bonds. Ultimately the classes or tranches of CMBS securities are retired sequentially. All principal payments are directed first to the shortest-maturity Class A bonds. When these bonds are completely retired, all principal payments are then directed to the next shortest-maturity bonds—the B class. This process continues until all the classes of bonds have been paid off. Investors typically like this type of structure as the tax benefits of a CMBS are generally structured like REMICs so that the interest is passed through without taxation at the security; rather, it is passed to the security holder.

CMBS have less prepayment risks and often contain lockout provisions after which they can be subject to "defeasance, yield maintenance, and prepayment penalties to protect bondholders."[10]

---

[10] Frank J. Fabozzi, *Bond Markets, Analysis, and Strategies* (Upper Saddle River, NJ: Prentice Hall, 2011), 311.

Questions for Discussion

1. Without a national mortgage exchange, how are mortgages traded in the United States?
2. Explain the relationship between the price and the yield on a mortgage loan.
3. Define the term "point" and explain how it is used, and list the different charges that can be quoted in points.
4. What market does Freddie Mac serve, and how does it raise money for the purchase of mortgage loans?
5. How can tax-exempt bonds offer lower-cost mortgage money and how is this money generally used?
6. Explain the two basic kinds of mortgage pools used to back securities and the two different methods used to generate the securities.
7. Describe the impact of the originate-to-distribute model on the growth of the subprime mortgage market.
8. Explain the differences between a CMO and a mortgage pass-through type of security.
9. Define a mortgage purchase "for portfolio."
10. Discuss the purpose and operation of Ginnie Mae.
11. What would be the price of a $100,000 loan if discounted by three points?

Multiple Choice Questions for Review

1. Which of the following is not one of the most common options available to mortgage lenders for the placement of mortgage loans they have originated?
   a. selling to GSEs like FNMA
   b. selling whole loans to pension funds
   c. selling parts of loans to consumers in a local area
   d. directly issuing mortgage-backed securities (MBS)

2. Which of the following three GSEs facilitate the workings of the secondary mortgage market by providing a network for the purchase, sale, and guarantee of existing mortgages and mortgage pools?
   a. GNMA, FmHA, and FHLMC
   b. FNMA, GNMA, and FHLMC
   c. FHLMC, FNMA, and VA
   d. FHA, FNMA, and GNMA

3. In the language of mortgage lending, the term "point" or "points" can best be described as which of the following?
   a. credit scoring system used to determine loan risk
   b. a reference system used in collateralized debt obligations
   c. the tax-deductible financing costs of a residential mortgage loan
   d. a loan fee that is illegal under the Truth-in-Lending Act

4. Which of the following is NOT one of the reasons that tax-exempt bond-supported financing of residential mortgages developed?
   a. The tax-exempt status from federal income taxes allows participating lenders to offer lower interest rates generally than the conventional mortgage market.
   b. State and federal support already existed for first-time and moderate-income borrowers.
   c. It provides a way to make direct loans to lower income families.
   d. Such financing has typically been easier to issue than conventional MBS.

5. Freddie Mac and Fannie Mae are regulated by:
   a. OFHEO
   b. HUD
   c. FHLB
   d. FHFA

6. The originate-to-distribute model of residential mortgage loan production has allowed originators to make loans without much consideration of risk of loss, creating a moral hazard revealed in the recent mortgage crisis. It was primarily driven by the development of which of the following secondary market tools?
   a. Ginnie Mae MBS
   b. private mortgage conduits
   c. Freddie Mac participation certificates
   d. Real Estate Investment Trust bonds

7. Which of the following are debt instruments that are issued using a pool of mortgages for security?
   a. commercial mortgage-backed bonds
   b. mortgage pass-through bonds
   c. collateralized mortgage obligations
   d. PO strip securities

8. Which of the following is NOT true regarding the purpose and operations of Ginnie Mae?
   a. It will commit to purchasing pools of FHA, VA, RHS, and state-authorized mortgage loans as part of its MBS commitments.
   b. It will implement special assistance for housing as may be required by Congress or the president.
   c. It issues guarantee certificates, which are backed by specific loan pools.
   d. It issues commitments backed by the full faith and credit of the United States.

9. A lender that is making mortgage loans for its own investment is often referred to as a:
   a. good lender
   b. originating lender
   c. portfolio lender
   d. residential lender

10. Real Estate Mortgage Investment Conduits have a unique structure that allows them to pass on untaxed income to investors, and typically use which of the following securitization types?
    a. participation certificates
    b. Fannie Mae bonds
    c. collateralized mortgage obligations
    d. Ginnie Mae II MBS

Information Resources

https://www.efanniemae.com/sf/formsdocs/forms/
Examples of the most current uniform documents can be found at this Fannie Mae-supported site.

http://www.investinginbonds.com/
The Securities Industry and Financial Markets Association has information about investing in bonds with specific links to the various securities that were introduced in this chapter on real estate finance.

http://www.intex.com/main/
This website is an excellent source of structured fixed-income cash flow models and related analytical software, along with a complete library of RMBS, ABS, CMBS, CDO, CLN, and covered bond deal models, created and maintained for accurate cash flow projections and price/yield analytics. It is maintained by Intex Solutions, Inc.

Chapter 5

SOURCES OF FUNDS

KEY TERMS AND PHRASES

application fee
bond
commercial paper
conduit
credit unions
Fraud Enforcement & Recovery Act of 2009 (FERA)
forward commitment
immediate commitment
life insurance companies
loan servicing
mortgage-backed securities
mortgage banker
mortgage broker
mortgage debt outstanding
Mortgage Disclosure Improvement Act of 2008 (MDIA)
mortgage loan originators (MLOs)
National Mortgage Licensing System (NMLS)
origination fee
pooler
Real Estate Investment Trusts (REITs)
SAFE Mortgage Licensing Act of 2008
servicing fee
yield spread premium

LEARNING OBJECTIVES

At the conclusion of this chapter, students will be able to:
- Understand the unique relationship of the mortgage companies and mortgage brokers to the real estate finance industry.
- Describe the purposes of a mortgage bank and how they differ from those of a mortgage broker.
- Understand the licensing and registration requirements for those engaged in making residential mortgage loans.
- Explain the basics of the various methods of funding mortgage-lending activities.
- Describe the principal source of income for mortgage lenders.
- Understand the role of the various government loan programs for the direct financing of real estate.
- Describe the other primary sources of real estate mortgage financing.

COMMERCIAL BANKS

The original purpose of U.S. commercial banks was to serve the business community and government. They were expected to provide the services of checking accounts, including the transfer of money, and the protection available in a depository institution.

Initially, states chartered their own banks and, prior to the Civil War, granted commercial banks the authority to issue their own currency. It was not until the passage of the National Bank Act in 1863 that issuance of currency was placed under the control of the federal government. The National Bank Act also authorized federally chartered banks to be organized under the regulatory authority of the Comptroller of the Currency. Interestingly, later amendments to this law prohibited national banks from making real estate loans, a restriction that was rescinded in 1913.

The creation of the Federal Reserve Bank (the Fed) in 1913 brought nationally chartered banks under the credit regulations of the Fed and established terms of cooperation between them. The Act establishing the Fed also allowed national banks to make real estate loans within certain specified limits. The regulatory authority over commercial banks is a separate system from those regulating savings associations and is also a dual system, with both federal and state governments issuing charters and regulations. In an effort to reduce conflicts between overlapping authorities, FIRREA placed all depository institutions that carry federal deposit insurance under federal regulation.

Limits on Real Estate Loans

In 1991, Congress passed the Federal Deposit Insurance Corporation Improvement Act, which, among other things, required the four federal banking regulators (Federal Reserve Bank System, FDIC, the Office of Thrift Supervision and the OCC) to establish limits for various categories of real estate loans. It should be noted that in 1980, the Bank Deregulation Act had eliminated loan-to-value limits for real estate loans that had been in place since the Depression years. The limits that became effective in March 1993 are as follows:

- There is no ceiling on one- to four-family property loans except that loans over 80% of the market value of the collateral must have private mortgage insurance.
- Certain loans are exempt from limits, such as those guaranteed by the federal government; a problem loan that must be renewed, refinanced, or restructured; and loans to facilitate the sale of foreclosed properties.
- Other limits are:

Loan Category	Loan-to-Value
Improved property	85%
One- to four-family construction	85%
Nonresidential construction	80%
Land development	75%
Raw land	65%

Note: A loan-to-value limit has not been established for permanent mortgage or home equity loans on owner-occupied, one- to four-family residential property. However, for any such loan with a loan-to-value ratio that equals or exceeds 90% at origination, an institution should require appropriate credit enhancement in the form of either mortgage insurance or readily marketable collateral.

The National Credit Union Administration, which administers the National Credit Union Insurance Fund, has joined in requiring the same loan-to-value limits for its credit unions.

Lending Policies

Because of the business orientation of commercial banks, the banks' lending policies have favored short-term loans for specific business purposes. These institutions have not been very active in the long-term home loan market.

Some only make mortgage loans through subsidiary mortgage companies, in part because substantial shares of a commercial bank's deposits are demand-type (checking accounts), and banks are limited in allowing such money to fund long-term loans. Growth in secondary mortgage market funding through the sale of mortgage-backed securities is changing this policy, however. The ability of large commercial banks to originate long-term residential loans and then fund them through the sale of securities is opening a new market that does not commit the banks' own deposit assets. Loan origination expands the use of a bank's credit expertise and provides additional income from origination charges and servicing fees.

Certain kinds of shorter-term mortgage loans (less than the older, 30-year standard term) are more suited to commercial banks, as are lines of credit for mortgage companies and construction loans. In addition, commercial banks may handle some medium-term mortgage loans as needed by their business customers. The four kinds of lending activities that can be found in a commercial bank's mortgage operations are as follows:

- **direct loans,** which are mortgage loans made for medium terms, such as 10 to 15 years, for good commercial customers;
- **construction loans** (The shorter-term, two- to three-year construction loans are attractive to banks due to higher returns. Larger banks are better able to employ the specialized talent necessary to monitor the disbursement of funds as construction progresses.);
- **warehouse lines of credit** (A warehouse line of credit is a short-term revolving line of credit secured by recently closed residential real estate loans that allows mortgage bankers to fund loans in their own names. This funding source, also known as the warehouse lender or bank, generally offers the necessary funds through a revolving purchase agreement to a mortgage banking company for funding mortgages at closing. The warehouse lender will want to see that these loans have been pre-sold or covered by a commitment agreement in the secondary market to large institutional investors, and that they are maintained on the warehouse line until they are purchased by the investor. Warehouse line funding usually covers an approximately 15- to 30-day period between loan closing and the sale of the loans to the institutional investor. Some credit lines can run as long as six to 12 months when dealing with some of the special commitments that Freddie Mac offers.); and
- **loan origination.** (Origination of home loans is a growing activity for commercial banks. Banks can initially fund these loans with their own

deposit assets and then sell them to secondary-market investors. Another path open to the larger banks is to create their own loan pools that then serve as collateral for the private issuance of mortgage-backed securities. These securities are not underwritten by the federal government.)

Regulation of Commercial Banks

Commercial banks can be chartered either by states or by the federal government. National charters (these are not called "federal charters" when commercial banks are involved) are issued by the Comptroller of the Currency, part of the U.S. Treasury Department. National charters must belong to the Federal Deposit Insurance Corporation (FDIC) and carry deposit insurance to protect depositors. State-chartered banks may join the FDIC system if they meet the necessary qualifications and accept such federal regulations as may apply; otherwise, they will not be granted a charter.

Commercial banks are responsible to an additional regulatory body. Besides the chartering agency and the deposit-insuring agency that normally provide regulation and periodic examination, commercial banks come under the jurisdiction of the Federal Reserve Bank Board as regards their credit policies. The Federal Reserve Bank is also responsible for setting reserve requirements for all depository institutions.

LIFE INSURANCE COMPANIES

While **life insurance companies** are not considered depository institutions, they are fully regulated by the various states that charter them. There are no federally chartered insurance companies, although Congress has explored the need for such from time to time. As new insurance companies have entered the health insurance and accident insurance business, an increase in consumer abuses has been noted. Further legislation is being examined at this time as their loan origination offices come under the provisions of the Secure and Fair Enforcement for Mortgage Licensing Act. However, in general, life insurance companies respond to older regulatory standards that have continued to offer sound protection for insured parties.

The cash that life insurance companies hold for investment comes from premium reserves and accumulated earnings. Because these reserves are not necessarily subject to demand withdrawal, life insurance companies have long favored the long-term nature of mortgage loans as investments. At one time, life insurance companies and savings associations held equal total investments in mortgage loans. But unlike savings associations, life insurance companies were not chartered for the purpose of providing mortgage money. Their primary interest in using their substantial investment funds is to provide the highest yield possible commensurate with the safety of their policyholders' money. This interest has dictated some flexibility in the movement of their investment funds from time to time to achieve better returns.

When a life insurance company sells an ordinary life policy or certain other kinds of life insurance, regulations normally require that a portion of the premium paid be set aside as a reserve to protect future obligations to the policyholder. The insurance company pays interest to the policyholder on the reserve amount (depending on the terms of the policy) and invests the money as it wishes—so long as it adheres to the regulatory limitations on investments of the state in which it is chartered. Over the years, this reserve pool has produced substantial returns for these companies while protecting the future payment of death benefits.

Casualty insurance companies—those that handle fire coverage, automobile insurance, and a host of other types of hazard insurance—have tremendous premium incomes but are not required to maintain the larger permanent reserves demanded of life insurance companies. Therefore, casualty companies hold their reserves in short-term investments due to the need for liquidity to pay claims. They negotiate practically no mortgage loans and we do not need to discuss them further.

In the United States, there are over 8,000 life insurance companies, including a few from Canada, selling policy contracts. These companies range in size from a very few million dollars in assets to the multibillion-dollar giants that have become household names, such as New York Life, Prudential, AXA, and Metropolitan Life.

Investment Policies

Although insurance companies invest most of their reserves in high-grade securities, they also make mortgage loans. The larger companies have generally confined their real estate activity to making loans for large commercial ventures in which they can acquire a participating interest. Smaller companies follow a different path and often look upon individual home loans in their local communities as good business and a way to make contacts for the sale of life insurance. This kind of loan is intended for holding in the insurance company's own portfolio.

Regulation of Life Insurance Companies

All insurance companies are chartered and operate under the control of state regulatory authorities. Since there are no federal charters for life insurance companies, they adhere to policies that vary from state to state, but the regulations are generally directed toward protecting the policyholders. State regulations also apply to out-of-state charters doing business within the state.

State regulations usually set limits on the types of investment that are permissible; the percentage of total portfolio that may be kept in stock, bonds, or mortgage loans; and the amount of liquidity that must be maintained for each policy dollar outstanding. Most states establish limits on the maximum amount of any one loan, or for any one property. Some states have limited their own chartered insurance companies to investments within their own states, and others have placed limits on out-of-state companies selling insurance within their state unless proportional investments are made within the state.

PENSION AND RETIREMENT PROGRAMS

Introduction

While the money that funds mortgage loans comes from a number of sources, most originates from private sources, including individual and company savings such as passbook savings accounts, money market accounts, and certificates of deposit, as well as premium reserves for policyholders held by life insurance companies, retirement programs such as IRA and Keogh accounts, and various mutual funds, plus the huge and growing pool of pension funds, sovereign funds, and liquidity interventions by central banks of large developed countries.

Up until about 2007, there was a common misconception that most funding for mortgages came from the federal government. Certainly the federal government did and still does have a number of direct-loan programs directed toward farmers, but this is only a very small percentage of the total loan market. Most states and some cities have housing agencies that offer direct loans and subsidy assistance, primarily for low-income home buyers. Various federal government agencies do offer underwriting programs that encourage private sources to fund loans, but these are in the form of guarantees rather than government money. The federal underwriting agencies charge fees for their guarantees with the expectation of making a profit and not burdening taxpayers. It should be noted that one of the biggest changes in the percentage of mortgage funding coming from the sources above has been that from financial institutions, investment funds, and individuals outside the United States during the period from 2001 to 2011. The recent financial crisis and the federal government's move to put Fannie Mae and Freddie Mac into conservatorship has made the Federal Reserve Bank the primary facilitator of funding for mortgage lending from 2008 to 2013. The significance of this change is more fully discussed in Chapter 1.

CREDIT UNIONS

The Mortgage Credit Market

In the credit market, the demand for mortgage money competes with all other demands for borrowed funds. While the mortgage share of this market fluctuates, it normally commands 20–25% of the total credit available each year. Total **mortgage debt outstanding** at the end of the 3rd quarter of 2014 totaled over $13,360 billion—the second largest single class of debt in this country. Only the total U.S. federal debt exceeds this demand for credit.

Credit Unions

Credit unions may be chartered by any group of people who can show a *common bond*. The bond has generally been that of a labor union, a company's employees, or a trade association. However, a recent interpretation of this rule allowed the American Association of Retired Persons (AARP), which has some 37 million members, to form a credit union. The common bond here is the fact that all members are over 50 years of age. There were 5,530 federally insured credit unions in the first quarter of 2018.[1]

Credit unions offer a special attraction as depository institutions because they pay no income taxes. Classed as nonprofit organizations, most credit unions are relatively small and often managed by nonprofessional personnel. Their primary lending consists of small loans to their members for such purposes as buying a car or furniture. When savings associations met with highly publicized reversals three decades ago, many individuals transferred their savings to credit unions, which now have over 90 million members.

---

[1]"NCUA Releases Q1 2018 Credit Union System Performance Data," National Credit Union Administration, 2018, https://www.ncua.gov/newsroom/news/2018/ncua-releases-q1-2018-credit-union-system-performance-data.

In 1978, federally chartered credit unions were authorized to make 30-year mortgage loans; prior to that date, the limit of their loan term was 12 years. That same year, credit unions were authorized to sell loans to secondary-market investors while retaining the loan servicing function. Even then, there was little growth in this particular activity for the smaller unions because of the specialized nature of mortgage lending. The larger unions with professional staff are capable of, and do engage in, the business of making long-term mortgage loans.

The 1980 Depository Institutions Deregulation Act increased credit unions' authority to make all types of loans and to accept all kinds of deposits. Furthermore, these institutions have expanded the services they offer to include some that were formerly available only through their competitors. These services include safe deposit boxes, credit cards, and money market accounts. These extra services plus the tax-exempt status of credit unions may not be their only advantages; many members feel they gain a closer personal touch.

Because of the tax-exempt status and other advantages found in credit unions, bankers have tried to limit credit union expansion through a lawsuit contesting what is meant by the *common bond* required of credit union members. The suit reached the U.S. Supreme Court, which ruled on February 25, 1998, that federally chartered credit unions are limited to membership as originally defined by law.

Though the banks were the victors in this lawsuit, Congress then passed legislation to restore credit union membership guidelines to employees of companies with total personnel of 3,000 or less. This legislation adds the requirement that credit unions must adhere to the Community Reinvestment Act but does not change their nonprofit status. Some credit unions have chosen to elect a change in status, asking their members to vote to re-charter as savings banks or banks. This movement, along with mergers of credit unions, has reduced the number of credit unions from a high of around 18,000 to a little more than one-third that number today.

Regulation of Credit Unions

Credit unions can be either state or federally chartered. An independent agency of the federal government, the National Credit Union Administration (NCUA) charters, regulates, and supervises the activities of federal credit unions. State charters adhere to their own state rules and laws.

Deposits in credit unions can be protected by the same kind of insurance as other regulated depository institutions. The federally chartered National Credit Union Share Insurance Fund, administered by the NCUA, covers deposits up to $250,000. Federal charters must offer this coverage, and state charters that qualify are eligible to join.

MORTGAGE BROKERS AND BANKERS

Mortgage Brokers

Mortgage brokers once operated in one of the high-growth areas in loan origination. The complex nature of mortgage lending has increased the need for knowledgeable experts to advise borrowers and open doors to the most effective lenders. The historic role of mortgage brokers as handling primarily commercial loans began to shift with financial deregulation in the 1980s. With the decline in the savings and loan industry as a primary source of residential mortgage funding and the need to save costs on brick-and-mortar branches, residential mortgage brokers came to the forefront. Many knowledgeable individuals formally trained at regulated institutions or independent mortgage companies began working as mortgage brokers, structuring loans and placing them with funding sources. Independent residential mortgage loan brokers are now referred to by their primary licensing regulator, the **National Mortgage Licensing System (NMLS)**, as **"mortgage loan originators" (MLOs)**. The NMLS was created to provide a uniform mortgage application for state mortgage regulatory agencies; a nationwide repository of licensed mortgage loan origination professionals; and a minimum education, experience, and testing requirement under the **SAFE Mortgage Licensing Act of 2008 (SAFE)**, also known by its full title, the Secure and Fair Enforcement for Mortgage Licensing Act of 2008.

More details on this entity are located in the section on the licensing of mortgage loan originators that follows. The SAFE Act requires all residential mortgage loan officers who work at federally regulated deposit-taking institutions who are exempt from provisions related to the new educational, experience, and testing requirements to have a unique identifier or registration number generated by the NMLS.

Mortgage brokers formed their own association in 1973—the National Association of Mortgage Brokers (NAMB)—and through this organization and other means, are expanding their influence within the industry.

NAMB offers its members a series of designations that define levels of expertise based on experience and education. The association works in cooperation with mortgage bankers and others to explain the needs of the industry and of the borrowing public to state legislatures and to Congress. It is helping to move regulatory practices into more effective channels.

A mortgage broker specializes in serving as an intermediary between the customer/borrower and the client/lender. While brokers are capable of handling all arrangements for the processing, or packaging, of the loan, they normally do no funding and they do not service the loan once it has closed. Some brokers serve as "retail" offices for large mortgage bankers or big institutional lenders, providing a lower-cost outlet than a branch office. Or they may serve as correspondents in the local area for a major lender that specializes in a particular category of loans, such as hotels or shopping centers. The broker earns a portion of the normal origination fee plus an application fee.

Large commercial loans are normally funded directly by the lending institution, such as an insurance company, and the monthly payments on debt service go directly to the lender. This procedure works very well for mortgage brokers. On the other hand, residential loans require an intermediary who assembles the smaller loans into larger blocks for easier selling to the big investors. Furthermore, residential loans produce relatively small monthly payments and require the substantial servicing capacity that can be found with a mortgage banker. However, the differences between commercial and residential loans have diminished in the present market, as many mortgage brokers have begun to operate in the "retail" market for residential loans, passing them on to various "wholesale" mortgage banking companies. The recent financial crisis has caused many regulated lenders to rethink their relationships with the retail, independent, licensed mortgage brokerage community for residential mortgage lending. One primary difference between commercial real estate lending and residential lending is the application and underwriting process. The concept of automated underwriting systems used for over 80% of residential mortgages is not a uniform technology used in commercial lending. Rather, in commercial real estate loan underwriting, the determination of the appropriate net operating income (NOI) is the first step in the process. The borrower will typically submit a rent roll and a pro forma, but the lender will almost always construct their own pro forma for loan underwriting purposes, which may result in a different NOI calculation. Possible lender adjustments to NOI include increasing the vacancy and credit loss factor to account for market conditions or tenant rollover risk, or deducting reserves for replacement from NOI.

The following list of data, reports, or analysis will be required for a lender to fulfill their normal lending guidelines used for underwriting. For commercial properties that are already producing income, they are the debt service coverage ratio and the loan-to-value ratio. Other documents that a mortgagor might expect to provide or have performed on behalf of the lender, besides historical and pro forma NOI financials, are listed below:

- discounted cash flow analysis
- financial stability of existing tenants
- creditworthiness of principals that represent the proposed mortgagor
- fair market valuation of property and the current rents charged
- full rent rolls with maturities and possibly sampling or full lease agreements in place

Development properties that are not being immediately developed into a subdivision, mini mall, or commercial office building will require a heavier emphasis on the valuation of the real estate property proposed for the loan and usually a personal guarantee of the borrower(s). The commercial real estate loan process is explained in detail in chapter 12.

Other types of mortgage brokers are companies operating on a national scale that primarily arrange purchases and sales of mortgage loans between originators and investors, or between investors and other investors. In so doing, they greatly aid the free flow of mortgages across state lines in the private mortgage market. These brokers seldom originate a loan and do not service them. However, they are part of the secondary market in some of their operations.

Occasionally, a commercial banker or savings association will broker a loan for a customer with another lender. Money may not be readily available through regular channels, or the loan request may be for something the local banker cannot handle with his or her own funds. The banker may then turn to other sources and earn a brokerage fee for handling the loan. This type of extra service is more commonly found in smaller communities. Many smaller, regulated lenders who are not FHA-approved will broker a mortgage loan in this way.

Mortgage Bankers

The distinction between "bankers" and "brokers" has diminished. Nevertheless, an essential difference between the two remains—the full-service facility offered by **mortgage bankers**. *Full service* means: (1) originating the mortgage loan, (2) funding the loan at closing, and (3) servicing the loan as it is paid off. But even this distinction between mortgage bankers and brokers is blurring as brokers divide themselves into those who close loans in their own names and those who close in another lender's name.

The need for a full-service facility developed from both the desire for a new approach to mortgage lending after the economic collapse of the 1930s and the implementation of the Federal Housing Administration (FHA) programs handled in conjunction with private industry. Economic pressures of the early 1930s had dried up lendable funds, new construction had halted, and many banks had closed their doors. The shortage of available funds made the mortgage banker an intermediary for the only remaining sources of cash: insurance companies, a few large savings banks, and the Federal National Mortgage Association.

In the 1930s, Federal Housing Administration programs were rejected by regulated depository institutions as a government intrusion into the field of banking. Within the industry, the extension of credit was then considered a banker's prerogative. The FHA's desire to work in cooperation with private industry was met by mortgage bankers. They offered the full-service facilities and market contacts that enabled the FHA to fulfill its purposes in meeting the needs of home buyers.

As early as 1914, mortgage bankers formed a trade association known as the Farm Mortgage Bankers Association, highlighting the original emphasis placed on farm loans. The name was changed to its present title of Mortgage Bankers Association (MBA) in 1923. MBA is a major communications and information center for the industry. It sponsors educational programs to keep the many people employed by mortgage bankers up to date in an ever-changing business. The MBA actively promotes legislation favorable to the industry and its borrowers.

With a better understanding of the variations among the businesses and individuals who serve those seeking mortgage loans, we can now examine the question, "What does it take to become a mortgage company?"

Qualifications of a Mortgage Lender

For many years, there were no federal requirements regarding the qualifications or licensing of an individual or company handling conventional mortgage loans. Most states had established some requirements, consisting mostly of registration and the posting of a bond. Many states had been exploring the possible need for further regulation, including licensing. In the past, any individual meriting the confidence of a lending institution could assist in arranging a loan, thereby earning a fee for his or her services. However, with the passage of the SAFE Act in 2008, the federal government signaled its intent to increase uniformity in the regulation and licensing of those making residential mortgage loans outside the employment of regulated financial institutions. The SAFE Act represents an attempt to ease regulatory burdens, enhance consumer protection, and reduce fraud by establishing the NMLS for the residential mortgage industry. This new regulation has had the greatest effect on the independent residential mortgage brokerage community. The SAFE Act did not replace the mortgage broker licensing requirements that were already in place in 38 states; rather, it created a uniform set of minimum licensing requirements that all states had to implement no later than April 1, 2010. In practice, mortgage company qualifications are set mostly within the industry itself, although many states require that mortgage companies be licensed to do business in that state. If a mortgage company elects to deal with a government agency involved with mortgage lending, that agency's standards must be met. These agencies include HUD/FHA, VA, Fannie Mae, Freddie Mac, Ginnie Mae, and Farmer Mac. Their requirements are similar: acceptable net worth and liquidity levels, experienced personnel, and adequate office facilities available to the general public. Even if these criteria are met, approval must be obtained from each agency with which a mortgage company wants to do business. The same is true of any other client-lender of a mortgage company. Approvals by either HUD/FHA or VA in the past were often accepted by conventional lenders as adequate qualification except for minimum capital requirements, which can be much higher for Fannie Mae and Freddie Mac. This will be no longer true after new minimum net worth and liquidity requirements for FHA-approved seller/servicers go into effect in 2015 (more about this in Chapter 5).

Licensing of Mortgage Loan Officers

Due to the complexity of residential mortgage lending, with its many guidelines and requirements, there has been a marked increase in the number of cases wherein consumers are misinformed—either as a result of a loan officer's lack of knowledge or through the dissemination of information known to be false. Several factors have increased the need for mortgage personnel with full knowledge of the mortgage lending industry. These include: problems with correct loan documentation, the existence of several hundred variations in repayment plans, confusion over the proper handling of escrow account money and loan closing costs covered by the Real Estate Settlements Procedures Act, the need for accurate advice on loan prepayments and disclosure of interest costs required by the Truth-in-Lending Act, along with the need for compliance with the Equal Credit Opportunity Act amid rising concerns about possible discriminatory lending and the new requirements of the Dodd-Frank Act.

Regulation of mortgage brokers was limited for many years. Early consumer protection laws enumerated above were enacted and regulated primarily by the Federal Reserve Bank, the Federal Deposit Insurance Corporation, the Federal Home Loan Bank, the Federal Trade Commission (FTC), and the Department of Housing and Urban Development. It was not that these laws did not apply to private mortgage brokers; rather, there was no official regulatory body with direct oversight of licensing, compliance, or enforcement powers except for the FTC. Mortgage loans made by independent retail or wholesale mortgage brokers increased from a small percentage of residential mortgage loans originated in 1972 to a 69% peak market share in 2004.[2] States began to react to the lack of federal regulation of the activity of these emerging mortgage loan originators. By 1996, all but eight states had some registration or licensing requirements for the mortgage industry, and by 2006, all but one state—Alaska—had some state regulatory oversight.[3] In addition to states' involvement with licensing and professional training, state governments also became more aggressive in opposing predatory lending and mortgage fraud abuses than did regulators at the federal level. But while there was a patchwork of state licensing requirements for those involved in residential mortgage loan origination, various Supreme Court decisions held that states did

---

[2] Lew Sichelman, "Loan Brokers Lose Share, but Still Rule the Market," *Realty Times*, June 18, 2007.
[3] Cynthia Pahl, *A Compilation of State Mortgage Broker Laws and Regulations, 1996–2006* (Minneapolis, MN: Federal Reserve Bank of Minneapolis, 2007).

not have regulatory oversight over national banks. These decisions left a large gap in regulatory control over mortgage lending within the commercial banking industry, a gap that contributed to the concentration of banking through consolidation and a lack of adequate regulatory oversight and enforcement resources at the federal level.[4,5]

As a result of these combined concerns, the Conference of State Bank Supervisors (CSBS) and the American Association of Residential Mortgage Regulators (AARMR) embarked on a four-year study that concluded that a uniform mortgage application for state mortgage regulatory agencies and a nationwide repository of licensed companies and professionals should be established. They made this recommendation to a Congressional House subcommittee in 2005.[6] Ultimately, at the continued urging of many industry experts, and as a result of additional pressure brought on by the financial crisis, state and federal officials determined that a uniform licensing method should be implemented, and Congress accordingly passed the SAFE Act. Consequently, all states have created licensing commissions that set minimum qualifications for those who handle consumer mortgage loans, which may exceed those established by the NMLS. The SAFE Act mandates minimum standards for mortgage loan originators, including that applicants pass, complete, or maintain the following five general requirements:

1. a criminal history and credit background check;
2. pre-licensure education, including:
    a. three hours of federal law and regulations;
    b. three hours of ethics;
    c. two hours of lending standards; and
    d. 12 hours of mortgage origination;
3. pre-licensure testing;
4. continuing education, including:
    a. three hours of federal law and regulations
    b. two hours of ethics;
    c. two hours of training related to lending standards for the nontraditional mortgage product market; and

---

[4]Chris Seabury, "The Causes and Effects of Credit Shocks," Investopedia, accessed December 28, 2014, http://www.investopedia.com/articles/economics/08/credit-shock-mortgages.asp
[5]Keith Harvey et al., "Disparities in Mortgage Lending, Bank Performance, Economic Influence, and Regulatory Oversight," *The Journal of Real Estate Finance and Economics* 23, no. 3 (November 2001).
[6]Teresa Dean, "CSBS Describes States' Plan for Mortgage Licensing and Registration at House Hearing," *CSBS Examiner*, September 30, 2005.

A LICENSED MORTGAGE PROFESSIONAL

    d. one hour of undefined instruction on mortgage origination; and
5. provide evidence of certain net worth and provide a surety bond or recovery fund.

In addition many states have specific education and testing requirements for licensing in their states.

More information about state specific licensing and compliance rules can be found at the NMLS website at http://mortgage.nationwidelicensingsystem.org/slr/Pages/default.aspx, which provides additional links for information on each state.

The requirements above apply to those residential mortgage loan originators who do not work for an institution that takes federally insured deposits or any agency that falls under the examination or supervision of the Farm Credit Administration. The NMLS grants national licenses and unique identifier numbers to individuals whom it refers to as mortgage loan originators or MLOs. But since states are within the dual licensing system established by the SAFE Act, many refer to their dual-licensed mortgage loan originators by different titles; for example, Texas uses the term "Residential Mortgage Loan Originator" to describe its licensees. As a result, the acronym RMLO has developed different meanings. It originally stood for the "Registered Mortgage Loan Originator," which was a term defined in the final rule in the Federal Register of July 2010[7] that directed federal depository regulators and the Farm Credit Administration to promulgate rules to enforce the registration of MLOs as defined by the SAFE Act. Later, various industry trade groups and individual independent loan originators—in an effort to differentiate themselves from banks or savings and loan mortgage loan originators—redefined RMLO as "Registered Mortgage Loan Officer" and began to refer to themselves as MLOs, now meaning Mortgage Loan Officer (Licensed and Trained). Neither of these is a regulatory term.

The new licensing requirements with the NMLS and state regulators caused the number of licensed mortgage brokers to fall dramatically, whether due to the new requirements of the NMLS or the general decline in the mortgage market, or a combination of both. As an example, the number of mortgage brokers licensed in Texas fell from over 30,000 to under 4,000 between 2008 and 2011. A slight recovery in the mortgage market began in 2012, and by the end of 2013, the number of mortgage loan originators in Texas had grown back to 24,743 with a growth rate in new MLOs of 14% in 2016 alone.[8]

Where Are We Now?

Who Needs to Register With NMLS?

If your institution is federally chartered or insured by one of the following agencies and your institution employs individuals required to be federally registered as mortgage loan originators, your institution must register with the NMLS.

- Office of the Comptroller of the Currency
- Board of Governors of the Federal Reserve System
- Federal Deposit Insurance Corporation
- Office of Thrift Supervision
- Farm Credit Administration
- National Credit Union Administration

---

[7] "Registration of Mortgage Loan Originators: Final Rule," Federal Register, accessed July 10, 2015, https://www.federalregister.gov/documents/2010/07/28/2010-18148/registration-of-mortgage-loan-originators

[8] Conference of State Bank Supervisors: 2017, 2016 NMLS Mortgage Industry Report, March 20th, 2017. Accessed September 11 2018, https://mortgage.nationwidelicensingsystem.org/about/Reports/2016%20Mortgage%20Report.pdf

Mortgage Company Operations

Although mortgage companies vary widely in their methods, the business organization common to most operates with three basic divisions: (1) administration, (2) loan servicing, and (3) loan acquisition.

The administrative group supervises and directs all operations and, using its sources of money, seeks out and maintains contact with lending institutions and, more recently, poolers of mortgages for issuance of mortgage-backed securities. The development of stable, continuing relations with a group of investors is a source of pride for mortgage companies. In the past, it was not considered good business for either a mortgage company or a lender to maintain an exclusive arrangement. Since the beginning of the current financial crisis in 2008, the number of investors has declined and those that remain tightened their credit standards initially. In early 2014, several lenders began to offer more relaxed requirements; for example, Wells Fargo began accepting 15% down payments for jumbo mortgage, reduced from 20%. Investors in residential mortgage loans are in and out of the market as their particular investment needs fluctuate, while mortgage companies must maintain a steady supply of funds. Mortgage company officers must know which sources are available for loans and the particular type of loan or loans that each lender or investor prefers. A mortgage company's secondary marketing department resides within the administrative group and works with investors to establish the pricing that the loan acquisition group will use to attract borrowers.

Loan servicing includes the record-keeping section that maintains customers' or borrowers' accounts. Larger companies have converted much of this accounting to computerized methods for more efficient handling. The escrow section holds the required insurance and tax deposits. Escrow account personnel must maintain a continuous analysis of taxes and insurance costs for each property to assure the company that sufficient money will be available when needed for payment. Another responsibility of the servicing section is to ensure prompt collection of borrowers' monthly payments and to send out notifications if delinquencies occur. All lenders insist on knowing borrowers' account statuses and depend on mortgage companies to use diligence in keeping their accounts current. Laxity in this area could jeopardize a lender's rights in a foreclosure action.

The loan acquisition group, the division best known to outsiders, consists of loan originator/officers or supervisor/managers who make the contacts with potential borrowers. These contacts are made through real estate agents, banks, accountants, and others. They help mortgage personnel seek out the best loans as well as handle actual loan applications. Loan processors normally work with these representatives to maintain files and to help collect required information on both the property and the borrower. Complete documentation of the loan must be included in the loan package. Any person who works directly with a mortgage loan applicant who recommends a product or discusses the applicant's credit or other qualifications for the loan is required to be a registrant with the Federal Registry maintained by the NMLS. While regulated financial institution personnel need not have or maintain NMLS mortgage originators' licenses, they must be registered with the NMLS Federal Registry to perform the function of making residential mortgage loans. The Federal Registry of the NMLS is set up under the law to maintain a record of all people involved in residential mortgage finance. If a person has committed fraud or had a mortgage license revoked, there will be a record of this revocation in the system, and the person who has lost the license cannot be employed or licensed in another location. The **Fraud Enforcement and Recovery Act of 2009 (FERA)** expanded the federal government's ability to prosecute mortgage fraud, securities and commodities fraud, and other types of fraud related to federal assistance and relief programs such as the Troubled Asset Relief Program (TARP).

How a Mortgage Company Funds Loans

As discussed earlier in this chapter, mortgage companies do not hold deposit assets that can be loaned the way regulated depository institutions do. Therefore, they must use somewhat different procedures to obtain an assurance of funds with which to make loans. When dealing with residential loans, mortgage bankers generally borrow money from a commercial banker on a **warehouse line of credit** to fund a loan at closing. The loan is pledged at the bank as collateral and held, or "warehoused," by the bank until it can be sold. The availability of warehouse lines of credit diminished during the Great Recession, but has since rebounded and is a very important component of mortgage liquidity in 2018.

Other methods are used by mortgage companies dealing with the larger commercial loans. These loans are more likely to be placed on a case-by-case basis with the most suitable lender available at the time. Mortgage bankers, and some brokers, use several methods to assure themselves of adequate funding at known costs, as the following section describes.

Sale of Loans to Secondary-Market Investors

A procedure long used by mortgage companies is the purchase of a **forward commitment** in advance of making any loans. This commitment is a promise by a lender (meaning a purchaser of loans or an investor) to have certain funds available for qualifying loans submitted to that lender over a limited period of time, such as 30 days to six months. With a forward commitment in hand, the mortgage company can give assurance to a commercial banker that loans pledged on a warehouse line of credit do have a ready market. A forward commitment generally includes an agreement for the mortgage company to service the loans that are delivered to the loan purchaser. The agreement between originator and purchaser is known as a *sales and servicing contract.* Savings associations, insurance companies, and some commercial banks, as well as Fannie Mae, Freddie Mac, and other loan poolers or mortgage conduits, buy loans from originators under commitments they have issued to originators. Mortgage companies maintain contact with various loan purchasers who are in and out of the market.

Both Fannie Mae and Freddie Mac are continuously in the market for the purchase of loans that conform to their requirements. This assurance gives their "conforming loan" parameters special importance for lenders seeking liquidity in loan portfolios. Like other secondary-market loan purchasers, Fannie and Freddie buy loans through the sale of forward commitments to make such purchases.

Large mortgage companies with substantial assets may make loans without a forward loan commitment, choosing instead to finance their operations through the issuance of commercial paper or by operating a conduit (described in Chapter 1). The mortgage companies can hold loans temporarily in their own portfolio or, more commonly, pledge them with a commercial bank on a warehouse line of credit. When a suitable buyer is found, the mortgage company can sell loans that have already been made on an **immediate commitment** basis. "Immediate" means that the loans do exist and can be delivered without delay. However, industry practice allows up to 60 days for delivery. The advantage of an immediate type of sale is that the purchaser's yield requirements will be slightly less (the purchaser's money is put to work right away) than for a forward commitment, which allows the mortgage company a little better margin of return.

Representative or Correspondent Basis

Insurance companies, pension funds, and other loan purchasers sometimes specialize in handling certain kinds of property loans, such as those for hotels or shopping centers. Rather than deal with a variety of loan originators, these companies often work through selected representatives throughout the country. These representatives, sometimes identified as agents and sometimes as correspondents, are commercial loan companies that understand the special requirements of each loan purchaser or investor. If a mortgage company customer is seeking a hotel loan, for example, the mortgage company will handle the contact with a secondary-market investor most interested in that particular kind of loan. In a situation such as this, the mortgage company serves as a loan broker, negotiating the loan for an investor. The investor then funds the loan at closing and usually handles the servicing.

Selling Mortgage-Backed Securities

These sales involve converting mortgage loans into mortgage-backed securities, which enjoy a broader market that is not practical for smaller mortgage companies. Prior to the mortgage crisis, most loan originators sold their loans to large loan poolers—like investment bankers—such as Morgan Stanley & Company, Inc., Goldman Sachs, or to government-sponsored enterprises such as Fannie Mae, which are more capable of dealing with financial market needs. However, a few of the larger mortgage companies had been successful in tapping financial markets for this purpose. One method is to place a multimillion-dollar block of mortgage loans in the care of a trustee, such as an authorized bank. Then the mortgage company issues a series of certificates backed by the block of loans, which is the collateral for the securities. The certificates are sold to investors and the money received from these certificates is used to reimburse the mortgage company. This procedure is often identified as *securitizing mortgages*. As the mortgage company that originally made the loans services them, it sends the principal and interest payments each month to the trustee. The trustee then passes these payments on to holders of the securities. The expression *pass-through securities* developed to describe this practice. When privately issued, as described here, mortgage-backed securities may or may not be guaranteed. Investment bankers entered the field of mortgage securities with a number of variations that will be discussed more fully in the next chapter.

Mortgage Company Income

Profit margins are narrow in handling mortgage loans. Mortgage companies make little, if any, money from the discount, since that amount passes to the loan purchaser as part of the cost of money. While the borrower measures the discount in a specific number of points, in practice the mortgage company originator does not receive that precise amount. What the mortgage company is really doing is buying a piece of paper—the mortgage note—when it funds the loan at closing. Then the note is sold to a secondary-market purchaser. The difference between what is funded at closing and what the mortgage company sells the note for is the amount it earns, measured in dollars. If the mortgage company has handled its commitments carefully, the margin covers its origination fee and maybe a small cushion. And if it makes a mistake or misjudges the secondary-market yield requirements, losses can result. Some lenders will charge a higher interest rate than market rates to add additional profits rather than charging discount points; this additional spread is called "yield spread premium."

The dependable income for loan originators comes from various fees: application fees, origination fees, yield spread premium, and servicing fees. These are more fully explained in the following section. When mortgage originators are at their most competitive in marketing, their firms may only break even when comparing their origination expenses, fee income, and yield spread premium, and may not realize a profit until after selling the servicing rights on each mortgage into the secondary market.

Application Fee

Loan originators normally charge a nonrefundable **application fee** at the time an application is taken. In the jargon of the industry, lenders will "entertain an application" for a loan if the application is in general conformance with the kind of loan the lenders make. The application fee covers certain costs incurred in screening an application, such as those involved in obtaining a credit report and a property appraisal, as well as that represented by the time it takes a loan officer to review the information. The fee is not regulated (except for HUD/FHA and VA) and is charged by almost all originators, not just mortgage companies. For residential loans, the fee is in the $150 to $500 range, while fees for commercial loans are often based on the size of the loan rather than on the work involved.

Origination Fee

An **origination fee** is sometimes combined with an application fee. However, in most cases, it is a separate charge amounting to 1–2% of the loan amount, payable if and when the loan closes. It is a charge incurred for assembling a loan package and making the decision to accept or reject the loan. The charge is for services rendered but is tax-deductible for the borrower if certain rules are followed. It is a separate charge from the discount, which is also tax-deductible, but the two are not always differentiated when loan costs are quoted. Mortgage personnel should disclose the distinction to borrowers so they may make more accurate comparisons of charges between lenders.

Mortgage companies usually split the origination fee, with about half going to the loan representative who contacts the borrower and takes the loan application. This fee is considered the commission earned by the representative and is not paid if the loan fails to close. In contrast, most savings associations and banks pay their loan officers on a salaried basis rather than on commission, with some paying bonuses based on a minimum level of monthly production and profitability.

Yield spread premium, or YSP, is the fee paid by the lender to the broker in exchange for a higher interest rate negotiated with the borrower at an above-wholesale rate. Though the borrower may qualify for a certain rate, the broker can charge this fee and give the borrower a slightly higher rate to make a higher commission. This practice was originally intended as a way to avoid charging the borrower any out-of-pocket fees. It can be abused, however, and used to charge inexperienced borrowers excessive fees for services rendered. Recent changes to the Real Estate Settlement Procedures Act occurred with the passage of the Mortgage Disclosure Improvement Act of 2008 (**MDIA**). MDIA requires that any yield spread premium be fully disclosed on the newly revised Loan Estimate disclosure form, pointing out this fee that was often hidden from consumers in the past. The method of disclosing mortgage broker compensation, including yield spread premium, continued to be a concern and was addressed in the Dodd-Frank Act. The CFPB has finalized new disclosure rules under the Truth-in-Lending Act that became effective in 2013 and will be modified under the new Qualified Mortgage (QM) rules, also part of the Dodd-Frank Act.

Servicing Fee

In mortgage lending, a **servicing fee** is the charge made for handling the loan after it has been funded. Services involve collecting and accounting for periodic loan payments, handling the escrow portion of the payments, and following up on delinquent accounts. The fee amounts to 0.25% to 0.50% of the loan balance and is collected by all loan servicers—mortgage companies, savings associations, banks, and others. Servicing charges are normally added to the interest rate for the loan and are not distinguishable to the average borrower. In the terminology of secondary-market investors, a yield requirement quoted as "net basis" means one that does not include a servicing fee; the loan originator must add that to the rate. Net basis rates are sometimes identified as the "wholesale rate." For example, the rate delivered to a loan purchaser might be 8.5%, while the charge to the borrower would be 8.75%; the 0.25% difference is the service fee.

Because the servicing of large blocks of mortgage loans can be a lucrative business by itself, specialized companies have developed in recent years to perform just this function. Sometimes a loan originator accumulates several billion dollars in loans to service and will sell a portion of the block to acquire cash. For example, if a $100 million block of loans is paying 0.25% in servicing fees, the total fees paid amount to $250,000 per year. The profit potential and cash flow could make the servicing alone worth $750,000 to $1.5 million in a sale.

The Great Recession or financial crisis from 2007 to 2009 led to the rise of a new breed of third-party mortgage loan servicing operation. These are known as special servicers or default servicers. Special servicers can be freestanding firms specializing in servicing hedge funds, mortgage assets, and those for other master servicers like Selene Finance LP, owned by Ranieri Partners. Another new type of mortgage loan special servicer is Carrington Mortgage Services, LLC. Carrington describes itself as a privately managed investment management company that provides integrated full lifecycle mortgage loan servicing support to borrowers and investors. These new special servicers and default servicers have a much higher fee structure than more traditional mortgage servicing operations.

Loan Servicing Disclosure Notice

As the residential mortgage market has expanded and changed, the older practice of making monthly payments to a loan originator has given way to a new trend. The servicing function may be transferred to a distant collection company that specializes in computer management of the cash flows. The ease with which a lender can now ask a borrower to send monthly checks to a new servicing agent has created an opportunity for some abuse. Scam artists using unauthorized or stolen lists of borrowers can direct payments to a post office box, skim the collections for perhaps a month or two, and disappear with the money.

To help give borrowers/consumers some protection from this kind of theft, Congress amended the Real Estate Settlement Procedures Act (RESPA). As of April 20, 1991, the Cranston-Gonzalez National Affordable Housing Act required loan originators to provide borrowers with a servicing disclosure notice. The notice must include an explanation of two points: (1) the possibility that loan servicing may be transferred to another company, and (2) the rights of a borrower, should such a transfer occur. The loan originator must provide a borrower with an estimate, expressed as a percentage, of the possibility of transfer. Furthermore, a notice of transfer must be sent to the borrower not less than 15 days prior to any transfer, and the new servicing company must confirm the change within 15 days after the date of transfer. A toll-free or collect telephone number must be provided for the borrower to contact the servicing company. Borrowers may collect damages and costs from companies that violate the requirements.

Automated Loan Underwriting

Since 1995, an explosive growth in mortgage originations has led to the use of computer programs using artificial intelligence in the analysis, and even the final approval, of residential loans. While it did not originate the idea, HUD has encouraged the greater use of computerized loan underwriting, as it can lower costs and provide more unbiased analysis. This method has brought an increase in the use of credit scoring and offers ways to expedite appraisals. Because of the many advances in technology, it is now possible for an individual to negotiate a mortgage loan on the internet. At this time, the vast majority of internet-based loan originators are fully focused on easy-to-close refinances.

Where Are We Now?

What is Automated Underwriting?

According to Freddie Mac, "automated underwriting is a technology-based tool that combines historical loan performance, statistical models, and mortgage lending factors to determine whether a loan can be sold into the secondary market. The most widely used automated underwriting services are Freddie Mac's Loan Prospector® and Fannie Mae's Desktop Underwriter®[9].

Mortgage originators use automated underwriting to help them:

- determine the terms under which the loan can be sold into the secondary market;
- evaluate the credit, collateral, and capacity of borrowers to make their monthly mortgage payments; and
- identify the appropriate type of loan for the borrower.

As the Freddie Mac website notes, "Automated underwriting improves the mortgage process by providing lower costs, expanded markets, and faster, fairer lending decisions."

"Automated underwriting also helps originators shed old guidelines that excluded too many borrowers from home ownership. By combining flexible, objective underwriting with a broad array of mortgage programs, originators can offer borrowers lowest-cost financing. This makes automated underwriting a big weapon against predatory lending."[10]

REAL ESTATE TRUSTS (REIT, REMT)

Real Estate Investment Trusts (REITs)

In 1960, when mortgage money was derived mostly from savings accounts, Congress passed the Real Estate Investment Trust Act. The intent was to make it more profitable and tax-efficient for the small investor to enter the real estate market, thus increasing available capital. To achieve this purpose, **Real Estate Investment Trusts (REITs)** are subject to strict qualifications and restrictions, as demonstrated in figure 5-1.

The points in figure 5-1 are general business observations of REIT structure. There can be harsh penalties for not meeting the required qualifications, including the loss of REIT status. Interested REIT holders or REIT licensees should always contact the IRS for the most current tax law involving REITs.

Two kinds of REITs developed. One made equity investments in real estate and derived its income from operation of properties. The other

---

[9]"Automated Underwriting," Freddie Mac, accessed July 10, 2015, https://stmpartners.com/manual/cor/general/1.04aus.pdf
[10]Ibid.

- A REIT must be structured as a corporation, trust, or association and be managed by a board of director or trustees.
- REITs must have transferable shares or certificates of interest.
- An REIT must be formed as an entity that is taxable as a corporation.
- Financial institutions and insurance companies cannot be formed as REITs.
- Joint ownership must be a key component, with at least 100 persons owning the REIT's stock.
- Additionally, a REIT must not have more than 50% of its shares held by five or fewer individuals during the last half of each taxable year.
- REITs must have at least 75% of total investment assets in real estate or in real estate–backed assets such as equity mortgage-backed securities.
- REITs must generate at least 75% of their gross income from rents on real property or mortgage interest.
- No more than 25% of a REIT's assets may consist of stock in taxable REIT subsidiaries.

FIGURE 5-1 Real Estate Investment Trusts.
Source: © 2021 Mbition LLC

arranged for mortgage loans, a lucrative business when interest rates were reaching peak levels. Both kinds of activity declined in the 1980s as the real estate market lost much of its luster. The 1990s saw the return of equity-type REITs as a sound method of raising investment capital.

In the mid-1990s, REITs began a large-scale operation of selling stock on the public markets. The stock was of interest to investors because of its tax advantages and the required distribution of any profit. REITs backed by the public markets were stronger than earlier REITs. Many showed equity of around 70% of capital, while earlier ones operated on about 30% equity with the rest borrowed. Now evolving as popular REIT alternatives are REITs with timberland or land with mineral interests. These might yield considerable income using the framework of pass-through special-purpose entities that build out the infrastructure for oil and gas production, as opposed to having a pure royalty income structure.

With cash raised in the public markets, REITs began buying real estate, ranging from prisons to apartment buildings. In 1997, REITs made several big hotel deals; the purchase of ITT (Sheraton Hotels) and LaQuinta Inns were two such deals. Because of an overload of stock on the market, the price stalled. In 1998, the Federal Reserve warned its banks to raise its credit standards on loans to REITs because such loans were dependent on real property, which could fluctuate downward. Unfortunately, the Fed did not give the same guidance on residential mortgage-backed securities, and these continued to flourish well into the current financial crisis.

Interestingly, more than a dozen new residential mortgage-backed security REITs have been formed since 2007, mainly secured by ARM loan portfolios of MBS freshly issued by Fannie Mae, Freddie Mac, and Ginnie Mae. Some of these new REITs, with names such as Invesco Mortgage Capital, Inc., Hatteras Financial Corp., and Two Harbors Investment Corp., have built their balance sheet assets to total holdings of over $20 billion in less than three years. The total new ARM RMBS put into these new and existing mortgage REITs, such as Capstead Mortgage Corporation, Annaly Capital Management, Inc., and MFA Financial, Inc., has been more than a quarter trillion dollars from January 2008 to December 2010. Much of this growth of the existing and new mortgage REITs was financed by U.S. Treasury's Troubled Asset Relief Program monies, private investors, and loans from the Federal Reserve's Term Asset-Backed Securities Loan Facility. The range in size of market capitalization of publicly traded mortgage REITs was $29.2 billion at the end of 2006 (a high at that time) to a low of $14.3 billion at year-end 2008, and by the end of 2017, they were $67.7 billion.[11]

A **public-private investment program** (PPIP) has two parts, addressing both the legacy loans and legacy securities that are clogging the balance sheets of financial firms by using $75 to $100 billion in TARP capital and capital from private investors. PPIPs are expected to generate $500 billion in purchasing power to buy legacy assets, with the potential to expand to $1 trillion over time, helping investors buy new RMBS securities with refinanced ARMs. This process allows those mortgage assets that were interest-only or option ARMs set at unaffordable pay rates for otherwise creditworthy borrowers to be reset. This reset has also allowed a limited number of potentially toxic mortgage assets to change characteristics and become performing assets.

In the past 10 years, the growth in specialized REITs has become a factor in this market. Some REITs concentrate their holdings specifically in one type of real estate, such as shopping centers, while others concentrate in a particular region of the country. Two examples of such

---

[11] "US REIT Industry Equity Market Cap," National Association of Real Estate Investment Trusts, accessed September 11, 2018, https://www.reit.com/investing/industry-data-research/us-reit-industry-equity-market-cap

specialized REITs are Associated Estates Realty Corp. and Post Properties, Inc., both of which are involved in the development, ownership, management, and sale for profit of upscale or luxury multifamily apartment communities.

There are also non-exchange-traded REITs that must still make filings with the SEC. These non-exchange-traded or private REITs are not freely traded, as they were never registered with the SEC. They differ from publicly traded REITs in the sense that investors pay a fixed price for each unit in a private REIT and anticipate receiving regular dividends from income produced by rents or mortgage interest. Investors in private REITs must be aware that these entities only trade during certain windows. It is only during these particular periods of time that investors can redeem units back to the issuer on terms set by the private REIT. Moreover, private REITs can have suspended redemptions. The biggest downside to private REITs is the fact that they do not have the disclosure requirements of other REITs, and there is typically no public or independent source of performance data on them available to investors.

REAL ESTATE BONDS

Stock Certificates

Shares of stock representing an ownership interest in a corporation are not relevant to the subject of real estate finance and will not be considered further in this text. The category is mentioned here only to distinguish it from bonds, which are debt instruments.

Bonds

A corporation can borrow money through the sale of bonds to investors. Thus, the corporation gains an additional source of funds not generally available to an individual or even to small, lesser-known corporations. To those unfamiliar with financial markets, the idea of "selling" a bond does not appear to relate to "borrowing" money. However, a **bond** is exactly that—a debt instrument representing borrowed money. Principal on bonds must be repaid with interest, and interest can be used as an expense for income tax purposes. Shares of stock carry no obligation for the corporation to repay the purchases' investment; nor are the dividends paid to shareholders tax-deductible. Bonds are offered in several categories:

- **debenture bonds**, which are an unsecured promise to repay; in effect, a corporate IOU (The sale of debenture bonds is widely used by the Federal National Mortgage Association (Fannie Mae) to raise most of the money it needs to buy mortgages for its own portfolio.);
- **mortgage bonds**, which are secured by a pledge of real estate;
- **equipment bonds**, which are secured by a pledge of equipment such as railroad cars or airplanes.
- **utility bonds**, which may be secured by a pledge of certain assets of a state-regulated utility company;
- **government bonds**, which are federal government promises to pay (no specific assets pledged) with maturity over 10 years;
- **municipal bonds**, which can be state or municipal issue, may or may not pledge tax or improvement revenue, and offer interest that is exempt from federal income tax with certain limitations (This category of bond may be used for the private purpose of financing home and apartment loans.); and
- **mortgage-backed bonds**, which are secured by the pledge of a large pool of mortgage loans. The loans are normally held by a trustee or a pooler that issues the mortgage-backed security.

A **pooler** is a corporation, such as investment banker Salomon Smith Barney, Inc., that buys loans to create these pools. This concept of pooling is used by those referred to as mortgage conduits. The earliest pooling was represented by collateralized mortgage obligations, or "CMOs," a special-purpose entity wholly separate from the institution(s) that created it. The entity is the legal owner of a set of mortgages, called a pool. From the early poolers, there evolved two general types of **conduit** lenders. The most popular during the last decade were those that simply purchased loans in order to securitize them. This is the basis of conduit lending. The other type of conduit lender also services loans. One example was Bear Stearns and Company, which, prior to its merger with JPMorgan Chase, was a major conduit that serviced the loans it securitized and sold as mortgage-backed securities (MBS) or real estate mortgage investment conduits, also called "REMICs." REMICs function somewhat like CMOs, piecing together mortgages into pools based on risk and issuing bonds or other securities to investors. These securities would then trade on the secondary mortgage market like MBS.

THE SECURITIES MARKET

To qualify for sale to the general public, securities must have prior approval by the federal Securities and Exchange Commission (SEC). Each state adds its own security requirements for the protection of consumers. Regulatory approval is based primarily on the disclosure of relevant financial information, not on an issue's potential value. Approved securities are bought and sold daily on major exchanges throughout the world, but sales are dominated by the New York markets. Stock exchanges deal in securities that trade in fairly large volumes and offer near-continuous price quotes.

Mortgage-backed bonds, more commonly called **mortgage-backed securities**, may bypass federal and state regulatory approval if underwritten by certain federal agencies, such as Fannie Mae and Freddie Mac. However, a growing category of privately issued, mortgage-backed securities must comply with SEC regulations.

Mortgage-backed securities are bought and sold every day in the financial markets and trade at fluctuating prices. Since almost all of them offer holders a fixed return on investment, value in a resale is sensitive to the fluctuation of interest rates. The fixed interest rate on such a security (the face rate or nominal rate) controls the price for which it may be sold. If market interest rates go up, the price falls. The reason is that a security purchased at the lower price still receives the fixed interest on the initial face amount, resulting in an increased return to match the higher interest rates. Thus, there is an inverse movement in the bond market. If bond prices rise, interest rates are falling; if bond prices fall, interest rates are rising.

Bonds and mortgage-backed securities are normally offered in $1,000 denominations or multiples of $1,000, and the price can be quoted in a dollar amount or as a percentage figure.

Example

A $10,000 bond offers a coupon interest rate of 5%, paying $500 each year to the holder of the bond. Assume that, for some valid reason, the bond is sold at a discount for $9,250 (the "price" could also be quoted as a percentage at 92.5%). The party paying $9,250 still receives an interest payment of $500 each year, which amounts to a return of 5.41% on the $9,250 invested. At maturity, the issuer of the bond is required to redeem the paper at its face amount of $10,000. Thus, the bond holder picks up an additional $750, which is the difference between the $9,250 paid and the face amount of $10,000 at which the bond was redeemed. Therefore, the total return, or yield, on the investment includes both the annual interest and the price differential when the bond is redeemed. However, if the bond is sold prior to maturity, the holder could sustain a loss if the market is down—meaning, in this instance, that interest rates have risen and a greater discount must be given to match the yield.

Commercial Paper

One other type of corporate borrowing should be mentioned, as it is used to finance construction by a few large builders. This is the sale of commercial paper. **Commercial paper** is a simple promise to pay that is unsecured (a corporate IOU). The term is short, generally between one day and 270 days. The largest issuer of commercial paper, General Electric Credit, uses it to finance its various financial services operations. Yields offered on commercial paper are usually competitive with short-term money market rates, running about .5% to 1% higher than 90-day Treasury bill yields. During the recent financial crisis, the Federal Reserve (the Fed) created the Commercial Paper Funding Facility (CPFF) to provide a liquidity backstop to U.S. issuers of commercial paper. This was critical for large corporations' liquidity, since the size of the market had shrunk to 1.7 trillion in 2008—down from $2.2 trillion a year earlier—imperiling the ability of companies to produce goods and services.[12] The CPFF was intended to improve liquidity in short-term funding markets and thereby contribute to the greater availability of credit for businesses and households. Under the CPFF, the Federal Reserve Bank of New York financed the purchase of highly rated, unsecured, and asset-backed commercial paper from eligible issuers via eligible primary dealers. The CPFF began

---

[12]Suzanne Woolley, "The Commercial Paper Squeeze: Why It Hurts," *Bloomberg*, September 29, 2008, accessed December 15, 2014, http://www.businessweek.com/stories/2008-09-29/the-commercial-paper-squeeze-why-it-hurtsbusinessweek-business-news-stock-market-and-financial-advice

operations on October 27, 2008, and ceased to operate on February 1, 2010. By 2014, the commercial paper market was well recovered, with rates on 90-day A2/P2 commercial paper hovering at 4/10th of 1% versus the astounding 4% seen in 2008.[13]

Competitive Market

A considerable variety of investments exist in the securities market. Each type of security must compete with other kinds based on their returns, or yields. Both the price at which a security is offered and the interest to be paid affect yield. The yield demanded by an investor varies with both risk and the length of time of the investment. The higher the risk, the higher the yield must be; the longer the term, the higher the yield required. Therefore, interest rates on mortgage loans must be competitive with other available security investments.

Investment Risk

For a mortgage-backed security, the risk is low. After all, each loan held in a pool usually carries some kind of default insurance (private mortgage insurance, FHA, or VA). In today's market, about half of mortgage-backed securities are guaranteed by a federal agency, and thus are doubly insured. Federal agency underwriting is a form of credit enhancement that reduces risk, allowing a lower yield requirement. This lower yield requirement is reflected in lower interest rates for the borrower.

PRIVATE LENDERS

Individuals

Individuals do not come under the legal restrictions and reporting requirements of institutional lenders. Therefore, good statistics on individual participation in the mortgage market are not readily available. However, many individuals make mortgage loans, albeit sometimes with considerable reluctance.

As a general rule, the individual lender has motives other than profiting from the loan itself. The most common motive is when a second mortgage (or a first mortgage) is accepted for the primary purpose of

---

[13]*Commercial Paper Rates and Outstanding Summary* (Washington, DC: Federal Reserve Bank, 2014).

consummating a house sale. In some cases, the motivation is to help a family member or perhaps to assist a valued employee in acquiring suitable housing.

Another area that individuals sometimes participate in is the second- and third-mortgage market for investment. The attraction is that junior mortgages offer higher yields than do first mortgages. The high yields are often obtained through substantial discounts that are due to the greater risk involved in junior mortgages, as prior lienholders must be satisfied first in the event of foreclosure. These loans have been a major source of investment losses for investors who made such second and third mortgages at the recent top of the residential real estate bubble.

MISCELLANEOUS OTHER SOURCES

In different parts of the country, various types of companies, institutions, and even state housing agencies have established themselves as sources of mortgage funds, usually limiting the geographic area in which they will loan money. As a general rule, this type of lender does little or no advertising because lending money is not its primary business. The following paragraphs identify the most important of these sources.

Title Companies

Because title companies have a close association with, and considerable knowledge of, the mortgage industry, these affiliated companies may act as primary sources in lending their own funds. They may also raise money from the sale of mortgage bonds or serve as correspondents or agents for other major lenders.

Endowment Funds Managed by Universities, Colleges, and Hospitals

As a group, endowment funds prefer to maintain their assets in high-grade stocks and bonds that have a good record for security are considered more liquid and, most importantly, require less administrative attention than a portfolio of mortgage loans. However, many endowments take the form of land and other real property, and these may require more expertise in the mortgage loan field.

Foundations

Foundations are established primarily by corporations or wealthy families as a means of continuing charitable or other activities through the use of income earned from the foundations' investments. Like endowment funds, foundations are primarily interested in high-grade stocks and bonds as investments but are not averse to mortgage loans, particularly if a purpose of special interest to the foundation can be served.

Fraternal, Benevolent, and Religious Associations

These funds are generally little known and very seldom advertised. Administration is usually handled on a careful, conservative basis with the security of the loan of greater importance than the yield. Some of these organizations limit lending to their own members and will provide low-cost loans to qualified members in good standing.

FOREIGN LENDERS

Foreign sources of investments are many, taking the forms of direct loans made to commercial real estate developers, investors by banks, or direct investments by foreign sovereign wealth funds. A good example is the Government Pension Fund Global of Norway, managed by Norges Bank Investment Management, an arm of the Central Bank of Norway. This firm has 5% of its investments in real estate and was the second largest investor in U.S. commercial real estate in 2014.[14] Most of the Norges Bank investments were leveraged to maximize investment returns by borrowings made from Nordic and other European banks. Many times, banks will form syndicates to make loans to REITs backed by commercial real estate in the U.S. and other locales. A good example is the recent syndicated loan made by Sumitomo Mitsui Banking Corporation; Mizuho Bank, Ltd.; Aozora Bank, Ltd.; Shinsei Bank, Limited; The Bank of Tokyo-Mitsubishi UFJ, Ltd.; and Resona Bank, Limited to the Ichigo Real Estate Investment Corporation in two loans of ¥5.5 million in December 2014.[15]

---

[14]"Norway jumps to second-biggest foreign buyer of U.S. real estate," Bloomberg, September 24, 2014.
[15]"Ichigo Real Estate Investment: New Loans and Interest Rate Swap," 4-traders, December 8, 2014, accessed December 27, 2014, http://www.4-traders.com/ICHIGO-REAL-ES-TATE-INVEST-6498170/news/Ichigo-Real-Estate-Investment--New-Loans-and-Interest-Rate-Swap-19508493/

Aegon Levensverzekering and Aegon Hypotheken are 100% indirect subsidiaries of Aegon N.V. ("Aegon NV"), an international life insurance, pension, and asset management company based in the Hague, the Netherlands, with businesses in over 20 markets in the Americas, Europe, and Asia. Historical performance of Aegon's total residential mortgage loan portfolio has been stable over the last 10 years when many other countries' mortgage markets were in disarray. Aegon NV also manages pension funds in the U.S. through some of its subsidiaries, such as Transamerica Retirement Solutions Corporation, and has purchased whole mortgages and mortgage-backed securities of single-family residential mortgages, and financed commercial real estate as well.

Recent Trends

In May 2018 Federal Reserve Bank regulators expressed concerns over the results of a Federal Reserve Bank quarterly survey of senior loan offices that seemed to indicate that regulators U.S. banks had relaxed standards on commercial real estate loans for the first time in almost three years[16]. It concluded that U.S. Banks had relaxed standards on three commercial underwriting criteria including: (1) the spread in basis points on the rate charged on the loan compared to their cost of funds; (2) maximum loan amount, and (3) debt coverage ratio requirements. These relaxed standards seemed to cover all the major commercial real estate loan types including multifamily loans, construction, land development, and nonfarm nonresidential loans. This has been driven by continued competition with foreign lenders who have continued to make funds for commercial real estate available at favorable terms to U.S. developers and investors. The foreign lenders that have been the most active in this market have been had somewhat of a natural advantage since over 31% of total international commercial real estate transactions in the U.S. in 2017 were made by Chinese and Mexico investors[17]. Other poorly regulated funding sources are coming on-line such as crowd funding via new

---

[16]Greg Robb, "U.S. banks Loosened Commercial Real Estate Lending Standards for First Time in 3 Years: Fed," MarketWatch, May 8, 2018, https://www.marketwatch.com/story/us-banks-loosened-commercial-real-estate-lending-standards-for-first-time-in-almost-3-years-fed-2018-05-08

[17]"Commercial Real Estate International Business Trends 2017,"National Association of REALTORS®, 2017, https://www.nar.realtor/sites/default/files/reports/2017/2017_REALTORS_CRE_International_Report.pdf

funders like: Patch of Land, Fundrise, RealtyMogul, and CrowdFunders, and this space is growing.

Earlier in 2018 Boston Federal Reserve Bank District President Eric Rosengren shared his views concerning a potential asset bubble in commercial real estate that has developed since late 2015[18]. President Rosengren went on to say in an interview that the problem of commercial real estate value inflation has continued to worsen not improve. Surveys by the National Association of REALTORS® and others for 2017 showed the main reason for foreign investors not purchasing U.S. commercial real estate were in order of highest percentage: (1) couldn't find a property, 36%; and (2) cost of the property, 21%. Both relate to causes and effects of higher pricing. Not surprising was that one of the lower reasons for not purchasing given by foreign investors was not being able to obtain financing at less than 6%.

Foreign lenders have been working with other nonbank lenders like the Blackstone Group that packaged the financing for the acquisition and renovation of RiverTower, an enormous Midtown East rental building in Chicago, for a total of $3 billion. Basel III effects on this type of transaction have made real estate loans less appealing and more expensive for banks. Banks conceded loan market share to private debt funds and other nonbank lenders. However, in the case of the RiverTown development, Blackstone sold the more senior portion of it to the Bank of China a few months later. This practice seems to have made an end run around U.S. banks, allowing the Bank of China to be largest commercial real estate loan holder in Chicago in 2016.

Questions for Discussion

1. Distinguish between the operations of a mortgage banker and a mortgage broker. What are the five major minimum standards that an independent mortgage broker or loan office must pass to be licensed with the NMLS?
2. What qualifications are necessary to become a mortgage banker? Are there any special requirements for mortgage lenders in your state?
3. What is meant by loan servicing?

---

[18]Greg Robb, "The Fed Official Most Concerned about Possible Asset Bubbles Presses the Alarm Button (Again)," MarketWatch, January 16, 2018, https://www.marketwatch.com/story/the-fed-official-most-concerned-about-possible-asset-bubbles-presses-the-alarm-button-again-2018-01-12

4. Identify the principal sources of mortgage company income.
5. Identify at least two kinds of shorter-term mortgage loans made by commercial banks.
6. The common business organization of a Mortgage Company involves what three divisions?
7. Explain the origin and purpose of Real Estate Investment Trusts.
8. Name three primary market lenders that are not subject to banking regulations.
9. Describe a warehouse line of credit and who may use it.
10. Are there any good sources of mortgage money available in your locality outside of mortgage companies and regulated lending institutions?

Multiple Choice Questions for Review

1. Which of the following minimum standards does an individual considering becoming a licensed mortgage broker under the SAFE Act not have to meet?
   a. pass a criminal background check
   b. pass a national licensing exam
   c. provide evidence of working as a mortgage loan officer for three years
   d. provide evidence of satisfactory net worth or a surety bond

2. Mortgage banking includes all of the following EXCEPT:
   a. the origination of loans secured by residential real estate
   b. the sale of mortgage loans
   c. the title insurance on mortgages
   d. the servicing of mortgage loans

3. Which of the following is NOT a typical function of a loan servicing department of a mortgage bank?
   a. collecting mortgage payments
   b. establishing escrow accounts for taxes and insurance payments
   c. issuing participation certificates to MBS pools for loans being serviced
   d. producing delinquency reports for investors

4. Who or what is referred to when a mortgage banker establishes a line of credit with a commercial bank?
   a. mortgage broker
   b. correspondent
   c. warehouse loan
   d. investor

5. The Rural Housing Development Service offers all of the following mortgage loan products EXCEPT:
   a. direct loans that can be made up to 100% of the appraised value of a house for a maximum term of 33 years
   b. loans to migrant workers to purchase mobile homes that can be permanently attached to a property
   c. guaranteed loan programs, in which applicants may have incomes of up to 115% of the median income for the area
   d. loans for the development and construction of waste disposal plants

6. Which of the following lenders is NOT exempt from most mortgage-lending regulation by the Federal Reserve, Comptroller of the Currency, and state banking and savings and loan regulators?
   a. home builders
   b. pension funds
   c. private finance companies
   d. insurance companies

7. REITs must have at least _____ of total investment assets in real estate or in real estate-backed assets such as equity mortgage-backed securities.
   a. 10%
   b. 25%
   c. 50%
   d. 75%

8. Which of the following is not a principal type of real estate trust?
   a. hybrid
   b. mortgage
   c. equity
   d. leveraged

9. Real Estate Investment Trusts have all the following characteristics EXCEPT:
   a. They pass through income to their owners without it being taxed.
   b. They are corporations.
   c. They are partnerships.
   d. They must be owned by 100 or more investors.

10. Which of the following might not be a good local source for alternative funding of a residential mortgage loan?
    a. local foundation
    b. state down payment assistance program
    c. title company
    d. hard money lender

Information Resources

http://mortgage.nationwidelicensingsystem.org/Pages/default.aspx

Some of you will wish to find out more about how to become licensed mortgage brokers. One of the best places to start is the National Mortgage Licensing System Resource Center.

https://www.reit.com/

This site, maintained by the National Association of Real Estate Investment Trusts, provides information about related programs, statistics, publications, and research.

http://www1.snl.com/Sectors/RealEstate/Default.aspx

For readers with some knowledge of REIT structures or who want to learn more about how professionals look at investing in new or existing REITs, this website provides fundamental financial data on more than 240 REITs, REOCs, and homebuilders with timely information about FFO estimates, proprietary AFFOs, and NAV consensus estimates.

http://cc-bc.com/grants.html

One of the better independent sources of information about grants and down payment assistance programs is part of the nonprofit organization Consumer Credit and Budget Counseling, Inc., accessible via the URL above.

Chapter 6

INSTRUMENTS OF REAL ESTATE FINANCE

KEY TERMS AND PHRASES

- acceleration clause
- alienation clause
- assumption
- blanket mortgage
- construction loan
- contract for deed
- deed of trust
- deficiency judgment
- hazard insurance
- junior mortgage
- lien theory
- mortgage
- open-end mortgage model
- package mortgage
- prepayment
- principal
- promissory note
- purchase money mortgage
- recording
- redemption
- subordination
- security instrument
- title theory

CHAPTER 6 Instruments of Real Estate Finance

> **LEARNING OBJECTIVES**
>
> At the conclusion of this chapter, students will be able to:
> - Describe the development of lien theory as a key requirement for real estate lending.
> - Describe mortgage procedures related to priority importance of recording, releases and subordination use in mortgage origination.
> - Understand the key mortgage instruments for securing real estate and the effects of state real estate ownership laws on their application.
> - Describe the types of real estate financing contracts.
> - Explain the insurance requirements relevant to financing various types of real estate.
> - Describe the evolution, benefits, and types of uniform mortgage documents.

INTRODUCTION

The use of real estate as the collateral security in loans related to the acquisition of land, homes, and farms can be traced back as far as the ancient businessmen of Ur, the Pharaohs of Egypt, and the Romans of the pre-Christian era. Even then, some form of promise or assignment of the property was used to ensure repayment of an obligation to the lender. The development over many centuries of this type of property assignment illustrates interplay between the rights of a borrower and the rights of a lender.

History and Development

In its earliest incarnation, the mortgage instrument as security for a loan actually granted title to the collateral property to the lender to assure repayment. As time passed and the means to borrow became more readily available, the rights of borrowers became a concern. Another form of mortgage pledge was introduced, granting the lender a lien on property pledged as collateral. This meant primarily that foreclosure would be subject to a court's determination. Both basic forms of mortgage pledges are in use today and their use is determined by state law.

State Laws Control Property Rights

Property rights in the United States are spelled out primarily under state laws, not by the federal government. Each state has written into its code of law specific rights and procedures that must be adhered to with regard to land ownership and its conveyance. The local variations and shadings in these laws reflect the background and origins of the particular region. For example, the great body of English parliamentary law and common law guided the New England and Mid-Atlantic states in setting up their constitutions and subsequent statutes. French legal codes were reflected in the Louisiana Territory and were especially evident in the growing city of New Orleans. Spanish heritage colored the laws, recognizing Catholic religious ties in marriage as well as patriarchal protection of wife, children, and family relationships in the southwestern states; one result is community property statutes that give special protection to both parties in a marriage. All states, however, require some **security instrument** that gives a creditor the right to sell the security property to satisfy the debt if the debtor fails to pay the debt according to the terms of the agreement.

The Mortgage as a Grant of Title

Initially, as noted above, a loan secured by real estate involved granting legal title to the lender. During the term of the loan, the lender might even have the physical use of that land and be entitled to any rents or other revenues derived from it. The borrower held equitable rights to the property, meaning that title must be returned upon satisfactory repayment of the loan. However, due to the primitive conditions of communications and transportation then in existence, the practice of granting lenders title to properties in exchange for loans tended to foster some abuses by lenders. For example, a slight delay in payments, which might even be encouraged by the lender, could easily create a default and forfeit the borrower's rights to any recovery of the land. Dispossession could be made without notice, with no return of money already paid to the lender.

Sometimes borrowers who felt they had been unjustly deprived of their property appealed to an official to seek a hearing for their grievances and to petition for just redress. If it was subsequently determined that a wrong had been committed, the borrower might be given a chance to redeem the land with a late payment of the obligation. Thus, the right of **redemption** came into being. Additional discussion of the use of the right of redemption will be covered in Chapter 10.

ENCUMBRANCES AND LIENS

The Mortgage as a Lien

As the law has developed in the United States, the rights of borrowers have become of greater concern; less than half of all states have adopted the **lien theory** for a mortgage pledge. With this method, the borrower retains legal title to the property and grants a lien to the lender as security for repayment of a loan. In law, to *hypothecate* property is to pledge it as security for an obligation without surrendering possession of it. As we noted in chapter 1, hypothecation, as it applies to mortgages, operates in the following way: The borrower hypothecates when he or she pledges property as security/collateral for payment of a mortgage in order to borrow against the value of the real estate. In both situations, the borrower retains the use of the real estate or home but the lender has the right to take possession (that is, foreclose) if the borrower fails to pay the debt service obligations when they are due.

A *lien* constitutes an encumbrance on property. It is a declaration of a claim to a parcel of land for some purpose and is recorded in the public record. In states where the lien form of mortgage is prevalent, a defaulted borrower retains possession and legal title until the lien is perfected through court action by the lender. Usually in a lien theory state, the lender must sue to foreclose and gain title to sell the secured property to obtain repayment if a borrower has defaulted.

The concept of a mortgage as a lien shifts considerable power from the lender to the borrower. It is possible for defaulted borrowers to remain in possession of the property for substantial periods of time without making loan payments. Coupled with statutory redemption periods, the result has been numerous problems for lenders trying to recover their losses within a reasonable period of time.

Some states have modified borrowers' rights under the **title theory** and allow lenders to take possession of collateral property in the event of a loan default, without waiting for the conclusion of foreclosure proceedings.

While there is obvious variation in the precise usage of the lien as a form of pledge versus the limited assignment of title as another form of pledge, mortgages can be classified into either of the two forms. The advantages and disadvantages of each can be weighed in terms of their legal significance, but for purposes of finance, it is important mainly to be aware of the existing differences and to know under what laws a particular property can be mortgaged. Lenders have learned to live with various requirements and can obtain adequate security for their loans by adapting mortgage pledges to state-specific laws. The conforming loan documentation required by Fannie Mae and Freddie Mac varies the mortgage instrument for each state.

As a review, when a lender is in a title theory state, the borrower will not hold the title to the property in their name; rather, the lender will be a beneficial holder to title to the property using a deed of trust that places the title to the property in trust with a third party trustee. In a lien theory state, the title to the real property will remain in the name of the borrower and the lender takes a mortgage or security interest that allows them to foreclose using the courts. Some states have hybrid forms of these theories, but a slight majority of states are title theory states.

THE NOTE AND DEED OF TRUST

Mortgage Variations

The underlying purpose of the mortgage instrument is to provide a pledge of property as collateral to secure a promissory note. In order to properly serve the needs of lenders and borrowers, there are variations in how loans are used that create differences in the wording of mortgage instruments. These are not the same as the special differences that derive from how a mortgage is repaid, an issue that will be considered in the next chapter. The following section identifies the principal kinds of mortgages and describes their purposes and unique features.

Regular Mortgage

A regular mortgage is a two-party legal document used to secure the performance of an obligation. The borrower, or mortgagor, grants certain rights to the lender, or mortgagee, pledging property as collateral. The rights granted may be in the nature of a lien or a conditional grant of title. Foreclosure with a regular mortgage is usually handled through court action. The mortgage is a conveyance instrument that creates rights in real property and should be recorded.

Deed of Trust

A **deed of trust**, sometimes called a *trust deed*, is a loan in which title to property is conditionally conveyed to a third-party trustee as security for an

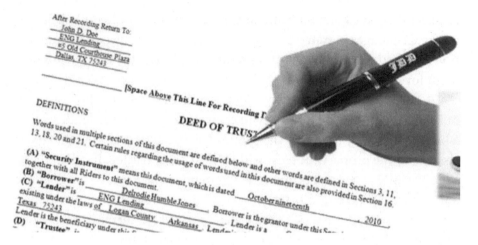

obligation owed to the lender, who is called the *beneficiary*. The trustee can be an individual (usually an attorney), a trust company, or a title insurance company, as selected by the lender. The trustee in this instrument is normally granted the right to undertake foreclosure through its "power of sale" clause. A deed of trust (an example of which appears in the appendix) is the security instrument used in title theory states, as discussed earlier in this chapter, and foreclosure proceedings can be implemented without benefit of court action. In the event of a default, the lender notifies the trustee to request that action be taken to protect the lender's interest. The trustee then notifies the debtor, in accordance with the relevant state law, that foreclosure is pending. On the date of foreclosure, the trustee offers the property to the highest bidder and has the authority to deliver title to the property in a nonjudicial action. In those states that allow it, this procedure is much faster and of lower cost than a judicial procedure, which requires court action to convey title in a foreclosure action.

THE NOTE AND MORTGAGE

While the broad field of real property law exceeds the scope of this text, it should be noted that a mortgage is a conveyance instrument, as it transfers certain property rights. The transfer of property rights should be handled by qualified attorneys, skilled in interpreting these rights according to the laws of each state. Most states limit any conveyance of property rights solely to written agreements, and all states require certain procedures to record conveyances of land in the public records. One result has been an increasingly accurate record of land titles, with a corresponding increase of protection for the rights of property owners and other interested parties.

Some basic instruments used in real estate loans have essentially the same purpose throughout the country. One of these, the **mortgage**, is the pledge of collateral that has given its name to the entire field of real estate finance. A mortgage is simply a pledge of property to secure a loan. It is not a promise to pay anything. As a matter of fact, without a debt to secure, the mortgage itself becomes null and void by its own terms; it is, as the French origin of the word indicates, a "dead pledge." Due to the differences in state laws, the precise definition varies somewhat, but for our purposes, a mortgage can best be defined as a conditional conveyance of property as security for the debt recited therein, which can only be activated by failure to comply with its terms.

Mortgage Instrument

A conforming loan mortgage instrument is divided into two major sections: (1) uniform covenants that are standard across the country, and (2) nonuniform covenants that cover special requirements of state law. While some of the details vary, the underlying purposes of mortgage covenants are very similar. These will be discussed next.

Parties Involved

The mortgage instrument must identify the names of all parties involved who have an ownership interest in the property being mortgaged. These parties may not be the same as those obligated on the promissory note. Since the mortgage is a conveyance-type instrument, it is necessary to have all owners indicate agreement by signature. The rules of contract law apply to mortgages, so they must be in writing, and the parties must be legally competent to contract. Whether the marital status of the parties involved needs to be stated depends upon state law. If the parties are married, both signatures may be required, as marital rights, homestead rights, and/or community property rights may be at stake.

Identification of Property

Identification of the property offered as collateral to secure the promissory note must be accurately described so as to distinguish it from any other property in the world. A street address is never acceptable because it can change over the years. Nor are boundary lines based on physical features—for example, "the big live oak by the river bend"—acceptable as long-term identification. Several methods are used to legally define real property. One is by "metes and bounds," using a surveyor's description of boundary lines from a fixed starting point, thence proceeding in specific compass directions and distances around the property back to the starting point. In urban areas, the most common method is by a "lot and block" description taken from a subdivision plat, which must be registered and approved by a local government authority. A third method, found mostly in western states, is by geodetic survey. By this method, large tracts of land were surveyed, marked by stakes in the ground, and designated by townships of 36 square miles that can be used to identify land. Legal description of real property is more fully explained in Chapter 11, "Property Analysis."

An erroneous description of the property, even a typographical error, can render the mortgage instrument void, but does not necessarily invalidate the promissory note. If a loan has been funded and the promissory note properly signed, there is an obligation to repay whether or not the mortgage is valid. If the mortgage is not valid, a properly signed and funded note becomes an unsecured obligation.

Principal Amount Due

Most mortgage notes are paid on an installment plan wherein each payment includes all the interest due to that payment date, plus a portion of the principal due. Thus with each payment, the total amount owed is reduced. When mortgage notes are transferred, only the principal balance then due can be conveyed. Business practice places confidence in the seller of a note to deliver accurate information on the precise balance due at the time of transfer. However, when a large commercial loan is transferred, some kind of legal assurance of the amount conveyed is usually required.

Estoppel

The term *estoppel* is sometimes applied to a mortgagee's information letter. This letter is a statement from the mortgage lender to the borrower giving information on the current status of that loan, including the amount of principal balance due at that time. Such information is normally obtained as part of the property listing process. An older practice, and one still used sometimes with large commercial loans, is to require an estoppel agreement when a note is transferred. The purpose of the agreement is an acknowledgment by both borrower and lender of the loan amount due at that time. In effect, it "stops" a subsequent purchaser of the note from claiming any greater amount. The legal doctrine of estoppel has a broader application in that it prevents a person from asserting rights that are inconsistent with a previous position.

CONTRACT FOR DEED

A **contract for deed** is a sale and financing agreement that allows the purchase price of property to be paid in installments. It is not a mortgage, although it is often misunderstood as one. Under a contract for deed, the buyer receives only the rights of possession and enjoyment, much the same as in a lease with option to buy. However, it is distinguished from a lease by the fact that a contract for deed grants the buyer an **equitable title** to the property during the payment period. This means that after a part, or all, of the payments have been made as agreed, the seller is obligated to deliver legal title to the property. State law varies as to how it treats the buyer/borrower under a contract for deed. Some states grant the buyer certain rights to the property as payments are made. Others recognize only the ownership rights retained by the seller to the extent that such contracts may not even be recordable.

The following are the risks that most concern a buyer in a contract for deed transaction:

1. The greatest risk for the buyer involves the fact that title is not delivered until after payment has been made. During the payment period, it is possible that the seller will become unable to perform. While legal title remains in the seller's name, it is subject to any adverse claim that may accrue against the seller. The seller may suffer a legal disability, file bankruptcy, or die. Or the seller may be a corporation with only limited liability for the directors and shareholders. Holding an executed deed in escrow pending final payment does not remove this risk because the deed would not be recorded.
2. If there is an underlying mortgage on the property, a payment escrow account should be used to assure the buyer that payments are properly made to the mortgage holder.

The following are the risks that most concern a seller in a contract for deed transaction:

1. If a buyer defaults or becomes bankrupt, there could be a problem of clearing title, which might be costly.
2. A contract for deed is subject to contract law, which offers differing interpretations.
3. If the seller has an existing lien on the property that is not going to be paid off by the transaction, he or she will mostly be in default under the due-on-sale clause provisions in most mortgage and deed of trust documents used over the past 30 years.

Although there are special problems with a contract for deed transaction, the procedure serves some valid purposes. One would be to allow someone who has difficulty qualifying for a mortgage loan to possess a home. A problem might arise if a person is laid off, then finds a new job but is unable to meet a lender's length of time on the job requirement. If the time requirement is met and a proper mortgage loan can be obtained, the buyer has possession of the home. Another possibility is that a property may have a known title defect that is curable, but the cure will take time. The present condition of the title disqualifies the property as collateral. A contract for deed could convey possession, however, while allowing time for the title to be cleared. Once good title is achieved, a mortgage loan could then be obtained to pay off the seller.

Contracts for deed are often used in the sale of lots in resort areas, or when the purpose is to achieve a fast sale under high-pressure tactics. With legal title to the property held by the seller, there is less need to fully qualify a buyer. It is easier to push for a quick closing. And because title is not conveyed at closing, there appears to be less need to assure good title with a search of the abstract, or to require title insurance. An unwary buyer may be in danger in this situation, as title defects can just as easily interfere with a later delivery of title as with an immediate delivery.

Contracts for deed can be found under an assortment of names, causing some confusion for buyers. They may be called land contracts, installment contracts, agreements of sale, conditional sales contracts, or even just real estate contracts. Properly handled and in the right circumstances, a contract for deed (an example of which appears in the appendix) is a practical procedure for transferring property, but legal counsel is advisable before entering into such an agreement, regardless of its name.

SUBORDINATE FINANCE INSTRUMENTS

Open-End Mortgage

An **open-end mortgage** sets a limit on the amount that may be borrowed and allows incremental advances up to that amount secured by the same mortgage. It reduces closing costs and appraisal costs. Nevertheless, new money advanced under an open-end mortgage may be at a different, current rate of interest. This type of mortgage is often used in farm loans to meet seasonal needs, much like a line of credit. Maintaining some balance due on the mortgage obligation can retain the priority of the mortgage lien. Even so, it is a good idea for the lender to require a title search when an incremental advance is made as certain claims, such as property taxes, can create a higher priority claim than the mortgage.

Construction Loan

A **construction loan** is a short-term loan used to cover the costs of building. It is sometimes called an "interim" loan, although that term also describes a broader range of loans. A construction loan differs from other mortgage loans in that it is funded through periodic advances as construction progresses. The loan may be funded by either of two different methods: (1) after certain stages of construction are completed, or (2) after certain time periods (such as each month) for work completed up to that point. It takes a construction-wise loan officer to ensure that funds are released as building progresses. Following this procedure of loan inspection and advances, the value of the building used as collateral increases at approximately the same rate as the amount of the loan. Nevertheless, the risk of a construction loan lies in the ability of the borrower/builder to complete the project within the budget, or the total amount of money available. Failure to complete the building precludes release of the permanent loan, the amount of which is normally used to pay off the construction loan. There are two types of construction loans: one-time closings and two closings. One-time closings are offered by many lenders that offer construction loans. These loans are also called "construction-to-permanent loans" because what occurs is a simple "rollover" from a construction loan to a standard mortgage once the building is completed. Taking one loan means one application and only one set of closing fees. Two-closing construction loans involve the simple construction loans discussed next (interim loans), where borrowers pay only the interest accrued on the cost of the build. Upon completion of construction, the borrower, if the same as the end-use homeowner, must re-qualify and pay the closing costs associated with taking a mortgage on the cost of the build.

Interim Loan

The term *interim* is often used synonymously with the term *construction loan*. While the jargon varies somewhat, an interim loan has a broader meaning. It is any loan that is expected to be repaid from the proceeds of another loan. A home loan is expected to be repaid from the borrower's personal income; an income property loan is expected to be repaid from income derived from the property itself; and an interim loan is expected to be repaid from other borrowed money. An interim loan is sometimes used for short-term financing until regular financing has been completed.

When used for this purpose, the financing is also called a *gap loan* or a *bridge loan*. Since most construction loans are made with the expectation of repayment from a permanent loan when the building is completed, they easily qualify as an interim type of financing.

Mortgage with Release Clauses

When money is borrowed for the purpose of land development, specific release procedures are necessary to enable the developer to sell lots, or portions of the land, and deliver good titles to those portions. This is the purpose of a release clause. Conditions are structured so that a developer can repay a portion of the loan and obtain a release of a portion of the collateral from the original mortgage. In a subdivision of building lots, loan repayment would be based on a percentage of the sales price of the lot or a minimum dollar amount for each lot released. The lender normally calculates partial payoffs so that the loan would be fully repaid when around 60% to 80% of the lots are sold.

With regular mortgages, partial sale of the collateral is normally not an option. So a development loan requires considerable negotiation to work out all the details necessary for success. The lender will want some control over the direction of development; that is, lots must be completed and sold in an orderly manner that will not undermine the value of any remaining land. A time pattern must be negotiated to allow realistic limits on how fast lots must be sold. The clause that permits release of a portion of the mortgaged land is also called a *partial release clause*, since the remainder of the land continues to be held as security for the remaining balance on the loan.

Junior Mortgage

The term **junior mortgage** applies to those mortgages that carry a lower priority than the prime or first mortgage. These can be second, third, or even fourth mortgages. The lower priority carries higher risk and requires corresponding higher interest rates. No mortgage instrument carries a designation in its title or text describing its lien position. The order of lien priority, which determines the exact order of claims against a piece of property, is established by the time of its recording. This order becomes of extreme importance in a foreclosure proceeding.

> ### Example
>
> Assume a property valued at $200,000 carries a first mortgage of $130,000 and a second mortgage of $40,000. If this property is forced into a foreclosure sale that results in a recovery of $135,000 in cash after payment of court costs and legal fees, how should the money be distributed? Assuming that no other liens, taxes, or other claims have shown priority, the first mortgage holder is in a position to recover the full $130,000 from the $135,000 in proceeds. The remaining $5,000 is awarded to the second mortgage holder, leaving that payment $35,000 short of recovering the $40,000 loan. Due to the promissory note, the second mortgage holder may have the right to seek a deficiency judgment against the borrower to recover that $35,000. However, the land serving as collateral has been wiped out by the foreclosure.

Later in this chapter, we will discuss in more detail the subject of recording as it relates to the question of establishing priority of mortgage liens.

Purchase Money Mortgage

A **purchase money mortgage** is one taken by the seller of property as all or part of the consideration. Such a mortgage carries certain priorities over other claims because the delivery of a deed occurs simultaneously with the taking back of the purchase money mortgage, allowing no time for any other lien to intervene. A purchase money mortgage of this kind carries the special status of a vendor's lien. A *vendor's lien* may be defined as an equitable lien of the grantor upon the land conveyed. It is an implied right held by a seller until all purchase money due the seller is repaid. Also, depending on state law, a defaulting buyer may or may not be subject to a deficiency judgment upon default of a purchase money mortgage. During the recent financial crisis, many lenders have offered delinquent borrowers the opportunity to simply deed the property back to the lender in a procedure referred to as a *deed in lieu of foreclosure* transaction. A deed in lieu of foreclosure is more desirable than a straight foreclosure for the borrower, as it will not have as negative an effect on a borrower's credit as a foreclosure. In addition, a deed in lieu of foreclosure is less expensive and far quicker for a lender in obtaining title to a distressed property than a foreclosure procedure.

A second definition of a *purchase money mortgage* is a mortgage in which the loan proceeds are used exclusively to buy the property secured by that mortgage.

Chattel Mortgage

Chattel is tangible personal property and it can be mortgaged to secure a debt; this is called a *chattel mortgage*. The procedure is more likely to be used when additional security is needed for a loan. It could also be used as part of a loan on real property when it is important to identify certain personal property assets. In the acquisition of personal property, chattel mortgages have been replaced by the *bill of sale* as a security agreement that is regulated by the Uniform Commercial Code.

Package Mortgage

A **package mortgage** pledges both real and personal property to secure a loan. It is often found in the acquisition of a new house. The buyer/borrower includes in the collateral package a number of essential furnishings and appliances needed for the house, and is thus able to pay for them over an extended period of time. Most package mortgages also require the borrower to sign and file a financing statement in accordance with the provisions of the Uniform Commercial Code. A package mortgage normally calls for simple interest rather than the add-on interest found in many installment-type loans.

Blanket Mortgage

A mortgage is not limited to pledging a single parcel of land as collateral. Sometimes the security pledged for a loan may include several tracts of land. When more than one tract is pledged, the security instrument is called a **blanket mortgage**.

"Subject To" Mortgage

In the conveyance of property, it is possible for title to be delivered *subject to* an existing mortgage. The phrase has a legal intent and means that the buyer is not accepting personal liability to the lender for payment of that mortgage note. It in no way changes the claim of a lender holding the mortgage. Rather, it means that the new buyer does not accept the liability. It also means that the new buyer's rights to the property could be wiped out if the grantor of the property fails to make mortgage payments. In the event of a default, the lender holds whatever rights were granted by the mortgage but has no additional right to pursue the new buyer for any deficiency. Such liability remains with the original debtor.

The "subject to" procedure may be used for a number of different transactions, such as when property is acquired for the purpose of rehabilitation and resale. Such a transaction does not create a contingent liability and would not be shown on a financial statement. However, "subject to" clauses are most commonly found when a wraparound mortgage is used.

Transferring property with a "subject to" procedure is definitely a transfer of interest, and could trigger a due-on-sale clause even though the loan itself is not assumed. A *wraparound mortgage* is a new mortgage that encompasses, or "wraps around," one or more existing mortgages and is subordinate to them. The purpose is to acquire additional funding from a loan while retaining the priority of lien of existing mortgages. In periods of escalating interest rates, this design has the additional benefit of retaining an older, lower-interest-rate loan that could benefit both buyer and seller. Lenders and most states' attorneys general have held that if mortgagees enter into wraparound mortgages without notification to the existing lender on the property of the transfer of title, even if it is only placed in escrow, they have committed fraud.

The wrap procedure can be used when an owner borrows additional money with the wrap as a junior mortgage, or it can be used in financing the sale of property. While declining interest rates limit usage of this procedure, it carries some attraction for seller-financed transactions. Since seller financing entails a transfer of interest, the existing mortgage must be assumable in order to consummate a wrap procedure even though the property is transferred "subject to" an existing mortgage. Following is a hypothetical example of how a wrap might fit into a seller-financed transaction that is advantageous to both parties.

> ## Example
>
> A property worth $350,000 has a mortgage with a $240,000 balance at 4% interest. In some future period, the market rate of interest on a 30-year, fixed-rate mortgage new financing costs might be 7%. To acquire the property, the buyer is willing to pay $60,000 down and is seeking $290,000 in financing. The buyer has three options:
>
> 1. Accept all new financing of a $290,000 first-mortgage loan at an interest rate of 7%.
> 2. Assume the existing loan of $240,000, and from a regular lender borrow the additional $50,000 (the difference between $240,000 and $290,000) needed on a second-mortgage loan. This second loan would carry a higher interest rate of, say, 9%.
> 3. Arrange a wraparound loan with the seller for $290,000 at, say, 6%—a loan that would include the existing $240,000 loan. Net new cash is $50,000.

Further examination of the wrap procedure illustrated in the preceding example shows that it could be advantageous to both buyer and seller. The advantage to the buyer, obviously, is lower-cost (6%) financing than otherwise would be possible. For the seller accepting a wraparound mortgage, the advantage is 6% on the new funding of $50,000 plus 2% additional earned interest on the existing $240,000 loan that requires no new cash. The net yield to the seller would thus be greater than 6%. In effect, the buyer makes payments to the seller on a $290,000 loan at 6% interest, while the seller passes on payments to the existing mortgage holder on the $240,000 at 4% interest.

SPECIAL PROVISIONS IN MORTGAGE LENDING INSTRUMENTS

Prepayment Penalty

If all or part of the principal balance of a loan is paid before it becomes due, there is a possible additional charge involved. The purpose of the **prepayment** penalty (some lenders call it a prepayment premium) is to allow the lender to recoup a portion of the interest that the lender had expected to earn when the loan was made. The following example serves to explain the lender's viewpoint.

> ## Example
>
> A loan of $200,000 for 30 years at 6% interest is expected to earn the lender $231,676 in interest over the life of the loan. (The monthly payment of $1,199.10 multiplied by 360 payments equals $431,676. The principal is $200,000; the balance is interest.)

Lenders do not loan money for the purpose of recovering the principal. There is a contractual right to the interest and some claim to compensation for a forfeiture of this right.

On the other hand, the borrower views the repayment as placing cash in the hands of the lender that can easily be loaned to another and continue to earn interest plus additional origination fees. So there is no compensable loss to the lender.

In mortgage instruments today, there are a variety of compromises on these conflicting views. First, no prepayment charges are permitted on HUD/FHA, VA, or conforming loans. On other residential loans, the prepayment penalty might range from 1% to 3% of the loan amount that is prepaid. For instance, if the charge is 3% and the amount prepaid is $20,000, the borrower would owe an additional $600 at the time of prepayment. Another fairly common solution to the prepayment question, sometimes found in commercial loans, is to allow up to 20% of the original loan amount to be prepaid in any one year with no additional charge. Under this option, the borrower could repay the loan in full within five years at no extra cost. Prepayment requirements must be clearly specified in the residential real estate loan documents, and specifically disclosed on the Truth-in-Lending document the lender must give a potential borrower within three business days of taking a mortgage loan application.

Lock-In Provisions

Another kind of prepayment requirement found in some commercial loans is the "lock-in." Commercial loans do not fall under the same kind of regulatory protection for borrowers that can be found in residential loans, making it easier for lenders to set harsher terms. A lock-in is one example. What it does is lock in the interest charge for a certain minimum number of years. For example, a loan for an apartment project might require all interest to be paid for the first eight years of the loan term. Prepayment at any time during the first eight years would require the borrower to pay all interest otherwise due for that time period and most likely would make any prepayment too costly.

Mortgage Covenants

These are promises made by the mortgagor or borrower. By signing the mortgage or deed of trust, the borrower agrees to uphold certain promises that fall into two broad categories: positive covenants and negative covenants. Examples of a positive covenant might include a mortgagor's promise to keep the property covered by hazard insurance or to make monthly mortgage payments. An example of a negative covenant might include a mortgagor's agreement to the restriction of his or her ability to rent the property for profit.

Generally, not complying with a mortgage covenant can result in foreclosure proceedings against the property mortgaged.

Acceleration Clause

The **acceleration clause** in a mortgage instrument, or promissory note, gives a lender the right to call the entire balance due, in full, in advance of its due date upon the occurrence of a default. The most common type of default is a failure to make timely payments, but there are other kinds of defaults that can trigger an acceleration clause, including destruction of the premises, an encumbrance placed on the property, or the unauthorized sale or assignment of the property. The acceleration clause is a very important part of an installment obligation because without it, the alternative could be to foreclose each month as the payments actually come due. The uniform mortgage language for Fannie Mae/Freddie Mac-conforming loans uses broad terminology to apply the acceleration clause in the Covenant 19 provision in both its mortgage security documents and deed of trust security instruments, and this clause is also incorporated by reference in Fannie Mae/Freddie Mac's common promissory note documents.

Right to Sell/Due-On-Sale Clause—Assumption

As a general rule, mortgaged property can be freely sold by the owner, or mortgagor, either with an **assumption** of the existing debt by the new buyer or, if that is not permitted, by paying off the balance due on the existing mortgage. The popularity of loan assumptions follows the rise or fall of interest rates; in a period of increasing rates, an older, lower-interest loan is attractive to a potential buyer. In 1982, the contract rate on mortgage loans as reported by regulated savings associations reached 15.01%. During the following 25 years, 30-year, fixed-rate, self-amortizing mortgage loan contract rates slowly declined to nearly 4%. Obviously, the assumption of older, higher-interest loans has not been so attractive. This trend may shift as the economy recovers over the next few years; interest rates are expected to go up as the demand for credit increases with the needs of an expanding economy and continuing demands by the states and federal government to finance deficits.

The last time interest rates saw a large rise, in the late 1970s, assumptions became very popular. Lenders took the position that any change in collateral ownership gave them the right to allow assumptions only at higher interest rates; borrowers countered that an increase in interest rates restricted their right to sell. The contention was that this amounted to an unreasonable restraint on the owner's right to sell. In legal terminology, this restraint on a sale is called a *restraint on alienation* (meaning the right to transfer an interest in real estate to another). Thus a right-to-sell clause in a mortgage is sometimes referred to as the **alienation clause**.

Most states prohibit any unreasonable restraint on alienation—a limitation that has been mostly concerned with discrimination. For example, a restrictive covenant in a property deed that forbids any sale to a woman would be classed as an unreasonable restraint on the owner's right to sell. The question of whether or not a lender's right to increase an interest rate on an assumption, or otherwise deny the right to sell, amounts to an unreasonable restraint was the subject of much controversy and many court battles during the early 1980s. In 1982, the U.S. Supreme Court decided that a federally chartered institution does have the right to enforce a due-on-sale provision rather than accept a loan assumption, thereby upholding the Garn Act, which allowed banks to enforce **due-on-sale** provisions for which the banking industry had lobbied hard. Since that time, the practice has been for the assumption of a conventional loan to be cleared with the lender before any title is conveyed.

Mortgage instruments now carry more specific language regarding the lender's right to change an interest rate, or call the loan due, in the event of an assumption effort. The uniform mortgage language for Fannie Mae/Freddie Mac-conforming loans uses broad terminology to apply its due-on-sale provision. Covenant 18, titled "Transfer of the Property or a Beneficial Interest in Borrower," simply prohibits any such transfer of interest without prior written consent of the lender. Failure to comply can result in a call for immediate payment of the entire loan balance. Both FHA and VA have limitations on assumptions that vary by date of loan origination, an issue that will be explored in greater detail in Chapter 8.

Even though there have been some rational arguments on both sides of the assumption/due-on-sale question, there is no obligation on the part of any lender to allow a loan assumption today. However, there is a need to disclose this fact in the loan agreement. This fact is particularly important when a home seller helps finance the sale of a house. Home sellers are not normally in the business of making loans, and they can include a more stringent clause simply forbidding any loan assumption; that is, if the buyer subsequently resells the house, the existing loan must be paid in full.

REVIEW OF PROMISSORY NOTE FORM

The Promissory Note

The **promissory note** is a debt instrument, and is the lender's basic evidence of the amount owed and who owes it. It creates the obligation to repay a loan. Both promissory notes and mortgage instruments must contain certain standard words and phrases to assure the accomplishment of their purposes, and as such, they are interlocking documents. A lender must have both a promissory note as a written promise to pay and a mortgage or deed of trust to evidence the lender's right to force the sale of the real estate securing the promissory note if the borrower defaults on his or her obligations under the promissory note or mortgage or deed of trust. Nevertheless, the balance of the terms and conditions can be worded in whatever way the attorney preparing the documents deems proper. The variations can be substantial, and in years past, such variations made the selling of conventional mortgage loans very difficult. HUD/FHA and VA have always required their standardized forms to be used if they underwrite a loan. But there is no such requirement for conventional loans—meaning those not underwritten by government agencies such as the FHA and VA. Conventional loans underwritten by federal agencies such as Fannie Mae are known as conforming loans because they must meet, or conform to, the requirements set by the underwriting agencies.

> ## Where Are We Now?
>
> ### Lien Theory vs. Title Theory
>
> **Under lien theory:**
>
> The borrower has title (ownership) to the property.
>
> - In most cases, the borrower has the right of redemption.
> - A lender can secure his or her interest in a property by designating a trustee to act on his or her behalf in the event of default by borrower.
> - The lender must go through due process by having the property sold at auction to recover the debt.
> - Lien theory is generally advantageous to the borrower.
>
> **Under title theory:**
>
> The lender holds title to the property.
>
> - The borrower can be evicted in the event of default without any judicial procedures.
> - Title theory is generally advantageous to the lender.
>
> **Deed to Secure Debt**
>
> A type of mortgage used in a few states; the title to the property is transferred to the lender until the debt is paid in full. Contrast this with deeds of trust, which are employed in states called title theory states, and with true mortgages, which are employed in states called lien theory states. The deed to secure debt is a hybrid of the two theories.

CONFORMING LOANS

In 1970, Fannie Mae was authorized to purchase residential conventional loans. Prior to that time, it was still an agency and was limited to purchasing HUD/FHA and VA loans. To develop standards to guide the purchase of conventional loans from lenders across the country, Fannie Mae worked in cooperation with Freddie Mac to create a series of uniform conventional mortgage documents. Since both entities are quasi-government, public hearings were required before formal approval could be given. Consumer advocates participated in the hearings to help decide what should and should not be included in these important documents.

No single mortgage form could be used throughout the country because of the variations in state property laws. So the result of this work has been a series of standardized mortgage instruments designed specifically to meet each state's requirements. Conforming mortgage instruments contain a section that covers universal standards and another section that covers state-specific requirements.

However, promissory notes are unilateral promises to pay and convey no property rights, so they contain fewer differences between the states' laws. This fact has allowed greater standardization of promissory note instruments, with one note serving a number of states as a multistate document. Examples of a note and a mortgage instrument appear in the appendix of this text.

Ongoing work to create uniform mortgage documents for residential loans has formed the basis for a standardized conventional loan known as a *conforming loan*. Besides uniform documents, which will be discussed in detail at the end of this chapter, a conforming loan must meet Fannie Mae/Freddie Mac standards for qualification of borrowers, preparation of an appraisal, and limits on the dollar amount of a loan. As a standardized conventional loan, the conforming loan has achieved wide acceptance. Since both agencies are always in the market to purchase loans, albeit at their own yield requirements, many primary-market lenders adhere to conforming loan standards to make sure their loans can be sold when money is needed.

While the preparation of mortgage instruments is a legal matter, real estate professionals use them in negotiations, and therefore the following section will provide an overview of important points regarding these instruments. The *promissory note* is almost always a separate instrument but is sometimes included as part of a mortgage document. The Uniform Commercial Code sets standards for drafting an enforceable and negotiable promissory note. In general, to be valid, a promissory note must contain the following basic provisions:

- It must name the parties to the promissory note—that is, the maker (borrower) and the payee (the lender).
- It must name the amount of the debt (**principal** borrowed).

- It must specify how and when the money is to be paid, including maturity date.
- It must contain an acceleration clause.
- It must contain a description of the payee's remedies if the money due is not repaid.
- It must be signed by the maker.

If, in foreclosure, the collateral securing the note (as pledged by the mortgage instrument) proves insufficient to cover the indebtedness, the holder of the note may obtain a **deficiency judgment**—an unsecured money judgment—against the debtor for the balance due. (State laws vary as to borrowers' and lenders' rights in a claim for deficiency judgment.) As discussed earlier, mortgagees attempting to obtain a deficiency judgment will generally follow the lien theory of mortgages requiring judiciary foreclosure procedures that usually allow deficiency judgments against the debtor. In the title theory states, mortgages typically allow nonjudicial foreclosure procedures but do not allow deficiency judgments. If the note is labeled "nonrecourse," the borrower cannot be held personally liable.

Use of the wording "or order" or "or bearer" in defining the payee is important, as it is these words that make it possible for the note to be endorsed and transferred, thus becoming negotiable. Most mortgage promissory notes are negotiable, to allow transfer to secondary-market investors. If the note is negotiable, only one copy should be executed. If other copies are made, the note maker may initial them, but should not sign them. It is imperative to secondary-market investors that they receive both the properly executed promissory note and mortgage or deed of trust that has been filed showing the security interest of the holder of the promissory note, since one cannot foreclose on a property with a promissory note alone.

REVIEW OF TRUST FORM

Let's take a practical view of the deed of trust discussed earlier in this chapter. The deed of trust, mortgage, or mortgage bond will normally detail:

- that the deed of trust/mortgage places a lien on the property;
- the specific property being pledged for the deed of trust/mortgage;

- that the borrower cannot sell the property without paying off the loan; and
- that the borrower must maintain hazard insurance on the property.

Property Insurance

If a building is included in the mortgage pledge rather than only raw land, the mortgage will require property insurance coverage for both the lender's and the borrower's protection. This is also termed **hazard insurance**. Principally, it includes fire and extended coverage and is required by the lender in an amount at least equal to that of the loan (even though the loan amount usually includes the value of the land). To make certain that collateral property is insured, the lender generally requires a full year's paid-up insurance policy before releasing loan proceeds. To assure future payment of premiums, the lender requires two months of the annual premium to be paid into an escrow account as a cushion at closing. (The Real Estate Settlement Procedures Act, RESPA, limits this escrow cushion to not more than two months' premiums.) Then, added to each monthly payment, one-twelfth of the annual premium must be paid. The original policy is held by the lender, and it is part of the lender's servicing responsibility to maintain the coverage with timely payments from the borrower's escrow account.

Minimum Requirement for Hazard Insurance

Insurance companies in most states must comply with another requirement controlling the minimum amount of coverage that can be carried to establish full repayment in case of a partial loss. Since most fire losses are partial in extent, it is not unusual for a property owner to want to carry only partial coverage, hoping that any fire would be brought under control before the damage exceeds the amount of insurance coverage. To distribute the cost of insurance more equitably over all policyholders, insurance company regulators set some minimum standards for coverage. Therefore, insurance companies generally include a required minimum coverage if the policyholder expects full recovery for a partial loss stemming from a claim on a home.

Such a clause will require an amount of insurance coverage not less than a given percentage of the actual cash value of the building at the time of loss. These clauses are known variously as *coinsurance clauses*, *average clauses*, and *reduced rate contribution clauses*. A common minimum amount of insurance to assure full payment of partial losses is 80% of the actual cash value of the building at the time of loss. By carrying less than the minimum percentage of insurance, the property owner cannot collect in full for a loss but will have to bear a part of the loss personally.

If coverage is below the required minimum, the insurance company's liability is limited to the same percentage of the loss that the amount of insurance carried bears to 80% of the property's actual cash value.

In areas of the country where property values tend to undergo substantial increases, any failure to maintain proper insurance coverage can expose the lender, as well as the property owner, to uninsured losses.

Disbursement of Hazard Insurance Proceeds

Another insurance problem to be considered with mortgaged property involves determining just how the proceeds should be paid in case of an actual loss. Earlier mortgages required payment of the insurance money to the lender, who in turn decided how to apply the funds, determining whether to permit the funds to be used for restoration of the property (the usual procedure for smaller losses), or instead to apply the proceeds to pay off the loan. Today, most residential mortgage instruments give the borrower a stronger position in the distribution of insurance proceeds, as is apparent in the Fannie Mae/Freddie Mac-conforming mortgage covenants. This instrument, in Covenant 5, states, "Any insurance proceeds, whether or not the underlying insurance was required by Lender, shall be applied to restoration or repair of the Property, if the restoration or repair is economically feasible and Lender's security is not lessened."

Flood Insurance

Property located in a flood-prone area serving as collateral for a loan handled by a federally related institution or agency must carry flood insurance. This requirement stems from the 1994 National Flood Insurance Reform Act, which became effective as of September 23, 1995, creating our current National Flood Insurance Program (NFIP). The NFIP places responsibility on the *lender* to force-place the necessary insurance if it is required and the borrower fails to buy the coverage. The borrower is allowed 45 days to purchase the required insurance when notified by the lender. The lender may rely on information provided by the director of the Federal Emergency Management Agency (FEMA) stating whether or not the building is in a special flood hazard area.

While National Flood Insurance has been in existence since 1968, the 1994 Act made nonpayment more difficult, requiring lenders and servicers to escrow flood insurance premiums for covered loans along with taxes and other insurance premiums. This placed both a responsibility and a liability on lenders to make sure loan collateral in flood-prone areas was insured for at least the loan amount.

The Disaster Mitigation Act of 2000 was passed to better coordinate state and local disaster alleviation efforts by requiring states and local government to have plans in place in order to continue to be allowed to participate in the federal flood insurance program. Lenders should know the basics of their state's plans to be able to coordinate claims should a disaster occur.

In 2004, the Bunning-Bereuter-Blumenauer Flood Insurance Reform Act was passed to reduce losses to properties for which repetitive flood insurance claim payments have been made. This development is important to real estate professionals because this restriction on future coverage runs with the property. It has generally been interpreted as meaning that after two claims have been paid on a subject property, it is no longer eligible for the program.

On July 16, 2010, the House of Representatives approved a flood insurance reform bill designed to extend the NFIP through September 30, 2015. The Flood Insurance Reform Priorities Act would have ensured that current policyholders would retain their coverage and that new policies could be written. However, it could not pass muster in the Senate due to lingering concerns over the program's losses from Hurricanes Katrina, Rita, and Wilma. These disasters caused almost $23 billion in NFIP losses—almost double the cumulative losses experienced by the program in its entire history prior to 2005. A real possibility exists that NFIP, even with the provision of the 2004 Act restricting future benefits, may eventually be a casualty of attempts to reduce the federal deficit. This was feared to occur after the term of its extension under the National Flood Insurance Program Act of 2010 expired, which was to occur on December 16, 2011. However, the Biggert-Waters Flood Insurance Reform Act of 2012 (FIRA of 2012) was passed, reauthorizing and reforming the National Flood Insurance Program (NFIP) for five years through September 30, 2017. The main impact on the real estate buyer community will be that premium rate structure reforms will phase out subsidies for second homes, business properties, severe repetitive loss properties, or substantially improved/damaged properties. Rates for these properties will increase by 25% per year until premiums meet the full actuarial cost. Real estate professionals must be aware that the FIRA of 2012 will require that any premiums for new flood insurance on property not currently covered must be based on actuarial rates. There are several other important provisions that can be found at the link to Floodsmart.gov provided at the end of this chapter.

Property Taxes

Property tax, also known as **ad valorem tax** ("according to value" tax), becomes a specific lien on real property on the date the tax is assessed by an authorized taxing authority. Release of lien is automatic upon payment of the tax. Tax records are normally filed in each county as a separate section of information. Property subject to tax (some land is exempt) must stand good for its payment. If the tax is not paid, the property is subject to foreclosure by the state. In some states, an assessment by a properly authorized neighborhood maintenance or homeowners association carries the same status as a property tax. A tax assessment is a high-priority claim in a foreclosure action, preceded only by the administrative costs of the sale. Thus, property taxes hold a higher priority than other secured claimants; regardless of the date their claims are recorded.

Property taxes take precedence over a first mortgage lien even though the mortgage may be filed of record earlier. Therefore, lenders normally require the protection of handling tax payments as a part of escrow requirements. A cushion of one-sixth of the annual tax is usually deposited with the lender at loan closing. In addition, the tax escrow at closing includes the amount of taxes that have accrued to that date (payable by the buyer or seller as may be owed by each). Then, one month's worth (one-twelfth of the annual amount due) of taxes is added to each monthly payment of the mortgage loan. Once the money is in escrow, the lender is responsible for making tax payments directly to the tax authority as part of its loan servicing function.

One of the most common errors on estimating closing costs for a residential mortgage loan is the amount that should be paid to begin the tax escrow account. Many misguided loan officers and real estate professionals, trying to "help" borrowers close more quickly, understate this amount, which lowers the amounts due at closing. Some go even further, offering an 80% LTV loan with a simultaneous closing of a second loan for 10% to 20%. These simultaneous loans avoid the requirement of a tax escrow account altogether. In states with higher real estate taxes, like California, New York, and Texas, borrowers who cannot come up with the money to pay their taxes on subprime mortgages caused servicers to advance funds and add this to the borrowers' payments. Subsequently, many of these borrowers had trouble making regular payments without consideration for paying back these taxes, advanced by the servicer.

Federal Tax Claims

A tax claim by the federal government is considered a general lien,[1] but only when it is filed of record. While a taxpayer may be delinquent in payment of taxes, such debt is not a lien until a claim is recorded. Such a lien may be assessed against any taxpayer's property, real or personal, and under the federal claim of supremacy, it would carry a higher priority than other liens or a mortgage lien in a foreclosure proceeding. If there is still equity in the property, the Internal Revenue Service has 120 days to redeem the property. If there is a great deal of equity in the property, the IRS can use that money to satisfy any tax liens. This is a rare but possible occurrence. However, the property tax would not necessarily be satisfied in such a foreclosure action; it simply rides with the land as a continuing claim unless title actually passes to the federal government, in which case the property tax must be satisfied. State property taxes have priority over all other claims regardless of when they were recorded.

Another problem has surfaced regarding federal tax liens. If a buyer has a federal lien against him or her, it would become a prior claim on any property acquired. As a result, title companies are now checking tax records for federal liens on buyers and sellers.

During the financial crisis that began in 2008, lenders started accepting settlements of troubled mortgages using a loss mitigation technique called a short sale. A short sale occurs when a borrower in or near default, with the mortgagor's permission, sells property for less than the mortgage loan balance. The lender agrees to this process

---

[1] A *general lien* is a claim against all assets of the target of the lien; a *specific lien* is a claim against one specific asset, such as a tract of land.

because the property has declined in value below the mortgage balance, and the lender prefers to get most of the value of the property rather than getting none.

The amount of debt not recovered, if no deficiency judgment is obtained, has historically been viewed by the federal government as debt forgiveness and, as such, is considered a taxable event to the borrower. However, to help facilitate a recovery of the residential real estate market and to provide some relief to already distressed borrowers, Congress passed the Mortgage Forgiveness Debt Relief Act of 2007, which removed taxation of forgiven debt to borrowers who received debt forgiveness on home sales for discharges of indebtedness on or after January 1, 2007, and before January 1, 2010.

Congress then passed Federal Bailout Legislation H.R. 1424 on October 3, 2008, extending this relief through December 31, 2012. This new law excludes qualified principal residence indebtedness forgiven by lenders from taxable income. The reduction in taxable income is limited to $2,000,000 for the exclusion ($1,000,000 for the mortgage interest deduction) and $1,000,000 for married persons filing a separate return for the mortgage interest deduction.

Congress habitually waits until the eleventh hour to make decisions. Real estate professionals or lenders may be asked whether a contemplated short sale, loan modification, or foreclosure is covered by the extension made by Congress through 2017 or any future time period. These clients should contact a tax professional familiar with the law for advice. The limits on taxable income and interest owed, as mentioned above, still apply. However, it seems that if a portion of the mortgage debt forgiven was used for purposes other than improving or construction of the mortgaged home, then that portion may not qualify for the exclusions. For example, it is unlikely that cash used to refinance or buy a car would qualify for the exclusion.

An example of the most commonly used deed of trust form and mortgage used by Fannie Mae can be found at the end of this chapter in the Additional Online Resources section.

MORTGAGE PROCEDURES

Several important procedures associated with mortgage instruments merit further discussion. While legal practices do differ between the states, the purpose or reason for certain procedures is generally the same, as we will see in the next section.

Recording

Modern society protects land ownership with the help of its public records, which are open to anyone with an acceptable instrument to file. **Recording** is the act of entering into the public record a written instrument that affects title to property. Other sets of public records, separate from that for real estate, have a bearing on the quality of title to real estate. These include records regarding taxes, probate, marriage, and judgments.

State laws define what is necessary for an instrument to be recorded; generally, it must be in writing and properly acknowledged. The instrument must be recorded in the county in which the land is located. Recording a document gives constructive notice to the world of the existence of the document and its contents. Failure to record a document does not invalidate the agreement between the parties thereto. Nor does a failure to record invalidate the agreement for any other parties who have notice of its existence. But recording laws specify that if a document is not recorded, it generally is void as against any subsequent purchaser, lessee, or mortgagee acting in good faith who does not have knowledge of the unrecorded document. This means, for example, that if a deed transferring property ownership is not recorded, the record title remains with the seller insofar as innocent third parties are concerned. A subsequent judgment against the seller could result in a valid claim against a property that has already been sold. The purchaser who did not bother to record the deed would most likely be left with a difficult lawsuit and possible loss of the property to the judgment claimant.

One more point should be noted on the nature of recording. If a recorded document is, for some reason, void, recording it does not make it valid.

Priority

From a practical point of view, recording gives priority to documents based on the time they are recorded; for example, a mortgage filed on October 15, 2015, has priority over a mortgage filed on October 16, 2015. However, there is a separate class of liens whose priority is not based on time of filing. This class includes tax liens, mechanic's liens, and special-assessment liens that are a matter of public record. Property taxes become liens when assessed. This is not true of federal income and payroll taxes, which must have claims of record filed to take a priority position as liens. One other way to alter the priority of a claim is a subordination agreement, which we will discuss in a later section.

Releases

Recording is so often thought of in terms of conveying property, or asserting a claim, that the reverse procedure is sometimes overlooked. It is also important to record a release when a claim has been satisfied. If a claim is based on a written document, so should the release be a written document.

Recording a release is most important when dealing with a mortgage. While it is true that payoff of a mortgage note voids the mortgage pledge, the document remains a matter of record and a cloud on the title unless released. Depending on state law, two releases may be needed: If there is a vendor's lien (a claim that derives from a purchase-money debt), a release is needed when it is paid off. And if there is another mortgage claim against the property, it too requires a release.

Releases must be in a recordable form. Sometimes return of original lien instruments to the grantor, or the note marked "paid in full," are thought to satisfy release requirements. That kind of release is valid between the parties involved, but it takes recorded documents to actually clear title to property.

Subordination

Subordination is a method of altering the priority of claims to property by a written agreement. It is a method commonly used in development projects when the land is seller-financed, or even when the land is leased. In a typical transaction, the land seller would hold a purchase-money mortgage on the land sold. Then, to facilitate development, the land seller would agree to subordinate that mortgage in favor of a construction lender. This allows the developer/purchaser to obtain a first mortgage loan to build the intended improvement. Thus, the subordination agreement alters the normal rule of giving priority to the mortgage that is recorded first.

If land is leased to a developer for a development project rather than sold, the landowner could subordinate the fee in favor of a construction loan (or other mortgage claim). Technically, the fee cannot be subordinated to a leasehold mortgage; the procedure is more properly called *encumbering* the fee. But the end result is the same. The construction lender holds a prior claim on the property for repayment of the loan.

A subordination clause can be included in a mortgage instrument permitting a subsequent mortgage to take a higher priority. This is a fairly standard type of clause found in a junior mortgage when an existing prior mortgage is recognized in the junior instrument.

GSE-Conforming Loans as a Catalyst for Uniform Loan Documentation

While neither Fannie Mae nor Freddie Mac are limited to purchasing only conforming loans, use of the procedures allows loan originators to avoid the time-consuming examinations necessary for nonconforming or nonuniform documented loans. Conforming loans require more than simply submitting uniform documentation. To be acceptable, a loan must also meet the not-to-exceed loan limits set annually, plus property standards and borrower qualification guidelines. In addition to use of the three standardized documents listed in the preceding section, Fannie Mae and Freddie Mac require the use of their own forms for conforming loans not previously outlined, as follows:

- Verification of Employment (Fannie Mae Form 1005 and Freddie Mac Form 90)
- Verification of Deposit (Fannie Mae Form 1006)
- a uniform state-specific mortgage instrument
- a uniform promissory note that complies with state requirements

Examples of all the forms listed above appear in the appendix.

It is not uncommon to find conforming loan standards explained to a borrower as "government limits." And in a general sense they are, as both Fannie Mae and Freddie Mac are quasi-government agencies. But the limitations are not in the same class as a government regulation. The standards apply only if the loan originator sells the loan to either Fannie Mae or Freddie Mac. Many investors will buy loans that are sold under the title of conforming except for some provision. The current maximum conforming limits were applied to all conventional mortgages delivered to Fannie Mae in 2018. In prior years, the conforming limit changed every year in response to gradual increases in home values. However, up until 2016 general conforming loan limits were identical to those of the previous eight years, reflective of the steep decline of home prices nationwide during the Great Recession and slow recovery in home prices since 2008. The high-cost areas are established by the Federal Housing Finance Agency and may vary depending on geographic location and loan origination date. The Housing and Economic Recovery Act of 2008 changed Fannie Mae's charter to expand the definition of a "conforming" loan, creating two sets of limits for first mortgages: general conforming loan limits and high-cost area conforming loan limits. See table 6-1 for a breakdown of these new limits.

TABLE 6-1 Maximum Original Principal Balance for Loans Closed in 2018*

Units	Contiguous States, District of Columbia, and Puerto Rico		Alaska, Guam, Hawaii, and Virgin Islands	
	General	High-Cost*	General	High-Cost*
1	$453,100	$679,650	$679,650	$1,019,45
2	$580,150	$870,225	$870,225	$1,305,325
3	$701,250	$1,051,875	$1,051,875	$1,577,800
4	$871,450	$1,307,175	$1,307,175	$1,960,750

* The limit may be lower for a specific high-cost area; use the Loan Limit Look-Up to see limits by location. These limits apply to all loans originated on or before January 1, 2018. High-cost area loan limits have increased in 2018 for all counties due to a high-cost area adjustment or the county being newly assigned to a high-cost area. Amounts shown listed above are maximum limits allowed by the provisions of the Housing and Economic Recovery Act of 2008. The specific high-cost area loan limits are established for each county (or equivalent) by FHFA. Lenders are responsible for ensuring that the original loan amount of each mortgage loan does not exceed the applicable maximum loan limit for the specific area in which the property is located. Some counties and states have been removed from high-cost status such as Puerto Rico, which is no longer a listed as high-cost.
Source: © 2021 Mbition LLC

Loan Document Mandate

In practice, loan originators retain considerable freedom in loan documentation because there are many secondary-market purchasers who do not require conforming loan standards. Basically, residential loans need only two mandatory forms: (1) the Uniform Residential Loan Application, and (2) the HUD-1 settlement statement. Standardized documents become important when a loan originator wants to sell a loan; at that point, it becomes necessary to meet the requirements of whoever purchases the loan.

Questions for Discussion

1. What procedure is used in your state to handle a pledge of collateral for a mortgage loan?
2. Explain the relationship and purpose of a promissory note and the two primary forms of security instruments.
3. In a foreclosure, how are priorities determined among lien claimants on the collateral property?
4. What is the underlying purpose of requiring a borrower to escrow money each month for the payment of property taxes?
5. Describe the difference between a buyer taking title subject to the mortgage versus assuming the mortgage.
6. Explain the difference between the equity right of redemption and the statutory right of redemption.
7. Explain the differences between a regular mortgage and a deed of trust.
8. What is the principal risk for the buyer/borrower in a contract for deed?
9. Describe a conforming loan.
10. What is the purpose of recording documents?

Multiple Choice Questions for Review

1. Which of the following would be a quick resource most lenders would use to locate an appropriate security agreement for use in their state for a loan closing?
   a. the secretary of state of the state in which the property is located
   b. the Fannie Mae business-to-business website
   c. the local attorney used to do loan closings
   d. the county clerk's office

2. When defining the parties to a formal promissory note, the borrower is referred to as the:
   a. trustee
   b. payee
   c. maker
   d. cosigner

3. In title theory states a foreclosure that does not have to be approved by court action is referred to by which of the following terms?
   a. judicial
   b. nonjudicial
   c. voluntary conveyance procedure
   d. strict foreclosure

4. When a portion of a mortgagor's monthly payment goes towards property taxes and insurance it will be held in a/an:
   a. balloon fund
   b. recovery fund
   c. trustee account
   d. escrow account

5. Conforming security agreements such as a deed of trust or mortgage include a due-on-sale clause; if a borrower sells the property subject to that security agreement, the lender may take which of the following actions?
   a. renegotiate the interest rate on the promissory note
   b. accelerate the promissory note and require immediate repayment
   c. agree and grant the assumption of the promissory note by the buyer
   d. all of these

6. The right of a mortgagor to redeem his or her property from default is described by which of the following terms?
   a. judicial foreclosure
   b. statutory redemption
   c. friendly redemption
   d. equity of redemption

7. Which of the following best describes how mortgages and deeds of trust are used?
   a. Mortgages are used to create a security agreement related to owner-occupied property, and deeds of trust are used in connection with commercial income producing real property.
   b. Each represents an internal unique clause within a security agreement covering real property, and both must be present for the security interest to be valid.
   c. They are two different legal documents that allow a lender to perfect a security interest in the real property of the borrower.
   d. They are two names for the same recordable security agreement, and thus can be used interchangeably.

8. Which of the following might be deemed a disadvantage for a home buyer who enters into a contract for deed agreement?
   a. If a buyer defaults or becomes bankrupt there could be a problem of clearing title, which might be costly.
   b. Liens that arise against the seller could cloud the title.
   c. IRS amounts owed by the buyer would allow a lien to be placed on the property purchased under the contract.
   d. A contract for deed is subject to contract law, which offers differing interpretations.

9. Which of the following best describes a conforming mortgage loan?
   a. a mortgage presented to potential mortgagors who do not meet the underwriting standards of Fannie Mae or Freddie Mac
   b. a loan in excess of $453,100 on a single-family residence that must be underwritten as a "jumbo mortgage"
   c. a mortgage that follows the underwriting criteria set by Fannie Mae and Freddie Mac for loans they purchase and place in their standard MBS
   d. a mortgage that meets the standard loan criteria for Ginnie Mae MBS

10. What is the primary reason for mortgage security agreements to be recorded with the county government where the real estate pledged as security is located?
    a. for disclosure of who holds the ownership interest in the mortgage on a piece of property
    b. to provide a public record of who holds an interest in a piece of property
    c. to provide the county tax assessor with key valuation information
    d. to provide data required by the Home Mortgage Disclosure Act

Information Resources

https://scholarship.law.missouri.edu/cgi/viewcontent.cgi?article=3745&context=mlr
   An online resource explaining the importance of uniform documents in the development and streamlining of underwriting, and providing access to uniform documents. Uniform documents and forms for Freddie Mac, can be found at the following URL: http://www.freddiemac.com/singlefamily/guide/

https://krscpas.com/tag/wrap-around-mortgage/
   This website provides an example of a common structure of a wraparound mortgage.

http://www.bankrate.com/mortgage.aspx
   Bankrate.com is a good source for basic information on mortgage products.

https://www.fanniemae.com/singlefamily/loan-limits
   Since 2015, "conforming" loan limits have not been as fully uniform as they were for high-cost areas. Now their use is limited to certain states, and 46 counties did see an increase in their high-cost status from 2014 to 2015. The website above is a handy guide for determining the exact limit for real estate professionals to use.

https://www.floodsmart.gov/
   The National Flood Insurance Program (NFIP) has developed a valuable tool designed to assist consumers and real estate professionals in an effort to educate and inform communities about the importance of flood insurance and precautions in the event of floods.

https://www.fanniemae.com/singlefamily/security-instruments
    Go to the website above and scroll down to form 3044 to see the most common deed of trust used for securing real estate loans.

https://www.fanniemae.com/content/legal_form/3244.1.pdf
    Follow the URL above to see the standard fixed-rate note for a Fannie Mae Conventional mortgage for the state of Texas Form 3244.1.

CHAPTER 7

LOAN TYPES, TERMS, AND ISSUES

KEY TERMS AND PHRASES

ad valorem tax
adjustable-rate mortgage
amortization
balloon payment
biweekly payment
buydown mortgage
caps
conforming loan
Fair Housing Amendments Act of 1988
graduated-payment mortgage
growing equity mortgage
home equity loan
home equity conversion mortgage (HECM)
income ratio method
interest
interest-only mortgage

interest rate indicators
participation loan
pension funds
piggyback loan
pledged-account mortgage
private mortgage insurance
prime rate
rate index
red flags
refinancing
reverse annuity mortgage
shared appreciation mortgage
shared equity mortgage
shorter-term loans
straight note
subprime loans
usury laws

LEARNING OBJECTIVES

At the conclusion of this chapter, students will be able to:
- Describe interest and how interest rates relate to several sectors of the investment marketplace.
- Define "usury" and explain how it has been regulated over time.
- Understand the concept of amortization and negative amortization.
- Describe how the components of an adjustable-rate mortgage work, including the rate index, margin, and caps.
- Understand the key mortgage products and their features.
- Describe how a home equity revolving line of credit mortgage works.
- Explain the function and costs of a reverse annuity mortgage.
- Understand the development of private mortgage insurance products and their current features.

INTRODUCTION

Beginning with the passage of the National Housing Act in 1934, the fixed-interest-rate, constant-level, fully amortized payment plan dominated mortgage lending. This type of mortgage repayment plan was used by nearly all primary market mortgage originators. It evolved as a result of unsettled economic events, specifically high inflation followed by high interest rates, and the poorly constructed deregulation of the savings and loan industry. This progression of events caused the fall of the savings and loan industry from preeminence as the leading source of fixed-rate mortgage credit and encouraged the development or adoption of alternative methods of repaying mortgage loans.

A number of the mortgage repayment plans commonly used in the past 10 years now appear to have been poorly thought out, and indeed appear to have been contributing factors in the recent financial crisis. At the same time, many trade group executives argue that interest-only, option ARM, and piggyback mortgage repayment plans were used in ways not intended by their creators and should not be dismissed as having no value simply because they were improperly "sold" to uninformed or unwary consumers.[1] Today, in a market with historically low fixed rates, mortgages are available due to Federal Reserve Bank intervention. But if and when interest rates rise, alternative repayment

---

[1] Paul Broadhead, "BSA Hits Out at Interest-Only Changes," *Mortgage Strategy*, September 30, 2010.

plans may be useful in helping borrowers qualify for larger loans than fixed rates may allow, as well as keeping interest rates and payment amounts low in the short term. Alternative plans may make sales happen that otherwise would not be possible. Secondary markets will find a way to reemerge with products that satisfy the new risk parameters of the mortgage investors. But only time will tell if some of the more outrageous excesses of the alternative mortgage products invented during the run up to the financial crisis—products such as "stated income" loans, also known as "liar loans" (mortgages approved without requiring proof of the borrower's income or assets)—will reemerge in new forms. The worst of these liar loans merited their nickname, "NINJA loans," short for "no income, no job, and (no) assets." These loans were made by major banks as late as 2007 to borrowers with credit scores as low as 500.[2]

Stated income loans have been around a long time, but they were historically used for borrowers for whom such a loan made sense—for example, for someone with a large amount of income, but whose tax returns were so complex that it was difficult to calculate the person's effective income, or for a borrower who could make a down payment of, say, 30% to 50% and perhaps had a large stock portfolio combined with a high credit score. The Dodd-Frank Act, along with other state regulations passed since 2010, makes it illegal to make a loan on a personal residence without determining if the borrower has the capacity to repay the mortgage under the loan terms. This is aimed at keeping predatory lenders from taking advantage of less financially literate borrowers who might have large amounts of equity in a home, but due to changes in financial circumstances, cannot pay back a larger mortgage or take out a loan on an inherited home.

Repayment plans can be classed as follows: (1) fixed-interest, constant-level plans, (2) adjustable-rate mortgages, (3) graduated-payment mortgages that allow lower early monthly payments, and (4) mortgages that can reduce total interest cost. Each one of these four major classifications of repayment plans can be referred to as *mortgage-product features* or offerings. A discussion of the four repayment plan types, as well as the mortgage products that fit within each of them are discussed later in this chapter. First, we will cover interest as a topic, as a deeper understanding of interest will make the discussion of mortgage-product features come into better focus.

---

[2] "Wells Fargo Absolutely Did Subprime, Stated, Interest Only, No Ratio, Etc." *Daily Mortgage*, October 8, 2008, accessed August 7, 2011, at http://mrmortgage.ml-implode.com/2008/10/03/wells-fargo-absolutely-did-subprime-stated-no-ratio-etc/

Yes, here at Last National Bank there is a fixed rate mortgage that can be made on your home that will mortgage your future for a very desirable low rate of interest.

INTEREST

In Chapter 2 we examined the U.S. monetary system, including the Federal Reserve Bank and the U.S. Treasury and their importance in establishing monetary policies and their impact on the rate of interest in the market place. While the Fed has substantial influence on short-term rates, long-term rates follow additional influences. So what is interest and how are interest rates determined?

Interest is the cost of using another's money, and that cost reflects supply and demand factors somewhat similar to the way commodity prices do. However, fluctuations in the cost of money differ from those of commodities in that demand does not always respond to a change in price. If, for instance, sugar, oil, or copper decline in price, the tendency is for demand to increase. Housing follows a similar pattern, primarily because borrowed money has become an integral and major part of the housing cost. If borrowing costs decrease, the cost of housing is reduced, with an obvious increase in the potential market. However, if money goes down in price, many other kinds of demand may not respond at all because additional factors influence money.

The reason for borrowing money is not simply to acquire the money itself. For instance, people borrow money to build a building, buy a car, or expand a business, but if the economy is in a decline, there may be no need for that building, the car, or even the business expansion. So what determines interest rates? It is a complex mix of influences, not the least of which is generated by the government's needs, clearly colored by the government's unique power to create money.

There are four major influences on interest rates: supply of money, demand for credit, monetary policies of the Federal Reserve, and fiscal policies of the United States government. Each of these will be discussed in the pages to follow.

Supply of Money

Thirty years ago, dependence on savings accounts as a source of mortgage money caused periodic shortages in the availability of funds. These shortages occurred when savings were withdrawn from depository institutions and placed in higher-yielding investments such as money market funds. As real estate financing shifted to the use of mortgage-backed securities, the capacity to tap huge financial markets for funds accelerated, bringing ample cash into the mortgage market. Just prior to the recent financial crisis, it seemed that a shortage of mortgage money had become a thing of the past. Now the supply of money derives from a much broader base of sources including pension funds, money market funds, and mutual funds, all in addition to savings deposits in the banking system. As discussed in Chapter 2 and later chapters, any current shortages in mortgage money availability have been made up by the intervention of the Federal Reserve Bank.

Demand for Credit

The demand for credit comes from the following four categories of borrowers:

1. government—which includes net debt increase for federal, state, and local governments;
2. corporate—which includes business borrowing for inventory requirements, capital needs, and longer-term investment;
3. mortgage loans—which includes housing, construction, industrial, and other investment purposes; and
4. consumer—personal loans for such things as automobiles, furniture, appliances, or other personal needs.

A normal balance between the four categories of credit demand exists when each takes about one-quarter of the available supply of funds each year. However, the demand for borrowed money by business and consumers is generally less in an economy with slow to modest growth. That was the situation in the 1990s and the early part of the twenty-first century.

Although mortgage money competes with all other demands for credit—they are all seeking essentially the same pool of funds—that pool has been large enough in recent years to supply each of their requirements even at declining interest rates.

Table 7-1 compares credit demand in 2007 with credit demand in 2009 and 2013. This table shows a decrease in total demand for credit from 2007 to 2009. The year 2007 had peak credit demand just before the recent financial crisis, with all categories taking a lesser share of demand except the government. By 2013 there had been a recovery in demand for credit including mortgage loans with real mortgage demand increasing rapidly in 2014. Mortgage lending decreased because of the recession. Note that the federal government borrows substantially more than the publicized amounts in order to pay for off-budget items. In 2007, mortgage loans took $1,062 billion in net credit, which means new money. The loan origination market growing threefold over the decade of 1997 to 2007 was only exceeded by federal, state, and local borrowing. With the financial crisis that began in the fall of 2007, the government slowly became the dominant borrower in the U.S. credit markets by 2009, and continued to have almost a one-third share in 2017.

An interesting feature of **credit markets** is the position of federal borrowing. Since there are no legal limits on what the government can pay for its money, it is capable of driving all other demands for credit out of the market. Of course, such an action is extreme, but it did occur in 1944 at the peak of World War II, when the government took 99% of available credit. This scenario was exceeded, however, in 2008 and 2009—a fact that exposes the full

TABLE 7-1 Funds Raised in U.S. Credit Markets* (in billions of dollars)

	2007		2009		2013	
	Amount	Percent	Amount	Percent	Amount	Percent
Total Net Borrowing	$4,483	100%	($ 644)	100%	$1,945	100%
Government (Fed, local)	358	30	1,515	335	716	37
Corporate	1,055	24	(540)	(84)	388	20
Mortgage loans	1,062	24	(293)	(45)	100	05
Consumer	139	03	(115)	(18)	174	09
Other	869	19	(1,211)	(188)	567	29

*Figures interpolated from "Funds Raised in U.S. Credit & Federal Reserve Statistical Release," *Federal Reserve Bulletin*, December 9, 2010, Table F.4, and "Credit Market Borrowing, All Sectors, by Instrument Markets," *Federal Reserve Bulletin*, December 11, 2014, Table F.4.

scope of the financial crisis that still haunts the U.S. credit markets. The only period when the federal government was not a net borrower over the past 50 years occurred between 1998 and 2001, when the federal government was, for the first time since the 1950s, not in a deficit spending position. Recent decades with the highest increases in federal deficit spending are 1981–1990 and 2001–2014.

Monetary Policies of the Federal Reserve

A substantial influence on interest rates is the Fed's ability to increase the money available in this country at any time, as described earlier in this chapter. The other "tools" available to the Fed can also be used to effectively change short-term interest rates.

Fiscal Policies of the United States Government

The way in which the federal government handles its tax and spending policies is called its *fiscal policies*. Fiscal policies represent a key factor in the competitive markets that control interest rates. If Congress and the president decide to spend more than the available income (tax revenues), the difference must be made up by either borrowing or printing money, thus forcing the U.S. Treasury and the Fed to act almost regardless of the effect on interest rates.

Interest Rate Indicators

There are a number of different interest rates published daily in leading business magazines and newspapers. All of these give good clues as to the direction in which money costs are moving. Following is a discussion of the four rates that represent important **interest rate indicators** for the real estate mortgage business.

Treasury Bill Rate

The cost of short-term borrowing by the federal government is determined each week at the auctions of three-month and six-month Treasury bills. T-bills are sold by the Federal Reserve Banks every Monday in minimum denominations of $10,000, and can be purchased from banks or through authorized security dealers. The return on this type of investment is expressed not as an interest rate but as a yield because it is determined by the difference between the purchase price and the face value of the bill. The auctions provide an accurate indication of current short-term rates, and the trend, up or down, yielding a clue to the future.

Prime Rate

The prime rate is often defined as the interest rate charged by a commercial bank to its most creditworthy customers. Each bank may set its prime rate by any method it chooses, as the rate is not regulated. Some banks use complicated formulas, while others depend on the wisdom of their boards of directors. In practice, most banks simply follow the lead of one of the major commercial banks.

Today, the prime rate is used more as a base upon which to float an interest rate for many kinds of loans than as an actual lending rate. For example, a construction loan may be quoted at two points over prime; if the prime rate is 3.25%, the construction loan will be 5.25%. If the prime rate moves up to 6%, the construction loan automatically will be increased to 8%, and is calculated from the date the prime rate change is announced. Another direct effect of the prime rate on the mortgage field is that warehouse lines of credit held by mortgage companies with commercial banks are usually quoted at prime or a point over prime.

Where Are We Now?

The History of 10-Year Treasury Rate

MONTHLY 10-YEAR RATE	
2017–June	2.21%
2017–May	2.33%
2017–Apr	2.35%
2017–Mar	2.46%
2017–Feb	2.48%
2017–Jan	2.45%
2016–Dec	2.45%
2016–Nov	1.83%
2016–Oct	1.63%
2016–Sept	1.57%
2016–Aug	1.51%
2016–July	1.46%

HISTORICAL 10-YEAR TREASURY RATE	
Average (Last 12 Months)	2.12%
Average (Last 10 Years)	3.06%
High (Last 12 Months)	2.48% (February 2017)
Low (Last 12 Months)	1.46% (July 2016)
High (Since April 1953)	15.32% (September 1981)
Low (Since April 1953)	1.44% (June 2012)

Recent rates are close to the all-time lows.

Fannie Mae/Freddie Mac–Administered Yield Requirements

During the early 1980s, the Federal National Mortgage Association (FNMA)—"Fannie Mae"—and the Federal Home Loan Mortgage Corporation (FHLMC)—"Freddie Mac"—phased out their frequent auctions for loan commitments to their seller/servicers. The auctions have been replaced by daily access to these secondary-market purchasers by seller/servicers through indicative pricing processes. When an approved Fannie Mae seller/servicer sells whole loan products to Fannie Mae for cash, this action generates immediate funds for additional mortgage originations. During 2004, Fannie Mae developed new technology to replace the old manual management of pipeline risk (covered in Chapters 4 and 5), which in a faster-paced mortgage market had become too difficult and required too much attention from key employees, taking them away from other value-added tasks. The system Fannie Mae calls **eCommitting**™ was developed to allow approved conventional mortgage lenders more time to focus on growing their business. eCommitONE™ is an easy-to-use, web-based application that provides automated pricing information and best efforts committing processes.

eCommitONE™ has been through nine upgrades over the past seven years; it now allows a mortgage lender to pass pipeline management risk onto Fannie Mae. Many lenders prefer the eCommitONE™ software application to commit loans in their mortgage loan pipeline to be purchased by Fannie Mae. If the committed loan does not close, lenders will not have "pair-off" fees like they have in mandatory commitments, as long as the committed loans that the lender closes are delivered to Fannie Mae before the commitment expiration date and receive the commitment price. These approved seller/servicers use one or both of two execution options to meet business objectives: mandatory committing (through Fannie Mae's eCommitting™ application) and best efforts committing (through Fannie Mae's eCommitONE™ application). When approved sellers/servicers enter into mandatory commitment with Fannie Mae, they agree to sell a specified dollar amount of mortgage loans to Fannie Mae at an agreed-upon price within a specified time frame. Because these commitments are mandatory, if the approved seller/servicer is not able to fulfill the terms of his or her commitment to Fannie Mae, he or she will be required to pair out of the contract, and may be subject to a pair-off fee. A best efforts commitment, conversely, allows an approved seller/servicer to enter into an agreement to sell the loan to Fannie Mae, but if the loan does not close, he or she will not be charged a pair-off fee for nondelivery. Both options are available to Fannie Mae's approved seller/servicers. Required net yields and indicative prices are typically updated once a day at approximately 8:15 a.m. Eastern time. While these rates can fluctuate during any one working day, an approved seller/servicer has online access to current pricing. Fannie Mae does post a historically required net yield by day online on all currently offered loan products.[3] The yield requirements of both Fannie Mae and Freddie Mac are quoted in what might be called the "wholesale" market rate for mortgage loans at that time. Within the industry, this wholesale rate is referred to as a *required net basis yield*, or a yield that must be delivered to the loan purchaser. Loan originators add 0.25% to 0.375% for servicing the loan, and the cost of private mortgage insurance is often combined as a part of the gross rate quoted to a borrower.

U.S. Treasury Security Rates

Shorter-term (one- to five-year) Treasury rates have become more important as an indicator of mortgage rates. Not only do they accurately reflect the shorter-term money market rates that affect mortgage money, but they are also being used as a major index for setting adjustable-rate mortgage (ARM) loan interest rates. Because the market for Treasuries is constantly changing to reflect the money markets, the rates reported are usually averages of daily rates for weekly or monthly time periods. All financial publications carry information on U.S. Treasury yields, and the Federal Reserve Board now offers a weekly release covering selected interest rates.[4]

---

[3] Approved seller/servicers can obtain this information online by logging into the eCommitting™ or eCommitONE™ system or this can be accessed at https://www.fanniemae.com/singlefamily/historical-daily-required-net-yields

[4] For further information, contact Publications Services, Mail Stop 138, Board of Governors of the Federal Reserve System, Washington, DC 20551, and ask for selected interest rates and bond prices (weekly). The St. Louis Federal Reserve Bank offers these reports online at http://www.federalreserve.gov/releases/h15/

London Interbank Offered Rate

More commonly referred to as **LIBOR**, the London Interbank Offered Rate is a daily reference rate based on the interest rates at which banks borrow unsecured funds from other banks in the London wholesale money market (or interbank lending market). LIBOR rates are a favorite referenced rate for adjustable-rate mortgages. The divergence of these more market-based rates from those set or affected by Federal Reserve Bank monetary policy helped trigger problems with many adjustable-rate mortgage products during the subprime loan crisis. LIBOR rates remained higher than rates based on Treasury bills, Treasury notes, and the Eleventh District Monthly Weighted Average Cost of Funds Index (COFI) from 2004 to 2009. Therefore, ARM products based on LIBOR caused higher mortgage delinquencies as borrowers struggled with higher payments.

Usury

Usury laws are state laws, not federal statutes, limiting the amount of interest that may be charged on different kinds of loans and to various categories of borrowers. For the first 70 years of the twentieth century, market interest rates remained generally below the various state limits, and there was little concern for this particular restriction. But as interest rates continued to climb in the late 1970s, usury limits began to surface and restricted mortgage lending in some states. The rising cost of money made it more and more difficult to make loans at interest rates within the statutory limits and still retain a safe operating margin. Furthermore, states with higher interest limits were able to attract the big secondary market investors that can purchase mortgages anywhere. Many states were simply excluded from the national market by restrictive usury laws. To help resolve the dilemma, Congress preempted state usury limits for first-mortgage residential loans as of March 31, 1980.

The concept supporting usury laws is that the individual borrower should have some protection from the substantial power represented by a lender. In earlier times, and perhaps in some smaller communities today, that protection may be appropriate. But where mortgage loans are concerned, the growth of lending across state lines, coupled with the big national markets for loans, has made restrictive usury laws somewhat counterproductive. In July 2010, the Dodd-Frank Wall Street Reform and Consumer Protection Act was signed into law. It provides for a Consumer Financial Protection Agency to regulate some credit practices, including notices for rate changes on credit cards, but does not have an interest rate limit.

> ## Where Are We Now?
>
> ### Implications for the Real Estate Market
>
> Why is the real estate industry so concerned about interest rates? Imagine that someone wants to buy a home priced at $300,000. The buyer makes a 20 percent down payment and, therefore, needs to borrow the balance of the purchase price, $240,000. If the interest rate is 5 percent, her monthly payment will be $1,288.37. Monthly income required to qualify for a 30 year fixed rate mortgage loan – specifically a conventional mortgage – requires a housing to income ratio of 28 percent, making it necessary that this borrower would earn at least $4,600 per month to qualify for the mortgage. If mortgage interest rates go up to 6 percent, in order to buy the same house, this purchaser will need monthly income of $5,139. The buyer will need a $539 raise (after taxes) just to buy the house. If interest rates climb to 7 percent, an increase in income to $5,703 will be required, the equivalent of a raise of almost $1,103 per month after all payroll taxes are withheld.
>
> For a 90 percent LTV loan, the variations are even more dramatic. The monthly income requirement for that loan at 5 percent would be $5,177 while at 7 percent it would be $5,781, a difference of a little over $600 per month. There has been a small uptick in mortgage rates during 2017 and 2018, but the worry of even higher rates and the effect on the housing market have been subsumed in the worry about the lack of first time buyer home supply and the rapid increase in housing cost over the past 2½ years.

Fixed-Interest, Constant-Level Plan

The repayment schedule for a fixed-rate mortgage (FRM) involves a constant payment for the life of the loan. Each payment is calculated so that all interest due to payment date is included, plus a portion of the principal. The periodic reduction of the principal balance is called **amortization**. This mortgage design gives assurance to home buyers that the loan payment will not increase during the life of the loan. As mentioned earlier, by the 1970s, it became obvious that more flexible repayment plans were needed to meet changing market requirements.

Nevertheless, the FRM product has remained a very popular design, holding well over half the new loan origination market. This is true even though it is normally offered at interest rates about two percentage points higher than adjustable-rate mortgages. There are several reasons for its continuing popularity, as follows:

1. In periods of relatively low interest rates, borrowers are reluctant to commit to an adjustable-rate mortgage that might start increasing in cost. So the FRM offers a sense of protection.

2. The growing use of mortgage pools to raise lendable funds in the financial markets tends to encourage fixed-rate loans. One of the problems for an investor in a mortgage-backed security is the uncertainty of cash flows: How frequently will borrowers prepay the principal? When you add to that the uncertainty of an adjustable-rate pool of mortgages, the projection of an accurate return to the investor becomes even more difficult. A short rule of thumb method for estimating a 30-year, fixed-rate mortgage is presented at the end of the chapter, along with websites for several monthly mortgage payment calculators.

Adjustable-Rate Mortgage (ARM)

An adjustable-rate mortgage product design allows a lender to make a change in the rate of interest at periodic intervals without altering other conditions of the loan agreement. The term **adjustable-rate mortgage**, or ARM, is not always used in a precise manner. In media reports, the term has been used to indicate any mortgage wherein the payment amount can change. Another repayment plan, the graduated-payment mortgage, offers changes in payment amounts, but it is calculated on a very different basis and should not be confused with an ARM. With an adjustable-rate mortgage, the interest rate can be changed; with a graduated design, the interest rate is fixed.

Adjustable-rate mortgages are not new. Other countries with developed economies that allow long-term real estate financing have wondered how the United States has been able to stick with FRMs for so long, since ARMs allow depository lenders to take less asset liability duration risk. British mortgage lenders, called Building Societies, have offered only variable-rate mortgages since 1932. Similarly, Canada developed a pattern of short-term mortgage loans (with terms such as five years) that allow a lender to renew the note when it comes due and to make an adjustment in the interest rate with no rate cap. This renewal type of note has become known as the *Canadian rollover*.

When banking regulators first considered adjustable-rate mortgages, they were concerned with the potential impact on home buyers of possible increases in payment amounts, so approval to write this kind of mortgage included constraints on how an interest rate could be adjusted. A change in the rate must be justified by tying the adjustment to change with a regulator-approved **rate index**—one not under the control of the lender. The frequency of adjustment was limited to fixed time periods such as once a year. The interest rate change was limited at each time period and a ceiling was placed on the total amount of increase over the life of the loan, referred to as a *period cap* and *lifetime of mortgage cap*, respectively. At that time, interest rates were moving only one way—up. (We will discuss these rate **caps** more fully later in the chapter.)

The first such design, approved by the Federal Home Loan Bank Board in 1979 for federally chartered savings associations, was called a *variable-rate mortgage* (VRM). The initial VRM design limited interest rate changes to a maximum of .5% per year and not more than 2.5% over the life of the loan. Even though the intent was to assist lenders, it was not widely accepted, primarily because limitations on how much interest rates could be adjusted were too restrictive in an escalating market. Remember, no lender is required to make any kind of a loan. An "approved" mortgage plan only means that it is legal for a regulated lender to offer such a mortgage; the lender does not have to offer the plan.

TYPES OF LOANS

Other Primary Market Lenders

The opening of the secondary market and the wide acceptance of mortgage-backed securities as sound investments have encouraged many newcomers to enter the loan origination market. The next section discusses the major players in this field, who are not subject to banking regulations.

Nonbank Lenders

Companies with long experience in handling loan qualification and funding for other kinds of consumer-type loans have entered the mortgage market. These include such major operators as ING Group, Ally Financial, Honda Financial Services, GM Financial, and the retail finance division of GE Capital.

Investment Bankers

As many investment bankers expand into handling various money market accounts, retirement funds, and even checking accounts, some have entered mortgage loan origination. Edward D. Jones, Charles Schwab Company, Merrill Lynch, and Raymond James & Associates are all examples of this kind of lender.

Finance Companies

Many small loan companies such as HSBC Finance Corporation that formerly made mostly unsecured personal loans have expanded into mortgage lending as a better method of securing their loans. Other firms such as Discover—the credit card issuer—have now diversified into personal lending and online mortgage lending (e.g., Discover® Home Loans).

Home Builders

Several large home builders, including KB Home, Pulte Homes, D.R. Horton and others, have entered the origination market through subsidiaries that process loans and sell them into mortgage pools. By exercising some control over the mortgage money, home builders are able to structure loans that better suit their buyers' needs, thus enhancing sales potential.

Real Estate Brokerage Firms

Companies that have developed national real estate brokerage operations through direct acquisitions or franchise networks have entered the loan origination business. Such companies as Century 21 and Prudential Real Estate are now able to offer mortgage loan services in their own offices.

Internet

The newest method of negotiating a mortgage loan is through contacting a mortgage loan site on the internet. An individual who may have a tarnished credit record and wants to remain anonymous, a person living in a rural area who wants to avoid traveling a long distance, or maybe even someone with an excellent credit record who feels more comfortable with an impersonal interview are all lured to the internet. There are some downsides to this method of loan application, of course. Waiting periods are still necessary for certain verifications, fees and interest rates are about the same, and there is no real person to assist in the process. Also, the internet has its share of shady operators who may be harder to distinguish from legitimate mortgage professionals in cyberspace.

Computerized Loan Origination (CLO)

As a forerunner to computerized loan analysis, computers were first used as a means of transmitting loan information to a human underwriter who did the analysis work and, after proper verifications, approved or rejected loan applications. This process involves computer network tie-ins between independent agents and major money sources. Today, CLO is one method used by real estate brokers to assist buyers in negotiating a loan to purchase a property. Current HUD rules allow a person or company who initiates the loan and assists in helping a borrower furnish the necessary information to earn a fee that is reasonably commensurate with the work performed. Now with new consumer disclosure requirements, the next generation of CLOs currently supports regulatory reporting as well. The procedure is further discussed in Chapter 14.

Pension Funds

During the past decade, **pension funds** have become large investors in mortgage loans. By far, the most common method is through the purchase of mortgage-backed securities. In this way, investors avoid the management problems associated with individual mortgage loans and are able to treat such investments as just another kind of security.

However, a few pension groups, particularly those operated by state agencies and by labor unions, offer home loan programs as primary lenders. Some funds restrict participation to their own members, and some offer such loans to the general public if qualifying standards are met. Most of these direct loans are available to middle- and low-income families and offer attractive interest rates.

PRIVATE MORTGAGE INSURANCE

In 1972, the problem posed by the lack of default insurance was resolved. At that time, the Federal Home Loan Bank Board approved the writing of 95% loans (formerly, the limit was a 90% loan-to-value ratio) by federally chartered savings associations. Loans with a loan-to-value ratio higher than 90% required insurance against default. Prior to that time, there had been no default insurance requirement. Within a matter of a few months, the private mortgage insurance industry, which had been rather dormant, suddenly came alive. Within two years of the FHLB approval, one insurance company—Mortgage Guaranty Insurance Co. (MGIC) of Milwaukee—was writing more default insurance than the entire FHA.

With conforming loans providing uniform documentation and private mortgage insurance offering protection for the lender, the secondary market was able to expand beyond the limited market of trading in FHA and VA loans.

The recent mortgage crisis and resultant housing downturn in the United States represents the most adverse scenario for private mortgage insurers since the Great Depression. The first small private mortgage insurer went into liquidation in 2008, followed by several more, including PMI Insurance Company of Arizona, a subsidiary of PMI Group. The PMI Group is a large, publicly traded private mortgage insurer that was placed in receivership on October 20, 2011. Many of these liquidated firms have paid off claims as a percentage of the claims put forth. Several firms were forced to raise capital in order to remain on the approved list of private mortgage insurers for Fannie Mae and Freddie Mac. The lack of capacity of private mortgage insurance was for a while an additional inhibitor lengthening the down cycle in residential real estate in the recent recession. Some private mortgage insurers engaged in writing polices that guaranteed private MBS underlying mortgages. Their uncertain future was one of the contributing factors to the virtual halt of private MBS issuance in 2009.

The lack of clarity in the fate of Fannie Mae and Freddie Mac makes it difficult for the remaining private mortgage insurers to gain footing going forward, as many are still reeling from losses sustained in the period 2008–2013.

REFINANCING EXISTING CONVENTIONAL LOANS

A decline in interest rates usually brings many property owners back to the mortgage market to refinance loans at lower rates. Some homeowners have taken this step two and three times if rates continue to decline. At the end of May 2015, **refinancing** accounted for about less than 50% of all loan originations.[5] (Most lenders consider refinancing the payoff of an existing loan from the proceeds of a new loan.)

---

[5]"Mortgage Applications Decrease in Latest MBA Weekly Survey," Mortgage Bankers Association of America, June 3, 2015, https://www.mba.org/2015-press-releases/june/mortgage-applications-decrease-in-latest-mba-weekly-survey

The benefits of refinancing differ for each borrower. They have to do with the amount of interest rate reduction, the costs of renegotiating the loan (new closing costs and discount), the effect of tax laws on the borrower, and possible new lender requirements such as an adjustable-rate instead of a fixed-rate loan. There are no real standards for refinancing, and costs can vary substantially between lenders. A discussion of the major questions involved with refinancing follows.

Where to Refinance

The best place to start a refinance search is with the holder of the existing mortgage note. Most lenders (but not all) are aware that mortgage notes can be refinanced when rates drop and would rather accept a lesser rate than lose the customer. The market is very competitive and most borrowers have access to more than one source. If the note holder will not reopen a loan for refinancing in a lower interest market, other lenders may be willing to consider such an application.

Rate Reduction

An earlier guideline for refinancing was that a rate reduction of 2% or more was worth taking. However, rate reduction alone may not save money if the costs exceed the savings. So a more practical approach is to add the costs of refinancing, and then compare those with the savings to see how many months it will take to recover the costs.

Calculation of the savings is shown in the following example.

Example

A property financed at 7% on a 30-year fixed-rate loan is compared with a 5% fixed-rate loan. (Reduction in principal balance is not considered.)

At 7%, $220,000, 30 years: Monthly payment $1,463.67
At 5%, $220,000, 30 years: Monthly payment   1,181.01
Monthly savings $ 282.66

The important question is: How long will it take to recover refinancing costs? Several lenders should be contacted because their charges can vary substantially.

Refinancing Costs

No specific regulations apply to the charges that may be assessed in a refinancing transaction. Most lenders consider refinancing in the same category (cost-wise) as a new loan. They may require a new application fee, title insurance, attorney's fees, and an appraisal. Most require some discount that may be a cash requirement. Add up the costs assessed by each lender contacted and an easy comparison can be made.

For example, say the lowest cost offered amounts to $8,300. By dividing that sum by the monthly savings from the preceding example, the number of months it takes to recover the expenditure calculates as follows:

$$\$8{,}300 \div \$282.66 = 29.36 \text{ months}$$

If occupancy of the house is expected to continue longer than 29.36 months, a savings can be achieved.

Effect of Tax Law

Tax law treats refinancing differently from a new loan in terms of deductibility of a discount. Even though a discount may be paid in cash for refinancing, the IRS ruled in May 1986 that a discount for refinancing a home loan must be amortized over the life of the loan. This differs from a discount paid by the buyer at the time of purchase of the house, which may be deducted in the year paid, the same as interest. Another tax question that should be considered concerns the tax value of deducting interest on a home loan. The benefit differs with the taxpayer's tax bracket. Therefore, a taxpayer in a higher bracket would have greater possible deductions and would need a lower refinance rate to achieve the same benefit as a taxpayer in a lower bracket.

Restructuring the Loan

Refinancing is a negotiable transaction. If a lender agrees to an interest rate concession, it is possible that one bargaining chip would be a change from a fixed-rate to an adjustable-rate repayment plan. In this scenario, the lender is accepting a lower rate and may insist that the rate be adjustable, in case the market should rise in the years ahead.

Appraisal Problems

One major problem that some homeowners have encountered in attempting refinancing is that the market value of the house has declined to an amount less than the balance due on the loan. Or, in the case of some graduated-payment designs, the balance due on the loan, which increased with negative amortization in the early years, has exceeded the market value of the property. In general, a refinanced conventional loan cannot exceed 95% of the current market value of the property. This means that additional cash may be required at closing in order to reduce the loan amount to an acceptable level based on the newly appraised value of the property.

An escape from possible appraisal problems is available for holders of FHA and VA loans. Both agencies encourage their borrowers to seek refinancing if lower interest rates can be achieved. An appraisal is not required, and agency fees have been reduced. As underwriters of these loans (rather than lenders), the FHA and VA benefit from anything that makes loan repayment easier for borrowers.

SUBPRIME AND PREDATORY LENDING

Subprime loans are those made to persons who do not have a top-grade credit record as is required to qualify for a regular mortgage loan. While subprime loans are not specifically connected to automated underwriting, the many credit details that can be handled by computer analysis provide one reason why many lenders have undertaken loans in this field. Another reason is that subprime loans command higher interest rates and discounts, which add profitable business to a lender, provided the lender is careful in analyzing the higher risks involved.

With a conforming loan, rates are posted in newspapers and elsewhere. But subprime lending uses risk-based pricing. Rates are not publicly quoted; rates are found, or negotiated, to fit the risk profile. To determine a risk profile, start with a prime loan. A prime loan is made to a good-to-excellent borrower who has perfect credit, which means no derogatories and no 30-, 60-, or 90-day delinquencies in his or her mortgage history, or few derogatories/delinquencies.

Below this level of risk are the subprime borrowers. To underwrite this type of loan, the underwriter does not examine whether or not the borrower is worthy of credit, but rather where the borrower belongs on the risk scale. Credit scoring is a helpful factor in this determination. Appraisals are also critical. It takes an astute underwriter to sort out the various risks involved and to properly evaluate the greater risk.

The borrower is matched to one of a series of risk profiles. Unfortunately, lenders differ in defining these profiles, as the process involves some gray areas. Following is an example of what may be included in determining the risk of an A, A-, B, C, D, or F mortgage borrower by a typical mortgage lender. Comparisons can be made to an "A" borrower with a delinquency rate of 7.8% as rated by many lenders.

"A" borrower has no late mortgage payments and no credit card payments over 30 days delinquent in the last year. "A" or prime borrowers have a low default rate and underwriters can allow a higher loan-to-value ratio. (The national delinquency rate, according to the Federal Reserve Bank of New York was 7.8% in the fall of 2010[6] and 3.18% by the fall of 2014.[7])

"A-" borrower is sometimes referred to as having an Alternate A or Alt-A mortgage. The borrower has no late mortgage payments and one or two credit card payments 30 days late. (The current national delinquency rate, according to CoreLogic, Inc., is 26.89%.)

"B" borrower is 30 days late on a mortgage payment and 60 days late on one or more charge account debts, and has satisfactory credit but high debt ratios. Reasons for delinquencies are important, as the record may indicate problems that can, or have been, overcome. This borrower may be self-employed and have trouble documenting income. The underwriter first looks for explainable delinquencies, then at secondary credit and revolving credit over a two-year period. (The current national delinquency rate was 36.57% in the fall of 2010 and fell to 4.09% in the 2nd quarter of 2013.[8])

"C" borrower is 30 days late two or three times on a mortgage payment and has several charge accounts 60 days or more in arrears. A C borrower has only fair credit and high debt ratios. A 500 credit score is typically a "C" borrower. These borrowers may have had employment problems or health and accident problems and are over their heads in debt. They want to consolidate the indebtedness. Underwriters look for both the willingness and ability to repay. (The current national

---

[6] Federal Reserve of New York, "U.S. Credit Conditions," Regional Outreach Research Data, October 2010.
[7] Federal Reserve of New York, "Consumer Debt Panel," Data Tables, December 2014.
[8] Transunion, "TransUnion: National Mortgage Loan Delinquency Rate Continues Torrid Decline in Q2," Transunion, press release, August 6, 2013, accessed February 1, 2015, http://finance.yahoo.com/news/transunion-national-mortgage-loan-delinquency-100000136.html

delinquency rate was 36.57% in the fall of 2010 and fell to 6.07% in the 2nd quarter of 2013.)

"D" borrower has poor credit and high debt ratios. These borrowers are not likely to become "A" borrowers very soon. Such loans have a good chance of going into foreclosure and the lender must depend on the collateral to guarantee repayment. (The current national delinquency rate was 51.26% in the fall of 2010 and fell to 9.67% in the 2nd quarter of 2013.)

"F" borrower is currently in bankruptcy or foreclosure. With the help of state-of-the-art information-gathering systems, subprime lending was burgeoning, but recently, most lenders and investors have not been doing very well with this category of loans. Subprime "B & C" mortgage lending became a growing field leading up to 2007, but had not had enough time to develop quality experience factors.

The current mortgage crisis has shown results very different from the past. Average delinquency and foreclosure rates were useful in predicting past delinquencies and foreclosures. In 2001, "A" loans had serious delinquency rates of 1.96%, "B" loans were at 3.73%, "C" loans at 4.99%, and "D" loans at 8.07%. However, as can be seen from the current delinquency rates, the numbers from 10 years ago did not provide sufficient data to predict the current mortgage failures. The subprime mortgage market has now completely collapsed.

PARTICIPATION AGREEMENT

Large Residential Loans

As the average cost of homes increases in certain areas above the $400,000 level[9], the need for larger loans becomes more important. Loans that exceed the conforming loan limit (the Fannie Mae/Freddie Mac limit) are more difficult to sell. While there is a growing secondary market for so-called "jumbo loans," the yield requirements are slightly higher. Attracted by higher yields, some of these larger loans are held in portfolio by lenders. Even so, the amounts may exceed the lender's own limits for a single loan. To overcome this problem, two or more lenders may combine to fund the loan. This is called a **participation loan**. One lender services the loan and accounts to the other participant(s) as the assigned percentage of the loan

---

[9]U.S. Census Bureau, (2018). Median and Average Sales Prices of New Homes Sold in United States – July 2018, Accessed September 17, 2018 at: https://www.census.gov/construction/nrs/pdf/uspricemon.pdf

may require. Prior to the ascendance of the commercial mortgage-backed and residential mortgage-backed securities markets, loan participation syndications were quite popular, allowing a lead bank to move loan assets off its balance sheets. Purchasers of participations found that such syndications were a source of a reasonably steady stream of new loan product. Syndicated pools of participated mortgage loans allowed purchasers to gain access to new markets without having to establish an office or underwriting expertise for that market. Both the lead bank and participation interest owners must ensure that the loan meets the underwriting requirements established by a participation term sheet. There is still an active market where smaller banks outgrown the legal lending or exposures limits as the originating lender and must sell a portion of the loan or loans.

Other Reasons for Residential Mortgage Loan Participation Packages

Packages of participation loans are often put together with the originating lender retaining 5 to 10% as a first loss position with a slightly higher yield that the average of the participation loan package as a way to recover lendable funds and increase yield on the loans made adjusted for the additional risk taken.

Sharing or reducing the risk of loss may not seem to be that important in the case of a single mortgage loan on a single family residence, but it is certainly important in a large package of residential loans or a package of loans secured by properties concentrated in one housing development project or in one geographic area.

Financial institutions involved in this market must make sure that participation agreement are well thought out and understood by both parties to avoid later litigation if problems arise with the participation package performance. Vital requirements of the participation agreements will consist of seller representations and warranties, voting and other rights and obligations of each party involved in the participation, transfer provisions, and reclaiming or buying back the transferred fund.

The underwriting due diligence with respect to the borrowers in the package is often guaranteed by the originating lender and the underlying real estate collateral is a necessity to mitigate risk for the loan participant. Those banks involved in this type of business must assure that the FDIC's Financial Institution Letter 492015 (FIL492015) that provides due diligence guidance for banks in managing risks associated with these transactions is followed.

TAX IMPACTS IN MORTGAGE LENDING

Property Taxes

Property tax, also known as ad valorem tax ("according to value" tax), becomes a specific lien on real property on the date the tax is assessed by an authorized taxing authority. Release of lien is automatic upon payment of the tax. Tax records are normally filed in each county as a separate section of information. Property subject to tax (some land is exempt) must stand good for its payment. If the tax is not paid, the property is subject to foreclosure by the state. In some states, an assessment by a properly authorized neighborhood maintenance or homeowners association carries the same status as a property tax. A tax assessment is a high-priority claim in a foreclosure action, preceded only by the administrative costs of the sale. Thus, property taxes hold a higher priority than other secured claimants; regardless of the date their claims are recorded.

Property taxes take precedence over a first mortgage lien even though the mortgage may be filed of record earlier. Therefore, lenders normally require the protection of handling tax payments as a part of escrow requirements. A cushion of one-sixth of the annual tax is usually deposited with the lender at loan closing. In addition, the tax escrow at closing includes the amount of taxes that have accrued to that date (payable by the buyer or seller as may be owed by each). Then, one month's worth (one-twelfth of the annual amount due) of taxes is added to each monthly payment of the mortgage loan.

Once the money is in escrow, the lender is responsible for making tax payments directly to the tax authority as part of its loan servicing function.

One of the most common errors on estimating closing costs for a residential mortgage loan is the amount that should be paid to begin the tax escrow account. Many misguided loan officers and real estate professional, trying to "help" borrowers close more quickly, understate this amount, which lowers the amounts due at closing. Some go even further, offering an 80% LTV loan with a simultaneous closing of a second loan for 10% to 20%. These simultaneous loans avoid the requirement of a tax escrow account altogether. In states with higher real estate taxes, like California, New York, and Texas, borrowers who cannot come up with the money to pay their taxes on subprime mortgages caused servicers to advance funds and add this to the borrowers' payments. Subsequently, many of these borrowers had trouble making regular payments without consideration for paying these taxes, advanced by the servicer, back.

Interest Expense and Real Estate Tax Deductions for Home Residence Loans

The provisions of the Tax Cuts and Jobs Act of 2017 (TCJA) put limits on the deductibility of state income and sales taxes. They have been capped at $10,000. This will cause as-yet-unresolved disparities in federal income tax burdens in high real-estate-market-value states with state income taxes like New York and California. The TCJA for 2018 through 2025 placed an acquisition indebtedness limit on the qualified residences. The Indebtedness deduction has been lowered to $750,000 for loans incurred after Dec. 15, 2017, and the separate deduction for home-equity indebtedness has been suspended. The TCJA also altered the rules concerning the deduction of qualified residence interest. The TCJA will decrease the amount of acquisition interest that is deductible, and now there are two sets of rules that apply for qualified residence interest.

1. For years before 2018:
    A. Interest is deductible on acquisition indebtedness up to $1,000,000 for single taxpayers, heads of household, and married taxpayers filing jointly; and up to $500,000 for married taxpayers who file separately. Interest on home-equity indebtedness is deductible to the extent that the debt does not exceed the lesser of:
        1. the fair market value (FMV) of the residence, reduced by acquisition indebtedness, or
        2. $100,000 ($50,000 for married taxpayers who file separately).
    B. Therefore the total amount of acquisition indebtedness and home-equity indebtedness (the interest on which is deductible) cannot exceed $1,100,000 ($1,000,000 + $100,000).
2. For years 2018 through 2025:
    A. Interest is deductible on acquisition indebtedness up to $750,000 ($375,000 for married taxpayers filing separate returns). Conversely the lower limitation does not apply to

acquisition indebtedness incurred on or before December 15, 2017. A taxpayer who has entered into a written binding contract before December 15, 2017 that has closed on the purchase of a principal residence before January 1, 2018, and who purchases that residence before April 1, 2018, is treated as having incurred the acquisition indebtedness on the residence on or before December 15, 2017.

B. However, the separate deduction for home-equity indebtedness interest is barred in the years 2018 through 2025. Should a home-equity loan be used to purchase, build, or significantly improve the taxpayer's main home or second home that secures the loan and the loan is less than the purchase price of the home, the interest on that loan will be considered as acquisition indebtedness and therefore deductible (subject to the $750,000/$375,000 acquisition indebtedness limits).

Fair Housing Requirements

The **Fair Housing Amendments Act of 1988** extended the prohibitions against discrimination in the 1968 Fair Housing Act to all residential real estate transactions and represents the only amendment to the Act to date. Prior law considers unlawful any discrimination in housing because of race, color, religion, gender, or national origin. The new amendment added two new categories for protection against discrimination: disability and familial status. The additional restrictions are of particular importance in the rental of multifamily dwellings.

The new category of "disability" protection requires proper accommodation in the design and construction of multifamily dwellings. The building and its facilities must provide accessibility and usability for physically disabled people. This includes such items as doors and hallways wide enough to handle wheelchairs, light switches and elevator buttons at a level accessible to those in wheelchairs, and alarm signals in both light and sound to protect those with hearing and visual impairment. People with AIDS are now included in this protected category as well.

Protection for familial status prohibits discrimination on the basis of family composition. Housing must be open to people with children 18 years and under. Parents with children or guardians with children cannot be denied housing. "Adults-only" apartments are no longer permissible. There are exceptions for housing occupied by elderly persons only.

Tax Deductions

As residential rental property, apartments have always offered some special tax advantages for investors. The purpose, of course, is to encourage suitable housing in this country. Under current law (the 1993 Tax Act), as renewed under President George W. Bush, residential property has retained its 27.5-year recovery period, while nonresidential property maintains its 39-year recovery period. Another tax advantage is that since the building—not the land—is depreciable, an apartment offers a favorable combination of values. The building portion of the investment is relatively high compared with the nondepreciable land. Also, items classed as personal property, such as any drapes, appliances, and carpeting necessary for apartment operation, are eligible for even greater depreciation deduction rates than the building, and the calculation can be made using accelerated rates.

Revisions to the 1986 Tax Act changed the tax nature of certain kinds of property formerly considered real estate to the class of "other tangible property," and thus eligible for greater depreciation deductions. Such land improvements as roads, fences, and landscaping are now placed in the 15-year class and eligible for either straight-line or accelerated depreciation deductions. Qualified real property does not share in the expensing benefits allowed under the Tax Relief, Unemployment Insurance Reauthorization, and Job Creation Act of 2010 (Tax Relief Act of 2010). Under the 2010 Small Business Jobs Act, a taxpayer can elect up to $250,000 of the $500,000 Code Sec. 179 deduction limit (subject to the investment limit) for qualified real property (qualified leasehold improvement property, qualified restaurant property, and qualified retail improvement property) for tax years beginning in 2010 and 2011. The Tax Relief Act of 2010 does not extend this treatment. Another possible tax break is that sewer pipe is listed in the 20-year class.

While tax deductions have grown fewer since the early 1980s, there remain important benefits for real estate investors. Depreciation deductions are based on the total value of a building, not just the equity interest in it. Since this kind of deduction represents a noncash item, it protects cash flows, allowing more money for debt service if necessary. The Jobs and Growth Tax Relief Reconciliation Act of 2003 reduced capital gains tax rates from 10% to 5%, and from 20% to 15% for asset sales after May 5, 2003, for assets held a year or longer. Gains from property purchased after 2000 and held more than five years are taxed at an 8% capital gains rate.

The Tax Relief Act of 2010 extended the Bush-era individual and capital gains/dividend tax cuts for all taxpayers for two years and also extended the 100% exclusion of gain realized from qualified small business stock held for more than five years—a provision that is particularly important for small commercial and farm real estate investor consortiums. Nevertheless, lenders are generally skeptical of any cash flow that depends on the unstable nature of tax law.

REVIEW OF FIXED-/ADJUSTABLE-RATE NOTE

Borrower Protection

The right to change an interest rate during the term of a mortgage loan can cause hardship for a borrower. Also, borrowers have been easily confused with indexes and the issue of how an adjustment might be calculated. Because these problems concern both lenders and regulators, a number of protective measures have been added to residential ARM requirements. These go beyond simply limiting how interest rates can be changed. The Federal Reserve Bank Board amended its Regulation Z (the Truth-in-Lending regulation), effective as of October 1, 1988, requiring lenders to provide more extensive information to consumers/borrowers on the characteristics of adjustable-rate mortgages. These rules have been adopted by federal agencies and other lending authorities and provide more uniform requirements. The requirements fall into two categories: up-front information and subsequent disclosures, as explained next.

Up-Front Information Required

Certain information must be provided to the consumer at the time an application form is provided or before a nonrefundable fee is paid, whichever comes first. The following requirements must be met:

1. An educational brochure about ARMs must be given to the applicant. This can be either the Consumer Handbook on Adjustable-Rate Mortgages published jointly by the Federal Reserve Bank Board and the Office of Thrift Supervision, or a suitable substitute.
2. The applicant must be shown by historical example how payments on a $10,000 loan would have changed in response to actual past historical data on the index to be applied. A required addendum to the

standard Truth-in-Lending disclosure document must be provided to each applicant for a residential mortgage loan.
3. A statement must be given to the applicant showing the payment amount on a $10,000 loan at the initial interest rate (the most recent rate shown on the historical example), and the maximum possible interest rate that could apply to the loan during its term.

Subsequent Disclosure Requirements

Notices must be given to the borrower during the term of the loan showing any adjusted payment amount, interest rate applied, index rate, and the loan balance at the time of adjustment. This notification must be made once each year during which there is a rate adjustment, whether or not there is a payment change. The notice must be mailed no less than 25 days and no more than 120 days before the new payment is due. Furthermore, the disclosure must indicate the extent to which any increase in the interest rate has not been fully implemented (meaning how much the index rate plus margin would exceed the rate cap). The notice must also state the payment required to fully amortize the loan if that payment is different.

The next section contains a more detailed explanation of the meaning of these requirements.

Use of an Index

One of the major protections offered to borrowers who accept an ARM loan is that any change in the rate of interest must be tied to the change in an index. An index is a published rate or yield approved by the lender's regulatory authority. The rule applies to regulated lenders making residential loans. Unlike the well-known banker's prime rate of interest, which is determined by each lender, an ARM index cannot be controlled by the lender. While a number of indexes have been approved by authorities across the country, five have achieved the greatest popularity. These are:

1. *cost of funds* (The national median cost of funds is derived each month from reports of SAIF-insured savings associations, as reported by the Office of Thrift Supervision. This figure is the average cost of all interest paid to depositors on passbook savings accounts, savings certificates, and certificates of deposit.);

2. *contract rate* (The national average contract interest rate for major lenders as reported by the Federal Housing Finance Board. Each month, insured savings institutions report the interest rate charged for mortgage loans made the previous month. The rate reported covers new and existing home loans.);
3. *Eleventh District cost of funds* (The cost of funds for the Eleventh District as released by the Office of Thrift Supervision in San Francisco. California is the largest single market for residential loans in the country.);
4. *1-year Treasury securities* (The 1-year constant maturity yield on U.S. Treasury securities is as reported by the Federal Reserve Bank Board.); and
5. *LIBOR.* (This is the interest rate that banks charge each other for 1-month, 3-month, 6-month, and 1-year loans. LIBOR is an acronym for London Interbank Offered Rate. This rate is charged by London banks; it is published and used as the benchmark for bank rates all over the world.)

Historical Record of Indexes

Table 7-2 illustrates the differences that can be found in the most popular indexes.

Application of an Index

Indexes are applied differently. Of the four indexes described in the previous section, only the "contract rate" would normally be applied directly as the rate charged to the borrower. That is, if the contract rate indicated 6.23% in December 2007 (as shown in table 7-2) at the time of loan origination, that would become the rate charged to the borrower. Assuming a one-year adjustment period, the rate shown in the index for December 2008 as 5.51% would apply for the second year. Then, for the third year, the rate would become 4.92%, as shown in the table for December 2009. Lenders normally adjust these rates to the nearest quarter percentage point; thus, the 4.92% rate would become 5.00% for the new period.

Rate Based on Index Plus Margin

Indexes other than the contract rate, as illustrated in the previous section, require the addition of a **margin**. The margin is determined by the lender and is not a regulated amount. Normally, it amounts to between 2 and 2.5 percentage points and is added to the index amount. The margin remains fixed for the life of the loan; it is the index that changes. The most widely used index today is the 1-year Treasury security rate. Its application is illustrated in the following example.

Example

Applying a 1-year Treasury security rate as shown in table 7-2, plus a 2.5% margin, to a 30-year loan of $100,000, we show the following:

Loan Year	Index Rate + Margin =		Rounded Rate	Remaining Term	Monthly Payment $100,000 Loan
2006 First	4.94	2.5%	7.44%*	30 yrs.	$695.11
2007 Second	3.26	2.5%	5.75%*	29 yrs.	$591.18
2008 Third	.49	2.5%	3.00%*	28 yrs.	$440.27

*Remember the method of rounding to nearest ¼ percent mentioned earlier.

TABLE 7-2 Historical Record of Indexes

Year*	Cost of Funds	Contract Rate	11TH Dist. COF	1-Year Treasury Securities	3-Month LIBOR**
1983	9.90	11.94	10.192	10.11	N/A
1984	9.92	12.26	10.520	9.33	N/A
1985	8.48	10.70	8.867	7.67	N/A
1986	7.28	9.29	7.509	5.87	N/A
1987	7.11	8.86	7.645	7.17	7.438
1988	7.44	9.61	8.022	8.05	9.313
1989	7.73	9.69	8.476	7.72	8.375
1990	7.54	9.58	7.963	7.05	7.758
1991	6.25	8.25	6.245	4.38	4.250
1992	4.51	7.53	4.432	3.71	3.453
1993	4.44	7.41	4.305	3.43	3.375
1994	4.31	7.26	4.218	5.32	6.500

(Continues)

TABLE 7-2 (Continued)

Year*	Cost of Funds	Contract Rate	11TH Dist. COF	1-Year Treasury Securities	3-Month LIBOR**
1995	4.38	7.65	4.329	5.94	5.657
1996	4.34	7.56	4.291	5.52	5.586
1997	4.39	7.26	4.314	5.63	5.985
1998	4.12	6.76	4.223	4.52	5.172
1999	4.52	7.55	4.852	5.84	6.005
2000	5.13	7.59	5.617	5.60	6.403
2001	4.27	6.69	3.074	2.22	1.883
2002	3.10	6.04	2.375	1.45	1.383
2003	2.28	5.74	1.902	1.31	1.157
2004	2.16	5.71	2.118	2.67	2.558
2005	2.74	6.29	3.296	4.35	4.530
2006	3.57	6.40	4.396	4.94	5.360
2007	3.83	6.23	4.072	3.26	5.131
2008	2.95	5.51	2.757	.490	2.217
2009	2.17	4.92	1.828	.370	.256
2010	1.62	4.49**	1.571	.300	.303
2011	1.22	4.15	1.201	.182	.557
2012	1.04	3.35	1.071	.175	.309
2013	.94	4.21	.784	.132	.244
2014	.93**	4.00	.671**	.114**	.233**

*Figures are as of December of each year.
**Exception: These figures are from November of the year shown.
Source: Federal Home Loan Bank Board, Federal Housing Finance Board Interest Rate Surveys and ERATE. The 3-month LIBOR began being tracked in U.S. currency in 1987. The Cost of Funds Index had been taken from the Office of Thrift Supervision that was merged into the Office of Comptroller of the Currency in 2011 and since then the index is the Federal Cost of Funds Index.

Rate Based on Index Movement

Another way to apply an index is to originate the loan with an agreed rate, then add or deduct the *movement* of an index.

It is important to note that the initial rate charged is not a regulated or controlled rate. This allows the lender greater flexibility in setting an initial interest rate while still complying with the requirement to tie any change to a regulator-approved index. The following example applies the same index as used in the previous example. The difference is that an origination rate of 9% is applied, rather than the 7.44% rate in the previous example. Then the change in the index each year is added or deducted from the previous year's rate.

Example

Using the 1-year Treasury security rate shown in table 7-2 and applying the movement of that index to a $100,000, 30-year loan that is originated at a 9% rate, the following higher monthly payments result:

Year	Rate Last Year	Previous Rate	Present Rate	Percentage Change	Rate Next Year	Monthly Payment
2006 First					9.00%	$804.63
2007 Second	9.0%	7.44%	5.76%	–1.68%	7.25%*	$684.14
2008 Third	7.32%	5.75%	2.99%	–2.78%	4.50%*	$514.93

*Remember the method of rounding to nearest ¼ percent mentioned earlier.

Obviously, there can be a difference in the rate and amount paid by a borrower even though the identical index is applied. It is important to read the repayment clause in a mortgage document very carefully. While disclosure of the key provisions is mandatory, the terminology can be confusing.

Regulations require that a rate be reduced if the index declines. However, an increase to match an index is optional for a lender. The fairly steady decline of index rates over the past decade has meant that homeowners with adjustable-rate mortgages made lower payments almost every year. More recently, the expectation that interest rates may fluctuate upwards has discouraged many from undertaking adjustable-rate loans.

Limitations on Changes (Caps)

Since the introduction of adjustable-rate mortgages in the 1970s, there has been a shift in who sets limits on how much an interest rate might be changed during the life of a home loan. Initially, regulatory authorities were concerned with the potential of catastrophic increases in mortgage payments hurting both home buyers and lenders alike. Limitations were tight in the introductory years, especially during the 1979–1981 time period when mortgage interest rates jumped about 2% each year over the course of only three years. The result was little encouragement for lenders to offer the new designs. In the next year or two, regulators backed off the tight limitations in an effort to encourage the use of adjustable plans. Some caps were eliminated, others increased.

Since the design is basically a lender-benefit plan, lenders began to show more support for ARMs, recognizing the inherent advantage of being able to adjust the rate on a long-term loan. Lenders realized that some of the risk of fluctuating rates could be passed on to the borrower, and ARMs became competitive. Initial interest rates on ARMs were lowered to between 1.5% and 3% less than rates on fixed-interest loans.

Burgeoning foreclosures in 1984 and 1985 brought renewed interest in limitations on rate changes—this time from lenders hurt by foreclosures. At the same time, secondary-market purchasers began to set limits on the kinds of ARM loans they would buy. While regulations vary, and lenders' self-imposed limitations vary, the caps as an added feature now offered on many ARM loan products center on the following four aspects of adjustable-rate plans:

1. *periodic interest rate change* (Almost all ARM loans limit the amount of change that can be made at each adjustment period; therefore, these are sometimes referred to as period caps. A 1% cap is commonly used, but some plans permit 2%. The use of a 1% cap means that even though an increase in the index rate would allow, say, a 1.75% increase, the new rate can only be increased by 1%.);

2. *interest rate change over the life of loan* (Sometimes called a limit on "rate swings," or a "life of the loan" cap, it is commonly at 5% (in the case of FHA, for example), though some (such as Fannie Mae) use a 6% cap. These prior two life of the loan caps are a general rule. Therefore, over the life of the loan, regardless of index fluctuation, the payment cannot be increased, or in some loans decreased, more than 5% (or 6%);

A mortgage loan originator or underwriter must check state-specific rules. For example, the Texas Home Equity 50(a)(6) specifies that mortgages on Texas homesteads have dozens of restrictions, including one that states the life of the loan cap cannot be more than 5% even if it is a Fannie Mae mortgage.

3. *frequency of rate change* (This is a limit on how often a rate can be changed. It is a distinguishing feature of residential mortgage lending

that does not permit a rate change every time the lender so desires. Federal regulations permit a change at least once a year, and up to once every five years. Some states permit changes as often as every six months. By far, the most popular adjustment period is once a year.); and

4. *mortgage payment amount.* (A more recent popular limitation has to do with the payment amount itself. This kind of cap limits any increase in the payment amount to a percentage of the payment. The most common limit has become 7.5%. Therefore a $1,000-per-month payment could not be increased to more than $1,075 in the second year, regardless of what the index might show on the interest rate. The problem with this process is that it can result in a borrower having periods of negative amortization, as discussed in the following caveat. Negative amortization is a periodic increase in the principal balance due on a mortgage loan, usually resulting from unpaid interest being added to the principal.)

A very important point to keep in mind regarding all limitations is that the cap may apply to the amount the borrower pays during the year, but may not limit the amount owed. There is no real standard on how the limits may be applied. Therefore, even though a rate change, or a payment amount, may show a specific limit on what the borrower pays, if the index shows a greater amount is actually due, the lender may add the unpaid amount to the principal balance. This procedure is another method of creating **negative amortization**. Fannie Mae, for one, will not buy this kind of loan. Like all other repayment conditions, this, too, must be disclosed and agreed to in the mortgage terms. Careful reading of these clauses is absolutely critical.

Another condition, perhaps of lesser concern, is the fact that some limitations apply to both increases and decreases in the application of an index. For example, a 5% life-of-loan limit could stop a 13% loan from ever falling to less than 8%. (This is not a big problem when market rates are in the 6% to 7% range.)

Continued Evolution of ARM Product Offerings

The "option ARM" came into being over 20 years ago and was developed by Washington Mutual. An option ARM is typically a 30-year ARM that initially offers the mortgage loan consumer the following four monthly payment options:

- The biggest payment is on a 15-year payoff schedule.
- The next-biggest payment is on a 30-year payoff schedule.
- There is an interest-only payment based on a 30-year payoff schedule.
- The minimum payment, which will not necessarily cover all the interest accrued during the month. In this "negative amortization" option, the mortgagor owes more at the end of the month than at the beginning, even after making a payment.

These types of loans are also called "pick-a-payment," "pick-a-pay," or "pay-option ARMs." They grew in popularity during early 2001 and 2002, with demand and acceptance peaking in 2007. The option ARM's decline in use has to do with the unusual risks to the mortgagor and mortgagee if the product is used by a mortgagor who is not suited to the product's unique characteristics.

When a mortgagor makes a pay-option ARM payment that is less than the accruing interest, "negative amortization" occurs, meaning that the unpaid portion of the accruing interest is added to the outstanding principal balance. For example, if the mortgagor makes a minimum payment of $1,200 and the ARM has accrued monthly interest in arrears of $1,500, $300 will be added to the mortgagor's loan balance. Moreover, the next month's interest-only payment will be calculated using the new, higher principal balance.

Option ARMs are often offered with a very low teaser rate (often as low as 1%), which translates into very low minimum payments for the first year of the ARM. Unfortunately, in the past, many lenders have underwritten consumers based on mortgage payments that are below the fully amortizing payment level. This practice enables potential mortgagors to qualify for a much larger mortgage than would normally be possible with a conventional mortgage. When evaluating an option ARM, vigilant consumers know not to focus on the teaser rate or initial payment level, but instead to consider the characteristics of the index, the margin that will be added to the index, and the other terms of the ARM. The various considerations that many consumers fail to consider are the possibilities that long-term interest rates may go up, or that their home value may not go up or could even lose value, or even that both risks may materialize. As of the end of 2014, no lenders had resumed making option ARMs. This may be because these loans are not allowed into Ginnie Mae, Fannie Mae, or Freddie Mac residential mortgage-backed securities (RMBS).

Graduated-Payment Mortgage (GPM)

The **graduated-payment mortgage** product concept was first tested by the FHA as a method of allowing home buyers to pay lower initial monthly payments in the earlier years of a mortgage term, with payments rising in successive years to a level sufficient to amortize the loan within a 30-year term. With a lower initial monthly payment, the buyer with a lower income might qualify for a loan, or conversely, be able to buy a larger house with the same income.

An added requirement for qualification is that the borrower must show reasonable expectation of an increase in annual income so as to meet the annual increase in monthly payments. It was this near-impossible prediction of continuing income increases that helped undermine the viability of the GPM design. Nevertheless, the option ARM is a type of loan that might make a deal possible that otherwise would be lost.

An inherent problem with the GPM is that even a constant-level payment, long-term mortgage loan allows very little money to be paid on principal in the early years. So, with only a modest reduction in the payment amount, any allocation to principal may easily be eliminated along with a portion of the interest payment due. This situation is illustrated in the following example.

Example

The constant-level payment on a $150,000 loan at 5% with a term of 30 years amounts to $805.23. The average amount of this monthly payment allocated to pay off principal is about $184.42 per month during the first year. Thus, a reduction of the monthly payment below $620.81 per month would not allow for any reduction of principal and would result in a probable accumulation of unpaid interest. When the graduated-payment plan allows for payments so low that not all the interest is paid, each year's unpaid interest is added to the principal balance for repayment in later years.

For most of the plans currently in use, there is an accumulation of unpaid interest, called *accrued interest*, in the early years of the mortgage term; thus, the borrower ends the year with larger principal balances owing than when the loan was first undertaken. As mentioned previously, this is called *negative amortization*—i.e., the loan balance increases instead of decreasing with each payment. To avoid the possibility that the increasing amount of the loan balance could exceed the initial value of the property serving as collateral, GPMs generally call for higher down payments than are necessary for constant-level payment plans. Down payments for this type of loan are calculated so that the loan balance will not exceed the limits permitted, which is 96.5% of the initial property value for an FHA (Section 245(a)) type mortgage.

A legal qualification is necessary in some states for this type of loan. The Act authorizing the FHA program specifically preempts any state law that prohibits the addition of interest to the principal of a mortgage loan as it pertains to the manner in which the loan is repaid. This preemption is also claimed by federally chartered institutions that come under federal banking rules.

The FHA Section 245 GPM program has been the most popular "graduated-payment mortgage" over the past several years. (See Chapter 8 for more details on the FHA program.) The graduated-payment design has been approved by federal regulators for conventional loans for over 30 years. Essentially, the procedures are the same as those developed by the FHA, but they have seldom been used by conforming lenders. Fannie Mae stopped purchasing Veterans Administration Section 3703(d) of Title 38 for graduated-payment mortgages. Under different market conditions, there could be greater interest in this mortgage design, as it fulfills a need. Young families buying their first homes do not have the benefit of a growing equity interest in an existing house. So, permitting lower initial monthly payments enables more family incomes to qualify for loans. It is a viable mortgage repayment plan, for example, for a couple with immediate prospects for future income growth, such as a young accountant who has passed her CPA exam and is about to become licensed, or a young licensed practical nurse who has nearly completed his educational requirements to become a registered nurse.

Buydown Mortgage

An older repayment plan that has been used successfully to sell houses is the **buydown mortgage** product, often referred to as a *temporary buydown mortgage* or payment abatements agreement. It has greater appeal when interest rates are high, but it can still be a useful procedure when lower rates are in effect. Its attraction is the same as those for other graduated-payment designs: the borrower may obtain qualification of income based on a lower initial monthly payment. The normal procedure is for the seller—usually a home builder—to "buy down" the initial payment amounts. This is simply a variation on the normal discount procedure. The major difference is that a buydown is a prepayment of interest costs for only a few years, whereas the discount is normally considered a prepayment of interest costs over the life of a loan. Buydown mortgages have historically been popular with builders and new construction purchases and have been most frequently offered through builder finance subsidiaries.

Buydowns can span any period, but are generally offered for periods of one to five years. The average buydown, and the one generally accepted for purchase by Fannie Mae, is for three years, amounting to a 3% less-than-market rate in the first year, 2% in the second, and 1% in the third. The procedure is sometimes called "3-2-1." By encouraging easier loan qualification, the seller opens a larger market of qualified buyers.

What the seller is actually doing is paying a portion of the interest cost in the early years. The following example illustrates the cost reduction of interest on a $50,000 loan at a nominal interest rate of 9% with a three-year buydown. The *nominal rate* is the one named on the note and is the only interest rate shown.

Example

First, consider the round-figure cost of a buydown. To reduce the interest cost from 9% to 6% for the first year, the seller must pay 3% of the cost:

$$.03 \times \$50,000 = \$1,500$$

For the second year, the cost is 2%:

$$.02 \times \$50,000 = 1,000$$

For the third year, the cost is 1%:

$$.01 \times \$50,000 = 500$$

Total cost of buydown $3,000

With a portion of the interest paid in advance, the buyer makes reduced monthly payments on a 30-year loan in the following amounts:

Year 1: $50,000 @ 6% = $299.78
Year 2: $50,000 @ 7% = $332.66
Year 3: $50,000 @ 8% = $366.89
Year 4 and on: $50,000 @ 9% = $402.32

These figures do not take into account the time value of money paid in advance or the declining balance of the loan amount, both of which are important considerations. As a result, the cost of a buydown is not always uniform. Lenders vary somewhat in how they make the calculation; it is not a regulated procedure.

While buydown mortgages are an attractive inducement for buyers, they have lost favor with secondary-market purchasers. Buydowns have caused more than their share of home foreclosures, and some limitations have been added. One is to qualify the buyer at the note rate, not the first year's payment amount. Another, similar limit is to require borrower income qualification to be based on the payment amount that will amortize the loan within its term. Currently, mortgages with payment abatements of any type are not eligible for delivery to Fannie Mae regardless of whether they are disclosed on the HUD-1 settlement statement. This prohibition applies to transactions in which an interested party is directly funding the abatement and/or if the funding for the abatement is flowing through another entity such as a nonprofit down payment assistance program.

Pledged-Account Mortgage

Some conventional lenders will offer a variation on the graduated-payment mortgage that provides similar benefits for a borrower called a **pledged-account mortgage**. As in the temporary buydown product described above, a part of the down payment is placed in an escrow account with the lender, rather than paid to the seller. Then the lender makes a loan of sufficient size to cover the purchase. The lender considers the escrow deposit as additional collateral, which allows a larger loan amount.

The borrower makes monthly payments in the early years of less than the full amortization payment amount. Then each month, the lender withdraws sufficient cash from the pledged account, adds the interest earned on that pledged account, and supplements the mortgage payment so that it equals a fully amortizing amount. The purpose of the procedure is the same as that of the GPM: to establish a lower initial monthly payment that can be used to qualify a lesser income for a larger house. It has the advantage of not creating negative amortization, and provides the lender with a new savings account.

All loans that have the effect of changing the current yield on a mortgage being sold to Fannie Mae or Freddie Mac must still conform to the maximum weighted-average coupon of the pooled mortgages set by the GSE seller/servicer guides.

Balloon Payment Note

The word *balloon* as used in the mortgage business now has two meanings. An older use of the term indicated payments less than those necessary to amortize the loan within its term, resulting in a substantial balance still due at maturity. A more recent application of the word indicates a loan with a lower initial interest rate that allows renewal at a market rate after five or seven years. The distinction is more fully explained next.

Balloon Due to Amortization

A balloon installment note product is only partially amortized over its term since it reaches maturity with a balance due. (The periodic installments are insufficient to fully repay the loan during its term.) Therefore, a final payment larger than the previous installment payments comes due. The final payment is called a **balloon payment** because of its greater size.

The purpose of a balloon note is to keep the periodic installment payment smaller than would otherwise be required. One fairly common way of handling this kind of note is to set a term of, say, 10 years for repayment. Then the periodic payments are calculated as if the term were 30 years.

Example

A $200,000 loan is made at an interest rate of 5.5% for a term of 10 years. To fully amortize the loan over 10 years requires a monthly payment of $2,170.53. To allow a lesser payment, the amount is calculated as if the term is 30 years, thus offering a monthly payment of $1,135.58. At the end of 10 years, the balance due amounts to a balloon payment of $165,081.98.

If the federal Truth-in-Lending provisions apply to the loan, the amount of the balloon payment must be clearly stated in the contract.

Balloon Allowing an Adjusted Rate

In 1990, as a compromise between low interest rates and payment predictability over a relatively long term, a new mortgage repayment design was introduced to attract borrowers: a "five or seven-year balloon." This was a Fannie Mae and Freddie Mac mortgage repayment product offered with payments based on a 30-year amortization schedule at an initial rate of 1.5 percentage points below the current 30-year market rate. On a $100,000 mortgage at this rate, savings could reach $3,000 per year. At the end of five or seven years, the mortgage would be refinanced at the current market rate—a rate that would remain fixed for the remaining term of the loan. This plan is also called a *two-step mortgage*.

The refinancing is not automatic, as there are some requirements that differ a bit among lenders. While the Fannie Mae seven-year balloon product was retired in April of 2010, Fannie Mae and Freddie Mac will allow a balloon mortgage reaching its balloon maturity date to be refinanced as a product feature of loans they purchase if the loans conform to the following requirements:

- The borrower must still be the owner/occupant.
- No payment for the preceding 12 months can be more than 30 days late.
- No other liens may exist on the property except taxes and special assessments not yet due.
- The new interest rate cannot be more than five percentage points above the original note rate.

Straight Note (More Popularly Advertised as an Interest-Only Mortgage)

A **straight note** is one that calls for payment of the interest only at periodic intervals and the principal balance due in full at maturity. It is also known as an **interest-only mortgage**, an *interest-only note* or a *term loan*. A straight note is a non-amortized note usually made for a short term, such as three to five years. It may allow renewal at the end of the term. If this kind of note is secured by a mortgage, it is called a *term mortgage*. Some ARM versions of this loan with payment caps discussed earlier can result in negative amortization under certain economic conditions.

Prior to the 1930s, straight loans were very common in residential mortgage lending, but they have generally been replaced with fully amortized notes. Today, this repayment plan product has reemerged as a product selection in the residential mortgage finance business, but it is more common in certain business loans and in personal bank loans.

Interest-only mortgages tied to LIBOR began to adjust in early 2005 at twice the rate that mortgagors had been income-qualified for just six months to a year earlier, and many of these borrowers very quickly defaulted on their loans. These defaults occurred for three reasons: (1) there is insufficient income to meet the debt service; (2) home price appreciation had stopped in many markets, thus choking off the use of equity to pay the closing costs of a refinancing; and (3) fixed interest rates for 15- and 30-year mortgages were higher than their adjusted rate.

Soon afterward, "teaser rates" proliferated. As late as 2007, the worst of the subprime lenders would loudly advertise rates of only 7% or so, with notices made visible only in the fine print that these were adjustable-rate mortgages. Often, interest rates would explode to 11% or more after a couple of years, causing families' monthly payments to double, or worse. Over 90% of subprime loans were made as ARMs, many with the mortgagor's income qualified at the lower rate. In the most extreme cases, some lenders would use a teaser rate to finance a builder loan where the builder offered a 3-2-1 temporary buydown so that the 7% teaser rate was 4% to start.

Where Are We Now?

Home Equity Line of Credit Caveat

A concern about the home equity line of credit results from the fact that borrowers may not be able to draw down on their line of credit to the amount originally agreed upon.

For example, imagine that George and Georgina have been granted a line of credit on their residence by a major bank. The original amount was $100,000. They only needed $40,000 at the time they arranged the line of credit, but knew they would need the remaining $60,000 in the near future. They did not draw down on the entire agreed-upon loan amount ($100,000) because they did not want to pay the interest on money they did not need at the time. Typically, line of credit interest is substantially higher than basic mortgage rates.

> Unforeseen things occurred, however. When Hurricane Ike blew through the area, the lender reappraised the line of credit and not only canceled the remainder of the commitment but "called" a portion of the outstanding balance due.

The Piggyback Loan

A **piggyback loan** is a residential mortgage financing option where a property is purchased using more than one mortgage from two or more mortgagees.

The most common three types of piggyback loans are the 80-10-10 loan, the 80-20 loan (also known as the 80-20-0 loan), and the 80-15-5 loan. The first number indicates that 80% of the home's purchase price will be financed by a mortgage from lender number one; the second number indicates the percentage amount of a loan secured by a second mortgage with a different lender; and the third number indicates the down payment percentage.

For instance, the once popular 80-20 loan is a feature in which 80% of the home loan is financed by one lender, 20% of the loan is financed by another lender, and the home buyer has no down payment. An 80-10-10 loan means that 80% of the home purchase price is financed by lender number one, 10% of the purchase price is financed by lender number two, and 10% of the purchase price is paid for in cash by the home buyer in the form of a down payment. Since Fannie Mae and Freddie Mac were prohibited from owning 100% of any mortgage they purchased, they were the most likely targeted purchaser of the 80% first mortgage loan. The recent financial crisis has raised the question: If a GSE was sold the 80% first mortgage without full disclosure of the piggyback structure, does the action constitute a misrepresentation to induce the GSE to purchase the mortgage under a commitment program?

The Advantages and Disadvantages of Piggyback Loans

Piggyback loans allow home buyers to qualify for more expensive homes. When more than one lender is involved in a single loan transaction, the entire loan risk is spread between two lenders. A home buyer with little or no down payment should have better luck with the loan approval process on a piggyback loan than he or she would with a single conventional loan.

A piggyback loan allows a home buyer to purchase a home with less than 20% down. These mortgages typically do not have a private mortgage insurance premium as a component. Up until recently, such premiums were not tax-deductible, unlike the interest on the second mortgage. A pure 80/20 mortgage where the borrower has no cash equity in the loan can no longer be sold to the major GSEs.

These mortgages are advertised as a means of leveling the playing field, making home ownership a possibility for more potential buyers, especially first-time home buyers who have little equity to use as a down payment. In addition, lenders note that piggyback lending programs allow homeowners to use a second mortgage in the amount of 10% to 15% in the current market environment; the first mortgage would not require a private insurance monthly payment component that was not tax deductible, as in the case of the interest expense on the second mortgage. This was true until the tax laws were changed in 2007, as we will discuss in Chapter 9. In certain instances, the interest costs of the second mortgage, when compared to the interest costs with a PMI payment component, were actually less without the tax-deductible feature[10] as you will see in table 7-3 below.

TABLE 7-3

$300,000 Home	FHA	Conventional	Piggyback 80/15/5	Piggyback 80/10/10
First Mortgage Loan Amount	$274,725 ($270,000 + 1.75% UFMIP)	$270,000	$240,000	$240,000
Interest Rate	4.15%	4.65%	4.65%	4.65%
First Mortgage Payment	$1,335.45	$1,392.22	$1,237.53	$1,237.53
2nd Mortgage or Mortgage Insurance Cost	FHA MIP: $286	PMI: $113	$45,000 second mortgage at 5.35%: $251.29	$30,000 second mortgage at 5.35%: $167.52
Est. Taxes	$452	$452	$452	$452
Est. Insurance	$90	$90	$90	$90
Estimated Totals	$2,163.45	$2,047.22	$2,030.32	$1,947.02

Source: © 2021 Mbition LLC

---

[10] C. Garriga et al., "Recent Trends in Homeownership," *Federal Reserve Bank of St. Louis Review* 88, no. 5 (September/October 2006): 397-411.

The disadvantages of piggyback loans in comparison with standard home mortgage programs are many. One is the fact that the combined rates for piggyback loans are often higher than those for standard loans. This is because of the risk amounts that each lender is assuming. The first lender, who is only financing 80% of the loan amount, might be willing to drop his or her rates a bit, but the second lender—the one who is only financing 5% to 15% of the loan—does not see much benefit from lending the money unless he or she can actualize a high interest return. Moreover, in certain instances, the originating lender may not correctly disclose to the purchaser of the 80% first mortgage that the loan was made to an applicant with little or no down payment. Many piggyback loans attach a large balloon payment at the end of a loan, an end-of-term payment that is substantially larger than the standard mortgage payments. Piggyback loans are based on the idea of dual mortgages; if an emergency were to arise; getting an additional mortgage or home equity loan could be difficult, if not impossible. But loan modification or settlement problems should a borrower later become delinquent are greatly complicated due to having to deal in some cases with as many as three lenders, two of whom are subordinate to the first mortgage holder. Despite losses taken by investors in the second line position of these loans, these types of loans have become available in 2015 from lenders that advertise, "80/10/10s are also available for conforming loans, but credit score and debt ratio requirements are tighter than regular agency guidelines."[11]

Mortgages that Can Reduce Total Interest Cost

Shorter-Term Loans

The 30-year loan became so deeply embedded in mortgage lending that many thought it was the best of all terms. During the escalation of interest rates in the 1980s, HUD even encouraged 40-year loans as a method of reducing monthly payments. The longer terms do achieve smaller monthly payments, but at a dramatic increase in the interest cost. It is difficult to believe today, but an older theory of home ownership was to maintain a low equity in a property so that it could be more easily sold. Certainly, one good way to preserve low equity is to make payments on a 30-year loan!

---

[11] Lisa Prevost, "'Piggyback' Loans Revisited," *New York Times*, December 19, 2014, http://www.nytimes.com/2014/12/21/realestate/piggyback-loans-revisited.html

For many years, little thought was given to the cost of long-term loans. After all, were housing prices not enjoying a fairly steady increase in value that more than offset loan costs? But during the 1980s, housing prices flattened and actually began to decline in some areas of the country. As the value of equity lost part of its allure, home buyers began looking for other ways to reduce housing costs. One way was to reduce, rather than increase, the loan term. Cost-conscious borrowers began to look favorably on **shorter-term loans**.

Another factor that increased concern for shorter-term loans was the wave of refinancing that occurred in the early 1990s. To capture even lower interest rates, many homeowners shifted from 30-year loans, refinancing with 15- and 20-year loans. Rather than taking advantage of lower monthly payments, many opted to pay about the same amount as before and take shorter-term loans.

The substantial cost of a long-term loan derives from the very small reduction of principal in the early years of repayment, not from interest compounding. Interest for almost all mortgage loans is calculated as simple interest. Table 7-4 indicates the interest cost for mortgage loans of differing terms. As buyers have become more aware of the true cost of long-term loans, attention has focused on the savings that can be achieved with shorter-term loans.

A brief examination of table 7-4 indicates that a reduction in the term of the loan from 30 years to 20 years increases the payment amount by $120.10, or 21%. The savings in interest amounts to $39,311, or 38% using a 20-year term versus a 30-year term. In today's market, a 15- or 20-year loan offers an interest rate of at least one-half to three-quarters of a percentage less than a 30-year loan, creating an even larger savings for the home buyer.

TABLE 7-4 Cost Comparison by Term for a $100,000 Mortgage Loan at 5.5%

Term	Monthly Payment	Months Paid	Total Cost	Interest Cost
40-year	$ 515.77	480	$ 247,569	$ 147,569
30-year	$ 567.79	360	$204,404	$104,404
20-year	$ 687.89	240	$ 165,094	$ 65,093
15-year	$ 817.08	180	$ 147,074	$ 47,075
10-year	1,085.26	120	130,231	30,231

Source: © 2021 Mbition LLC

Biweekly Payment Plan

Another method of accelerating the payment of principal to reduce total interest costs is the **biweekly payment** mortgage product. For borrowers who are paid every other week, this method might be easier to budget. The calculation for such a payment amount is normally just one-half of a monthly payment, paid biweekly. For example, if the monthly payment for a 30-year loan amounts to $1,000, the borrower would pay $500 every other week. This amounts to 26 biweekly payments over the span of one year, amounting to $13,000. Compare this to 12 monthly payments, which would total $12,000. The additional payments applied to principal reduction in the biweekly plan will pay off the loan in about 17 to 20 years, depending, of course, on the rate of interest.

An important encouragement for this type of loan is that it is a loan approved for purchase by Fannie Mae. Loan originators can offer this kind of loan and be assured of funding.

Growing Equity Mortgage

Still another method that can be used to shorten a loan term, thus reducing interest costs, is called a **growing equity mortgage**, or a graduated equity mortgage product, both having the acronym of GEM. Many variations may be found, but the basic pattern is to make certain increases in the payment amount each year. Then, the entire amount of the increase is applied to repayment of the principal. Depending on the interest rate, an increase of, say, 4% in the payment amount (not the interest rate) each year can reduce the term of a 30-year loan to 18 or 20 years. And the impressive reduction in total interest costs is similar to that described for the 15-year loan.

Both the FHA and VA have approved this concept for early payment of a loan. For the FHA, acceptance comes under its Section 245 program (the graduated-payment program) because it authorizes insurance on mortgages with varying rates of amortization.

Opportunity Cost

Critics of the 15- or 20-year loan, the biweekly loan plan, and GEM mortgages contend that any increase in the payment amount creates a loss for the borrower from the amount that might be gained had the payment increase been invested in order to earn interest. From a mathematical point of view, there is no question that making a larger mortgage payment than may be necessary to pay off a loan does reduce the opportunity to invest that money elsewhere. Table 7-4 illustrates that the difference between the monthly payment on a 30-year loan and a 15-year loan amounts to $249.29 (817.08 − 567.79 = 249.29). If that sum is deposited monthly into an interest-bearing account earning compound interest, then in 15 years, depending on the interest rate, it could easily total a sum sufficient to pay off the balance due on that loan if one could earn 5% interest on your monthly investment. Whether or not a net savings would result varies with each borrower, as the analysis must include any gain or loss of savings resulting from the tax-deductible nature of home loan interest. In the current interest rate environment for deposit accounts, refinancing to reduce interest paid would make more economic sense.

Home Equity Revolving Loans

Pledging the equity in a home, or other property, to borrow money on a second mortgage has been a common procedure for many years. What is new is pledging the property to secure a revolving line of credit. Unlike a traditional second mortgage, which provides a single lump-sum payment, a home equity credit line stays in place for years. It gives the borrower more flexibility to finance everything from a child's education to a trip around the world. Interest is paid only on the portion of the credit that is used, just like a credit card account. Generally, the interest rate on the loan is adjusted periodically and floats without a maximum ceiling other than usury limits.

Equity credit lines have grown since the concept was first launched in California in the 1970s. Today, *home equity lines of credit*, most commonly referred to as **home equity loans**, are a major component of total outstanding second mortgages and one of the prime reasons for reduced net worth of individuals before the financial crisis. Many borrowers used home equity loans as a way of consolidating other debts not secured by real estate with the idea of the improved tax deduction of interest expense on this type of credit extension. Since the collateral is a home, it is eligible for the same tax treatment for interest deductions as a home loan, but with certain limitations.

Not all financial institutions offer home equity revolving credit lines. The concept presents some risks in that collateral may be adequate, but the borrower's income may become too easily overextended. It is this kind of credit line that gives some justification to the comment, "I bought the house on my credit card!" Some states refer to home equity revolving mortgage loans as open-end home equity loans because the balance on the loan can go up and down, as would the balance of a credit card. This fact has caused increasing concerns about abusive practices against consumers. A closed-end home equity loan operates like a traditional second mortgage in that it has a definite payoff plan organized into a series of payments to pay off the amount initially borrowed. Over the last decade, the ease of obtaining a closed-end second mortgage has increased abusive practices. The new Mortgage Disclosure Improvement Act of 2008 (MDIA), an amendment to the Truth-in-Lending rules, prohibited the seven most common deceptive or misleading practices in advertisements for closed-end mortgage loans.

The home equity loan market was virtually shut down during the mortgage crisis, but in late 2012, gradually increasing through 2014; many lenders would look at the LTV on the home being proposed as collateral for a home equity mortgage. If the LTV was below 75% after you added the existing first lien position to the proposed home equity loan, then a borrower with good credit could be approved.

Other Alternative Plans

Several other basic concepts need to be considered in the many variations now available in mortgage repayment plans. Two are shared financing methods and the other is borrowing against home equity with a reverse annuity mortgage that allows payments to the borrower.

Shared Appreciation Mortgage (SAM)

The **shared appreciation mortgage** product became practical when interest rates reached all-time highs in the early 1980s. While it is rarely used these days, the concept is another alternative mortgage method that resurfaces from time to time. A brief review of the procedure will explain how it functions. A portion of the collateral's appreciation is accepted as "contingent interest." When home values showed a prolonged appreciation in value and interest rates were in the 12% to 15% range, some lenders found it profitable to take a portion of the expected return of their money from the appreciation. Some lenders active in this type of lending between

1998 and 2001 have had problems getting title insurance with the proper endorsement for appreciation coverage, and charges of equitable interest calculation when these mortgages have gone into foreclosure.

Shared Equity Mortgage

Shared equity is sometimes confused with shared appreciation, but the two are quite different. In a shared appreciation mortgage, a lender or other investor subordinated to the mortgagee holds a claim, a lien, on that portion of the property value that represents an increase from the time of loan origination in return for their consideration in making the loan or for contributing to the down payment. But this claim or lien falls short of title to the property. The shared equity might be used in a family if a parent wants to help a son or daughter purchase a house. Or an employer may wish to attract a new employee at a time when starting salaries are insufficient to purchase houses in a high-cost area. Or shared equity might be used as an added inducement to encourage an employee to move to a remote or less desirable area. Normally, the employee in such cases is given an option to buy out the employer's share within a limited number of years. Or, in case of a transfer, the employer would be obligated to purchase the entire property at a fair price.

Recently, net investment income has been redefined to include the shared equity interest in a **shared equity mortgage** on the part of an individual investor or trust. The Health Care and Education Reconciliation Act of 2010 imposed an unearned income Medicare contribution in 2013 on wages in excess of $200,000 for single taxpayers and $250,000 for married couples. Also, for the first time ever, a Medicare tax was applied to the net investment income of high earners. The 3.8% levy hits the lesser of (1) their net investment income, or (2) the amount by which their adjusted gross income exceeds the $200,000 or $250,000 threshold amounts. The new law defines net investment income as interest, dividends, capital gains, annuities, royalties, and rents, other than such income derived in the normal course of business, which would include the gains from an investment in a shared equity mortgage. Tax-exempt interest is not included, nor is income from retirement accounts.

Reverse Annuity Mortgage (RAM)

The **reverse annuity mortgage** product is another of the mortgage forms approved by the Federal Home Loan Bank Board as of January 1, 1979.

It does not finance the acquisition of real estate. Rather, the reverse annuity utilizes the collateral value of a home as a means of financing living expenses for the owner. The basic purpose is to assist older homeowners who are pressed to meet rising living costs on fixed retirement or pension income. With the use of a reverse annuity, the equity value of a home may be utilized without the owner being forced to sell the property.

Where state laws permit (an owner's homestead rights may preclude this form of mortgage), a lender can advance monthly installment payments to the homeowner (instead of a lump sum) using a mortgage on the home as collateral. Federal agency rules governing the writing of RAMs require extensive disclosures to reduce the possibility of misunderstandings by the homeowner. Among the requirements is that the borrower must be given a seven-day rescission period. Another is that a statement must be signed by the borrower acknowledging all contractual contingencies that might force a sale of the home. Repayment of the loan must be allowed without penalties and, if the mortgage has a fixed term, refinancing must be arranged at market rates if requested at maturity of the loan.

Interest on this type of loan is added to the principal amount along with each monthly payment made to the borrower. For a savings institution, the monthly payout of loan proceeds with interest added to the principal presents an altogether different cash flow problem.

Reverse annuity mortgages present the lender with a concern for repayment. If the borrower needs more money for living expenses now, what would enable repayment in later years? The early result of this conundrum was the fact that this type of loan was not offered extensively. In 1989, HUD/FHA introduced an experimental program to insure a limited number of "reverse mortgages," and both Fannie Mae and Freddie Mac agreed to purchase them for their own portfolio investments. The amount of the loan is based on the equity value of the home, but for HUD/FHA approval, it cannot exceed the maximum loan permitted for that geographic area. The monthly advances, plus accrued interest added each month, are designed to reach the maximum loan amount in terms of three to 12 years. Several different repayment plans are offered, including a sale of the property at time of death. To qualify, borrowers must be 62 years or older and living in the home, and have little or no mortgage debt. A loan origination fee of up to $2,500 can be charged on loans of $125,000 or less, with origination fees of up to 2% of the first $200,000 of amounts borrowed and 1% on balances above $200,000, not to exceed a total of $6,000. Loan borrowers have a choice of two up-front premiums:

1. The HECM Standard option has a 2% mortgage insurance premium (MIP), and the HECM Saver option has a .01% MIP.
2. The HECM second option is 1.25% of the mortgage balance each year.

With an FHA policy insuring loan repayment, an obvious problem was alleviated. Furthermore, in 1997, Fannie Mae introduced its own Home Keeper for Home Purchase Mortgage, which is similar to the FHA's reverse annuity mortgage, called the **Home Equity Conversion Mortgage (HECM)**. The market for this type of loan has been expanding as more seniors take advantage of its possibilities.

Where Are We Now?

What You Should Know about the HECM Program

Transaction Types

- traditional (The equity in current property is used to obtain a new HECM loan.)
- purchase (HECM loan proceeds are used to purchase a principal residence.)
- refinance (An existing HECM loan is refinanced with a new HECM loan.)

Borrower Eligibility

- The borrower must be 62 years of age or older.
- The property used as collateral must be a primary residence.
- The borrower must not be delinquent on any federal debt.
- The borrower must complete HECM counseling.

Eligible Properties

- single-family residences
- HUD-approved condominiums
- manufactured homes built after June 15, 1976
- planned unit developments (PUDs)
- 1–4 units; borrower(s) must occupy one of the units

> All existing mortgages must be paid off at closing because the HECM has to be in first position. The home must meet FHA minimum property standards; HECM may be used to make required repairs/updates if the cost is within program limits.

Fannie Mae's Home Keeper for Home Purchase Mortgage

In 1997, Fannie Mae introduced another type of mortgage aimed at the senior citizen market that activates a reverse annuity type of mortgage at the time a home is purchased. It allows senior citizens (62 or older) to obtain a mortgage against the equity in a home if they make a substantial down payment. In June of 2011, Fannie Mae effectively ended this program and now will only buy FHA HECM originated reverse mortgages that are underwritten under FHA guidelines and insured by FHA.[12]

MORTGAGE FRAUD

The Closing Disclosure and Red Flags

Unfortunately, some borrowers, financing firms, or their employees may practice certain fraudulent practices to obtain a loan. The responsibility of any lender's quality control or compliance procedures should include someone independent of the loan originator and processing staff checking the following items to make sure that they do not raise concerns about the loan quality during the settlement process.

Common Closing Disclosure **red flags:**[13]

- The names and addresses of property seller and buyer vary from other loan documentation.
- The seller's mailing address is the same as another party to the transaction.
- There are excessive real estate agent commissions paid, or real estate commission paid, but no real estate agents are listed on the purchase contract.
- The sales price differs from the price on the sales contract.

---

[12]"*Selling Guide* Updates," Fannie Mae, June 28, 2011, accessed Dec. 31, 2013, https://www.fanniemae.com/content/announcement/sel1105.pdf

[13]"Fraud Mitigation Best Practices—Single Family." Freddie Mac, January 2015, February 19, 2015, http://www.freddiemac.com/singlefamily/pdf/fraudprevention_practices.pdf

- Reference is made to undisclosed secondary financing or double escrow.
- The rent is prorated on owner-occupied transactions.
- A zero amount is due to/from buyer.
- The Closing Disclosure form or escrow instructions contain unusual credits, disbursements, related parties, delinquent loans paid off, or multiple mortgages paid off.
- The payoffs for items are not consistent with the liens listed on title commitment.
- There are excessive seller-paid marketing, administrative, assignment, or trust fees.
- There are payouts to unknown parties.
- The terms of the closed mortgage differ from the terms approved by the underwriter.
- The date of settlement is delayed without explanation.

Most of these red flags point to the most common types of fraud in the loan origination process, as the following examples will show:

- **Appraisal Fraud** – This occurs when a home's value is deliberately or fraudulently overstated so that more cash can be obtained, or the value could be understated in order to get a lower price on a foreclosed home.
- **Employment Fraud** – When a borrower claims to be self-employed in a nonexistent company or claims a better paying position in a real company in order to falsify his/her income for purposes of acquiring a mortgage.
- **Fraud for Profit** – Some of these are simple, while others can be complex, such as when the fraud involves multiple real estate professionals in an effort to deceive the lender of cash. Those that might be involved in arranging an undeserved mortgage may include an unethical appraiser, settlement agent, or loan originator who might all be working with a straw borrower.
- **Income Fraud** – For a time, firms allowed borrowers with highly over-collateralized proposed mortgages to not have their income verified. This caused a huge increase in this type of mortgage fraud which simply consists of the borrower overstating his or her income, allowing the borrower to qualify for a greater mortgage amount.

- **Gift Loan Fraud** – Frequently, individuals will borrow money from their family in order to make a down payment on a property. This allows the underwriter to treat this as a gift, and subsequently as a reduction in the amount of debt that the borrower appears to have, to gain the approval of a mortgage that the lender would otherwise deny.
- **Occupancy Fraud** – Borrowers often will use the claim of purchasing a home for their use as a primary residence when their true intent is to use it as an investment property. This is done because lenders usually charge higher interest rates for investment property mortgages and demand lower LTVs, as investment real estate is considered higher risk.

Lenders can also use inappropriate products for potential borrowers, including many that became prohibited after the passage of the Dodd-Frank Act as well as other legislation since the financial crisis of 2007–2012. For a review of red flags or prohibited practices now considered as predatory or no longer allowed, see the listing in the appendix of this text.

PITI WORKSHOP–CONVENTIONAL

Defining "Principal, Interest, Taxes, Insurance (PITI)"

Simply stated, PITI is the sum total of a mortgage payment that includes the principal reduction amount, loan interest, property tax, homeowner's property insurance and private mortgage insurance premiums.

PITI is normally the basis of calculating if a borrower's monthly gross income for computing the individual's front-end and back-end ratios is sufficient to approve a mortgage loan. Normally, conventional mortgage lenders require PITI to be equal to or less than 28% of a borrower's gross monthly income for the front-end ratio and 36% of a borrower's gross monthly income for the back-end ratio.

Since the PITI stands for the total monthly mortgage payment, it aids the lender and borrower in the determination of the affordability of an individual mortgage. This is true since a mortgage banker can use the PITI to qualify the borrower from a risk perspective and borrowers can use the back-end ratio to determine if they can afford to purchase a specific price range of a home before beginning their home search.

An example of this back-end ratio calculation contrasts PITI and other monthly debt obligations with the gross monthly income of the borrower. Conventional mortgage underwriting typically requires a maximum back-end ratio of 36% or less. Therefore if a borrower has a $500 car payment, a $150 credit card payment, and a $240 student loan payment, and the proposed PITI is $1,500, and $8,500 gross monthly income, the back-end ratio would be 33% (PITI: $1,950 + $500 +$150 + $240/$8,500 = 33%), which would satisfy the average conventional mortgage lender.

Refer to the PITI workshop and exercise session included with this text.

VA Income Ratio Method of Qualification

As of October 1, 1986, the VA introduced the **income ratio method** of qualifying an applicant's income. It is used in conjunction with the residual method. If the income ratio is not met, an applicant may still be approved, provided the excess residual is at least 20% of minimum required residual. The income ratio method uses some different measures—one being that the applicant's income is gross income (i.e., income taxes and Social Security taxes are *not* a recognized deduction). Other differences in definitions for the income ratio method follow.

Shelter Expenses

The same expenses apply for the income ratio method as for the residual method, with the exception of utility and maintenance costs. These are not included when calculating the income ratio method. Unlike FHA or conforming-loan guideline procedures, VA draws no line that requires any percentage limit on shelter expenses.

Other Monthly Payments

There is no difference in defining other monthly payments between the two methods. Recurring monthly obligations include other loan repayments, installment obligations, and other obligations such as child support. Federal tax obligations are not included in this method because they are expected to be paid from income that remains after all mandatory deductions are taken.

Income Ratio

The sum of housing expenses plus other monthly payments (as briefly defined above) is then compared with the applicant's gross income.

The limitation is 41%—that is, the listed expenses should not exceed 41% of gross income. In this example, the total monthly obligations amount to 39% of the applicant's gross income. Since this number falls within the VA's 41% guideline, the applicant would meet the test for adequate income.

Comparison with Residual Guideline

As a final step in qualifying an applicant's income, the underwriter must review the results of the residual method qualification. This becomes most important if the income ratio method exceeds the 41% guideline limit. Should that occur, the underwriter then reviews the amount by which the applicant's residual exceeds the minimum residual, as required by the VA cost-of-living figures. As explained earlier, if the excess residual ratio is 20% or greater, the applicant may still qualify.

Other Qualification Considerations

While the VA considers the income available for family support a significant factor, it is not the sole criterion for approving or rejecting a loan. Other important considerations for qualification are as follows:

1. applicant's demonstrated ability to accumulate liquid assets such as cash and securities
2. applicant's ability to use credit wisely and refrain from incurring excessive debt
3. the relationship between proposed housing expenses and the amount applicant is accustomed to paying
4. the number and ages of applicant's dependents
5. the likelihood of increases or decreases in income
6. applicant's work experience and history
7. applicant's credit record with other obligations
8. the amount of any down payment made

Conventional/Conforming Loan Qualification

A **conforming loan** is a conventional loan that meets the requirements of either Fannie Mae or Freddie Mac. Both of these secondary-market agencies, while publicly owned, are subject to a HUD oversight committee and must have congressional approval for any major change in their operating procedures. Congress has set the policy on the maximum loan amount that these agencies may purchase, which amounted to $453,100, with a few exceptions for high-costs areas of the country in 2018 for a single dwelling unit. Because Fannie and Freddie are continuously in the market to purchase mortgage loans, this loan limit has set a benchmark for pricing loans. Loans that do not exceed the limit are more readily salable and can be delivered at lower cost than larger loans.

While Fannie Mae and Freddie Mac use the same basic documents (application, verification forms, mortgage, and note) in processing their loan applicants, there are some differences in the standards applied and the kinds of repayment plans that are acceptable. For instance, Fannie Mae will not accept either ARMs with negative amortization or GPMs if combined with ARMs, while Freddie Mac will accept both but requires at least a 10% down payment. There are no restrictions on who is eligible for a conforming loan other than meeting the minimum standards set by each agency. What makes the procedures a bit confusing is that loan originators may set requirements that are more stringent than those acceptable to the agencies, but they cannot exceed the limitations if the loan is to be sold through either agency.

Like both FHA and VA, a conforming loan must meet certain percentage guidelines covering an applicant's income. The mortgage payment cannot exceed 28% of an applicant's gross income, and other obligations when added to the mortgage payment cannot exceed 36%. Note that for conforming loans, the applicants' gross combined income is used to measure adequacy.

Mortgage Payment

For a conforming loan, the mortgage payment amount is defined as principal, interest, taxes, and insurance (PITI), plus any special assessments that may hold the power of a lien on the property.

Other Monthly Payments

Recognized obligations include installment debt that extends for six months or longer, revolving account payments, and other payments that represent a fixed claim on the applicant's income. Like both FHA and VA, the definition of what comprises a fixed claim on an applicant's income is subject to some interpretation. Many real demands on income, such as food, clothing and taxes, are not included. This does not mean that these costs are overlooked. It is simply that these costs represent considerable flexibility and are expected to be paid from the 64% of an applicant's income that is not designated for mandatory payments.

Example

Conforming Loan Qualification

Applicant's total gross income		$3,000
Mortgage payment (PITI)		
Mortgage principal and interest	$660	
Taxes and insurance	$165	
Total mortgage payment		$825
Other monthly payments		
Car payment	$240	
State and local taxes	$90	
Total other payments		$330
Total mortgage plus other payments		$1,155
Ratios:		
Total mortgage payment	$825/3,000 = 27.5%	
Total mortgage and other payments	$1,155/3,000 = 38.5%	

The figures in this example would disqualify an applicant from a conforming loan. The total mortgage payment ratio of 27.5% falls within the 28% limit for a 90% loan. However, the total of the mortgage payment plus other monthly payments at a 38.5% ratio exceeds the 36% limit for total fixed payments. If either ratio exceeds the limit, the applicant's income does not qualify.

Where Are We Now?

Comparing HUD/FHA, VA, and Conventional Qualifying Housing Ratios

Sam and Sally Summers want to buy a house priced at $200,000 and will make a 10% down payment. They have total monthly obligations in the amount of $645. They are both veterans living in the South, so they will examine all available programs. The interest rate for all programs is 5%. The following table lists the minimum family income required to qualify for each program.

HUD/FHA	$5,150	Ratios 31/43
VA Residual	$5,275	
VA Income Ratio	$5,634	Ratio 41
Conventional	$6,418	Ratios 28/36

Other Conventional Loan Qualifications

With the exception of a fairly new set of standards for "affordable housing" loans, there are few fixed guidelines for conventional loan qualification. When a lender is offering its own deposit assets to fund a loan, it is free to set standards that meet its own requirements. There are some general limitations such as nondiscrimination laws and state usury laws, but perhaps the biggest constraint is the need to attract borrower/customers. Borrowers usually investigate more than one source for loans, and if the qualification standards are unreasonable, there are other sources available. Even when making conventional loans intended to be held in portfolio, many lenders prefer to follow the guidelines for conforming loans in case there is a need to sell the loans at a later date.

Questions for Discussion

1. What are the advantages to a home buyer of a graduated-payment mortgage?
2. What is the major constraint on lenders in setting new interest rates for an adjustable-rate mortgage?
3. Discuss the quality of the major indexes cited in the text.
4. Identify the limits or caps placed on changes in the interest rate on an adjustable-rate mortgage.
5. What is the difference between amortization and negative amortization?
6. Define "discount rate of interest" and "prime rate."
7. What is the difference between a permanent and temporary buy-down mortgage?
8. Discuss the advantages and disadvantages found in shorter-term mortgage loans.
9. What is a home equity line of credit?
10. Describe the FHA/HUD reverse mortgage program.

Multiple Choice Questions for Review

1. Which of the following types of mortgages provides for a series of mortgage payments that are lower in the initial years of the loan than they would be with a standard mortgage loan, as an advantage to a borrower?
   a. constant amortization mortgage
   b. graduated-payment mortgage
   c. reverse annuity mortgage
   d. constant payment mortgage

2. ARM agreements have maximum increases allowed in payments, interest rates, and maturity extensions, and they can lead to negative amortization between adjustment intervals or over the life of the loan. They are referred to as:
   a. floors
   b. indexes
   c. caps
   d. margins

3. When contrasting the key indexes below, which has historically had the higher cost at the adjustment date for consumers?
   a. Cost of Funds
   b. contract rate
   c. Eleventh District COF
   d. 1-year Treasury securities

4. What is the maximum allowed increase in interest rate over the life of a Fannie Mae conforming loan, regardless of index fluctuation?
   a. 3%
   b. 4%
   c. 5%
   d. 6%

5. Which of the following mortgage repayment plans would have the possibility of causing negative amortization?
   a. FRM plan
   b. ARM plan
   c. graduated-payment plan
   d. biweekly plan

6. The loan has a fixed interest rate and level monthly payments; a portion of each month's payment is applied to interest and the remainder is applied to principal. However, a balloon payment will be due at the end of the term. This loan is:
   a. unamortized
   b. negatively amortized
   c. fully amortized
   d. partially amortized

7. A mortgage loan with a 3-2-1 buydown and a starting interest rate of 4.5% would have a payment based on what interest rate in month 23?
   a. 4.5%
   b. 5.5%
   c. 6.5%
   d. 7.5%

8. For which type of mortgage repayment plan does the portion of the payment that is applied to the principal increase regularly over time?
   a. pledged-account mortgage
   b. reverse annuity mortgage
   c. interest-only mortgage
   d. growing equity mortgage

9. A mortgage repayment plan that creates a "reusable loan" with a balance that can fluctuate up and down according to the amount used is known as a/an:
   a. graduated-payment mortgage
   b. installment mortgage
   c. credit card
   d. home equity line of credit

10. Which of the following mortgage repayment plans provides the mortgagor with a monthly check instead of the borrower paying a monthly payment?
    a. graduated-payment mortgage
    b. reset mortgage
    c. reverse mortgage
    d. fixed-payment mortgage

Information Resources

https://www.fanniemae.com/singlefamily/mortgage-products
https://www.efanniemae.com/sf/mortgage-products/index.jsp
http://www.freddiemac.com/singlefamily/mortgages/
   These websites allow you to see the mortgage repayment plans of Fannie Mae and Freddie Mac respectively.

https://www.newretirement.com/retirement/reverse-mortgage-interest-rates/
   This website provides the most recent updated retirement blog provides up-to-date information on reverse annuity mortgages.

http://www.mortgage-x.com/library/loans.htm
http://www.owners.com/mortgage
   These two websites allow a review of the mortgage repayment product features explained in consumer-friendly language.

Chapter 8

GOVERNMENT LOANS

KEY TERMS AND PHRASES

203(B) home mortgage insurance
203(k) rehabilitation home mortgage insurance
acquisition cost
American Recovery and Reinvestment Act (ARRA)
annual premium
certificate of reasonable value (CRV)
Department of Housing and Urban Development (HUD)
Department of Veterans Affairs (VA)
Economic Stimulus Act of 2008 (ESA)
eligibility
entitlement
Federal Housing Administration (FHA)
FHA new minimum credit scores
formal assumption
prepaid items
release of liability
simple assumption
up-front mortgage insurance premium (UFMIP)

LEARNING OBJECTIVES

At the conclusion of this chapter, students will be able to:
- Understand the difference between a Veterans Administration mortgage loan and the primary FHA mortgage loan programs.
- Describe the components of an FHA loan, including its unique requirement of mortgage insurance as a part of the closing costs and continuing mortgagor obligations.

- Outline basic mortgage assumption rights of borrowers who have FHA or VA mortgage loans.
- Understand the purposes and features of, as well as the mortgagor and property qualification approval process for, the popular FHA single-family mortgage products.
- Describe how a veteran can qualify for a residential home loan under the guidelines of the Veterans Administration.

INTRODUCTION

There are many federal agencies with programs that provide assistance to people buying homes, rehabilitating homes, renting apartments, applying for farm loans, or needing housing following a natural disaster. All involve government help in the form of a loan, a grant, or an underwriting guarantee that insures private lenders against loss. Several of the government agencies that make direct loans to borrowers were discussed in Chapter 3 as part of the discussion of primary-market lenders. This chapter is limited to two major agencies with home loan underwriting programs that have helped many people to buy and/or rehabilitate their homes. Neither is in the business of making direct loans, although they do offer financial assistance when disposing of repossessed properties. One is the Federal Housing Administration (FHA), which is under the **Department of Housing and Urban Development (HUD)**, and the other is the Department of Veterans Affairs (called the "VA").

The oldest and probably the best-known of all government housing agencies is the FHA, and its most popular mortgage insurance programs will be outlined in this chapter. The VA was granted authority during World War II to offer housing assistance to qualified veterans in the form of a partial guaranty of a home loan.

Both agencies have one feature in common: the fact that their underwriting activities are not expected to be funded by tax revenues, but rather by fees charged to those who use the programs. The FHA has always charged an insurance premium for its underwriting commitment. The VA loan program was initially a veteran's benefit at no charge, but today a funding fee is required. The increased closing costs of both agencies' programs, plus the higher loan-to-value programs offered by conventional lenders, has made them less competitive with conventional loans, causing the FHA's market share to slow erode to 15% between 1985 and 1993. Between 1998 and 2005, the FHA's market share declined even further, with the ascendance of alternative mortgage types such as Alternate A and subprime. Conventional mortgage lending declined to less than 6% nationwide and to nearly zero in some states, such as California.

With the subprime market collapse in 2008, however, the FHA program has seen a huge increase in origination volume. It is expected that the FHA's market share topped out at 40% of all mortgage insurance premiums written in 2010. This was caused by three factors: (1) the FHA offered the only remaining alternative for moderate-income, first-time home buyers with less than perfect credit or little credit history; (2) HUD expanded the maximum loan limits to reach deeper into the housing market in states with higher average housing costs; and (3) Congress passed the Housing and Economic Recovery Act of 2008, which revised the National Housing Act to do the following:

1. require that the mortgagor shall have paid, in cash or its equivalent, an amount equal to not less than 3.5% of the appraised value of the property;
2. eliminate the variable loan-to-value limits that were based on the combination of the property value and the average closing costs of the state where the property is located (also known as "down payment simplification"); and
3. limit the total FHA-insured first mortgage to 100% of the appraised value, and require the inclusion of the up-front mortgage insurance premium (UFMIP) within that limit.

In 2011, the FHA tightened credit standards, incorporating minimum credit scores into the underwriting process and increasing mortgage insurance premiums. The effect is that borrowers with credit scores below 500 are not eligible. Moreover, the level of required up-front mortgage insurance premiums are now as high as 1.75%—up from 1%—and annual MIP is up to 1.35% from only .55% in 2009. Thus, the market share of FHA has declined in total mortgages made from a high of 32% of all mortgages made in 2009 to 22.3% at the end of 2013.[1]

Since June 4, 2013, all new FHA-insured mortgages that require MIP payments no longer allow the cancellation of MIP payments when the loan drops below 78% of the property value or initial LTV, whichever is higher.

Congress occasionally approves housing subsidy programs that may be handled through HUD/FHA, but these fall into a separate category from the underwriting programs discussed in this chapter.

---

[1] "FHA Single Family Market Share 4th Quarter 2014," Office of Risk Management and Regulatory Affairs, Office of Evaluation, Reporting & Analysis Division, Department of Housing and Urban Affairs, September 30, 2014, accessed January 3, 2015, http://portal.hud.gov/hudportal/documents/huddoc?id=FHA_SF_MarketShare_2014Q2.pdf

FEDERAL HOUSING ADMINISTRATION

The **Federal Housing Administration (FHA)** was one of the many agencies created by the federal government during the Great Depression to help resolve the economic problems that plagued the nation. It is one of the very few that survived, and it has proven its value over nearly seven decades of operation.

The reasons for which the FHA was formed in 1934 are still valid today, although its area of operations has expanded substantially from its origin as an initial assistance program for home buyers.

The purposes of the FHA are to: (1) encourage wider home ownership, (2) improve housing standards, and (3) create a better method of financing mortgage loans. All these aims have been successfully realized, even beyond original hopes. This was accomplished without making a single loan, simply by the sound use of government credit to insure mortgage loans. After its initial widespread rejection by many private lenders, a government-insured commitment is now readily salable to a large number of investors. Even in the tightest money markets, there has always been funding available for a government-insured loan.

First-Time Home Buyer with HUD-Approved Prepurchase Counseling

The National Housing Act, as amended by the Housing and Economic Recovery Act of 2008, authorizes upfront premiums of up to 3%, except these premiums cannot exceed 2.75% for first-time home buyers who complete HUD-approved prepurchase counseling. Since the up-front premium rate of 1%, effective October 4, 2010, remains below the statutory cap, no variable rate is provided for first-time home buyers who receive HUD-approved counseling.

Home Equity Conversion Mortgage (HECM) Loans

Effective for all HECM loans for which the case number is assigned on or after October 4, 2010, the FHA will increase the annual premium that is collected on a monthly basis. This policy change will not affect the up-front premiums collected. The annual premium, shown in basis points below, is to be remitted on a monthly basis, and will be charged according to the following schedule:

Premium Type	Basis Points or % of Mortgage Balance
Up-front (UFMIP)	200 BPS or 2%
Annual (MIP)	50 BPS or .5%

Premium Refund

The UFMIP is subject to partial refund when a loan is paid off prematurely. The FHA Commissioner determines how much of the up-front premium is refunded when loans are terminated. Refunds are based on the number of months the loan is insured. For any FHA-insured loans with a closing date prior to January 1, 2001, and endorsed before December 8, 2004, no refund is due the homeowner after the end of the seventh year of insurance. For any FHA-insured loans closed on or after January 1, 2001, and endorsed before December 8, 2004, no refund is due the homeowner after the fifth year of insurance. For FHA-insured loans endorsed on or after December 8, 2004, no refund is due the homeowner unless he or she refinanced to a new FHA-insured loan, and no refund is due to homeowners in this second category after the third year of insurance. Mortgagee Letter 2005-03 provides additional information on the recent policy changes regarding refunds of up-front mortgage insurance premiums. It behooves an owner or sales agent to contact the local HUD/FHA office for current information on a possible refund when a transaction involves property with an existing FHA loan. A sales agent should also be aware that no refund will be made on an FHA loan assumption, and if an FHA loan is made to refinance an existing FHA loan, any refundable portion of the previously paid UFMIP can be applied to the UFMIP due on the refinanced loan.

Assumption of an FHA Loan

From its beginning in 1934 and through to 1986, an FHA loan was classed as "freely assumable." This meant that a borrower holding an FHA mortgage loan had the right to sell the property, deliver title, and assign repayment of the loan to a new buyer without either FHA's or the mortgagee's approval. While this right did exist, what was overlooked was the fact that an assignment by the mortgagor resulted in no release of liability for the mortgagor/seller. Therefore, the seller remained fully liable for repayment for the remaining life of the loan. So long as house prices escalated, as they did in the 1970s and the early 1980s, this was not a big problem. The few foreclosures that occurred generally resulted in repossession of a house of greater value than the mortgage obligation.

However, this situation began to change in the mid-1980s, when repossessions increased as house values declined in some depressed areas of the country. (We would see a similar pattern in the condition of the residential market during the financial crisis.) What the FHA encountered when defaults occurred was houses occupied by persons unknown to them. The effort to notify an original obligor who remained liable was difficult since he or she most likely had moved away. Further trouble resulted when original obligors contended that they had not been notified of any default. They felt no further responsibility since the house had been conveyed along with the mortgage in accordance with what they believed to be an acceptable procedure.

To correct the situation, HUD/FHA changed the assumption rules. In fact, the rules were changed twice between 1986 and 1989, and there are now three separate sets of requirements. The differing requirements are distinguished by date of loan origination (which is the date of the FHA-insured commitment) and are not retroactive. To better understand the changes, we will first examine the two methods that have always applied to FHA loan assumptions. One is called a simple assumption and the other a formal assumption.

Simple Assumption

With a **simple assumption**, property may be sold and the loan assumed without notification to the FHA or its agent (the mortgage lender). However, with this method, the seller remains fully liable to the FHA and the lender for repayment of the loan, regardless of the buyer's assumed obligation.

Formal Assumption

With a **formal assumption**, the property is not conveyed to a new buyer until that person's creditworthiness has been approved by the FHA or its agent. With a creditworthy buyer assuming the loan, the seller may obtain a full release of liability from the FHA. This is the method that the FHA has always recommended, but the agency did not require it until 1989.

The three separate categories of FHA loans for assumption purposes, distinguished by date of origination, are as follows:

1. **For loans originated prior to December 1, 1986,** the original rules still apply. The borrower has an option to sell the mortgaged property by simple or formal assumption rules. It should be noted that in this category, using a formal assumption, a release of liability from the FHA is available but is not automatic. The release should be obtained

as one of the documents delivered when the transaction is closed and should also be filed of record.

2. **For loans originated between December 1, 1986, and December 15, 1989,** there is a restriction on early assumptions, after which time the loan can be freely assumed by simple assumption. Specifically, an owner/occupant cannot sell the property with an assumption during the first 12 months after execution of the mortgage except to an approved buyer—meaning by formal assumption. If the seller is an investor (in rental property), a simple assumption sale cannot be made during the first 24 months after execution of the mortgage. Failure to comply with this restriction can result in acceleration of the loan balance.

   After the one- or two-year period, this category of loans may be assumed without prior approval of the buyer. However, should a simple assumption be undertaken, both the seller and buyer remain fully liable for five years after the new mortgage is executed. If the loan is not in default after five years, the seller is automatically released from further liability.

3. **For loans originated on or after December 15, 1989,** creditworthiness approval of the new buyer must be obtained prior to conveyance of title for all assumptions. Failure to comply can result in acceleration of the note. If an acceptable borrower assumes the mortgage loan, the lender cannot refuse to release the original borrower from further liability.

In addition to regular mortgage loans, the rules on assumptions apply to subsequent sale transactions consummated with a contract for deed, a lease purchase agreement, or a wraparound note. An exception applies if properties are transferred by operation of law, such as devise or descent.

The additional time necessary to meet qualification standards for a new buyer can be irritating to both buyer and seller, but it is a safer course to follow. This is particularly true now that the FHA policy is to pursue collection of defaulted loans to the original obligors if they remain liable.

Between November 2003 and May 2005, FHA developed a system to allow assumption data to be input into an assumption case tracking system, allowing the case to be tracked online to see the status of the case. The potential case statues are:

1. *success updates allowed,* which indicates that the case assumption request was processed—that is, the case has been successfully reassigned to the new lender and/or new sponsor/agent;
2. *unavailable,* which indicates that the system is down; or
3. *error,* which indicates that an error has occurred during the case assumption process and that the case has not been assumed successfully (the data were either missing or in error).

In today's market, some servicing organizations are authorized to service FHA loans but are not "supervised originators." This means that they do not have the rights to underwrite the credit-qualifying assumptions as would an authorized seller/servicer with Direct Endorsement underwriters on staff approved by the FHA.

Investor Mortgagors Eliminated

Since its origin, a primary purpose of HUD/FHA has been to provide suitable housing to qualified people. To promote this goal, rental housing has been encouraged as a means of increasing available dwelling units in this country. Unfortunately, in the late 1980s, investor loans experienced a much higher rate of default than owner-occupied housing loans, and it became necessary to limit the FHA's risk exposure. As a result, insured loans for investors were eliminated as of December 15, 1989.

While new loans to investors were eliminated, loans made prior to December 15, 1989, may still be assumed by investors, although some restrictions apply. Essentially, additional cash could be required so that the balance due on a loan assumed by an investor does not exceed 75% of the value of the property.

A procedure that is considered an attempt to circumvent the restriction on investor financing is sometimes referred to as a *friendly foreclosure.* In this process, an investor "lends" a portion of an FHA mortgagor's equity to the owner and places a second lien on the property. This step in itself does not violate HUD requirements. The next step, however, is a preplanned default by the owner on the second mortgage and a foreclosure transferring title to the investor, and this step *does* violate the provision barring investors from acquiring HUD-financed properties. This second provision provides for acceleration of the note if all or part of the property is transferred (other than by devise or descent) to a purchaser who does not occupy the property.

Exceptions to Restrictions on Investor Financing

There are two important exceptions that allow investors to acquire property with an FHA-insured commitment, as follows:

1. **HUD foreclosures** (Investors may still purchase HUD-foreclosed properties with a 25% down payment and the balance financed with an FHA-insured commitment, or within the guidelines of any special program.); and
2. **Section 203(k) rehabs.** Section **203(k) Rehabilitation Home Mortgage Insurance** is available to investors. This program combines a purchase money mortgage with a construction loan. It targets the restoration of rundown houses as a practical means of adding to the country's housing stock. More details on the 203(k) program are provided in a later section of this chapter.

FHA Loan Limits

Federal Housing Administration (FHA) single-family loan limits have changed frequently over the past 20 years. The most dramatic is the result of the **American Recovery and Reinvestment Act (ARRA)**, signed into law on February 17, 2009. The dual concept of maximum loan amount limitation based on high- and low-cost geographic areas is still a factor, and one that we will more fully discuss later in this chapter, as these limitations have been affected by the various new federal laws passed in 2008 and 2009 that have now been merged into one common listing.

The announced methodology used and allowed by HUD was developed using the following criteria:

- The minimum FHA national loan limit "floor" is at 65% of the national conforming loan limit ($417,000 for a one-unit property for the period January 1, 2015, through December 31, 2015). The "floor" applies to those areas where 115% of the median home price is less than 65% of the national conforming loan limit.
- The maximum FHA national loan limit "ceiling" is at 150% of the national conforming loan limit. In areas where 115% of the median home price (of the highest cost county) exceeds 150% of the conforming loan limit, FHA loan limits remain at 150% of the conforming loan limit.

- Mortgage Letter 2014-25 sets the FHA loan limits for 2015 that are effective for all Title II FHA forward insurance programs except for Streamline Refinance loans and loans made in Special Exceptions for Alaska, Hawaii, Guam, and the Virgin Islands.

Exceptions to loan limits and a county-by-county listing of loan limits can be found at the following HUD/FHA website: https://entp.hud.gov/idapp/html/hicostlook.cfm

Value of Property, Down Payment, and Closing Costs

The FHA values the property itself as the lesser of the appraised value or the purchase price. The 2009 change requires the borrower to pay 3.5% of the acquisition cost in cash to close. The cash requirement can be met with the down payment plus closing costs. The older rules allowed closing costs to be added to the property value, thus increasing the amount that could be borrowed. New rules do not allow this. Closing costs are those listed in the Loan Estimate (the same Loan Estimate required by RESPA to be furnished to a loan applicant) but cannot exceed certain FHA limitations, as determined in the local area. Acceptable closing costs include attorney's fees, credit report, appraisal costs, origination fee, and title insurance.

Example

For houses priced higher than $150,000:

Acquisition cost	$200,000
Loan amount (96.5%)	− $193,000
Down payment & closing costs	$ 7,000

To meet the $7,000 cash required to close (i.e., 3.5% of acquisition cost in the preceding example), the borrower may add the money paid for closing costs to the down payment.

In addition, to meet the 3.5% requirement, the borrower may also use proper gift money if supported by a gift letter. A seller may pay up to 6% in costs, but anything over that amount is considered a reduction in selling price. The 3.5% cash requirement cannot consist of discount points or prepaid expenses, or any portion of such charges. Borrowers can still finance the up-front mortgage insurance premium.

> (Using the example above, multiply the amount that can be borrowed ($193,000) by the current 1.75% UFMIP, or $3,378. Therefore, if they choose to do so, the borrower could finance up to $196,378, or over 98% LTV.)
>
> The 2015 revised mortgage amount calculation applies to the following programs: 203(b) home mortgages and condominium mortgages; 203(i) outlying areas; 203(n) cooperative units; 203(k) rehabilitation home mortgage insurance; and 223(e) home mortgages in older, declining urban areas. The new calculation does not apply to 203(h) housing for disaster victims or 221(d)(2) low-cost and moderate income.

Secondary Financing with HUD/FHA-Insured Commitments

If the mortgagor uses any funds that require a lien to be placed on the property, it is considered secondary financing and must be taken into account when determining the maximum insurable amount. This is true whether or not the note may be forgiven at some future date depending on the borrower's continued employment. HUD/FHA will insure first mortgages on property with secondary financing under the following conditions:

1. The sum of the first and second mortgages cannot exceed the applicable loan-to-value ratio or maximum mortgage limit for that area.
2. The payments under the insured first mortgage and the second mortgage do not exceed the mortgagor's reasonable ability to pay.
3. Any periodic payments on the second mortgage are collected monthly and are substantially in the same amount.
4. The repayment terms of the second mortgage: (a) do not provide for a balloon payment before 10 years or such other terms not acceptable to HUD/FHA, and (b) permit prepayment by the mortgagor without penalty.

Analyzing the Loan Application

In the past decade, the various government agencies involved with underwriting home loans have made a concerted effort to simplify procedures, including the use of standard forms by all agencies plus the acceptance of each other's appraisals and general procedures. The present form used by lenders to apply for government underwriting is a uniform version that combines HUD Form 92900, VA Form 26-1802a, and the Rural Development Services (formerly FMHA) Home Loan Guaranty form. This is the form that a mortgage company submits to HUD/FHA to apply for mortgage insurance. It is based on information obtained from the borrower's loan application and subsequent verifications. The borrower's application to the lender for a loan is also a standard form that has been made mandatory for all residential loans, as will be explained more fully in the next chapter.

One of the standardization chores that the industry is working on is to make the various computerized loan analysis systems compatible. As they were originated, each system was designed to operate with different software, making it more difficult for lenders to work with more than one system. It is the intention of major lenders to offer systems that can be used by others with similar software.

When computerized analysis of loan applications was introduced in 1995 by several major lenders, FHA did not approve any one system. Its procedure at first was to approve an FHA lender's use of an automated system, but not the system itself. Then in 1996, FHA gave approval for a joint pilot project for its lenders to use Freddie Mac's Loan Prospector (LP) system for loan analysis. The agency hoped to reduce processing time and to qualify some borrowers who would not have qualified through ordinary lender underwriting. Now, approved seller/servicers can use either Fannie Mae's automated underwriting system, Desktop Underwriter (DU), or Freddie Mac's LP and further speed the underwriting loan approval process.

In 2009, the FHA introduced its "Technology Open To Approved Lenders" (TOTAL) underwriting scorecard that was tied into DU and LP. TOTAL, it was announced, was to be a tool to assist approved FHA seller/servicers in the management of their workflow and in expediting the endorsement process, and was particularly helpful for those lenders that had direct endorsement underwriters on staff. TOTAL should not be considered a substitute for the lender's responsibilities in the consideration of risk and creditworthiness. Direct endorsement lenders using TOTAL remain solely responsible for the underwriting decision.

Since TOTAL works through various automated underwriting systems (AUS), it primarily evaluates the overall creditworthiness of the applicants based on a number of credit variables and determines an associated risk level of a loan's eligibility for insurance by FHA. It is the FHA's policy that no borrower is to be denied an FHA-insured mortgage based solely on a risk assessment generated by TOTAL. In certain instances and circumstances, TOTAL cannot be used, so manual underwriting must be done instead.

TOTAL does not:

- reject applications;
- review the loan for compliance;
- review maximum mortgage amounts;
- compute debt-to-income ratios;
- review property eligibility;
- determine LTV; or
- complete additional functions typically performed by an AUS.

The agency requires that all transactions be scored through TOTAL except transactions involving borrowers without credit scores and streamline refinance transactions. Lenders should not use TOTAL on streamline refinance transactions, as the results are considered invalid. Direct endorsement-approved seller/servicers must keep up with all Mortgagee Letters that change full eligibility considerations for those using TOTAL. An example is Mortgagee Letter 2013-05, effective April 1, 2013, advising all approved seller/servicers that when underwriting loans where the borrower has a decision credit score below 620 and the debt-to-income ratio exceeds 43.00%, these loans must be manually underwritten. HUD had its TOTAL scorecard system modified to issue a scoring recommendation of "refer for loans" when such criteria are entered.

Analysis of Property and the Borrower

The property and the borrower are processed separately in determining qualification. Procedures that are followed for approval of the property are outlined in the sections that follow.

FHA INSURED LOAN PROGRAM

HUD/FHA Terminology and Basic Procedures

All underwriting programs are implemented by the issuance of a certificate of insurance that protects the lender against default. The differences between the programs are based on the kind of property involved and the qualifications of the individual who needs the help. There may be lower cash requirements for some and, in certain programs, an actual subsidy of interest costs. Also, the property must meet certain standards to qualify as collateral for an insured commitment.

To handle qualification of borrowers and the property offered as collateral, HUD/FHA follows certain procedures as detailed in its *Underwriter's Guide*. There are some words and phrases with special meaning in the world of HUD/FHA loan qualification. For example, a conventional lender measures the loan amount against the property value almost regardless of its sales contract value or certain types of deferred maintenance. In the past, with an FHA loan, a distinction was made between loans of $50,000 or less and those exceeding $125,000. That changed with the passage of the **Economic Stimulus Act of 2008 (ESA)**, which we will discuss later. The conventional lender focuses its cash requirement on a down payment; the FHA requires 3.5% in cash at closing, which may come from the down payment plus closing costs. Regardless of the details, the basic qualification procedures are the same—whether FHA, VA, or conventional—and their purpose is to distinguish a creditworthy borrower and evaluate the property to make sure it serves as adequate collateral for a loan. Nevertheless, to understand FHA procedures, it is necessary to understand their basic requirements. These are detailed in the following sections.

Acquisition Cost

The amount of mortgage insurance available under any HUD/FHA program is limited to a percentage of the acquisition cost. **Acquisition cost** is the *lesser* of the purchase price or the appraised value.

Calculation of Down Payment

For the purposes of this calculation, there are only two categories of loans: (1) those in the amount of $50,000 or less, and (2) those for more than

$50,000. For loans of $50,000 and less, the FHA insures 98.75%. For loans over $50,000, the FHA insured commitment is 97.75%.

The amount of cash required to close is now at 3.5%, a combination of down payment plus closing costs. Previous rules allowed closing costs to be included in the insured commitment; new rules do not allow this, but the buyer can add closing costs to the down payment to achieve the 3.5% cash requirement to close.

On March 1, 2011, requirements for down payments under standard FHA Section 203(b) purchase money mortgages became tied to the borrower's credit score. The HUD Handbook 4155.1 4.A.1.c was changed to state that, if the borrower's minimum decision credit score is equal to or above 580, the loan is eligible for maximum financing and an LTV of 96.5%. If the credit score is between 500 and 579, the loan is limited to a maximum LTV of 90%, and if the credit score is less than 500, the loan is not eligible for standard Section 203(b) FHA-insured financing. Exceptions to this new tightening of underwriting standards are:

- Section 223(e)
- Section 238
- Section 247
- Section 248
- Section 255 home equity conversion mortgages (HECM)
- Title I
- HOPE for Homeowners

There are still provisions for borrowers with nontraditional or insufficient credit histories to be eligible for maximum financing, but they must meet the underwriting guidelines in HUD Handbook 4155.1 4.C.3.

Prepaid Items

HUD/FHA distinguishes between closing costs and **prepaid items**. Closing costs are described more fully in the above paragraph. Prepaid items are property taxes, insurance premiums (including the FHA mortgage insurance premium), and possibly subdivision maintenance fees, most of which must be placed in an escrow account with the lender. It also covers *per diem interest*. The lender must use a minimum of 15 days of per diem interest when estimating prepaid items. To reduce the burden on borrowers whose loans were scheduled to close at the end of the month, but did not due to unforeseen circumstances, lenders and borrowers may agree to credit the per diem interest to the borrower and have the mortgage payments begin on the first day of the succeeding month.

Property Taxes

The borrower must pay whatever pro rata share of property taxes may fall due for the first year plus one month in escrow at closing. HUD/FHA requires one month of all annual prepays to be held by the lender, but allows two months to be held at lender's option as a cushion.

Subdivision Maintenance Fees

In some areas, maintenance fees are considered to be in about the same category as taxes. That is, nonpayment can result in foreclosure of the property. To protect the lender, such charges may be required to be paid into escrow.

Hazard Insurance Premium

A full year's premium for property insurance must be paid in advance of closing, plus one month of premium placed in escrow. The same requirement applies to flood insurance, if applicable.

Flood Insurance and FHA Requirements

Effective March 1, 2011, FHA required that all mortgagees obtain a flood zone determination on all properties instead of simply strongly encouraging such action. Such a determination is obtained from a review of the Federal Emergency Management Agency (FEMA) flood maps. In addition, FHA is now consistent with the Coastal Barrier Resources Act (CBRA), prohibiting FHA mortgage insurance for properties located within designated coastal barriers. Mortgagees will be required to obtain life-of-loan flood zone determination services for all properties that will be collateral for FHA-insured mortgages, as determined by FEMA flood maps. Authorized FHA lenders and servicers must comply with provisions that any property located within a designated Coastal

Barrier Resource System (CBRS) unit is not eligible for an FHA-insured mortgage.

> ## Where Are We Now?
>
> ### Avoiding Foreclosure
>
> Whether you are in foreclosure now or worried about it in the future, HUD.gov has information that can help. The HUD.gov website provides links that allow homeowners to do the following:
>
> - Learn about the U.S. Treasury's Hardest-Hit Fund Initiative.
> - Talk to a foreclosure avoidance counselor.
> - Talk to their lenders.
> - Find state and local foreclosure resources.
> - Contact HOPE NOW.
> - Contact the Homeownership Preservation Foundation.
> - Learn whether they are at risk of foreclosure.
> - Obtain a *Save Your Home* brochure.
> - Discover tips for avoiding foreclosure.
> - Learn about foreclosure scams.

FHA MORTGAGE INSURANCE PREMIUMS

There have traditionally been two types of FHA mortgage insurance premiums: (1) an **up-front mortgage insurance premium (UFMIP)**, and (2) a continuing **annual premium** paid monthly and typically called the mortgage insurance premium (MIP). These two premiums have changed considerably over the years, including three times in 2010, so it is important that the reader always check the current UFMIP and MIP for each of the 11 individual FHA residential mortgage loan programs.

On August 12, 2010, Public Law 111-229 was passed, providing the Secretary of Housing and Urban Development (HUD) with additional flexibility regarding the amount of the premiums charged for Federal

Housing Administration (FHA) single-family housing mortgage insurance programs. Specifically, the new law permits HUD to increase the amount of the annual mortgage insurance premium that HUD is authorized to charge. This allowed HUD/FHA to change the UFMIP and MIP for loans with different loan-to-value ratios, based on the loan terms and the amount of the loan being insured. For most FHA loans, the UFMIP is 1.75% of the insured amount of the original principal balance of the mortgage. The Act authorizes HUD to adjust the amount of the annual mortgage insurance premiums through Federal Register Notice or Mortgagee Letter.

Now FHA is in a better position to address the increased demands of the marketplace and return the Mutual Mortgage Insurance (MMI) fund to congressionally mandated levels without disruption to the housing market. Based on the new authority—effective for FHA loans for which the case number is assigned on or after April 1, 2013, or June 3, 2013, based on Mortgagee Letter 2013-04 issued on January 31, 2013—the FHA will require all the following new enhancements to raise funding for the MMI:

- revision to the period for assessing the annual MIP;
- removal of the exemption from the annual MIP for loans with terms of 15 years or less and LTVs of less than or equal to 78% at origination; and
- increase in the annual MIP for mortgages with terms less than or equal to 15 years and LTV ratios less than or equal to 78% at origination.

Mortgage Letter 2013-04 also:

- rescinds the automatic cancellation of the annual MIP collection announced in MLs 2000-38 and 2000-46;
- rescinds ML 2011-35, under which mortgages with terms of 15 years or less and LTVs of less than or equal to 78% at time of origination were exempt from the annual MIP; and
- rescinds and updates Sections 7.3.a, 7.3.c, 7.3.d, 7.3.e, 7.3.f, and 7.3.g of HUD Handbook 4155.2 as appropriate.

Programs Not Affected by the Premium Changes

The following up-front and annual premium programs were not affected by Mortgagee Letter 2013-04:

- streamline refinance transactions of existing FHA loans that were endorsed on or before May 31, 2009 (see ML 2012-04);
- Title I;
- home equity conversion mortgages (HECM);
- Section 247 (Hawaiian homelands); and
- Section 248 (Indian reservations).

Up-front Premiums and Annual Premiums

For all FHA loans that are assigned a case number on or after June 3, 2013, including both FHA traditional purchase products and refinance products, the up-front premium (shown in basis points below) will be charged for all amortization terms. The following schedule shows the most common UFMIP and MIP percentage rates, according to HUD Mortgagee Letter 2013-04:

Loan Term > 15 Years				Loan Term ≤ 15 Years					
>95.00% LTV		≤95.00% LTV		>90.00% LTV		78.01%–90.00% LTV		≤78.00% LTV	
UFMIP	ANNUAL	UFMIP	ANNUAL	UFMIP	ANNUAL	UFMIP	ANNUAL	UFMIP	ANNUAL
1.75%	1.35%	1.75%	1.30%	1.75%	0.70%	1.75%	0.45%	1.75%	0.45%

FHA Mortgagee Letter 2015-01, effective for case numbers assigned on or after January 26, 2015, reduces annual MIP rates for FHA Title II forward mortgages and provides FHA lenders the opportunity for cancellation of existing case numbers in order to utilize the MIP rates contained in ML 2015-01. See reduced rates below:

Loan Term > 15 Years				Loan Term ≤ 15 Years					
>95.00% LTV		≤95.00% LTV		>90.00% LTV		78.01%–90.00% LTV		≤78.00% LTV	
UFMIP	ANNUAL	UFMIP	ANNUAL	UFMIP	ANNUAL	UFMIP	ANNUAL	UFMIP	ANNUAL
1.05%	.85%	1.00%	.80%	.95%	0.70%	.70%	0.45%	.45%	0.45%

Practice Exercise: UFMIP and Annual MIP Calculation

Calculate the minimum FHA down payment amount by multiplying the cost of the house by 3.5%. (The minimum down payment for an FHA loan is 3.5%.) For example, if the home costs $300,000, the minimum down payment is $10,500.

- Calculate the initial loan amount by subtracting your planned down payment from the price of the home. Using the minimum down payment in the example, the loan amount is $289,500.
- Multiply the loan amount by 1.05% to calculate the up-front MIP. In the example loan, $289,500 multiplied by 1.05% yields an up-front MIP of $3040.

Next, calculate the annual MIP using the following five steps:

1. Calculate the amortization schedule of the loan. If the up-front MIP will be financed, it should be added to the loan amount. Use an online loan amortization calculator.
2. Calculate the average outstanding balance for the first year of the mortgage. The average balance is calculated by adding together the original loan amount plus the loan balance after the first 11 payments and dividing the total by 12. In the example loan, the initial loan amount is $294,566; at a 4.5% rate, the average outstanding balance is $292,392.10.[2]
3. Multiply the average outstanding balance by the annual MIP rate of .85%. In the example, $292,392.10 times .85% is $2,485.33.
4. Reduce the annual MIP amount by dividing by 1 plus the up-front MIP factor, if the up-front MIP was added to the loan amount. The up-front MIP is 1.05%, so the annual MIP result from above is divided by 1 plus 0.0085, or 1.0085. The result is $2.517.64. This is the annual MIP amount for the first year of the example FHA loan.
5. Divide the annual MIP amount by 12 for the amount that will be added to the monthly mortgage payment. In the example, $209.80 is added to each monthly loan payment.

---

[2] Go to www.Bankrate.com and click on the calculator at the top of the page.

UNDERWRITING GUIDELINES

TABLE 8-1 The Compensating Factors that FHA Underwriters May Use to Justify Approval of Mortgage Loans with Ratios that Exceed FHA Benchmark Guidelines

Compensating Factor	Guideline Description
Housing Expense Payments	The borrower has successfully demonstrated the ability to pay housing expenses greater than or equal to the proposed monthly housing expenses for the new mortgage over the past 12 to 24 months.
Down Payment	The borrower makes a large down payment of 10% or higher toward the purchase of the property.
Accumulated Savings	The borrower has demonstrated an ability to accumulate savings and a conservative attitude toward using credit.
Previous Credit History	A borrower's previous credit history shows that he/she has the ability to devote a greater portion of income to housing expenses.
Compensation or Income Not Reflected in Effective Income	The borrower receives documented compensation or income that is not reflected in effective income, but directly affects his/her ability to pay the mortgage. This type of income includes food stamps, and similar public benefits.
Minimal Housing Expense Increase	There is only a minimal increase in the borrower's housing expense.
Substantial Cash Reserves	The borrower has substantial documented cash reserves (at least three months' worth) after closing. The lender must judge if the substantial cash reserve asset is liquid or readily convertible to cash, and can be done so absent retirement or job termination, when determining if the asset can be included as cash reserves, or cash to close. Funds and/or "assets" that are not to be considered as cash reserves include equity in other properties, and proceeds from a cash-out refinance. Lenders may use a portion of a borrower's retirement account, subject to the conditions stated below. To account for withdrawal penalties and taxes, only 60% of the vested amount of the account may be used. The lender must document the existence of the account with the most recent depository or brokerage account statement. In addition, evidence must be provided that the retirement account allows for withdrawals for conditions other than in connection with the borrower's employment termination, retirement, or death. If withdrawals can only be made under these circumstances, the retirement account may not be included as cash reserves. If any of these funds are also to be used for loan settlement, that amount must be subtracted from the amount included as cash reserves. Similarly, any gift funds that remain in the borrower's account following loan closing, subject to proper documentation, may be considered as cash.
Substantial Nontaxable Income	The borrower has substantial nontaxable income. This applies if no adjustment was previously made when computing ratios.
Potential for Increased Earnings	The borrower has a potential for increased earnings, as indicated by job training or education in his/her profession.
Primary Wage-Earner Relocation	The home is being purchased because the primary wage-earner is relocating, and the secondary wage-earner has an established employment history, is expected to return to work, and has reasonable prospects for securing employment in a similar occupation in the new area.

Source: © 2021 Mbition LLC

MOST FREQUENTLY USED FHA LOANS

HUD/FHA Program Details

There are now over 50 different programs offered by HUD/FHA. They include multifamily housing, manufactured home parks, nursing homes, and planned unit developments (PUDs), as well as the better-known single-family housing programs. Their utilization varies somewhat across the country according to local situations. Some programs have become inactive due to loan limitations or qualification standards that no longer fit the changing housing market.

This section examines the qualifications needed and the restrictions placed on several of the more popular programs, including:

1. Section 203(b)—home mortgage insurance (including the special assistance offered veterans) and condominiums;
2. Section 203(k)—rehabilitation home mortgage insurance;
3. Section 245—graduated-payment mortgage; and
4. Title 1—home improvement loan insurance.

Section 203(b)—Home Mortgage Insurance

The basic 203(b) program authorized in the initial Act of 1934 is still the most widely used home mortgage insurance program. Experience gained from this program has been used extensively in the development of many succeeding plans. It is used as a standard with some of the other housing assistance programs, which refer to qualification requirements simply as "same as 203(b)."

As with all HUD/FHA programs, the property to be acquired and used as collateral for the loan must meet applicable standards. While there are no special requirements for the individual borrower under 203(b), he or she must have an acceptable **FHA new minimum credit score** as defined next, and demonstrate an ability to make the required investment as well as to handle the monthly mortgage payments.

Section 203(b) offers the simplified calculation of the down payment (FHA loan commitment of 96.5% of acquisition value with 3.5% cash required to close). A borrower's credit score can now affect the maximum allowed LTV. As previously discussed, those with credit scores between 500 and 579 are required to make a 10% investment.

As part of the Housing and Economic Recovery Act of 2008 (HERA), the Federal Housing Administration (FHA) implemented an approval process for condominium projects and insurance requirements for mortgages on individual units under Section 203(b) of the National Housing Act. HUD/FHA insures mortgages for the purchase of individual family units in multifamily housing projects now with the change under Section 234(c). It also insures loans for the construction or rehabilitation of housing projects intended for sale as individual condominium units under Section 234(d). The approved units under the old 234(d) have all been phased out, and now condominiums are covered by Section 203(b).

A *condominium* is defined as joint ownership of common areas and facilities by the separate owners of single-family dwelling units in the project. To be acceptable for FHA insurance, the project must include at least four dwelling units. At least one other unit in each project must be acquired under a government-underwritten program.

Before a loan can be insured for a single condominium, the entire project must meet HUD/FHA minimum standards, just as a new subdivision must meet compliance standards. The agreement under which a homeowners association may function comes under scrutiny, as do the rights of the developer. The question of when the developer vacates the premises becomes more important with a condominium, as it affects control of the common areas. Under FHA requirements, the developer may not claim a right of first refusal to offer condominiums for resale.

Section 203(b)(Veteran)

Under 203(b), HUD/FHA has a special concession for qualified veterans, allowing an insured commitment of 100% of the first $25,000. Regular 203(b) limits apply to all loans over that amount.

The FHA veterans' program has additional value, as it offers broader **eligibility** measures than those available under the VA program. The basic differences are as follows:

1. The FHA qualification requires 90 days of active duty and a discharge other than dishonorable. The VA has longer time spans of required service at different periods of time; for example, hot war/cold war distinctions. (See VA requirements later in this chapter.)
2. The FHA does not take into consideration any prior commitment of the veteran's entitlement, while the VA must deduct any previous usage of the entitlement if the loan has not been paid off or assumed by another qualified veteran.

Veterans using FHA for their home loans can in some circumstances receive 100% financing and do not pay monthly mortgage insurance premiums.

Section 203(k)—Rehabilitation Home Mortgage Insurance

To help restore and preserve the nation's existing housing stock, the 203(k) program has been revised and expanded. In June 1993, this kind of loan was made eligible for "direct endorsement," which means lenders can underwrite them without prior HUD field office approval. Further stimulus for the program was given by allowing the loans to be sold to secondary-market investors when the loan is originated and before rehabilitation is completed.

Unlike any other HUD-insured program, 203(k) combines a purchase money mortgage with a construction loan. The new revision offers an insured commitment (with the same limits as 203[b]) that allows the purchase of an existing house over one year old, plus sufficient additional money to rehabilitate the property. The program is limited to one- to four-family dwellings and can be utilized as follows:

1. Purchase and rehabilitate an existing one- to-four-family dwelling (completed for more than one year) that will be used for residential purposes.
2. Refinance and rehabilitate an existing one- to-four-family dwelling and refinance the outstanding indebtedness (not applicable for Streamline [k]).
3. Rehabilitate a dwelling after it has been moved from one site to a new foundation (excluding manufactured homes).

Section 203(k) should not be used unless the rehabilitation or improvement costs total a minimum of $5,000 (not applicable for Streamline 203[k], which has no minimum, but does have a $35,000 maximum).

A single insurance commitment combines the funds needed to purchase the property or refinance existing indebtedness, the costs incidental to closing, and the money needed to complete the proposed rehabilitation. If the 203(k)-insured commitment involves insurance of advances, which would be normal when rehabilitation is required, then a rehabilitation loan agreement must be executed by the lender and the borrower. As part of this agreement, there must be an inspection and release schedule that details the amount of escrowed money that can be released at each stage of completion.

Before any release of funds can be made by the lender holding the escrow account, an inspection must be made to determine satisfactory completion of the work to that stage. Inspection is made by HUD-approved fee inspectors from a list provided by the HUD field office. The number of inspections required will vary with the complexity of the rehabilitation but cannot exceed four plus the final one.

The current maximum mortgage calculation for a 203(k) is based on:

1. the estimate of as-is value or the purchase price of the property before rehabilitation, whichever is less, plus the estimated cost of rehabilitation and allowable closing costs; or
2. 110% of the expected market value of the property upon completion of the work, plus allowable closing costs, if the subject property to be rehabilitated is to be the principal residence (owner-occupied).

The maximum mortgage amount is based on 96.5% of (1) or (2) above. Should the rehab loan be for an investment property (non-occupant mortgagor or builder/rehabber), the maximum mortgage amount will be based on 85% of (1) or (2) above. The dollar difference between the maximum mortgage amount (96.5% of the fair market value for an owner/occupant) and the mortgage amount available to an investor (85% of acquisition cost) will remain in escrow with the lender until the property is assumed by an owner/occupant acceptable to the Commissioner of the Federal Housing Administration. The qualifying housing and debt ratios are the same as in the 203(b) program.

Because this program is fairly complex and requires additional supervision by the mortgage lender, higher charges are permitted. Lenders may add one percentage point to the normal 1% origination fee for a purchase money mortgage, and 1.5% more than normal for the rehabilitation loan, with a minimum or $350 plus some other modest fees for plan review inspection.

Mortgage Limits and the Insured Commitment

Both the maximum amount of mortgage loan permitted and the calculation of the maximum insured commitment are determined on the same basis as that for the 203(b) program described earlier in this section.

Section 245—Graduated-Payment Mortgage (GPM)

Several years of experimental testing provided the groundwork for HUD/FHA to offer an insurance program for graduated-payment mortgages, which was approved nationally in November 1976. The purpose of the program is to reduce monthly payments in the early years of the mortgage term so that families with lower incomes, but reasonable expectation of future increases, can qualify for suitable housing in a higher-cost market.

The program was well received through the early 1980s, as it enabled many young families to purchase their first home. Initially, the program was targeted at first-home buyers, so the original program guidelines were more lenient. The key benefit for the applicant is that income qualification is based on the monthly payment required for the first year, which is normally much less than necessary to fully amortize the loan. The repayment plan worked well in times when housing prices escalated and inflation was an accepted fact of life. However, the GPM and its borrowers faced difficulties when the economy reversed into a downslide in the late 1980s. To avoid further problems, qualification guidelines were tightened a bit.

Section 245 is limited to owner-occupant applicants; there are no other special qualifications such as income limitations. As in other programs, the applicant must have an acceptable credit record, demonstrate ability to make the required down payment, and be able to handle the monthly mortgage payments. In addition, the applicant must have reasonable expectation of an increased annual income in future years.

The lower monthly payments in the early years under most of the HUD/FHA Section 245 plans are insufficient to pay anything on principal and do not cover all of the interest due each month (see table 8-2). Consequently, each year the unpaid interest is added to the principal balance due. Since the loan balance is increased, rather than reduced or "amortized," the result is called negative amortization. To prevent an increase in the loan balance from exceeding the value of the property, higher down payments may be required.

TABLE 8-2 HUD/FHA Floor and Ceiling Limits*

Property Size	Low Cost Area "Floor"	High Cost Area "Ceiling"
One Unit	$294,515	$679,650
Two Units	$377,075	$870,225
Three Units	$455,800	$1,051,875
Four Units	$566,425	$1,307,175

*Based on HUD/FHA Mortgagee Letter 2017-16
Source: © 2021 Mbition LLC

Mortgage Limits

The maximum amount of the insured commitment for Section 245 is derived as the lesser of two calculations, a process that we will describe more fully later. Section 245 plans make it possible for the loan amount (that is, the principal balance due on the loan) to increase due to the negative amortization feature (adding unpaid interest to the principal balance each year). Thus the loan balance can increase to an amount greater than the initial authorized loan amount. This possibility is recognized and does not constitute a violation of the National Housing Act so long as the down payment computations are made in accordance with Section 245 instructions.

Section 245—Repayment Plans

HUD/FHA insures graduated-payment mortgages with five different repayment plans. These are differentiated by the rate of payment increases each year and the duration of the escalation period. Three plans offer 2.5%, 5%, and 7.5% annual increases for the first five years; two plans offer 2% and 3% increases for the first 10 years. Stated another way, the initial monthly payment amount is calculated so that it can be increased each year at a fixed, or predetermined, rate until it reaches a constant-level payment amount by the sixth year for the five-year plans, and by the 11th year for the 10-year plans. The amount of monthly payment, the mortgage insurance premium, and the down payment required depend on the interest rate and the term of the loan. To simplify the calculation of these amounts, the FHA has published a series of tables that give factors to be used in the calculation of payment requirements.

Calculating the 245 Insured Commitment

To comply with the requirements, it is necessary to make two separate calculations to establish the correct maximum insured commitment. Since the insured commitment almost always becomes the amount of the loan, the difference between the commitment and the contract price is the required down payment. The first calculation that determines the insured commitment, called Criterion I in the example that follows, is the same as that required for Section 203(b) qualification. The second calculation, Criterion II, is in accordance with the Section 245 formulas. The lesser of the two results is the amount of the insured commitment.

Under Criterion II for the nonveteran applicant, the procedure is to take 97% of the property value (including closing costs) and divide the result by the highest outstanding balance factor for the applicable plan and interest rate. Different procedures apply for veterans and for properties constructed without prior FHA approval that are less than one year old.

Example

To calculate the down payment and monthly mortgage payments for a HUD 245 loan, the applicant refers to a HUD/FHA Graduated Payment Factor Table. This is available at any HUD/FHA office and provides factors with differing interest rates and the HUD payment plan that applies. Table 8-3 illustrates these factors for three plans and two different interest rates. For this example, assume a property value of $190,000 and closing costs of $3,800, a total value for mortgage insurance purposes of $193,800. Assume that the loan requested has a 30-year term and an interest rate of 8% using Plan III. (Plan III offers payment amounts increasing at 7.5% each year for the first five years.) The calculation must be made by two separate criteria to determine which offers the lesser loan amount.

Criterion I [same as 203(b)]

Value of property (acquisition cost)	$190,000
Insured commitment (96.5%)	183,350

Criterion II (245 Calculation)

Value of property	$193,800 × .97 =	187,986
	$187,986 ÷ 1030.9550 =	182.34162
	182.34162 × 1,000 =	182,341.61

Per these calculations, Criterion II offers the lesser loan amount of $182,341.61 and, therefore, the applicable number is rounded down to $182,300. The difference between the loan amount and the purchase cost is the down payment; thus, $193,800 minus $182,300 equals $11,500. The cost of the mortgage insurance premium must be added as a one-time charge at closing. For this example, consider that 100% of current UFMIP (always check for current status of percentage of loan amount), which is 1.75% UFMIP, will be financed (that is, added to the loan amount at closing). Calculate as follows:

For the first year:
  ($185,490 ÷ 1,000) × 5.5101 = $1,022.07 (first year's P&I payments)

And for the second year:
  ($185,490 ÷ 1,000) × 5.9233 = $1,098.71 (second year's P&I payments)

Complete the computation for each successive year, always applying the P&I factor to the initial loan amount. The amount of the sixth-year payment in this example remains constant for the remaining life of the loan.

TABLE 8-3 HUD/FHA Section 245 GPM Factors

	Principal Balance Factor	Monthly Principal and Interest (P&I) Factors (per $1,000 of original loan balance)					
		Year 1	Year 2	Year 3	Year 4	Year 5	Year 6+
		INTEREST RATE: 8.00%					
Plan I	1000.0195	6.6651	6.8317	7.0025	7.1775	7.3570	7.5409
Plan II	1012.8612	6.0579	6.3608	6.6789	7.0128	7.3634	7.7316
Plan III	1030.9550	5.5101	5.9233	6.3676	6.8452	7.3585	7.9104
		INTEREST RATE: 9.00%					
Plan I	1002.3085	7.3244	7.5075	7.6952	7.8876	8.0848	8.2869
Plan II	1021.0154	6.6706	7.0042	7.3544	7.7221	8.1082	8.5136
Plan III	1043.5617	6.0788	6.5347	7.0248	7.5517	8.1181	8.7269

Source: © 2021 Mbition LLC

Title 1—Home Improvement Loan Insurance

One of the more popular programs offered by HUD/FHA is insurance on loans to finance home improvements. The money may be used for major or minor improvements, alterations, or repairs of individual homes and nonresidential structures, whether owned or rented. Lenders determine eligibility for these loans and handle the processing themselves. The smaller loans in this category are usually handled as unsecured personal loans (recording of a mortgage instrument is not required).

Any creditworthy property owner is eligible for a Title I loan. Loans may also be made to tenants for improvement of leased apartment units, provided the lease term is at least six months longer than the term of the loan. In addition, Title I covers the insurance of loans on mobile homes (manufactured housing) that do not qualify as real estate. Whether or not a mobile home qualifies as real estate depends on state laws, the nature of its title, and how it is taxed. States generally claim an ad valorem property tax if the unit is permanently attached to the ground.

Where Are We Now?

When visiting the HUD/FHA website (http://portal.hud.gov/hudportal/HUD?src=/topics), you have access to these topics:

- avoiding foreclosure
- buying a home
- economic development
- energy
- environment
- fair lending
- the Freedom of Information Act (FOIA)
- grants
- home improvements
- homelessness
- homes for sale
- the Housing Choice Voucher Program (Section 8)
- housing discrimination
- housing research and data sets
- HUD Homes
- information for disabled persons
- information for senior citizens
- limited denials of participation
- rental assistance
- veteran information
- volunteering
- working with HUD

DIRECT ENDORSEMENT
HUD/FHA Qualification Procedures

Since its beginning, HUD/FHA has trained its own valuation and mortgage credit staff to handle the qualification of loan applicants so as to assure compliance with the special requirements of the various programs. Guidelines are furnished in a comprehensive *Underwriter's Guide*, supplemented with an almost continuous flow of updated information to keep readers abreast of changing needs and new laws.

While the process has been difficult to fit into a computerized analysis program, in 1996, the FHA approved the use of Freddie Mac's Loan Prospector as a system to analyze loan applications. The purpose is to expedite loan processing and reduce costs, and possibly to qualify some applicants who might otherwise be rejected. As pointed out earlier, the computer does not reject an applicant, but rather, asks the lender's underwriting department for further information to help process the loan application.

No two applications are alike, and judgment calls sometimes become necessary to determine proper approval or rejection. The system has always permitted sufficient flexibility to allow a review of the decision if the applicant feels an error has been made.

In 1983, HUD established the Direct Endorsement Program in an effort to both reduce costs and simplify the process for mortgagees (mortgage lenders) to secure insurance endorsements. Under this program, the mortgagee underwrites and closes a mortgage loan without prior HUD review or approval. The authority to participate in this program is a privilege granted to mortgagees on the basis of demonstrated qualifications, experience, and expertise.

In this procedure, the mortgagee is given sufficient certainty of HUD approval to justify undertaking the responsibility. Essentially, HUD requires compliance with its rules and does not "second guess" the underwriters' decisions. HUD does make a post-endorsement review, and if underwriting deficiencies are discovered in the loan documents, an underwriting report is sent to the mortgagee. However, the insurance contract is incontestable except in cases of fraud or misrepresentation. If the mortgagee continues to submit marginal-type loans under this program, its authority under Direct Endorsement may be withdrawn.

FHA CONTRIBUTIONS TO REAL ESTATE FINANCE

Early History

When the FHA stepped into the housing picture in 1934, houses had been financed for 50% to 60% of their sales price on a first mortgage of three to five years, with a small second and even a third mortgage at increasingly higher interest rates. The average loan was a three- to five-year balloon note with interest only due every six months, and it was callable at the option of the bank even if payments were current should the bank need the cash to meet deposit withdrawals. The FHA introduced a better way. By offering to insure a single large loan up to 80% of value (an extremely high ratio in those days), the FHA was able to insist that the down payment be made in cash, permit no secondary financing, and command a moderate interest rate. The loans were for long terms—up to 20 years at first—and fully amortized over the life of the loan. Equal monthly payments covered principal and interest. Escrow accounts were established for hazard insurance and property taxes, requiring payment of one-twelfth of the yearly cost each month. Each monthly payment also included a premium to cover the cost of the FHA's mortgage default insurance. Most of these features were later incorporated into the loan guaranty program of the Veterans Administration and have now become normal procedure for conventional loans as well. While none of these ideas actually originated with the FHA, this agency gave them wide usage for the first time and brought about a sweeping reform in the field of residential financing.

As the FHA gained strength in its housing assistance, more titles and sections were added to its operations. While the FHA has over 50 different programs in its portfolio of assistance to borrowers for home loans, improvement loans, nursing home loans, mobile home park loans, multifamily project loans, and land development loans, our concern in this chapter is primarily with the 11 loan programs for single-family residences. Under the assistance programs for home loans, the FHA provides special help for members of the armed services, civilian employees of the armed services, and disaster victims, as well as programs in experimental housing, urban renewal, and condominium housing.

In 1993, HUD Secretary Henry Cisneros undertook a major overhaul of all multifamily housing programs, which had suffered accumulated losses in excess of $6 billion. By then, single-family programs had recovered from a period of substantial foreclosures, and the Mutual Mortgage Insurance Fund that sustains the programs was again operating in the black. Few people really understand that the FHA mortgage program is one of the most successful, self-sustaining government programs in U.S. history—unlike so many others that have drained taxpayer resources.

VA LOAN GUARANTY PROGRAM
Department of Veterans Affairs (VA)

The Veterans Administration was elevated to cabinet rank in 1989 as the **Department of Veterans Affairs**. Title and mortgage documents now reflect conveyance to the "Secretary of Veterans Affairs" rather than the "Administrator of Veterans Affairs." While the VA administers a number of programs for the benefit of eligible veterans, our interest is confined to the home loan program that was created in 1944 as part of the "G.I. Bill of Rights." Section 501 of this Act provides for a first-mortgage real estate loan that is partially guaranteed by the VA and is subject to strict rules covering all phases of the loan: the borrower, the lender, the property, the loan charges, the term and loan amount, collections, and foreclosures. The primary interest of the VA is to assist the veteran, and it is to this end that the rules are directed.

While HUD/FHA insures 100% of its approved loans, the VA guarantees only a portion of the loan amount. Since the guarantee reduces the risk exposure for a lender, it has been considered an acceptable loan. The VA does not have a cash requirement for a veteran to qualify—meaning no down payment is required. Even the VA funding fee can be added to the loan amount rather than paid in cash. However, the "no cash" rule describes what is acceptable to the VA for its loan approval. It does not apply to a lender who may require a down payment and an origination fee paid by the veteran. Thus, even though a VA loan may be found with no cash required of the veteran, many lenders believe some investment on the part of a borrower makes a more acceptable loan, and this practice is permitted by the VA.

Not all veterans are eligible for a home loan guarantee. They must meet certain minimum requirements of time served on active duty. Eligibility for a loan is different from "entitlement," although the terminology is often confused. The differences between what is meant by these two terms are more fully described next.

Eligibility of a Veteran

To be eligible for a home loan guarantee, the veteran must have served on active duty a minimum amount of time that varies during different periods—lesser time during periods of "hot wars," and longer for other types of conflict. Military service requirements for VA loan eligibility almost always require that a veteran has had an honorable discharge. When dealing with VA loan eligibility, applicants with other than honorable discharges will usually require further investigation by the VA. This is necessary to determine if the service was performed under other than dishonorable conditions. For many years, service eligibility was broken down into "Wartime" and "Peacetime" service based on the criteria presented in table 8-4.

Active Duty Service Personnel

For military currently on active duty defined as regular duty (not active duty for training), applicants are eligible after having served 181 days (90 days during the Gulf War) unless discharged or separated from a previous qualifying period of active duty service.

Selected Reserves or National Guard and Other Qualifying Military or Service Personnel

If an applicant not otherwise eligible has completed a total of six years in the Selected Reserves or National Guard (member of an active unit, attended required weekend drills and two-week active duty for training) and received an honorable discharge *and* been placed on the retired list, been transferred to the Standby Reserve or an element of the Ready Reserve other than the Selected Reserve after service characterized as honorable service, or continues to serve in the Selected Reserves, he or she may be considered eligible for the program.

Individuals who completed less than six years may be eligible if discharged for a service-connected disability.

Under certain circumstances, current United States citizens who served in the armed forces of a government allied with the United States in World War II are also considered eligible. So are some individuals with service as members in certain organizations, including Public Health Service officers; cadets at the United States Military, Air Force, or Coast Guard Academy; midshipmen at the United States Naval Academy;

TABLE 8-4 Veteran Home Loan Guarantee Eligibility Requirements

Status	Qualifying Wartime & Peacetime Periods	Qualifying Active Duty Dates	Minimum Active Duty Service Requirements
Veteran	WWII	9/16/1940–7/25/1947	90 total days
	Post-WWII	7/26/1947–6/26/1950	181 continuous days
	Korean War	6/27/1950–1/31/1955	90 total days
	Post-Korean War	2/1/1955–8/4/1964	181 continuous days
	Vietnam War	8/5/1964–5/7/1975 *For Veterans who served in the Republic of Vietnam, the beginning date is February 28, 1961.	90 total days
	Post-Vietnam War	5/8/1975–9/7/1980 *The ending date for officers is October 16, 1981.	181 continuous days
	24-month rule	9/8/1980–8/1/1980* The beginning date for officers is October 17, 1981.	24 continuous months, OR the full period (at least 181 days) for which you were called or ordered to active duty
Currently on Active Duty	Gulf War	8/2/1990–Present	24 continuous months, OR the full period (at least 90 days) for which you were called or ordered to active duty
Currently on Active Duty	Any	Any	90 continuous days
National Guard & Reserve Member	Gulf War	8/2/1990–Present	90 days of active service

Other Eligibility based on:
- six years of service in the Selected Reserve or National Guard; AND
- were discharged honorably; OR
- were placed on the retired list; OR
- were transferred to the Standby Reserve or an element of the Ready Reserve other than the Selected Service after Service characterized as honorable; OR
- continue to serve in the Selected Reserve.

Exceptions for Gulf War Service from 8/2/1990 forward to dates to be determined are for those who have:
- completed at least 90 days of active duty and have been discharged under the specific authority of 10 USC 1173 (Hardship), or 10 USC 1171 (Early Out), or have been determined to have a compensable service-connected disability; or
- been discharged with less than 90 days of service for a service-connected disability; individuals may also be eligible if they were released from active duty due to an involuntary reduction in force, certain medical conditions or, in some instances, for the convenience of the government.

Source: © 2021 Mbition LLC

officers of the National Oceanic and Atmospheric Administration; and merchant seamen with World War II service.

Owner-Occupied

The VA guaranty can be used by a veteran only to buy a house to live in as a principal residence. The guaranty cannot be used to purchase rental property, except for an approved one- to-four-family dwelling that is also occupied by the veteran/buyer. The definition of an owner/occupant has been expanded to include a qualified veteran's spouse during the time a veteran is on active duty out of the country.

Eligibility of Spouses of Otherwise Qualifying Veterans

Any not-remarried spouse of a veteran who died while in service or from a service-connected disability, or any spouse of a service person missing in action or a prisoner of war, is eligible. A surviving spouse who remarries on or after attaining age 57, and on or after December 16, 2003, may be eligible for the home loan benefit as well. However, a surviving spouse who remarried before December 16, 2003, and on or after attaining age 57, must have applied no later than December 15, 2004, to establish home loan eligibility. The VA must deny applications submitted after the December 15, 2004 deadline from surviving spouses who remarried before December 6, 2003.

For any veteran considering the purchase of a home and the use of a VA loan, it is a good idea to ask the VA regional office to confirm eligibility. This is done by submitting VA Form 26-1880, "Request for Determination of Eligibility and Available Loan Guaranty Entitlement." The VA response to this request answers two questions: Is the veteran eligible? And if so, how much is available in the entitlement?

Sliding Scale Guaranty

Prior to 1988, the VA applied the same maximum permissible amount as the guaranty portion of a loan regardless of the amount of the loan. As the size of loans continued to increase, the single-figure guaranty became disproportionate for a smaller loan as compared with larger loans. The VA introduced a sliding scale of loan guaranties on February 1, 1988, when the limit was increased to $36,000. The new guaranty limits are a mix of loan percentages and fixed amounts, as shown in table 8-5.

Where Are We Now?

Illustrations of Guarantee Calculation

Illustration 1

If a veteran has not previously used an entitlement and now wishes to purchase a home that would qualify for a loan of $300,000, the loan would fall in the guaranty category of 25% (see table 8-5). To calculate:

300,000 × 25% = $75,000 (guaranty applied to the loan)

Illustration 2

Assume a veteran with full entitlement is purchasing a home for $700,000 where the county loan limit is $625,500. The loan would fall into the guaranty category of 25% (See table 8-5).

$625,500 × 25% = $156,375 maximum guaranty and entitlement available for the loan

$156,375 ÷ $700,000 = 22.34% maximum guaranty

To be able to sell the loan, lenders will require $700,000 × 25% = $175,000 guaranty. The veteran will need a down payment combination requirement of $175,000 minus $156,375, the maximum guaranty. This yields a required down payment of $18,625.

Illustration 3

Assume a second veteran has used $54,000 of entitlement on a prior loan (which cannot be restored) and plans to purchase a home for $405,000 in a county with a loan limit of $625,500.

$625,500 × 25% = $156,375; maximum guaranty $156,375 − $54,000 = $102,375 entitlement available

$102,475 × 4 = $409,500 maximum loan amount with 25% guaranty

Since the proposed loan amount will be less than $409,500, the lender will receive a 25% VA guaranty on the loan of $405,000, and a down payment will not be required.

TABLE 8-5 Sliding Scale Guaranty

Loan Amount	Guaranty Amount Range
$45,000 and less	50% of loan
$45,001 to $56,250	$22,500
$56,251 to $90,000	40% of loan not to exceed $36,000
$90,001 to $144,000	$36,000
$144,001 to $453,100	25% of loan not to exceed the maximum loan guaranty of $113,275*

*Always refer to the VA county-specific loan limit. Note that effective January 1, 2018, VA's 2018 loan limits are the same as the Federal Housing Finance Agency's limits. For purposes of determining the VA guaranty, lenders are instructed to reference only the One-Unit Limit column in the FHFA table titled "Fannie Mae and Freddie Mac Maximum Loan Limits for Mortgages Acquired in Calendar Year 2018 and Originated after 10/1/2011 or before 7/1/2007." The highest county four-family limit in 2018 is $1,307,175; that amount, if multiplied by 25%, would equal a maximum guaranty of $326,795.
Source: © 2021 Mbition LLC

Tier 1 or Partial Entitlements

If a veteran sells a house with assumption of a VA loan, the Department of Veterans Affairs remains liable to the holder of that note (the lender) until it is paid off. This is true whether or not the selling veteran has obtained a release of liability from the obligation to the VA. So when this occurs, the veteran's entitlement for that existing loan remains committed insofar as the VA is concerned. This means that the amount of entitlement previously committed cannot be used to acquire another property. However, when the entitlement limit itself is increased, the additional amount becomes available for further use. Under such circumstances, a veteran may be eligible for partial entitlement.

Example

A veteran purchased a home in 1977 using a VA guaranty that amounted to $17,500 at that time (refer to table 8-4). The home was sold in 1992 with an assumption of the old loan by the new buyer. If the veteran seller did not obtain a restoration of full entitlement at the time, there is still a new entitlement that can amount to the difference between the $17,500 that remains committed and the current limit of $104,250. But there is now a limit on partial entitlements.

Limit on Tier 1/Partial Entitlements

Except in the case of eligible loans in excess of $144,000, the maximum amount of the guarantee remains $36,000. For example, a veteran who previously used a $17,500 entitlement that has not been restored has $18,500 available ($36,000 minus $17,500 equals $18,500) for use in connection with any eligible purpose. However, in the event of a new loan in excess of $144,000, the remaining entitlement used to guarantee the loan amount will be based on the difference between $46,000 and the previously used guaranty amount. Thus, the same veteran with a previously used guaranty amount of $17,500 would have a $28,500 entitlement for use if the purpose of the new loan is to acquire a home or condominium with a loan in excess of $144,000. A real estate agent or loan officer dealing with a partial entitlement question should understand whether the veteran is in a high-cost county before attempting to advice about his or her remaining entitlement, and would benefit by contacting the local VA office or by visiting this page on the Veterans' Administration website: http://www.benefits.va.gov/HOMELOANS/purchaseco_loan_limits.asp

Practical Value of an Entitlement

In the marketplace, the amount of entitlement is a key determinant of the maximum size of a VA loan because almost all VA loans are now sold into Ginnie Mae loan pools. It is a Ginnie Mae, not a VA, requirement that in order for any VA loan to be accepted into a Ginnie Mae-underwritten pool, it must have guaranty and/or cash covering at least 25% of the loan amount. Since VA loans can be approved with no cash down, the market puts emphasis on the amount of a veteran's entitlement, meaning at least 25% of the loan amount must be a VA guaranty. In other words, a VA loan cannot exceed four times its guaranty. The VA's limit-on-loan amount is quite different; in this case, the loan cannot exceed the appraised value of the property. The appraised value in VA terminology is **the certificate of reasonable value (CRV)**.

Restoration of Entitlement

Restoration of entitlement is often confused with a release of liability. They are quite different and require two separate procedures if both are to be accomplished. One way of distinguishing between the two is to think of restoration of entitlement as help in obtaining a new loan. Release of liability, as will be explained later, has to do with responsibility for an old loan. Restoration is important for a veteran desiring to purchase a new house, and this question should be considered in any contract when a veteran sells a house that has a VA loan.

There are two ways for a veteran to regain the right to full entitlement. These are as follows:

1. **Pay off the loan through sale of the property.** This means not allowing an existing VA loan to be assumed. Once the loan is paid off, the obligation of the VA terminates for that loan and the veteran's entitlement rights can be restored. One further requirement is that the house must be vacated, as a veteran can only own one house, which must be his or her own principal residence.

2. **Substitute another veteran's entitlement.** To qualify under this procedure, the veteran may sell his or her home on an assumption basis, but only to another qualified veteran. The purchasing veteran must: (a) have at least as much entitlement as the selling veteran, (b) meet the normal income and creditworthiness requirements, and (c) agree to permit the entitlement to be substituted.

For many years, the VA also required that there be a compelling personal reason for the sale—for example, a job transfer—to restore a veteran's entitlement. This is no longer necessary.

Other Special Veterans Rights

The American Recovery and Reinvestment Act of 2009 (ARRA) included a temporary expansion of the Homeowner's Assistance Program benefits for private home sale losses of both military and civilian Defense Department personnel. The program may provide benefits for those with military affiliation that lose money on a home purchased before July 1, 2006, and must sell due to a service-forced relocation or certain other service-related circumstances. The circumstances covered by the ARRA allow for compensation for service members with or without VA loans who sell their homes and suffer a loss due to declines in fair market value if the sale was made necessary by relocation after a military base closure; reassignment ordered between July 1, 2006, and September 30, 2012; or a combat wound requiring relocation for further medical assistance.

The ARRA also provides protection for surviving spouses of those killed in the line of duty. The ARRA allows for appropriation to be used by the secretary of defense in a number of alternative ways, such as by acquiring title to a military person's property or reimbursing a military person for losses after a private sale.

Under the ARRA provisions, the federal government is prepared to cover part of a veteran's loss if the veteran was effectively forced to sell as a result of any of the above. The government could buy the home, and the price or payment would be determined by a formula. Generally, the government would cover the difference between 95% of the prior fair market value and the fair market value at the time of the event that resulted in a loss.

Non-Spouse Co-Ownership

A veteran wanting to use their VA home loan benefit to purchase a home along with a non-spouse/nonveteran often is not realistic if the veteran does not intend to use the home as their primary residence. When taking a VA home loan, the occupying borrower has to be an eligible veteran. While the VA does not specifically prohibit non-occupying co-borrowers, it does require that such a loan be sent to them for prior authorization. Although both incomes can be used to qualify for the loan, the borrower's (veteran's) income must be sufficient to repay his/her portion of the loan. Also, the VA guaranty covers only the veteran's portion of the loan. The outcome will be that few or possibly no VA lenders will issue a loan without a full guaranty.

Release of Liability

The above-stated rules underline the importance of selling a house to someone who is capable of making payments on the loan if it is to be assumed. While it will take many years for the older, more easily assumed loans to work their way out of existence, selling veterans continue to have the right to obtain a release of liability in a sale with a loan assumption. A selling veteran is entitled to a **release of liability** if the following conditions are met:

1. The loan must be current.
2. The purchaser/assumptor must qualify from the standpoint of income and be an acceptable credit risk.

3. The purchaser must agree to assume the veteran's obligations on the loan.

The veteran need not sell the house to another veteran in order to obtain a release of liability for a loan assumption. The purchaser need only meet the above-listed requirements. Release of liability is a separate form and should be completed at the time the transaction is closed.

Loan Default and Foreclosure

Even though the VA guaranty covers only a portion of the loan amount, historically, in the event of foreclosure, VA followed a policy of paying off the principal balance with interest due and taking title to the property. This practice enhanced the value of a VA guaranty for the lender. However, as foreclosures escalated in the late 1980s, increased losses were sustained by the VA. To better protect the programs and reduce potential cost to taxpayers, the VA changed its procedures when faced with a foreclosure.

Similar to the practice followed by HUD/FHA, the VA now requires notification of a pending foreclosure so that it can have the property appraised. On a case-by-case basis, the VA then decides what action is in the best interest for the agency; that is, the VA must decide whether or not it is best for the VA to pay off the loan and take title to the property, or simply pay only the guaranty amount to the lender. If the latter method is followed, the VA pays the guaranty and declines to bid for the property at foreclosure, or "no-bids" the property. This means the lender takes title in foreclosure and must arrange for whatever disposition it can find.

The "no-bid" procedure has substantially altered the risk level of a VA loan for lenders and is one of the reasons why lenders encourage veteran applicants to consider competitive conventional loans.

Funding Fee

Initially, the VA home loan program was handled as part of the country's ongoing commitment of service to veterans. For many years, there was no charge for processing the loan application or for issuing the guaranty certificate. However, increasing costs and growing losses caused Congress to add a .5% funding fee in 1982 for issuance of a VA guaranty. Since then, the fee has been raised and lowered several times, the latest increase becoming effective in 2012 based on the changes from the Honoring America's Veterans and Caring for Camp Lejeune Families Act of 2012 ("Honoring Veterans Act"). There are still three categories of eligible veterans with differing fees. The fee is reduced as down payment is increased, as shown in table 8-6.

The fee is payable at closing and may be included in the amount of the loan. There are a few exceptions. For example, the fee is not paid by veterans receiving compensation for service-connected disabilities or surviving spouses of veterans who died in service or as a result of service-connected disabilities. The Honoring Veterans Act grants exemption from paying the funding fee for:

- veterans receiving VA compensation for service-connected disabilities;
- veterans who are entitled to receive compensation for service-connected disabilities if they do not receive retirement pay;
- veterans who are rated by the VA as eligible to receive compensation as a result of pre-discharge disability examination and rating or on the basis of a pre-discharge review of existing medical evidence (including service medical and treatment records) that results in issuance of a memorandum rating;
- veterans entitled to receive compensation, but who are not presently in receipt because they are on active duty; and
- surviving spouses of veterans who died in service or from service-connected disabilities (whether or not such surviving spouses are veterans with their own entitlement and whether or not they are using their own entitlement on the loan).

TABLE 8-6 VA Funding Fees (Funding fee is based on the amount of down payment)

Down Payment	First Time	Multiple User	Nat'l Guard	Nat'l Guard	Stmline Refi	Cashout Refi	Cashout Refi	Cashout Refi
		Purchase Multiple			Regular Res/Nat'l Multiple Use*			
(%)	(%)	(%)	(%)	(%)	(%)	(%)	(%)	(%)
None	2.15%	3.30%	2.40%	3.30%	.50%	2.15%	2.4%	3.3%
5–<10%	1.50%	1.50%	1.75%	1.75%	.50%	2.15%	2.4%	3.3%
10% or more	1.25%	1.25%	1.50%	1.50%	.50%	2.15%	2.4%	3.3%

*Multiple Use Cash Out Refinance Funding Fee is the same for Regular Military and Reserve/National Guard.
Source: Veterans Benefits Administration, *Lender's Handbook*, VA Pamphlet 26-7 (Revised), 8–21.

Fees apply to all types of VA-guaranteed loans, but they vary for different categories. For instance, the fee for interest rate reduction/refinancing loans was reduced to .5% as of October 28, 1992, and was extended to December 31, 2017, under the Honoring Veterans Act. The VA accepts the possibility that the addition of a funding fee may make the loan in excess of the property value.

Negotiated Interest Rate and Discount

In a historic change for the VA, Congress passed legislation in 1992 to allow market interest rates and discounts to be applied to VA loans. (The FHA made this change in 1982.) Before this change, the VA set a maximum permissible rate for issuance of its guaranty and allowed no discount to be paid by a veteran borrower. Even though the VA interest rate was changed periodically to stay abreast of market fluctuations, the cost of a loan to the borrower was adjusted by lenders to meet current market yields through a change in the discount. The burden was placed on the seller, who was required to pay any discount, and this cost was often shifted into the price of the property.

The new law, which became effective October 28, 1992, allows loans to be guaranteed by the VA at an interest rate agreed upon between the veteran and the lender. In addition, discount points as agreed between veteran and lender may be paid by the veteran, but may not be added to the loan amount.

Adjustable-Rate Mortgage (ARM)

ARMs have had an on-again, off-again relationship with the Veterans Administration. Just a decade ago, a three-year test period to underwrite ARM mortgages expired on September 30, 1995. The reason given for the elimination at that time was that the program had cost the VA money. Currently, the VA allows traditional ARMs, hybrid ARMs (3/1, 5/1, 7/1, and 10/1), graduated-payment mortgages (GPM), and growing equity mortgages (GEM) for veteran loans.

Interest Rate Reduction Refinancing Loans (IRRRLs)

In times of low interest rates, such as what occurred during the 1990s, both the FHA and the VA take steps to encourage refinancing existing loans. It is not their money that is at stake, but their underwriting guarantees of loan repayment. The easier it is for their borrowers to repay loans, the lower the risk for the underwriting agencies. Refinancing loans to obtain lower interest rates results in lower monthly payments and easier repayment, and reduces default risk.

Inducements to refinance include eliminating an appraisal, extending loan terms, and reducing funding or insuring fees. For VA loans closed after January 21, 1988, the term may be extended for up to 10 years longer than the remaining term of the original loan, but not longer than a maximum of 30 years and 32 days. The veteran need not occupy the house to secure refinancing but must certify that the house was occupied by the veteran when the loan was secured. The funding fee for refinancing has been reduced to .5 points.

The rules applicable to refinancing a VA-guaranteed loan at a lower interest rate were modified in May 1999. In a final rule on the issue, the VA will not permit refinancing if a loan is delinquent. Furthermore, the payment must be reduced on the refinanced loan and the veteran seeking refinancing must meet certain credit standards. The purpose of requiring a payment reduction is to prevent unscrupulous lenders from lowering the interest rate while still packing the refinanced loan with excessive fees so that the payment is actually increased.

Other VA Requirements and Procedures

To assure the veteran that the home loan will be properly handled and that the government guaranty will not be abused, the VA has a number of specific requirements relating to the loan and how it is handled. Essential areas of VA concern are discussed next.

The Lender

To protect against any unscrupulous activity, the VA distinguishes between supervised and nonsupervised lenders. A *supervised* lender is one who is subject to periodic examination and regulation by a federal or state agency. Savings associations, commercial banks, savings banks, and insurance companies all qualify as supervised lenders. As such, they can process loans on an automatic basis.

Under this procedure, the supervised lender takes all the necessary steps to qualify a borrower, asks for a VA appraisal, and then makes its own underwriting decision. If favorable, the information is submitted to the VA in a loan report that the VA is obliged to honor with the issuance of a guaranty certificate.

A *nonsupervised* lender is anyone who does not qualify as a supervised lender. Mortgage companies, fraternal associations, and individuals are examples of nonsupervised lenders. To obtain a certificate of guaranty from the VA, the nonsupervised lender must first obtain approval from the VA to make a loan to the veteran applicant, and would have to submit all required information to the VA office for underwriting approval.

A third category of lender is a *nonsupervised lender that qualifies for automatic loan processing*. Mortgage companies that are wholly-owned subsidiaries of a supervised lender, subject to the same periodic examination as their parent firm, are listed in this category. If the VA qualifications are met, the nonsupervised lenders may submit their own approved applications for guaranty in the form of a loan report, and receive the same automatic issuance of a VA guaranty certificate as a supervised lender.

Term of the Loan

A VA home loan can be obtained for up to 30 years. Shorter terms are approved by the VA if required by the lender and accepted by the veteran. The veteran has the right to repay all or any part of the principal balance due on the loan at any time with no additional interest charges or penalties.

Loan Servicing

The administration of a VA loan is not prescribed by the VA. Approved lenders are expected to follow the normal standards and practices of prudent lenders. The VA expects a veteran/obligor to meet the obligations fully and on time; however, it does encourage reasonable forbearance on the part of the lender with enforcement of its collections. The lender is required to notify the VA of a default within 60 days after nonpayment of an installment. Failure to file the default notice within the prescribed time limits can result in a reduction of the guaranty allowed for the lender. Additional VA notification processes are discussed in Chapter 10.

Manufactured Home Loans

The Veterans Housing Act of 1970 (updated in 1974) authorized the VA to guarantee loans made by private lenders to veterans for the purchase of new and used mobile homes. (Mobile homes constructed on or after June 15, 1976, are called *manufactured homes,* as defined by HUD.) The same VA rules apply to a manufactured home as for a site-built house; it must be occupied by the veteran as his or her principal residence. The unit so acquired may be a single-wide or a double-wide, and the authorization to guarantee also covers a lot suitable for a manufactured home.

Because the status of a manufactured home as real versus personal property is not always clear, the VA now offers two categories under which lenders may request guarantees. The older procedure, identified as Section 1819 (of Title 38), offers a guaranty at the lesser of 50% of the loan amount up to a maximum of $20,000. Effective on March 2, 1984, a new provision was added to Section 1810 increasing the maximum guaranty for a manufactured home permanently affixed to a lot, provided the manufactured home is considered real property under laws of the state where the lot is located. A Section 1810 loan allows longer repayment terms and may be guaranteed on the same sliding scale entitlement as for site-built houses.

Section 1810 permits a veteran to purchase a manufactured home already permanently affixed to a lot, or a home and a lot to which the home will be permanently affixed, or to refinance an existing loan secured by a manufactured home permanently affixed to a lot. The veteran is allowed to pay a reasonable discount on the refinancing portion of the loan. The term of these loans can be for as long as 30 years and 32 days. Interest rate and discount can be negotiated between the veteran and lender.

Manufactured home loans are not an additional entitlement for the veteran, as the privilege is reduced by the amount of entitlement already committed, similar to a regular home loan. The same rules that apply to regular VA house loans regarding a veteran's entitlement, negotiated interest rate, and liability for repayment also apply to a manufactured home loan.

Analyzing the Loan Application

Both the property to be pledged as collateral and the veteran applicant must meet VA qualification standards. Because both HUD/FHA and the VA have similar underwriting goals (that is, a sound building as collateral and a creditworthy borrower), their qualification standards are similar. And each agency now accepts the other's qualifications of applicants with a few exceptions. Property qualification is considered next. The process of qualifying a veteran applicant is examined in the next chapter to allow comparisons with other loan-qualifying procedures.

ADDITIONAL VA LOAN PROGRAMS

The Loan Guaranty Entitlement

The amount of money that the VA will guarantee for a veteran is called an **entitlement**. At its origin in 1944, the maximum entitlement amounted to $2,000. As housing prices increased over the years, Congress has periodically adjusted the entitlement limit, as shown in table 8-7.

Assumption of a VA Loan

Prior rules allowed the assumption of a VA loan by any purchaser—veteran or nonveteran—without approval by the VA. What became lost in

TABLE 8-7 Entitlement Increments

Date of Increase	Maximum Entitlement
Original Act, 1944	$ 2,000
December 28, 1945	$ 4,000
July 12, 1950	$ 7,500
May 7, 1968	$ 12,500
December 31, 1974	$ 17,500
October 1, 1978	$ 25,000
October 7, 1982	$ 7,500
February 1, 1988	$ 36,000
December 18, 1989	$ 46,000
October 13, 1994	$ 50,750
December 27, 2001	$ 60,000
December 10, 2004	$ 89,913*
January 1, 2006	$104,250*
January 1, 2018	$ 113.275

*The Veterans Benefits Improvement Act of 2004 began an expansion of VA maximum loan amounts to the levels of those of Fannie Mae and Freddie Mac, and its guarantee amount to 25% of that maximum. This was to be indexed through 2008, but the Veterans Housing Opportunity and Benefits Act of 2006 eliminated the $80,000 maximum loan amount, in addition to the need for Secretarial determination of higher loan amounts in high-cost areas. Instead, the new limit on Native American Direct Loan (NADL) is the same as the Federal Home Loan Mortgage Corporation (or Freddie Mac) single-family conventional conforming loan limit. That limit is currently $417,000 for loans located in the 48 contiguous states and $625,000 for loans in Alaska, Guam, Hawaii, and the U.S. Virgin Islands. Increases in these loan limits will be published annually, based on the annual adjustment in the Freddie Mac conventional conforming loan limit, which is $417,000 for 2015. In 2015, high-cost area loan limits have increased for 46 counties due to a high-cost area adjustment or the county being newly assigned to a high-cost area, and are as high as $938,250 for a single-family residence.

Source: © 2021 Mbition LLC

the long upswing in the housing market into the early 1980s, however, was the fact that the seller remained primarily liable for repayment of that assumed loan; the loan could be transferred, but not the responsibility for its repayment. Unless the selling veteran took the available steps to find a creditworthy buyer and then obtain a release of liability, the obligation remained. When the economy in certain areas of the country began to decline in the mid-1980s, defaults and foreclosures became far more prevalent. Many problems resulted when a private mortgage lender was forced to foreclose on properties that had been conveyed to buyers unknown to the VA or the lender.

A claim for repayment of a defaulted VA loan is a debt owed to the federal government (as is an FHA claim) and subject to collection from the debtor(s) through the U.S. government's right of indemnification and/or subrogation. To reduce any recurrence of this kind of problem, the VA changed the assumption rules for all VA-guaranteed loans underwritten after March 1, 1988.

Assumption by Creditworthy Buyers Only

For loans underwritten after March 1, 1988, assumptions are not permitted without prior underwriting approval by the lender or the VA. This rule is not retroactive and does not apply to loans underwritten before that date, meaning that older loans may still be freely assumed. But without a release of liability from the old loan, the seller remains fully liable.

Veterans holding VA loans underwritten after March 1, 1988, must follow specific procedures if a loan assumption is anticipated. Specifically, a selling veteran must notify the mortgagee before the property is transferred. The mortgagee must then determine if the prospective buyer meets credit standards. If the selling veteran fails to notify the mortgagee before transferring the property, or if the property is transferred to a buyer who has failed the creditworthiness test, the lender has the right to accelerate the note. There exists a right of appeal for the selling veteran: Should the lender determine that the prospective buyer is not creditworthy, the seller has 30 days to appeal the decision. The nonveteran that assumes the loan must meet the same underwriting requirements as if a new VA loan were being made. If the VA overrides the lender's determination, the lender must then approve the assumption.

To protect the veteran and to make sure assumption requirements are fully disclosed, mortgage instruments underwritten after March 1,

1988, must show in capital letters on the first page the following sentence: "THIS LOAN IS NOT ASSUMABLE WITHOUT THE APPROVAL OF THE DEPARTMENT OF VETERANS AFFAIRS OR ITS AGENT."

A transfer fee of one-half of 1% of the balance due on the loan shall be payable at the time of transfer to the loan holder, or its authorized agent, as trustee for the secretary for the Department of Veterans Affairs. In the event the fee is not paid, it shall be added to the debt secured by this instrument.

FHA CASE STUDY/WORKSHOP

Your clients want to use FHA financing to purchase a home. They have asked you to help them look for a house. As a professional, you go through a short pre-qualification process to determine how much of a home they might qualify for based on their income and current recurring debt. The following is the information your clients provide:

- Yearly income as a salary is $60,000.
- Other monthly debt payments are $275.
- The client wants a home that will meet FHA's energy efficiency standards.
- Interest rates for a 30-year fixed-rate FHA mortgage are assumed to be 4.25%.
- Taxes and insurance on an average FHA mortgage loan in your county are running $255 a month.
- Since your client wants to use the minimum cash down and closing costs, you will assume about a $300-per-month annual MIP.

Requirement 1: Using the assumptions above, how much of a PI of the PITI can your client afford?

Requirement 2: How large a mortgage will the PI get on a 30-year fixed-rate mortgage at 4.25% interest?

Requirement 3: What would be your estimate of the UFMIP for this client to help them calculate estimated closing costs prior to them contacting a bank or mortgage company?

SUGGESTED SOLUTION TO FHA CASE STUDY

Requirement 1:

Client's annual gross income:	$60,000
Monthly gross income: $5,000	($60,000 ÷ 12 = $5,000)
Other monthly debt payments:	$275

Max. monthly housing expense: (MHE) plus other debt expense based on 45% Back-end debt-to-income ratio for FHA energy efficient homes:	$2,250 ($5,000 × 45% = $2,250)
Estimated max. monthly housing expense (principal, interest, property taxes, property insurance, mortgage insurance premium):	$1,975 ($2,250 − $275 [other monthly debt] = $1,975)
Estimated monthly property taxes and insurance:	$255
Estimated ongoing monthly FHA mortgage insurance premium:	$300
Estimated monthly mortgage payment:	$1,420

Requirement 2: Estimated mortgage amount for which the borrower qualifies (based on a 30-year fixed-rate mortgage with an interest rate of 4.250%) is approximately $285,400.

Requirement 3: $285,400 × 1.75% = $4,495.

VA CASE STUDY/WORKSHOP

Lois Marie Hazard, a qualified Navy veteran, is trying to decide if she can use her remaining eligibility of her VA loan benefits to purchase new home. Ms. Hazard knows she has used $27,500 of entitlement on a prior loan, which may not be restored, and wants to purchase a home for $320,000 where the county loan limit is $417,000.

Requirement 1: Assuming Ms. Hazard's credit and income will qualify for a loan of this type, can she still use her remaining entitlement to obtain a new VA mortgage loan?

Requirement 2: Ms. Hazard has stated that she has two children still to put through college and wants to use the least amount of cash to get into this new home. Will the VA loan or an FHA mortgage loan fulfill this requirement of cash conservation the best?

Requirement 3: If the PITI for the loan described above totaled $2,101, and the other monthly obligations of Ms. Hazard are $1,050, what would her monthly income need to be to qualify for the loan above?

SUGGESTED SOLUTION FOR VA CASE STUDY

Requirement 1: Answer: Yes, with a small down payment requirement.

$417,000 × 25% = $104,250	maximum VA loan guaranty
$104,250 – $27,500 = $76,750	VA loan entitlement available
$76,750 ÷ $320,000 = 23.98%	guaranty
$76,750 × 4 = $307,000	maximum loan amount with 25% guaranty

Since the VA loan's guaranty will be less than 25%, a down payment will be required.

$320,000 × 25% = $80,000
$80,000 – $76,750 = $3,250 down payment

Requirement 2: Since the minimum required investment that FHA now requires is 3.5%, or over $11,000, the down payment requirement of the VA loan meets Ms. Hazard's requirements better than an FHA loan.

Requirement 3: The $2,101 and the $1,050, and that would total $3,151, which would represent the maximum amount of monthly gross income that could represent 41% of the veteran's income. So $7,685 (obtained by dividing $3,151 by .41) represents the gross monthly income requirement that Ms. Hazard would have to demonstrate.

Questions for Discussion

1. How has the FHA achieved the goals for which it was established?
2. Explain the two different dollar limits that apply to HUD/FHA-insured commitments.
3. In HUD/FHA settlement requirements, what rules apply to the handling of the down payment? To the handling of the closing costs?
4. Explain the difference between loan underwriting commitments made by the VA and those made by HUD/FHA.
5. What charges must a borrower pay for a HUD/FHA-insured commitment?
6. How are interest rates determined on HUD/FHA loans? On VA loans?

7. What are the assumption requirements now in effect for HUD/FHA loans? For VA loans?
8. Distinguish between the release of liability for a veteran and the restoration of entitlement.
9. What is the purpose of the HUD/FHA 203(k) Rehabilitation Home Mortgage Insurance program?
10. What charges, if any, must a veteran pay for a loan guaranty?

Multiple Choice Questions for Review

1. What is the main purpose of FHA?
   a. to set standards for construction
   b. to insure residential mortgage loans made by individual or private lenders
   c. to set standards for underwriting
   d. to provide loans to borrowers

2. Which of the following best describes first-time home buyers' use of FHA loans?
   a. A borrower can qualify with no down payment and get cash at closing.
   b. It is the only loan for which a first-time home buyer can be approved.
   c. It has the lowest interest rates available on the market.
   d. It allows small down payments and has generous qualifying guidelines.

3. The statutory down payment requirements for an FHA loan are:
   a. 2%
   b. 3%
   c. 3.5%
   d. 5%

4. One of the differences between an FHA and a VA mortgage is the:
   a. down payment requirements
   b. application forms and addendums
   c. maximum loan origination fees
   d. all of these

5. An FHA borrower is:
   a. not allowed to pay discount points
   b. not required to make a down payment
   c. required to make minimum cash investment, which may include closing costs paid by the borrower in addition to the down payment
   d. required to make a minimum cash investment, which may include closing costs, discount points, and prepaid expenses

6. For a lower-income buyer with high debt ratios, a preferred loan choice would be a(n):
   a. conventional loan
   b. FHA loan
   c. REIT
   d. VA loan

7. Who is eligible for VA home loan benefits?
   a. U.S. military personnel
   b. honorably discharged veterans
   c. active military
   d. all of these

8. For which of the following reasons could a potential FHA borrower not utilize the 203(k) program?
   a. to move an existing home to a new foundation at a different location and ready it for use as a residence
   b. to purchase and rehabilitate an older home
   c. to purchase a tear-down and rebuild in its place
   d. to refinance an existing mortgage and roll in repairs that rehabilitate the home

9. Which of the following is a way that a veteran can have his or her entitlement restored and used again?
   a. The veteran's home was destroyed by a tornado.
   b. The previous loan was assumed by another veteran's widow.
   c. The veteran has been put on a work-release program.
   d. The veteran has sold his or her old home.

10. Can a VA loan still be obtained with no money down?
    a. no
    b. yes
    c. no, for a loan over $240,000
    d. yes, but the borrower may have to pay a funding fee unless he or she has a service-related disability

Information Resources

http://portal.hud.gov/hudportal/documents/huddoc?id=DOC_14599.pdf
   Additional information on the changes in the method of insuring a FHA condominium loan and how such loans are processed can be found at the Question and Answer HUD website above.

http://portal.hud.gov/portal/page/portal/HUD
   For definitive information on FHA programs, visit the official Department of Housing and Urban Development site.

http://www.benefits.va.gov/homeloans/
   The Veterans Administration has set up an excellent website for its Loan Guaranty Home Loan Program.

https://www.whatsmypayment.com/VA-Entitlement-Calculator/
   Questions about the calculation of VA loan guaranty amounts and how to calculate remaining available entitlement can be found at the URL above.

https://msc.fema.gov/portal/search
   Federal Emergency Management Agency flood maps can be found at the URL above.

http://portal.hud.gov/hudportal/documents/huddoc?id=13-26ml.pdf
   To find more about the FHA Back to Work program see the guidance in Mortgagee Letter 2013-26 that covers how this may be applied for borrowers that experienced extenuating circumstances related to an economic event.

Chapter 9

LENDER LOAN PROCESSES

KEY TERMS AND PHRASES

cost-of-living expenses (VA)
credit report
credit scoring
effective income
Equal Credit Opportunity Act (ECOA)
FHA new minimum credit scores
FICO
housing expense
income ratio method (VA)
loan application
percentage guideline method
principal, interest, taxes, and insurance (PITI)
private mortgage insurance (PMI)
ratio method (VA)
residual method (VA)
title insurance

LEARNING OBJECTIVES

At the conclusion of this chapter, students will be able to:
- Describe how the Equal Credit Opportunity Act was the first step towards equalizing the availability of credit.
- Understand similarities and differences in borrower qualification between Veterans Administration, primary FHA, and conventional mortgage loan programs.
- Describe how the application process differs between conventional, Veterans Administration and FHA residential mortgage loans, and commercial mortgage loans.

> - Identify how mortgage insurance has extended the residential mortgage market.
> - Understand the development of private mortgage insurance products and their current features.
> - Describe how a home equity revolving line of credit mortgage works.
> - Identify the need for title insurance and use of a title commitment.

INTRODUCTION

For the purpose of analysis, mortgage loans may be divided into two categories: those made to individuals and families to buy homes, and those made to individuals and companies to acquire commercial properties. Because the basic source of loan repayment is not the same, the analysis differs in emphasis. For a home loan, the analysis focuses first on the applicant's income. It is the buyer's personal income—essentially, income unrelated to the property itself—that will be used to repay the loan. For a commercial property loan, the lender normally expects repayment from income produced by the property, and that source takes priority in the analysis.

This chapter examines, first, the individual as a borrower for the purpose of buying a home. **Residential loans** comprise over two-thirds of the mortgage loan market and may be classed in four major categories: (1) insured by a government agency such as HUD/FHA, (2) having some complete or limited government-agency guaranty from an entity such as VA or RHS, (3) conventional/conforming, and (4) other conventional. (A conventional loan is one without government underwriting.) Of the four, both HUD/FHA and VA or RHS offer fairly clear standards and guidelines for the industry and the consumer.

The third category, conventional/conforming, covers loans made with the expectation of selling them to either Fannie Mae or Freddie Mac. Both of these secondary-market purchasers have developed uniform documents and some common limitations (but not always the same standards) on the loans they can accept.

The fourth category, other conventional, offers few uniform procedures with many minor variations, and includes those residential loans characterized as alternate A and subprime. The latter classifications of subprime and alternate A are a recent variation of a conventional loan originally designed to better fit the needs of lower-income families and will be explained later under the umbrella term of *affordable housing loan*. In sum, the field of loan

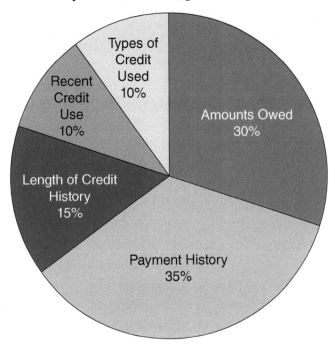

Source: © 2021 Mbition LLC

qualification does not offer standards used by everyone. (Some of the variations appear in table 9-1 later in this chapter.)

We will examine the similarities and the differences between the four major categories of borrower qualification in this chapter. Examples are given for each, using the same basic applicant's income and loan amount. Generally, the analyses arrive at similar conclusions but use slightly different methods to reach that point.

A requirement for all borrowers is to furnish a credit report, and we will examine the information found in these reports in this chapter. Also, we will discuss the qualification of corporate borrowers. Finally, because private mortgage insurance has become an essential part of mortgage lending practices, we will review this kind of underwriting.

Loan analysis begins with the loan application. Lenders no longer have the freedom to ask whatever questions they may wish of an applicant, for in the past this practice has led to some discriminatory lending practices. As a step toward reducing discrimination in all kinds of credit transactions, Congress passed the Equal Credit Opportunity Act, which had an important effect on mortgage lending procedures, as we will discuss next.

EQUAL CREDIT OPPORTUNITY ACT

The basis for analysis of a borrower is the loan application. As a step toward equalizing the availability of credit, the **Equal Credit Opportunity Act (ECOA),** passed in 1974, limits the information that may be required in an application. Questions that could lead to discriminatory lending practices have been eliminated, and new questions have been added that need only be answered on a voluntary basis. The Act was implemented under the direction of the Federal Reserve Board and is administered by the Consumer Affairs Office of the Federal Reserve.

Initially, the Act prohibited discrimination in the granting of credit on the basis of sex or marital status. On March 23, 1976, the ECOA was amended to expand the prohibition against discrimination in credit transactions by adding race, color, religion, national origin, age, receipt of public assistance income, and the exercise of rights under the Consumer Credit Protection Act, of which the ECOA is a part, as protected categories.

The restrictions covering information on sources of an applicant's income do not apply if the applicant expects to use that income as a means of repaying the loan. For example, no questions may be asked regarding alimony, child support, or separate maintenance payments *unless* the borrower plans to use this money to make the loan payments.

No discounting of income is allowed because of sex or marital status or because income is derived from part-time employment. In earlier years, it was not uncommon to discount the income of a wife of child-bearing age by as much as 50%. In regard to a credit history, an applicant must be permitted to show evidence that facts in a joint report do not accurately reflect his or her individual ability or inclination to repay the loan. If credit is denied, the lender must provide the reasons for denial upon request of applicant.

ECOA preempts only those applicable state laws that are inconsistent with the federal requirements. Lenders in states that may impose additional requirements, such as additional prohibitions on what may be in a loan application, must also comply with state laws. It should be noted that the requirement for separate liability for separate accounts (i.e., married persons can demand that separate credit records be maintained in either a married name or a maiden name) cannot be changed by state laws. However, any action taken by a creditor in accordance with state property laws directly or indirectly affecting creditworthiness will not constitute discrimination.

In general, the law does not specify how or to whom loans should be made, but does call for lenders to be much more specific with reasons for rejection of a loan applicant. Generalizations and categories of persons not eligible for credit are no longer permissible. For example, at one time a married person who was separated could be denied credit by lenders as a customary policy. Or a single person might not be accepted as a loan applicant. This kind of blanket denial is no longer permitted because each person must be considered as an individual and judged by the same standards.

There can be a difference in the standards that a lender may use for long-term mortgage credit as opposed to a short-term installment-type of credit, but the standards must be applied uniformly to all applicants.

THE LOAN APPLICATION

A mortgage **loan application** offers information for qualification of both the borrower and the property. If the loan is residential, as explained earlier, the information requested on an application must conform to the requirements of ECOA. For this purpose, the Federal Reserve has prepared model application forms for five different types of credit, one of which is residential real estate. On the basis of the Federal Reserve model, Fannie Mae and Freddie Mac designed their own standard form (FNMA 1003 and FHLMC 65, respectively). As the need for greater standardization developed, this form became mandatory for use after November 15, 1986, by all lenders with all residential loans. The latest revision, dated June 2009, appears in the appendix.

The information required in a residential loan application may be summarized as follows:

1. identification of borrower (and co-borrower)
2. cost of house, down payment, financing requested
3. employment and income data
4. anticipated monthly housing expenses
5. list of assets and liabilities
6. permission to obtain a credit report
7. details of the transaction, including an estimate of cash needed to close the loan
8. applicant's certification as to accuracy of information

Commercial Loan

If a loan is for commercial property, the lender is more likely to use its own application form because considerably more information is needed.

Further, federal laws regarding application information designed to better protect an individual generally do not apply to commercial loans.

Since most commercial loans are expected to be repaid from the property income, rather than from the borrower's personal income, specific information is needed on that property. An appraisal, market information with a review of competition, and substantial financial data on anticipated operations would be required. More detailed information on commercial loans will be considered in this chapter after the examination of residential loan qualification.

QUALIFYING THE BORROWER

All lenders have the same underwriting goal: a borrower capable of repaying the loan plus a property providing adequate collateral. As examined earlier in this chapter, more than income is involved in borrower qualification for a residential loan. This is only one of the elements that falls under "ability to pay," albeit a crucial one. Greater emphasis is being given to income qualification today, as it involves numbers that provide easier comparisons between applicants. Comparison between applicants is one method of screening the mortgage market for discriminatory practices.

A residential loan applicant's personal income is examined carefully since that is where the money will come from to repay the loan. Other obligations against that income must be weighed to determine if an additional burden can be undertaken. It does neither party—the lender nor the borrower—any good to place an overload of debt on a home buyer. Several different paths are used to reach a judgment on qualification, but in the final analysis, the decision has to be a judgment call. The decision can be made by a human underwriter or by a computer with a software program that uses artificial intelligence to evaluate the information submitted.

Following are explanations of the qualification guidelines—income and other measures—as applied to each of the four principal kinds of home loans: (1) HUD/ FHA, (2) VA and RHS, (3) conventional/conforming, and (4) other conventional loans, with special attention given to affordable housing loans. While each procedure is slightly different, the thrust is the same: to set a measure that limits other obligations to a percentage of the applicant's effective income. An underlying problem is defining what should be included as "other obligations."

HUD/FHA Borrower Income Qualification

HUD/FHA uses a percentage guideline method to measure the adequacy of an applicant's income. As part of an ongoing effort within the industry to standardize residential loan procedures, the measures used to qualify FHA loan applicants have been simplified and are now similar to those used for conventional loans.

Taxes, maintenance, and utilities are now considered payable from "residual income"—that income remaining after the required mandatory expenses have been deducted.

Percentage Guideline Method

The **percentage guideline method** considers an applicant's monthly liabilities in two separate categories and measures each amount against the applicant's effective income. The two categories and limits applied are as follows:

1. Housing expense should not exceed 31% of the applicant's effective income.
2. Housing expense plus other recurring charges are identified and should not exceed 43% of effective income.

How HUD/FHA defines the measures that are used is important. Following is a brief explanation of the major items considered.

Effective Income

This includes gross income from all sources, including borrower and co-borrower that can be expected to continue for the first three years of the mortgage. Even though an applicant's income has been properly verified, HUD/FHA reserves the right to adjust, or disallow, unacceptable income. A bonus or unusually large commission should be supported by a record of equivalent previous earnings. The owner of a business is allowed the amount he or she withdraws as salary, provided this amount does not exceed actual earnings. Money reimbursed for travel expenses cannot be accepted, nor can any repayment of principal on a capital investment. The HUD Handbook Section 4155.1 4.D.1.a defines "**effective income**" in detail, assisting with the understanding of how to handle more unique income sources. Examples of acceptable income sources, if verified, are rental property income, royalty income, or annuity payments.

PITI or Housing Expense

These expenses include the mortgage payment of principal, interest, real estate taxes, and hazard insurance, plus flood insurance if applicable. (In conventional loans, this payment is often identified simply as **PITI**.) The **housing expense** also includes the FHA annual premium charge and homeowners association or condo fees if applicable.

How might a real estate professional or loan officer easily explain the maximum PITI for which an applicant would qualify? She would multiply the applicant's effective or gross monthly income by the debt-to-income ratio described on the next few pages.

Example

Determine Maximum Debt Ratio

Borrower's Income	$6,000.00 monthly
Multiply by Total Debt Ratio	× 36%* (or actual amount)
Maximum Monthly Payments	$2,160.00**

* This is the maximum debt ratio for conventional residential mortgages.
** This is the maximum amount the borrower can afford for all monthly obligations.

A quick prequalification for a home buyer may be performed by learning the home buyer's nonhousing monthly debt and subtracting it from the $2,160 calculation to arrive at an amount that could approximate the PITI. This provides the amount of mortgage loan the borrower could afford and, thus, the price range of home for which the home buyer should be shopping.

Recurring Obligations

In addition to the monthly housing expense, when computing the debt-to-income ratios for recurring obligations the lender must include any additional recurring charges extending 10 months or more, such as:

- payments on installment accounts;
- child support or separate maintenance payments;
- revolving accounts; and/or
- alimony.

Debts lasting less than 10 months must be included if the amount of the debt affects the borrower's ability to pay the mortgage during the months immediately after loan closing, especially if the borrower will have limited or no cash assets after loan closing.

Monthly payments on revolving or open-ended accounts, regardless of the balance, are counted as a liability for qualifying purposes even if the account appears likely to be paid off within 10 months or less.

Fixed Payment

A *fixed payment* is an FHA-defined term that equals the sum total of the housing expense and the recurring charges (such as car payments and student loan payments) and is used in the calculation of the "back-end" or "debt" ratio covered later.

Residual Income

This is effective income minus fixed payment. Because residual income is affected by tax liabilities, Social Security deductions, and utility and maintenance expenses, HUD/FHA does not establish a required residual income amount as is found in VA procedures.

Ratios

The measure of adequacy is determined by ratios. Dividing the housing expense by the applicant's effective income determines a ratio. Housing expense, as defined earlier, should not exceed 31% of income (take PITI and divide it by gross effective income). The second ratio is for the total fixed payment. This ratio, obtained by dividing fixed payment by gross effective income, should not exceed 43% (also referred to as the back-end ratio or debt ratio).

These ratios are guidelines and subject to an underwriter's judgment. If compensating factors are present, the ratios may be exceeded. Table 9-1 describes the compensating factors that may be used to justify approval of mortgage loans with ratios that exceed FHA benchmark guidelines.

The underwriter must document the availability of potential employment.

The following simplified example serves to illustrate the key elements of an applicant's income qualification.

Example
Percentage Guideline—Monthly Basis

Gross effective income		$3,500
Housing expense		
Mortgage principal and interest	$695	
Taxes and insurance	180	
Total housing expense		$875
Recurring charges		
Car payment	$290	
Revolving account payments	170	
Total recurring charges		$460
Total fixed payment		$1,355
Ratios:		
Housing expense	855/3,500 = 25.6%	
Fixed payment	1,355/3,500 = 38.7%	

In this example, the housing expense or front-end ratio shows 25.6% of effective income, which falls within the HUD ceiling of 31%. The other measure—fixed payment or back-end ratio—shows a 38.7% ratio of effective income, which also falls within the HUD 43% guideline. If either exceeds the guidelines, the underwriter would look for other compensating factors that might justify the granting of an insurance commitment. For those borrowers who qualify under FHA's Energy Efficient Homes (EEH), the ratio is set at 33% for the front-end ratio and 45% for the back-end ratio (sometimes referred to as the debt-to-income ratio).

Borrower Rating

Income qualification alone is not the final determinant. One further judgment must be made by a HUD/FHA underwriter, and that is a *borrower rating*. An older method using a five-point gradient scale (from excellent to reject) has been replaced with only two grades: acceptable or rejection. A rejection on any one of the ratings is cause for denial of the loan commitment. The four elements that are rated are: (1) credit characteristics, (2) adequacy of effective income, (3) stability of effective income, and (4) adequacy of available assets.

RECENT ADDITIONAL CREDIT SCORE REQUIREMENTS FOR HUD/FHA

FHA Institutes Minimum Credit Scores and Loan-to-Value Ratios

The older construct of borrower rating has been affected due to the **FHA new minimum credit scores** and loan-to-value (LTV) ratio requirements for FHA-insured loans, effective March 1, 2011. In accordance with the final Federal Register Notice (FR-5404-N-02) on minimum decision credit scores and LTV ratios for FHA-insured single-family mortgages, the new requirements are now as follows:

- Borrowers with a minimum decision credit score at or above 580 are eligible for maximum financing.
- Borrowers with a minimum decision credit score between 500 and 579 are limited to 90% LTV.
- Borrowers with a minimum decision credit score of less than 500 are not eligible for FHA-insured mortgage financing.
- Borrowers with a nontraditional credit history or insufficient credit are eligible for maximum financing but must meet the underwriting guidance in HUD 4155.14.C.3.

- Borrowers using 203(h), Mortgage Insurance for Disaster Victims, are eligible for 100% financing and no down payment is required, provided that the borrowers have a minimum credit score of 500 (borrowers with decision credit scores below 500 are not eligible for FHA financing).

These new requirements are applicable to all single-family programs *except* Title I, home equity conversion mortgages; HOPE for Homeowners; Section 247; Section 248; Section 223(e); and Section 238.

It is important to note that for temporary *minimum credit scores* and LTV requirements for *refinancing* conventional mortgages, borrowers must meet all the requirements of that program and have a minimum credit score of 500.

By taking credit scores into consideration and using the four-element process in determining eligibility for FHA mortgages, underwriters no longer enjoy the same level of discretion in decision making that they had in the past.

VA BORROWER QUALIFICATION

In chapter 8, we discussed how the VA qualifies property offered as collateral, including the need to obtain a VA form 26-1843, Certificate of Reasonable Value, if the lender has not been approved by the VA for its Lender Appraisal Processing Program. This section examines the methods used by the VA to qualify an applicant who is a veteran. In addition to meeting the requirements for eligibility and entitlement stated in Chapter 8, the applicant must show an income adequate to repay the loan and have an acceptable credit record with other creditors. To qualify an applicant's income, the VA requires two separate sets of calculations. One, called the **residual method**, has been used for many years. The other, a procedure using income ratios, became effective October 1, 1986. Explanations, examples, and guidelines for each of the two methods follow.

Residual Method of Income Qualification

The VA's residual method of qualifying an applicant's income might be called a summation process. It starts with the applicant's *gross monthly income*, which means gross pay before any deductions are taken. Then, mandatory deductions start with the applicant's monthly tax liabilities, continue with shelter expenses and other fixed obligations, and result in what the applicant has left. What remains after the applicable mandatory obligations have been deducted is called *residual income*. How the VA underwriter defines the various items is discussed next.

Gross Income

The recognized income of both borrower and spouse are combined; that income should have a reasonable expectation of continuing.

Tax Liabilities

The applicant's tax liabilities include federal and state income taxes, Social Security tax, and any other tax liabilities that may be due. The amount of tax is based on that shown by tax tables applicable to an applicant's recognized income and may not be the same as what the taxpayer pays. Tax liabilities are deducted from the gross income, resulting in the applicant's net take-home pay. Take-home pay is not a critical number with the VA because it is not used as a basis for qualification.

Shelter Expenses

For the residual method only, the VA adds certain shelter expenses not found in either FHA or conforming loan qualification calculations. In addition to the standard mortgage payment (principal, interest, taxes, and insurance, or PITI) and any special assessments, the VA adds estimated costs of maintenance and utilities for the house to be acquired. (These two expenses are not included in the VA's income ratio method.) The costs of maintenance and utilities are developed by the VA Regional Office from experience with various neighborhoods.

Other Monthly Obligations

Under other monthly obligations, the VA lists installment obligations (such as a car payment) with six or more monthly payments still due, revolving account payments, alimony and/or child support, and job-related expenses (such as union dues). If the applicant is obligated for other state and local taxes or life insurance premiums, these should also be listed.

Residual Income

After deducting the taxes, shelter expenses, and other monthly obligations from the applicant's gross monthly income, what remains is called *residual income*. For qualification, the residual income must be sufficient to cover the applicant's required *minimum residual income*. The minimum residual income is a cost-of-living amount that varies by region, by family size, and loan amount. It is adjusted periodically by the VA to meet changing conditions.

Cost of Living Expense

Unlike any other underwriting procedure, the VA residual method uses a calculated figure for determining the **cost of living expense**. These costs include food, clothing, transportation, personal and medical care, and other consumption items. Since 1986, these costs have been determined by the standards for the four Census Bureau regions: West, South, Midwest, and Northeast. The actual figures are developed by the VA from Department of Labor data on consumer expenditure surveys.

The applicant's residual income (what remains after total monthly obligations have been deducted) must be sufficient to cover the applicable cost of living amount. Whatever remains of the applicant's income after total obligations and cost of living expenses are deducted is called *excess residual income*. The "excess," if any, may be used to help qualify marginal applicants, as shown below.

Example

Residual Guideline Method: Monthly Basis

Gross salary or earnings		$3,000
LESS:		
Federal income tax	330	
Social Security tax	205	
Total tax liabilities		535
Net take-home pay		2,465
LESS:		
Principal and interest	660	
Realty taxes	105	
Hazard insurance	60	
Maintenance	55	
Utilities	125	
Total monthly shelter expenses		1,005
LESS:		
Installment obligation	240	
State and local taxes	90	
Total other obligations		330
Applicant's residual income		$1,130

If the applicant in the example is a family of two living in the South region and the loan amount is less than $79,999, the minimum required residual (see VA website for residual income limits by region at http://www.benefits.va.gov/warms/pam26_7.asp; click on chapter 4, and look starting on pages 4–56) amounts to $738. The applicant's residual income of $1,300 is adequate to meet the requirements. It may be worth noting that the VA process favors single people and small families. By applying the cost of living table as family size increases, an applicant is less likely to qualify.

Excess Residual Income

There is one more piece of information to be derived from this method of calculation, and that is how much the applicant's residual income exceeds the minimum required amount. To continue using the same example, the *required* residual amounted to $738. Subtracting that amount from the applicant's residual income of $1,300 leaves an "excess residual" of $562 ($1,300 minus $738 equals $562). It is not the amount, but the ratio, that is significant. To find this ratio, divide the applicant's excess residual by the minimum required residual. The result is the *excess residual ratio*. In the preceding example, dividing $562 by $738 gives a ratio of .76, or 76%. This ratio fits into the qualification measure if there is a problem with the income ratio qualification calculation. If the excess residual ratio is 20% or greater, the applicant may still qualify even though the income ratio guidelines are not met. The income ratio method of calculation is explained next.

QUALIFYING THE COLLATERAL

Qualifying the Property

The FHA requires an appraisal to be made of property offered as collateral by one of its staff appraisers or by an FHA-approved fee appraiser. Following are the distinctions made for four basic categories of property:

- **proposed construction** (To qualify, plans and specifications are submitted to HUD/FHA prior to the start of construction. If found acceptable, the approved plans and specifications are certified and returned to the mortgagee.)
- **low-ratio properties** (For loans of 90% of the value, not approved by HUD or VA prior to construction and not covered by an acceptable warranty plan, and for properties that are less than one year old at the date of application, HUD requires an appraisal by its own staff or a HUD-assigned fee appraiser to determine the value.)

- **existing construction** (Property completed at least one year prior to the date of application must be appraised by a staff appraiser or a fee appraiser assigned by HUD/FHA.)
- **warranty plan** (If a property is covered by a warranty plan approved by HUD, a conditional commitment by HUD/FHA or a VA CRV (certificate of reasonable value) may be used to qualify the property.

Property Value

HUD/FHA defines *proper value*—that is, the value of the house and land—as the lesser of the FHA-appraised value or the purchase price. Since it is possible for an earnest money contract to be signed prior to making an appraisal, the value in an appraisal can be different from the agreed-upon price. Should the appraised value be *less* than the agreed-upon price, FHA rules permit a buyer to withdraw from the earnest money contract (unilaterally rescind it) and recover the earnest money in full. Or, should the buyer prefer, the purchase can be consummated at the contract price, but any amount paid over the appraised value must be in cash. The amount of the loan is calculated as a percentage of the appraised value in such a case. Another frequently used option is to renegotiate the contract to reflect the appraised value.

Determining Value

HUD/FHA appraisals are made in the same manner as other appraisals, with possibly one slight difference: Because of the volume of FHA activity, the agency retains substantial records of previous transactions that can be used for making good comparisons with other sales. HUD field offices can usually quote a current value per square foot of house in most of its neighborhoods.

However, the FHA has the same problem as the VA and conventional loan underwriters, with the impact of seller loan buydowns on the price of a house that may be used as a comparable. Over a period of time, it is quite possible for a home builder to offer an attractive buydown for a loan, add its costs to the price of the house, and develop an inflated "market value" that could be used as a sale comparable. HUD/FHA addresses this problem in two steps: (1) all appraisals must now include as additional information the amount of loan discount when the house was acquired, and (2) excessive buydowns must be deducted from the value of any house used as a comparable.

> ### Example
>
> Say that a $200,000 loan was made to the homeowner with an eight-point discount and buydown tied in. Say that in the region involved, the FHA considers anything over five points to be "excessive." This would mean that three points, amounting to $6,000 of the $200,000 loan amount, is considered a reduction in the sales price for that property. Thus, if the listed sale price had been $218,000, its true price for use as a comparable would be $212,000 ($218,000 minus $6,000 equals $212,000).

Scope of Appraisal

The HUD/FHA appraisal contains other important information. In addition to placing a dollar value on the property, an appraiser also determines what repairs may be needed to restore the property to acceptable FHA standards. Special inspections may be called for to examine the roofing, plumbing, electrical system, heating/air conditioning system, and water heater.

If deficiencies are found, the property must be brought up to standard before the loan can be funded. The seller may make the repairs or, in some cases, the buyer may do the work as part of the buyer's cash contribution—a "sweat equity" contribution.

In 1995, HUD advised its underwriters to delete "conditions that have little or nothing to do with safety or soundness of the property" from repair requirements stipulated by an appraiser.

Qualifying the Property

The VA uses both its own staff and approved independent fee appraisers to inspect and evaluate property that may serve as loan collateral. While the appraisal form has been standardized (see appendix for an illustration), the VA refers to its appraisal analysis as a certificate of reasonable value (CRV). A CRV represents the maximum amount a lender may loan and still obtain an underwriting guarantee from the VA. A veteran may purchase a house at a price exceeding the CRV, but any amount in excess of the CRV must be paid in cash. Or, if the CRV comes in at less than the agreed price, the veteran has the right to withdraw from the contract and recover the earnest money in full.

The requirements mentioned are for VA qualification and are not necessarily the same as a lender might require. Lenders are not required to make a loan at the VA-permissible limits. Simply put, a lender cannot exceed those limits and still obtain a VA guaranty. But if the lender's policy is more limited than that allowed by the VA, the lender is free to apply its own limitations and still obtain a VA guaranty commitment. For instance, many lenders will not accept 100% loan-to-value loans regardless of VA permission. Nevertheless, so long as the loan does not exceed VA limits, the guaranty can be issued. The same concept applies to all other underwriting programs—FHA, GNMA, and all conforming loans—and the lender is free to offer a loan at lower than the designated limits and may still qualify the loan for whatever underwriting program is sought. The point is that loan applicants should not expect government agency maximum limitations to be uniformly accepted by all private lenders.

Scope of the VA Appraisal

Like the HUD/FHA appraisal procedure discussed earlier in this chapter, there are other pieces of information needed beyond the property evaluation. The VA is the only agency that still requires information on the maintenance and utility costs of the house to be acquired. Both of these costs are considered in an applicant's income qualification under the residual guideline method, as more fully described in the next chapter. And like the FHA, VA appraisers are expected to make the necessary adjustments in valuation that will more closely reflect the property's real value rather than an inflated value caused by excessive financial inducements.

The appraiser's responsibility extends to inspecting the property to make sure that it meets VA minimum property standards. If not, repairs may be required to upgrade the property before the loan can be funded.

COMMERCIAL LOANS

As explained earlier, commercial loans follow a different pattern than residential loans. In most instances, repayment of the loan is expected from the property's income rather than from the borrower's personal income. A creditworthy borrower is still important, but greater emphasis is placed on the property. Furthermore, commercial loans are made primarily to businesses rather than individuals, and detailed financial statements are normally required. These are scrutinized as to the company's profitability and the accumulation of assets over a period of time. Ownership of the company must be examined and information submitted on the principal owners and/or officers and directors. A loan agreement is usually required that spells out certain limitations on the company's operations during the term of the loan. Even though quite different, like all loans, the process for obtaining a commercial loan begins with a loan application.

Commercial Loan Application

No consumer-based protective restrictions on what questions may be asked apply to commercial loan applications. Lenders may develop their own forms to fulfill their need for information since there are no standards. This is one of the reasons why commercial lenders often specialize in the kind of loans they will undertake. Knowledge of a particular kind of property and the business operation involved is crucial to making sound commercial loans. So knowing what kind of information is necessary is reflected in the questions on the application.

The general areas of information covered in a commercial loan application may be listed as follows:

1. company name, address, and business structure
2. information on owners or corporate officers and directors
3. name of contact person
4. purpose of the loan requested
5. financial statements for past three to five years, including a balance sheet, a profit and loss statement (P&L), and a pro forma statement showing the impact of the loan on profitability
6. names of suppliers and banks for credit references
7. appraisal of the property to be pledged as collateral
8. an environmental assessment of the property
9. possibly a feasibility study if project is new construction

The listed information above would suffice for a preliminary review of the loan application, but more detail may be required later.

With commercial loans, it is normal for a lender to require an upfront charge to review the application. Some set a rather high fee for new applicants simply to discourage frivolous requests. All costs of information are paid by the borrower.

The review necessary for a commercial loan can be very broad, covering management, sales, production, purchasing, research and planning, and personnel policies, plus the physical plant and equipment. The loan underwriter expects to have current, preferably audited, financial statements presented with the loan application. An *audited statement* is one in which all pertinent data are verified by the certified public accountant preparing the report.

When examining a financial statement, the underwriter looks for a record of profitable use of existing assets; the accumulation of cash, property, and other assets versus outstanding obligations; and the very important working ratio of current assets to current liabilities. A favorable ratio would be at least $2 of assets for every $1 of liabilities. The ratio indicates both the manner of operation and the immediate cushion of assets available to protect the company against a temporary reversal.

Creditworthiness of a commercial loan applicant can be determined by contacting the firm's suppliers and bank references (an applicant's permission is required to do so). Also, various credit reporting agencies are sources of commercial credit information. One of the largest is Dun & Bradstreet, which can provide something of a history on some companies as well as a credit rating.

Where Are We Now?

Qualifying a Commercial Loan: The Wistful Vista Apartments

Pro Forma

Gross scheduled	$1,200,000
Vacancy and credit loss (5%)	60,000
Adjusted gross income	1,140,000
Operating expenses	684,000
Net operating income (NOI)	456,000
Debt coverage ratio (DCR) required by lender for apartments of this quality	1.20
Loan constant (K) for this type of loan	7.25%

Debt service (DS) = NOI/DCR = 456,000/1.2 = 380,000

Maximum loan amount = DS/K = 380,000/.0725 = 5,241,379

$5,240,000 (rounded)

To evaluate the results of the loan on the company's finances, it is customary to prepare pro forma statements: both a balance sheet and a profit and loss statement. These statements are a projection of what the loan will do for the company—such as enable it to increase the investment in productivity, add a new product line, provide an additional service, or enter a new market—as well as an estimate of the expected effects on profitability. It is the long-range ability of a company to operate profitably that is the real key to the trouble-free recovery of a loan.

Loan Agreement

Since the ownership and/or management of a company may change during the term of a commercial loan, a separate agreement is usually a part of the loan commitment. The agreement may state how the proceeds of a loan are to be used and can provide penalties for noncompliance. In addition, certain restrictive covenants are often added that limit company policies during the term of the loan. These would include such actions as loans or advances to officers or employees, control over the amount of salary increases, restrictions on the payment of dividends, and limits on any other borrowing. Furthermore, the agreement might require lender approval before any major assets, patents, or leasehold interests could be sold. All terms of a loan agreement are negotiable and are designed primarily to protect a lender's interest in the company until the loan is repaid in full.

PRIVATE MORTGAGE INSURANCE

Many, many years ago, in the jargon of the mortgage industry, an "insured loan" was simply another name for either an FHA or VA loan. These government-backed insurance programs created a standardization of loan practices and uniform documentation that produced loans readily salable to investors throughout the country. Investors knew in advance what they were buying. Conventional loans—those not covered by government insurance—were not standardized; they remained localized in their procedures and documentation for many years.

During that time period, the lack of standardization was no big handicap because prior to the 1980s, major funding for conventional loans was found in local savings associations and a few banks. As this source of funds declined in the early 1980s, the need for alternate sources to fund conventional loans helped fuel the growth in **private mortgage insurance**. As sources of funds became national, and thus further removed from the geographic location of a mortgage loan, the need for protection against loan defaults increased.

History of Private Mortgage Insurance

The idea of writing an insurance policy to protect a lender against loss in the event of loan default began with the creation of the Federal Housing Administration in 1934. It was not until the 1950s that several entrepreneurs began testing the market for private default insurance coverage for conventional loans. Progress was slow at first, as few lenders required the coverage; after all, if an insured loan was needed, one could simply contact the FHA or VA.

It was not until 1971 that private mortgage insurance became a requirement for higher-ratio conventional loans. In that year, regulatory authorities expanded lending limits for conventional residential loans and required the use of default insurance coverage. The new limits allowed federally chartered savings and loan associations to make loans up to 95% of the appraised value of a house, compared with 90% previously, provided that loans over 90% were insured. The result was a tremendous growth in private mortgage insurance.

One major pioneering insurance company, Mortgage Guaranty Insurance Corporation (MGIC, called "Magic"), based in Milwaukee, increased its loan coverage volume from almost nothing in 1970 to $7.5 billion in 1972, with about 40% in 95% loans. The private sector topped the FHA coverage in that year and retained its lead until the financial crisis beginning in 2008.

By the end of the 1970s, private mortgage insurance companies had become popular growth companies on the nation's stock markets. More growth meant higher stock values, and many companies overlooked loan quality in the competitive surge for more premium income. The fallout came in 1982 and 1983 when loss ratios increased dramatically due to more foreclosures. A few companies withdrew from the mortgage insurance market, but most tightened their loan qualification requirements and raised premium rates to rebuild their resources, a strategy that was effective until the industry's recent test, the most difficult since the Great Depression, when all private mortgage insurers failed, as discussed in Chapter 5.

Private Mortgage Insurance Companies

The very specialized nature of default risk has limited the number of companies offering this kind of coverage. The insurance companies work through various loan originators to sell their coverage. The originator must meet company requirements to be designated as an agent. Agents obtain the necessary qualifying information from a loan applicant for submission to the insurance company underwriter.

Qualifying Information Required

Loan originator/agents use information taken from a borrower's application to prepare a request for coverage to the private mortgage insurance company. The decision to approve or disapprove is made by the insurance company's own underwriters. The insurance company relies on loan originators to submit complete and accurate information on an applicant because response time is fast—within 24 hours—allowing no time for verification. A request for coverage includes submitting: (1) a copy of the loan application, (2) a property appraisal made by an approved appraiser, (3) a credit report on the borrower, (4) several verifications, and (5) any other data helpful in analyzing the loan.

Amount of Coverage Offered

While private mortgage insurers, FHA, and VA all offer protection against the same risk of default, the amount of coverage differs. HUD/FHA insures 100% of the loan amount, while the VA guarantees only a portion of the loan. Private mortgage insurance carriers issue a variety of policies for residential loans that range from a low of 12% of the loan amount insured to a high of 35%. For example, a 12% insurance commitment limits the insurer to paying only 12% of the original loan amount should default occur.

Term of PMI

Furthermore, there is a difference in the term of insurance coverage. HUD/FHA and VA offer their commitments for the life of a loan, while private mortgage insurers limit their coverage to a shorter term of years. The range varies from three to 15 years. This means that insurance coverage would terminate at the end of the term regardless of the balance due on the loan.

Types of Property that Can Be Covered

Private mortgage insurance is available for a greater variety of property than with government programs. Residential loans that can be insured include primary residences, second or leisure homes, multifamily properties, mobile homes (if permanently secured and classed as real estate by state law), and modular housing. Commercial loan coverage is available for hotels, motels, shopping centers, office buildings, warehouses, and others. The loans may be participation loans, loans secured by junior liens, and seller-financed mortgages. Each insurance company may set its own standards for the loans it will cover, as there are no national requirements.

Premiums Charged

Because private mortgage insurance usually covers less than the full amount of a loan for a shorter term, the premiums are less than those found with a HUD/FHA loan. As a type of insurance, PMI comes under the regulation of state insurance commissions in those states with that kind of authority. These states determine insurance premiums, including PMI, as a protective measure for their citizens. The state in which the property is located controls.

Premiums on PMI may be paid as a single premium at time of closing or in installments as an annual premium plan. The premium amount is expressed as a percentage of the original loan amount, measured in "points." If the premium is paid in installments, the charge is simply added to the interest rate.

Because they are a type of insurance, it has been customary to treat PMI premiums the same as other insurance charges—that is, to require two months' worth of premiums to be paid at closing, plus the cost for one year placed in escrow. By 1993, competition had brought a change in this policy. In an effort to reduce the up-front cash requirement for some loans, several companies began offering to drop the one-year escrow requirement and make charges only on a monthly basis.

Up until 2007, the premiums charged for PMI were not deductible from individuals' federal or state income tax returns if they had sufficient itemized deductions to include a Schedule A with their IRS Form 1040. For loans originated in 2006, the federal government, as a way to discourage piggyback mortgage exposure to the GSE, allowed premiums to be tax-deductible for those mortgages made in 2007. This provision was set to expire after one year, but it has been extended to cover loans made in 2007 through 2014 as an allowed deduction through 2014, and seems to be renewed annually since it was to have expired in 2011. The homeowner will usually find the amount of private mortgage insurance premiums shown in Box 4 of Form 1098.

Cancellation of PMI Coverage

The normal PMI policy has allowed for payment of premiums for the life of the loan. This has been true even though the coverage may no longer be needed. Lenders have been able to legally collect premiums even though Fannie Mae, for one, has had a rule that allows dropping the insurance when a mortgage balance is paid down to 80% of the original value of the property. A U.S. district court ruled in 1996 that the Fannie Mae rule is a set of instructions from a lender/principal to a servicer/agent, not a contract between borrower and lender.

Federal legislation passed in 1998, effective July 29, 1999, changed this policy. The law exempts FHA and VA loans and does not preempt any state statutes in effect before January 2, 1998. Lenders are required to notify consumers of their right to cancel PMI when the equity in their homes reaches 20%, if requested by the borrower. In addition, the law provides for automatic cancellation of PMI when the loan reaches 78% of the original LTVR for a conventional loan with private mortgage insurance. FHA has its own new statutes, as discussed in chapter 8, effective since HUD Mortgagee Letter 13-4 was issued. To cancel the MIP for FHA mortgages, the following criteria must be met:

- Loans with terms less than or equal to 15 years and LTVs of less than or equal to 78% require MIP in place for 11 years.
- Loans with terms less than or equal to 15 years and LTVs of greater than 78% or less than 90% require MIP in place for 11 years.
- Loans with terms less than or equal to 15 years and LTVs of 90% or greater require MIP in place until to the end of the loan term, or when it is paid off.
- Loans with terms greater than 15 years and LTVs of less than or equal to 78% require MIP in place for 11 years.
- Loans with terms greater than 15 years and LTVs of greater than 78% or less than 90% require MIP in place for 11 years.
- Loans with terms greater than 15 years and LTVs of 90% or greater require MIP in place until the end of the loan term, or when it is paid off.

Private Mortgage Insurance

Who Determines the Need for PMI?

The answer is lenders, not borrowers. The need is based on risk: the larger the down payment, the lower the risk. A general rule of lenders is that loans with 20% or more down payment (80% loan-to-value) are not required to carry PMI. (The federal regulator limit is that loans over 90% loan-to-value must carry PMI.)

In practice, the borrower has little voice in the selection of coverage or the insurance carrier, as that decision is made by the loan originator. This is because it is the lender who is protected by the insurance, not the borrower. What the borrower gains is an easier qualification for perhaps a larger loan and a lower down payment than might otherwise be available.

PMI Obligations in the Event of Foreclosure

Even though PMI coverage is limited to a percentage of the loan amount, insurance companies have generally followed a practice of reimbursing the lender in full on a mortgage loan should foreclosure become necessary. By taking title to the foreclosed property, the insurance company relieves a lender of any further problems. This is one of the settlement options offered by PMI carriers. The purpose, of course, is to make the insurance coverage more competitive in a market that places a high value on service. As foreclosure problems escalated in some parts of the country, many insurers were forced to limit their exposure to the legal obligation contained in the insurance contract—that is, to reimburse the lender for the amount of the loan actually covered.

Lenders and borrowers should be assured that the mortgage insurance companies with which they do business are highly rated both from a financial standpoint and from a claims paying ability. The recent financial crisis has seen the demise of several large private mortgage insurance firms as a result of the large number of failed mortgages and lower market price of residential real estate during that time. Many of the companies taken over by their state insurance regulators have only paid a percentage of legitimate claims made. Investors that counted on the insurance to shield them from losses failed.

Indemnification Clause

Another obligation often overlooked, and not very well understood by borrowers, is the indemnification clause in many private mortgage insurance policies. What this clause means is that if the insurance company suffers a loss in the settlement of a claim with a lender (when the loan balance due exceeds the value of the property), the borrower is liable for reimbursement of the loss. Remember, the insurance protects the lender against loss. And unlike many other kinds of insurance, the insurance company holds the borrower responsible for repayment of any loss. While the indemnification clause is clearly stated in the body of policies, it is not usually carefully explained to a possibly unwary borrower. However, recovery of such a loss against a borrower/debtor who has just lost his or her home is not always feasible.

REVIEW OF SAMPLE CREDIT REPORT

Credit Scoring

The increased use of computer analysis has brought greater use of credit scoring to mortgage lending. Credit scoring is the assignment of a numerical rating to consumers based on their credit history. Credit scores continue to have a rising influence by residential mortgage lenders, auto lenders, credit card issuers, and other extenders of credit. Credit scoring is calculated by credit bureaus using information from one or more of the three major credit repositories: Equifax, Experian, and TransUnion. Therefore, they can report different ratings.

As mentioned in previous chapters, a **credit score** is a snapshot that objectively assesses a borrower's credit history and current usage at a given point in time based on credit bureau reports. An individual borrower's credit score may vary somewhat across repositories if there are differences in the amount or content of information contained in credit records. A credit score may be generated even if a repository's file includes only one tradeline, so lenders try to make sure that multiple files are included, probably at least three.

While credit scoring has recently received publicity, it is not a new phenomenon. One of the principal procedures was begun in 1956 by Fair, Isaac, and Company of San Rafael, California, and is known as **FICO**. What has brought credit scoring into wider usage is its easy adaptability to computerized loan analysis. The "score" is a number that shows a person's credit history and helps in the analysis of a borrower's probability of paying off another loan. Or, as some lenders interpret, the score is indicative of the risk of foreclosure.

Today, credit scoring is offered using two major methods. Both are approved and recommended for use with either manual or automated underwriting of mortgage loans. Both have shown a good predictive power in loan analysis. One is the FICO "bureau scores" that run from about 350 to 900, with the *lower* number showing the greater risk of default. Scores over 660 will generally have credit histories acceptable to Fannie Mae, but 660 is not a cutoff point and lower scores can be approved. Freddie Mac recommends a cautious and detailed review for loan files that score less than 660 but not less than 620. The recent credit crisis has uncovered some weaknesses in employing too great a reliance on the credit score. The first of several alternatives was developed in 2011, called VantageScore 2.0®. VantageScore 2.0® has worked as it was intended, which was to have the ability to score a broad population, including those who use credit infrequently.

The VantageScore® was created by a joint venture with the three major credit reporting companies: (1) Experian, (2) Equifax, and (3) TransUnion. It has been widely adopted as a credit scoring engine by combining cutting-edge, patented, and patent-pending analytic techniques to produce a model that offers more consistency across bureau platforms, along with the ability to score a broader population. This new lending ecosystem brings with it a revitalized emphasis on:

- model governance to ensure regulatory compliance;
- consumer education, transparency, and inclusive lending practices;
- controlled growth that balances expansion with risk mitigation; and
- agile and flexible operational processes without single-threaded dependencies.

The credit reporting industry has begun to embrace a single model across all three credit reporting companies, hoping that it will reduce credit score variances. In addition, VantageScore utilizes easier-to-understand reason codes to indicate why a consumer's credit score is not higher. The latest new credit scoring engine is VantageScore 4.0®. It will include some new features, like accounts that were collected and that have been reported as paid in full will no longer factor into the calculation. Explanations and methods for resolving them are described. (See the sample credit tri-merged report in the appendix of the text.)

Suppressed for several years by the financial crisis of the late 2000s, savings and loans, credit unions, credit card companies, and other financial institutions have seen increased demand for loans. Improvements in scoring approaches encapsulate a wider consumer population concurrent with reevaluation of credit policies to prevent past errors and provide orderly growth.

Credit scoring is used in conjunction with many other criteria, such as an applicant's income, other assets, total indebtedness, and future possibilities. It is only one criterion, and though it shows good predictive powers, it is seldom used by itself for underwriting purposes. It has been a big help in setting prices for subprime loans.

A number of other factors enter into judging a person's creditworthiness; scoring is just one.

For a detailed walk-through of a typical credit report, with explanations from the issuer, browse to https://www.experian.com/blogs/ask-experian/credit-education/report-basics/understanding-your-experian-credit-report/ and take the time now to review the detailed sample. Each page begins with a description of what you will see. There is also a sample three-party credit report included in the appendix of this text.

REVIEW OF UNIFORM RESIDENTIAL LOAN APPLICATION

Most of you will be using a loan origination package or a proprietary employer-based computerized loan application that will print off a copy for you to have your client sign, after you have entered all the information necessary. A cautionary note—systems fail, computers crash, and internet connections can temporarily stop communicating. When you make your living as a residential mortgage lender, you will need to know how to fill out a manual paper application. Remember all Uniform Residential Loan Applications must be filled out completely and legibly. Loan officers and loan processors should know that most of the information listed on the URAR form is required. Submission of the URAR without the requested and optional information completely filled in with correct dates, account numbers, addresses, Social Security numbers, etc., will normally cause a delay in the processing or underwriting of the applications, resulting in a delay in closing (not good for customer relationships) and delays in being paid for your work.

The good thing is that Fannie Mae's Uniform Residential Loan Application lists all the information it requires. The bad news is it can be nine pages in length. Lenders should give a broad explanation of each section of the application to the applicant before starting and fill in the details during the interview.

With the introduction of the first new Uniform Residential Loan Application in January 2019, nine years after the last revision, you would explain that the following sections will need to be completed:

- **Section 1: Borrower Information** collects the personal information, income, and employer of the borrower and co-borrower (if any).
- **Section 2: Financial Information – Assets and Liabilities** collects information about a borrower's financial assets, personal financial obligations, and debts the borrower owes.
- **Section 3: Financial Information – Real Estate** collects information about property a borrower may own, along with debts and expenses related to the property.
- **Section 4: Loan and Property Information** collects information about the loan purpose and the property the borrower is buying or refinancing.
- **Section 5: Declarations** asks specific questions about the property, how the property will be financed, and the borrower's past financial history.
- **Section 6: Acknowledgments and Agreements** informs the borrower of their legal obligations related to the mortgage application, and provides the borrower with an acknowledgment that certain information will be obtained, used, and shared.
- **Section 7: Demographic Information** requests information the lender is required by law to ask the borrower.
- **Section 8: Loan Originator Information** provides the borrower with information about the loan originator.

Compliance topics to remember from Regulation B:

- Do not discourage an applicant from completing an application, even if a prequalification review shows they most likely would not qualify and the prospective borrower insists on going on with the completion of an application.
- Do not discriminate on a prohibited basis.
- Remember the limitations of questions that can be asked, such as marital status.
- Remember that the application should use only terms that are neutral as to sex, except in government monitoring section of the URLA. Note: A borrower can choose to request that the lender use a

courtesy title (Mr., Mrs. etc.) in correspondence, but the applicant must first be told that the designation of such a title is at their option, not a requirement of the lender.

- Remember not to exclude any income on a prohibited basis, or income because of its source (retirement income, part-time work, public assistance, etc.).
- Ask prospective mortgage applicants to sign a Borrower's Signature Authorization (see a copy on page XX) to allow you to access their credit. While a signed Uniform Residential Loan Application will give this permission, it is necessary to have this information at hand while taking the application.

While the following sections will provide some appropriate reminders of things to remember by section when filling out the application, they are suggestions, not an all-inclusive list. A lender needs to commit the federal, state, and local compliance regulations to memory and actively maintain that knowledge through continued reading and education about any changes.

The Top Section and Section I of the URLA are displayed with detailed explanations below.

Section 1: Borrower Information

To be completed by the Lender: Lender Loan No./Universal Loan Identifier 7654321 (1)		Agency Case No. GFF-1234567 (2)

Uniform Residential Loan Application

Verify and complete the information on this application. If you are applying for this loan with others, each additional Borrower must provide information as directed by your Lender.

Section 1: Borrower Information. This section asks about your personal information and your income from employment and other sources, such as retirement, that you want considered to qualify for this loan.

1a. Personal Information

Name (First, Middle, Last, Suffix) Jose Fernando Andrews (3)	Social Security Number 123 - 45 - 6789 (or Individual Taxpayer Identification Number)
Alternate Names – List any names by which you are known or any names under which credit was previously received (First, Middle, Last, Suffix) Jose Andrews	Date of Birth (mm/dd/yyyy) 04 / 01 / 1961 ⦿ U.S. Citizen ○ Permanent Resident Alien ○ Non-Permanent Resident Alien
○ I am applying for **Individual credit.** (4) ⦿ I am applying for **Joint credit.** Total Number of Borrowers: 2 Each Borrower intends to apply for joint credit. *Your Initials:* ___	List Name(s) of Other Borrower(s) Applying for this Loan (First, Middle, Last, Suffix) Luci Mae Andrews
Marital Status ⦿ Married (5) ○ Separated ○ Unmarried* *Single, Divorced, Widowed, Civil Union, Domestic Partnership, Registered Reciprocal Beneficiary Relationship	**Dependents** (not listed by another Borrower) Number 2 Ages 8 & 10	**Contact Information** Home Phone (804) 555 - 1212 (6) Cell Phone (804) 555 - 2121 Work Phone (804) 555 - 5557 Ext.___ Email jfandrews111@gmail.com

(1) The lender's case number will be filled in by the loan processor, unless it is provided at the time of application from the lender's automated loan origination system.

(2) The agency case number field will be filled in if the loan has been assigned by FHA, VA, or RHS.

(3) Fill out all borrower contact and identification information, including verified Social Security number, marital status (notice that these comply with ECOA), DOB (date of birth) in MM/DD/YYYY format, and the borrower's current status as a citizen or other category must be filled out. Most permanent resident aliens will not be barred from borrowing and few nonpermanent resident aliens might be barred from some types of mortgages due to enforceability on diplomatic personnel of a foreign embassy.

A lender cannot refuse to extend credit due to life, or accident/health insurance not being carried or its lack of availability due to the applicant's age.

(4) Should there be more than one borrower, information for the co-borrower(s) will be required for the application as well. A spouse or a relative typically provides the information; should the borrowers not be related (except in the rare cases where 100% of all debts and assets are co-mingled), an additional URLA must be completed.

(5) As a loan originator, only ask if an applicant is "married, unmarried, or separated." In essence you may not ask directly, "Are you divorced?" "What is your marital status?" or "Have you been divorced?" While the originator cannot ask any questions about future plans for children or parenthood under ECOA, it is permissible to ask about the number and ages of dependents or about dependent-related financial obligation or expenditures.

(6) A loan originator, processor, or underwriter cannot take into account the existence (or absence) of a telephone listing in the applicant's name nor the existence of an email address. This should not affect a decision of creditworthiness. It is appropriate to require a business phone contact that is carried in the businesses name, unless the applicant is self-employed, in which case a listed home phone number may be appropriate.

Item 1a. (Continued)

```
Current Address
Street  13108 Burninglog Lane          (1)                                                              Unit #
City    Dallas          State T.  Zip 75243        Country United States of America
How Long at Current Address?  2  Years  9  Months   ○Own  ●Rent ($ 1,300 /month)  ○No primary housing expense

If at Current Address for LESS than 2 years, list Former Address   ☐ Does not apply
Street  N/A                                                    (2)                                      Unit #
City           State  ▼ Zip          Country
How Long at Former Address?  ___ Years ___ Months  ○Own  ○Rent ($___ /month)  ○No primary housing expense

Mailing Address – If different from Current Address   ☑ Does not apply
Street                                                (3)                                               Unit #
City           State  Zip          Country

Military Service – Did you (or your deceased spouse) ever serve, or are you currently serving, in the United States Armed Forces?  ●NO  ○YES
If YES, check all that apply:  ☐ Currently serving on active duty with projected expiration date of service/tour ___/___ (mm/yyyy)
                               ☐ Currently retired, discharged, or separated from service
         (4)                   ☐ Only period of service was as a non-activated member of the Reserve or National Guard
                               ☐ Surviving spouse
```

(1) Fill in current address (where the borrower currently resides) and how long they have resided there.

(2) The last space in this section is for the borrower's former address; fill this address out if the borrower has lived at her current address less than two years.

(3) If the applicant has a mailing address that is different from the residence address, put that here. Insert all employment information on the borrower and co-borrower.

(4) If either borrower had military service, fill out which applies; otherwise just check no.

No blanks will be left unfilled, unless one of the borrowers is not employed (or in the case of a married couple who will qualify with only one spouse's income). If the borrower(s) has not held his current job for two years; prior employment history must be provided. If the applicants are self-employed, they will need to furnish copies of federal income tax returns with all schedules for the last two full years, along with a profit and loss statement and balance sheet for the current year to date. All the self-employment documents provided should be signed and dated, as many investors require original signatures.

Item 1b.

1b. Current Employment/Self Employment and Income ☐ Does not apply

Employer or Business Name: Hard Sidewalk, LLC (1)
Address: 11048 Jar Head Way (2)
City: Richmond
Phone: (804) 555-5557 (3)
State: VA Zip: 23369

Position or Title: Estimator/Engineer (4)
Start Date: 07/2014 (mm/yyyy)
How long in this line of work? 2 Years 10 Months

Check if this statement applies: (6)
☐ I am employed by a family member, property seller, real estate agent, or other party to the transaction.

☐ Check if you are the Business Owner or Self-Employed (7)
○ I have an ownership share of less than 25%.
○ I have an ownership share of 25% or more.
Monthly Income (or Loss): $ (8)

Gross Monthly Income
Base (5) $ 4,000 /month
Overtime $ /month
Bonus $ /month
Commission $ /month
Military Entitlements $ /month
Other $ 500 /month
TOTAL $ 4,500 /month

(1) Under "Employer or Business Name," identify the borrower's employer. If the borrower owns a business, enter the name of the business. If the borrower is self-employed and does not operate under a business name, enter the borrower's name.

(2) Enter the mailing address of the business.

(3) Enter the main phone number of the company the borrower works for. Do not enter the borrower's personal work phone number as it is reported under Contact Information in Section 1a.

(4) Enter the job or position title of the borrower at the business where they work, along with the start date at the current employer and how long they have been in that line of work/profession.

(5) For "Gross Monthly Income," enter all income earned from the borrower's employer. If the borrower is self-employed or owns a business, enter the income in the "Monthly Income (or Loss)" field (not the "Gross Monthly Income" section). In the spaced titled "Military Entitlements," enter income received for Active, Reserve, or National Guard duty that is in addition to base pay [e.g., Basic Allowance for Subsistence (BAS), Basic Allowance for Housing (BAH), and other military entitlements shown on the Leave and Earnings Statement (LES)].

(6) It is considered fraud if a borrower or their lender knows of a relationship that exists between a family member, property seller, real estate agent, or other party to the agreement, but does not disclose this. If this is true and disclosed, there may be no problem.

(7) Fill out "Business Owner or Self-Employed Ownership Share" should a borrower own the business.

(8) Check the radial button that reflects the borrower's corresponding percentage of ownership.

Item 1c. is to be filled out using the same methodology as (1b.) above.

1c. IF APPLICABLE, Complete Information for Additional Employment/Self Employment and Income ☐ Does not apply

Employer or Business Name	Phone ( ) -	Gross Monthly Income
Address		Base $ /month
City	State Zip	Overtime $ /month
		Bonus $ /month
Position or Title	Check if this statement applies:	Commission $ /month
Start Date / (mm/yyyy)	☐ I am employed by a family member, property seller, real estate agent, or other party to the transaction.	Military Entitlements $ /month
How long in this line of work? Years Months		Other $ /month
☐ Check if you are the Business Owner or Self-Employed	○ I have an ownership share of less than 25%. Monthly Income (or Loss) ○ I have an ownership share of 25% or more. $	TOTAL $ /month

1d. Previous Employment/Self-Employment and Income ONLY IF your Current Employment is LESS than 2 years. ☐ Does not apply

Employer or Business Name	☐ Check if you were the Business Owner or Self-Employed	Previous Gross Monthly Income
Address		$
City State Zip		
Position or Title		
Start Date / (mm/yyyy) End Date / (mm/yyyy)		

Item 1d. is only filled out when a self-employed borrower has not owned or run the present business for more than two years.

1e. Income from Other Sources ☐ Does not apply

Include income from other sources below. Under Income Source, choose from the sources listed here:
- Alimony
- Automobile Allowance
- Boarder Income
- Capital Gains
- Child Support
- Disability
- Foster Care
- Housing or Parsonage
- Interest and Dividends
- Notes Receivable
- Public Assistance
- Mortgage Credit Certificate
- Mortgage Differential Payments
- Retirement (e.g., Pension, IRA)
- Royalty Payments
- Separate Maintenance
- Social Security
- Trust
- Unemployment Benefits
- VA Compensation
- Other

NOTE: Reveal alimony, child support, separate maintenance, or other income ONLY IF you want it considered in determining your qualification for this loan.

Income Source – use list above	Monthly Income
Interest and Dividends	$ 100
	$
	$
Provide TOTAL Amount Here	**$ 100**

Item 1e. is filled out using the titles for sources listed any other income and its monthly amount. If no other sources exist, then check the box "Does not apply."

Section 2: Financial Information — Assets and Liabilities. This section asks about things you own that are worth money and that you want considered to qualify for this loan. It then asks about your liabilities (or debts) that you pay each month, such as credit cards, alimony, or other expenses.

2a. Assets – Bank Accounts, Retirement, and Other Accounts You Have

Include all accounts below. Under Account Type, choose from the account types listed here:
- Checking
- Savings
- Money Market
- Certificate of Deposit
- Mutual Fund
- Stocks
- Stock Options
- Bonds
- Retirement (e.g., 401k, IRA)
- Bridge Loan Proceeds
- Individual Development Account
- Trust Account
- Cash Value of Life Insurance (used for the transaction)

Account Type – use list above	Financial Institution	Account Number	Cash or Market Value
Checking	Treasury CU	554466	$ 9,000
Money Market	Treasury CU	554468	$ 100,000
Bonds	Treasury CU	554467	$ 2,500
			$
			$
		Provide TOTAL Amount Here	**$ 111,500**

Item 2a. is where the borrower enters the current value of asset accounts. Include the amount of any cash gift or grant that has been received and deposited in the asset account balance (see Section 4d).

2c. Liabilities – Credit Cards, Other Debts, and Leases that You Owe		☐ Does not apply				
List all liabilities below (except real estate) and include deferred payments. Under Account Type, choose from the types listed here: • Revolving (e.g., credit cards) • Installment (e.g., car, student, personal loans) • Open 30-Day (balance paid monthly) • Lease (not real estate) • Other						
Account Type – use list above	Company Name	Account Number	Unpaid Balance	To be paid off at or before closing	Monthly Payment	
Revolving	Visa	1111222233334444	$ 1,350	☐	$	50
Revolving	Mastercard	9999888877776666	$ 800	☐	$	35
Open 30-Day	American Express	5555666644443333	$ 2,500	☑	$	
			$	☐	$	
			$	☐	$	

Item 2c. is where the borrower enters all debts including those that may not be listed on the borrower's credit report. Enter the details of personal debt obligations that the borrower currently owes or will owe before this mortgage loan closes. Include debt on which the payments are currently deferred. Do not include household expenses for phones, utilities, or insurance unless instructed, or unless it's determined that it's needed for credit support. Identify any personal debt obligations that will be paid off at or before closing, whether or not the payoff is a result of this loan application.

2d. Other Liabilities and Expenses	☐ Does not apply	
Include all other liabilities and expenses below. Choose from the types listed here: • Alimony • Child Support • Separate Maintenance • Job Related Expenses • Other		Monthly Payment
		$
		$
		$

Item 2d. is where the borrower lists other liabilities with monthly payments such as alimony, child support, separate maintenance, and job-related expenses.

Section 3: Financial Information — Real Estate. This section asks you to list all properties you currently own and what you owe on them. ☐ I do not own any real estate

3a. Property You Own	If you are refinancing, list the property you are refinancing FIRST.					
Address Street **(1)**		Unit #	City		State ▾ Zip	
				For Investment Property Only		
Property Value	Status: Sold, Pending Sale, or Retained	Monthly Insurance, Taxes, Association Dues, etc. Not Included in Mortgage Payment	Monthly Rental Income	For LENDER to Calculate: Net Monthly Rental Income		
$ **(2)**	**(3)** ▾	$ **(4)**	$ **(5**	$		
Mortgage Loans on this Property	☐ Does not apply					
Creditor Name	Account Number	Monthly Mortgage Payment	Unpaid Balance	To be paid off at or before closing	Type: FHA, VA, Conventional, USDA-RD, Other	Credit Limit (if applicable)
(6)	**(6)**	$ **(7)**	$	☐	▾	$ **(8)**
		$	$	☐	▾	$

(1) This section applies to any property (including land) in which the borrower has an ownership interest and/or on which the borrower has a mortgage. If the borrower is refinancing a mortgage loan, list the property that is the subject of the refinance first.

(2) Provide an estimate of the current property value. When the property is the subject of the refinance at time of closing, this is the property value used for underwriting purposes, generally obtained from the appraisal report.

(3) Specify the status of the property the borrower owns: either Sold—for a recently sold property; Pending Sale—for a property currently under contract for sale; or Retained—for a property you will continue to own after this mortgage loan closing.

(4) Complete the Monthly Insurance, Taxes, Association Dues, etc. section only if the amount of these expenses is not included in the Monthly Mortgage Payment (in a mortgage loan listed in the next section). Association dues (condo, PUD, or co-op fees) are not generally included in the mortgage payment and must be entered here.

(5) When a borrower owns an investment property, identify the gross monthly rental income the borrower receives from that property. You as the lender will calculate the net monthly rental for income for qualification purposes.

(6) Write the full account number here, unless your firm allows the use of the last four digits of account numbers.

(7) Monthly mortgage payment is entered as the mortgage payment the borrower is obligated to pay. If insurance and taxes are not identified separately under "Monthly Insurance, Taxes, Association Dues, etc.," include their cost in this amount.

(8) Should the borrower have an open-ended line of credit for a loan on the property, put the maximum credit line here even if it is the maximum of a home equity line of credit.

Item 3b. is to be completed if the borrower owns more than one property.

Section 4: Loan and Property Information. This section asks about the loan's purpose and the property you want to purchase or refinance.

4a. Loan and Property Information

Loan Amount $ 210,000 **(1)** Loan Purpose **(2)** ⦿Purchase ○Refinance ○Other _____
Property Address Street 123 Anywhere Street **(3)**
                  Unit # _____ City Washington _____ State DC ▾ Zip 12345
                  County _____ Number of Units 1 **(4)** Property Value $ 275,000 **(5)**
Occupancy **(6)** ⦿Primary Residence ○Second Home ○Investment Property ○FHA Secondary Residence

1. **Mixed-Use Property.** If you will occupy the property, will you set aside space within the property to operate your own business? (e.g., daycare facility, medical office, beauty/barber shop) **(7)** ⦿NO ○YES
2. **Manufactured Home.** Is the property a manufactured home? (e.g., a factory built dwelling built on a permanent chassis) ⦿NO ○YES

(1) "Loan Amount" is the total amount the borrower intends to borrow using the subject property as collateral.

(2) Under "Loan Purpose," "Purchase" is chosen generally for a transaction where the borrower acquires ownership of the property. "Refinance" is chosen generally for a transaction where the borrower already owns the property. Note: A refinance can include a transaction for which there are no mortgages currently on the property (e.g., a property owned free and clear where the borrower takes out equity/cash). "Other" is chosen for a transaction that is neither a purchase nor a refinance. Examples include a construction loan that is temporary in nature and is not intended to serve as permanent financing, or a new subordinate lien for which the proceeds will not be used for a purchase or refinance transaction. Note: If your borrower is unsure which loan purpose to enter, as the lender you can help the borrower make the determination.

(3) Enter the subject property street address. When applicable, enter how the unit is identified, such as the unit number and/or letter. Include any unit number that is part of the legal property address, such as A, 1, 1A, or 123.

(4) Write the number of units represented by the subject property (2 for a duplex for an example).

(5) Property value is the estimated value of the property at the time of the application. At the time of closing, this is the property value used for underwriting purposes, generally obtained from the appraisal report.

(6) For Occupancy, specify the intended use of the property. The choices include:

- primary residence (At least one borrower intends to occupy the property as his or her primary residence.);

- second home (The property will be occupied by a borrower but not as the borrower's primary residence (e.g., a vacation home).); or
- investment property. (The property will be owned, but not occupied, by any borrower on the loan application. The borrower can occupy the property in addition to their principal residence, but for less than a majority of the calendar year. It does not apply to a vacation home.)

(7) For "Mixed-Use Property," select "YES" if a business will operate within the property. A mixed-use property is a property that has a business use in addition to a residential use; for example, when a portion of the residence is used as a dental office. Retail spaces within a multiunit property or a room in the property used as a home office are not considered mixed-use properties.

For "Manufactured Home," select "YES" if the home is delivered to the property site on wheels and a permanent chassis. A modular home is not considered a manufactured home.

If you are unsure whether the property is a manufactured home, your lender can assist you in answering this question.

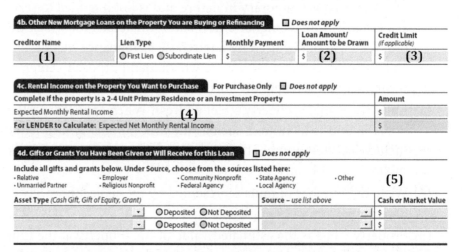

(1) If your borrower is obtaining more than one new mortgage loan to purchase or refinance this property, enter it here.

(2) Under "Loan Amount to be Drawn," if the loan is a line of credit and you are drawing funds at closing from the line, enter that amount. If it is a closed-end loan (no additional funds can be drawn), enter the loan amount.

(3) If the loan is a line of credit, identify the maximum amount of credit that will be permitted to borrow.

(4) For "Rental Income on the Property You Want to Purchase," identify the estimated gross rental income the borrower expects to receive on the property being purchased. As the lender, you will calculate the expected net rental income. Note: Rental income derived from properties you already own should be entered in Section 3: Financial Information – Real Estate.

(5) "Gifts and Grants – Item 4d" is where any cash gift or grant has been deposited. The borrower should select "Deposited," if the gift or grant has been received and is reflected in the balance of one of the borrower's asset accounts disclosed on this application in Section 2a. Note: "Deposited" or "Not Deposited" only applies to cash gifts or grants and does not apply to gifts of equity.

Section 5: Declarations

5a. About this Property and Your Money for this Loan	
A. Will you occupy the property as your primary residence? (1) If YES, have you had an ownership interest in another property in the last three years? If YES, complete (1) and (2) below: (1) What type of property did you own: primary residence (PR), FHA secondary residence (SR), second home (SH), or investment property (IP)? (2) How did you hold title to the property: by yourself (S), jointly with your spouse (SP), or jointly with another person (O)	○NO ●YES ●NO ○YES
B. If this is a Purchase Transaction: Do you have a family relationship or business affiliation with the seller of the property?	●NO ○YES (2
C. Are you borrowing any money for this real estate transaction (e.g., money for your closing costs or down payment) or obtaining any money from another party, such as the seller or realtor, that you have not disclosed on this loan application? If YES, what is the amount of this money?	●NO ○YES (3) $
D. 1. Have you or will you be applying for a mortgage loan on another property (not the property securing this loan) on or before closing this transaction that is not disclosed on this loan application? 2. Have you or will you be applying for any new credit (e.g., installment loan, credit card, etc.) on or before closing this loan that is not disclosed on this application?	●NO ○YES ●NO ○YES (4)
E. Will this property be subject to a lien that could take priority over the first mortgage lien, such as a clean energy lien paid through your property taxes (e.g., the Property Assessed Clean Energy Program)?	●NO ○YES (5)

(1) This series of questions about recent home ownership is to determine if the borrower qualifies for first-time home buyer status under various programs.

(2) Borrowers must disclose any family or business relationship with the seller of the subject property on a purchase money mortgage.

(3) For C, if the borrower is borrowing any money for this real estate transaction (e.g., money for closing costs or down payment) or obtaining any money from another party, such as the seller or real estate agent, this must be disclosed on the loan application. This

may include a rebate of real estate agent commission on or after closing or guaranteed cash payments from the seller.

(4) Here is where a borrower notes if he/she will be applying for a mortgage loan on another property (not the property securing this loan) on or before closing of this transaction. As the lender, you must see that the borrower is asked to disclose all applications for credit made with another lender or creditor during the mortgage process.

(5) Will this property be subject to a lien that could take priority over the first mortgage lien, such as a clean energy lien paid through the borrower's property taxes (e.g., the Property Assessed Clean Energy program)? This question refers to energy liens on the property that is being purchased or refinanced. These types of liens are repaid through the property taxes the borrower is obligated to pay (or will pay) on the property. This question is not asking about standard real estate property taxes or homeowners association liens.

5b. About Your Finances

F. Are you a co-signer or guarantor on any debt or loan that is not disclosed on this application? **(1)**	○ NO ○ YES
G. Are there any outstanding judgments against you? **(2)**	○ NO ○ YES
H. Are you currently delinquent or in default on a federal debt? **(3)**	○ NO ○ YES
I. Are you a party to a lawsuit in which you potentially have any personal financial liability? **(4)**	○ NO ○ YES
J. Have you conveyed title to any property in lieu of foreclosure in the past 7 years? **(5)**	○ NO ○ YES
K. Within the past 7 years, have you completed a pre-foreclosure sale or short sale, whereby the property was sold to a third party and the Lender agreed to accept less than the outstanding mortgage balance due? **(6)**	○ NO ○ YES
L. Have you had property foreclosed upon in the last 7 years? **(7)**	○ NO ○ YES
M. Have you declared bankruptcy within the past 7 years? If YES, identify the type(s) of bankruptcy: ☐ Chapter 7 ☐ Chapter 11 ☐ Chapter 12 ☐ Chapter 13 **(8)**	○ NO ○ YES

(1) A co-signer is jointly liable on any debt or loan; a guarantor is only liable if primary borrower cannot pay. If the response is yes, then this will be used as qualifying for monthly debt payments and used in the debt to income calculation.

(2) Any outstanding judgments will normally show up on a standard credit report, but you should ask your borrower to confirm whether he or she does or does not have any unresolved judgments.

(3) Federal debt refers to any debt owed to the federal government, such as a federally-backed student loan, FHA loan, USDA-RD loan, or a VA loan. As a lender, you need to know if a borrower has an unresolved government debt, as it might preclude the borrower from qualifying for some federally sponsored loans.

(4) This disclosure will allow the lender to make a determination of the added risk that an active case might have on the credit decision.

(5) This is also called "deed in lieu of foreclosure." Select "Yes" for a property in which the borrower was on title and was foreclosed upon or conveyed through a deed in lieu of foreclosure, whether or not the borrower was responsible for repayment of the mortgage loan.

(6) Has the borrower been foreclosed on in past 7 years? Choose yes or no.

(7) If yes, select each applicable bankruptcy type.

(8) If yes to (7), then check which type of bankruptcy was declared.

CHAPTER 9 Lender Loan Processes

Uniform Residential Loan Application

This application is designed to be completed by the applicant(s) with the Lender's assistance. Applicants should complete this form as "Borrower" or "Co-Borrower," as applicable. Co-Borrower information must also be provided (and the appropriate box checked) when ☐ the income or assets of a person other than the Borrower (including the Borrower's spouse) will be used as a basis for loan qualification or ☐ the income or assets of the Borrower's spouse or other person who has community property rights pursuant to state law will not be used as a basis for loan qualification, but his or her liabilities must be considered because the spouse or other person has community property rights pursuant to applicable law and Borrower resides in a community property state, the security property is located in a community property state, or the Borrower is relying on other property located in a community property state as a basis for repayment of the loan.

If this is an application for joint credit, Borrower and Co-Borrower each agree that we intend to apply for joint credit (sign below):

_____   _____
Borrower   Co-Borrower

I. TYPE OF MORTGAGE AND TERMS OF LOAN

Mortgage Applied for:	☐ VA ☐ FHA	☐ Conventional ☐ USDA/Rural Housing Service	☐ Other (explain):	Agency Case Number	Lender Case Number
Amount $	Interest Rate %	No. of Months	Amortization Type:	☐ Fixed Rate ☐ GPM	☐ Other (explain): ☐ ARM (type):

II. PROPERTY INFORMATION AND PURPOSE OF LOAN

Subject Property Address (street, city, state & ZIP)	No. of Units
Legal Description of Subject Property (attach description if necessary)	Year Built

| Purpose of Loan | ☐ Purchase ☐ Refinance | ☐ Construction ☐ Construction-Permanent | ☐ Other (explain): | Property will be: ☐ Primary Residence | ☐ Secondary Residence | ☐ Investment |

Complete this line if construction or construction-permanent loan.

Year Lot Acquired	Original Cost $	Amount Existing Liens $	(a) Present Value of Lot $	(b) Cost of Improvements $	Total (a + b) $

Complete this line if this is a refinance loan.

Year Acquired	Original Cost $	Amount Existing Liens $	Purpose of Refinance	Describe Improvements ☐ made ☐ to be made Cost: $

Title will be held in what Name(s)	Manner in which Title will be held	Estate will be held in: ☐ Fee Simple ☐ Leasehold (show expiration date)

Source of Down Payment, Settlement Charges, and/or Subordinate Financing (explain)

III. BORROWER INFORMATION

Borrower	Co-Borrower
Borrower's Name (include Jr. or Sr. if applicable)	Co-Borrower's Name (include Jr. or Sr. if applicable)
Social Security Number	Home Phone (incl. area code)	DOB (mm/dd/yyyy)	Yrs. School	Social Security Number	Home Phone (incl. area code)	DOB (mm/dd/yyyy)	Yrs. School
☐ Married ☐ Unmarried (include ☐ Separated single, divorced, widowed)	Dependents (not listed by Co-Borrower) no. ages	☐ Married ☐ Unmarried (include ☐ Separated single, divorced, widowed)	Dependents (not listed by Borrower) no. ages
Present Address (street, city, state, ZIP) ☐ Own ☐ Rent ___No. Yrs.	Present Address (street, city, state, ZIP) ☐ Own ☐ Rent ___No. Yrs.
Mailing Address, if different from Present Address	Mailing Address, if different from Present Address

If residing at present address for less than two years, complete the following:

Former Address (street, city, state, ZIP) ☐ Own ☐ Rent ___No. Yrs.	Former Address (street, city, state, ZIP) ☐ Own ☐ Rent ___No. Yrs.

IV. EMPLOYMENT INFORMATION

Borrower	Co-Borrower
Name & Address of Employer	☐ Self Employed	Yrs. on this job	Name & Address of Employer	☐ Self Employed	Yrs. on this job
		Yrs. employed in this line of work/profession			Yrs. employed in this line of work/profession
Position/Title/Type of Business	Business Phone (incl. area code)	Position/Title/Type of Business	Business Phone (incl. area code)

If employed in current position for less than two years or if currently employed in more than one position, complete the following:

Uniform Residential Loan Application
Freddie Mac Form 65   7/05 (rev.6/09)

Fannie Mae Form 1003   7/05 (rev.6/09)

Review of Uniform Residential Loan Application

IV. EMPLOYMENT INFORMATION (cont'd)

Borrower		Co-Borrower	
Name & Address of Employer ☐ Self Employed	Dates (from – to)	Name & Address of Employer ☐ Self Employed	Dates (from – to)
	Monthly Income $		Monthly Income $
Position/Title/Type of Business	Business Phone (incl. area code)	Position/Title/Type of Business	Business Phone (incl. area code)
Name & Address of Employer ☐ Self Employed	Dates (from – to)	Name & Address of Employer ☐ Self Employed	Dates (from – to)
	Monthly Income $		Monthly Income $
Position/Title/Type of Business	Business Phone (incl. area code)	Position/Title/Type of Business	Business Phone (incl. area code)

V. MONTHLY INCOME AND COMBINED HOUSING EXPENSE INFORMATION

Gross Monthly Income	Borrower	Co-Borrower	Total	Combined Monthly Housing Expense	Present	Proposed
Base Empl. Income*	$	$	$	Rent	$	
Overtime				First Mortgage (P&I)		$
Bonuses				Other Financing (P&I)		
Commissions				Hazard Insurance		
Dividends/Interest				Real Estate Taxes		
Net Rental Income				Mortgage Insurance		
Other (before completing, see the notice in "describe other income," below)				Homeowner Assn. Dues		
				Other:		
Total	$	$	$	Total	$	$

* Self Employed Borrower(s) may be required to provide additional documentation such as tax returns and financial statements.

Describe Other Income

Notice: Alimony, child support, or separate maintenance income need not be revealed if the Borrower (B) or Co-Borrower (C) does not choose to have it considered for repaying this loan.

B/C		Monthly Amount
		$

VI. ASSETS AND LIABILITIES

This Statement and any applicable supporting schedules may be completed jointly by both married and unmarried Co-Borrowers if their assets and liabilities are sufficiently joined so that the Statement can be meaningfully and fairly presented on a combined basis; otherwise, separate Statements and Schedules are required. If the Co-Borrower section was completed about a non-applicant spouse or other person, this Statement and supporting schedules must be completed about that spouse or other person also.

Completed ☐ Jointly ☐ Not Jointly

ASSETS Description	Cash or Market Value	Liabilities and Pledged Assets. List the creditor's name, address, and account number for all outstanding debts, including automobile loans, revolving charge accounts, real estate loans, alimony, child support, stock pledges, etc. Use continuation sheet, if necessary. Indicate by (*) those liabilities, which will be satisfied upon sale of real estate owned or upon refinancing of the subject property.		
Cash deposit toward purchase held by:	$			
List checking and savings accounts below		LIABILITIES	Monthly Payment & Months Left to Pay	Unpaid Balance
Name and address of Bank, S&L, or Credit Union		Name and address of Company	$ Payment/Months	$
Acct. no.	$	Acct. no.		
Name and address of Bank, S&L, or Credit Union		Name and address of Company	$ Payment/Months	$
Acct. no.	$	Acct. no.		
Name and address of Bank, S&L, or Credit Union		Name and address of Company	$ Payment/Months	$
Acct. no.	$	Acct. no.		

Uniform Residential Loan Application
Freddie Mac Form 65 7/05 (rev. 6/09)

Fannie Mae Form 1003 7/05 (rev.6/09)

VI. ASSETS AND LIABILITIES (cont'd)

Name and address of Bank, S&L, or Credit Union		Name and address of Company	$ Payment/Months	$
Acct. no.	$	Acct. no.		
Stocks & Bonds (Company name/ number & description)	$	Name and address of Company	$ Payment/Months	$
		Acct. no.		
Life insurance net cash value Face amount: $	$	Name and address of Company	$ Payment/Months	$
Subtotal Liquid Assets	$			
Real estate owned (enter market value from schedule of real estate owned)	$			
Vested interest in retirement fund	$			
Net worth of business(es) owned (attach financial statement)	$	Acct. no.		
Automobiles owned (make and year)	$	Alimony/Child Support/Separate Maintenance Payments Owed to:	$	
Other Assets (itemize)	$	Job-Related Expense (child care, union dues, etc.)	$	
		Total Monthly Payments	$	
Total Assets a.	$	Net Worth ▶ $ (a minus b)	**Total Liabilities b.**	$

Schedule of Real Estate Owned (If additional properties are owned, use continuation sheet.)

Property Address (enter S if sold, PS if pending sale or R if rental being held for income) ▼	Type of Property	Present Market Value	Amount of Mortgages & Liens	Gross Rental Income	Mortgage Payments	Insurance, Maintenance, Taxes & Misc.	Net Rental Income
		$	$	$	$	$	$
Totals		$	$	$	$	$	$

List any additional names under which credit has previously been received and indicate appropriate creditor name(s) and account number(s):

Alternate Name	Creditor Name	Account Number

VII. DETAILS OF TRANSACTION

a.	Purchase price	$
b.	Alterations, improvements, repairs	
c.	Land (if acquired separately)	
d.	Refinance (incl. debts to be paid off)	
e.	Estimated prepaid items	
f.	Estimated closing costs	
g.	PMI, MIP, Funding Fee	
h.	Discount (if Borrower will pay)	
i.	Total costs (add items a through h)	

VIII. DECLARATIONS

If you answer "Yes" to any questions a through i, please use continuation sheet for explanation.

	Borrower		Co-Borrower	
	Yes	No	Yes	No
a. Are there any outstanding judgments against you?	☐	☐	☐	☐
b. Have you been declared bankrupt within the past 7 years?	☐	☐	☐	☐
c. Have you had property foreclosed upon or given title or deed in lieu thereof in the last 7 years?	☐	☐	☐	☐
d. Are you a party to a lawsuit?	☐	☐	☐	☐
e. Have you directly or indirectly been obligated on any loan which resulted in foreclosure, transfer of title in lieu of foreclosure, or judgment? (This would include such loans as home mortgage loans, SBA loans, home improvement loans, educational loans, manufactured (mobile) home loans, any mortgage, financial obligation, bond, or loan guarantee. If "Yes," provide details, including date, name, and address of Lender, FHA or VA case number, if any, and reasons for the action.)	☐	☐	☐	☐

Uniform Residential Loan Application
Freddie Mac Form 65   7/05 (rev.6/09)

Fannie Mae Form 1003   7/05 (rev.6/09)

Review of Uniform Residential Loan Application

VII. DETAILS OF TRANSACTION		VIII. DECLARATIONS				
		If you answer "Yes" to any questions a through i, please use continuation sheet for explanation.	Borrower		Co-Borrower	
			Yes	No	Yes	No
j. Subordinate financing		f. Are you presently delinquent or in default on any Federal debt or any other loan, mortgage, financial obligation, bond, or loan guarantee?	☐	☐	☐	☐
k. Borrower's closing costs paid by Seller		g. Are you obligated to pay alimony, child support, or separate maintenance?	☐	☐	☐	☐
		h. Is any part of the down payment borrowed?	☐	☐	☐	☐
l. Other Credits (explain)		i. Are you a co-maker or endorser on a note?	☐	☐	☐	☐
m. Loan amount (exclude PMI, MIP, Funding Fee financed)		j. Are you a U.S. citizen?	☐	☐	☐	☐
n. PMI, MIP, Funding Fee financed		k. Are you a permanent resident alien?	☐	☐	☐	☐
o. Loan amount (add m & n)		l. Do you intend to occupy the property as your primary residence? If Yes," complete question m below.	☐	☐	☐	☐
p. Cash from/to Borrower (subtract j, k, l & o from i)		m. Have you had an ownership interest in a property in the last three years? (1) What type of property did you own—principal residence (PR), second home (SH), or investment property (IP)? (2) How did you hold title to the home— by yourself (S), jointly with your spouse (SP), or jointly with another person (O)?	☐	☐	☐	☐

IX. ACKNOWLEDGEMENT AND AGREEMENT

Each of the undersigned specifically represents to Lender and to Lender's actual or potential agents, brokers, processors, attorneys, insurers, servicers, successors and assigns and agrees and acknowledges that: (1) the information provided in this application is true and correct as of the date set forth opposite my signature and that any intentional or negligent misrepresentation of this information contained in this application may result in civil liability, including monetary damages, to any person who may suffer any loss due to reliance upon any misrepresentation that I have made on this application, and/or in criminal penalties including, but not limited to, fine or imprisonment or both under the provisions of Title 18, United States Code, Sec. 1001, et seq.; (2) the loan requested pursuant to this application (the "Loan") will be secured by a mortgage or deed of trust on the property described in this application; (3) the property will not be used for any illegal or prohibited purpose or use; (4) all statements made in this application are made for the purpose of obtaining a residential mortgage loan; (5) the property will be occupied as indicated in this application; (6) the Lender, its servicers, successors or assigns may retain the original and/or an electronic record of this application, whether or not the Loan is approved; (7) the Lender and its agents, brokers, insurers, servicers, successors, and assigns may continuously rely on the information contained in the application, and I am obligated to amend and/or supplement the information provided in this application if any of the material facts that I have represented herein should change prior to closing of the Loan; (8) in the event that my payments on the Loan become delinquent, the Lender, its servicers, successors or assigns may, in addition to any other rights and remedies that it may have relating to such delinquency, report my name and account information to one or more consumer reporting agencies; (9) ownership of the Loan and/or administration of the Loan account may be transferred with such notice as may be required by law; (10) neither Lender nor its agents, brokers, insurers, servicers, successors or assigns has made any representation or warranty, express or implied, to me regarding the property or the condition or value of the property; and (11) my transmission of this application as an "electronic record" containing my "electronic signature," as those terms are defined in applicable federal and/or state laws (excluding audio and video recordings), or my facsimile transmission of this application containing a facsimile of my signature, shall be as effective, enforceable and valid as if a paper version of this application were delivered containing my original written signature.

Acknowledgement. Each of the undersigned hereby acknowledges that any owner of the Loan, its servicers, successors and assigns, may verify or reverify any information contained in this application or obtain any information or data relating to the Loan, for any legitimate business purpose through any source, including a source named in this application or a consumer reporting agency.

Borrower's Signature X	Date	Co-Borrower's Signature X	Date

X. INFORMATION FOR GOVERNMENT MONITORING PURPOSES

The following information is requested by the Federal Government for certain types of loans related to a dwelling in order to monitor the lender's compliance with equal credit opportunity, fair housing and home mortgage disclosure laws. You are not required to furnish this information, but are encouraged to do so. The law provides that a lender may not discriminate either on the basis of this information, or on whether you choose to furnish it. If you furnish the information, please provide both ethnicity and race. For race, you may check more than one designation. If you do not furnish ethnicity, race, or sex, under Federal regulations, this lender is required to note the information on the basis of visual observation and surname if you have made this application in person. If you do not wish to furnish the information, please check the box below. (Lender must review the above material to assure that the disclosures satisfy all requirements to which the lender is subject under applicable state law for the particular type of loan applied for.)

BORROWER	☐ I do not wish to furnish this information			CO-BORROWER	☐ I do not wish to furnish this information		
Ethnicity:	☐ Hispanic or Latino	☐ Not Hispanic or Latino		Ethnicity:	☐ Hispanic or Latino	☐ Not Hispanic or Latino	
Race:	☐ American Indian or Alaska Native ☐ Native Hawaiian or Other Pacific Islander	☐ Asian ☐ White	☐ Black or African American	Race:	☐ American Indian or Alaska Native ☐ Native Hawaiian or Other Pacific Islander	☐ Asian ☐ White	☐ Black or African American
Sex:	☐ Female ☐ Male			Sex:	☐ Female ☐ Male		

To be Completed by Loan Originator:
This information was provided:
- ☐ In a face-to-face interview
- ☐ In a telephone interview
- ☐ By the applicant and submitted by fax or mail
- ☐ By the applicant and submitted via e-mail or the Internet

Loan Originator's Signature X		Date
Loan Originator's Name (print or type)	Loan Originator Identifier	Loan Originator's Phone Number (including area code)
Loan Origination Company's Name	Loan Origination Company Identifier	Loan Origination Company's Address

Uniform Residential Loan Application
Freddie Mac Form 65   7/05 (rev.6/09)

Fannie Mae Form 1003   7/05 (rev.6/09)

CONTINUATION SHEET/RESIDENTIAL LOAN APPLICATION			
Use this continuation sheet if you need more space to complete the Residential Loan Application. Mark **B** for Borrower or **C** for Co-Borrower.	Borrower:		Agency Case Number:
	Co-Borrower:		Lender Case Number:

I/We fully understand that it is a Federal crime punishable by fine or imprisonment, or both, to knowingly make any false statements concerning any of the above facts as applicable under the provisions of Title 18, United States Code, Section 1001, et seq.

Borrower's Signature	Date	Co-Borrower's Signature	Date
X		X	

Uniform Residential Loan Application
Freddie Mac Form 65 7/05 (rev.6/09)

Fannie Mae Form 1003 7/05 (rev.6/09)

REVIEW OF REQUEST FOR VERIFICATION OF DEPOSIT

Fannie Mae Form 1006, Request for Verification of Deposit, is found on page 441. This form is divided into two sections. The first section is completed by the lender from information supplied by the applicant and is signed by the applicant, authorizing the financial institution to release the information to the lender. The second section of the form is to be completed by the financial institution. The financial institution is asked to give information about the deposit accounts and outstanding loans of the applicant. In the section dealing with deposit accounts, the financial institution is asked to give the current balance and also the average balance for the previous 2 months. There is reason for such a request. For example, if the present balance in the account is $15,000 and the average balance for the previous two months has been only $5,000, the lender will ask the applicant to explain the reason for the radical increase. The applicant can do this by writing a source of funds letter. In item 12, the institution is asked to give any additional information that may aid the lender in determining the credit worthiness of the applicant. This should include information about loans that have been paid in full.

The FHA/VA form titled "Request for Verification of Deposit" requests similar information as the Fannie Mae form, but once again the form is somewhat different. As with the employment verification form, the lender is required to certify that the verification was sent directly to the bank and that the form did not pass through the hands of the applicant or any other interested party.

When processing loan document or disclosure request, the loan processor should mail all verifications directly. Verifications must not be hand-delivered or mailed by the applicant because of the potential for fraud.

A lender must verify the source of funds for accounts opened within the last 90 days of the application date, and account balances that are considerably greater than the average balance reflected on the VOD. One of the most important functions of the loan processor is to clearly verify all the sources of funds that the applicants(s) will use to close the mortgage loan. It may be that Uncle Joe has signed a gift letter that the applicant(s) brought when applying for the loan. What if Uncle Joe does not have the money in the bank, spends it prior to closing in 45 days, or has a falling out with the applicant(s)?

Lenders will also use any of the following types of documentation to verify that a borrower has sufficient funds for closing, down payment, and/or financial reserves other than those that can be covered by the use of Form 1006 and 1006(S). These include:

1. copies of bank statements or investment portfolio statements (The statements must cover the most recent full two-month period of account activity (60 days, or, if account information is reported on a quarterly basis, the most recent quarter). The statements must:
   - clearly identify the borrower as the account holder;
   - include at least the last four digits of the account number;
   - include the time period covered by the statement;
   - include all deposits and withdrawal transactions (for depository accounts);
   - include all purchase and sale transactions (for financial portfolio accounts); and
   - include the ending account balance.);
2. copies of retirement account statements (They must be the most recent statements, and they must identify the borrower's vested amount and the terms.); and
3. stocks and mutual funds where copies of recent statements can be used initially, but if the lender or holder of the borrower's account, the lender or holder may produce a printout or other alternative verification of the asset(s) directly from its system. The printout or alternative verification is acceptable as long as all required data (above) is supplied and documented.

Should the automated underwriting system like DU or LP require multiple verifications of assets to be used for closing costs or down payment, then (to ease the verification) a Form 1005 Blanket Authorization Form can be used for all accounts or assets held by that single lender or holder.

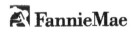

Request for Verification of Deposit

Privacy Act Notice: This information is to be used by the agency collecting it or its assignees in determining whether you qualify as a prospective mortgagor under its program. It will not be disclosed outside the agency except as required and permitted by law. You do not have to provide this information, but if you do not your application for approval as a prospective mortgagor or borrower may be delayed or rejected. The information requested in this form is authorized by Title 38, USC, Chapter 37 (If VA); by 12 USC, Section 1701 et.seq. (If HUD/FHA); by 42 USC, Section 1452b (if HUD/CPD); and Title 42 USC, 1471 et.seq. or 7 USC, 1921 et.seq. (If USDA/FmHA).

Instructions: Lender — Complete Items 1 through 8. Have applicant(s) complete Item 9. Forward directly to depository named in Item 1.
Depository — Please complete Items 10 through 18 and return DIRECTLY to lender named in Item 2.
The form is to be transmitted directly to the lender and is not to be transmitted through the applicant(s) or any other party.

Part I — Request

1. To (Name and address of depository)	2. From (Name and address of lender)

I certify that this verification has been sent directly to the bank or depository and has not passed through the hands of the applicant or any other party.

3. Signature of lender	4. Title	5. Date	6. Lender's No. (Optional)

7. Information To Be Verified

Type of Account	Account in Name of	Account Number	Balance
			$
			$
			$

To Depository: I/We have applied for a mortgage loan and stated in my financial statement that the balance on deposit with you is as shown above. You are authorized to verify this information and to supply the lender identified above with the information requested in Items 10 through 13. Your response is solely a matter of courtesy for which no responsibility is attached to your institution or any of your officers.

8. Name and Address of Applicant(s)	9. Signature of Applicant(s)

To Be Completed by Depository
Part II — Verification of Depository

10. Deposit Accounts of Applicant(s)

Type of Account	Account Number	Current Balance	Average Balance For Previous Two Months	Date Opened
		$	$	
		$	$	
		$	$	

11. Loans Outstanding To Applicant(s)

Loan Number	Date of Loan	Original Amount	Current Balance	Installments (Monthly/Quarterly)		Secured By	Number of Late Payments
		$	$	$	per		
		$	$	$	per		
		$	$	$	per		

12. Please include any additional information which may be of assistance in determination of credit worthiness. (Please include information on loans paid-in-full in Item 11 above.)

13. If the name(s) on the account(s) differ from those listed in Item 7, please supply the name(s) on the account(s) as reflected by your records.

Part III — Authorized Signature
Federal statutes provide severe penalties for any fraud, intentional misrepresentation, or criminal connivance or conspiracy purposed to influence the issuance of any guaranty or insurance by the VA Secretary, the U.S.D.A., FmHA/FHA Commissioner, or the HUD/CPD Assistant Secretary.

14. Signature of Depository Representative	15. Title (Please print or type)	16. Date
17. Please print or type name signed in item 14	18. Phone No.	

Fannie Mae
Form 1006   July 96

Instructions

Verification of Deposit

The lender uses this form for applications for conventional first or second mortgages to verify the cash deposits that the applicant listed on the loan application.

Copies
Original only.

Printing Instructions
This for must be printed on letter size paper, using portrait format. When printing this form, you must use the "shrink to fit" option in the Adobe Acrobat print dialogue box.

Instructions
The applicant must sign this form to authorize his or her depository to release the requested information. Separate forms should be sent to each depository named in the loan application. However, rather than having the applicant sign multiple forms, the lender may have the applicant sign a borower's signature authorization form, which gives the lender blanket authorization to request the information it needs to evaluate the applicant's creditworthiness. When the lender uses this type of blanket authorization, it must attach a copy of the authorization form to each Form 1006 it sends to the depository institutions in which the applicant has accounts.

For First Mortgages
The lender must send the request directly to the depositories. We will not permit the borrower to hand-carry the verification form. The lender must receive the completed form directly from the depositories. The completed form should not be passed through the applicant or any other party.

For Second Mortgages
The borrower may hand-carry the verification to the depositories. The depositories will then be required to mail this form directly to the lender.

The lender retains the original form in its mortgage file.

Instructions Page

REVIEW OF REQUEST FOR VERIFICATION OF EMPLOYMENT

Fannie Mae Form 1005, Request for Verification of Employment, is on page 444. The form is divided into four sections. The first section is to be completed by the lender. This section is usually completed at the time of application and is signed by the applicant. Normally the lender will have the applicant sign several of the forms in Line 8, just in case the original form that is sent to the employer is lost. The second section of the form is to be completed by the present employer. The employer states that the applicant or co-applicant is still in his employment. Part II of the form is divided into two parts.

First is the employment record and pay data. Line 14 of the employment section inquires about the existence of overtime and/or bonuses, if they are paid, and the likelihood of their continuance in the future. Part III of the form, Verification of Previous Employment, is to be filled out by the employer only if the person signing the request is no longer an employee. This form will be forwarded directly to the employer, and the employer will return the completed form directly to the lender. The broker or lender should not ask the borrower to hand carry the verification to help speed up approval; the statement at the bottom specifies that the form must be transmitted directly to the lender without passing through the hands of the applicant or any other party. It is important to make sure that the employer has filled out Section IV when reviewing the returned document.

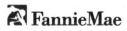

Request for Verification of Employment

Privacy Act Notice: This information is to be used by the agency collecting it or its assignees in determining whether you qualify as a prospective mortgagor under its program. It will not be disclosed outside the agency except as required and permitted by law. You do not have to provide this information, but if you do not your application for approval as a prospective mortgagor or borrower may be delayed or rejected. The information requested in this form is authorized by Title 38, USC, Chapter 37 (if VA); by 12 USC, Section 1701 et. seq. (if HUD/FHA); by 42 USC, Section 1452b (if HUD/CPD); and Title 42 USC, 1471 et. seq., or 7 USC, 1921 et. seq. (if USDA/FmHA).

Instructions: Lender — Complete items 1 through 7. Have applicant complete item 8. Forward directly to employer named in item 1.
Employer — Please complete either Part II or Part III as applicable. Complete Part IV and return directly to lender named in item 2.
The form is to be transmitted directly to the lender and is not to be transmitted through the applicant or any other party.

Part I — Request

1. To (Name and address of employer)	2. From (Name and address of lender)

I certify that this verification has been sent directly to the employer and has not passed through the hands of the applicant or any other interested party.

3. Signature of Lender	4. Title	5. Date	6. Lender's Number (Optional)

I have applied for a mortgage loan and stated that I am now or was formerly employed by you. My signature below authorizes verification of this information.

7. Name and Address of Applicant (include employee or badge number)	8. Signature of Applicant

Part II — Verification of Present Employment

9. Applicant's Date of Employment	10. Present Position	11. Probability of Continued Employment

12A. Current **Gross** Base Pay (Enter Amount and Check Period)
☐ Annual ☐ Hourly
☐ Monthly ☐ Other (Specify)
☐ Weekly
$ _____

12B. Gross Earnings				13. For Military Personnel Only		14. If Overtime or Bonus is Applicable, Is Its Continuance Likely?		
Type	Year To Date	Past Year	Past Year	Pay Grade		Overtime ☐ Yes ☐ No		
	Thru _____			Type	Monthly Amount	Bonus ☐ Yes ☐ No		
Base Pay	$	$	$	Base Pay	$	15. If paid hourly — average hours per week		
				Rations	$			
Overtime	$	$	$	Flight or Hazard	$	16. Date of applicant's next pay increase		
				Clothing	$			
Commissions	$	$	$	Quarters	$	17. Projected amount of next pay increase		
				Pro Pay	$	18. Date of applicant's last pay increase		
Bonus	$	$	$	Overseas or Combat	$	19. Amount of last pay increase		
Total	$ 0.00	$ 0.00	$ 0.00	Variable Housing Allowance	$			

20. Remarks (If employee was off work for any length of time, please indicate time period and reason)

Part III — Verification of Previous Employment

21. Date Hired	23. Salary/Wage at Termination Per (Year) (Month) (Week)
22. Date Terminated	Base _____ Overtime _____ Commissions _____ Bonus _____
24. Reason for Leaving	25. Position Held

Part IV — Authorized Signature - Federal statutes provide severe penalties for any fraud, intentional misrepresentation, or criminal connivance or conspiracy purposed to influence the issuance of any guaranty or insurance by the VA Secretary, the U.S.D.A., FmHA/FHA Commissioner, or the HUD/CPD Assistant Secretary.

26. Signature of Employer	27. Title (Please print or type)	28. Date
29. Print or type name signed in Item 26	30. Phone No.	

Fannie Mae
Form 1005   July 96

Review of Request for Verification of Employment

Instructions

Verification of Employment

The lender uses this form for applications for conventional first or second mortgages to verify the applicant's past and present employment status.

Copies
Original only.

Printing Instructions
This form must be printed on letter size paper, using portrait format.

Instructions
The applicant must sign this form to authorize his or her employer(s) to release the requested information. Separate forms should be sent to each firm that employed the applicant in the past two years. However, rather than having an applicant sign multiple forms, the lender may have the applicant sign a borrower's signature authorization form, which gives the lender blanket authorization to request the information it needs to evaluate the applicant's creditworthiness. When the lender uses this type of blanket authorization, it must attach a copy of the authorization form to each Form 1005 it sends to the applicant's employer(s).

For First Mortgages:
The lender must send the request directly to the employers. We will not permit the borrower to hand-carry the verification form. The lender must receive the completed form back directly from the employers. The completed form should not be passed through the applicant or any other party.

For Second Mortgages:
The borrower may hand-carry the verification to the employer. The employer will then be required to mail this form directly to the lender.

The lender retains the original form in its mortgage file.

REVIEW OF UNIFORM RESIDENTIAL APPRAISAL REPORT

An appraisal is an estimated value—an opinion—of property by a trained professional to indicate whether the property is adequate to serve as security for a loan. Most mortgage bankers and investors consider the property appraisal one of the most important documents contained in the loan file since it establishes the value of the property securing the mortgage loan. In fact, many investors consider the review of the appraisal on the same level as the review of credit.

The FHA defines an appraisal as "the act or process of estimating value." In addition, the FHA states that an appraisal shall be taken to mean a written statement independently and impartially prepared by a qualified appraiser setting forth an opinion of defined value of an adequately described property as of a specific date, supported by the presentation and analysis of relevant market information.

Appraisers are legally considered professionals (i.e., they issue opinions for which they are legally liable, as are doctors, lawyers, CPAs, etc.). They follow professional standards and practices to ensure that they do not commit malpractice. Some must do their work in conformity with other standards and obtain additional approval to perform work for agencies such as the FHA. Most states require a person holding him or herself out as a real estate appraiser to have a license and meet some minimal standards of knowledge.

An appraisal is an appraiser's estimate or opinion of value. It may or may not correspond to the asking price, offer, or reproduction costs of the property. The appraiser will use a Uniform Residential Appraisal Report (URAR) to document their assessment of the market value of the property. The appraiser must also consider the condition of the property for insurability.

Any appraiser should assess the home's physical condition. They will be looking for things that may impair the safety, sanitation, or structural soundness of the dwelling. Some GSEs or government-sponsored insured programs, such as FHA, will often not insure a building if the appraisal uncovers: (1) shoddy construction; (2) poor workmanship; (3) foundation settlement; (4) excessive dampness; (5) leakage; (6) decay; or (7) termite damage.

FHA mortgage compliance requirements for dealing with the situation where the borrower has not been informed of the appraised value by receiving a copy of the HUD-92900.5B form require an amendatory clause to be made part of the sales contract. This statement, often referred to as the FHA escape clause, states that if the appraised value is less than the sales price, the purchaser can cancel the contract.

A property's description from an appraisal point of view includes more than the property's address, legal description, and tax assessor's parcel number. It includes an analysis of: (1) the neighborhood; (2) site description; (3) improvements analysis, and (4) different approaches to valuation.

Three Value Methodologies

The three methodologies for determining a property's value are:

1. the cost approach (Under current criteria for residential properties, this approach is given the least emphasis and is used primarily for substantiation purposes. The cost to rebuild or replace the existing structure and site improvements will be based on the construction industry estimates in this approach. It is found to be the most suitable when appraising a proposed construction or remodel.);

2. the income approach (This is used for income-producing investment properties. This process will include a review of market rents and must consider future rental revenue and expenses of the proposed subject property. The appraiser is also required to capitalize the property to determine if the property will recapture the cost of the subject property.); and

3. the market approach. (This has been the approach that has been given the most weight in valuation by the appraisal community and the underwriting requirements of the government-sponsored enterprises. This approach is the comparison of the subject property to recent sales of similar properties and uses the theory of substitution. These "comparable sales" start with the proposed sales price of the subject property and reduce or increase each comparable sale by the relative value of the comparable sale based on the aspects of the subject property that may be superior or inferior. These are used to adjust the value of the comparable sales and aid the appraiser in determining a value of the subject property that is more systematic.)

TABLE 9-1 Appraisal Report Forms

Form	Property	Inspection	Fannie Mae #	Freddie Mac #
Uniform Residential Appraisal Report	Single-Family PUD	Interior & Exterior	1004	70
Exterior-Only Inspection Residential Appraisal Report	Single-Family PUD	Exterior Only	2055	2055
Manufactured Home Appraisal Report	Manufactured Home	Interior & Exterior	1004C	70B
Individual Condominium Unit Appraisal Report	Condominium	Interior & Exterior	1073	465
Exterior Only Inspection Condominium Unit Appraisal Report	Condominium	Exterior Only	1075	466
Small Residential Income Property Appraisal Report	Two- to Four-Unit Property	Interior & Exterior	1025	72

- Uniform Residential Appraisal Report (URAR) (FNMA form 1004 or FHLMC Form 70)—These provide a complete summary appraisal report for a single-unit property with interior and exterior inspections.
- Quantitative Analysis Appraisal Report (FNMA form 2055 and FHLMC form 2055)—This is a report used only for loans approved by either the Desktop Underwriter or Loan Prospector Automated Underwriting (AU) system. These will prove only market data (not cost or income approach); they will give an adjusted value of each of the comparables and may be based on an exterior inspection only.
- Desktop Underwriter Qualitative Analysis Appraisal Report (FNMA form 2065)—This is a report that only is used for loans approved by the Desktop Underwriter AU system. It provides only market data (not cost or income approach), and it does not provide dollar adjustments to the comparables and usually requires only and exterior inspection.
- Desktop Underwriter Property Inspection Report (FNMA form 2075 or FHLMC's Loan Prospector Condition and Marketability Report—These forms are not appraisal reports; rather they are used by the appraiser to provide the information on the condition and marketability of a single-unit property. They are only used for loans approved by either the DU or LP AU systems.

- There are also separate reports for small-income properties and condominium appraisals called FNMA 1025 and 1073 and FHLMC 72 and 465 respectively.
- The Residential Appraisal Field Review Report (FNMA form 2000 and FHLMC form 1032)—These are provided to lenders to use when requesting review appraisals for quality control or other purposes.

Automated underwriting has changed the ways that appraisals or collateral assessments are performed. An example of this is Freddie Mac's beginning to call its appraisal process on its AUS Loan Prospector (LP) a "collateral assessment." LP uses two methods for property evaluation. They are both available to the lender. These are:

1. the expedited assessment that can be done in as little as two hours (It is a physical assessment to see if any obvious problems exist. This type of evaluation is intended to reduce unnecessary work and time when it serves no useful purpose.); and
2. a nonexpedited assessment where a full appraisal is offered in a time frame of 72 hours. (Freddie Mac selects one of three appraisal management firms, which in turn selects a local appraiser to make the assessment.)

How are Automated Underwriter System Findings Indicative of Property Values?

The Automated Underwriter system (AUS) indicates its findings in the following ways.

1. The Automated Underwriter system states that it returned the following standardized address and census tract. This is the address that will be used in its property valuation and fieldwork.
2. The AUS collateral assessment model indicates that the submitted value estimate for this transaction may be excessive.
3. The AUS collateral assessment model indicates that the property appears to have an excessive rate of appreciation.
4. The subject property has been identified as being located in either an area of declining home prices or in an area where it may be difficult to assess home values.

5. The AUS conducts a review for accuracy: The estimated value of property or net purchase price submitted for this transaction may have a higher rate of appreciation than the local market.
6. Fannie Mae's AUS will determine whether the use of Form 2055, 2065, or 2075 is the minimum assessment required; otherwise Form 1004 or a variant will be required.

Other reasons for an appraisal include: (1) insurance losses; (2) legal proceedings (divorces, judgments, etc.); (3) IRS proceedings; (4) estate taxation; and (5) determining a reasonable value for pricing property.

Historically there have been four primary "forces" that affect real estate values:

1. physical or environmental forces, meaning the physical layout of the property (literally: location, size, frontage, topology, etc.);
2. economic (market) forces, primarily referring to what are called "macro-economic" forces, including general employment, tax rates, labor supply, and credit terms and availability;
3. social forces (or non-market-driven social forces), which include political trends, demographic trends, and of course the economic tradition of the society; and
4. governmental forces, which largely come down to a simple question—To what degree does the population allow the government to restrict their property rights? The best examples are zoning, green zones, and government demands for easements.

Uniform Residential Appraisal Report

File #

The purpose of this summary appraisal report is to provide the lender/client with an accurate, and adequately supported, opinion of the market value of the subject property.

SUBJECT

Property Address		City		State	Zip Code
Borrower		Owner of Public Record		County	
Legal Description					
Assessor's Parcel #		Tax Year		R.E. Taxes $	
Neighborhood Name		Map Reference		Census Tract	
Occupant ☐ Owner ☐ Tenant ☐ Vacant	Special Assessments $	☐ PUD	HOA $	☐ per year ☐ per month
Property Rights Appraised ☐ Fee Simple ☐ Leasehold ☐ Other (describe)					
Assignment Type ☐ Purchase Transaction ☐ Refinance Transaction ☐ Other (describe)					
Lender/Client		Address			
Is the subject property currently offered for sale or has it been offered for sale in the twelve months prior to the effective date of this appraisal? ☐ Yes ☐ No					
Report data source(s) used, offering price(s), and date(s).					

CONTRACT

I ☐ did ☐ did not analyze the contract for sale for the subject purchase transaction. Explain the results of the analysis of the contract for sale or why the analysis was not performed.

Contract Price $ ____ Date of Contract ____ Is the property seller the owner of public record? ☐ Yes ☐ No Data Source(s)
Is there any financial assistance (loan charges, sale concessions, gift or downpayment assistance, etc.) to be paid by any party on behalf of the borrower? ☐ Yes ☐ No
If Yes, report the total dollar amount and describe the items to be paid.

NEIGHBORHOOD

Note: Race and the racial composition of the neighborhood are not appraisal factors.

Neighborhood Characteristics	One-Unit Housing Trends	One-Unit Housing	Present Land Use %
Location ☐ Urban ☐ Suburban ☐ Rural	Property Values ☐ Increasing ☐ Stable ☐ Declining	PRICE AGE	One-Unit %
Built-Up ☐ Over 75% ☐ 25-75% ☐ Under 25%	Demand/Supply ☐ Shortage ☐ In Balance ☐ Over Supply	$ (000) (yrs)	2-4 Unit %
Growth ☐ Rapid ☐ Stable ☐ Slow	Marketing Time ☐ Under 3 mths ☐ 3-6 mths ☐ Over 6 mths	Low	Multi-Family %
Neighborhood Boundaries		High	Commercial %
		Pred.	Other %

Neighborhood Description

Market Conditions (including support for the above conclusions)

SITE

Dimensions		Area		Shape		View	
Specific Zoning Classification			Zoning Description				
Zoning Compliance ☐ Legal ☐ Legal Nonconforming (Grandfathered Use) ☐ No Zoning ☐ Illegal (describe)							
Is the highest and best use of the subject property as improved (or as proposed per plans and specifications) the present use? ☐ Yes ☐ No If No, describe							

Utilities	Public	Other (describe)		Public	Other (describe)	Off-site Improvements—Type	Public	Private
Electricity	☐		Water	☐		Street	☐	☐
Gas	☐		Sanitary Sewer	☐		Alley	☐	☐

FEMA Special Flood Hazard Area ☐ Yes ☐ No FEMA Flood Zone ____ FEMA Map # ____ FEMA Map Date
Are the utilities and off-site improvements typical for the market area? ☐ Yes ☐ No If No, describe
Are there any adverse site conditions or external factors (easements, encroachments, environmental conditions, land uses, etc.)? ☐ Yes ☐ No If Yes, describe

IMPROVEMENTS

General Description		Foundation		Exterior Description	materials/condition	Interior	materials/condition
Units ☐ One ☐ One with Accessory Unit		☐ Concrete Slab ☐ Crawl Space		Foundation Walls		Floors	
# of Stories		☐ Full Basement ☐ Partial Basement		Exterior Walls		Walls	
Type ☐ Det. ☐ Att. ☐ S-Det./End Unit		Basement Area ____ sq. ft.		Roof Surface		Trim/Finish	
☐ Existing ☐ Proposed ☐ Under Const.		Basement Finish ____ %		Gutters & Downspouts		Bath Floor	
Design (Style)		☐ Outside Entry/Exit ☐ Sump Pump		Window Type		Bath Wainscot	
Year Built		Evidence of ☐ Infestation		Storm Sash/Insulated		Car Storage ☐ None	
Effective Age (Yrs)		☐ Dampness ☐ Settlement		Screens		☐ Driveway # of Cars ____
Attic ☐ None		Heating ☐ FWA ☐ HWBB ☐ Radiant		Amenities	☐ Woodstove(s) #	Driveway Surface	
☐ Drop Stair ☐ Stairs		☐ Other ____ Fuel ____		☐ Fireplace(s) # ____ ☐ Fence		☐ Garage # of Cars ____	
☐ Floor ☐ Scuttle		Cooling ☐ Central Air Conditioning		☐ Patio/Deck ____ ☐ Porch ____		☐ Carport # of Cars ____	
☐ Finished ☐ Heated		☐ Individual ☐ Other		☐ Pool ____ ☐ Other ____		☐ Att. ☐ Det. ☐ Built-in	

Appliances ☐ Refrigerator ☐ Range/Oven ☐ Dishwasher ☐ Disposal ☐ Microwave ☐ Washer/Dryer ☐ Other (describe)
Finished area **above** grade contains: ____ Rooms ____ Bedrooms ____ Bath(s) ____ Square Feet of Gross Living Area Above Grade
Additional features (special energy efficient items, etc.)

Describe the condition of the property (including needed repairs, deterioration, renovations, remodeling, etc.).

Are there any physical deficiencies or adverse conditions that affect the livability, soundness, or structural integrity of the property? ☐ Yes ☐ No If Yes, describe

Does the property generally conform to the neighborhood (functional utility, style, condition, use, construction, etc.)? ☐ Yes ☐ No If No, describe

Freddie Mac Form 70 March 2005   Fannie Mae Form 1004 March 2005

Uniform Residential Appraisal Report

File #

There are	comparable properties currently offered for sale in the subject neighborhood ranging in price from $					to $	
There are	comparable sales in the subject neighborhood within the past twelve months ranging in sale price from $					to $	

FEATURE	SUBJECT	COMPARABLE SALE # 1		COMPARABLE SALE # 2		COMPARABLE SALE # 3	
Address							
Proximity to Subject							
Sale Price	$		$		$		$
Sale Price/Gross Liv. Area	$ sq. ft.	$ sq. ft.		$ sq. ft.		$ sq. ft.	
Data Source(s)							
Verification Source(s)							
VALUE ADJUSTMENTS	DESCRIPTION	DESCRIPTION	+(-) $ Adjustment	DESCRIPTION	+(-) $ Adjustment	DESCRIPTION	+(-) $ Adjustment
Sale or Financing Concessions							
Date of Sale/Time							
Location							
Leasehold/Fee Simple							
Site							
View							
Design (Style)							
Quality of Construction							
Actual Age							
Condition							
Above Grade Room Count	Total Bdrms. Baths	Total Bdrms. Baths		Total Bdrms. Baths		Total Bdrms. Baths	
Gross Living Area	sq. ft.	sq. ft.		sq. ft.		sq. ft.	
Basement & Finished Rooms Below Grade							
Functional Utility							
Heating/Cooling							
Energy Efficient Items							
Garage/Carport							
Porch/Patio/Deck							
Net Adjustment (Total)		☐+ ☐-	$	☐+ ☐-	$	☐+ ☐-	$
Adjusted Sale Price of Comparables		Net Adj. % Gross Adj. %	$	Net Adj. % Gross Adj. %	$	Net Adj. % Gross Adj. %	$

I ☐ did ☐ did not research the sale or transfer history of the subject property and comparable sales. If not, explain

My research ☐ did ☐ did not reveal any prior sales or transfers of the subject property for the three years prior to the effective date of this appraisal.
Data source(s)
My research ☐ did ☐ did not reveal any prior sales or transfers of the comparable sales for the year prior to the date of sale of the comparable sale.
Data source(s)
Report the results of the research and analysis of the prior sale or transfer history of the subject property and comparable sales (report additional prior sales on page 3).

ITEM	SUBJECT	COMPARABLE SALE # 1	COMPARABLE SALE # 2	COMPARABLE SALE # 3
Date of Prior Sale/Transfer				
Price of Prior Sale/Transfer				
Data Source(s)				
Effective Date of Data Source(s)				

Analysis of prior sale or transfer history of the subject property and comparable sales

Summary of Sales Comparison Approach

Indicated Value by Sales Comparison Approach $

Indicated Value by: Sales Comparison Approach $ Cost Approach (if developed) $ Income Approach (if developed) $

This appraisal is made ☐ "as is", ☐ subject to completion per plans and specifications on the basis of a hypothetical condition that the improvements have been completed, ☐ subject to the following repairs or alterations on the basis of a hypothetical condition that the repairs or alterations have been completed, or ☐ subject to the following required inspection based on the extraordinary assumption that the condition or deficiency does not require alteration or repair:

Based on a complete visual inspection of the interior and exterior areas of the subject property, defined scope of work, statement of assumptions and limiting conditions, and appraiser's certification, my (our) opinion of the market value, as defined, of the real property that is the subject of this report is
$, as of   , which is the date of inspection and the effective date of this appraisal.

Freddie Mac Form 70   March 2005   Fannie Mae Form 1004   March 2005

Review of Uniform Residential Appraisal Report

Uniform Residential Appraisal Report   File

ADDITIONAL COMMENTS

COST APPROACH TO VALUE (not required by Fannie Mae)

Provide adequate information for the lender/client to replicate the below cost figures and calculations.
Support for the opinion of site value (summary of comparable land sales or other methods for estimating site value)

ESTIMATED ☐ REPRODUCTION OR ☐ REPLACEMENT COST NEW | OPINION OF SITE VALUE ....= $
Source of cost data | Dwelling   Sq. Ft. @ $ =$
Quality rating from cost service   Effective date of cost data | Sq. Ft. @ $ =$
Comments on Cost Approach (gross living area calculations, depreciation, etc.) | Garage/Carport   Sq. Ft. @ $ =$
| Total Estimate of Cost-New   = $
| Less   Physical   Functional   External
| Depreciation   =$(   )
| Depreciated Cost of Improvements   =$
| "As-is" Value of Site Improvements   =$
Estimated Remaining Economic Life (HUD and VA only)   Years | Indicated Value By Cost Approach   =$

INCOME APPROACH TO VALUE (not required by Fannie Mae)

Estimated Monthly Market Rent $ _____ X Gross Rent Multiplier _____ = $ _____ Indicated Value by Income Approach
Summary of Income Approach (including support for market rent and GRM)

PROJECT INFORMATION FOR PUDs (if applicable)

Is the developer/builder in control of the Homeowners' Association (HOA)? ☐ Yes ☐ No Unit type(s) ☐ Detached ☐ Attached
Provide the following information for PUDs ONLY if the developer/builder is in control of the HOA and the subject property is an attached dwelling unit.
Legal name of project
Total number of phases _____ Total number of units _____ Total number of units sold _____
Total number of units rented _____ Total number of units for sale _____ Data source(s)
Was the project created by the conversion of an existing building(s) into a PUD? ☐ Yes ☐ No If Yes, date of conversion
Does the project contain any multi-dwelling units? ☐ Yes ☐ No Data source(s)
Are the units, common elements, and recreation facilities complete? ☐ Yes ☐ No If No, describe the status of completion.

Are the common elements leased to or by the Homeowners' Association? ☐ Yes ☐ No If Yes, describe the rental terms and options.
Describe common elements and recreational facilities

Freddie Mac Form 70   March 2005   Fannie Mae Form 1004   March 2005

Uniform Residential Appraisal Report

File #

This report form is designed to report an appraisal of a one-unit property or a one-unit property with an accessory unit; including a unit in a planned unit development (PUD). This report form is not designed to report an appraisal of a manufactured home or a unit in a condominium or cooperative project.

This appraisal report is subject to the following scope of work, intended use, intended user, definition of market value, statement of assumptions and limiting conditions, and certifications. Modifications, additions, or deletions to the intended use, intended user, definition of market value, or assumptions and limiting conditions are not permitted. The appraiser may expand the scope of work to include any additional research or analysis necessary based on the complexity of this appraisal assignment. Modifications or deletions to the certifications are also not permitted. However, additional certifications that do not constitute material alterations to this appraisal report, such as those required by law or those related to the appraiser's continuing education or membership in an appraisal organization, are permitted.

SCOPE OF WORK: The scope of work for this appraisal is defined by the complexity of this appraisal assignment and the reporting requirements of this appraisal report form, including the following definition of market value, statement of assumptions and limiting conditions, and certifications. The appraiser must, at a minimum: (1) perform a complete visual inspection of the interior and exterior areas of the subject property, (2) inspect the neighborhood, (3) inspect each of the comparable sales from at least the street, (4) research, verify, and analyze data from reliable public and/or private sources, and (5) report his or her analysis, opinions, and conclusions in this appraisal report.

INTENDED USE: The intended use of this appraisal report is for the lender/client to evaluate the property that is the subject of this appraisal for a mortgage finance transaction.

INTENDED USER: The intended user of this appraisal report is the lender/client.

DEFINITION OF MARKET VALUE: The most probable price which a property should bring in a competitive and open market under all conditions requisite to a fair sale, the buyer and seller, each acting prudently, knowledgeably and assuming the price is not affected by undue stimulus. Implicit in this definition is the consummation of a sale as of a specified date and the passing of title from seller to buyer under conditions whereby: (1) buyer and seller are typically motivated; (2) both parties are well informed or well advised, and each acting in what he or she considers his or her own best interest; (3) a reasonable time is allowed for exposure in the open market; (4) payment is made in terms of cash in U. S. dollars or in terms of financial arrangements comparable thereto; and (5) the price represents the normal consideration for the property sold unaffected by special or creative financing or sales concessions* granted by anyone associated with the sale.

*Adjustments to the comparables must be made for special or creative financing or sales concessions. No adjustments are necessary for those costs which are normally paid by sellers as a result of tradition or law in a market area; these costs are readily identifiable since the seller pays these costs in virtually all sales transactions. Special or creative financing adjustments can be made to the comparable property by comparisons to financing terms offered by a third party institutional lender that is not already involved in the property or transaction. Any adjustment should not be calculated on a mechanical dollar for dollar cost of the financing or concession but the dollar amount of any adjustment should approximate the market's reaction to the financing or concessions based on the appraiser's judgment.

STATEMENT OF ASSUMPTIONS AND LIMITING CONDITIONS: The appraiser's certification in this report is subject to the following assumptions and limiting conditions:

1. The appraiser will not be responsible for matters of a legal nature that affect either the property being appraised or the title to it, except for information that he or she became aware of during the research involved in performing this appraisal. The appraiser assumes that the title is good and marketable and will not render any opinions about the title.

2. The appraiser has provided a sketch in this appraisal report to show the approximate dimensions of the improvements. The sketch is included only to assist the reader in visualizing the property and understanding the appraiser's determination of its size.

3. The appraiser has examined the available flood maps that are provided by the Federal Emergency Management Agency (or other data sources) and has noted in this appraisal report whether any portion of the subject site is located in an identified Special Flood Hazard Area. Because the appraiser is not a surveyor, he or she makes no guarantees, express or implied, regarding this determination.

4. The appraiser will not give testimony or appear in court because he or she made an appraisal of the property in question, unless specific arrangements to do so have been made beforehand, or as otherwise required by law.

5. The appraiser has noted in this appraisal report any adverse conditions (such as needed repairs, deterioration, the presence of hazardous wastes, toxic substances, etc.) observed during the inspection of the subject property or that he or she became aware of during the research involved in performing this appraisal. Unless otherwise stated in this appraisal report, the appraiser has no knowledge of any hidden or unapparent physical deficiencies or adverse conditions of the property (such as, but not limited to, needed repairs, deterioration, the presence of hazardous wastes, toxic substances, adverse environmental conditions, etc.) that would make the property less valuable, and has assumed that there are no such conditions and makes no guarantees or warranties, express or implied. The appraiser will not be responsible for any such conditions that do exist or for any engineering or testing that might be required to discover whether such conditions exist. Because the appraiser is not an expert in the field of environmental hazards, this appraisal report must not be considered as an environmental assessment of the property.

6. The appraiser has based his or her appraisal report and valuation conclusion for an appraisal that is subject to satisfactory completion, repairs, or alterations on the assumption that the completion, repairs, or alterations of the subject property will be performed in a professional manner.

Freddie Mac Form 70   March 2005   Fannie Mae Form 1004   March 2005

Uniform Residential Appraisal Report   File

APPRAISER'S CERTIFICATION: The Appraiser certifies and agrees that:

1. I have, at a minimum, developed and reported this appraisal in accordance with the scope of work requirements stated in this appraisal report.

2. I performed a complete visual inspection of the interior and exterior areas of the subject property. I reported the condition of the improvements in factual, specific terms. I identified and reported the physical deficiencies that could affect the livability, soundness, or structural integrity of the property.

3. I performed this appraisal in accordance with the requirements of the Uniform Standards of Professional Appraisal Practice that were adopted and promulgated by the Appraisal Standards Board of The Appraisal Foundation and that were in place at the time this appraisal report was prepared.

4. I developed my opinion of the market value of the real property that is the subject of this report based on the sales comparison approach to value. I have adequate comparable market data to develop a reliable sales comparison approach for this appraisal assignment. I further certify that I considered the cost and income approaches to value but did not develop them, unless otherwise indicated in this report.

5. I researched, verified, analyzed, and reported on any current agreement for sale for the subject property, any offering for sale of the subject property in the twelve months prior to the effective date of this appraisal, and the prior sales of the subject property for a minimum of three years prior to the effective date of this appraisal, unless otherwise indicated in this report.

6. I researched, verified, analyzed, and reported on the prior sales of the comparable sales for a minimum of one year prior to the date of sale of the comparable sale, unless otherwise indicated in this report.

7. I selected and used comparable sales that are locationally, physically, and functionally the most similar to the subject property.

8. I have not used comparable sales that were the result of combining a land sale with the contract purchase price of a home that has been built or will be built on the land.

9. I have reported adjustments to the comparable sales that reflect the market's reaction to the differences between the subject property and the comparable sales.

10. I verified, from a disinterested source, all information in this report that was provided by parties who have a financial interest in the sale or financing of the subject property.

11. I have knowledge and experience in appraising this type of property in this market area.

12. I am aware of, and have access to, the necessary and appropriate public and private data sources, such as multiple listing services, tax assessment records, public land records and other such data sources for the area in which the property is located.

13. I obtained the information, estimates, and opinions furnished by other parties and expressed in this appraisal report from reliable sources that I believe to be true and correct.

14. I have taken into consideration the factors that have an impact on value with respect to the subject neighborhood, subject property, and the proximity of the subject property to adverse influences in the development of my opinion of market value. I have noted in this appraisal report any adverse conditions (such as, but not limited to, needed repairs, deterioration, the presence of hazardous wastes, toxic substances, adverse environmental conditions, etc.) observed during the inspection of the subject property or that I became aware of during the research involved in performing this appraisal. I have considered these adverse conditions in my analysis of the property value, and have reported on the effect of the conditions on the value and marketability of the subject property.

15. I have not knowingly withheld any significant information from this appraisal report and, to the best of my knowledge, all statements and information in this appraisal report are true and correct.

16. I stated in this appraisal report my own personal, unbiased, and professional analysis, opinions, and conclusions, which are subject only to the assumptions and limiting conditions in this appraisal report.

17. I have no present or prospective interest in the property that is the subject of this report, and I have no present or prospective personal interest or bias with respect to the participants in the transaction. I did not base, either partially or completely, my analysis and/or opinion of market value in this appraisal report on the race, color, religion, sex, age, marital status, handicap, familial status, or national origin of either the prospective owners or occupants of the subject property or of the present owners or occupants of the properties in the vicinity of the subject property or on any other basis prohibited by law.

18. My employment and/or compensation for performing this appraisal or any future or anticipated appraisals was not conditioned on any agreement or understanding, written or otherwise, that I would report (or present analysis supporting) a predetermined specific value, a predetermined minimum value, a range or direction in value, a value that favors the cause of any party, or the attainment of a specific result or occurrence of a specific subsequent event (such as approval of a pending mortgage loan application).

19. I personally prepared all conclusions and opinions about the real estate that were set forth in this appraisal report. If I relied on significant real property appraisal assistance from any individual or individuals in the performance of this appraisal or the preparation of this appraisal report, I have named such individual(s) and disclosed the specific tasks performed in this appraisal report. I certify that any individual so named is qualified to perform the tasks. I have not authorized anyone to make a change to any item in this appraisal report; therefore, any change made to this appraisal is unauthorized and I will take no responsibility for it.

20. I identified the lender/client in this appraisal report who is the individual, organization, or agent for the organization that ordered and will receive this appraisal report.

Uniform Residential Appraisal Report   File

21. The lender/client may disclose or distribute this appraisal report to: the borrower; another lender at the request of the borrower; the mortgagee or its successors and assigns; mortgage insurers; government sponsored enterprises; other secondary market participants; data collection or reporting services; professional appraisal organizations; any department, agency, or instrumentality of the United States; and any state, the District of Columbia, or other jurisdictions; without having to obtain the appraiser's or supervisory appraiser's (if applicable) consent. Such consent must be obtained before this appraisal report may be disclosed or distributed to any other party (including, but not limited to, the public through advertising, public relations, news, sales, or other media).

22. I am aware that any disclosure or distribution of this appraisal report by me or the lender/client may be subject to certain laws and regulations. Further, I am also subject to the provisions of the Uniform Standards of Professional Appraisal Practice that pertain to disclosure or distribution by me.

23. The borrower, another lender at the request of the borrower, the mortgagee or its successors and assigns, mortgage insurers, government sponsored enterprises, and other secondary market participants may rely on this appraisal report as part of any mortgage finance transaction that involves any one or more of these parties.

24. If this appraisal report was transmitted as an "electronic record" containing my "electronic signature," as those terms are defined in applicable federal and/or state laws (excluding audio and video recordings), or a facsimile transmission of this appraisal report containing a copy or representation of my signature, the appraisal report shall be as effective, enforceable and valid as if a paper version of this appraisal report were delivered containing my original hand written signature.

25. Any intentional or negligent misrepresentation(s) contained in this appraisal report may result in civil liability and/or criminal penalties including, but not limited to, fine or imprisonment or both under the provisions of Title 18, United States Code, Section 1001, et seq., or similar state laws.

SUPERVISORY APPRAISER'S CERTIFICATION: The Supervisory Appraiser certifies and agrees that:

1. I directly supervised the appraiser for this appraisal assignment, have read the appraisal report, and agree with the appraiser's analysis, opinions, statements, conclusions, and the appraiser's certification.

2. I accept full responsibility for the contents of this appraisal report including, but not limited to, the appraiser's analysis, opinions, statements, conclusions, and the appraiser's certification.

3. The appraiser identified in this appraisal report is either a sub-contractor or an employee of the supervisory appraiser (or the appraisal firm), is qualified to perform this appraisal, and is acceptable to perform this appraisal under the applicable state law.

4. This appraisal report complies with the Uniform Standards of Professional Appraisal Practice that were adopted and promulgated by the Appraisal Standards Board of The Appraisal Foundation and that were in place at the time this appraisal report was prepared.

5. If this appraisal report was transmitted as an "electronic record" containing my "electronic signature," as those terms are defined in applicable federal and/or state laws (excluding audio and video recordings), or a facsimile transmission of this appraisal report containing a copy or representation of my signature, the appraisal report shall be as effective, enforceable and valid as if a paper version of this appraisal report were delivered containing my original hand written signature.

APPRAISER

Signature _____
Name _____
Company Name _____
Company Address _____

Telephone Number _____
Email Address _____
Date of Signature and Report _____
Effective Date of Appraisal _____
State Certification # _____
or State License # _____
or Other (describe) _____ State # _____
State _____
Expiration Date of Certification or License _____

ADDRESS OF PROPERTY APPRAISED
_____
_____

APPRAISED VALUE OF SUBJECT PROPERTY $ _____
LENDER/CLIENT
Name _____
Company Name _____
Company Address _____
_____
Email Address _____

SUPERVISORY APPRAISER (ONLY IF REQUIRED)

Signature _____
Name _____
Company Name _____
Company Address _____

Telephone Number _____
Email Address _____
Date of Signature _____
State Certification # _____
or State License # _____
State _____
Expiration Date of Certification or License _____

SUBJECT PROPERTY

☐ Did not inspect subject property
☐ Did inspect exterior of subject property from street
  Date of Inspection _____
☐ Did inspect interior and exterior of subject property
  Date of Inspection _____

COMPARABLE SALES

☐ Did not inspect exterior of comparable sales from street
☐ Did inspect exterior of comparable sales from street
  Date of Inspection _____

REQUIRED LENDER NOTICES

Federally mandated notices include:

- The Loan Estimate is a form that lays out important information about the loan applied for. The lender must send this Loan Estimate within three business days of receiving a borrower's application.
- Lenders must still give out a Good Faith Estimate and Truth-in-Lending disclosure for a reverse mortgage.
- The Closing Disclosure must be sent out by the lender at least three business days before closing.
- The Notice of the Right to Rescind is used for loans not used to purchase a home, for example, a refinance or home equity line of credit. This notice informs the borrower that they have three business days from the lender's fulfillment of certain conditions to cancel the loan and it provides a form for cancelling the loan.
- An Initial Escrow Statement, which lists the estimated taxes, insurance premiums, and other charges the lender anticipates paying from a borrower's escrow account during the first year of their loan.
- A lender must provide a Servicing Disclosure Notice of the Mortgagor's Right of Disclosure and Notice of Servicing Rights Being Transferred to a New Servicer under RESPA.
- Since the right to a service mortgage loan can be transferred to a new servicer, the existing servicer will be required to send a borrower two notices:
    - a notice from the current mortgage servicer at least 15 days before the effective transfer date; and
    - a notice from the new servicer not more than 15 days after the effective date of the transfer.
- The current servicer and the new servicer may send a single notice, in which case it must be provided to the borrower at least 15 days before the servicing transfer date. The notice(s) will include:
    - the date on which the transferring servicer will stop accepting payments on the loan; and
    - the date on which the new servicer will begin to accept payments.
- The Real Estate Settlements Procedures Act requires that a lender provide a notice disclosing the mortgagor's right to receive a copy of the appraisal report and credit report.

- Lenders must also provide a Flood Insurance Notice that informs a borrower if the subject property is or is not in a flood zone and that they might be required to purchase a flood insurance policy.

Examples of State-Mandated Notices

Texas legislators passed several laws covered within Chapter 343 of its Finance Code that require a three-day notice "cooling off" period before closing any mortgage product with single premium insurance such as credit life, disability or unemployment income replacement insurance. Chapter 343 of the Texas Finance Code piggybacked onto the regulations in HOEPA and adds a requirement of a notice of mortgage **counseling** for home loans that are **12%** or higher.

Texas requires its credit unions to provide each applicant for a home loan a written notice that states that intentionally or knowingly making a materially false or misleading written statement to obtain property or credit, including a mortgage loan, is a violation of § 32.32, Texas Penal Code.

Another example is the recent Alabama Supreme Court decision that requires a mortgage servicer's strict compliance with the acceleration remedies notice provisions contained within a security instrument. The Supreme Court found that absent strict compliance, a foreclosure sale is potentially subject to being declared void, even if notice to the borrower satisfied key requirements by providing notice of a default under the mortgage.

California under its recently passed Homeowner Bill of Rights legislation requires written explanation for denial of loan modification: If a first loan modification application is denied, "the mortgage servicer shall send a written notice to the borrower identifying with specificity the reasons for the denial and shall include a statement that the borrower may obtain additional documentation supporting the denial decision upon written request to the mortgage servicer."

California requires that prior to the required counseling for a reverse mortgage, the applicant must receive the list of HUD-approved counseling agencies as well as the required Reverse Mortgage Worksheet Guide and Important Notice to Reverse Mortgage Loan Applicant disclosures.

It is therefore imperative that lenders be aware of not only all the state and federal laws concerning required notices for real estate finance transactions, but also the timing of those notices to protect the interest of the lender, investor, and borrower.

QUALIFYING THE TITLE

Mortgage lenders have a unique need to qualify the title of the property if they are using it as collateral security for a loan they are going to make. Mortgage lenders want to assure themselves and the ultimate investor in the mortgage that the buyer/owner is getting a "good" title, meaning that it is insurable and saleable. Mortgage lenders obviously are concerned with the insurability of a property since a seller's title insurance policy is typically required on a mortgage loan. There are, however, three means to getting title protection that a title is clear of any claims that would worry a buyer or lender. The lender can obtain assurance by:

- ordering an abstract and attorney title opinion;
- ordering a preliminary title insurance binder; or
- (in some states, like New York) verify the chain of ownership using the Torrens system.

Title Protection

A standard requirement for approval of a mortgage loan is that the title to pledged property must be valid. The lender wants some assurance that the parties granting the mortgage are the true owners and hold valid title to the property pledged. Many problems can occur in a chain of title ownership that may impair present ownership rights. These include the possibility of forged documents, undisclosed heirs, mistaken legal interpretation of wills, misfiled documents, confusion resulting from a similarity of names, and incorrectly stated marital status. It is critical that a purchaser of real property take the necessary steps to assure good title, whether or not a mortgage loan is involved.

Three methods are commonly used to protect both a purchaser and a lender from future title problems. One is an opinion by a qualified attorney based on the research of an abstract; another is the purchase of title insurance; and the third is a land registration system used in a few areas of the country called the Torrens system. Each will be discussed further below.

Attorney's Opinion Based on Abstract

The older method—and still the only one available for assuring valid title in oil and gas sale or lease transactions—is a research of the abstract by a qualified attorney.

Abstract of Title

The chronological collection of all recorded documents that affect land title is called an abstract of title. It is prepared by an abstracter who specializes in researching county land records. Early recorded instruments affecting land title were all handwritten and provide a fascinating history of the people and events involved with a particular tract of land. Modern abstracts can be drawn from computerized files. The record includes conveyances, wills, judicial proceedings, liens, and encumbrances that affect title to land. It is simply a history of the instruments that affect title and, by itself, does not assure the validity of title. The status of title comes from an opinion given by a qualified attorney.

Attorney's Opinion

After careful research of an abstract, a qualified attorney can issue an opinion as to the validity of title. By examining the chain of events that affect title, the attorney can reach a conclusion as to the identity of the present owners, and report any instruments that have an adverse effect on the ownership rights. Furthermore, the attorney may state what curative steps must be taken to clear the title if there is an adverse claim or a break in the chain of ownership. An attorney's favorable opinion may be accepted by a lender as adequate proof of title.

In large real property transactions, an attorney's opinion may be a lower-cost procedure. In recent years, some large office buildings have been conveyed based on an attorney's opinion of title as lower cost than the purchase of title insurance. This is more likely when no mortgage loan is involved. However, this approach does have some disadvantages. This method provides no insurance against an adverse claim, leaving the purchaser with only the seller as recourse against future loss. Furthermore, it can take more time than the issuance of a title policy, since title insurance companies usually maintain continuous records of all recorded documents subject to rapid recall. Ignoring for the time being the lower cost of a attorney's opinion, some transactions demand that both a title policy and attorney's opinion is obtained with the attorney's opinion coming from a firm with a high professional liability insurance coverage. The reason for this is if an expensive property is going to have a development that might have a value four to 10 times the value of the raw land (like a mall), then taking a loss on the full value of the developed value might exceed the title insurance policy limits.

Title Insurance

The most popular method used to assure valid title in real estate transactions is the purchase of **title insurance**. It is a specialized type of insurance that protects a policyholder against loss from something that has already happened, such as a forged deed somewhere in the chain of title. Title companies examine the chain of title to make sure the title is insurable (that is, that there are no defects that could cause a subsequent claim). This is important because the title company also agrees to defend the policyholder's title in court should any lawsuits arise with adverse claims.

Title insurance policies normally list certain exclusions that are not covered by the insurance protection. These exclusions include such things as the rights of parties in possession, unrecorded easements, encroachments, zoning laws, and other governmental restrictions. What is insured is sometimes called a marketable title, meaning one not necessarily perfect but free from plausible or reasonable objections. There are two different kinds of title insurance: one indemnifies an owner against loss, and the other indemnifies a lender against loss.

Owner's Policy

An owner's policy protects him or her as long as the insured party has an interest in the property. This protection can extend beyond the period of actual possession. When an insured owner sells the property, it is often conveyed with a general warranty deed. The warranty clause in that kind of deed makes the seller liable to "forever defend" against possible defects in the title at the time of conveyance, even though the claim may not arise until long after the property has been conveyed. State limitation statutes normally limit this exposure to a period of 20 to 30 years, after which time the insurance policy itself lapses. The important point is that the owner's title insurance does not "run with the land"—i.e., it does not transfer to a new owner and is not assignable. The reason is that the previous owner remains liable and holds the protection of that policy.

An owner's policy is issued in the amount of the property value at the time of the transaction. In certain instances, it is possible to increase the coverage should substantial improvements be made or appreciation occur in the property value.

Lender's Policy

At the time that an owner's policy is issued, the property can also be insured against the same defects for the benefit of a lender—through a different kind of policy, however. The lender's, or mortgagee's, policy is issued in the amount of the mortgage loan and declines with each reduction in the principal balance. When the loan is paid off, the lender's policy becomes void. Also, unlike the owner's policy, a lender's policy automatically transfers to whoever holds the mortgage note. If the property is foreclosed and purchased by the mortgagee, the policy automatically becomes an owner's policy.

Who Pays for Title Insurance?

Practice varies throughout the country in regard to who pays for an owner's title policy. A fairly common procedure is for the owner selling the property to pay. The reasoning is that it proves the seller is delivering valid title, even though the coverage protects the buyer. In some parts of the country, the buyer pays for title insurance as the one gaining protection. It is the lender's policy that is most consistently paid for by the buyer as a cost of borrowing money.

Torrens System

Some states permit the use of the Torrens system, a method of registering the ownership of land and encumbrances, except for tax liens. It might be compared with the registration system used for automobiles. The system was developed in 1857 by Sir Robert Torrens of Australia, who took the idea from how titles to ships were registered.

To initiate a Torrens system registration, the landowner petitions a state court to register the subject property. Necessary title information must be filed with the court and notice given to all interested parties. The court's determination is made in the form of a decree somewhat similar to that used in a quiet title suit. Once a property is registered following the court's decree, title cannot pass to another, nor are encumbrances or conveyances effective until they also are registered on the certificate of title. Initial use of the Torrens system is optional, but once property is registered, all subsequent transfers must follow the registration procedures. In some states, Torrens-registered property is not subject to general judgment liens, nor can title be lost through adverse possession.

One of the problems with the use of the Torrens system as a method of protecting title to property is that the cost of court action to simply register a title may easily exceed the cost of purchasing title insurance.

REVIEW OF THE TITLE COMMITMENT

A **title commitment** is the end result of using public records to establish rights of real property ownership. This is a way of establishing that the person who is selling the property actually has the right to sell it and that the buyer is getting all the rights to the property (title) for which he or she is paying.

Title commitments are important documents in real estate transactions. The real estate agent and lender must carefully read the title commitment so that any errors or problems listed are properly addressed. Some problems can hold up a closing or perhaps ruin the transaction or financing.

The American Land Title Association recommends reviewing the following information on each title commitment as a best practice for real estate agents and lenders to prepare the way for a smooth transaction at the closing table.

The Delivery Slip

Professionals should not ignore the delivery slip as just a convenience. Rather, they should perform a rapid review for the following important information:

1. Are the buyers and/or sellers listed on the delivery slip? If not, they are not receiving copies of the commitment from the title company. It is incumbent upon the real estate agent to deliver a copy.
2. Make sure all parties to the transaction are listed on the delivery slip. The lender and any attorneys involved will want to receive copies of the commitment.
3. Keep a copy of delivery slips handy because they list the closer and the title contacts—information you might need in case questions or issues arise prior to closing.

Schedule A

Upon receipt of the title commitment, carefully review the following information on Schedule A:

1. Are the buyers' names spelled correctly?
2. Is the purchase price correct?

3. Does the legal description match the one on the contract?
4. Are the sellers listed on the commitment the same parties who executed the contract?
5. Is the property address correct?
6. Does the title premium reflect a reissue rate if a seller is entitled to one?
7. If the contract calls for an owner's extended coverage (OEC) policy, check the premium to make sure that the correct policy type is being paid for and provided.
8. Review the endorsements and make sure they apply to the property. Lender endorsements are requested by the lender and may not be removed by any other party.

If there are discrepancies between Schedule A and the contract, contact the closer immediately.

Schedule B-1

As soon as you receive the title commitment, carefully review the following information on Schedule B-1 (Requirements):

1. Are any of the parties using a power of attorney? Even though there will not be a requirement listing this, it is very important to get a copy of the POA to your closer for review well in advance of the closing.
2. Is the seller or buyer a corporation, limited liability company, or partnership? If so, requirements may call for a trade name affidavit, partnership agreement, or articles of incorporation. The sooner these are obtained from the customer, the sooner the title department can review them.

Sometimes the title commitment shows two deeds of trust on a property, yet the seller has only a single loan. The lender should let the closer know right away, as the title insurer can probably obtain a Release of Deed of Trust from the previous lender or a Letter of Indemnity from the previous title company.

LENDER CLOSING COSTS

Permissible **closing costs** are defined by regional FHA insuring offices in accordance with local practices, and therefore are not always uniform.

These costs include the HUD/FHA application fee, a lender's origination fee, costs of the title search, legal fees to prepare necessary closing instruments, and miscellaneous costs such as notary fees, recording costs, and a credit report charge. New rules were released in November 2010 that gave more flexibility in determining acceptable closing costs. Lenders may charge and collect from borrowers those customary and reasonable costs necessary to close the mortgage loan. For example, borrowers may not be forced to pay a tax service fee that lenders collect when they use a third-party vendor to determine current real estate tax payment status and annual costs rather than calling or checking with the county clerk's office themselves. FHA no longer limits the origination fee to 1% of the mortgage amount for its standard mortgage insurance programs. However, both home equity conversion mortgage (HECM) and Section 203(k) Rehabilitation Mortgage Insurance programs retain their statutory origination fee caps of 2% for HECM mortgage loans, and as of May 2009, when the Section 203(k) mortgage involves insurance of advances and partial disbursements of the rehabilitation escrow account, the lender may collect from the borrower a supplemental origination fee that compensates the lender for the additional cost of disbursements and inspections of the work, limited to 1.5% of the portion of the mortgage allocated to rehabilitation or $350, whichever is greater.

CREDIT SCORE CASE STUDY/WORKSHOP

Go to the URL below, and print out the tri-merged credit report with credit scores. Use the information from earlier in this to evaluate the credit report, listing all areas reviewed.

http://www.avantus.com/samples/AvantusCreditReport.pdf

If you feel you need a little more practice or information, navigate to the web address below for tutorials on how to read and interpret a credit report. This same site offers several good webinars on credit reports and credit scoring:

http://wn.com/consumer_credit_myfico_transunion_credit_report_tutorial

Additional review can be performed at the following link with a sample credit report, where you can get explanations as you go through it:

http://www.creditcards.com/credit-card-news/help/interactive-sample-credit-report-6000.php

Questions for Discussion

1. How does the Equal Credit Opportunity Act reduce discrimination?
2. List the essential information that a prospective borrower must provide in a residential loan application, and in a commercial loan.
3. Discuss "ability to repay" a loan as may be indicated by type of income and stability of income.
4. What are the major rights of borrowers as they relate to how their credit is reported, protected, and accessed?
5. Define willingness to pay and how it can be evaluated.
6. Explain why PMI can offer lower premiums than Government Programs.
7. In analyzing corporate credit, what further investigation would an underwriter employ beyond a careful study of the company's financial statements?
8. What is the risk insured by private mortgage insurance?
9. Who pays for title insurance?
10. How are liabilities usually measured in the analysis of an applicant seeking a home loan?

Multiple Choice Questions for Review

1. What is the primary purpose of the Equal Credit Opportunity Act?
   a. to collect information for monitoring purposes
   b. to prevent discrimination in the granting of credit by requiring banks and other creditors to make extensions of credit equally available to all creditworthy applicants with fairness and impartiality and without discrimination on any prohibited basis
   c. to verify the applicant's permanent residence and immigration status
   d. to request information concerning the applicant's plan or expectations of having children and his or her childbearing capabilities or birth-control practices

2. Of the following, which is not a primary determinant in the amount of mortgage credit to extend?
   a. credit history
   b. income
   c. likelihood of continuing employment
   d. education

3. The two underlying relationships that must be assessed by a lender when considering the risk of a mortgage are:
   a. payment-to-debt ratio and loan-to-value ratio
   b. front-end-payment-to-income ratio and loan-to-value ratio
   c. payment-to-debt ratio and loan-to-price ratio
   d. front-end-payment-to-income ratio and loan-to-price ratio

4. A consumer has the right to:
   a. dispute the accuracy of credit report information
   b. file a statement setting forth the nature of disputed credit report information
   c. have obsolete information removed from a credit report
   d. all of these

5. The borrower's history of willingness to pay obligations is key to underwriting decisions, so an underwriter is going to do a more deliberate study of the borrower's credit by using all of the following EXCEPT:
   a. payment histories and amount of time credit accounts have been open
   b. the frequency of requests for credit
   c. results of any legal proceedings and a careful review of personal data for relevance and consistency
   d. results of collateral review with appraiser

6. A title commitment is the end result of using public records to:
   a. establish current municipal bonds taxes
   b. establish rights of real property ownership
   c. establish criminal liability claims
   d. all of these

7. Other than the analysis of a corporation's financial statements, which of the following would NOT be a question a commercial underwriter could ask when a corporation is borrowing to purchase real estate?
   a. Can the company's stock price reflect the value of the real estate?
   b. Are the best interests of the shareholders being met by holding real estate?
   c. Does the corporation have the expertise to manage the property?
   d. All of these are relevant questions.

8. Which of the following will help control the risk of loss in the event of a default by a mortgagor?
   a. secondary financing to obtain equity to pay for a delinquency
   b. a loan-to-value ratio of 90%
   c. private mortgage insurance
   d. a graduated-payment mortgage

9. One of the problems with the use of the Torrens system as a method of protecting title to property is that:
   a. it is similar to the system of registration used for automobiles
   b. the cost of court action to register a title may easily exceed the cost of purchasing title insurance.
   c. it is difficult to find the original title holder.
   d. the system was established in 1857 and is archaic.

10. Understanding the liabilities of a potential mortgagor is important in determining whether or not he or she would meet certain acceptable debt ratios established by the investor. Which of the following are the maximum acceptable ratios for conforming loans?
    a. 25/35
    b. 28/36
    c. 29/42
    d. 31/43

Additional Online Resources

http://www.makinghomeaffordable.gov/pages/default.aspx
   The link above provides the most current information about the HAMP and HARP temporary Affordable Housing Programs that existed at the time of publication.

https://www.fanniemae.com/singlefamily/uniform-residential-loan-application
   New Redesigned Fannie Mae Form 1003 eLearning Tutorial is available at the link above.

Chapter 10

DEFAULTS AND FORECLOSURES

KEY TERMS AND PHRASES

Credit Alert Interactive Voice Response System (CAIVRS)
deficiency judgment
Home Affordable Foreclosure Alternatives Program (HAFA)
Home Affordable Mortgage Program (HAMP)
Home Affordable Refinance Program (HARP)
Housing Finance Agency Innovation Fund (HHF)
judicial foreclosure
loan modification
nonjudicial foreclosure
redemption period
strict foreclosure

LEARNING OBJECTIVES

At the conclusion of this chapter, students will be able to:
- Explain the ways in which mortgage loans default and advance into a foreclosure.
- Learn the tax effect of foreclosure on the borrower and the calculation of gains and losses on a foreclosed property.
- Learn the use of advances, modifications, and forbearance for changes in loan terms.

> - State reasons why a lender would want to avoid foreclosing on a mortgage loan.
> - Describe the effects of delinquent mortgage loans on lost income and increased costs.

DEFAULTS

Loan Default and Foreclosure

The insured commitment on a HUD/FHA loan covers 100% of the loan amount since lenders normally loan exactly the insured amount. In the event of a default and foreclosure action, previous practice has been for the FHA to pay off the loan balance, with interest, in exchange for an assignment of the mortgagee's claim to the foreclosed property. The property becomes federally owned and subject to rehabilitation and resale as permitted under FHA rules.

With the substantial escalation of foreclosures beginning in the mid-1980s, HUD/FHA undertook a new policy in an effort to stem depletion of its Mutual Mortgage Insurance Fund (the back-up fund for single-family insurance programs). The new policy calls for a case-by-case review of each foreclosure prior to taking action. When a foreclosure becomes necessary, HUD/FHA appraises the property to determine its fair market value. If this value proves to be less than the amount due on the loan, the FHA will pay the difference between the fair market value of the property and the balance due on the loan to the lender. The lender is then asked to make its claim for that difference without a conveyance of the property. The practice is known within the industry as a *claim without conveyance.*

Its purpose, of course, is to limit both the cash payout on claims and the number of properties returned for the FHA to manage, rehabilitate, and resell. So long as the determination of fair market value by HUD/FHA is accurate, losses to the lender could be minimized. Nevertheless, lenders have been skeptical of the practice, as it allows the FHA to set its own value on the amount of an insured commitment. Furthermore, lenders feel much better served if they never have to undertake repossession of a foreclosed property. Claim without conveyance is one of the changes that has increased the risk of an FHA loan for a mortgage lender.

How Delinquency and Defaults Impact Lenders

Delinquent or defaulted mortgages receive a substantial amount of attention by the lenders. Sometimes the public believes that lenders just wait for a loan that is delinquent to get to a point that they are in default and then just foreclose. There are two reasons that this is not true. The first is that foreclosure without collection efforts runs counter to the main purposes of being a mortgage lender to allow a borrower to attain home ownership. Secondly, foreclosure is full of risk that the sale of the property will not raise enough funds to pay off the outstanding mortgage. The following items are also in play to explain the effects of delinquency and foreclosure on a lender:

1. Critically delinquent loans may affect the company's operations.
2. Collection activities increase administrative costs and employee time.
3. Ineffective collection attempts will exacerbate poor public perceptions and possibly a bad public image of the lender.
4. Lenders lose income no matter whether a third party is servicing the loan.
5. The opportunity cost of not being able to reinvest the funds from income lost or principal amortization into more profitable mortgages is lost.

Successful troubled asset managers for delinquent mortgages have superior processes for examining the reasons for nonpayment and work with the borrower to accomplish a recovery to a fully paying status. This is often accomplished with a loan modification that will be discussed later in this chapter.

Reporting Defaults and Foreclosures

Another change in practices since late 1986 is that the FHA, having been faced with massive foreclosure problems, requires mortgagees to notify credit bureaus of defaults and foreclosures. This report must include the names of original obligors who allowed loans to be assumed without obtaining a release of liability.

In 1987, HUD introduced the **Credit Alert Interactive Voice Response System (CAIVRS)** to collect and furnish credit data from its own files for lenders' and borrowers' use. These data are primarily detailed reports on borrowers who might owe amounts to the government or its agencies or guaranty programs. By maintaining a file of information on those who default on its loans, HUD is able to minimize the problem of borrowers obtaining a second or third HUD loan after defaulting on an earlier obligation. In 1992, the system was expanded to include default information on guaranteed loans made by the Rural Development Services (formerly, the Farmers Home Administration program), Small Business Administration, Department of Veterans Affairs, and the Department of Education.

HUD reported on their website that "The use of CAIVRS has allowed participating agencies to better monitor their credit programs and to reduce the credit extended to individuals with outstanding delinquencies on Federal debts. CAIVRS has allowed participating agencies to avoid potential losses in excess of $12 billion in 2012."[1]

For any federally guaranteed loan, as evidence that screening was performed, the lender must enter a CAIVRS response code on the loan analysis sheet. If a claim was caused by unavoidable circumstances, or if a satisfactory repayment plan has been arranged, the applicant may still be approved.

VA Default and Foreclosure

Once notification of a default has been filed with the VA, there is no time limit that dictates when a lender must take action to foreclose on the property. If foreclosure does become necessary, the VA must first appraise the property and set a "specified value." This value becomes the minimum amount for which the property can be sold and serves as a protection for all parties involved.

In years past, the VA has followed the practice of paying a lender in full on a foreclosed loan and taking title to repossessed property. It was not legally obligated to do this but believed assurance to a lender of full recovery of its loan balance with interest provided greater credibility for the VA guaranty. And certainly it did so.

More recently, as foreclosure problems escalated, the VA altered its policies into what is commonly called a "no-bid" action in foreclosure proceedings. This means that the VA now appraises the property's net value to the VA prior to a lender foreclosure action. If it would cost the VA less to pay off the guaranty to the lender (rather than the balance due on the loan), it simply chooses not to bid at the foreclosure auction (no-bid) and forfeits any further claim to the property. This possibility has lessened the value of a VA guaranty for many lenders.

---

[1] *The FHA Solvency Act of 2013: Hearing, Before the Committee on Banking, Housing, and Urban Affairs,* United States Senate (July 24, 2013), http://www.gpo.gov/fdsys/pkg/CHRG-113shrg82782/pdf/CHRG-113shrg82782.pdf

ADJUSTMENTS AND MODIFICATIONS

Temporary "Making Home Affordable" Programs

Starting in 2006, poor credit and underwriting practices combined with overly aggressive origination-to-distribute mortgage programs were just two of many factors that led to the recent financial crisis. After placing Fannie Mae and Freddie Mac into conservatorship, the federal government was suddenly faced with the need to work in concert with the Federal Reserve Bank and the commercial banking industry to come up with innovative programs not aimed at making new affordable mortgages, but rather, trying to keep existing homeowners in their homes during a prolonged slump in the economy and one of the most severe downturns in residential real estate prices since the Great Depression. The programs listed below only apply to mortgages that are owned or guaranteed by Fannie Mae and Freddie Mac or serviced by over 100 servicers participating in HAMP™. These programs have been developed over the period 2008–2014. While the life of these programs is coming to a close, they can be broken down into the following broad categories, followed by a few of the more common programs:

- lowering borrower payments
- Programs in effect as of January 2015 are:
  - Home Affordable Modification Program™ (HAMP™);
  - Second Lien Modification Program (2MP);
  - FHA Home Affordable Modification Program (FHA-HAMP); and
  - Veteran's Administration Home Affordable Modification (VA-HAMP).
- lowering borrower mortgage interest rates
- Programs in effect as of January 2015 are:
  - Home Affordable Refinance Program (HARP); and
  - FHA Refinance for Borrowers with Negative Equity (FHA Short Refinance).
- assistance for unemployed borrowers
- A program in effect as of January 2015 is:
  - Housing Finance Agency Innovation Fund for the Hardest-Hit Housing Markets (HHF).
- assistance for borrowers with poorly constructed second mortgages
- A program in effect as of January 2015 is:

- Second Lien Modification Program (only available to those borrowers with mortgages modified through the Homes Affordable Modification Program listed above).
- assistance for borrowers with negative equity
- Programs in effect as of January 2015 are:
  - Home Affordable Refinance Program (HARP);
  - FHA Refinance for Borrowers in Negative Equity (FHA Short Refinance); and
  - Housing Finance Agency Innovation Fund for the Hardest-Hit Housing Markets (HHF).
- foreclosure alternative programs for borrowers
- A program in effect as of January 2015 is:
  - Home Affordable Foreclosure Alternatives (HAFA™) Program.

Each of the programs above has unique eligibility requirements and provisions, and many are under sunset provisions that are set to expire. Many of the programs below have a requirement that the mortgage be made prior to 2009. These programs will naturally wind down over time since the average mortgage pays off within 12 to 15 years. The success of many of these programs has been the subject of much criticism in the financial press and among industry professionals and investors. For aforementioned reasons, only the most widely used programs—HAMP™, HARP™, HHF, and HAFA™—will be discussed in detail below.

HAMP™

The **Home Affordable Modification Program** is intended to help borrowers lower their monthly mortgage payment to 31% of their verified monthly gross (pretax) income to make their going-forward mortgage payments more affordable. The typical HAMP™ modification results in a 40% drop in a monthly mortgage payment. The Department of Housing and Urban Development reported in April of 2011 that 18% of HAMP™ homeowners had reduced their payments by $1,000 or more. The eligibility requirements for a borrower are as follows:

- The mortgagor must occupy the house as their primary residence.
- The mortgage must have been obtained on or before January 1, 2009.

- The current mortgage payment must be more than 31% of the mortgagor's monthly gross (pretax) income.
- The mortgagor can owe up to $729,750 on the home.
- The mortgagor must show that he or she has a financial hardship and is either delinquent or in danger of falling behind.
- The mortgagor must have sufficient, documented income to support the modified payment.
- The mortgagor must not have been convicted within the last 10 years of a felony, larceny, theft, fraud or forgery, or money laundering or tax evasion, in connection with a mortgage or real estate transaction.

HARP™

The **Home Affordable Refinance Program** is intended to help borrowers who are current on their mortgages and have been unable to obtain a traditional refinance because the value of their homes has declined. HARP™ was designed to help mortgagors refinance into new, affordable, and more stable mortgages. The HARP™ mortgage is a new loan and will require mortgagors to make a loan application with normal loan refinancing fees. Applicants must meet all of the following criteria:

- Mortgagor must have a mortgage owned or guaranteed by Fannie Mae or Freddie Mac.
- Mortgage cannot be a FHA, VA, or USDA loan.
- Mortgagor must be current on his or her mortgage payments and have not been more than 30 days late in making a payment over the past year.
- Mortgagor can owe more than the home is worth, but the mortgage cannot exceed 125% of the current market value of the home.
- As refinanced, the mortgage must improve the long-term affordability or stability of the new mortgage (a fairly subjective process).
- Mortgagor must have the ability to make the new mortgage payments.

HHF

The **Housing Finance Agency Innovation Fund** for the Hardest-Hit Housing Markets was a new program established by the U.S. Treasury Department in early 2010 to provide at least $7.6 billion in targeted aid to states hit hard by the economic crisis. This program continues to be coordinated with various state housing finance agencies to develop innovative programs to stabilize the local housing markets and help borrowers avoid foreclosure. The Hardest-Hit Fund programs complement the Making Home Affordable® Program, but are not limited to homeowners eligible for Making Home Affordable. The HHF program fund has been allocated to just 18 states plus the District of Columbia[2]. The programs vary greatly by state but commonly include the following benefits:

- mortgage payment assistance for unemployed or underemployed homeowners;
- principal reduction to help homeowners get into more affordable mortgages;
- funding to eliminate homeowners' second lien loans; and/or
- help for homeowners who are transitioning out of their homes and into more affordable places of residence.

HAFA™

The **Home Affordable Foreclosure Alternatives Program** is targeting those borrowers who have a mortgage payment that is unaffordable and borrowers who are interested in transitioning to more affordable housing. The typical borrower is eligible for a short sale or deed in lieu of foreclosure through HAFA™. The benefit of a HAFA™ short sale is that the mortgagor will no longer be responsible for the difference between what he or she owed on the mortgage and the amount for which his or her home sells. The mortgagor will also receive $3,000 in relocation assistance upon successful closing of any arranged and approved short sale or deed in lieu of foreclosure. For a mortgagor to be eligible for a HAFA™, he or she must meet all of the following criteria:

---

[2] "Hardest Hit Fund," Making Home Affordable Program, https://www.makinghomeaffordable.gov/need-help/Pages/need-help-options-hhf.aspx

- Mortgagor must have lived in the home for the last 12 months.
- Mortgagor must be able to document financial hardship.
- Mortgagor must not have purchased a new house within the last 12 months.
- The first mortgage must be less than $729,750.
- Mortgagor must have received the mortgage on or before January 1, 2009.
- Mortgagor must not have been convicted within the last 10 years of a felony, larceny, theft, fraud or forgery, or money laundering or tax evasion, in connection with a mortgage or real estate transaction.

The requirements and existence of the programs above are handled by the U.S. Treasury Department and the Department of Housing and Urban Development.

Comparison of Qualification Guidelines

Table 10-1 provides a summary of the percentage guidelines found in the four types of loans just discussed.

Other major changes to loan terms include the following:

1. **additional advances**, a formally approved increase in the amount of loan principal;
2. **loan modification**, a permanent change in the repayment amount of interest rate, often for the purpose of reducing monthly payment; or
   a. this might be a restructuring of a loan to shorten the original maturity date through the use of accelerated amortization; or
   b. extending the term of the loan from the original maturity to fit a borrower's special needs; or
   c. allowing prepayments to reduce the monthly payment (sometimes called riding prepayments).

TABLE 10-1 Summary of Percentage Guidelines

	Housing Ratio	Fixed Payment Ratio
HUD/FHA	31%	43%
VA	(Not limited)	41
Conforming/conventional	28	36
Affordable housing	33	45

Source: © 2021 Mbition LLC

> [Space Above This Line For Recording Data]
>
> ## SPECIMEN - LOAN MODIFICATION AGREEMENT
> (Providing for Fixed Interest Rate)
>
> This Loan Modification Agreement ("Agreement"), made this 5th day of May, 2018, between Jonnie I Jones ("Borrower") and XYZ Mortgage Company ("Lender"), amends and supplements (1) the Mortgage, Deed of Trust, or Security Deed (the "Security Instrument"), and Timely Payment Rewards Rider, if any, dated January 4, 2016 and recorded in Book or Liber E-TOSTIDOS AII, at page(s) 666, 667 & 668, of the County Clerks Records of Pope County State of Arkansas and (2) the
> (Name of Records) (County and State, or other Jurisdiction)
> Note, bearing the same date as, and secured by, the Security Instrument, which covers the real and personal property described in the Security Instrument and defined therein as the "Property", located at
>
> 112 West Mockingbird, Mt. Nebo, Arkansas 72803
> (Property Address)
> the real property described being set forth as follows:
>
> Lot 6 & 7 Block 7 of the 2nd improvement addition to the city of Mount Nebo, plat record Book 8308 – 88.

3. **forbearance** – a temporary change in the loan repayment plan generally made because the borrower is experiencing financial difficulties. Forbearance agreements:
    a. unlike a loan modification can be written or oral agreements
    b. typically are used when a loan has become delinquent
    c. with different loan types have differing rules, for example:
        i. FHA forbearance rules where the opportunity to bring the account current is made verbally, the mortgage insurance settlement in the event of a foreclosure is limited, so most FHA forbearances agreements are in writing and tend to be complicated.
        ii. FHA has expectations that a servicer will allow borrowers an opportunity to bring their loan current, therefore foreclosure cannot begin until at least three full installments are due and unpaid.

TYPES OF FORECLOSURES

Foreclosure practices are determined by state laws. They fall into three categories: judicial, nonjudicial, and strict foreclosure.

Judicial Foreclosure

A **judicial foreclosure** is normally used when a regular mortgage is the security instrument. A default is handled by filing the required notices to the debtor, followed by a suit in court to foreclose the mortgage claim. If the court agrees with the claim, it can order that the property be sold to satisfy the debt. The sale is handled through a public auction, usually called a *sheriff's sale*.

The Bankruptcy Abuse Prevention and Consumer Protection Act of 2005 (BAPCPA) was enacted to make it more difficult for some consumers to file bankruptcy under Chapter 7 by establishing means-testing criteria for both Chapter 7 and Chapter 13. Bankruptcy filers are consequently required to prove that they would be unlikely to ever have the means to pay back creditors. BAPCPA also lengthens the time between Chapter 7 and 13 bankruptcy filing from six to eight years. However, BAPCPA contributed to the surge in subprime foreclosures during the recent mortgage crisis by shifting risk from unsecured credit card lenders to secured mortgage lenders. Before BAPCPA, a borrower could file Chapter 7 bankruptcy and have credit cards and other unsecured debts discharged. The prior ability to eliminate unsecured debts left more income to pay the borrower's mortgage. BAPCPA stopped this tactic by the new means test that forces better-off households who demand bankruptcy to file Chapter 13, where they must continue paying unsecured creditors. Since the means test is binding, cash-strapped borrowers who might have saved their homes by filing for Chapter 7 now are more likely to face foreclosure or to have to sell their homes.

Nonjudicial Foreclosure

Nonjudicial foreclosure is the method by which foreclosure is accomplished when a power of sale clause is contained in a mortgage or deed of trust. No court action is required, as the instrument contains a clause granting power of sale to a third-party trustee. The lender notifies the trustee of a default and requests foreclosure action to protect the lender's interest. Depending on the applicable state laws, proper notification must be given to the debtor prior to the property being offered for sale. Then the trustee, who is the third party in a deed of trust, may sell the property at public auction. The trustee is authorized to bid for the property on behalf of the lender (called the *beneficiary* in a deed of trust), usually up to the amount of the mortgage debt. Title to the property can be transferred to the winning bidder by the trustee with no court action involved.

Strict Foreclosure

Strict foreclosure is possible in only a few states because it results in the borrower losing all equity invested in the property. After appropriate notice is given to a delinquent borrower and proper papers are filed in court, the court establishes a specific time period during which the entire defaulted debt must be paid. If full payment is not made within the time period, the borrower's redemption rights are waived and the court awards full legal title to the lender. There can be no deficiency judgment claimed under strict foreclosure.

Mortgagor Redemption Rights in Foreclosure

A **redemption period** is a specific time period given to borrowers in foreclosure during which they can buy back, or "redeem," their property. "Redeeming" or "redemption" of the home can refer to one of the following situations:

- repaying the total debt, including the principal balance, plus certain additional costs and interest, before the sale in order to stop the foreclosure, or
- repaying the purchase price, plus certain costs and interest, after the foreclosure sale to reclaim the property.

In all states, the borrower can redeem the home before the foreclosure sale, but only certain states provide a redemption period following the foreclosure sale. Go to the following website to see how your state handles redemption rights: http://www.nolo.com/legal-encyclopedia/free-books/foreclosure-book/chapter11-1.html

However, lenders were not happy with this redemption privilege and initiated a countermove, inserting a clause into subsequent loan agreements that specifically waived the right of redemption. The borrower had to accept this clause or be denied the loan. As written codes of law developed and the unchallenged rule of an absolute monarch slowly declined, the granting or refusal of redemption became a matter of law called statutory redemption. This right to redemption of property after foreclosure action that existed in various forms from medieval times has now been incorporated into the laws of a few more than half the states in this country. Most of these states are in the old South or Midwest where state constitutions from reconstruction and losses of farms during the

Great Depression prompted a rise in progressive issues to change the laws that were slanted in favor of lenders. Redemption periods vary among the states from three months to two years. Redemption periods can be different for different types of property and loan terms. In some cases, the redemption period is longer in the states with statutory redemption periods for farm land. In Michigan, for example, if a borrower has borrowed less than two-thirds of the value of a single-family home, the redemption period will be one year; if he or she has borrowed more than two-thirds, the period will be six months, as long as the property has less than three acres and is not more than a three-family dwelling. The equity right of redemption is the right of a borrower to redeem their real property from default during the period of time of notice of default and the time foreclosure proceedings have begun. The equity right of redemption exists in all states, and generally once the foreclosure sale has been confirmed, the borrower can no longer redeem property except in those states with a statutory right of redemption.

There are procedural steps involved in a foreclosure procedure and these vary by state law. In a typical judicial foreclosure state with redemption rights, the formal foreclosure process would be generally as follows:

1. The loan servicer would send a formal foreclosure notice, either by certified mail, or in many states, by the local sheriff.
2. The lender begins foreclosure action in court.
3. Legal notices are published in local papers.
4. You still have not been able to reach a payment or settlement arrangement with the mortgagor.
5. The notice and waiting periods expire.
6. The court holds a hearing regarding the investor's claim.
7. The court issues a foreclosure order. This gives the servicer on behalf the legal right to sell the home.
8. Legal notice of actual foreclosure sale and advertisements published in local papers.
9. You still have not been able to reach a payment or settlement agreement with the mortgagor.
10. The house is sold at auction to the highest bidder or not sold and the investors take possession of the home.
11. The mortgagor either moves out or the servicer/investor evicts the mortgagor.

Should the sale of the home bring less than the mortgagor owes, then you notify of any debt still outstanding as a result of the sale (i.e., the home is sold for less than they the mortgagor owed). This remaining balance is called a deficiency, and often a separate action for a deficiency must be filed within a statutory period (often four or five years) after the foreclosure sale.

Where Are We Now?

What You Should Know about Rampant Foreclosures

What follows is an excerpt from a 2011 *New York Times* article on foreclosure:

Revelations that mortgage servicers failed to accurately document the seizure and sale of tens of thousands of homes caused a public uproar and prompted lenders like Bank of America, JPMorgan Chase, and GMAC Mortgage to temporarily halt foreclosures in many states. In October 2010, all 50 states' attorneys general announced that they would investigate foreclosure practices. The nation's largest electronic mortgage tracking system, MERS, has been criticized for losing documents and other sloppy practices, and JPMorgan Chase has announced that it no longer used the service.

Mortgage documents of all sorts were treated in an almost lackadaisical way during the dizzying mortgage lending spree from 2005 through 2007, according to court documents, analysts, and interviews. Now those missing and possibly fraudulent documents are at the center of a potentially seismic legal clash that pits big lenders against homeowners and their advocates who are concerned that the lenders' rush to foreclose flouts private property rights.

In early 2011, the attorneys general and the newly created Consumer Financial Protection Bureau began pressing for a settlement that would involve banks paying penalties of up to $20 billion, and for steps to drastically alter the foreclosure process and give the government sweeping authority over how mortgage servicers deal with millions of Americans in danger of losing their homes.[3]

By February 2012, 49 state attorneys general and the federal government announced an historic, joint state-federal settlement with the country's five largest mortgage servicers, including Bank of America Corporation, JPMorgan Chase & Co., Wells Fargo & Company, Citigroup, Inc., and Ally Financial, Inc. (formerly GMAC).

---

[3]Orson Aguilar and Tunua Thrash, "Hopeful Signs in Settlement Talks," American Banker 176, no. 53 (April 6, 2011).

The settlement provides as much as $25 billion in relief to distressed borrowers, and direct payments to states and the federal government. This agreement settles state and federal investigations. Interestingly, data observed shows that the country's five largest mortgage servicers routinely signed foreclosure-related documents outside the presence of a notary public and without really knowing whether the facts they contained were correct. Both of these practices violate the law. The settlement provides benefits to borrowers whose loans are owned by the settling banks as well as to many of the borrowers whose loans they service.

Some of the terms of the agreement required that the government and borrowers preserved the following claims:

1. The release does not grant any immunity from criminal offenses or affect criminal prosecutions.
2. The release does not include claims relating to securitizations of mortgage loans.
3. The release does not include the Mortgage Electronic Registration Systems (MERSCORP, Inc.), a privately held company that operates an electronic registry designed to track ownership of mortgage loans and servicing rights.
4. State attorneys general and the federal agencies signing onto this agreement agree to release the servicers only from servicing; foreclosure and origination liability claims (note that many origination claims are now time-barred by statutes of limitation).
5. This agreement does not prevent homeowners or investors from pursuing individual, institutional, or class action civil cases against the servicers.

Because of these preserved claims, settlements have continued in the following years, including the following:

6. JPMorgan Chase agreed to a $13 billion settlement that included paying $6 billion to compensate investors, $4 billion to help struggling homeowners, and the remainder as a fine in early November 2013.
7. A $1.9 billion settlement between the FHFA and Deutsche Bank Structured products was announced in December 2013. The agreement resolved ongoing securities fraud-related litigation as well as certain repurchase claims.

8. Ocwen Financial Corporation and its subsidiary, Ocwen Loan Servicing, agreed to a $2.1 billion dollar joint state-federal settlement on December 20, 2013.
9. Bank of America reached a comprehensive settlement with the U.S. Department of Justice, certain federal agencies, and six states. The settlement includes releases on the securitization, origination, sale, and other specified conduct relating to residential mortgage-backed securities for $9 billion in August 2014.

During the same period, the CFPB fined over 30 large firms over half a billion dollars, and ongoing investigations will continue until all the statutes of limitation expire. There were government penalties, criminal charges, and civil suits that lasted for 10 years after the savings and loan crisis and the formation of the Resolution Trust Corporation back in the late 1980s.

DEFICIENCY JUDGMENTS

The sale of property at a foreclosure auction may or may not produce sufficient recovery to satisfy all claimants. The lender is entitled only to the defaulted debt (principal balance plus interest) and costs incurred. If, for example, the debt at foreclosure amounts to $42,000 and the property is sold for $35,000, there remains $7,000 due to the lender as a deficiency. Since the borrower may be obligated to the lender for the balance due on the note, the lender may have the right to seek a **deficiency judgment** for the remaining $7,000. However, some states limit the lender's right to a deficiency claim if the property is a person's homestead. In such a case, the lender could only recover the amount realized in the foreclosure sale.

Another protective law found in some states is granting a foreclosed debtor the right to cite the market value of foreclosed property as a defense against a deficiency claim. This kind of protection forces a lender to bid more realistically on the value of a foreclosed property and not resort to deficiency judgment claims that can be abusive.

Until late 1986, there was little action taken against borrowers who might owe a deficiency claim after foreclosure had been taken. There were two practical reasons for this seeming leniency. First, during most of the

1970s and the early 1980s, property generally increased in value, thus limiting the potential loss for a lender. Second, during that time period, people tried to hold onto their mortgaged property as it increased in value, enlarging their equity. If a default did occur, the debtor seldom had sufficient other assets to allow collection of such a claim.

This situation began to change in the mid-1980s. Substantial loss in real property values in certain areas of the country caused some debtors to "walk away" from both their property and the obligation to pay the remaining debt. With the property value substantially less than the balance due on a mortgage note, continued payments seemed a bad deal to some. As losses mounted, lenders began to take steps to enforce their claims. In October 1986, all federal agencies involved with underwriting home loans required that mortgagees report defaults and foreclosure action to credit bureaus. A further stipulation was that deficiency judgments must be pursued if the debtor holds other assets that may be subject to attachment.

If the claim against a defaulted borrower is made by a private mortgage insurance company, a deficiency judgment must be sought against the debtor through the courts. This judgment, when filed of record, operates as a general lien on the debtor's assets and is collectible in the same manner as any other judgment. As such actions became more common by the early 1990s, debtors fought against such claims, primarily on the basis that the indemnity obligation to the insurer was not fully disclosed when the policy was issued. Results so far have been mixed and the amounts involved have not been great enough to justify much litigation.

The problem is different if the loss is sustained by either HUD/FHA or the VA. Since both are federal agencies, an obligation to them becomes an obligation to the government, allowing a federal lien to be filed against a debtor. Recent Justice Department rules consider federal debt as preempting all other claims to property, including first mortgage liens. And such debt is more difficult to wash through bankruptcy. Furthermore, the 1992 expansion of HUD's Credit Alert Interactive Voice Response System (CAIVRS) added a number of government lending agencies to the list with access to the files. This means that default on any of these government-related loans will be on record with CAIVRS and will prevent use of government credit until acceptable resolution is made.

Settlement of a federal lien depends on the debtor's circumstances and is handled on a case-by-case basis. Generally, the obligation can be mitigated only in cases of proven hardship.

TAX IMPACTS OF FORECLOSURE

Relief of Debt

There can be unpleasant tax consequences for the borrower after foreclosure. This can occur if a borrower is granted relief from payment of any unsatisfied obligation. Income tax law treats relief of debt as income to the person granted relief. If a lender grants such relief, Form 1099 must be filed with the IRS, reporting the amount that the debtor is no longer obligated to pay. To a homeowner who has suffered the loss of a home, an additional tax obligation seems particularly unfair. Nevertheless, current IRS rules consider borrowed money that is not repaid as simply another source of income for the relieved debtor. The Emergency Economic Stabilization Act, enacted October 3, 2008, created three new tax provisions: (1) an extension for home mortgage debt forgiveness relief, (2) tax relief for community banks that invested in Fannie Mae and Freddie Mac preferred stock, and (3) a tax crackdown on compensation and severance pay for certain financial executives. Under 2007 tax legislation, taxpayers are generally allowed to exclude up to $2 million in mortgage debt forgiveness on their principal residence. However, this relief provision was scheduled to expire at the end of 2008. Under the new law, this debt relief provision is extended through 2017 as discussed in detail in Chapter 6. Some states that have similar rules for state income taxes did not match state rules for debt forgiveness with the federal law extension. California is one example.[4]

The Internal Revenue Service considers a foreclosure the same as the sale of a property. The outcome of which is that what was once was yours is no longer yours. Interestingly enough a foreclosure or short sale cant can produce a capital gain or loss. More importantly, should any portion of the mortgage debt be forgiven or canceled, income tax may be owed on that sum in addition to the capital gain (if any).

---

[4] "Mortgage Forgiveness Debt Relief," State of California Franchise Tax Board, July 25, 2014, accessed February 10, 2015, https://www.ftb.ca.gov/aboutFTB/newsroom/Mortgage_Debt_Relief_Law.shtml

Dealing with Foreclosure Capital Gains and Losses

As discussed in the "Types of Foreclosures" section of this chapter, most sales of real property typically go through an escrow process. Then the seller receives statements showing how much the home was sold for. There is no escrow with foreclosures; the owner of the loan just takes possession of the home. As pointed out earlier in the chapter, the Internal Revenue Service declares that a foreclosure is still counts as a sale or "disposition" of property.

Capital gains are calculated using the formula whereby you subtract the basis or cost of the property from the sales price. The product of this calculation is how much profit a former owner has made or lost in the transaction. In a foreclosure situation without escrow statements, the selling price used for tax purposes isn't at once clear-cut as there is no jointly agreed-on sales price. Commonly the "sales price" for tax purposes will be the fair market value of the property, or the outstanding loan balance immediately prior to the foreclosure is determined by the type of loan the borrower used. The foreclosed-on borrower will have these amounts reported to them and the IRS by the owner of the loan on IRS Form 1099-A.

Other considerations are whether a mortgage was a recourse or a nonrecourse loan. Depending on the property rights laws of the state the mortgage property is in, generally the mortgages used to acquire a house tend to be nonrecourse loans. However; in many states refinanced loans and home equity loans tend to be recourse loans. A borrower, having entered into a recourse loan, is personally liable for the debt, and the lender can pursue the borrower for repayment even after the property has been foreclosed on and disposed of. The formula for calculating the capital gain or loss is the outstanding loan balance immediately before the foreclosure minus any debt for which the borrower remains personally liable after the foreclosure or the fair market value of the property being foreclosed. The borrower can have taxable income from any debt canceled from this type of loan foreclosure.

In those cases where a borrower is not personally liable for the repayment of the loan, a "nonrecourse loan" is satisfied and the lender cannot pursue the borrower for further repayment after it repossesses the property. Since the sales price is considered the outstanding loan balance just before the foreclosure, the Internal Revenue Service considers this essentially selling the house back to the lender for complete financial consideration of the outstanding debt. Therefore, a borrower will not have any canceled debt income because the lender is prohibited by law from pursuing them for repayment.

A borrower normally will calculate a capital gain or loss and report this on Schedule D and Form 8949 (if the foreclosed property was a borrower's primary home) only after determining the nature of the loan (recourse or nonrecourse) and determining the sales price. A borrower might qualify to exclude up to $500,000 of gain from income tax subject to certain rules: (1) The home was your primary residence; (2) you lived in it for at least two of the last five years; and (3) individual taxpayers can exclude $250,000, and married taxpayers filing jointly can double that amount. Some care must be exercised if the foreclosed property was at first a primary home and then later a secondary residence, as in some cases they might qualify for an exclusion under modified rules used to calculate gains and losses.

As a reminder, the Tax Cuts and Jobs Act of 2017 allows federal income tax rate on long-term capital gains for properties owned a year or longer to be 15% for taxpayers who fall in the 25–35% tax bracket. For those who fall into the 39.6% tax bracket, the capital gains rate is 20%. Should a homeowner have owned a property for less than a year, the gain will be taxed at the ordinary rate for his or her regular income.

Sometimes an income-producing property is foreclosed on; this sale will be reported on Form 4797. If the foreclosed property was a rental property, report the sale on Form 4797. The difference between the Form 1099-A and the 1099-C is the latter is used for debt forgiveness on a recourse loan. Form 1099-A reports the fair market value, the date of foreclosure, and the remaining balance on the mortgage on the day before the foreclosure.

Questions for Discussion

1. Describe the use of advances, modification, and forbearance for changes in loan terms.
2. Define the legal process of foreclosure.
3. Describe the most common methods of foreclosure that lenders commonly use.
4. List the main four IRS forms used by lenders to deal with debt forgiveness.

5. List the common data repository for most federally sponsored loan programs to assure that federal debts that were not paid in the past are cleared before a borrower can participate in any new federal credit program.
6. Contrast nonjudicial foreclosure with the judicial foreclosure process.
7. Describe the importance of the Emergency Economic Stabilization Act for consumers.
8. Describe the formula for calculating the amount of a deficiency judgment.
9. Define the redemption period as used in the mortgage foreclosure process.
10. Describe a federal lien and list the mortgage loan products to which it can be applied.

Multiple Choice Questions for Review

1. A loan modification in one or more of the terms of a loan agreement/note is a change that is:
   a. temporary
   b. permanent
   c. required
   d. compliant

2. A deed in lieu of foreclosure is a voluntary conveyance of the property securing a debt from a borrower to the lender in return for:
   a. deficiency judgment
   b. forgiveness of debt
   c. support for Chapter 7 bankruptcy
   d. property redemption rights preservation

3. Part of lending on residential mortgages is the acceptance of a certain amount of risk; this risk can be managed in two ways:
   a. foreclose and forget
   b. loan origination and underwriting
   c. before and after the loan is made
   d. a review of credit and collateral

4. One of the most difficult issues to deal with when faced with a foreclosure incident is the:
   a. notice period required by state law
   b. mortgage insurance policy claim
   c. sheriff's sale
   d. establishment of the subject property's value

5. For a HAFA mortgage program, which of the following must a homeowner have as a condition for a short sale solution to be used?
   a. death of a grandparent
   b. short-term job loss
   c. financial hardship
   d. unexpected repairs on home

6. With a mortgage document, in lien theory states, since the borrower holds the title of the property, the foreclosure sale must be under court oversight. However, with a deed of trust, in either lien theory states or title theory states, because the trustee holds the title of the property, the property could be sold through nonjudicial foreclosure sale if it's allowed by the state laws. These statements:
   a. describe the difference between mortgage document and deed of trust in terms of the foreclosure
   b. explain the relationship between discount point and contract rate for a mortgage loan.
   c. describe the difference between judicial foreclosure and power of sale
   d. explain the defeasance requirement

7. Which of the following is a risk of a lender entering into a loan modification versus a foreclosure?
   a. The original security agreements acceleration clause is extinguished.
   b. Loan modification may impair a lender's lien position because in some states, the court may interpret loan modification as creating a new mortgage loan.
   c. They typically stop the foreclosure process temporarily.
   d. These agreements usually don't allow for the payment of a prepayment penalty.

8. When does a lender issue Form 4797?
   a. on a vacant lot debt forgiveness
   b. on a single family residential primary residence foreclosed on with debt forgiveness
   c. deficiency for a rental property
   d. for Chapter 11 bankruptcy foreclosures

9. Which of the following is NOT one of the more common alternatives to foreclosure for a mortgage in default status?
   a. short sale
   b. a deed in lieu of foreclosure
   c. a loan modification agreement
   d. use of contract for deed

10. A prolonged delinquency defined as the failure of a borrower to meet the terms and conditions of a note is referred to as:
    a. defeasance
    b. default
    c. Chapter 13 bankruptcy
    d. forfeiture

Information Resources

http://www.lonestarlandlaw.com/Deeding-Property.html
    This webpage provides an excellent overview of some of the more esoteric issues that can occur with deed in lieu process.

http://www.makinghomeaffordable.gov/pages/default.aspx
    The link above provides the most current information about the HAMP and HARP temporary Affordable Housing Programs that existed at the time of publication.

Chapter 11

PROPERTY ANALYSIS

KEY TERMS AND PHRASES

appraisal principles
apparent age
balance sheet
broker price opinion (BPO)
capitalization
common areas
condominiums
cooperative apartment
discount analysis
effective interest

homeowners association
income approach
land survey
physical characteristics
property appraisal
redlining
remaining useful life
underwriting
Uniform Collateral Data Portal®

LEARNING OBJECTIVES

At the conclusion of this chapter, students will be able to:
- Describe how the appraisal works as a key component of the analysis of any real estate financing credit decision.
- Understand the development and importance of the professional qualifications of appraisers of residential and commercial real estate.
- Describe the difference between a commercial condominium and a cooperative apartment.

- Understand the use of legal descriptions and survey's in commercial construction lending.
- Explain the draw or disbursement process for commercial construction real estate loans.
- Describe how property value is estimated using one of the three key approaches to valuing commercial real estate.

INTRODUCTION

The process of analyzing and approving a loan is called **underwriting**. The individual who assembles and analyzes the necessary data and is authorized to give a company's consent to a specific loan is referred to as the *underwriter*.

Properly underwriting any loan requires a complete analysis of all pertinent factors, including: (1) the borrower's ability and willingness to pay; (2) the property's condition, location, and usage; (3) all relevant economic influences; (4) laws controlling foreclosure procedures and assignments of rent; and (5) any unusual conditions that may exist.

An underwriter must examine the future, estimate the continued stability of the borrower, and try to judge the future value in a specific property. The underwriter must look beyond a normal appraisal, which provides an estimate of past or present value, and weigh the forces that affect the future based on his or her experience in this field. Many underwriting professionals were not in the business the last time residential real estate had a major decline in value—during the mid-1980s in the Oil Belt states and more generally in the 1991 recession—so this has proved a daunting task to many during the recent mortgage crisis.

A loan analysis covers a wide assortment of information, and from these diverse elements, an underwriter must determine the degree of risk involved. There is no such thing as a risk-free mortgage loan. It is the underwriter's primary responsibility to determine the magnitude of the risk and to compensate for it in the terms and conditions of the loan. The degree of risk determines the ratio of loan to value, the length of time for repayment, and the interest and discount points required by the lender.

As one of the essential elements in underwriting any mortgage loan, the property to be pledged must be examined for suitability. As discussed in the previous chapter, for a residential loan, it is the borrower's personal income that is expected to repay the loan. For commercial loans, it is the income from the property that becomes more important. So the analysis of property that will be pledged as collateral differs somewhat between residential and commercial loans. For a residential loan, the property serves as a backup, a pledge of something of value that better assures repayment of the loan. It is not something the lender expects to use for repayment of the loan. Therefore, the thrust of a property analysis for a residential loan is simply to determine the property's market value and whether that value serves as adequate collateral for the loan. Some of the new requirements being placed on the appraisal community due to changes in the data collection process will be daunting. We will discuss these changes later in the chapter.

For a commercial loan, the property analysis must look further. Generally, the loan is expected to be repaid from income generated by the property. While the property does serve as collateral—a backup in case of loan default—it is more important for the underwriter to make sure the property income can sustain loan repayment. While the underlying purposes differ, both rely on professional appraisals as a starting point for property analysis.

PROPERTY APPRAISAL

An appraisal may be defined as an *estimate* of value of an adequately described property as of a specific date. It is the considered opinion of a knowledgeable and qualified professional, supported by an analysis of relevant data. An appraisal can be an evaluation of a full ownership, a partial ownership interest, or leasehold rights.

A **property appraisal** provides information that has several uses in financing real estate. It is used as an important measure of the loan amount. Lenders limit loan amounts to a percentage of property value. However, for commercial loans, the loan amount may have an alternate limit as a percentage of the property's income. But a property's income is also a direct reflection of the property's value. In addition, an appraisal serves as a support document for institutional lenders when they undergo regulatory examinations.

Determination of appraised value is made by individuals specially qualified in the field. In the past, a lending institution's loan officer might have estimated the property value based on personal knowledge and experience in the area. However, as mortgage lending increased in volume and complexity, almost all appraisals were shifted to professionals who specialized in this work. Some work as employees of a lending institution and some as independent fee appraisers.

Federal/State Certification

In the past, both the qualification of professional appraisers and the determination of what comprises acceptable content in an appraisal have been the province of various independent appraiser associations. These are primarily peer groups organized to develop quality standards among themselves and to award designations to eligible members meeting their requirements. Prior to 1989, there was no federal regulatory involvement in this field.

While many must share the blame for the collapse of savings and loan associations in the 1980s, Congress felt the quality of appraisals carried some of the responsibility. As a result, legislation was passed creating a system to set proper standards for both appraisers and the content of appraisals.

In 1989, Congress passed the Financial Institutions Reform, Recovery, and Enforcement Act (FIRREA), of which Title XI spelled out a system for setting federal appraiser and appraisal standards to be used as a guideline for each state to develop its own system of qualification. Title XI is applicable to both residential and commercial loans. FIRREA established a council called the Federal Financial Institutions Examination Council with a subcommittee known as the Appraisal Subcommittee. The law applies to a loan made by a federally related lender and is applicable to both residential and commercial loans.

The purpose of the Subcommittee was to develop suitable criteria for state licensure of appraisers and standards for appraisals that would assure credible information for federally related lenders. *Federally related* is a broad-brush definition of any lender with some relation to the federal government, including those carrying federal deposit insurance, and covers quasi-government entities such as Fannie Mae and Freddie Mac.

Since its creation, the Appraisal Subcommittee has set standards that are now reflected in every state's requirements for certification and licensing of individuals qualified to perform appraisals in federally related transactions. The Subcommittee continues to monitor requirements of federal regulatory agencies with respect to appraisal standards. It also maintains a national registry of state-certified and state-licensed appraisers eligible to appraise in federally related transactions. The Appraisal Foundation (TAF) is the congressionally appointed writer of the Uniform Standards of Professional Appraisal Practice (USPAP) and sets qualification standards for appraisers.

Standards for Appraisers

FIRREA's Title XI calls for the qualification of appraisers through appropriate testing and experience requirements to be established by state law. As of January 1, 2008, the new examination criteria became effective. The new education criteria, including the college degree requirement, were effective January 1, 2010, as announced by the Appraisal Qualifications Board (AQB). It should be noted that state requirements may exceed AQB minimums. The four categories of appraisers and their qualifications are below.

1. **A Certified General Real Property Appraiser** is qualified to evaluate both residential and commercial property of any size. A general appraiser must demonstrate knowledge of the profession and understand the documents involved. To qualify, the applicant for the Certified General license must hold a bachelor's degree or higher from an accredited college or university, and have 300 hours of AQB-approved education, including 15 hours of USPAP, plus 14 hours per year of continuing education and 3,000 hours of experience (1,500 hours must be obtained in nonresidential appraisal work), during the past 30 months.

2. **A Certified Residential Real Property Appraiser** can appraise one- to four-unit residential properties without regard to value or complexity. To qualify, the appraiser must hold a bachelor's degree or higher from an accredited college or university, and have 200 hours of education, including 15 hours of USPAP, in addition to 14 hours per year of continuing education. The appraiser must have passed the AQB-approved Certified Residential Real Property Appraiser examination and have 2,500 hours of experience during the past 24 months.

3. **A Licensed Residential Real Property Appraiser** is qualified to appraise noncomplex one- to four-unit residential properties having

a transaction value of less than $1,000,000, and complex one- to four-unit residential properties having a transaction value less than $250,000. LRRPA applicants for the Licensed Residential credential shall successfully complete 30 semester hours of college-level education from an accredited college, junior college, community college, or university. The college or university must be a degree-granting institution accredited by the Commission on Colleges, a regional or national accreditation association, or by an accrediting agency that is recognized by the U.S. Secretary of Education. In addition to the 30 semester hours, applicants must also complete 150 hours of education, including 15 hours of USPAP, in addition to 14 hours per year of continuing education and 2,000 hours of experience over the course of no fewer than 12 months.

4. **An Appraiser Trainee** must complete 75 hours of education and pass the Core Curriculum examinations and the 15-hour national USPAP course, in addition to completing 14 hours of continuing education in the third and successive years. Appraiser Trainees are not required to pass a state exam (as all other categories are) and must finish these requirements within five years of starting.

The Appraisal Foundation sets the criteria for who can reproduce the approved USPAP materials for training and education; this is limited to the firms referred to as Appraisal Sponsors.

Standards for Appraisers and FHA Mortgages

HUD/FHA requires that licensed qualified appraisers also be approved for FHA mortgage appraisal work. FHA Mortgagee Letter 1996-26 specifies that FHA Roster appraisers must avoid conflicts of interest and the appearance of conflicts of interest. In order to help appraisers avoid actual conflicts or the appearance of conflicts, no members of a lender's loan production staff or any person (i) who is compensated on a commission basis upon the successful completion of a loan, or (ii) who reports, ultimately, to any officer of the lender not independent of the loan production staff and process, is allowed to have substantive communications with an appraiser relating to or having an impact on valuation, including ordering or managing an appraisal assignment. FHA Mortgagee Letter 2009-28 is effective for all case numbers assigned on or after January 1, 2010. The existing requirements will remain in effect.

The new requirements are as follows:

- Mortgage brokers and commission-based lender staff are prohibited from participating in the appraisal process.
- Historically, the FHA prohibited mortgagees from accepting appraisal reports completed by an appraiser selected, retained, or compensated, in any manner by real estate agents. To ensure appraiser independence, FHA-approved lenders are now prohibited from accepting appraisals prepared by FHA Roster appraisers who are selected, retained, or compensated in any manner by a mortgage broker, or any member of a lender's staff who is compensated on a commission basis tied to the successful completion of a loan. FHA Mortgagee Letter 2009-28 lists those practices in which lenders, brokers, or other originators are prohibited from engaging. These practices might be construed as attempting to influence appraisers' independence.
- Compliance by December 31, 2011, with the Uniform Appraisal Dataset (UAD) was required for FHA appraisals reported on the 1004 (URAR) form and the 1073 (Condo) form. Appraisals reported on other forms, such as the 1025 and 1004C, may not be required to be UAD compliant. More specifics on the UAD will be covered later in this chapter.

Appraiser Selection in FHA Connection

Lenders are responsible for assuring that the appraiser who actually conducts the appraisal used for an FHA-insured mortgage is correctly identified in FHA Connection (discussed further in Chapter 14). The FHA has found that on numerous occasions, the name of an appraiser appearing in the appraiser log-in screen is not the appraiser who actually completes the appraisal. Lenders who fail to assure that FHA Connection reflects the correct name of the appraiser are subject to administrative sanctions.

Use of an Appraisal Management Company (AMC) and Appropriate Third-Party Fees

FHA does not require the use of AMCs or other third-party organizations for appraisal ordering, but recognizes that some lenders use AMCs and/or other third-party organizations to help ensure appraiser independence.

To address several questions that have already been raised regarding compensation, this document corrects and expands existing fee requirements set forth in Mortgagee Letter 1997-46.

FHA-approved lenders must ensure that:

- FHA Appraisers are not prohibited by the lender, AMC, or other third party from recording the fee the appraiser was paid for the performance of the appraisal in the appraisal report.
- FHA Roster appraisers are compensated at a rate that is customary and reasonable for appraisal services performed in the market area of the property being appraised.
- The fee for the actual completion of an FHA appraisal may not include a fee for management of the appraisal process or any activity other than the performance of the appraisal.
- Any management fees charged by an AMC or other third party must be for actual services related to ordering, processing, or reviewing appraisals performed for FHA financing.
- AMC and other third-party fees must not exceed what is customary and reasonable for such services provided in the market area of the property being appraised.

Standards for Appraisals

As stated earlier in the chapter, FIRREA's Title XI requires that the content of appraisals meets the standards set by the Appraisal Standards Board, which is a part of the Appraisal Foundation. The Appraisal Foundation was created in 1987 by eight active private appraisal associations. Prior to passage of federal legislation in 1989, professional appraisers recognized a need for better qualification for both appraisers and appraisals, and established the Appraisal Foundation to develop practical standards and requirements. Federal recognition of their work is an indication of FIRREA's continued acceptance of their standards.

Federal standards require appraisals to conform to the USPAP as adopted by the AQB. A standardized appraisal form has been developed in a cooperative effort between the industry working group, Fannie Mae, Freddie Mac, HUD, and the VA. The form, called the Uniform Residential Appraisal Report (URAR), is a revision of Fannie Mae Form 1004/Freddie Mac Form 70. It became mandatory for use after January 1, 1994. The last major revision of the standards of appraisal review of residential properties and the revision of Form 1004 and Form 70 took place in March 2005. (A copy of the current form in use as of February 2011 is reproduced in the appendix.) Federal requirements also set a minimum level of certification based on the value and kind of property appraised.

New Quality Mortgage (QM) Appraisal Issues

The Truth-in-Lending Act (TILA) of 1968 and its implementing rules under Regulation Z seek to promote the informed use of consumer credit by requiring disclosures about its costs and terms. In 2010, TILA was amended by the Dodd-Frank Act and now requires appraisals on principal residences securing higher-priced loans. The Consumer Financial Protection Bureau (CFPB) under the Dodd-Frank Act was to implement these TILA amendments in partnership with five other federal regulatory agencies that are adopting a new rule, the Higher-Priced Mortgage Loans (HPML) Appraisal Rule. The rule is part of Regulation Z.

A residential mortgage is defined as an HPML if it is secured by a consumer's principal dwelling and has interest rates above the following thresholds:

- It is a first-lien mortgage (other than a jumbo loan) with an annual percentage rate (APR) that exceeds the Average Prime Offer Rate (APOR), published by the Bureau at the time the APR is set, by 1.5 percentage points or more.
- It is a first-lien jumbo loan with an APR that exceeds the APOR at the time the APR is set by 2.5 percentage points or more. A loan is a jumbo loan when the principal balance exceeds the limit in effect as of the date the transaction's rate is set for the maximum principal obligation eligible for purchase by Freddie Mac.
- It is a subordinate-lien with an APR that exceeds the APOR at the time the APR is set by 3.5 percentage points or more.

When you originate a higher-priced, first-lien, or subordinate-lien loan covered by the HPML Appraisal Rule, you must:

- Use a licensed or certified appraiser who certifies that the appraisal complies with the Uniform Standards of Professional Appraisal Practice (USPAP) and the Financial Institutions Reform, Recovery, and Enforcement Act (FIRREA) of 1989, as amended, 12 U.S.C. 3331 et seq., and any implementing regulations.

- Have the appraiser physically visit the property, view the interior, and produce a written appraisal report.
- Obtain an additional appraisal at your own expense if the property's seller acquired the dwelling within the past 180 days and is reselling it for a price that exceeds certain thresholds, which can be found in the October 2017 Small Entity Compliance Guide. (See the web address at the end of this chapter.)
- Provide a disclosure within three business days of application explaining the consumer's rights with regard to appraisals.
- Give consumers free copies of the appraisal reports performed in connection with the loan at least three days before consummation of the transaction.

Appraisal Associations

Federal certification standards for appraisers have not changed the existence of a number of private professional organizations offering appraisal designations to those who qualify under each organization's standards. These are peer groups made up of appraisers who are interested in maintaining and improving the quality of their profession. Each organization offers certain designations that indicate qualification in a particular area of appraisal work. The requirements differ somewhat, but all are based on a minimum prescribed level of education and experience, in addition to successful performance on some rather difficult tests. What follows is a brief listing of some of the better-known organizations and the designations granted by each:

Appraisers Association of America, Inc. (1)
    AAA—Certified Member

The Appraisal Institute (2)
    MAI—Member of Appraisal Institute
    SRA—Senior Residential Appraiser
    SRPA—Senior Real Property Appraiser

American Society of Appraisers (1)
    ASA—Senior Member of the Society
    FASA—Fellow of the Society

American Society of Farm Managers and Rural Appraisers (the oldest group in the United States) (1)
    AFM—Accredited Farm Manager
    ARA—Accredited Rural Appraiser

International Association of Assessing Officers (1)
  RES—Residential Evaluation Specialist
  AAS—Assessment Administration Specialist
  CAE—Certified Assessment Evaluator

National Association of Independent Fee Appraisers[1] (1)
  IFA—Independent Fee Appraiser (Residential Only), Member
  IFAS—Independent Fee Appraiser, Senior Member
  IFAA—Independent Fee Agricultural Appraiser, Specialist
  IFAC—Independent Fee Appraiser, Counselor

National Association of Real Estate Appraisers (2)
  CREA—Certified Real Estate Appraiser
  CCRA—Certified Commercial Real Estate Appraiser
  RTA—Registered Trainee Appraiser

1. On January 19, 2015, was an Approved Sponsor of the Appraisal Foundation and had the right to reproduce USPAP materials.
2. On January 19, 2015, was not an Approved Sponsor of the Appraisal Foundation without the rights to reproduce USPAP materials.

Peer designations are good indicators of expertise in a specialized area of appraisal work, and they give some assurance of an appraiser's interest in maintaining professional standards. But there is no requirement that a person belong to any peer group in order to qualify as a state-certified or licensed appraiser.

Principles of Appraising

How do appraisers approach their problems? What are they looking for in determining values? What analytical details should lenders or borrowers expect to find in professional appraisals? Considerable study has been given to the theory that underlies all sound appraisals, resulting in specific **appraisal principles** that guide professional thinking in evaluating property. What follows are descriptions of several of the more important principles:

1. **supply and demand,** the theory underlying all economic practice is that scarcity influences supply, and that what people want and can purchase controls the demand;

---

[1] The American Association of Certified Appraisers merged with the National Association of Independent Fee Appraisers for those members with the former professional designations of CA-R (Certified Appraiser, Residential), CA-S (Certified Appraiser, Senior), CA-C (Certified Appraiser, Consultant), and CA-F&L (Certified Appraiser, Farm and Land).

2. **substitution,** which means that the value of replaceable property will tend to coincide with the value of an equally desirable substitute property;
3. **highest and best use,** which says it is the use of land at the time of the appraisal that will provide the greatest net return (This requires the proper balance of the four agents of production (labor, coordination, capital, and land) to provide the maximum return for the land used.);
4. **contribution,** which applies to the contributory market value added by an improvement, such as an elevator in a three-story building, or the value added to a building lot by increasing the depth of that lot;
5. **conformity,** which says that to achieve maximum value, land use must conform to the surrounding area (An over-improvement, such as a $300,000 house built in a neighborhood of $60,000 homes, will lower the value of the larger house. Conversely, a $60,000 home in a neighborhood of $300,000 homes might see its value increase.);
6. **anticipation,** which says that since value is considered to be the worth of all present and future benefits resulting from property ownership, the anticipation of future benefits must be evaluated; and
7. **arm's length transaction,** which is a transaction in which the parties involved are not related or previously involved. Transactions between family members and relatives are normally not considered arm's length. Transactions between friends, colleagues, or individuals with previous or existing relationships may or may not be arm's length. Appraisers must be careful to know individual state laws relating to licensed appraisers' responsibilities to disclose transactions that are not arm's length.

TYPES OF APPRAISALS

In 1994, the Uniform Standards of Professional Appraisal Practice (USPAP) was changed to include a Departure Provision that permits a limited appraisal, the rules of which are classified as specific guidelines rather than binding requirements. The burden of proof is placed on the appraiser to decide before accepting an assignment that the departure from the Uniform Standards will not confuse or mislead those relying on the appraisal.

The appraiser must advise the client that the assignment calls for something less than a full appraisal and that departures will be explained. The client must agree that a limited appraisal would be appropriate.

The USPAP Departure Provision now lists two types of appraisals:

1. a *complete appraisal*, defined as the act of estimating value without invoking the Departure Provision; and
2. a *limited appraisal*, defined as the act of estimating value resulting from invoking the Departure Provision.

If an appraisal is being used for purposes of valuation in any circumstance involving the Internal Revenue Service (IRS), the appraiser should not invoke the Departure Provision under SR 9-4, the "Market Approach and Methods" section of the USPAP. The appraiser should generally follow the eight factors found in Revenue Ruling 59-60, which states that when the IRS is the intended user of the valuation, the person performing the valuation should follow all of the specific guidelines of SR 9-4 without invoking the Departure Provision for any part of SR 9-4.

USPAP now defines two different levels of reporting requirements. These are as follows:

1. the *appraisal report,* where the appraiser's responsibility to determine whether greater "detail or explanation" is required based on the intended use and the intended user(s) of the report (The minimum standards for an appraisal report are:
   a. when there are intended users in addition to the client;
   b. when the client may need to understand the appraiser's rationale for options and conclusions; and/or
   c. when the client may not have specialized knowledge about the subject property.); and
2. the *restrictive report*, which is the least detailed of the reporting options. (There is a minimal presentation of information and it is intended for the client only. The report must contain a use restriction that clearly limits reliance on the report on the part of the client, and warns that the report cannot be properly understood without additional information from the appraiser.)

These two levels of appraisals may be found in practice in roughly the following formats:

1. The *restrictive report* is often in *letter form.* In its simplest form, an appraiser can submit a letter to the client detailing only the most

important points and reaching a conclusion of value. No background information or supporting data are given, although the appraiser must have developed these prior to issuing the estimate.

2. The *appraisal report* is often in *standard form*. For residential appraisals, a standard printed form is now required. It is Freddie Mac Form 70/Fannie Mae Form 1004, called the Uniform Residential Appraisal Report. The most recently revised form was mandated for use in May 2005.

Note: Due to new reporting rules issued by the USPAP in 2014, when an appraiser uses the standard Form 1004 they will have to deal with the label "built-in" to the form; there may be no way to delete the "Summary Appraisal Report" label from the form, but it should be viewed as an unnecessary [2nd] label and the USPAP "Appraisal Report" label should be prominently displayed somewhere near the beginning of the report. Since official form reports cannot be changed, the USPAP seems to believe that relying on the fact that the phrase "Summary Appraisal Report" includes the words "Appraisal Report" is NOT adequate to properly identify the report option used and the term "Appraisal Report" should be prominently displayed by itself or within a longer identifying sentence. Most have just used: "Appraisal Report; Prepared in Accordance with USPAP Standards Rule 2-2(a)" or "This report was prepared in accordance with the requirements of the Appraisal Report option of USPAP." As of July 14, 2015, the Fannie Mae Form 1004 called the Uniform Residential Appraisal Report had not been updated to reflect the new language requirement of 2014–2015 USPAP Report Options (Standards 2 & 8).

Appraisal Report

To better explain major information found in an evaluation of property, a more detailed discussion of the appraisal report is in the following section.

Description of Property

The property should be defined in accurate legal wording, and the precise rights of ownership must be described. The rights may be a leasehold interest, mineral rights, surface rights, or the full value of the fee simple rights in the land and buildings thereon.

The Date and Purpose of the Appraisal

Appraisals can be made for times other than the present, such as when needed to settle an earlier legal dispute. The date of the appraised value must be clearly shown. Also, the purpose of the appraisal should be stated, as it will influence the dominant approach to value. In professional appraisals, there is no such thing as the buyer's or seller's value; this is not a "purpose" as identified here.

An example of purpose would be to estimate value for an insurance settlement, emphasizing a cost approach to value, as claims are adjusted on the basis of cost. If the purpose is a condemnation action, the most relevant approach is the market value approach.

The Background Data

While the standard form and simple letter report will not provide any economic background data, the narrative report discloses economic information as clues to value. An overall study of the market region is made, which may include an area as large as an entire state. The focus is then narrowed down to the local area—the town or that portion of a city where the property is located. From there, the analysis narrows even further, to the specific neighborhood and then to the actual site under appraisal.

The Approaches to Value

Appraisers use three common approaches to estimate value: (1) cost, (2) sales comparison, and (3) income. All approaches should be used wherever possible, and all should reach approximately similar values, although these values are seldom the same. In certain appraisals, only one approach may be practical, such as valuing a city hall building for insurance purposes. In such an analysis, only a cost approach would be practical, as there is not much buying or selling of city halls to provide sales comparison data, nor is there a true income from the building itself to provide figures for an income approach. A single-family residence may appear to lack any income for analysis, but certain neighborhoods have sufficient houses rented to provide enough data to reach an income-approach conclusion. We will discuss the three approaches to value in greater detail later in the chapter.

Qualifying Conditions

If, in the analysis of property, the appraiser discovers any material factors that will affect the property's value, these can and should be reported as further substantiation of the value conclusion.

Estimate of Value

This is the real conclusion of the study, the figure most people turn to first when handed a finished appraisal. Each of the approaches to value will result in a firm dollar valuation. It is the purpose of this estimate to explain why one of the approaches to value is favored over the others. For example, with an income property such as a motel, the value judgment would rest most heavily on the income analysis. The final conclusion is a single value for the property and represents the considered knowledge and experience of the appraiser making the report.

Certification of the Appraiser and His or Her Qualifications

The professional appraiser certifies his or her opinion by signature and disclaims any financial interest in the property being appraised that could influence a truly objective conclusion. A recitation of the appraiser's educational background, standing within the profession as indicated by professional ratings, and previous experience—such as appraisals previously made and for whom—is included. The certification serves to substantiate the quality of the appraisal for an underwriting officer.

Addendum

Depending on the need for clarification, the appraisal will include maps of the area under consideration with the site pointed out, plus the location of comparable properties referred to in the analysis. Charts may be used to indicate such things as the variables in a market analysis. Photos of the subject property are usually mandatory.

THREE APPROACHES TO PROPERTY VALUE

The three approaches to value, the essence of an appraisal, are discussed in the sections that follow.

Property Value as Estimated by Cost Approach

The **cost approach** is developed as the sum of the building reproduction costs, less depreciation, plus land value. The reproduction costs can be developed the same way a builder would prepare a bid proposal—by listing every item of material, labor, field burden, and administrative overhead. Reproduction cost estimates have been simplified in active urban areas through compilation of many cost experiences converted to a cost-per-square-foot figure. The offices of active appraisers collect such data in depth for reference.

Depreciation, by definition, detracts from the value and must be deducted from the reproduction costs. However, **external obsolescence** can be either a deduction or an addition, depending on its nature. Three separate types of adjustments must be made in the cost approach:

1. **physical deterioration** (Wear and tear on the building is the type most commonly associated with the word *depreciation*. Examples would be the flaking paint, a worn-out roof needing new shingles, and rotting window casements. These are curable items and, under the breakdown method, should be deducted from value as rehabilitation costs. Other items of physical deterioration are incurable—meaning not economically feasible to repair. For example, the aging of the foundations or of the walls is incurable, and this kind of deterioration should be charged off as a certain portion of the usable life of the building. Another method of handling physical deterioration, in contrast to the breakdown method, is the engineering or observed method wherein each major component of the building is listed and a percentage of its full life is charged off. This method recognizes that each major component of a building may have a different life and the percentage of depreciation would vary at any point in time.);

2. **functional obsolescence** (As important as physical deterioration is that category of loss in value resulting from poor basic design, inadequate facilities, or outdated equipment. These elements, too, can be curable or incurable. An example of incurable functional obsolescence would be an aging building that no longer meets the needs of modern business with its demands for greater flexibility in its office arrangements. There could be an excess of walls or partitions in an office building, which would cost money to remove and modernize, but might be curable. Lack of air conditioning in a hotel or office building is an older example of curable functional obsolescence.); and

3. **external obsolescence.** The third type of depreciation has a more elusive quality and is actually not part of the building at all. External obsolescence is the set of factors outside and surrounding the property that affect its value, requiring the determination of the plus or minus effect of these forces. Some are very obvious influences—

for example, a new freeway bypassing an existing service station, or the construction of an undesirable industry in an area adjacent to residential property—and would certainly lower value. However, the bridging of a stream to open new land for development would create a substantial increase in value. A more difficult problem is ascertaining the economic impact of a possible decline in a specific neighborhood. While landowners are able to exercise some voice in protest or encouragement of these outside forces, for the most part, what is done with neighboring properties is not controllable and is not curable. And it will always be a latent force that can affect the value of an individual property.

After determining building reproduction cost, then depreciation adjustments, the third factor to be considered under the cost approach is value of the land. Land value, which varies with local economic conditions, affects demand, and to a lesser extent, supply. More recently, environmental problems have affected the value and availability of land. Land value is best determined through an examination of recent sales of similarly located properties—i.e., the sales comparison method as discussed in the next section.

However, there are sometimes specific reasons for changes in the appraised value of land. Buildings can and do deteriorate, while land can continue to increase in value due to the same outside factors noted in the preceding discussion of external obsolescence. For example, as urban areas expand, certain intersections become more and more valuable, new throughways and freeways concentrate greater flows of traffic, and huge shopping centers add to the value of all surrounding land. As suburban sprawl moves outward, former farmland increases in value as it becomes potential residential subdivisions. Another example can be found in some older sections of a city when the land becomes more valuable than the building. The building may represent such poor usage of the land that it becomes a liability to the property value, and its removal costs should be deducted from the stated value of the land. By ascertaining these fluctuations in land value, the appraiser can bring a cost analysis into step with a changing market value.

Property Value as Estimated by Sales Comparison Analysis

Also known as a market analysis, the estimated value by a **sales comparison approach** is determined by prices paid for similar properties in the neighborhood. This approach is most commonly used with residential property because it offers sufficient sales information to make comparisons useful. Since no two properties are ever precisely **comparable**, much of the analysis under this method concerns itself with detailing major characteristics and whether these add to or subtract from the value of the property. For example, if a similar property was sold two years earlier, the appraiser could assume that the subject property would show an increase, or decrease, in that time span, depending on the nature of the neighborhood. A fireplace in the subject property would give it a plus factor in comparison with a similar property lacking a fireplace. Comparisons are comprehensive, covering such points as location, size, physical condition, and amenities.

Some confusion does exist in the relationship between sales prices and asking prices. An appraiser is primarily concerned with completed sales and with sales uncomplicated by extraneous pressures such as forced sales, estate disposals, or transfers within a family. The willing-buyer-and-willing-seller standard of a free market sale is lacking in a forced sale. An asking or offering price is considered by most to represent a ceiling or maximum value for the property. Appraisers usually recognize the inherent inaccuracy of an asking price, especially one set by homeowners. This figure is often arrived at by adding together the original purchase price, the full cost of all improvements that have been made, the selling commission, and the owner's amateur notion of general market appreciation. But every so often, an owner actually receives such a sales price from a willing buyer, and this makes the professional feel a bit foolish!

Sales price as a sound basis for comparing market values of property came under question in the mid-1980s. By that time, it had become common for home sellers, particularly home builders, to offer attractive financing plans as a sales inducement. By paying a lender part of the interest cost up front, as in a buydown, a seller could offer lower-than-market "effective" interest rates to a buyer during the early years of a mortgage. The lower payment amount made loan qualification easier, which attracted more buyers. The cost of the buydown of interest was usually added into the price of the house. Since the sales price thereby included a built-in finance cost, it was no longer an accurate indication of true market value. Most lenders have since added a requirement that any market value used as a basis for sales comparisons be adjusted downward to reflect any excessive finance costs. Between 2007 and 2010, the use of a special code in the Multiple Listing Services (MLS) around the United States which allowed sales prices to be reported as listing prices caused distortions in the use of MLS data for the sales comparison approach. RE InfoLink (REIL)—the MLS serving the counties of Monterey, San Benito, San Mateo, Santa Clara, and Santa Cruz in Northern California—approved adoption of a new policy enabling buyers or sellers to withhold the sale price of a property as a condition of a transaction. With completion of an "Authorization to Withhold Sale Price" form and payment of a $500 fee, the listing price, rather than the actual sale price, can be entered into the "sale price" field at close of escrow.[2] The listing agent will be required to enter a code in the Confidential Remarks (agent only) field, indicating that the sales price was withheld. Some referred to this as the "Z" code. Both Fannie Mae and Freddie Mac have revised their definition of *market value* to "the most probable price [that] a property should bring."

In June 2010, in response to the issues discussed above and the continuing crisis in residential finance, Fannie Mae and Freddie Mac, at the direction of the Federal Housing Finance Agency (FHFA), developed the **Uniform Collateral Data Portal®** (UCDP®), which is a single portal for the electronic submission of appraisal data files. Lenders are required to use UCDP® to submit electronic appraisal data files that conform to all GSE requirements, including the Uniform Appraisal Dataset (UAD) when applicable, before the delivery date of the mortgage to either Fannie Mae or Freddie Mac. The goal of the UCDP is to allow lenders to take a more consistent approach to appraisal definitions and requirements through the use of a common portal for submitting appraisal data files.

UCDP became available in June 2011. To facilitate a smooth transition to the electronic submission of appraisal data files, lenders were encouraged to begin using UCDP for their live production immediately.

- Appraisal report forms for all conventional mortgages delivered to the GSEs on or after March 19, 2012, have been submitted to UCDP prior to the delivery date of the mortgage if:
    - the loan application is dated on or after December 1, 2011; and
    - an appraisal report is required.

Appraisals must be submitted before the delivery date of the mortgage to Fannie Mae or Freddie Mac and must include the applicable required

---

[2] Kris Berg, "How Timely—Northern California MLS Allows Sales Price to Be Withheld," *San Diego Home (blog)*, August 8, 2007, accessed May 11, 2011, http://sandiegocastles.com/sandiegohome-blog/how-timely-northern-california-mls-allows-sales-price-to-be-withheld/.

appraisal report forms listed below for all conventional appraisal reports issued on the dates listed above.

- Uniform Residential Appraisal Report (Fannie Mae 1004/Freddie Mac Form 70)*
- Manufactured Home Appraisal Report (Fannie Mae 1004C/Freddie Mac Form 70B)
- Small Residential Income Property Appraisal Report (Fannie Mae 1025/Freddie Mac Form 72)
- Individual Condominium Unit Appraisal Report (Fannie Mae 1073/Freddie Mac Form 465)*
- Exterior-Only Inspection Individual Condominium Unit Appraisal Report (Fannie Mae 1075/Freddie Mac Form 466)*
- Exterior-Only Inspection Residential Appraisal Report (Fannie Mae 2055/Freddie Mac Form 2055)*
- Individual Cooperative Interest Appraisal Report (Fannie Mae Form 2090)
- Exterior-Only Inspection Individual Cooperative Interest Appraisal Report (Fannie Mae Form 2095)

The Direct Sales Comparison Approach uses the sales price of a comparable property and makes any positive or negative adjustments in that price to more accurately compare it to the value of the subject property. The URAR requires that at least three comparables be used. This is the only required approach by Fannie Mae unless otherwise directed by its automated underwriting system. This is a departure from the appraisal approach in effect prior to 2005, and the Appraisal Standards Board of the Appraisal Foundation has required that (1) appraisers do a cost approach when it is necessary for credible assignment results, and (2) the appraiser must always explain the omission of the comparison approach, cost approach, or income approach.[3] It is unclear as to how the USPAP and the Appraisal Foundation will aid in the transition to the new UAD, which requires 50 additional data collection points and standardizes definitions and responses for a key subset of the fields now in use. The Appraisal Foundation met with the Federal Housing Finance Agency, Fannie

---

[3]Danny Wiley, "USPAP in the Real World" (Presentation at Appraisal Standards Board, the Appraisal Foundation Annual Meeting, August 1, 2006).

*These forms are uniform in appearance and are required content; only the form numbers vary from Fannie Mae to Freddie Mac.

Mae, and Freddie Mac on February 17, 2011, and March 10, 2011, to discuss the Uniform Mortgage Data Processing (UMDP) initiative and the Uniform Appraisal Dataset (UAD) and express its concerns with the implementation of the new regulations and their effects on the appraiser community, and submitted its concerns in writing on April 29, 2011.

After introducing the UCDP® in 2011, Fannie Mae followed up by launching proprietary appraisal messages in the UCDP® in January 2013. These messages have assisted lenders in detecting data inconsistencies and improving the overall reasonableness and quality of appraisal data.

On December 13, 2014, numerous other Fannie Mae proprietary appraisal messages were retired in order to focus lenders' attention on eligibility and compliance messages, and to better align with appraisal policy. In addition, Fannie Mae implemented additional changes to the proprietary messages in UCDP® to provide more information and help lenders identify potential defects during the appraisal review process. The changes included the introduction of an appraisal risk score, flags, and new messages in UCDP® from Collateral Underwriter™ (CU™), a new proprietary appraisal risk assessment application developed by Fannie Mae in January 2015 to support proactive management of appraisal quality.

On January 26, 2015, the severity level for 21 Fannie Mae proprietary appraisal messages that relate to eligibility violations was modified. The severity level changed from a warning message that is automatically overridden to a hard stop requiring a lender action (a manual override or the submission of a corrected appraisal) to obtain a "Successful" submission status in the UCDP®.

Property Value as Estimated by Income Approach

Because the **income approach** examines the actual return per dollar invested, it is the most important method for any investment property. When people buy investment property, they normally expect to recover, or *recapture* in appraisal terminology, their money with a profit. The money comes from two sources: (1) the annual *earnings* (excess income over all costs) and (2) the proceeds from a resale at the end of the term of ownership, called the *residual value*.

There are several acceptable methods used to estimate value with an income approach. However, any method based on the value of future income suffers from the same problem: Real estate does not offer the certainty of future income that other kinds of investment may provide. Nevertheless, once an income stream has been developed for analysis purposes, two methods are more widely used to convert the income stream into a value of the income-producing asset: the capitalization method and the discount analysis method, described next.

Capitalization Method

Probably the oldest, and the simplest, method of converting an income stream into an asset value is **capitalization** of the income. This is done by using the following formula:

$$\text{Income Stream} \div \text{Rate of Return} = \text{Value}$$

In the formula, the income stream is the expected profit derived from the property for the year. The rate of return is the return, expressed as a percentage that the investor expects to receive from the property. The return is determined by the investor, or the analyst, as one commensurate with current market conditions and the degree of risk involved.

Example

A property shows an income stream* of $20,000. A fair rate of return for the present market, including comparable risks involved, is 9%. Using the formula:

$$\$20{,}000 \div .09 = \$222{,}222$$

If you are offered a property showing the foregoing returns, you can place a value of $222,222 on the cash flow. Add to that amount the residual value of the property at the end of a holding period, and it will give the property value by one income approach.

Value of income stream	$222,222
Value of residual (estimated)	85,000
Total value	$307,222

*The term *income stream* is not precisely defined; it can mean different things to different analysts. However, when making comparisons between properties, whatever measure is used, the same measure must be applied to each property.

Discount Analysis Method

Another method of analysis—this one derived from financial markets—is **discount analysis**. This procedure takes each year's future cash flow and reduces it to its present worth. The investor receives a return on the investment delivered at intervals in the future. Yet payment for the income-producing asset is expected at time of purchase, either in cash or by borrowing money to deliver the cash at closing. So the question is: How much are the future cash flows worth in dollars today? By referring to the "Present Worth of a Dollar" (the third column in table 11-1), we can easily calculate the discount. Using the same numbers as in the previous example leads to the result shown in table 11-1.

The figures in table 11-1 are hypothetical and intended only to illustrate the discount calculation. In practice, the holding period would most likely be much longer. And the annual cash flows would be projected to take into account such variations as might be anticipated in occupancy and rental-rate adjustments. This kind of calculation can be made easily with a computer using any of several available software programs.

Where Are We Now?

Which Approach Has the Most Significant Weight?

While all three appraisal approaches are used in evaluating most properties, more weight is given to a specific approach depending on the property being appraised. The following table shows the approach being given the most weight as a function of the property:

TYPE OF PROPERTY	APPRAISAL APPROACH
Abandoned fire station	Cost
House in zoned residential subdivision	Sales Comparison
Stand-alone operating drugstore	Income
Tract of raw land	Sales Comparison
Condominium unit	Sales Comparison
Office building	Income
House in unzoned industrial area	Cost
Mini storage complex	Income
School facility	Cost

TABLE 11-1 Present Worth of Cash Flow Plus Residual

At End of Year	Annual Cash Flow		Present Worth of a Dollar Factor* at 9% Rate		Present Worth of Cash Flow
1	$20,000	×	0.91743	=	$18,349
2	20,000	×	0.84168	=	16,834
3	20,000	×	0.77218	=	15,444
			Sum of annual cash flows	=	$50,627
At the end of year 3, the property is sold for $250,000, discounted to its present worth equals $250,000 × 0.77218				=	193,045
	Total present worth of cash flows plus residual			=	$243,672

*Present worth factors are obtained from financial tables such as "An Introduction to Statistics for Appraisers," provided by the Appraisal Institute.
Source: © 2021 Mbition LLC

PROPERTY CHARACTERISTICS

There are several considerations concerning the property's **physical characteristics** that may be used as "go/no-go" determinants in the approval of a mortgage loan. Commentary follows on several of the more common distinctions.

Dwelling Units

Statistical references class one- to four-family housing as residential. However, many lenders in the conventional loan market separate this group into single-family housing (which qualifies for prime loan rates) and multiunit commercial property (which is rated for higher risk loans). Both the FHA and the VA issue commitments for two-, three-, and four-family housing, but the requirements are not as favorable as those for single-family units.

Number of Bedrooms

Conventional lenders no longer view the number of bedrooms as an important consideration. Years ago, it was not unusual to restrict loans to housing that had more than one bedroom. But the market has changed so that a number of buyers prefer limited bedroom space. As long as the lender believes a reasonable market exists for the property should foreclosure become necessary, the collateral is acceptable. (The FHA does base some of its loan limits in certain programs on the number of available bedrooms.)

Square Footage

Minimum house size based on square footage is no longer used as a loan determinant. As builders have endeavored to reduce housing costs, the size of houses has been reduced. The old standard of "not less than 1,000 square feet of living area" is simply not applicable in today's markets. Actually, the importance of square footage is more relevant to the value of the house in an appraisal. There are a few exceptions for permanently installed mobile homes where the minimum square footage requirement for FHA and RHS is 400 square feet. An extremely small but growing housing trend known simply as the "tiny house" movement has taken advantage of this FHA small-home financing outlet.

Paved Streets

While most cities have managed to pave their streets, there are some smaller communities and new subdivisions that have not. Lenders have used the lack of paving as a "no-go" situation for a loan if it can result in a lessening of the collateral value. For example, the cost of paving is often handled in the form of an additional assessment on the property fronting the new pavement. If the assessment's amount is unknown, it is difficult to make adequate provision for the charge.

Utilities

A loan application may be rejected if the property offered as collateral does not have adequate sewer and water facilities. Top preference is given to a municipally operated or a regulated private operation furnishing both sewer and water services. The use of septic tanks or private water wells may be a cause for rejection. Some lenders will permit a septic tank if the percolation tests of the soil surrounding it meet certain minimum requirements. Also classed as utilities are the services of electricity, natural gas, and telephone. Lack of electricity would be a negative factor for urban and suburban properties, but could be accepted in rural areas. Lack of natural gas or telephone is not detrimental for a loan. Also, there are no requirements for electricity or phones to be furnished through underground systems at the present time.

Building Materials

As important as building materials would seem to be, only the use of asbestos is considered a negative factor in underwriting a loan. Whether the building is sheathed in aluminum, wood, brick, or stone is important to an appraiser in evaluating the building, but not to a lender in determining a "go/no-go" situation. The quality of building materials is expressed in terms of both the value of the building and in its estimated life or apparent age.

Amenities

The extra niceties that exist in some buildings are reflected in the value of the property, but are not considered critical for the underwriter. A swimming pool, fine landscaping, exterior lighting, a neighborhood club, or a recreational area are all added features that increase property value, but are never considered requirements for loan approval.

Hazardous Waste Areas

A more recent concern in the evaluation of real property as collateral for a loan is whether or not the land is on or near a hazardous waste area. While the problem is more likely to be found in a commercial area, residential developments may also be involved. The importance of all environmental requirements has become a major factor in loan determination and will be discussed more fully in a later chapter.

Location of Property

Lines are drawn by most conventional lenders among urban, suburban, and rural housing. The differences are not always clearly delineated, but they do provide a broad classification that is useful in describing packages of loans.

Due to the sprawl of metropolitan areas, the term *suburban* now means almost any location in a recorded subdivision of land in the general area surrounding cities—still the region of greatest growth in our country. *Urban* means the downtown and near-downtown areas of our cities. *Rural* identifies farm housing and, to many lenders, houses existing in the smaller towns. "Rural" may also be used to identify housing without access to a central water and sewer system.

Neighborhoods

Lenders no longer specify areas or neighborhoods within a city as acceptable or unacceptable for making loans. The practice is known more commonly as **redlining**, from lines drawn on city maps to guide loan officers. Such identification has been interpreted as leading to possible discrimination in violation of the Fair Housing Act. Obviously, a neighborhood that is allowed to deteriorate does not make an attractive location for a 30-year loan. Nevertheless, lenders are asked to qualify houses on their individual merit rather than on the basis of the neighborhood in which they are located.

As assistance in monitoring compliance with these rules, federally regulated lenders are required to disclose the geographic areas in which they have made loans by census tract or by postal zip code number.

Interesting problems are arising in older neighborhoods that have declined but are now recovering due to a phenomenon called "gentrification." This occurs in areas where older homes have been removed and townhomes are built in their place. Just a few blocks away, however, other older homes remain that have market values sometimes as low as 25% of the level of the new townhomes being built and sold.

Flood-Prone Areas

The federal government has designated certain areas of the country as flood plain zones. These are areas that either have been flooded in the past 100 years or that, if records do not exist, are calculated to have a 1% or greater chance of being flooded. Flood plain elevation lines have been determined by the U.S. Geological Survey, and land at lower elevation comprises a flood plain area. While houses may be built in a designated flood plain, they may not be financed by lenders subject to any federal regulatory body unless minimum elevation requirements are met. Essentially, this means that buildings in flood-prone areas must either be flood-proofed or have the ground floor raised at least one foot above the elevation of the 100-year flood plain line.

Since 1968, the federal government has offered assistance to property owners with subsidized flood insurance through the National Flood Insurance Program. For a homeowner to be eligible for such coverage, the community must agree to participate in flood management and regulate development in its flood-prone areas. The subsidized insurance is offered in cooperation with selected private insurance companies in approved areas.

In 1973, Congress passed the Flood Disaster Protection Act, which required communities to participate in the National Flood Insurance

Program as a condition of receiving federal financial assistance. And it required property owners in flood hazard areas to purchase flood insurance as a condition of obtaining financing through a federally regulated, supervised, or insured financial institution. Even so, many borrowers, probably believing they would not be flooded, stopped paying premiums during the term of the loan.

To help make such nonpayment of premiums more difficult, the National Flood Insurance Act of 1994 imposed new obligations on lenders and servicers, including mandatory escrow requirements for flood insurance and mandatory provisions for "forced placement" of flood insurance if the borrower fails to pay premiums. The borrower must be notified if the required coverage is not purchased and kept in force. If no action is taken within 45 days of notification, the lender or servicer must purchase the insurance on behalf of the borrower, charging the cost to the borrower. Lenders and servicers may now rely on a determination by the director of the Federal Emergency Management Agency (FEMA) stating whether or not the building is in a special flood hazard area.

Other Disaster-Prone Areas

As new real estate developments increase in areas that are subject to certain kinds of natural disasters, many lenders are refusing to consider loans for such properties. The potential for disasters includes earthquakes, volcanic eruptions, swelling soils, subsidence of the land, landslides, firestorms, and geographic faulting. Where adequate hazard insurance is available, however, most lenders will make the loans.

Age of Property

The age of a house is a simple, frequently used criterion for determining acceptable and unacceptable loans. The range varies from an insistence by a lender on exclusively new houses—which is unusual—to no fixed limit. Many lenders couple the age of property with the location of the house. Some neighborhoods maintain their desirability over the years, and 30- to 40-year-old homes may qualify for prime loans. Older houses that are not in prime neighborhoods may still qualify for mortgage loans, but at higher interest rates and for shorter terms. The originator of a loan must always keep in mind the specific requirements of various secondary-market sources of money in regard to property age.

Regarding the question of age, conventional loans are considered in two ways: One is the actual age of property; the other is its years of remaining useful life. If actual age is the criterion, a "no-go" limit is set at a specific maximum age—such as 15 years, for example. A lender may commit to take loans on new houses only or perhaps on houses not over three years old or not over 20 years old. Determining the actual age is the responsibility of an appraiser, and some flexibility is allowed in his or her professional opinion. It is not necessary, in most cases, to report the date of a building permit or the exact day of commencement of construction. Rather, the appraiser can make a judgment call on the **apparent age** of the house. Obviously, a well-kept house and yard would indicate a lower "apparent" age than would one that has been allowed to deteriorate.

The second method of using the age of a property as an underwriting guideline for a conventional loan is the appraiser's judgment of its **remaining useful life**. For this purpose, both FNMA and FHLMC use the same standard as the FHA and the VA to qualify loans that they will purchase—that is, the term of the loan cannot exceed 100% of the remaining useful life of the property pledged as collateral. Prior to 1986, the limitation was 75% of remaining useful life, which is why many older appraisals show an estimate of 40 years of remaining life rather than the 30-year estimate now in more common usage. There are still strict requirements concerning an appraiser's opinion for remaining useful life on any unit that is a condo conversion.

Usage of Property

Residential properties fall into four categories of usage insofar as mortgage loans are concerned. These are:

1. **owner-occupied** (This usage of property is considered the best, and generally commands lower interest rates and discounts than apply to other usages.);

2. **tenant-occupied** (For loan purposes, rental property is classed in the commercial loan category. The rationale is that rental property would not have a first call on the owner's personal income should a troubled financial situation arise. This means a loan at a little higher interest rate and discount and for a shorter term than that for owner-occupied property. This is true even though residential rental properties classify as "residential loans" for savings association tax purposes and insofar as banking regulations are concerned.);

Where Are We Now?

Sample Items From Fannie Mae/Freddie Mac Uniform Residential Appraisal Report

Item	Subject	Comparable No. 1	Comparable No. 2	Comparable No. 3
Proximity to Subject		1.42 Miles	0.32 Miles	0.60 Miles
Sales Price	$449,000	$417,000	$540,000	$595,000
Price/Gross Area	$161.98	$210.61	$205.32	$230.00
Financing		CONV	CONV	CONV
Concessions		N/A	N/A	N/A
Date of Sale/Time		xx/yy DOM 35	xx/yy DOM 62	xx/yy DOM 328
Location	Good	Good	Good	Good
Site	7,603 Corner	8,669 Inside	14,586 C-Sac-40,000	6,895 Inside
View	Canal/Ocean View	Ocean View	Canal/Ocean View	Ocean View
Room Count	8-4-2.5	8-4-3 -1,500	7-3-3.5 -3,000	8-4-3 -1,500
Gross Living Area	2,772 sq ft	1,980 sq ft + 39,600	2,630 sq ft + 7,100	2,587 sq ft + 9,250
Rooms Below Grade	Boat Slip	None	+ 7,000 Boat Slip	None + 7,000
Garage/Carport	1 Bl GAR	2 Bl GAR	2 Bl GAR–2,500	3 Bl GAR–5,000
Fence, Pool, Etc.	Fence, Pool	None + 7,000	None + 7,001	Fence, Pool
Net Adj. (Total)		52,100	–31,400	9,750
Adj. Sales Price		469,100	508,600	604,750

3. **resort housing** (Not too many years ago, resort houses could be described as cottages, sometimes poorly built of nonpermanent materials and generally not acceptable as security for loans. The locations often lacked proper fire and police protection, were subject to vandalism and excessive storm damage, and were often not connected to municipal utility systems. In recent years, the growth of new, higher-class subdivisions in lakefront or mountainous areas has greatly improved the quality and thus the acceptability of these homes

as collateral. Lenders do, in fact, make many resort home loans, but they adjust the loan amount downward, ranging from, perhaps, 90% to as low as 65% loan-to-value ratio. In resort-type developments, it is not unusual for a developer to buy a loan commitment, paying the discount fee necessary to provide potential customers with a dependable, economical source of mortgage money.); and

4. **second homes.** (Second homes are a close corollary to resort homes, though they differ in several ways. The more affluent society has produced a growing number of families that are financially able to own and utilize two different houses. On occasion, the house in the city might be less lived in and less occupied, on the whole, than the so-called second home in the country. In financing these homes, a lender usually makes a careful determination as to which house might be considered the primary housing entitled to preferential treatment and which one should be downgraded as a second home, receiving a 75% or 80% or smaller loan. A decision such as this would be required where the borrower was making a purchase based primarily on a substantial annual income and not much in other assets. The lender must then consider risk from the viewpoint of a sudden decrease in income due to job loss or working disablement. Which house, then, would most likely have to be forfeited under adverse circumstances?)

CONDOMINIUMS

Changes in lifestyles have supported a growth in demand for **condominiums** in place of freestanding houses. The advantages include less maintenance responsibility, access to more amenities, and the same tax advantages that go with all home ownership. Those most interested in this type of dwelling are singles, young married couples, and senior citizens, together comprising over half the adult population.

Classifying a unit of space remote from attachment to the land as a piece of real estate has required new state property laws. All states passed such enabling legislation prior to 1960, making it possible to pledge this type of property as collateral for mortgage loans. Generally, these laws state how condominiums can be legally described so that they can be classified as real property. Nevertheless, from a lender's viewpoint, a condominium loan involves more questions than does a freestanding house loan because of **common areas** usually owned jointly by all unit owners.

Management of common areas is generally handled by a **homeowners association**, or perhaps through a management agreement. Lenders need to know how maintenance costs are managed and how they are allocated to the unit owners because with an imprecise agreement or under inadequate management, costs could suddenly escalate, creating an early loan default. One example of possible problems is with new properties. A developer may hold maintenance costs to a minimum during the sell-out period, but this may leave an overload of maintenance costs for unit owners later on.

While a lender has little voice in the continuing operation of a condominium project, careful screening of the management agreement may point out other troublesome provisions. Besides maintenance costs, the rights associated with collecting these charges can present real problems. In some states, a maintenance assessment may carry lien rights similar to those of property taxes—that is, they can take priority over a mortgage lien.

Lenders generally require a copy of the management agreement or the homeowners association operating contract for the condominium as part of the loan documentation. A review of this agreement takes time, so to spread the cost, lenders usually require more than one loan in a project before undertaking examination of a condominium loan application. To avoid this problem, some builders ask a lender for project approval prior to offering any units for sale. However, complicating this issue is the fact that the maximum time that an approved FHA appraisal is valid was reduced on construction loans from one year to 120 days in the HUD/FHA Mortgagee Letter 2009-30. This project approval is done to obtain an FHA Certification. The certification process is the method used by HUD to ensure that condominium complexes meet comprehensive criteria to ensure that they are fiscally stable and properly managed. The certification process is used by HUD as a risk management tool to reduce the possibility of foreclosures on FHA-insured loans on condominiums and condo communities everywhere. Prior to 2010, condo communities were either previously approved as FHA condos (by the developer) or could be purchased using an "FHA Spot Approval." The "Spot Approval" process has since been eliminated, and all condos were given expiration dates for their FHA condo approval and certification and they must be re-certified every two years. Now all FHA-approved appraisers will first check to see if the subject property is on the FHA's approved list. (See website at end of chapter.)

Several pitfalls occurred in some of the earlier condominium projects, but with hindsight, these have been mostly overcome. These problems involved both apartment conversions and new developments in which developers held onto management control too long. Examples of this kind of problem include retention of exclusive rights to all future sales of the units, controlling distribution and resale of utilities to the individual units, and holding an unlimited right to expand the project that could overburden existing amenities.

While property qualification for a condominium differs as outlined, qualification for a borrower buying a condo is the same as for any other mortgage loan.

The following is a summary of all the basic "regulations/requirements" that must be in place before an FHA lender can endorse a condominium loan commencing in 2015:

- All units and facilities and phases inside the project must be 100% complete.
- At least 50% of total units must be sold prior to endorsement.
- At least 50% of the project must be owner-occupied.
- There can be no more than 50% of the units with FHA loans.
- Any investor/entity (single- or multiple-owner entities) may own up to 50% of the total units, only if at least 50% of the total units in the complex are owner-occupied as principal residences. (The previous limit was 10%.)
- No more than 50% of property can be used as commercial space.
- No more than 15% of units can be arrears in dues payments more than 60 days.
- Right of first refusal can be present in the "Covenants, Conditions, and Restrictions" (defined as limitations and rules placed on a group of homes by a builder, developer, neighborhood association and/or homeowner association). These CCRs cannot violate "Discriminatory Conduct," as defined under the Fair Housing Act Regulation 24 CFR part 100.

Commercial Condominiums

While the condominium concept has been most widely applied to residential units, a number of applications have been made for the use of condos as rental properties or as business locations. In some condo projects, a number of the dwelling units are owned by investors and are subject to rental. This fact has caused additional problems in that the motivation among occupants differs. Those owning their own condos consider the entire project, including common areas, as an asset to be maintained and protected to assure future value. Those renting units may consider occupancy a temporary situation and have little interest in maintaining the property's future value. Differing motivations present difficult problems for a homeowners association. This conflict of interests is sometimes created unintentionally when a developer is unable to sell all finished units and resorts to rentals as preferable to vacancies.

The economic advantages of a multiple-occupancy building have encouraged groups of businesspeople to utilize the condominium concept for owner-occupied office space. The group can be one with similar interests, such as doctors, or it can be a diverse group of professionals or possibly a variety of sales offices. A developer or builder undertaking such a project may emphasize the presale of the units to assure acceptable construction or rehabilitation financing. Individual condos used for business purposes may be purchased with long-term financing at commercial loan rates and conditions. They are eligible for the same basic tax treatment as any freestanding building used for business.

COOPERATIVE APARTMENTS

A **cooperative apartment** is one in which the ownership of the entire project is vested in an occupant-owned corporation or trust that leases the dwelling units. The concept originated in the eastern part of this country before condominium ownership was fully developed. It provides the advantages of multifamily dwellings along with certain ownership rights. In addition, co-op apartments offer owners some degree of control over who may occupy the units and a legal means to enforce compliance with their rules. This is accomplished through control over the ownership of stock.

To purchase an apartment unit, it is first necessary to buy shares of stock in the owning corporation or a beneficial interest in the trust, depending on how ownership is held. Then the apartment is leased from the corporate owner. The purchase price of the stock covers the basic cost of acquiring the unit, while the lease payment covers ongoing maintenance costs. Thus the occupant holds no title to the apartment unit.

To sell a unit, an occupant must sell the stock held in the ownership entity. The occupant would be subject to certain restrictions on this right to sell. The difficulty of freely marketing a co-op unit has made this type of ownership less desirable than that of a condominium. In contrast, a condominium unit is classed as real property, and legal title can be conveyed to an owner upon acquisition. The right to sell is not subject to approval by other condo owners.

Nevertheless, cooperative apartments may offer an owner similar tax advantages as those available to the owner of a condominium. There are some minor differences in tax questions, though, as the common areas of a co-op are owned by the corporate owner rather than jointly by the unit owners, as would be true of a condominium unit.

Financing the construction of a cooperative apartment (or a condominium project) has the disadvantage of requiring a number of units to be built with the initial commitment of money. Unlike a single-family housing development, this allows houses to be constructed at about the same rate as they are sold; the cooperative apartment must be planned and built as a complete project. One method that is sometimes used to assure a construction lender of loan repayment is to presell (or prelease) a certain number of the units. Release of construction funding can be made contingent on the presale of a specified number of units.

MANUFACTURED HOUSING/MOBILE HOMES

The only difference between a mobile home and a manufactured home is that the latter has been constructed on or after June 15, 1976. Otherwise, the same description applies. The date for the change of names derives from the Federal Manufactured Home Requirements imposed by the U.S. Department of Housing and Urban Development. The HUD description of such a unit is that it must be transportable in one or more sections not less than 8 feet wide and 40 feet long. When assembled, such a home must contain no less than 400 square feet. It must be built on a permanent chassis and may or may not have a permanent foundation.

Unless the unit can be classed as real property, it does not qualify for a regular mortgage loan. Financing for these units, when considered other than real property, may be accomplished with a chattel mortgage as security for the loan. However, in most areas, the chattel mortgage has been replaced by a bill of sale with a security agreement that is regulated by the Uniform Commercial Code.

An FHA-approved appraiser must be aware of the maximum loan amounts that can be made on manufactured homes attached to real property. These are as follows:

Maximum Loan Amounts

Manufactured home only	$69,678
Manufactured home lot	$23,226
Manufactured home and lot	$92,904

The maximum dollar limits for lot loans and combination loans may be increased up to 85% in designated high-cost areas. For further information on high-cost area limits, contact (800) CALL-FHA.

Conversion of Manufactured Homes to Real Property

State laws control the definition of real property, and there are some differences from state to state. Nevertheless, a manufactured home is initially sold by a manufacturer as personal property with an instrument asserting title similar to that of a car. Liens may be included in the title instrument to accommodate purchase financing. Conversion of the unit to real property normally requires several steps. First, liens attached to the initial title normally must be released. The initial title must be canceled, an action that, in effect, releases the unit from its title as personal property. Then, to become real property, the unit must be permanently attached to the land. Depending on state law, in general, prior liens on the manufactured home do not attach to the land, but liens against the land will attach to the manufactured home upon permanent attachment.

Use of Broker Price Opinion (BPO)

The **broker price opinion (BPO)** is a common way of estimating the value of a property. Typical reasons for ordering a BPO include estimating value prior to purchase or sale, understanding collateral value when securing a new loan or refinancing, estimating liquidation value, and buying out a partner's interest in a property, among many others. The major difference between a BPO and an appraisal is cost. Because a BPO is less comprehensive, it's normally a small percentage of the cost of a full appraisal. Appraisals are provided by a third party and are not biased in their estimate of market value. A BPO is normally done by a real estate broker who often is hoping to gain a listing of the property being valued and ultimately win the listing, and as such, the primary incentive behind a BPO may well differ from that of an appraisal. Regulated depository institutions or those approved as mortgage originators by Fannie Mae, Freddie Mac, or the Federal Housing Administration can use a BPO in lieu of a formal appraisal for a single-family residential mortgage they are in the process of underwriting. However, many financial institutions will use BPOs for the following types of valuation issues:

- due diligence for investors or investment bankers;
- foreclosures;
- low-balance home equity lines of credit;
- mark to market—a method banks/lenders use to assess the current value of assets (homes) on their books and for accounting purposes;
- REO listings;
- requests to remove PMI (private mortgage insurance); and
- short sales.

SURVEYS

One of the recurring problems in passing land titles and in ensuring that a lender is actually receiving a mortgage on the proper land is the identification of that land. Improper identification of the property to be mortgaged, through field error or typographical error, will invalidate the mortgage instrument (but not the obligation to repay the loan). A survey is made to physically identify a parcel of land. A **land survey** is an accurate measurement of the property, not a legal description of it.

An example of an error in property description occurred in a motel loan several years ago. In this case, the property described in the mortgage was identified by the perimeter of the building rather than by the boundaries of the land on which the building stood. The parking areas surrounding the building, which provided the only access to the premises, were not included in the mortgage indenture. When it became necessary to foreclose, the mortgagee learned the hard way that there was no access to the building.

For our purposes, a survey is the physical measurement of a specific piece of property certified by a professionally registered surveyor. In processing a mortgage loan, no lender will accept any measurements other than those taken by a professional. It is a precise business, and the loan package requires an accurate description of the land being mortgaged.

When a licensed surveyor physically defines a piece of property, it is customary to drive stakes or iron rods into the ground at the corners and to "flag" them with colored ribbons. It is not unusual for a lending officer to physically walk the land, checking corner markers, thus making sure of the shape of the parcel and whether or not there might be any encroachments that could infringe on the mortgage lien. Any purchaser of land is well advised to follow the same procedure. Walking the land prior to closing is a prudent exercise. However, the prime responsibility for locating encroachments belongs to the surveyor, which is one of the reasons why a survey is necessary.

LEGAL DESCRIPTIONS

A completed survey is a map showing each boundary line of the property with its precise length and direction. A survey should not be confused with a legal description. A legal description uses words, while a survey uses illustration. Legal descriptions are most commonly found in the following three formats.

Lot and Block

Probably the best-known type of legal description is that found in incorporated areas that have established procedures for land development. To obtain city approval to build streets and connect utilities, a developer will submit a master survey of the entire tract of land, showing how the area is to be divided into lots. The lots are each numbered and may be grouped into "blocks" for easier identification. Once the subdivision plat is approved, it can be recorded in the county offices and becomes a readily available legal reference to any lot in the plan.

For lending purposes, where the need is to identify a specific property over a period of 30 or even 40 years, the recorded subdivision plat is a much better method than a street address. Street names change and numbers can be altered, but the lot and block numbers remain secure because they are recorded. It may be argued that a street address gives a much better picture of where the property lies in discussing various houses or properties, but such identification is not sufficiently accurate to be acceptable to a lender. The common method of clearly identifying property in real estate transactions is, first, to give the legal description, followed by a phrase such as "also known as," and then to provide the street address. To illustrate, a property identification might be spelled out as, "Lot 6, Block 9, Nottingham Addition, Harris County, Texas, also known as 1234 Ashford Lane, Houston, Harris County, Texas."

Metes and Bounds

When recorded plats are not available for identification of land (and sometimes when plats are available), it becomes necessary to use an exact survey of the boundary lines for complete identification. This might be true of a recorded lot that has a stream or river as one boundary, the precise boundary being subject to change through erosion or realignment.

The method used is to define a starting corner with proper references to other marking lines, then note the direction in degrees and the distance to the next marking corner, and so on around the perimeter of the property back to the starting point. These descriptions can be quite lengthy and involved. An example of the wording used to describe several boundary lines might be, for example, ". . . and thence along said Smith Street south 61 degrees 32 minutes 18 seconds west 948 and 25/100 feet; thence continuing along said Smith Street south 64 degrees 45 minutes 51 seconds west 162 and 80/100 feet to the point of beginning."

It is obvious that considerable accuracy is required to figure the necessary directions down to a second of a degree and to measure the distances over highly variable and often rough terrain in order to close the boundaries properly. Such a description is acceptable only if certified by a registered surveyor.

In some rural areas, land is identified in the form of metes and bounds by the use of monuments. A *monument* may be something tangible—such as a river, a tree, rocks, fences, or streets—or an intangible—such as a survey line from an adjoining property. Physical monuments such as these are subject to destruction, removal, or shifting and do not provide lasting identifications for long-term loans.

U.S. Geodetic or Government Survey

As long ago as 1785, the federal government adopted a measurement system for land based on survey lines running north and south, called *meridians*, and those running east and west, called *base lines*. The system eventually applied to 30 western states, with the exception of Texas. A number of prime meridians and base lines were established. Then the surveyors divided the areas between the intersections into squares called *checks*, which are 24 miles on each side. These checks are further divided into 16 squares, each measuring 6 miles by 6 miles, called *townships*. The townships are then divided into one-square-mile units (36 to a township), called *sections*, which amount to 640 acres each. These sections are then divided into halves, quarters, or such portions as are needed to describe individual land holdings. An example is shown in figure 11-1.

During the growth years of this country, much of the western land was laid out in this fashion by contract survey crews. Marking stakes were duly placed to identify corners, and these same markers are frequently used today. The fact that many of the surveys accumulated errors, including the failure to close lines, has created some confusion. It is a concern primarily for oil and mining companies, which must identify their land rights, and ranchers claiming property lines against a neighbor. However, these faulty descriptions have not constituted a serious problem for lending institutions. Land described, for example, as "Section 16, Township 31 north, Range 16 east, New Mexico Prime Meridian," could effectively collateralize a farm or ranch loan. A minor inaccuracy in describing such a tract would not undermine the basic security of the collateral.

In pledging property where there is the possibility or probability that some slight inaccuracy has occurred as to the exact amount of land involved, it is customary to use a qualifying term such as "comprising 640 acres, more or less." Any variation in property size should be considered in light of what might be termed "reasonable." A few acres out of line among 640 acres would not matter a great deal, but a few feet in a downtown city property could well be of critical importance.

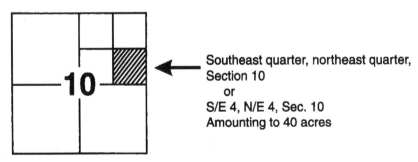

FIGURE 11-1 Section of Township Divided into Quarters

Source: © 2021 Mbition LLC

Questions for Discussion

1. Define an appraisal.
2. What qualifications does a mortgage lender require of an appraiser?
3. Name the three most common appraisal report formats and how they differ in content and use.
4. Describe each of the three approaches to value and give examples of the property type for which each would be most applicable.
5. Identify the three categories of depreciation associated with real property.
6. How would you capitalize an income stream so as to show a property value? What is the advantage of a discounted or present-worth analysis over capitalization?
7. Discuss how the occupancy status of a home might affect the appraisal and lender maximum loan-to-value ratios, the two methods of using age of property as a criterion for loan approval.
8. Why is a loan for a condominium more difficult to analyze than one for a freestanding house?
9. Distinguish between a survey and a legal description.
10. Give an example of a physical characteristic of a house that could cause loan rejection.

Multiple Choice Questions for Review

1. Which of the following might best define an appraisal?
   a. a report prepared by a valuation expert
   b. an estimate of the book value of a home
   c. an estimate of value of an adequately described property as of a specific date
   d. a report prepared by a qualified appraiser holding a license from the USPAP

2. An "appraiser" considered by Fannie Mae to be qualified to perform an appraisal for a conforming loan must, at a minimum:
   a. meet minimum educational requirements of the Appraisal Institute
   b. meet the examination requirements of the USPAP
   c. be licensed or certified by the state in which the property to be appraised is located
   d. all of these

3. A property owner is interested in simply knowing the current value of her property. She does not intend to share the appraisal with anyone or use it for any other purpose. As such, she would like an appraisal report that is as brief as possible, providing only a minimal discussion of the appraisal and the property value. Which appraisal report best satisfies these criteria?
   a. a self-contained appraisal report
   b. a narrative appraisal report
   c. a summary appraisal report
   d. a "letter"/restricted appraisal report

4. In which of the following approaches does the appraiser typically use sales of a rental property similar to the subject property and calculate the ratio of sale price to monthly rental income?
   a. sales comparison approach
   b. market value approach
   c. income approach
   d. cost approach

5. An adjustment for any loss in value within a structure due to changes in tastes, preferences, and technical innovations is called:
   a. physical obsolescence
   b. external deterioration
   c. functional obsolescence
   d. consumer preference obsolescence

6. The estimation approach used by appraisers that is called the income approach is based on:
   a. a property's depreciated value
   b. discounted gross annual cash flows
   c. a property's ability to generate net income
   d. adjustments of the sales prices of comparable properties

7. What is the maximum LTV that can be made on a conforming loan where the subject property is used as a second home?
   a. 50%
   b. 75%
   c. 85%
   d. 90%

8. Which form is used for condo appraisals for Fannie Mae and FHA?
   a. Form 1003
   b. Form 1004
   c. Form 1073
   d. Form 2055

9. A legal description of a property is best served by which of the following?
   a. the street address of the property
   b. the boundaries of the property at the present
   c. the system of metes and bounds
   d. the unique title described in words of the subject property

10. Which of the following characteristics, if found in an appraisal of a conforming residential loan, might cause a loan to be rejected?
    a. The subject property is less than 1,000 square feet.
    b. The subject property has only one bedroom.
    c. The subject property has a septic tank system in an urban area.
    d. The subject property is in a bad ZIP code.

Information Resources

http://www.appraisalfoundation.org/imis/TAF/How_to_Become_an_Appraiser.aspx
　This website provides information about the Appraisal Foundation and how to become an appraiser.

https://entp.hud.gov/idapp/html/condlook.cfm
　This website makes it possible to see if a condominium is on the FHA's DELRAP Approval (Direct Endorsement Lender Review and Approval Process) or HRAP Approval (HUD Review and Approval Process) list.

https://entp.hud.gov/idapp/html/apprlook.cfm
　Many mortgage loan types require that approved originators use specifically approved appraisers. FHA mortgages are one such loan type, and the website above lists approved FHA appraisers in every area of the country.

https://www.fanniemae.com/content/fact_sheet/appraiser-independence-requirements.pdf
　Fannie Mae's basic requirements for appraisers are that they are licensed and in good standing and that they meet Fannie Mae's Appraiser Independence Requirements; these latter are available at the website above.

http://files.consumerfinance.gov/f/documents/201710_cfpb_KBYO-Small-Entity-Compliance-Guide_v5.pdf
　The TILA Higher-Priced Mortgage Loans (HPML) Appraisal Rule, in the *Small Entity Compliance Guide* issued by the CFPB in January 2014. Its last amendment was on October 10, 2017 and can be used to find the price thresholds that would trigger a second appraisal.

https://www.fanniemae.com/content/guide/selling/b3/2/02.html
　Fannie Mae has a validation service as part of its automated underwriting system Desktop Underwriter that offers lenders an opportunity to deliver loans with more certainty. Specific components of the loan file such as: (1) income; (2) employment; and other assets. The website above enumerates those who are eligible for validation by DU, using electronic verification reports obtained from vendors.

Chapter 12

COMMERCIAL LOANS: CONSTRUCTION AND LAND LOANS

KEY TERMS AND PHRASES

audited statement
balance sheet
Certified Public Accountant (CPA)
commercial loan
construction loans
feasibility study
land development loans
land loans
net operating income
Office of Interstate Land Sales
operating statement
pro forma statement
profit and loss statement
release clauses
takeout commitment

LEARNING OBJECTIVES

At the conclusion of this chapter, students will be able to:
- Understand key aspects of commercial real estate finance analysis.
- Describe the commercial real estate loan application process and documentation requirements.
- Understand how the property evaluation process relies on more than the appraised value of the property, and how the type of commercial loan will affect the approach to valuation and maximum loan considerations.

- Explain the draw or disbursement process for commercial construction real estate loans.
- Describe the approach used for considering commercial loans for residential properties versus other types of commercial real estate loans.

INTRODUCTION

In mortgage financing, the term **commercial loan** has a broad and ill-defined meaning. One major discrepancy in the standard accepted definition is that an apartment loan is considered a commercial type of loan. Yet for tax purposes, such as calculating depreciation, an apartment is classed as residential property. Perhaps the best definition of a commercial loan would be simply "those loans that are not classed as residential." Generally, loans on one- to four-family residential units are not considered commercial, while any housing unit that has five or more units is considered commercial. It is a broad category with considerable variety in the handling of each major class of property.

A practical distinction between residential and commercial loans can be drawn from the anticipated source of loan repayment. A residential loan is expected to be repaid from the personal income of the borrower—that is, income unrelated to the property offered as collateral. The commercial loan is a business loan and in most instances repayment is expected from income generated by the property pledged as collateral. The individual involved with seeking a commercial loan is certainly important, but not crucially so as with a residential loan. Some very large commercial loans may not have any personal liability for the principals as individuals, since the property securing the commercial real estate provides both the loan collateral and the anticipated source of loan repayment. Most community banks and smaller local lenders still make a practice of obtaining the personal guarantee of the principals on smaller commercial real estate projects. Many of the risks of investing in commercial real estate still must be addressed by the owner and lender. The following are some of the more common of these risks:

- **business risk** (This is a form of risk due to fluctuations in economic activity/economic conditions, including changes in interest rates.);
- **financial risk** (This is the use of debt or leverage, which can magnify business risk.);
- **liquidity risk** (Many believe this risk has to do with the lack of ability to sell rapidly or into a distressed market. However, it also includes the risk that a business will have inadequate cash flow and/or

working capital to satisfy ongoing expenses, pay creditors and lenders, and maintain capital facilities in proper working order, and the possibility that tenants will relocate when their leases expire.);

- **management risk** (Poor management of a commercial property or development project can cause unnecessary delays or tenant dissatisfaction; poor record keeping can cause rating agency, investor, or debt covenant problems.); and
- **risk management,** which includes identifying material sources of risk; measuring and monitoring those risks; and devising approaches to control, mitigate, or hedge those risks (e.g., purchase of liability insurance, completion bonds, hazard insurance, and building security).

Commercial loan evaluation focuses first on the property, then on the business applicant who expects to own the property. The following section discusses the type of information needed for commercial loan analysis and several of the tools that are used to make such an analysis.

INFORMATION SOURCES

The underwriter of a commercial loan has more sources of information than are normally found with home loans. The home loan evaluation is based primarily on an applicant's personal income and a market appraisal of the property offered as collateral. Proper underwriting of a commercial loan usually involves a business operation and property expected to produce sufficient income to repay the loan. So, to evaluate a commercial loan, the underwriter examines the financial statements offered by the business (or individual) applicant, studies the income-producing capability of the property offered as collateral, and conducts an investigation of the local market for that property's particular product or service. In addition, analysis of a commercial loan application can include extensive interviews with the principals involved in the business operation, who should have provided resumes or background documentation covering their relevant commercial operations experience prior to this interview. Finally, it includes a thorough inspection of the property itself. Other underwriting requests might include an inspection of the rent rolls, tenant lease agreements, and credit quality of the tenants.

THE LOAN APPLICATION

All loans commence with an application. However, unlike residential loans, a commercial loan application is not a standardized form. It is designed by lenders to suit their own specific requirements. Often, the application has specialty sections that focus on different classes of properties—for example, the distinctive information needed for a hotel loan, which differs from that needed to evaluate an apartment loan application. Knowing what questions to ask about specific kinds of properties is one reason commercial lenders tend to specialize in their lending practices.

Depending on market conditions, it is normal for the lender to charge a reasonable fee in order to pay for the appraisal, the environmental report, the engineering report, and the title commitment. This fee defrays the cost of studying an extensive, and usually "one-of-a-kind," body of information that supports sound applications. It also discourages frivolous applications. Some mortgage brokers charge an application fee, typically less than $1,000, which can be considered reasonable due to the time and effort the broker must invest in order to see if the loan is marketable. Some lenders will only charge an application fee if the loan is made, while in some market conditions, lenders may not charge a fee.

Information Required for a Commercial Loan Application

There are few standards and little regulation guiding how financial information is presented. The design of the principal kinds of statements comes closest to being standardized, but even this information can vary considerably. Regulations that apply to this type of information are directed almost entirely at those real estate companies that offer securities to the general public. At the end of the chapter, there are several links to different commercial real estate loan applications from a sampling of existing lenders. Next, we will examine the specific information most likely to be required in a real estate loan application.

Operating Statements of Property

If the property has been operating, statements for the past two or three years are required. These include annual balance sheets and profit and loss statements. A third statement—an operating statement—reports on an individual property and does not show income tax or depreciation figures. While tax and depreciation figures are very important, they are not considered as operating expenses, but rather, as costs that vary with the owner's personal situation. More detail on the three principal financial statements follows.

Balance Sheet

The **balance sheet** is the most standardized of all the financial statements. It is a listing of a company's (or individual's) assets in a column at the left of the page, and a listing of the liabilities plus the net worth in a column at the right of the page. The difference between the assets (what is owned) and the liabilities (what is owed) amounts to the net worth of the company. This makes the sum of liabilities and net worth on one side of the sheet equal in amount to the assets listed on the other side—thus, a "balance" sheet.

The figures that are of most concern to an analyst as regards the balance sheet are the valuation of assets. This is particularly important when major assets consist of real estate. A distortion in value can easily present an erroneous picture of true worth. The careful underwriter will need to know how asset values, particularly land and buildings, are derived. Therefore the underwriter is faced with the following questions:

- Is it a book value representing the original cost of the property?
- Is it based on a professional appraisal?
- Might the value be an owner's concept of market value?

Most other figures found in a balance sheet are more easily verified with simple auditing procedures.

Profit and Loss Statement

The **profit and loss statement** (P&L) is a statement of income and expense; it has nothing to do with assets and liabilities. An underwriter or a buyer doing due diligence must be aware that a set of audited financial statements prepared by a Certified Public Accountant (CPA) will be titled either the "income statement" or the "statement of operations," which are the terms professional accountants use and which constitute a different basis of presentation from the profit and loss statement. These differences will be discussed later in the chapter. The basic format is simple. Start with the revenues (usually rental income), then deduct expenses, and the bottom line shows a profit or loss for the time period covered. The figures may be presented in excruciating detail, covering several pages, or may be reduced to three lines: one for gross revenues (all items of income), one for total expenses, and the third representing the difference between the two, which is the profit (or loss). Most statements fall between the extremes.

Normally, the P&L statement gives some detail as to what items comprise the operation's income, as several sources are often involved. The same is true of expenses that provide information on where the money has been spent. The result of subtracting the operating expenses from income is commonly called **net operating income**, not to be confused with a term by the same name in the more formal CPA-audited income statement. Using the P&L statement, operating expenses are those costs necessary for the day-to-day operation of the business. Operating expenses in the P&L do not include such important deductions as debt service, depreciation, and reserves for payment of income taxes, as would the more formal audited income statement. This is why net operating income best reflects the true operation of a property.

To explain further, the other costs mentioned (debt service, depreciation, and tax reserves) are determined by the owner's decisions and have little to do with the efficiency of day-to-day management of operations (fixed costs are not really considered controllable). Debt service is the cost of financing and has nothing to do with operations. To put it another way, if the property is overloaded with debt, firing the manager is not a solution. As identified on a P&L statement, debt service is the payment of principal and interest only. It does not include insurance premiums and property taxes (these are deducted as expenses), as is customary with home loans. (Home loans identify this cost as a *mortgage payment* that includes principal, interest, taxes, and insurance—or PITI.)

The choice of depreciation procedures allows an owner some flexibility and reflects tax decisions rather than operations. After the 1986 tax reform, income tax policy settled on straight-line depreciation methods (which imply an increasing rate of depreciation for older buildings), with the depreciation rate based on 27.5 years for apartments and 31 years (subsequently increased to 39) for nonresidential commercial buildings.[1] And in today's world of income taxes, there is no standard that can be applied to any particular income. Such taxes, particularly when real estate is involved, must reflect all sources of income. Therefore, having identical dollar amounts of income no longer results in identical taxation.

Because of the questions just raised, a profit and loss statement should deduct debt service, depreciation, and tax reserves from the net operating

---

[1] Sheharyar Bokhari and David Geltner, "Characteristics of Depreciation in Commercial and Multifamily Property: An Investment Perspective," *Social Science Research Network*, modified January 26, 2016, https://papers.ssrn.com/sol3/papers.cfm?abstract_id=2464164.

income after that figure has been determined. This gives an important "bottom line" for an owner or analyst to make informed decisions on future property rehabilitation, expansion, possible disposition, and tax matters. This information is often considered proprietary and not readily available to potential buyers of the property. Instead, for potential buyers a shortened form of the P&L is commonly used, which is better known as an *operating statement*.

Operating Statement

Because it is similar in format, an **operating statement** is often confused with a profit and loss statement. As a shortened P&L, it limits information to income and expenses. It does not include debt service, depreciation, or income taxes. Furthermore, both income and expenses should be presented in sufficient detail to give a reader good knowledge of the property's operation.

An operating statement contains the kind of information most commonly found in real estate transactions. It gives some detail on the income that can be made (the potential gross income), reduced by vacancy and credit losses. Operating expenses are then listed as a deduction from income. The expenses are given in considerable detail and include property taxes and insurance premiums. As explained earlier, these items are not included in debt service when considering commercial loans. The information, subject to verification, can be used as part of an offering package for prospective buyers.

A helpful addition found on some operating statements is a percentage column that gives the ratio of an expense to the property's gross operating income. For example, to use round figures for simplicity, a property that shows a gross operating income of $100,000 where the cost of electricity is $8,000 would represent an 8% (8,000 divided by 100,000 equals .08) measure.

Key expenses should be shown in a percentage column for two reasons: (1) for comparison of operating expenses between potential acquisitions, and (2) to single out those expense items that appear inordinately high compared with local norms. Percentages are a more accurate reflection for comparing costs than dollar amounts because of variation in size of properties. They help to show whether or not expenses may be increasing because of increased revenue or for some other reason.

Pro Forma Cash Flow Statements

A **pro forma statement** is a projection of both income and expenses. It is not a record of what has happened, but of what might be expected.

Pro forma statements are most frequently used as an analysis for new developments. They may be found in a prospectus for an offering of a real estate security. Because the figures are all projections, a pro forma statement should be very clearly labeled. In the hands of a professional analyst, the pro forma can provide very helpful information on a proposed investment project. In the hands of a sales enthusiast, however, it can be misleading. New technologies are available for forecasting and pro forma statement preparations, including software tools such as ARGUS Valuation-DCF™, ARGUS Developer™ and ARGUS Property Budget™, which we will discuss further in Chapter 14. Cash flow projections like the one that follows can often be developed and supported with ARGUS Valuation-DCF software that documents and projects assumptions while supporting the resulting financial conclusions with its standard reporting of all input data, property and portfolio-level summary reports, and detailed tenant-by-tenant supporting schedules.

Where Are We Now?

Cash Flow Projections

PROPERTY:	CITY LIGHTS SHOPPING CENTER
YEAR END DATE:	mm/dd/yyyy
INCOME AND EXPENSE ITEMS:	$1,240,000
Gross Scheduled Income	$83,500
Miscellaneous Income	$1,323,500
Gross Possible Income	$62,000
Less: Vacancy and Credit Loss	$1,261,500
Adjusted Gross Income	$1,240,000
OPERATING EXPENSES:	$300,000
NET OPERATING INCOME:	$961,500
LESS DEBT SERVICE	$758,302
NET CASH FLOW	$203,198

Business Financial Statements

If the real estate borrower has a business, or is a business, lenders will require two or three years' worth of signed and dated statements. Audited statements are usually preferred; however, depending on the loan amount, the lender may accept compiled or reviewed statements.

Personal Financial Statements

The principals involved are expected to furnish personal financial statements for at least the past year. Many lenders want these statements to have been updated within the past 60 days.

Business and Personal Income Tax Returns

A complete loan package will include two or three years' worth of tax returns for both a business and the principals involved. A typical lender will ask for any extensions of tax filings that are outstanding and the expected disposition of each.

Current Rent Roll

The rent roll is a list of the space available for rent and, if available, should include current tenants, vacancies, current rent (gross and effective rate per square foot per year), escalation clauses, maturity of rent contracts, options for renewal, type of rent (single tenant net lease, double net lease, or triple net lease), rent concessions and their timing, and square footage currently under lease. Copies of all leases are normally required. Creditworthiness of current tenants is reviewed, and the lender may require an assignment of leases and rental agreements as additional collateral.

Accounts Receivable and Accounts Payable Aging Reports

Some lenders may require this information to help analyze the overall financial health of the business.

Purchase Contract or Warranty Deed

If the property is to be purchased, the lender will require a copy of the purchase contract and all addendums. If the property is already owned, the lender will want a copy of the recorded warranty deed.

Insurance

Lenders require that the property have hazard and general liability insurance. Depending on the location of the property, other types of insurance (such as flood insurance) may be required.

Current Real Estate Appraisal

Lenders usually order the appraisal because they have their own list of acceptable appraisers. A narrative-type appraisal is normally required, giving cost, market, and income approaches to value. Depository lending institutions will not use appraisals prepared by the borrower or the appraiser selected by the mortgage broker. They select an appraiser using their own list, which has been approved by their board of directors.

Survey

Lenders require a current survey of the land, made by a registered surveyor.

Property Tax Bill

Some lenders require a copy of the tax bill to verify the legal description, the owners, and the tax assessment on the land and any buildings.

Resumes of Principals

The borrower should supply a lender with a brief resume of all principals' work history. Also, if a business is involved, a brief history is helpful.

Articles of Incorporation

If the borrower is a corporation, the lender will require a copy of the articles of incorporation and a corporate borrowing resolution.

Authorization to Release Information

A commercial loan package should contain an authorization for the lender to request credit information on all principals and the business if one is involved.

Environmental Audit

All commercial loans require an environmental site assessment. The audit should be made by a professional acceptable to the lender.

Permits Obtained or Zoning Requirements Met

It is important for the applicants for any development loan to have completed their due diligence on any permits that are needed or to have obtained zoning variances or have researched zoning restrictions to ensure that no violations will be committed based on planned use. A completed file on this type of information will typically be required by a commercial real estate development underwriter. For existing buildings or land that will be purchased for alternative uses, the loan can be allowed to go to closing with the permits or zoning requirements being a closing condition rather than a precondition of underwriting.

PREPARATION OF FINANCIAL STATEMENTS

The most important assurance of receiving complete and accurate information on a financial statement is the caliber of the person preparing the statement. The highest professional designation in this field is **Certified Public Accountant (CPA)**, a qualification that may be granted by each state. Some states offer lesser designations, such as "public accountant" for those meeting certain requirements, usually preparatory to reaching the CPA level. The requirements vary somewhat among the states, but all demand completion of educational courses, some experience in the field working for another CPA, and the passing of exhaustive qualification tests.

In practice, only a CPA may prepare an **audited statement**. This means that the information contained therein has been prepared in accordance with accepted accounting practices and that the numbers used have been verified by the preparer. The preparer then certifies that the statement accurately represents the financial condition of the subject. CPAs can also prepare statements without audit that do not offer the substantiation of data provided with an audit. For larger commercial loans, lenders may insist on audited statements.

The initial presentation of most commercial property investments as found in sales brochures often offers financial information that has not been compiled by professional accountants. If the preparer is an owner or a sales broker, the information given may be suspect because of the vested interest of the preparer. Nevertheless, such information can be verified to some degree by an interested investor and does provide a point of beginning. A major problem with these statements is that they lack consistency, do not have uniform account identification, can reach conclusions that defy easy comparison, and are not always accurate.

Prudent investors normally take the financial information supplied, verify essential details, and then restate all of the figures onto a standard form. A standard form is used to shift income and expense items into uniform accounts that allow easier comparison. The standard statement procedure also reveals accounting information that may be lacking, such as how replacement costs are handled. By restating information onto a standard form, an investor or analyst can make a better comparison between properties offering investment opportunities.

PROPERTY EVALUATION

In commercial loan analysis, the evaluation of property offered as collateral involves more than determining its present value. In most instances, it is the income produced by that property that is expected to repay the loan, so the study involves its potential for producing sufficient income to handle timely repayment. Each kind of property presents a different set of circumstances that affects its cash flows. Because of this, many lenders simply limit their participation in commercial lending to the types of properties they know best. Experience is a valuable teacher.

We will discuss the specialized problems of the major classes of income properties in the next chapter. More generalized information can be obtained from an appraisal and a feasibility study, as explained next.

Appraisal

Unlike residential loans, there are no standardized forms and few regulations that apply to how an appraisal must be prepared for a commercial loan. The most common practice is for a lender to require a narrative-type appraisal prepared by a recognized professional. If the loan is destined for handling by any federally-related lender, such as a multifamily housing loan, a state-certified or HUD/FHA-approved appraiser must be used. It is most important that the appraiser be acceptable to the lender. Or the lender requirement might be given as a minimum level of appraiser designation, such as an "MAI appraiser or the equivalent with state certification."

For a lender, an appraisal represents several things. It is used to confirm an applicant's opinion of value. It provides a professional opinion of what the property actually comprises in land and buildings. And it gives regulated lenders an acceptable basis for meeting maximum limits on loan-to-value ratios. An appraisal should be recognized as an estimate of value at approximately the time of loan origination, and not an assurance that value will remain unchanged over the life of the loan. Nevertheless, the appraisal industry has come under increasing scrutiny by regulatory authorities (see Chapter 10).

Feasibility Study

A **feasibility study** is a variation of the more standardized appraisal techniques in that it places much greater emphasis on a market study of the products and services offered by the subject property. Furthermore, while appraisers are professionally recognized with designations offered by various peer groups and state certifications, those who prepare feasibility reports are not. Even so, feasibility studies are usually prepared by various professionals such as appraisers, property managers, real estate brokers, and market analysts.

As its name implies, a feasibility study attempts to determine whether or not a proposed investment is likely to be successful. It estimates the cost of the project, whether new construction or rehabilitation. Potential income is measured with a market analysis of competing properties in the area. This involves a study of occupancy, amenities offered by the competition, and rental rates. Based on the proven experience of similar properties, the analysis will include a pro forma statement of the expected income and expense of the operation. It should also include a variance analysis that contains some adjustments to deal with the risk of ownership—in particular, the financial risk or leverage risk. Use and overuse of financial leverage occurs cyclically and in differing economic conditions. The overleverage in commercial real estate that took place in the late 1980s and early 1990s caused by, among other factors, easy access to low-cost debt, helped fuel the risk taking that eventually took property investment markets into unsustainable territory. While commercial real estate was not the direct cause of the problems that surfaced in 2007, the end result has turned out to be nearly the same as in the late 1980s, and potentially more destructive given the widespread nature of the ramifications of the financial credit crisis and resulting international recession. The build-up in easy credit was caused in part by the international market's excessive financial assets needing a place to be put to work. People have tended to forget the fact that real estate prices can go down, and there are various forms of liquidity risks inherent to commercial real estate investment and lending. Multifamily and commercial mortgage debt surged over the past 20 years from just over $1 trillion in 1997 (as the sector finally emerged from the early 1990s downturn) to $3.4 trillion in the third quarter of 2008, and was $3.3 trillion in the third quarter of 2014,[2] with a shift of $200 billion of that total to multifamily debt. The net effect of this surge was the growth of the mortgage market from about

---

[2] Federal Reserve Bank, "Mortgage Debt Outstanding," press release, December 14, 2014, accessed January 31, 2015, http://www.federalreserve.gov/econresdata/releases/mortoutstand/current.htm

14% in 2007 to 25% by the end of 2008, exceeding the 1980s peak of 20% of the nation's gross domestic product.[3] Commercial and multifamily mortgage debt outstanding grew $44.3 billion during the first quarter of 2018, the largest first-quarter gain since before the Great Recession, according to the Mortgage Bankers Association.[4]

Feasibility studies should also consider problems associated with environmental questions as they relate to the subject of property. In its conclusion (which is often presented at the beginning of the report), the study attempts to answer the practical question of whether or not the project will be successful. Obviously, the knowledge and ability of the preparer is critical in reaching reasonably accurate conclusions. Most feasibility studies consist of the following five broad topics: (1) market analysis, (2) location analysis, (3) analysis of usage concept, (4) competition analysis, and (5) risk analysis. Several good examples can be found at the following websites:

- http://graziadiovoice.pepperdine.edu/a-feasibility-study-for-developing-new-real-estate/
- https://www.rowan.edu/home/sites/default/files/Rohrer%20College%20of%20Business/feasibility-study.pdf

Where Are We Now?

Comparison of Debt Coverage Ratio (DCR) and Loan-to-Value (LTV) Methods

Consider the City Lights Shopping Center, which has been appraised at $12,000,000 and is expected to have a pro forma statement as shown in the earlier example. The loan constant (K) for this type of loan is 8.275% and the net operating income (NOI) is $961,500.

Debt Coverage Ratio Method:
Lender's DCR for this type of property is 1.2
The maximum debt service (DS) allowed by the lender:

NOI/DCR   =   961,500/1.2   =   801,250

---

[3] C. Allen Garner, "Is Commercial Real Estate Reliving the 1980s and Early 1990s?" Federal Reserve Bank of Kansas City, research study, October 2009, accessed May 31, 2011, http://www.kansascityfed.org/PUBLICAT/ECONREV/PDF/3q08Garner.pdf

[4] Ali Ahmad, "Commercial/Multifamily Mortgage Debt Outstanding Posts Largest Q1 Increase Since Before Great Recession." Mortgage Bankers Association Press Release, Jun 26, 2018, https://www.mba.org/2018-press-releases/june/commercial/multifamily-mortgage-debt-outstanding-posts-largest-q1-increase-since-before-great-recession

The maximum loan amount is:

$$DS/K = 841{,}250/.08275 = \$9{,}682{,}500 \text{ (rounded)}$$

Loan-to-Value Method:
The lender will lend 75% of value:

$$12{,}000{,}000 \times .75 = 9{,}000{,}000$$

The debt service will be:

$$DS = \text{Loan} \times K = 9{,}000{,}000 \times .08275 = \$744{,}750$$

LAND PURCHASE LOANS

Considered as a class, raw land acquisition loans are probably the most difficult of all mortgage loans to obtain. Undeveloped land offers no income that might be used to repay the loan. There is further concern in the need for additional cash each year to pay property taxes, possibly insurance, and various "standby" charges. A hindsight view of the serious decline of real estate values and the collapse of many savings institutions in the late 1980s points a heavy finger at raw land as the most serious real estate problem. As a result, not many lenders will even entertain an application for a **land loan**.

Lenders who do make this kind of loan are likely to restrict approval to those with (1) a good track record of repayment of other land purchase loans, (2) substantial other assets available, or (3) an assurance with some written commitment of a future resale of the land. Effective in March 1993, new loan-to-value limits were placed on regulated lenders at 65% for raw land loans. However, lenders can, and do, apply even lower limits as prudent policy. (This limit has not changed and updates dating from February 2011 can be found at FDIC Law, Regulations, Related Acts, under Section 2000, Rules and Regulations, PART 365—REAL ESTATE LENDING STANDARDS, Sec. 365.1 Purpose and scope; 365.2 Real estate lending standards; Appendix A to Part 365—Interagency Guidelines for Real Estate Lending Policies.)[5]

---

[5] "FDIC Law, Regulations, Related Acts: Appendix A to Subpart A of part 365," Federal Deposit Insurance Corporation, modified April 20, 2014, accessed January 31, 2014, https://www.fdic.gov/regulations/laws/rules/2000-8700.html#fdic2000appendixatosubapart365

Any mortgage loan that is expected to be repaid through the sale of its collateral carries a higher risk for the lender. A future sale is not always an assured condition. In certain situations, a future sale or use of the land might be known when the land is acquired, yet final disposition is not immediate. For instance, the land may be purchased for a housing development, or perhaps a shopping center, requiring time to complete plans and secure permanent financing. If such conditions exist, the attraction for a lender to assist in the immediate purchase of raw land is the potential to make the construction and permanent loans.

Sometimes a land broker or developer will locate a tract of land highly suitable for a particular purchaser. It could be a small tract for a service station or a larger parcel on which to erect a retail store outlet. But at the time the property becomes available, the ultimate user may not be in a position to consummate the land purchase. In such a circumstance, a binding letter of intent by a creditworthy buyer issued to a real estate broker or developer would greatly facilitate a raw land loan to acquire the chosen site. The land broker will present the lender with a reasonably sure sale for the land within a specified time period, with the land itself as collateral.

LAND DEVELOPMENT LOANS

The next logical step after purchase of raw land is its development. Land development for loan purposes means the building of streets and utilities to prepare lots for resale as home sites. In contrast, the land development work associated with the construction of an apartment or office building project is in the category of site development, or land preparation, and is an integral part of the project's construction costs.

For such projects, separate **land development loans** are not needed. Since the work called for in land development plans can easily identify the project for residential purposes, such a loan is much more acceptable to an insured deposit-taking financial institution or other lender than the land purchase itself. The reason is that the development loan classifies as "residential," which for regulatory and tax purposes may receive more favorable treatment for the lender than strictly commercial loans.

A development loan is limited for regulated lenders to a maximum of 75% of the property value. The property value normally used for this measure is the appraised value of the finished lots. This is one of several types of loans that generate what might be called a certain distortion in values due to the fact that the very development being financed greatly enhances the value of raw land. Normally, the appraised value of completed lots based on an existing market would be substantially greater than the development costs. In such a case, a 75% loan could permit the developer to borrow an amount in excess of the actual costs. In lending jargon, the amount of a loan that exceeds a borrower's actual costs is called *walking money*—that is, money the borrower can walk away with upon completion. The prudent lender is reluctant to permit a borrower to obtain cash "profit" from a development loan, since this has a tendency to lessen the incentive to sell the property as intended.

Release Clause

An integral part of a land development loan agreement is the **release clause**. This is the clause that spells out when, how, and at what price any lot or lots may be released from the mortgage pledge of the initial tract of land. The release terms may call for an order of priorities by which the land can be developed and will state in what manner lots may be released. The purpose of this kind of mandate is to assure overall development in a manner that realizes the most efficient utilization of the entire tract that is pledged.

Another important clause specifies the amount of money from each lot sale that must be paid to the lender to release that lot. The release itself is a specific release of the mortgage lien on the lot or lots being sold and is intended to permit delivery of a clear title to the lot purchaser—usually the home builder. The amount of money required to release a lot may be a percentage of the sales price of the lot, such as 75%, stating a minimum sales price. In this procedure, any increase in sales price over the minimum would increase the payment to the lender and amortize the loan more rapidly.

Another method is to set a flat sum on each lot for release and let the developer sell it at whatever price he or she can. The flat sum per lot is usually calculated to repay the development loan with interest in full when somewhere between 60% and 75% of the lots have been sold. Lenders are not interested in waiting for the last, perhaps least desirable, lots to be sold in order to recover the loan.

Office of Interstate Land Sales

Since 1968, the Department of Housing and Urban Development (HUD) has had an **Office of Interstate Land Sales** charged by Congress with the responsibility of establishing guidelines and procedures for land developers in an effort to minimize deceptive practices and outright frauds. Sales of lots—developed and undeveloped—and certain types of time-sharing condominiums have grown substantially in this country and have brought out some unscrupulous operators. Basically, the rules require a full disclosure of the essential facts for the land buyer and serve as protection for both buyer and seller. As one explanation goes, a developer can sell a lot that is completely under water but must state in writing that it is physically under water. The rules apply to any development with over 25 lots for sale. However, certain Statutory Exemptions from both *Anti-Fraud Provisions* and *Registration Requirements with HUD* are allowed. For example, If a seller wants to live dangerously, he or she can claim an exemption from the Registration Requirements, but only if the development has 99 or fewer lots for sale, or if each lot contains at least 20 acres each, and on which no construction is required. Failure to comply with HUD regulations can lead to fines and imprisonment for the lender, the developer, and the sales agents. Legal decisions handed down since 2007 have held that condominium purchase contracts on a lot on which a condominium will be built are only exempt if the completed unit is built and inhabited by the purchaser within a two-year period from the date of contract; otherwise, the developer must be in compliance with the Interstate Land Sales Full Disclosure Act (ILSFDA).

The Dodd-Frank Act placed enforcement under the Consumer Financial Protection Bureau and, due to the financial crisis, more enforcement actions were set into process as purchasers of lots and condominiums tried to get out of transactions using the ILSFDA noncompliance as their cause of action. One interesting action, as evidence of the breadth of the act's definition of "developer," in *Aaron v. The Trump Organization, Inc.*, 2011 WL 2784151 (M.D.Fla., July 15, 2011), the court found that The Trump Organization was liable under the Act as a "developer" because it had licensed the Trump name to the condominium project, including using the name on various sales and marketing materials. The Trump Organization had the authority to review various plans and specifications for the project.[6]

In a rare bipartisan action, the initial bill to remove condominiums from the Act passed with a 410-0 vote in the U.S. House of Representatives.

---

[6]Joseph Lubinski, "Interstate Land Sales Full Disclosure Act: 2012 Update," *American Bar Association Journal* (February 2012).

This was part of a bill to amend the ILSFDA to exempt condominiums from the Act and was signed into law in September 2014.[7] Therefore, condominiums developers are relieved, but consumers will need to become more aware that the ILSFDA no longer provides them the same amount of protection as before. It should be noted that CFPB, who now administers ILSA, has not adopted HUD Guidelines as of March 29, 2017.

CONSTRUCTION LOANS

The construction industry is a major employer in this country and it depends heavily on the availability of lendable funds. However, several large segments of the construction business are not so dependent on the regular commercial loan market. These are mostly government projects such as streets, highways, dams, and public buildings, which can be paid for from tax revenues. To finance these projects, various types of bonds can be sold that are often collateralized with a pledge of tax revenues. Another large segment of the construction market is the building of industrial plants and utility systems by large corporations. These projects are often financed from their own revenues, or perhaps through the sale of corporate securities, including mortgage bonds.

The type of construction lending discussed in this section concerns a building loan—that is, a loan of the money needed to construct a house, an office building, or a shopping center. While these loans vary substantially in size, there is a similarity in the risks involved. All are secured by a mortgage on the land and the building to be constructed, all are funded only after each stage of construction has been completed, and almost all require a permanent loan commitment or takeout of some kind to assure repayment of the construction loan immediately upon completion of the project. So where is the big risk?

The risk to the construction lender lies in whether or not the building can be completed with the available money and whether it meets all required specifications. Many factors that are difficult to foresee can hamper the successful completion of a building. Some of these problems include the weather, labor difficulties and strikes, delays in the delivery of materials, and changes in the plans or specifications. A more recent

---

[7]"H.R. 2600 (113th): To Amend the Interstate Land Sales Full Disclosure Act to Clarify How the Act Applies to Condominiums," GovTrac, 2015, accessed January 31, 2015, https://www.govtrack.us/congress/bills/113/hr2600

requirement involves meeting sometimes difficult-to-define environmental stipulations. These can result in time-consuming meetings, additional paperwork, and even litigation.

Definition

The definition of a **construction loan** focuses on the special requirements for this type of financing. A construction loan is initially a loan commitment that provides for the money to be disbursed at intervals during construction in a manner that ensures payment of all construction costs and finance charges. It requires completion of the building in accordance with the plans and specifications so as to deliver a valid first mortgage upon completion. Further explanation of each part of this definition follows.

Disbursement during Construction

Unlike other types of loans, a construction loan is not funded when the borrower signs the note. All the borrower has at the beginning is a commitment that funds will be released as construction progresses. There are two basic ways that progress payments are released: (1) on a time-interval basis, and (2) on a by-work-completed basis.

With the time-interval method (usually monthly), the building progress is inspected at specified intervals and the amount of work completed is duly noted. The lender then releases that portion of the loan that has been allocated to the work accomplished. Under the by-work-completed plan, the lender and borrower agree at the outset on about five stages of progress that, when reached, will release that amount of the loan proceeds. An example of a first stage might be the completion of all underground work and the pouring of the foundation.

Assurance of Payment of Costs

While it is the borrower's prime responsibility to use the loan proceeds for the payment of charges on the construction, the lender has an important stake in making sure that all labor and materials are paid as the money is released. Every so often, a builder, accidentally or by design, may mix the records and use the proceeds from one construction loan to pay charges accruing from another project. The result can be labor liens and material suppliers' liens filed on the property for loan funds that have already been released to cover those claimants.

Lenders can minimize the risk of improper disbursement in several ways. One is for the lender to handle the payments to contractors and subcontractors. Another is to require proof of payment for costs incurred by the borrower before any funds are released from the loan. Another is to require a waiver-of-lien form, signed by each contractor involved, with every progress payment. Many lenders have a real estate attorney do a lien search of the subject property prior to any disbursement. This search will reveal if there have been any mechanic's liens on the property due to nonpayment by the owner or contractor. Perhaps the most important protection for the lender in this regard is to know the borrower's reputation for handling building projects, then to make close inspection a standard procedure.

Completion in Accordance with Plans

Again, it is the borrower who is primarily concerned that the building be constructed according to the plans and specifications. But the lender also has a real interest in this question, as failure to meet the plans can be a cause for refusal by the permanent lender to release the loan for payoff of the construction loan. The problems are mostly technical, such as the size of pipes and wiring, the grade and thickness of concrete, the amount of reinforcing used, and the compaction of foundation and parking areas.

On small projects, the lender may rely on its regular staff for inspection approvals. On large projects, it is more common to employ an independent firm or professional to serve as the inspector. Architects and engineers are both used for this purpose, and the decision of the professional is usually accepted by both the borrower and lender as final determination of the acceptability of the project as it is built.

Delivering a Valid First Mortgage

Insofar as the lender is concerned, the goal of a successful construction loan is to complete the project within the money allocated, with all bills paid and no liens filed. The construction loan can then be repaid through funding of a permanent loan or the sale of the property.

Additional Comments

It is customary in a construction loan for the lender to withhold 10% from each progress payment until final completion. The purpose is to provide a reserve against unexpected claims. Some lenders will hold this reserve until the statutory lien period has expired (after construction completion) before releasing it to the borrower. If an unexpected cost is encountered that was not allowed for in the loan amount committed, the lender will ask, or demand, that the borrower make such payment. The same procedure is used if the borrower decides to make some changes in the plans after the loan has been committed. Such changes must be approved by the lender, and if they should cause an increase in the anticipated cost, the borrower will be expected to use his or her own funds for payment. The lender does not want to have a building only partially completed with all loan funds exhausted.

Personal endorsement by the borrower/owner is almost always required on a construction loan. The same lender may agree to make a long-term permanent loan with no personal endorsement required, but will refuse to do so on the construction loan for the same project. The reason is not just the added security given by another endorsement; it is to place personal responsibility on the borrower/owner, who is in a controlling position during construction to insist on changes in the plans or create costly problems that can upset orderly construction work. The lender just wants to make certain that the borrower/owner carries a full share of responsibility.

The principal sources for construction money are commercial banks with specialized construction loan departments, savings associations, mortgage companies or commercial mortgage brokers that represent life insurance companies, and other funding lenders such as sovereign funds. The commercial banks' interest is in the higher yield and short terms represented in construction lending; savings associations, sovereign funds, and mortgage companies prefer the higher yields, but also are usually in a position to pick up permanent loans at a minimum of expense to themselves.

Construction Loans for Residential Properties

Single-family detached houses and some townhouse projects are financed by builders on both a contract basis and a speculative basis.

Contract Basis

A house built for an owner under contract represents a reduced risk to the construction lender. The normal sales contract to the home buyer is a firm commitment by the purchaser and includes a permanent loan commitment for closing. Often, the permanent commitment is made to a home buyer by the same lender handling the construction financing as a sort of package deal, which minimizes paperwork. On such a loan, the risk to the construction lender is primarily in the builder's ability to complete the house within contract terms. The builder's track record must be known to the lender.

In smaller communities and rural areas, houses are often constructed under contract by a local builder, who may also operate a lumberyard or other supply facility, with the builder providing the construction financing from personal resources. A nearby savings association will have already agreed to make the permanent loan when the house is completed.

Speculative Basis

Many builders, mostly in growing suburban areas, build houses with the expectation of selling them by the time they are completed. Added to the risk of being able to complete the house within the projected cost figure is the risk of selling the house at a profit upon completion. A lender must look at the strength and capability of a speculative builder before accepting such a loan. As a builder proves satisfactory ability to the lender, the construction line of credit can be expanded.

When the housing market fluctuates downward, the speculative builder is the first to be hurt. He or she can be caught with many unsold houses on which the high interest of a construction loan can continue to eat at any profits. More and more, construction lenders are seeking to protect themselves against a soft market by demanding a takeout commitment before they will agree to the construction loan. This has created a whole new industry of placement firms selling the end (permanent) loan to specialty real estate investment trusts and hedge fund managers, who then place the permanent or takeout loan into the portfolio of the REIT or managed fund accounts of the hedge fund's clients.

Takeout Commitment

A **takeout commitment**, sometimes called a *standby commitment*, is a promise to the home builder by an acceptable mortgage lender to make a permanent home loan directly to the builder in the event that the subject house is not sold within a certain time limit—commonly, one year. The commitment is usually in the form of a simple letter agreement and costs the builder at least one point payable upon delivery of the letter agreement. The amount of the commitment would be the same as the construction loan—normally, 80% of the sales value of the house.

However, the commitment is not really expected to be used. It serves more as an insurance policy to protect the construction lender's loan. To encourage the builder to sell the house rather than rely on the takeout commitment, the rate of interest on the takeout is set at one to three percentage points over the going rate, and the term much shorter (probably 10 years) than if the loan had been made to the intended occupant/buyer. The builder still has the problem of selling the house, but has a little breathing room because he or she is facing a monthly amortization payment rather than full repayment of the construction loan, while the construction lender is clear with all money repaid.

Construction Loans for Income Properties

Apartments, office buildings, shopping centers, and warehouses all use construction financing, sometimes termed *interim financing*, to accomplish the building of the project. As noted earlier, only the strongest builder/developers are capable of commanding construction financing for any income property without a permanent loan commitment to pay off the construction loan at completion. The terms of the permanent loan influence the manner in which the construction money can be handled. Special requirements for funding the permanent loan, such as an 80% lease-up before release of the loan proceeds, place the construction lender in a far riskier position. If a permanent lender is currently unavailable, the developer may resort to a takeout commitment within the same framework as described earlier for a home builder. The construction lender must have a closing date for the takeout within a reasonable period (one to three years) for proper recovery of the construction loan.

Construction lending calls for highly experienced personnel who can work with builders and who understand construction progress and procedures, so as to make timely releases of the loan proceeds. Most lenders will not release a progress draw without physically inspecting the project or having an independent architect inspector submit an estimate of work accomplished. The trick is to be able to complete the project within the money available and still have 10% of the loan amount retained at completion to protect the lender against any unforeseen contingencies. When the lender is satisfied that all bills are paid and that no valid liens can be filed, this 10% retainer/holdback can be released. Commercial construction loan draws are somewhat more complex and can have many additional requirements if they are from a community or state development agency. Common mistakes made for draw requests can include any or all of the following:

- missing invoices and/or proper support documentation;
- invoices lacking sufficient information (e.g., type of work performed, periods covered);
- charging previous balances or accounts receivable balances (most lenders and state community development agencies will only approve "invoiced amounts");
- failure to properly carry forward approved work-in-place on the Mortgagor's Draw Requisition;
- development budget/sources on Mortgagor's Draw Requisition not agreeing with the approved development budget;
- support documentation not properly organized or identified on the Mortgagor's Draw Requisition;
- payment request and attachments not signed;
- request for soft/hard costs not preapproved;
- failure to provide any required supporting documentation; and/or
- lack of coordination between multiple lenders.

Loan Syndications or Participations

Many large commercial mortgage loans have been placed in commercial mortgage-backed securities (CMBS) over the past 20 years. This replaced the more common consortium of banks or other investors that put together loan syndications and/or large commercial banks or savings and loans selling 75% to 90% of a commercial mortgage loan to another investor such as a large insurance company. With the negative impact of the recent financial crisis on the CMBS market, more lenders have returned to the syndication market, and some private commercial mortgage bankers have started working with savings and loans and sovereign wealth funds in selling commercial loan participation on a more active basis.

Questions for Discussion

1. Discuss the differences in the loan application for a commercial loan and a home loan.
2. Describe the risks involved in commercial real estate investment and financing.
3. What type of work is covered in a land development loan?
4. Describe the information normally found in a profit and loss statement and in an operating statement.
5. What is a pro forma statement?
6. What is an audited statement and who can prepare one?
7. Describe the function of the Office of Interstate Land Sales.
8. Define construction loan.
9. How is a takeout commitment normally used?
10. List two ways in which a lender can be assured that release of construction money is delivered to the right contractor.

Multiple Choice Questions for Review

1. The primary difference between a residential mortgage loan application for an investment property and a commercial mortgage application is the:
   a. use of standardized forms
   b. pro forma operating statements
   c. survey
   d. audited financial statements prepared on behalf of the borrower

2. Real estate risk due to fluctuations in economic activity/economic conditions would be best described as:
   a. management risk
   b. inflation risk
   c. financial risk
   d. business risk

3. Which of the following is typically not one of the preliminary work processes done prior to loan application?
   a. feasibility study
   b. analysis of rental income
   c. analysis of the credit of the owner
   d. existence of an appraisal requirement

4. The typical P&L statement will include details of all the following EXCEPT:
   a. total revenues
   b. depreciation expense
   c. utilities expense
   d. net operating income

5. Which of the following is NOT true regarding pro forma statements?
   a. They are typically audited by a CPA.
   b. They include rental income.
   c. They include operating expenses.
   d. They are typically projections of future net operating income.

6. An audited set of financial statements is often required as part of the borrower's commercial loan application package. Which of the following persons or firms can issue an audit report?
   a. a Certified Management Accountant
   b. a Certified Lender Business Banker
   c. a Certified Public Accountant
   d. a Registered Investment Advisor

7. Which one of the following is a reason that the Office of Interstate Land Sales exists?
   a. to protect buyers against a seller of lots that are under water, who discloses that they are so located
   b. to protect against inadequate disclosures on land lot sales of more than 100 lots
   c. to protect against sales of lots for condos that will not be developed within two years
   d. none of these

8. Construction loans typically include the use of a retainer that is best defined as:
   a. a percentage of dollars usually held by the lender
   b. a percentage of dollars usually held by the developer
   c. a percentage of dollars usually held by the developer and the lender
   d. none of these

9. There are takeout commitments for both residential construction and commercial construction loans. Which of the following is most typical of a residential takeout commitment?
   a. It is called a standby commitment, whereas a commercial construction loan is called a takeout commitment.
   b. It is a promise to the home builder by an acceptable mortgage lender to make a permanent home loan directly to the builder in the event that the subject house is not sold within a certain time frame.
   c. It is typically issued by Ginnie Mae.
   d. None of these is typical.

10. All of the following are true of the monthly draw method of financing, EXCEPT:
    a. Draws requested are based on work completed.
    b. The collateral value of the loan will decrease with the disbursement of funds.
    c. This method is predominantly used on large-scale construction projects.
    d. It is used primarily on commercial developments.

Information Resources

http://www.norwoodbank.com/media_library/Comm-RE-loan-App.pdf

https://www.greenwichfirst.com/wp-content/uploads/2013/02/CRE-Application-Package-Full.pdf

> The first website features a shorter form of commercial real estate loan application and the second is in the form of a checklist as an application.

https://dhcd.maryland.gov/HousingDevelopment/Pages/default.aspx

> One good site covering replacement reserve requests for reserves is the Community Development Agency of the State of Maryland with its detailed requirements for multi-family development housing programs.

http://www.axiometrics.com/company.html

> Axiometrics, Inc., has an extensive database on apartments and apartment-related information from public REITs and private sources generated by trained researchers conversing with the on-site leasing agents, giving them additional information about a property's performance, current pricing by floor plan and unit, concessions, amenities, and renovations on 14,400 properties each month.

http://www.icsc.org/research/quickstats

> The Resource Research Center of the International Council of Shopping Centers is a good source of information on the commercial real estate lending environment.

Chapter 13

COMMERCIAL BUILDING AND FARM LOANS

KEY TERMS AND PHRASES

agricorporate farm loans
anchor tenant
apartment buildings
community center
endorsement
Fair Housing Amendments Act of 1988
family-resident farm loans
farm and ranch loans
future purchase contract
leasehold
mini warehouses
neighborhood center
net lease
office buildings
office/warehouses
percentage lease
regional center
religious facility financing
retail store buildings
shopping centers
special-purpose buildings
term lease
warehouse buildings

LEARNING OBJECTIVES

At the conclusion of this chapter, students will be able to:
- Understand importance of using leasehold interests as a key aspect of commercial real estate economics.
- Explain the nature of farm and ranch loans and how they differ from agricorporate farm loans.

- Describe the different approaches to application process and documentation requirements for special-purpose buildings compared to apartment and retail commercial real estate loans.
- Understand how the property evaluation process differs among property types such as the financing of a shopping center versus an office building.
- Describe the approach used for considering religious facility financing and the three dominant types of funding used for religious-use facilities.

INTRODUCTION

Commercial loans deal with a wide variety of properties and businesses. In this chapter, we will consider the major categories of buildings along with some information on the special conditions that lenders must examine to properly underwrite each loan. With certain categories of commercial buildings, different forms of leases are generally used. We will look at these leases along with the buildings that use them. For instance, a term lease is normally used for apartment rentals, net leases are often used in freestanding store buildings and warehouses, and percentage leases dominate shopping centers. Some leases will be defined as creating a **leasehold** interest and this can be for a residential or commercial property. A leasehold interest is a form of land tenure or property tenure where the lessee buys the right to use land or a building for a given length of time. In residential leasehold situations, the lender will require that the lease payment be escrowed like taxes and insurance payments are, and that the lease runs at least until the end of the loan term.

The chapter closes with some information on farm and ranch loans, which are not classed as commercial loans. While they are a most important category of loans and follow different guidelines, this text only gives some generalized information and does not address this kind of loan in any depth.

The study of commercial real estate loans is important as it is a very large, competitive market with highly fragmented ownership and carries many of the same risks as residential real estate in terms of overcentralization in a geographic area (e.g., the Texas Oil Belt recession of the mid- to late 1980s, when the collapse of oil prices affected both the commercial and residential markets) and concentration of risk (e.g., an overexposure to loans on financed properties with Blockbuster or Circuit City as the main tenants or owners). More recent trends reveal that some retailers typically found in malls have failed, such as Dots LLC, Ashley Stewart Holdings,

Inc., and Coldwater Creek Inc., all of which declared bankruptcy in 2014. These three firms account for over 1,000 stores. These key issues underpin commercial real estate financial analysis.

In some states, contracts covering commercial real estate space now show increased use of covenants intended to protect health or human safety against the presence of hazardous materials. Such claims may be recorded against a property, and remediation expenses can be enforceable even if they do not benefit the land of the party seeking to enforce the covenant. Environmental issues are a key focus of due diligence in nonresidential real property purchase and sale transactions, particularly in areas of current or historical manufacturing, dry cleaning, gasoline stations, auto body and repair shops, and landfill uses. Such uses commonly result in the discharge, release, or disposal of "pollutants" or "contaminants" that cause soil, groundwater, surface water, and indoor air contamination, which can create significant economic, environmental, and public health risks, have increasing impact on the viability and terms of a deal.[1] More detail on these emerging issues will be covered in Chapter 15.

The following commentary points out major differences in the various categories of commercial loans for buildings.

SPECIAL-PURPOSE BUILDINGS

In a sense, all buildings are "special purpose," as their design generally restricts use to a specific kind of occupancy. However, in the jargon of real estate, *special purpose* has a more precise meaning. **Special-purpose buildings** offer a specific kind of service and are more difficult to convert to any other usage. Examples of special-purpose buildings include fast-food restaurants, bowling lanes, service stations, recreational structures, theaters, and automobile dealerships. Because of the close relationship between the building and the specialized services offered, such buildings are often owned by the business operator. But many are built by investors for lease to professional operators.

Another feature of a special-purpose building is a much greater dependence on the ability of the operator/manager to achieve profitable operation. While management is important in other kinds of income property, such as apartments and office buildings, it is less critical than with special-purpose

---

[1] Lee Gotshall-Maxon and Sandi Nichols, "Key Issues in: Real Property Purchase and Sale Agreements" (Presented at the *Getting Ahead of the Deals Coming Your Way in 2012* conference, San Francisco, CA, January 24, 2012).

property. For instance, an office building, once fully leased, will continue to show a cash flow even with changes in the management. But an automobile dealership or a fast-food franchise is heavily dependent on the particular skills of management for its profitability. Therefore, lenders may limit the amount of loans in their portfolio for special-purpose buildings. They may also restrict loans for these types of buildings depending on their risk tolerance. In addition, there are also restrictions for public REITs under Regulation A and Rule 504 and Regulation S-B of the Securities Act—rules that have to do with disclosures and restrictions on holdings under certain REIT classifications related to special-purpose buildings.

Because of this emphasis on management, lenders must look beyond the building itself and examine the capabilities of those who will be managing the property. This is never an easy determination, and it is particularly difficult if the loan applicant is a newcomer to the business. Lenders may use several procedures to make such a determination, as we will see in the following section.

Earnings Record of Applicant

If the company requesting the loan has a record of steady earnings and is creditworthy, there is little problem with approval. Examples of this type of applicant include oil companies building service stations and fast-food franchisers expanding their operations, among others.

Endorsement

A method of credit enhancement sometimes used to expand automobile dealerships or recreational facilities is a manufacturer's **endorsement** of the obligation. This means that the manufacturer agrees to accept a contingent responsibility for repayment of the mortgage obligation on the special-purpose building. For the manufacturer, the purpose of undertaking such a risk would be to increase its sales outlets.

Future Purchase Contract

Yet another method of credit enhancement that has a broader application than just special-purpose buildings is a **future purchase contract**. Consider a situation where a large grocery chain desires assurance of a special product made or produced by a small local supplier. By offering the supplier a large continuing contract for its product, the supplier would have a proven source of cash flow to induce a lender's favorable decision on a loan. As additional security, the lender might ask that the purchase money for the product be paid through the lender's offices as delivery is made to the grocery chain. While such a contract, assigned to the lender or not, falls short of an endorsement of the obligation, it does give a lender some assurance as to how the loan will be repaid. And that is the key question in the minds of all lenders.

APARTMENT BUILDINGS

An **apartment building**, or *multifamily housing* as the federal government classifies it, represents an investment in residential property. In the past, residential property, particularly low-income housing, has enjoyed certain tax advantages, and it is subject to some restraints that serve to protect the rights of tenants. While tax advantages for a while tended to distort investment decisions, the principal determinant for sound apartment investment still remains the occupancy of such projects in each market area.

Underlying the achievement and maintenance of good occupancy are several qualifying factors. Experienced apartment operators judge three factors to be of almost equal importance in a successful operation: (1) location, (2) physical facilities, and (3) management. Obviously, a careful underwriting analysis must consider all three factors in determining the risk involved.

Location

Location is usually the first limiting requirement of an apartment seeker. A major consideration of location is easy access to jobs. Access to freeways improves accessibility for apartment dwellers, and many apartment seekers regard proximity to schools and churches as important. The availability of recreational facilities such as parks, golf courses, restaurants, and other entertainment is also an important consideration. Apartment dwellers as a group are not as burdened with exterior housework and yard maintenance as are single-family home residents.

Since location is a major determinant of the available market, it is necessary to evaluate the market in that area. For instance, does the proposed rental structure fit the requirements? Will it be competitive? Do the size and type of units meet these demands?

Physical Facilities

The physical plant must meet the market requirements, not only in size of units but also in architectural style and amenities available. Amenities include such factors as playground areas, tennis courts, swimming pools, club rooms, and entertainment facilities. If the market is primarily families, the two- or three-bedroom units would be the most popular choice; if intended for young singles, the one-bedroom and studio designs are often in greatest demand. The elderly, on the other hand, might prefer one or two bedrooms with a minimum of stairs to climb. Sometimes an assortment of units is used with the hope of covering all phases of the market. In smaller communities, this assortment may best fit local needs. However, in metropolitan areas, this "shotgun" approach is a poor substitute for careful analysis of the market, as it may result in one type or style of unit easily rented and maintaining good occupancy while others go begging for tenants. Before building begins on an apartment complex, knowledgeable operators (developers) study the market for particular requirements and then use their merchandising power to attract suitable occupants.

Management

Management is the third major factor in successful apartment operation. Its importance is well known to experienced owners but too often underestimated by newcomers to the field. Along with location and the physical plant, management, too, can be a "make-or-break" factor.

Larger cities throughout the country have companies that specialize in apartment management, offering a complete management service for a fee of 3–5% of the gross revenues. Good management involves maintaining routine cleanliness of the public areas, prompt repairs of equipment or damaged sections of the building, and fair enforcement of rules for the mutual well-being of the tenants; all are necessary to achieve and maintain a high occupancy rate. Experienced operators learn how to cope with the special requirements of rental properties, such as initial screening of tenants, the most effective methods of collecting rents and keeping them current, the special problems created by domestic pets, handling skip-outs, and dealing with tenants who create disturbances for other occupants. Consequently, an underwriter will look much more favorably, risk-wise, on a property under the management of competent individuals or companies.

As apartment-style living proliferates in cities, underwriters recognize that the better-planned, better-maintained facilities are those that will sustain occupancy in soft or competitive markets. And a continuous high occupancy rate is the key to survival in this business.

Analysis of Income and Expenses

For proposed apartment construction, a projected statement can be prepared to show anticipated gross revenues from each unit and all miscellaneous revenues (for example, from laundry rooms), less a vacancy factor and credit losses. This will produce an effective income from which deductions can be made for all expenses. Fixed operating expenses include such items as taxes and insurance and do not fluctuate with occupancy rates. Other operating expenses do fluctuate with occupancy rates, such as utilities, maintenance, supplies, and labor. A special expense that is frequently overlooked or underestimated is replacement cost. Items such as drapes and carpeting and equipment such as ranges or dishwashers, all in continuous use, have a tendency to wear out. Allowances must be set aside for their replacement. The cash remaining after these deductions then becomes available for debt service. Any remaining cash, after all expenses and debt service have been covered, serves as a cushion against a loss or a slow period.

Many of these costs estimated ahead of construction are subject to interpretation. For example, what occupancy rate may be reliably projected? The FHA uses a figure of 93%, with exceptions for 221(d) programs and 223(f) programs where lease-up requirements are less constricted. Conventional lenders generally tend to select an occupancy rate substantiated by actual rates prevailing in a particular area. Most lenders require proof of an occupancy rate near 90% before they will entertain an apartment loan application. Rental rates also must be in line with the going market. Expenses can be projected with reasonable accuracy. In general, total expenses range from 36% to 45% of the gross operating income, depending on the size of the operations and the efficiency of management.

The dramatic drop in commercial real estate values during the recent financial crisis has caused many projects to be put on hold. It has also caused many banks to have to put up additional capital for performing real estate loans as a result of downgrades in loans stemming from the recent and ongoing bank safety and soundness examinations. These examinations are quite vigorous; between 2010 and 2014, about $1.4 trillion in commercial real estate loans will reach the end of their terms, and some have estimated that half are currently "underwater."[2] As discussed in chapter

---

[2] "June Oversight Report: The AIG Rescue, Its Impact on Markets, and the Government's Exit Strategy," Congressional Oversight Panel, accessed January 31, 2015, http://cybercemetery.unt.edu/archive/cop/20110402010341/cop.senate.gov/documents/cop-061010-report.pdf

11, there was a renewal in the development of multifamily housing units as early as 2011, but by 2014, the interest moved more toward starts of development of industrial properties. The office building segment shows primary activity in redevelopment of holdings to address shifting tenant demands as well as to attract new tenants.

Debt service is the monthly or annual cost of the principal and interest payment, and should be tailored to ensure timely retirement of the full loan. By careful analysis of the cash available for debt service, an underwriter can determine the most effective loan for the proposed apartment. Adjustable and negotiable factors are the term, which ranges from 15 years upward to 30 years, and the loan-to-value ratio, which determines the equity cash required. The interest rate may be adjustable or fixed, is usually pegged to market rates, and is less subject to negotiation.

Recent data from Fannie Mae and Freddie Mac have shown that delinquency rates for single-family homes have been unprecedented; multifamily loans and leases have delinquency rates far lower than during the last major downturn at the end of 2010. Fannie Mae and Freddie Mac's new multifamily MBS was down over 60% between 2007 and 2010, while FHA multifamily originations had grown more than seven fold by October 2011 than in the previous three years.[3] As of the beginning of 2015, delinquency rates continued to abate to pre-recession levels. As of the beginning of 2015, due to the generation "Y" preference of housing in a more urban setting,[4] the multifamily commercial market should continue to see positive growth—at least in the near term. This will ultimately affect residential housing demand, because generation "Y" is putting off new household foundations to later decades. Moreover, they prefer urban living to suburban living.

Term Leases

Apartments are usually leased under the conditions of a **term lease**—that is, a short-term lease that may or may not be in writing. While state laws control how leases may be handled, a general rule is that a lease for less than one year need not be in writing. The short-term nature of the lease

---

[3] Jon Prior, "FHA multifamily origination breaks record," *HousingWire Magazine*, 2011, http://www.housingwire.com/articles/13997-fha-multifamily-origination-breaks-record

[4] Andrew Warren et al., "Emerging Trends in Real Estate 2014," Price Waterhouse/Coopers and Urban Land Institute, report, 2014, 7.

allows the landlord to make periodic increases (or decreases) in the rent, as the market may require. Occupancy is more volatile in an apartment property than in an office building or retail store, and this can create a lack of stability in its continuing income.

RETAIL STORE BUILDINGS

The freestanding **retail store building**, or strip of stores, is an interesting investment for individuals as well as large companies. The more conservative way to handle such an investment is to first obtain a lease for the premises, then build to suit the tenant. In good economic environments, many such buildings are constructed on a strictly speculative basis, with owners and developers expecting to attract tenants later. However, during times of economic stress, in order to be eligible for financing, properties will have to include either an anchored or unanchored retail store building, as well as net-leased, single-tenant properties with certain occupancy and sales requirements. At all times, the best commercial mortgage rates and terms are possible when a subject property meets some of following basic conditions:

- high visibility
- a profitable operating history
- direct access to major roadways

Analysis of Income and Expenses

A retail store building rented to a business tenant for a fairly long term—say, 10 or 15 years—offers a stability of income not found in apartment-type properties. A well-drawn lease agreement should allow periodic rental increases, either as a fixed amount every few years or as an escalation clause. The escalation clause ties an increase in rentals to increases in the landlord's operating expenses.

With this type of property, the payment of expenses is usually negotiable between the landlord and tenant and is spelled out in the lease agreement. A common division of responsibility for maintenance is that the tenant pays the costs of maintaining the interior of the building while the landlord is responsible for the exterior. And the landlord is responsible for handling building insurance coverage and payment of taxes.

Net Lease

Freestanding store buildings are often leased to major grocery chains and other retailers on a **net lease** basis. This means the tenant is responsible for maintaining the building, providing the insurance coverage, and paying property taxes. With the responsibility for paying maintenance, insurance, and taxes passed on to the tenant, this kind of lease is often identified as *triple net*. It is the kind of investment that is attractive to a person who wants to avoid management of the property; the rental rate is based on a fair return on the investment without the addition of a management cost. Financing for this kind of investment may be enhanced by the assignment of all or part of the rentals. A major tenant is an attractive source of loan repayment for lenders.

SHOPPING CENTERS

The development and leasing of **shopping centers** is a specialized business. Some developers not only build major centers but are retained to manage them. Many large retailers have entered the development business themselves to expand their own market reach. It is likely that shopping center owners work to prelease their centers' space more than the owners of most other types of property investment. To attract tenants to a new project, the developer can undertake a careful market analysis of the area to be served. Such a market study includes potential sales volumes for the various commodities that will be offered at the center. With this information in hand, the developer can better prove to a merchant the value of opening an outlet in the subject area. The market study would also be of benefit to prospective mall owners seeking a mortgage loan.

Anchor Tenant

Crucial to the successful operation of a shopping center is having a major tenant, or **anchor tenant**. The big merchant can attract shoppers that benefit the smaller merchants. Major retailers have learned that smaller stores can also attract customers on their own, thus benefiting all, as this arrangement offers greater convenience for the shopper.

The value of an anchor tenant is such that many major retailers have spearheaded their own projects. Some rely on experienced shopping-center developers to implement their plans and manage the center upon completion. Others, such as Sears, Roebuck & Company, have entered the development business themselves. Sears has built a number of major centers through its Homart Development Company subsidiary.

Shifts in consumer attitudes, along with consumer interests in better values, have caused mall owners and mall developers to embrace more discount stores as anchor tenants. For example, the Palisades Center, a 1.8 million sq. ft. regional mall located 20 miles north of New York City, has four levels that boast BJ's Wholesale Club, Home Depot, and Target built on top of one another.[5] The structuring has worked well because the section of the parking area was built on a slope, and each store has direct access to the lot, along with over 150 other retail stores and eateries.

Classification of Centers

Shopping centers defy easy classification, as most major developers try hard to be different. Something unique has more appeal, and the intent is to attract the general public. Centers fall into roughly three classes, based mostly on size and merchandise offered: neighborhood, community, and regional.

Neighborhood Center: Smaller **neighborhood centers** often consist of a large corner area with a strip of two or more stores. Merchandise offered is mostly daily essentials such as food, drugs, hardware, and other everyday services.

Community Center: A **community center** offers all the services found in the neighborhood center plus an anchor tenant, such as a general merchandise store, an apparel store, a furniture outlet, a professional service, or some recreational facility.

Regional Center: The largest category, a **regional center**, offers a full range of merchandise and services. It contains at least two anchor tenants as well as scores of lesser shops, and a variety of restaurants, theaters, and other recreational facilities. Often, there is a large mall that offers various kinds of entertainment to attract the general public. Hotels, office buildings, and apartment complexes are often found around these areas. Regional centers have become an attraction for business meetings of all kinds since they offer easy access to "off-duty" activities for those attending (or not attending) the meetings.

---

[5]Stan Luxenberg, "Redefining the Mall Anchor Tenant," *National Real Estate Investor*, accessed January 31, 2015, http://nreionline.com/mag/redefining-mall-anchor-tenant

Income and Expenses

The income from a shopping center depends to a considerable degree on the success of its tenants. High-volume sales attract and retain tenants. Management expertise can add to the success with advertising, crowd-attracting displays, and entertainment. The reason for the tie between center profitability and tenant success is that most leases are based on a percentage of the tenants' sales. To enhance promotion of the center, management usually organizes and spearheads a tenant/management association that meets regularly to plan and arrange financing for various sales events. Larger shopping malls are capable of offering rather lavish seasonal entertainment spectacles that boost sales. Some malls actively encourage senior citizen walking clubs that use the climate-controlled areas for exercise and perhaps spend a few dollars with the merchants as well.

Operating Expenses

The costs of operating and maintaining a shopping center are divided between landlord and tenant. There is no standard procedure, as negotiation plays an important role in attracting larger tenants. Typically, however, one finds that the higher the costs borne by the tenant, the lower the rental. Usually, all exterior maintenance of the building, grounds, and common interior areas are the responsibility of the landlord, while the tenant pays for interior maintenance of its space. Janitorial service normally follows the same pattern: the landlord pays for cleaning public areas while the tenant services its own space.

Utility service is usually separately metered to tenants. However, a recent trend in larger centers is to install their own electricity-generating plants, even selling surplus power back to the local utility company under a co-generation agreement. Some commercial operators have turned to new technology. For example, Bloom's Energy Server® provides a solid oxide fuel cell in a new class of distributed power generator, producing clean, reliable, affordable electricity at the customer site. This allows larger energy consumers to produce electricity using natural gas at 2.5 times less energy per kilowatt produced by the most energy-efficient natural gas electrical plant.

Heating and air conditioning may be either centrally furnished or supplied by each tenant with its own equipment. Shopping center management prefers that tenants furnish such equipment and take responsibility for its operation for several reasons. One is that maintenance and operating costs are not easily predictable, and providing the proper temperature often causes problems. Another reason is the potential for liability if sales are lost through failure of the equipment to maintain comfortable temperatures.

A growing practice is to separate the base rent from many of the operating costs. This is accomplished by billing such operating expenses as a separate "service fee" to the tenant. It allows a more stable rental structure yet provides the landlord with some protection against the uncertainty of future operating costs. An alternative method of allowing for fluctuating costs is to include an escalation clause in the lease agreement that allows for an annual rental adjustment based on changes in operating costs.

There is an emphasis on increased sustainability with regard to energy efficiency and environmentally sustainable design. Some state and local governments have implemented standards that govern future development or redevelopment of commercial property to meet energy-efficiency standards or environmentally sustainable design, or both. One well-known voluntary standard is Leadership in Energy and Environmental Design (LEED), an internationally recognized green building certification system. The LEED green building certification system is the leading third-party verification of construction designed and built using strategies aimed at increasing performance, reducing waste, and improving quality of life. This is covered in greater detail in Chapter 15.

Percentage Leases

Usually, shopping centers lease space at percentage rates based on the nature of the tenant's business, rather than as a flat percentage for the entire center. The rates vary from a low of 1% to 1.5% of gross monthly sales for large volume stores such as supermarkets and discount stores, to a high of 10% to 20% for smaller shops and boutiques.

Percentage leases usually require a base, or minimum, rental payment each month. Otherwise, it would be possible for a merchant to achieve a profitable operation on high-margin merchandise that could produce too low a gross volume for the landlord to pay its own expenses. The minimum may be stated as "amounting to 6% of gross sales each month but not less than $1,500." Or the base rental could be separated from the percentage with language such as "rental shall be $1,500 each month *plus* 3% of gross sales." The minimum rental payment may be subject to an escalation clause based on a landlord's cost experience.

Verification of the tenant's monthly sales volume is usually a requirement in the lease terms. It can be achieved through submission of a copy of the tenant's state sales tax report to the landlord each month. Or the landlord may require a periodic audit of the tenant's sales records.

> ### Where Are We Now?
>
> **Typical Percentage Rent Rates**
>
> The following table represents typical percentage rates for various types of tenants:
>
> | Type of tenant | Typical % rate |
> |---|---|
> | Grocery store (national credit) | 1% |
> | Drugstore (national credit) | 1% |
> | Variety store (regional credit) | 1.2% |
> | Video store (regional credit) | 2% |
> | Shoe store (local credit) | 4% |
> | Electronics store (local credit) | 4% |
> | Liquor store (local credit) | 5% |
> | Cleaners (local credit) | 5% |
> | Restaurant (local credit) | 6% |

Financing of Shopping Centers

Three categories of retail store facilities must be considered separately for loan purposes. The differences are based on whether or not a merchant wants to own or lease its premises. It is a top policy decision, and major retailers differ in their answers. Some prefer to lease their store space and use that capital for other business purposes, a practice that is fairly common for grocery chains. Others see an advantage in anticipating a market growth area and building their own facilities to maintain better control of operating costs. What follows is a discussion of the three categories: (1) owner-occupied buildings, (2) preleased space, and (3) speculative projects.

Owner-Occupied Buildings

An owner/occupant merchant seeking financing to buy or build a new facility has several options. The company may use its own cash flow as a source of funds or, if the company is large enough and well recognized, it may obtain funding through the sale of mortgage bonds in the financial markets. If the decision is to seek financing from a mortgage lender, the financial record of the company itself becomes as important as the value of the property pledged as security. While the property serves as collateral, the success of the company's operations is a key factor in loan approval.

In the current environment, many owners are attempting to obtain loan modifications to take advantage of historic low rates or to make necessary improvements to retain or attract new tenant stores. Lenders need to understand that a somewhat troubled existing borrower requesting a loan modification is usually told that he or she must keep payments current for the period leading up to the modified mortgage being finalized and closed. Sometimes to keep debt service current, a mortgagor may have ceased paying his or her vendors and suppliers, and by the time the lender finds out about the liens these vendors and suppliers have placed on the property, the modification has become much more difficult to execute.

Preleased Space

The method used by most shopping center developers is to prelease as much space as possible, and certainly this would include the major tenants. With leases in hand, the developer can show a lender exactly what kind of stores will be operating in the center and, more importantly, that there will be a commitment of rental income. It is not unusual for a lender to base the loan amount on the value of the leases rather than on the value of the buildings as collateral. Thus, the better the quality of leases, the greater the loan commitment, which reduces the equity cash required up front. Few centers are able to fully prelease their space, so usually some additional, speculative space is included. This space is easier to lease if the smaller merchants know who the other tenants will be and what kind of competition they will encounter.

Speculative Projects

Only financially strong builders/developers are able to construct speculative store space, either as freestanding buildings or neighborhood centers. The larger shopping centers cannot be financed without obtaining leases with substantial tenants. The risk of leasing speculative space is considerable, and the quality of the tenant is unknown to the lender. Nevertheless, a number of developers are quite capable of erecting smaller projects and have proven successful. One key is to keep up-to-date on the growth in market areas and select appropriate building sites. Another key is to maintain a sound list of prospective clients—that is, merchants who have proven records of success and are aggressively expanding their operations. A track record of successful development is essential for any loan approval in this field.

OFFICE BUILDINGS

The owners of all types of **office buildings**, ranging from the largest to the smallest, acquire or construct them for one of two purposes: (1) their own occupancy, or (2) for lease to others.

Business Owner-Occupied Buildings

Many owner-occupied office buildings are bought or built by companies or persons with a financial history that makes the decision on underwriting such a property somewhat easier for the lender. This is because the credit reputation of the owner is the major qualifying factor under consideration, whereas the real estate to be pledged is of secondary importance. Ultimately, the source of loan repayment is closely tied to the owner/occupant's record of profitability and the manner in which previous financial obligations have been met.

In financing large owner-occupied buildings, an alternative choice to straight mortgage financing is the sale of first-mortgage bonds (where a pledge of the property collateralizes the bond issue) through an investment banker or a mortgage banker. Acquisition of large office buildings by investing institutions such as banks or insurance companies is a common practice. To accomplish this, owners may simply finance the property from their own investment funds. On occasion, a firm needs to free up capital in an existing building that they occupy and will enter into a sale and leaseback.

Various local, state, and federal governments and their agencies build office buildings for their own use with legislative appropriations or through the sale of various types of bonds. Some government buildings, such as post offices, are built by private investors under long-term lease contracts and are financed through private sources.

Office Buildings for Lease to Others

The underwriting of buildings intended for lease to others calls for some specialized techniques of real estate mortgage financing and requires extensive analysis of the property involved. In this category, there are four main groups: (1) a builder-investor with preleased office space to build, (2) a speculative builder-investor hoping to attract tenants before the building is completed or soon thereafter, (3) an owner-occupied building with extra space for lease, and (4) a "stabilized income property" that is being acquired.

Preleased Office Space

A substantially preleased building is the more conservative method of making an office building investment. For financing, it provides the underwriter with a lease to analyze a tenant to examine for creditworthiness, and a building and location to study. If the building is specialized to meet a tenant's unusual requirements (such as heavy electrical gear, raised or lowered floors, or special wall patterns), the term of the lease should be sufficient to recover the extra investment. Most underwriters will limit loans to a percentage of the total lease payments, as this is the main source for loan recovery, or to at least secure sufficient preleased space to cover debt payments and forecast operating expenses.

Similar to a shopping center, a preleased office building faces an inflexible situation in regard to an overrun on construction costs. The building must be designed and constructed in a manner that meets projected costs, and the contractor must have the ability to complete the project within the contract terms. Bonding of the contractor is a normal requirement. Preleased office buildings for single tenants are usually "bare-wall" leases—that is, the tenant pays for finishing the interior (not added to the rental payment) and provides future maintenance.

Speculative Office Buildings

The speculative builder presents a greater risk to an underwriter, and this limits loans to only the more experienced and creditworthy builders. In addition to the usual analysis of the building and its location, consideration must be given to the market and the regional economic pattern. What are the chances of the speculative building becoming fully leased? However, the underwriter, by choice, is not in the business of chance, so a protective restriction is sometimes applied that would require the building to have a 75%, 80%, or perhaps 85% occupancy with bona fide tenants before the permanent loan will be released. A minimum rental provision clause used to protect the lender's repayments is often included in a speculative building loan. Of course, restrictions based on lease-up throw a real burden on construction financing and usually mean that the builder of a speculative building must have the credit strength or cash reserves to build and lease the building without an assured permanent loan commitment.

It is not unusual for a knowledgeable builder-contractor entity to build and lease a moderate-sized office building with its own funds, then mortgage out for more than the costs. In such a case, the loan security rests as much on an assignment of the lease income as on the mortgage pledge. One method of measuring loan size based on lease assignments is to calculate the current worth of future lease payments and loan 80% of that value. Innovators like Bluelofts are catering to speculative developers or owners of older properties with core vacancy issues, offering a a modular "box" for its apartments that includes the kitchen, the bathroom and all the plumbing. Bluelofts and firms like Peer Capital Advisors are using often dead space in the middle of commercial buildings where they can put co-working offices and other amenities for the tenants, creating a community where people can live, work and socialize.

Owner-Occupied Building with Space to Lease

A building constructed or acquired for owner-occupancy is often larger than needed at the time. The expectation, of course, is of future expansion. This would mean offering leases to others of shorter duration, like two- to five-year leases, or even including cancellation clauses in anticipation of future needs. Such limitations on occupancy could mean lower rental rates.

In periods of downsizing, owners may reduce their own use of office space. In an effort to attract new tenants, favorable rental rates may be offered in an effort to further reduce overhead expenses.

Regardless of how multitenant occupancy is created, owners tend to use contract management companies to handle operations rather than self-managing the property. Management is a specialized business, and building owners generally recognize the advantages of having experienced personnel handling lease-up and operation of a property.

On the first floor, because of the enlarged entrance area, the add-on factor is likely more, such as 1.20.

> ## Where Are We Now?
>
> ### Rent Calculations for Office Buildings
>
> Consider an 11-story multitenant office building. The size of floors 2 through 11 are 21,000 square feet. Of that space, 1,000 square feet are part of the "core" (elevator, stairwell), 3,000 square feet compose the "common area," and the remaining 17,000 square feet make up the leasable space.
>
> The quoted rental rate for the lease space is $30 per net rentable area (NRA). If a prospective tenant wants to rent 4,000 sq. ft. for a new office, the 4,000 sq. ft. is considered net useable area (NUA). To calculate the contract rent, multiply $30 × 4,000 × 1.15. The 1.15 is called the add-on factor (AOF). The actual rent, therefore, is 30 × 4,000 × 1.15 = $138,000.
>
> Another way to express the rent rate calculations would be:
>
> $$NRA = NUA \times AOF, \text{ or}$$
>
> $$\text{Contract rent} = NRA \times NUA \times AOF$$
>
> The landlord pays for the core and the tenants pay for their demised premises plus their pro-rata shares of the common area.

Stabilized income property is a property type in which the building has a longer operating history; it usually has an 85% or higher occupancy and is for sale by its current owner for varying reasons. One of the typical issues facing a lender on these types of loans is that the current owner may be selling due to a lack of funding for reseating tenants when existing leases expire, or the building may need renovation and the owner is a passive investor, such as a pension fund or certain types of real estate investment trusts, without the management expertise or authority to complete such a transition. Therefore, many borrowers interested in stabilized income property may want additional financing, not just for the purchase of the office building, but for rehabilitation costs as well. For this reason, this type of loan sometimes has similar characteristics to the speculative office mortgage in terms of final LTV and expected occupancy after all rehabilitation construction and reseating of tenants is complete.

WAREHOUSE BUILDINGS

The **warehouse building** is another type of income property that is preferred by many investors because of its relatively low maintenance and management requirements. The demand for warehouse space has grown substantially in the past decade for several reasons. Many types of companies use general warehouse space to store merchandise in peak seasons, to keep a product closer to its ultimate market, or to house an unusually large stock of a particular raw material.

Somewhat like office buildings, this type of facility can be built for use by an owner, such as a grocery chain operator; it can be built for use in part by an owner, such as a light manufacturer, with portions available for lease to others; or it can be built for speculative leasing as commercial warehouse space. It is the speculative warehouse that requires the most careful loan evaluation of the property. Owner-occupied or partially occupied buildings provide an established business with a source of income to substantiate and undergird the loan analysis. Warehouses are built fully preleased and partially preleased in much the same way as office buildings and shopping centers, so the analysis of the different types is similar.

General Warehouse

There are several basic requirements for general warehouse space that make it more easily rentable during the life of a loan. Like all other income properties, location is of paramount importance. Location should include accessibility by roads running in several directions that are able to accommodate large trucks or tractor trailers. The land need not be in high-density traffic zones as required by shopping centers and some office buildings, but neither should it be locked into small street patterns that limit the size of the truck that can transit through. Warehouses should also be accessible to rail spurs, if possible. Availability of a rail siding is not essential to every user, but lack of this facility may limit future marketability.

Because general warehouses may be built in older or less-developed areas of a community, it is important to check out the availability of adequate water lines and water pressure to support proper fire extinguisher installations. Without adequate fire protection, insurance rates skyrocket and greatly increase storage costs for the prospective tenant.

In the construction design of the building itself, provision should be made for loading docks capable of handling truck and freight-car loadings at the proper heights. The ceilings must be high (generally over 15 feet) for more efficient stack storage of merchandise. The costs of construction of a warehouse building are similar to those for a shopping center building insofar as both are fairly high-ceiling buildings with little or no interior finishing provided by the builder. Warehouses require heavier floors to support more weight but use much less parking space than a shopping center building. Furthermore, the cost of land suitable for a warehouse is much lower than that required for freeway-accessible shopping sites.

Net Lease

Warehouse leases often provide for a triple net return to the owner, which means the tenant pays all maintenance and operating costs, plus all insurance and taxes on the building. In such a lease, management expenses are held to a bare minimum. The cash available for debt service is therefore very easy to calculate. For general warehouses with multitenant occupancy, the owner may provide some services and most likely will be responsible for taxes and insurance costs.

Office/Warehouses

A variation of the general warehouse is the type of building that combines an office facility in front and larger warehouse-type space in the rear. These **office/warehouses** have many uses—for example, as sales and storage offices for such items as parts or distribution of equipment, small manufacturing operations, and repair facilities. Office/warehouses should be more accessible to general traffic than general warehouses and are more likely to be attractively landscaped, with parking available for the tenants' customers. Construction costs are about the same as for a general warehouse except for finish work in the office area.

Mini Warehouses

A growth segment of the warehouse market has developed in the building of one-story structures partitioned into small rental spaces. The market for these **mini warehouses** comes from the more affluent and mobile citizens who accumulate material goods but are unable to accommodate them in small apartments and houses. The structures usually contain from 100 to 300 rental spaces, each ranging in size from $5' \times 5'$ to $20' \times 20'$. The management requirement, depending somewhat on size, ranges from almost nil to full-time administrative personnel and security guards. Returns on investment have been good. Owners have reported that a completed warehouse averages about one-half the cost per square foot as that for an apartment building, and the rental rates per square foot are about the same.

FARM AND RANCH LOANS

Farm and ranch loans are distinctive and should not be classified as commercial loans. They require a very specialized knowledge of both the borrower and the property pledged to make a sound underwriting judgment. Almost all of these loans are analyzed in the local area. There are few, if any, national guidelines, as each local area presents its own distinctive soil, weather, crops, and markets. Because of the great importance of agriculture to the national economy, federal and many state governments have undertaken a number of helpful loan programs to support some stability within the industry. Government land and crop loans are the single most important source of farm loans, accounting for about half of all farm mortgage debt outstanding. The other half of the market is covered by commercial banks in rural communities and life insurance companies dealing through mortgage companies. The creation of Farmer Mac by Congress in 1989 and its expansion of powers in 1996 enhanced the willingness of regulated lenders to undertake farm loans. Farmer Mac is now authorized to buy agricultural loans and create its own mortgage pools very much like Fannie Mae and Freddie Mac.

The term of a farm loan varies as to need and may run from 10 to 40 years, with 33 years being a popular term partly because the Federal Land Bank formerly used 33 years. More leniency is given in the repayment of farm loans than other real estate loans. A farmer's income is subject to greater variation, and a rigid payment schedule can be self-defeating. But any long-term farm loan should have full amortization as a goal.

Some of the major government agencies handling direct farm loans were discussed in Chapter 3 as a part of the primary-mortgage market. This section addresses some of the questions that would be involved in conventional underwriting of farm and ranch loans. Two general categories of farm loans are (1) family-resident loans and (2) agricorporate loans.

Family-Resident Farm Loans

The **family-resident farm loan** has not changed a great deal in the past 30 years. It is still based on the three legs of any good mortgage loan: (1) a creditworthy borrower, (2) a property of sufficient value to provide good collateral, and (3) the ability of the property and the borrower to produce an income, assuring repayment of the loan. Judgments on farm land value require good knowledge and experience in the local area. A single-crop farm is the most vulnerable to failure and subsequent loan default. A diversified crop operation, plus some livestock, provides the best security. So the ability of the farm to produce a continued income, regardless of an occasional crop failure or a fluctuating market, is a prime consideration in making a sound farm loan.

The land value itself may be distorted by outside pressures such as a city developing nearby, a large neighboring farm desiring to expand, or possibly a new freeway providing much frontage acreage. But the farm underwriter should confine the analysis to the producing factors—soil conditions, weather, available irrigation, type of crops, nearness to markets, and condition of the markets—that will produce the income from which the loan can be recovered. To give any substantial weight to possibly increasing land values takes the loan into the speculative category of land development.

Agricorporate Farm Loans

Agricorporate farm loans show some similarity to special-purpose property loans. Large commercial farm companies control much of the nation's agriculture today and usually provide good business records to assist an underwriter in making an evaluation. Studies of land productivity with various crops and fertilizers, the most effective methods of breeding and feeding livestock, and management techniques in cost control have developed economies of operation. Equipment can be more fully utilized and better maintained than on smaller holdings. Along with the advantages, there is a word of caution: the dependency on hired labor and fixed management costs make commercial farms less flexible and more difficult to retrench in periods of declining prices.

Ranch Loans

A ranch loan presents only slight variations to a farm loan in that it produces livestock as a principal source of revenue. Because ranches are predominantly in the drought-prone southwestern regions, an underwriter must take care to analyze the water situation. Often, water rights can be of greater value than the land, since without water the land may be worthless. A common practice in ranching is to lease public lands for grazing. The acreage so leased becomes of value to the ranch only in terms of the productivity it can add to the ranch, and this can be limited by the term of the lease. But leased land or grazing rights do add value and should be included in the appraisal for loan purposes. Sometimes, ranches produce additional revenues from the sale of timber rights, from mineral leasing, and even from hunting leases and dude ranching. All income has its value, but must be considered according to its tenure and stability.

Religious Facility Financing

Church or other financing of buildings for the use of religious organizations requires the authorized officials of the organization to meet some unique prequalification requirements. For the typical church facility, for new construction or refinancing a lender will typically want, at a minimum, the following:

- a minimum of three years of financial statements (five years is preferable) and a year-to-date financial statement for the current year including both balance sheets and income statements;
- a minimum of three years' worth of average adult worship attendance;
- annual contributions from each of the largest 15 donors for the previous year (the names of the donors are not usually required);
- cash on hand in the building fund;
- the value of land or a building already owned;
- the current liabilities of the organization;
- a method of fundraising to finalize repayment; and
- current status.

A lender will also want to ask about the level of borrowing that will be needed, so a preliminary budget should be prepared and the authorized officials of the organization making the loan request should be able to answer the following question: Should your fundraising campaign not come to fruition, could the organization pay for a self-amortizing mortgage out of its existing budget?

There are three dominant types of funding for religious-use facilities. These are conventional loans from a bank or other financial institution, a bond offering, or a capital stewardship campaign. Conventional loans will run the gamut of types as the loan may be for new construction, remodeling, or acquisition of land or other facilities such as a daycare center or school, and as such will have many differing options, including funding projections, that might vary from those of a traditional new house of worship.

With conventional lending, borrowers might approach a direct lender such as a commercial bank or broker, usually obtaining a construction loan based on the future value of the facilities to be built, using available assets as collateral. Borrowers will generally obtain money from one lender; however, in some small communities, local banks will participate in making the loan, with one as the lead on the construction loan while the other becomes the servicer on the permanent loan at the end of the construction. The transfer is usually handled like the construction-to-permanent single closing procedure discussed for residential construction financing in Chapter 6.

The second source of funding is bonds. A religious organization would deal with a bond company that specializes in putting together and promoting the offering. As discussed earlier, lenders and bond underwriters will limit the amount of money that can be borrowed based on current income, membership trends, and cash flow trends. Many bond underwriters will tell a church it can only borrow three to four times its current earnings. For example, should a religious organization be able to demonstrate an annual income of $200,000 over the past three years, it might have a bond borrowing power of between $600,000 and $800,000, to be offset by expected cash flows from a capital stewardship campaign and/or the existing value of collateral, such as the land. Some more centralized religious organizations have developed their own bond underwriting and issuance capability.

Many religious organizations use capital stewardship campaigns for new facilities, schools, or other facilities. These capital stewardship campaigns will range in terms of need, funding between one and three times the organization's current total income over a three-year campaign period. Many religious organizations have carefully crafted professionally facilitated campaigns or templates for local use. This is a highly desirable way to fund any building program and aid in obtaining permanent funding from conventional lenders or bond issuers.

Most successful fundraising and financing programs for new construction start with plans developed by a professional architect, ideally based on a budget or bid from the expected contractor. The funds for the architect's fee must be paid for by the religious institution desiring funding, as this demonstrates the level of commitment and competency looked for by funding organizations.

Questions for Discussion

1. Describe a special-purpose building.
2. Compare and contrast two widely different types of commercial real estate loans discussed in this chapter that you had not previously had any experience with before reading about them.
3. Discuss each of the three factors in the operation of a commercial building: location, physical facilities, and management.
4. What part of the federal Fair Housing Act is applicable to an apartment project?
5. Define net lease.
6. Why does shopping center management promote shopper-attraction activities?
7. How does a shopping center utilize percentage leases?
8. Discuss who builds office buildings and why.
9. Evaluate preleased space as a factor in obtaining a building loan.
10. Distinguish between issues of valuation in commercial and farm loans.

Multiple Choice Questions for Review

1. Which of the following would best be described as a special-purpose building?
   a. strip mall
   b. atrium office building
   c. automobile dealer
   d. office tower

2. In this chapter, which of the following was NOT described as a key issue driving commercial real estate finance?
   a. It is a large market.
   b. It is highly decentralized.
   c. It is highly competitive.
   d. It consists primarily of fragmented ownership.

3. From an economic point of view, which of the following would be considered an action taken to forestall a loss in value, rather than an action taken to add value to a commercial real estate investment?
   a. rehabilitation
   b. maintenance
   c. remodeling
   d. renovation

4. Which of the following is NOT an act of discrimination under the provision of the Fair Housing Act that covers apartment developers and commercial multifamily property managers?
   a. failing to comply with installation of wheel chair ramps for the disabled
   b. not renting to persons of a particular racial group
   c. not allowing young families to rent in an elder care facility
   d. refusing to rent to persons of Iranian heritage

5. Net lease usually refers to the tenant paying all of the following expenses, EXCEPT:
   a. maintenance
   b. property taxes
   c. management fees
   d. building insurance

6. When a developer is planning to build a shopping mall, what is one of the more important factors that he or she must have in place to obtain funding?
   a. zoning variances cleared before construction begins
   b. a firm commitment from an anchor tenant
   c. an insurance binder for a construction bond
   d. a contract with a licensed architect

7. The name for the fixed component of a percentage lease, before adding the variable rent portion from sales, is the:
   a. gross rent
   b. rent stop
   c. base rent
   d. net rent

8. Which of the following is NOT one of the primary drivers for the construction of a new office building complex?
   a. need for expansion of space for a corporate headquarters
   b. speculative construction in a market with little commercial office vacancy
   c. a community need for a star-power building
   d. none of these

9. An underwriter of a commercial real estate loan would require a preleased occupancy rate at least at the level required to cover which of the following?
   a. forecasted vacancy rates and operating expenses
   b. debt-coverage ratio and forecasted vacancy
   c. expected debt-coverage ratio and operating expenses
   d. forecasted debt payments plus stub period

10. Which of the following might distort the valuation of farm land from its income-production potential?
    a. a drought
    b. its source of irrigation
    c. its proximity to a growing urban area
    d. the current rate of interest for crop loans

Information Resources

http://portal.hud.gov/hudportal/HUD?src=/program_offices/housing/mfh/mfhclosingdocuments
HUD has issued the documents for closing multifamily housing mortgages that must be used after September 1, 2011. These forms were available on the HUD website above at the time of publication.

http://www.leasingprofessional.com/lease-agreement/list-of-lease-agreements-and-lease-forms.htm
Leasing Professional Newsletter was a premier source of information on issues important to commercial real estate owners, tenants, attorneys, real estate consultants, leasing agents, and management agents. In 2000, its format changed; the new site is called leasingprofessional.com, and includes all the previous analyses of how a tightening office market at the time would likely affect the negotiation and drafting of a variety of clauses in office leases—notably expansion options. It now also includes sources of advanced specialized downloadable real estate documents, forms, and strategies.

https://www.reis.com/comps/form#r,s1=Apt

http://www.reis.com/our-solutions/commercial-real-estate-comps
Reis, Inc., provides commercial real estate performance information and analysis at the metro (city), submarket (neighborhood), and property level.

http://www.rentbluelofts.com/
Adaptive reuse is a new and innovative way to deal with commercial office building vacancy. This modular approach is a method of transforming excellent buildings to possibly accelerate lease-ups and boost value in appreciation by making properties come alive again. Learn how these modular apartments can be broken down and sent up building elevators and set up, plugging into the existing building systems.

http://uli.org/research/

http://uli.org/publications/
Urban Land Institute is a multidisciplinary real estate forum representing the entire spectrum of land use and real estate development disciplines working in private enterprise and public service.

Chapter 14

ENVIRONMENTAL ISSUES

KEY TERMS AND PHRASES

- asbestos
- ASTM International (ASTM)
- Brownfields Program
- Comprehensive Environmental Response, Compensation, and Liability Act of 1980 (CERCLA)
- electromagnetic forces (EMFs)
- Endangered Species Act
- environmental consulting
- Environmental Protection Agency (EPA)
- environmental site assessment
- formaldehyde gas
- hazardous materials
- innocent landowner defense
- Leadership in Energy and Environmental Design (LEED)
- lead poisoning
- Phase I assessment
- Phase II assessment
- Phase III assessment
- radon
- responsible parties
- secured creditor exemption
- superfund
- toxic waste sites
- transaction screen
- underground storage tanks (USTs)
- wetland

LEARNING OBJECTIVES

At the conclusion of this chapter, students will be able to:
- Understand the role of the Environmental Protection Agency in residential and commercial real estate development.
- Describe the principal environmental problems faced by real estate developers, owners, and lenders.
- Describe the types of liabilities for environment hazards, including the liabilities of parties that own a property when a hazard needs to be cleaned up versus those of an owner in "due course" who finds afterward that the real estate in question is on a hazardous site or, under a new definition, is considered a hazardous site works.
- Understand how indoor air quality can affect the health of occupants and the value of real estate.
- Explain the function of energy efficiency standards and their relationship to environmental laws.

INTRODUCTION

In addition to a property appraisal, a fairly recent requirement for loan qualification is an **environmental site assessment**. This has become a necessary procedure due to the potential for massive liabilities that can be assessed against a property owner should environmental problems be discovered. There are a number of different kinds of environmental issues that affect property; some can change its value, some limit usage of the property, and some affect both value and usage. However, of all these environmental issues, the one that harbors the greatest potential for liability is the cleanup of toxic waste sites as addressed by the federal government under the Superfund Act. A further complication is that these problems are addressed by federal, state, and local laws, which can make compliance complicated.

Environmental issues cover a number of important problems. This kind of assessment is commonly required for commercial loans, but not in such detail for home loans. Owner-occupied dwelling units usually hold certain exemptions from environmental rules, as explained next.

ENVIRONMENTAL ASSESSMENTS FOR HOME LOANS

Home loans are distinguished from residential loans in this section, as the latter category includes multifamily properties treated as commercial loans. A broad exemption from liability for cleanup of toxic waste sites was granted homeowners by the **Environmental Protection Agency (EPA)** in 1991. It has eased some concern for lenders considering home loans on or near hazardous waste sites.

In its policy statement, "Policy Toward Owners of Residential Property at Superfund Sites," issued in July 1991, the EPA stated that it would not hold homeowners liable for cleanup costs unless that owner knowingly contaminated the property or failed to cooperate with the EPA in its cleanup efforts (for example, by not permitting the EPA access to a Superfund site). Homeowners are only protected if they use their property solely for residential purposes. The policy also protects lenders who acquire residential properties through foreclosure (defined as one- to four-family dwellings in this policy statement).

The EPA's policy statement is not a statutory exemption. Rather, it is intended only as guidance for EPA enforcement employees. In other words, the EPA's policy does not amend the Superfund statute, meaning homeowners can still be held liable for cleanup costs. However, the EPA indicates that it will not exercise its right to pursue homeowners, but it remains free to rescind the policy or take actions at variance with the policy. This should not cause any less vigilance on the part of home buyers or the real estate professionals who support them in their home purchase evaluation decisions. Contaminants that may be found in homes such as lead-based paint, mold, and radon pose known health risks and are routinely evaluated by home inspectors and other professionals. Threats from pollution outside the home, such as groundwater and soil contamination, are often as hazardous and are gaining increased attention in residential real estate.

Should environmental contamination be discovered on, in, or near a residential property, the value of the home is usually lowered a larger percentage than would be the case for a commercial property facing similar conditions. The reason for this disparity is the few alternative land uses for such properties (i.e., zoning restrictions), and the potential for health impairment of any present or future occupants.

Freddie Mac and Fannie Mae multifamily housing loans require a Freddie Mac/Fannie Mae Phase I Environmental Site Assessment (ESA). There are two specialized types of Phase I ESAs that are required when a loan is financed through Freddie Mac or Fannie Mae. The scope of the work is based on the ASTM E1527-13 Standard, but each has specific requirements, including the following: the percentage and scope of the property inspection; requirements for radon testing; asbestos and lead-based paint testing and operations-and-maintenance (O&M) plans to manage the hazards in place; lead in drinking water; and mold inspection (only specifically required by Freddie Mac).[1] Descriptions of these hazards will be provided later in the chapter.

For residential properties, if the cost of radon gas remediation is in excess of $5,000, that amount can be financed using the FHA 203(k) program. If the cost of remediation is less than $5,000, it can be added to other FHA 203(k) streamline or standard mortgage loan program home modifications or repairs.

ENVIRONMENTAL ASSESSMENTS FOR COMMERCIAL LOANS

Almost all commercial loan applications must now include an environmental site assessment. This includes multifamily dwellings. The normal requirement is for a "Phase I assessment," more fully discussed later as defined under the Superfund Act. A properly completed Phase I assessment can offer a new owner an acceptable defense against claims for toxic waste cleanup costs.

A big problem with Phase I assessments is that the law defining this procedure fails to set standards as to precisely what constitutes contamination or exactly what qualifications are necessary for a person to prepare an acceptable assessment. Education programs and certain standards are being developed, so future resolution of this problem is likely. Another problem with Phase I assessments is that critical environmental problems, such as the presence of asbestos or lead-based paints, are not covered, as these dangers do not subject an owner to the same broad liabilities that stem from the Superfund Act.

Efforts to overcome these limitations have resulted in requirements for an environmental site assessment that is intended to cover all environmental problems, such as wetlands, endangered species, and the presence or nearness of any hazardous materials. This is in contrast to the more limited definition of a "Phase I assessment," which is defined in the Superfund Act and is identified as a possible defense against liabilities imposed for the cleanup of hazardous waste sites. While market jargon still uses both terms almost synonymously to identify the requirement, it is most important for a buyer or investor to clarify the terminology and to understand what the other party really means when requiring an assessment.

Lead-based paint remediation for commercial real estate endures as a topic of dialogue as Senator James Inhofe, a Republican from Oklahoma,

---

[1]ASTM International (ASTM), originally known as the American Society for Testing and Materials, is an international standards organization that develops and publishes voluntary consensus technical standards for a wide range of materials, products, systems, and services.

introduced the Lead Exposure Reduction Amendments Act of 2013, which includes a provision directing the EPA to collect requisite health data for a commercial lead paint rule. Currently, the EPA is collecting information in an effort to get a better understanding of the existence of lead paint in public and commercial buildings, and the extent of renovation and remodeling activities in these structures.

The National Association of REALTORS® informed its members in 2018 that the EPA is developing a federal strategy to reduce childhood lead exposure and update our nation's drinking water infrastructure.[2]

ENVIRONMENTAL REQUIREMENTS OF THE SECONDARY MARKET

While the secondary market is dominated by home loans, a few commercial loans, including multifamily loans, are moving into the hands of secondary-market investors. Since these investors place limits on the kind of loans that are acceptable, some requirements regarding environmental questions are in place and more will likely be forthcoming as the need arises. At this time, both Fannie Mae and Freddie Mac require that certain environmental information be included with any loan eligible for purchase. Primarily, both agencies rely on some added information derived from a property appraisal.

Freddie Mac requires that an appraiser comment on any known environmental conditions that may adversely affect a property's value. These include asbestos and urea-formaldehyde foam insulation. Further information is required on the proximity of the mortgaged house to industrial sites or waste- or water-treatment facilities, as well as to commercial establishments using chemicals or oil products in their operations. While appraisers are not considered to be experts on environmental hazards, they are expected to provide "early warnings" of properties harboring potential environmental problems. Freddie Mac also requires that an appraiser consider environmental factors in reaching a conclusion as to the property's value.

For multifamily loans, Fannie Mae requires its seller/servicers to perform an environmental assessment before submitting the loans for purchase. This assessment includes a review of available documents,

---

[2]Erin Stackley, Ken Wingert, and Russell Riggs, "NAR Meets with Lead Exposure Initiative," April 20, 2018, https://www.nar.realtor/washington-report/nar-meets-with-lead-exposure-initiative.

interviews with people familiar with the site, and an actual site inspection. If the Phase I assessment indicates potential problems, a Phase II assessment is required. (Both Phase I and Phase II assessments are explained in a later section of this chapter.)

Loan Documents

It is becoming more common for both residential and commercial lenders to include environmental covenants in their mortgage documents. For instance, the documents could prohibit a borrower from using hazardous substances on pledged property.

The Freddie Mac/Fannie Mae revised single-family mortgage requires the borrower to promise to abide by state and federal environmental laws and to refrain from storing or using hazardous materials on the mortgaged property. Furthermore, the borrower must promise to notify the lender if an investigation or lawsuit involving hazardous substances is filed against the property.

PRINCIPAL ENVIRONMENTAL PROBLEMS

The need for information on environmental problems is now crucial in any transaction involving commercial property. Some limits have been defined for homeowners as regards storing or using hazardous material. But exactly what comprises an environmental problem? What is the origin of these problems and what is being done to mitigate the dangers? The balance of this chapter is devoted to outlining the problems, explaining the principal federal laws and regulations that attempt to address these problems, and identifying the major impact these changes will have on lenders and property owners.

The principal laws, rules, and regulations designed to protect the environment—which also have a substantial impact on real estate transactions and future land value—are as follows:

1. laws concerned with the cleanup of toxic waste sites;
2. laws addressing indoor air pollution;
3. lead poisoning rules, including proper disclosure of lead-based paint in dwellings;
4. regulations designed to protect wetlands areas;
5. the Endangered Species Act;
6. laws and regulations governing the proper handling of underground storage tanks; and
7. regulations governing electromagnetic forces.

Other Environmental Issues

To give perspective to the subject matter, many more categories than those listed above are part of the broad subject of environmental problems. Among them are air and water pollution resulting from automobile and industrial discharges, changes needed in mining and forestry practices, the need to filter storm water runoff, and the proper treatment and disposal of sewage. Important as they are, these issues have more to do with providing a cleaner, safer world to live in, and go a step beyond the immediate problem of determining real property value. These problems, therefore, will not be further discussed in this text since the seven categories of laws and regulations mentioned above are the ones that most directly affect land value. Unfortunately, the information presented may raise as many questions as it answers, but that is the current state of the laws and knowledge of the problems.

TOXIC WASTE SITES

Poisonous contamination of land can occur without visible evidence on the surface since it can be located deep underground. If contamination is present, the cost of cleanup is the responsibility of all who might have had a hand in creating the problem, plus any unfortunate purchaser who may have acquired the land even a day or two before. A landowner, both unaware of and innocent of creating any contamination, is equally liable for cleanup as the party actually responsible for the danger. With such broad liability, the burden normally falls to the party with the "deepest pockets," almost regardless of responsibility.

Unfortunately, thus far much of the money spent on environmental problems has been consumed with litigation denying liability for any cleanup. The ill-defined liabilities are a major reason for uncertainty as to future land values, particularly in areas of the country that harbor chemical plants, oil refineries, tank farms, heavy manufacturing plants, mining operations, and government-owned nuclear manufacturing and storage facilities. Underground seepage of hazardous materials generated by this kind of activity can wreak havoc on neighboring properties.

Discovery of the Problem

The first national notice that **toxic waste sites** could endanger people's lives surfaced on August 3, 1978, in news reports on Love Canal, near

Niagara Falls, New York. For many years, the Hooker Chemical Company and others had dumped nearly 22,000 tons of chemical waste in what had once been Love Canal. The wastes included polychlorinated biphenyls (PCBs), dioxin, and long-lasting pesticides. In 1953, Hooker filled in the dump and sold it to the city of Niagara Falls for one dollar. Later, a road was built on top of the fill, making way for houses and a public school. Complaints of foul odors, the surfacing of a black sludge, and minor burn marks showing up on children in the area were not heeded until the late 1970s, when New York State began an investigation.

First Federal Action on Toxic Waste Sites

The public shock created by discovery of massive health problems found near Love Canal finally brought federal government action. The first result was passage of the **Comprehensive Environmental Response, Compensation, and Liability Act of 1980 (CERCLA)**. The Act set up a $1.6 billion Hazardous Waste Trust Fund, which became known as **Superfund**. Later, an amendment increased the Superfund to $8.5 billion. CERCLA and subsequent legislation provide a federal regulatory mechanism to identify, investigate, evaluate, and clean up inactive and abandoned waste sites throughout the United States. They further authorize states and private parties to take appropriate action to clean up contaminated sites and to seek reimbursement from the responsible parties. Implementation of CERCLA was assigned to the Environmental Protection Agency.

Environmental Protection Agency (EPA)

The EPA has defined over 700 **hazardous materials**. Wherever a concentration of such materials is found, the site can be designated for cleanup. The definition of what is hazardous, as well as what concentrations are considered dangerous, is left to the judgment of the EPA. The EPA has determined that some specific wastes are hazardous by definition. It publishes this information in lists that are organized into three categories:

1. **the F-list (nonspecific source wastes)** (This list identifies wastes from common manufacturing and industrial processes, such as solvents that have been used in cleaning or degreasing operations. Because the processes producing these wastes can occur in different sectors of industry, the F-listed wastes are known as wastes from

nonspecific sources. Wastes included on the F-list can be found in the regulations at 40 CFR §261.31.);

2. **the K-list (source-specific wastes)** (This list includes certain wastes from specific industries, such as petroleum refining or pesticide manufacturing. Certain sludge and wastewaters from treatment and production processes in these industries are examples of source-specific wastes. Wastes included on the K-list can be found in the regulations at 40 CFR §261.32.); and

3. **the P-list and the U-list (discarded commercial chemical products).** (These lists include specific commercial chemical products in an unused form. Some pesticides and some pharmaceutical products become hazardous waste when discarded. Wastes included on the P- and U-lists can be found in the regulations at 40 CFR §261.33.)

The EPA is responsible for administering the cleanup of these areas and recovering its costs from the **responsible parties.**

CERCLA specifically excludes a number of hazardous materials that fall under other environmental laws. These include petroleum and its derivatives, natural gas, mining wastes, cement kiln dust, and wastes generated from the combustion of coal and other fossil fuels. These exclusions are important since damage from such sources is separate from and not part of the liabilities cited in the Superfund Act.

Liability for Cleanup Costs

Liability for cleanup as determined by the Superfund Act is broadly stated to cover the release, or threatened release, of hazardous substances from a facility that causes the incurrence of response costs (investigating and testing) and remedial action (removal, neutralization, or containment). Responsibility for cleanup with strict, joint, and several liability falls on all who may have been involved in the waste site. *Strict liability* means liable regardless of fault. *Joint* and *several* mean that each party is both singularly and jointly liable for all costs. However, liability among the various responsible parties may be apportioned if there is a reasonable basis for doing so.

The Act offers no limits on the amount of cleanup, removal, or containment costs for which a responsible party may be held liable. However, liability for damages to natural resources is limited to $50 million.

No Minimum Quantity Required

Whether or not Superfund Section 101(14) requires a minimum quantity of a substance to be present for it to be considered hazardous is not clearly stated. Courts have generally ruled that in the absence of specific legislation to the contrary, no minimum quantity of a substance is necessary for it to be hazardous. The industry complaint is that the rules are ill defined and require monitoring of many harmless materials at substantial additional cost.

Responsible Parties

There are four categories of persons or companies specifically liable for cleanup costs under Superfund Section 107(a), as cited below:

1. the owner and operator of a vessel or a facility;
2. any person who at the time of disposal of any hazardous substance owned or operated any facility at which such hazardous substances were disposed of;
3. any person who by contract, agreement, or otherwise arranged for disposal or treatment, or arranged with a transporter for transport for disposal or treatment, of hazardous substances owned or possessed by such person, by any other party or entity, at any facility or incineration vessel owned or operated by another party or entity and containing such hazardous substances; and
4. any person who accepts or accepted any hazardous substances for transport to disposal or treatment facilities, incineration vessels, or sites selected by such person, from which there is a release, or a threatened release, [that] causes the incurrence of response costs, of a hazardous substance, shall be liable for:
    a. all costs of removal or remedial action incurred by the U.S. government or a state or an Indian tribe not inconsistent with the national contingency plan; and
    b. any other necessary costs of response incurred by any other person consistent with the national contingency plan.

Source: CERCLA Section 107(a)(4)(A) – (B), 42 U.S.C. §9607(a)(4)(A) – (B) (emphasis added)

A February 2009 U.S. Supreme Court decision in the case of *Burlington Northern & Santa Fe Railway Co. et al. v. the United States et al.* (i.e., the EPA) weakened the ability of the EPA to hold companies accountable for the actions of third-party disposal companies, as described in category three of responsible parties above.

The burden is heavy on the current owner or operator as the most visible party. However, there is no requirement that the current owner have any part in creating the hazard to be liable, only that the party be the owner or operator of the designated hazardous site.

Lender Liability

CERCLA allows a lender some protection from liability under the **secured creditor exemption.** The intent is to permit lenders to make mortgage loans without being included as a responsible party should toxic waste cleanup become a problem. However, a few subsequent court rulings placed cleanup liability on lenders if they have the "capacity to influence" a borrower's business.[3] The result has been much greater interest and diligence on the part of lenders making commercial loans to require an environmental assessment as part of a loan application.

Defenses to Cost Recovery Actions

There are very few statutory defenses that might be raised in a Superfund cost recovery action. Those available include a challenge to the quality of government evidence, a claim that liability is for events occurring prior to effective date of the law, or a claim that the statute of limitations applies. CERCLA itself provides some defenses, including such claims as an act of God or an act of war, or the claim that the damage was caused by a third party with whom the defendant had no contractual relationship.

Recent developments include the Supreme Court decision in the Atlantic Research case in 2007 that did provide a definitive "yes" answer to one key question created by the Supreme Court's 2004 *Cooper Industries v. Aviall* opinion.[4] Specifically, a potentially responsible party (PRP) may voluntarily perform necessary cleanup work at an environmentally impaired property and file suit in federal court to recover some or all of the costs of such work.

---

[3] *Chemical Manufacturers Association v. Environmental Protection Agency*, 15 F.3d 1100 (D.C. Cir. 1994).
[4] On Monday, June 11, 2007, the U.S. Supreme Court issued its long-awaited decision in *United States v. Atlantic Research Corp*. The Court's decision confirmed that private parties may sue other persons, including the United States and state governments, to recover costs spent voluntarily (i.e., without the party first being the subject of a cost recovery lawsuit or entering into a settlement with the government), to perform cleanup work at environmentally contaminated properties.

Innocent Landowner Defense

Another possible defense is available under CERCLA if certain steps are undertaken prior to acquisition of a property through what is called an **innocent landowner defense.** Such a defense may be sustained if the landowner makes an appropriate inquiry into the previous ownership and usage of the property before taking title. This constitutes an *environmental due diligence assessment,* also called a **Phase I assessment.** The purpose is to ascertain if any prior use would indicate the presence of environmental contamination or hazardous substances. If an adequate inquiry is made with proper records maintained and nothing of a hazardous nature is found, the buyer may be classed as an innocent landowner. This provides the landowner with a valid defense against future cleanup liability should contamination occur later through no fault of the landowner.

The EPA's "Final Rule" that sets federal standards for the conduct of all appropriate inquiries took effect on November 1, 2006 (except for changes in the standards for Phase I assessments that have new standards, which will be effective on October 16, 2015, as discussed earlier). The term "all appropriate inquiries," or AAI, means the process of evaluating a property's environmental conditions and assessing potential liability for any contamination prior to purchase. CERCLA imposes cleanup liability on owners of contaminated property. Since cleanup liability can exceed the value of the property, the stakes are high. In order for buyers to obtain protection from cleanup liability, they must have complied with the Final Rule prior to closing. The Final Rule applies to any party who claims protection from CERCLA liability for releases or threatened releases of hazardous substances and includes innocent landowners and bona fide prospective purchasers. The Final Rule defines an innocent landowner as one who has purchased property without knowledge of contamination and who "had no reason to know" of the contamination. Otherwise, a bona fide prospective purchaser who acquires previously contaminated property with the knowledge that it is contaminated can likely shield him- or herself from cleanup liability for any preexisting contamination, provided he or she has complied with the environmental site assessment requirements of the Final Rule prior to closing.

Some states have passed their own enabling legislation, such as the Model Toxics Control Act (MTCA) of Washington State that creates the standards for liability release, statute of limitations, and allocation of cleanup costs. The MTCA specifically includes language that in certain cases—such as trust/estate beneficiary liability where the MTCA is silent on the issue—that CERCLA case law is persuasive authority. So real estate professionals on both the lending and development side must also be aware of state laws that affect liability for toxic cleanup, even in cases where a buyer might find new contamination 10 or 15 years later when a new section of a property is being developed. This issue will need to be addressed by the qualified professional performing the Phase I assessment that includes all of the following:

- interviews with persons familiar with the property;
- reviews of historical information;
- searches for environmental cleanup liens against the property;
- reviews of waste disposal and underground storage tank records;
- reviews of hazardous waste records, including handling, generation, treatment, disposal, and spill records;
- visual inspections of the site and adjoining properties;
- a discussion of the specialized knowledge or experience of the defendant;
- an analysis of the relationship of the purchase price to the value of the property if the property were not contaminated;
- reviews of commonly known or reasonably ascertainable information;
- an opinion on the likely presence of contamination at the property;
- a discussion of the degree of obviousness of the presence or likely presence of contamination at the property; and
- an analysis of the ability to detect suspected contamination by appropriate follow-up investigation.

If a Phase I assessment turns up indications of actual or potential contamination, a **Phase II assessment** will be required. Unlike the Phase I assessment, the Superfund Act does not set specific requirements for Phase II. The purpose is to target those areas believed to be contaminated, and includes the collection and chemical analysis of soil samples, surface, and groundwater samples as well as other relevant investigations and analyses. Sampling must be undertaken pursuant to EPA or state regulatory procedures, or both.

A **Phase III assessment** essentially calls for a definition of the extent of contamination, determining the remedial action necessary, and the implementation of the most appropriate cleanup procedures.

Environmental Assessment Standards

One problem with site assessments as a defense against future liability is that no federal standards are provided for determining what comprises contamination, nor are there government requirements as to what authority might be qualified to make such an assessment. To help resolve these problems, a number of trade associations and other organizations have worked with the EPA Enforcement Council to develop better standards for enforcement actions. There is a need to protect property and also to clarify more precisely what comprises a contributing cause that creates liability. Several major universities have developed degree programs to provide qualified professionals who will be able to make more accurate environmental assessments. For example, Arizona State University established a school of sustainability in spring 2007, with an undergraduate degree added in 2008 and a master's degree shortly thereafter. In 2005, the Association for the Advancement of Sustainability in Higher Education (AASHE) was founded with the mission of inspiring and catalyzing higher education to lead the global sustainability transformation. The AASHE, 10 years later, has grown to more than 775 members and actively offers sustainability coursework and degrees.

Leadership in Energy and Environmental Design

One of the leading professional sustainability for-profit organizations is the U.S. Green Building Council (USGBC), a firm that provides top-quality educational programs on green design, construction, and operations for professionals from all sectors of the building industry. One of the company's largest endeavors has been the development and expansion of the **Leadership in Energy and Environmental Design (LEED)**, an internationally recognized green building certification system. The LEED green building certification system is the leading third-party verification of construction designed and built using strategies aimed at increasing performance, reducing waste, and improving quality of life. USGBC has a network of over 80 local affiliates and over 16,000 member companies and organizations, and has put together a diverse group of builders, environmentalists, corporations, nonprofits, elected officials, educators, students, and members of the general public.

LEED professional credential holders number over 150,000; each has obtained one of the six separate levels or specialties listed below:

1. LEED® Green Associate
2. LEED® AP Building Design 1 Construction
3. LEED® AP Homes
4. LEED® AP Interior Design & Construction
5. LEED® AP Neighborhood Development
6. LEED® AP Operations 1 Maintenance

There are ratings systems and guidelines that match up with these six categories to allow buildings or communities to achieve LEED certification for energy use, lighting, water, and material use, as well as incorporating a variety of other sustainable strategies. As part of its certification process, LEED verifies environmental performance, occupant health, and financial returns.

Real estate professionals need to understand the new public commitment to eco-efficient, renewable, and sustainable energy solutions due to cost-effective savings, improvements in employee productivity and health, and value creation stemming from the use of green building technology, as noted below.

Savings

Green building is not just about helping the environment. It makes great economic sense. It yields substantial utility cost reductions—as much as 50% reduction in energy costs, 40% reduction in water use, 70% reduction in solid waste, and 39% reduction in CO_2 emissions.[5]

Productivity and Health

Worker productivity is dramatically increased in a green building. Improvements in indoor air quality and day lighting improve worker health and make a building a place people want to live and work in.[6] In the United States, people are indoors an average of 90% of the time, and green buildings provide a healthier indoor environment. In addition, worker and student productivity can increase as much as 16% in a green building.

---

[5] Bonni Kaufman et al., "Building Green in the Black: More Than Just the Right Thing to Do?" *The Real Estate Finance Journal* (Summer 2007).
[6] Ibid.

Value

The value of green buildings is substantially higher than those built using traditional construction methods.[7] According to the National Appraisal Institute, the value of a building increases by $20 for every $1 in energy savings. On average, one can expect the following results:

- 9% operating cost reduction;
- 7.5% increase in building value;
- 6.6% return on investment;
- 3.5% increase in occupancy; and
- 3% increase in rent ratio.

The value of green building is becoming clear to both builders and owners.

American Society for Testing of Materials' Standards

Another major step toward creating standards for environmental assessment has resulted from an extended study made by the prestigious **ASTM International (ASTM).** On March 16, 1993, ASTM released voluntary standards of practice for performing environmental assessments on commercial properties. The organization has been steadily updating these standards over the ensuing 18 years. The purpose of the standards is to better measure what is meant by an "appropriate inquiry" that would satisfy CERCLA's requirements to support an innocent landowner's defense. The standards give definition to the CERCLA phrase "good commercial or customary practice." For instance, how can it be proven at the time of acquisition that the landowner did not know or have reason to know of any contamination?

CERCLA's broad terminology states that, to pass the "reason to know" test, the landowner must have exercised "all appropriate inquiry into the prior history and uses of the property consistent with good commercial or customary practice in an effort to minimize liability."

---

[7]Josh Partee, *"Shifts in Practice: How Green Building Design and Construction Have Changed the Industry,"* U.S. Green Building Council, Quantifying Sustainability series, 2012, accessed February 17, 2015, http://www.usgbc.org/resources/leed-stories-practice-article-shifts-practice.

ASTM Methods

ASTM has developed two alternative methods that set standards for an "appropriate inquiry," including: (1) a transaction screen process, and (2) a Phase I environmental site assessment (ESA).

The **transaction screen** comprises a series of about 23 questions (using Fannie Mae Form 4340) that examines a property's history. It is recommended that the preparer of the screen be an environmental professional, but this is not required. The screen requires answers from owners, occupants, and the preparer of the report, and may be sufficient for small commercial transactions. However, it is not an assured defense under the "innocent landowner" standards due to a revision to the ASTM Standard E 1528 in February 2006. The standard now states that if a driving force behind the environmental due diligence is a desire to qualify for CERCLA innocent landowner liability protection, then this practice should not be applied. Moreover, a Phase I ESA must be completed, which in the past meant meeting the AAI and ASTM Standard E 1527-05 standards. However, the EPA recently took its final step to phase out ASTM E1527-05, the standard for conducting Phase I environmental site assessments utilized by environmental professionals and parties since 2005. Starting October 16, 2015, environmental professionals and parties must use the updated 2013 version of the standard, ASTM E1527-13, or the federal rule, when conducting Phase I environmental site assessments to potentially qualify for the liability defenses available under the Comprehensive Environmental Response, Compensation, and Liability Act. Transaction screen ESAs, if conducted, are generally prepared for low-risk properties only, but they are a step in the right direction.

The much more extensive ASTM-named Phase I assessment must be prepared by a professional, defined as "a person possessing sufficient training and experience necessary to conduct activities in accordance with (the standard)." The report format contains seven sections covering past and current use of the property, studies of the surrounding properties, identification of information sources, and conclusions as to whether or not further inquiry is indicated.

One of the sections addresses "non-scope considerations." Since the purpose of a Phase I assessment is to limit potential CERCLA liability, the ASTM report is limited to only those substances that are included in

CERCLA's definition of hazardous materials. ASTM suggests that further assessments might be needed on such problems as asbestos-containing materials, radon gas, lead-based paint, wetlands, and possibly others.

One recently added assessment was due to the Drywall Safety Act of 2012, which went into effect on January 14, 2013. As a result, ASTM Committee C11 on Gypsum and Related Building Materials and Systems was given two years to develop or revise standards to satisfy the requirements of the law. This was accomplished by revising three drywall-related standards:

- Specification for Gypsum Board (C1396/C1396M-14A) that limits sulfur content to a level not associated with elevated rates of corrosion in the home;
- Test Methods for Chemical Analysis of Gypsum and Gypsum Products (Metric) (C471M); and
- Specification for Sampling, Inspection, Rejection, Certification, Packaging, Marking, Shipping, Handling and Storage of Gypsum Panel Products (C1264).

Environmental Consultants

A number of property appraisers are entering the field of **environmental consulting.** Their background in examining real property is helpful in making specific environmental assessments. However, much more analysis is involved than assessing value, so the need for specialized training becomes obvious. Persons seeking an environmental assessment from acceptable professionals should base selection on a review of the consultant's education, experience, and reputation rather than on a state certification, as none currently exists in this specialized area. If the purpose of an assessment is to support a loan application, the person selected should be acceptable to that lender.

Many lenders such as Royal Bank of Canada, a large commercial real estate lender in North America, has required that prequalified environmental consulting firms must have at least three full-time licensed professionals (Professional Engineer or Professional Geoscientist) with degrees in civil, chemical, environmental or geological engineering, hydrogeology, geology, or environmental science. At least one of those professionals should possess an advanced degree and 10 years of experience in order to be classified as an expert witness.[8]

---

[8]"Responsible Financing," Royal Bank of Canada, 2015, accessed on February 14, 2015, http://www.rbc.com/community-sustainability/environment/responsible-financing.html.

Private Insurance for Superfund Liabilities

Obviously, the risk level of toxic contamination is difficult to measure. Nevertheless, a few insurance companies have entered the field. They offer two kinds of limited coverage: (1) pollution coverage and (2) banker's environmental risk.

Pollution Insurance

After suffering substantial losses from earlier policies that were interpreted by courts to include coverage for environmental liabilities even though not intended to do so, newer, more limited policies have become available. The policies offer pollution coverage targeting low-risk operations, such as owners of office buildings, warehouses, and shopping centers. An example of the cost for a property valued at $1 million would be an annual premium of $10,000 to $12,000 for a three-year policy providing $2 million in protection.

Banker's Environmental Risk Insurance

Bankers have difficulty determining the risk level of loans that could entail environmental hazards. Extensive research on the property seemed to be the best answer. Recently, however, another option has become available: insurance that protects lenders when a loan goes into default and contamination is found on the property. The insurance either covers the cost of cleaning up the property or pays off the balance due on the loan. This helps avoid foreclosing on contaminated property and thereby becoming liable for cleanup costs.

The need for this type of insurance sharpens at every downturn in the economy, as losses tend to occur when foreclosing on property with environment problems. A trade association has grown out of problems and losses over the past 30 years. It is called the Environmental Bankers Association, and it is a nonprofit trade association that represents the financial services industry, including bank and nonbank financial institutions and insurers, as well as those who provide services to them. It is a good source of information on environment risk trends. Its members include lending institutions; property, casualty, and life insurers; the environmental consulting and appraisal community; and attorneys.

Brownfields Program

In many areas of the country, land that has been contaminated lies untouched by any further development. Several approaches have been made to return this contaminated land to a useful purpose. Under a voluntary program in Texas, for example, property owners can document their cleanup activities and, after inspection by state authorities, obtain a certificate that is placed on the property deed releasing future owners and lenders from liability. While it does not release the present owner from liability, it makes a sale possible by eliminating future liability to the purchaser. The EPA initiated a **Brownfields Program** to remove about 25,000 sites from the federal Superfund program. This reduction in liability has brought dormant sites back to useful life, improving former eyesores and making good use of well-located tracts. Under current law, lenders can conduct pre-loan activities, loan servicing activities, workout, reorganization, and foreclosure without becoming liable for the cost of cleanup. This is true provided the lender does not participate in management activities prior to foreclosure. Real estate professionals and developers should examine the tax-related benefits of this program, which include some relief for urban environmental cleanups in empowerment zones and allowance for deductions for the costs of cleaning up these brownfields. After cleanup, the sites may be used for new businesses that create jobs.

Where Are We Now?

Go Green and Keep More Green

Green home improvements can be quite significant. There may now be better ways to lower energy consumption and reduce monthly utility bills. Some improvements can also add value to the home and give advantages at tax time with federal tax credits. Some of the improvements that can save money include:

- fluorescent lamps and fixtures;
- duct sealing;
- high-efficiency (HE) clothes washer;
- programmable thermostat;
- water heater tank trap;
- refrigerator heat pump;
- high-efficiency dishwasher;
- air sealing to 0.5 air changes per hour;

> - increasing wall and attic insulation; and
> - ENERGY STAR appliances.
>
> The Home Energy Saver website will help the consumer determine the optimum improvements based on their zip code. Visit the website at http://hes.lbl.gov/consumer/.

The Brownfields Program has leveraging money for assessment, cleanup, and revitalization of brownfields based on data from grantee reporting and information available through the program's ACRES database. During the fiscal year 2010, $17.39 on average was leveraged for each EPA Brownfields dollar expended at a Brownfield from the Assessment, Cleanup, and Revolving Loan Fund cooperative agreements made since the program's inception.

Commercial real estate developers must be acutely aware of what has recently been described as High Volatility Commercial Real Estate (HVCRE) Exposures. HVCRE current issues include tenant hazards in commercial property ownership such as illegal drug manufacturing operations like methamphetamine production and indoor farming such as vertical indoor, involved in the production of cannabis and microbreweries. Both of these types of tenant activities tend to cause damage to walls, ceilings and floors due to prolonged exposure to moisture. Positive trends include urban dwellers' and developers' recent conversion of former industrial sites to mixed-use retail. One example is the SouthSide Works, built on the site of a former steel mill in Homestead, Pa. As this trend continues to grow not only in the U.S. but in the United Kingdom, it willl be important to keep in mind that these types of projects can come with impending environmental risks.

In the recent past and the current time natural disasters and climate change have resulted in property and environmental damage from events such as severe storms, wildfires, floods, earthquakes, volcanic activity, and rising sea levels. The most recent hurricane Harvey that hit Houston, Texas in 2017 had one chemical plant east of town release "nearly half a billion gallons of industrial wastewater"[9] alone. Three

---

[9]Matisons, Michelle (2018). Environmental fallout from 2017 hurricanes still ongoing, Multibriefs: Exclusive, April 11, 2018. Accessed at: http://exclusive.multibriefs.com/content/environmental-fallout-from-2017-hurricanes-still-ongoing/waste-management-environmental

know chemicals (benzene, vinyl chloride and butadiene) leaked into surging stormwater during Harvey.

INDOOR AIR POLLUTION

Recent studies by the Environmental Protection Agency have indicated that indoor air can be several times more polluted than outdoor air. The EPA has estimated that half of all illnesses are directly attributable to the following seven types of indoor air pollution:

1. formaldehyde gas;
2. asbestos used in building materials;
3. radon gas;
4. tobacco smoke;
5. biological pollutants such as bacteria, viruses, and fungi/mold;
6. volatile organic compounds found in cleaning products, repair work, and building materials; and
7. combustion by-products from wood, coal, or oil.

Of the seven types of indoor pollution, the first three—formaldehyde gas, asbestos, and radon gas—are among the most dangerous and difficult to assess.

Formaldehyde Gas

Formaldehyde gas is colorless, toxic, and water-soluble and has a strong, pungent, pickle-like smell. It can be emitted by a number of household materials such as urea-formaldehyde foam insulation, formaldehyde-based adhesives used in pressed wood, particle board, plywood, shelves, cabinets, and office furniture. It can also be found in some draperies and carpeting. The gas can cause health problems ranging from minor eye, nose, and throat irritation to such serious effects as nasal cancer.

Urea-formaldehyde foam was a popular insulating material in the late 1970s and early 1980s. By 1982, its health hazards were recognized and this kind of insulation is no longer in general usage. While the greatest danger of gas escaping is when the material is first drying, gas can also be released later if the material is dampened or exposed to high temperatures.

Such problems with insulation are not normally found in the average building, but urea-formaldehyde-based adhesives can be found in wood paneling and other construction materials. Formaldehyde poses greater problems in manufactured or mobile homes, very high energy-efficient houses, tightly constructed newer office buildings, and even in schools. Only manufactured homes are required to carry warning labels if they contain products made with formaldehyde, and buyers must sign statements acknowledging the presence of any such material. Other buildings have no such requirements.

Testing for formaldehyde may be done by a professional or by a commercial testing device. To remedy this type of problem, the gas-emitting material can be removed. A lower-cost procedure is to increase ventilation or lower the temperature and humidity within the building. A common remedy for adhesive-induced gas is to seal particle board and other wood products with paints or veneers.

Asbestos as Used in Building Materials

Asbestos consists of naturally occurring mineral fibers found in rocks. For many years, it has been added to such manufactured products as patching compounds, siding, roofing shingles, and vinyl floors. Asbestos has many advantages as a building material because it strengthens material, provides thermal and acoustical insulation, and fireproofs material. Its only real disadvantage is that it can kill you! Asbestos can cause asbestosis, a noncancerous disease that scars the lung tissues. It can also cause several different kinds of cancer in the lungs, esophagus, stomach, and intestines. The most well-known is called mesothelioma. Yet it is a difficult type of pollution to accurately assess. It can produce a health hazard in schools, office buildings, and dwelling units.

Nevertheless, recent studies indicate that the real danger lies in so-called "loose" asbestos rather than that occurring in "hard" form. Asbestos becomes dangerous only when it breaks down and its fibers are released into the air to be inhaled. To date, there have been no conclusive studies suggesting that a health hazard is caused from ingesting food or water containing asbestos, or that fibers can penetrate the skin. Testing for its presence should be done by an EPA-certified asbestos inspector when possible.

Many building owners have had asbestos removed to eliminate the hazards. However, this is costly and not always necessary. The EPA has "Building Owners' Guides" available on its website. Their objective is to reinforce the EPA's position that the most prudent option is in-place management of asbestos rather than removal. The EPA defines a management program as a plan of training, cleaning, work practices, air monitoring, and maintenance of asbestos-containing materials in good condition. Maintenance, custodial, and administrative staff must be trained on the problem, and tenants must be informed of the presence of asbestos in the building.

Discovery of asbestos in a building can be a nightmare to its owner. Aside from the problems associated with federal and state laws regarding the handling of asbestos-containing materials, another problem lies in the economic results of its presence. If it is found in a building, one result can be the potential of health-related lawsuits; another is a substantial loss in value of the contaminated building. This is true of both commercial and residential buildings.

The renovation and the demolition of an asbestos-bearing facility fall under the National Emission Standards for Hazardous Air Pollution (NESHAP) administered by the EPA and possibly a state agency. NESHAP requires that certain notices be filed with the EPA *prior* to work on a facility containing friable (loose) asbestos. *Friable asbestos* is defined as any material containing more than 1% asbestos by weight that hand pressure can crumble, pulverize, or reduce to powder when dry. The threshold level for reporting to the EPA is when at least 260 feet of friable asbestos-containing material is found on pipes, or at least 160 square feet of asbestos-containing materials is being stripped or removed.

As of February 2004, the EPA had promulgated all the maximum achievable control technologies standards required. The EPA developed 96 rules to reduce toxic emissions from over 160 categories of industrial sources. Compared to the 1990 baseline emissions, these rules will reduce 1.7 million tons per year of toxic emissions.

Radon Gas

In 1989, the head of the EPA at that time, William Reilly, pronounced radon "the second leading cause of cancer in this country." The EPA estimates that radon causes as many as 20,000 deaths each year. National and international public health agencies support the contention that radon is a leading environmental health risk, as asserted by R. William Field, PhD, an associate professor in the Departments of Occupational and Environmental Health and Epidemiology at the University of Iowa, in his presentation at the Fifteenth National Radon Meeting in 2005.

Radon is an invisible radioactive gas. You cannot smell it, feel it, or see it. Outside, it is virtually harmless as it is dissipated. It only becomes a big problem inside a building, when it can accumulate into dangerous concentrations. Radon comes from decaying uranium. Uranium can be found in many places—in the earth's soil, black shale, phosphatic rocks, and even granite. It can be found in areas that have been contaminated with industrial wastes, such as by-products of uranium or phosphate mining.

The danger arises when such materials are located directly underneath an inhabited building and the gas seeps inside. Radon gas can enter into a building through cracks in the slab or openings found around pipes. The gas can also enter through well water. In buildings that lack adequate ventilation and areas such as basements, the gas can become concentrated and dangerous.

Testing for radon can be managed with an activated charcoal canister available at hardware stores or home centers. After four to seven days in a suspected location, the canister should be sent to a laboratory for testing. If radon is found, remedies can include sealing cracks and other openings. Ventilation devices alone may be sufficient to reduce radon concentrations to a minimal level.

LEAD POISONING

Lead is a heavy, relatively soft, malleable, bluish-gray metal. It cannot be broken down or destroyed. Because of the ease with which it can be shaped, it has been used for centuries in the form of pipe and other building materials. More recently, it has been alloyed for use as solder that can secure pipe joints and as a component of paint. Paint containing high levels of lead was found to be more durable and to look fresher for a greater length of time.

Although lead has some advantages as a building material, its adverse effects for humans have been known as far back as early Greek and Roman civilizations. Lead has no beneficial function in the human body; its ingestion can only do harm. The damage from **lead poisoning** is most threatening to children in their formative years. Its symptoms are wide-ranging and can easily go undiagnosed and even unnoticed. Lead was reported as a cause of encephalopathy (inflammation of the brain) in a number of children in the United States in 1917. By 1930, more data became available on lead poisoning in children.

Lead can be more damaging to children than adults because of their higher rates of respiration and metabolism. Their bodies handle lead differently, as they are not as efficient at keeping lead in the bones, which leaves a higher percentage circulating in the bloodstream. Lead can be most damaging to the brain. Testing in the first and second grades found that children with the lowest IQs, academic achievement, language skills, and attention spans had the highest levels of lead.

The EPA was made responsible for implementing the Lead-Based Paint Poisoning Prevention Act passed in 1971. In 1975, under court order, the EPA evaluated atmospheric lead as a "criteria pollutant," as it was referred to in the Clean Air Act. That led to an examination of the lead problem everywhere in the environment.

Sources of Lead Poisoning

There are two ways that lead can be absorbed into the body: inhalation and ingestion.

1. **Inhalation:** Airborne lead is caused by emissions from certain industrial plants, internal combustion engines (primarily cars still using gasoline containing lead), and dust found in the household. Dust can derive from lead-based paint and other lead-containing items. Lead-containing dust can also be transported on clothing from the workplace. On the brighter side, the EPA reported in 1995 that about 88% of lead had been removed from the air because of various restrictive rules.

2. **Ingestion:** Household dust and the soil around a house can contain lead that may be ingested. Water passing through lead or copper pipes with soldered joints can contain lead. Lead-based paint flakes can be attractive to children. Other lead-containing nonfood items such as toys, cosmetics, and jewelry may end up in children's mouths, as can hands covered with dirt.

Testing for Lead

Lead poisoning is caused by high levels of lead in the blood. Since the greatest risk is with children age seven and under, it is logical to test them first. Since there is no known "safe level," any level of lead in the blood tests as positive. If positive, it means that lead is being released somewhere in the daily environment of that child and further testing is necessary.

How Lead Affects Property Value

The presence of lead on a property in any form can reduce its value. Generally, lead problems are curable and the cost of cleaning up the property can be determined, but as a contaminant, lead is not included in definitions of toxic waste substances and cleanup is not yet mandatory. However, lead-based materials, if found, require prompt remedial action to minimize future problems.

Lead-Based Paint Rule

HUD and the EPA require sellers and renters of houses *built before 1978* to disclose to potential buyers or renters the presence of lead-based paint hazards. The disclosure statement must be attached as a separate item to all sales and lease contracts on properties built before 1978. A federal lead hazard pamphlet on how to protect families must be distributed to potential buyers and renters. Buyers must be allowed an optional 10-day period before the contract is closed to conduct a lead-based paint inspection or risk assessment at their own expense. While real estate agents are not responsible for ensuring that people read or understand the brochure, they are responsible for compliance.

The rule does not require any lead paint testing, removal, or abatement. Nor does it invalidate leasing or sales contracts. Housing built after 1977 and zero-bedroom units such as efficiencies, lofts, and dormitories are not covered under this rule. Also not covered are leases for less than 100 days, housing for the elderly or handicapped (unless children live there), and foreclosure sales.

Handling Lead When Found

What follows is information on ways to handle lead found in paint and in water.

Lead in Paint

Lead-based paint was used until 1978 when its disadvantages became better known. Such paint is still not considered an immediate hazard if it is smooth and intact. Only damaged surfaces are considered dangerous, inside or outside, where the paint is blistering, peeling, scaling, or powdering. If any lead-containing paint is suspected, it should be tested. On

April 22, 2008, the EPA signed a new regulation regarding the renovation of child-occupied buildings built before 1978. The rule became effective April 22, 2010. Under the rule, contractors performing renovation, repair, and painting projects that disturb lead-based coatings (including lead paint, shellac, or varnish) in child-occupied facilities built before 1978 must be certified and must follow specific work practices to prevent lead contamination.

Lead in Water

Because there are no safe levels of lead, all drinking water should be tested. This is especially important if the property has lead pipes (most likely if the house was built before 1930). Lead-content solder was banned in 1986, but many houses built prior to that time have copper pipes with soldered connections. Local water utility companies or health departments may offer water testing for free or at a nominal charge. Also, the EPA has a list of approved testing labs.

One way to remedy possibly contaminated water is to install a filter system. Filters normally also reduce the acid level of water, making it less corrosive. Also, a "point of use" treatment device may be installed. Distillation units are available commercially, but can be a bit costly and must be maintained.

WETLANDS PROTECTION

In years past, swampy, marshy, or water-saturated soils were considered a source of sickness—a breeding place for disease-bearing mosquitoes. Farmers were encouraged to drain or fill such areas. In addition, large areas of wetlands were eliminated for federal flood control projects, canal building, and mosquito control projects. Too late in many cases, scientists learned that wetlands can help control flooding, filter out pollution, clean drinking water, and provide habitats for fish and other wildlife. Environmentalists were quick to expand on the new intelligence with rather far-reaching results.

The law covering wetlands stems from the 1987 Clean Water Act, which introduced a permit system to control the discharge of any pollutant into waters of the United States. This law does not define "waters of the United States." It is the Code of Federal Regulations (Section 328.3) that defines the term as including wetlands and adjacent wetlands.

Both the EPA and the U.S. Army Corps of Engineers (Corps) share responsibility for administering the Clean Water Act and the issuance of permits. This authority has been extended to include the issuance of permits that allow a landowner to disturb a wetland.

Wetlands is not a scientific term, and it lacks a good definition. A **wetland** may be natural or man-made. Decorative lakes or water hazards on golf courses, for example, may become protected wetlands. If an area containing a wetland is disturbed before discovering that it is so defined, the result can be enforcement action, including the assessment of administrative, civil, and/or criminal penalties.

To help guide landowners and others, in 1987 the EPA and the Corps combined to produce the *Federal Wetlands Determination Manual,* which explains the criteria for judging what comprises a wetland. Essentially, three criteria are described for making this determination:

1. The area must be inundated by surface water, groundwater, or rainwater.
2. The land must contain a predominance of vegetation typically adapted for life in water-saturated soils.
3. The soil must be under water long enough during the growing season to develop anaerobic conditions (meaning absence of oxygen). This usually occurs when the soil is saturated for a week or longer.

It is not clear yet whether just one or all of the criteria must be in place to declare an area as a wetland and subject to a permit before it can be disturbed. No distinction is made between natural and man-made wetlands. A wet area in a cornfield created by a farmer's leaky irrigation ditch would be classified in the same way as an ancient cypress swamp in the Florida Everglades.

The only way to be certain whether or not an area falls under the wetlands definition is to ask the Corps to make an inspection and issue its own determination. Each of the 26 Corps District Offices throughout the country is authorized to make these determinations, which are final unless landowners bring suit in federal court to overturn them. There is no right of administrative appeal.

A report titled *Clean Water Act: A Summary of the Law,* issued on April 23, 2010, by the Congressional Research Service, stated that authorization for appropriation to support the Clean Water Act generally expired at the end of the federal government's fiscal year ending in 1990. This report went on to say that "[t]he programs did not lapse, however, and Congress has continued to appropriate funds to carry out the [Clean Water Act]. Since the 1987 amendments, although Congress has enacted several bills that reauthorize and modify a number of individual provisions in the law, none comprehensively addressed major programs or requirements."

Break for Small Landowner

If a small tract of residential property contains one-half acre or less of wetlands area, the landowner may use an expedited process. Instead of going through the process of filing an individual permit to disturb the wetland area, the landowner may file a "Nationwide Permit 29" with the nearest Corps of Engineers office. Approval can usually be granted within 15 days, or if no word is heard, approval is automatic in 30 days.

Effect of Wetlands on Financing

Concern over additional risk resulting from wetlands problems is limited to land development loans. Even then, a lender would be primarily interested in the developer's awareness of the need to comply with the Clean Water Act. A violation could be damaging to completion of the development and jeopardize loan repayment if the developer suffers substantial financial penalties.

In some parts of the country, entrepreneurs have created wetlands areas, or banks, of 500 acres or more that are offered to developers as may be needed as an alternative to wetlands found on property to be developed. The developer may buy acreage in the newly developed wetland area—usually on a ratio of 1.5 acres of new wetland for every acre of wetland in the to-be-developed area. The developer can offer the newly developed wetlands acreage to the Corps as a substitute for what is to be developed. The method is known as *mitigation banking* and is gaining recognition as it offers an opportunity for commercial real estate developers to go forward with projects that involve disturbing a wetland area.

ENDANGERED SPECIES

Landowners have recently become more aware that the **Endangered Species Act** of 1973 can have a profound impact on the value of their land. One reason for the delay in recognizing its importance is that, since the initial Act was passed, it has been substantially expanded. The 1973 Act was limited to the protection of endangered species *on federal land* and passed Congress almost unopposed. Since then, regulators have focused on controlling land usage, including private land, if it might contain an endangered species' habitat.

The Endangered Species Act mandates that a protected species be determined by the "best scientific and commercial data available." Nevertheless, no standards were set, and the responsible agencies make their own determinations without peer review. The agencies specifically require that economic consequences *not* be a consideration in making the determination. The result has been a tremendous expansion of protected species.

Taking Is Prohibited

The Act prohibits the "taking" of endangered species as listed by the federal government. *Taking* means the killing of any listed plant, animal, fish, or insect. Also, U.S. Fish and Wildlife Service regulations prohibit any harm or harassment of an endangered species, including modification, damaging, or destroying their habitat even if the species is not currently present.

Challenge to Development

The Endangered Species Act authorizes citizen suits to enjoin violations or to compel the Secretary of the Interior to enforce its provisions. Anyone can sue the landowner for violations. It also allows recovery of awards and attorneys' fees in connection with private actions. The effect has been a substantial increase in the risk for any new development.

The Endangered Species Act's Net Effect on Loans

Similar to the question of wetlands, the risk falls primarily on a land development, but it can also affect rehabilitation and expansion. If a building permit is needed, the door may be opened to activists' challenges. There is a difference between wetland problems and endangered species questions in that a wetland is something visible, while an endangered species habitat can be difficult to discover.

The risk of not being able to complete a land development or rehabilitation project on schedule and within budget must be considered, as these can be increased by the open door to private challenges permitted under the Act. There are a growing number of areas in the country today that have been closed to development simply from fear of a shutdown even after a project is underway. Land development loans in these areas are close to nonexistent.

Recent Rulings Mitigating the Act

If an endangered species or its habitat is found on private land, it has been customary for the U.S. Fish and Wildlife Service to prohibit any further use of the land that might disturb the habitat. Because of this practice, it is believed that some landowners are encouraged to "shoot, shovel, and shut up." Recently, the Department of the Interior has offered a "safe harbor" procedure to reduce this possibility. For example, golf course developers in the Carolinas agreed to provide a habitat for the red-cockaded woodpecker, which likes the openness of a golf course, as long as the government promised to do nothing legally to impair the future use of their land. In Texas, a similar deal was arranged with Frank Yturria near Brownsville to encourage the return of the aplomado falcon on his 13,000-acre spread. Such safe harbor deals and a similar law-softening policy called "no surprises" have been encouraged. Former Interior Secretary Gale Norton reported that by 2005, about 325 such deals had been made with private landowners controlling more than 3.6 million acres.

In a 1997 case, the U.S. Supreme Court gave those hurt by an action to protect an endangered species the right to sue over how the federal law is enforced. Because of a drought in 1992, the government had cut off irrigation water to farms and ranches near Oregon's Lost River to preserve two species of fish. Lower courts had ruled that those claiming economic harm had no legal standing to sue over how the federal law was enforced. Justice Antonin Scalia, in the Supreme Court's majority opinion, said the lower courts were wrong and revived the lawsuit.

National Assn. of Home Builders v. Defenders of Wildlife in 2007 was a case about federal jurisdiction over anti-pollution statutes. Supreme Court Justice Samuel Alito wrote the majority opinion, holding that the Endangered Species Act did not require the Environmental Protection Agency to apply additional criteria when evaluating a transfer of pollution control jurisdiction under the Clean Water Act.

Recently, climate change—global warming—has become an important topic of discussion. Whether or not climate change can be cited as a reason for protection of a species, such as the polar bear, under the Endangered Species Act is an issue being vigorously debated.

> ## Where Are We Now?
>
> The EPA website, http://www.epa.gov/, offers extensive resources on many environmental issues, such as the following:
>
> - cleaning and care of air ducts;
> - cross-state air pollution;
> - car A/C;
> - climate change;
> - drinking water;
> - donating or recycling electronics;
> - Environmental Kids Club;
> - lead contamination;
> - mold and moisture;
> - pesticides;
> - radon;
> - toxic release inventory;
> - UV Index: UV ratings by zip code; and
> - toxic waste.

Private Property Rights

The underlying legal question resulting from the Endangered Species Act and other such laws is: Can prohibitions of land usage entitle the landowner to undertake an inverse condemnation suit against the government entities involved? The Fifth Amendment to the U.S. Constitution clearly states, "nor shall private property be taken for public use without just compensation." Earlier opinion interpreted this clause as meaning compensation is due only when title to private property is taken under the right of eminent domain. The difficult-to-define gray area that has since arisen concerns partial taking that leaves the landowner with full title but only limited rights to usage of the property. Only recently have the courts begun to recognize that private property rights can be taken through regulatory action and that, while the right to regulate is not challenged, the need to compensate landowners in certain cases may be necessary. In 2005, the House of Representatives passed a law giving additional protections against taking, but it failed to garner sufficient support in the Senate, so this remains a controversial issue.

UNDERGROUND STORAGE TANKS

For many years, hundreds of thousands of underground tanks have stored petroleum products or other hazardous materials and many have leaked. Using the "out of sight, out of mind" theory, little attention was given to possible contamination—until recently. Damage to the land became obvious with a focal point on petroleum product storage, particularly with service stations.

A later amendment to the Resources Conservation and Recovery Act of 1976 (RCRA) required the Environmental Protection Agency to develop a comprehensive program to prevent, detect, and correct releases from **underground storage tanks (USTs)**. The EPA defined a UST as any tank that has 10% or more of its volume below ground and contains either petroleum or hazardous substances.

The EPA estimates that 2 million USTs are covered by the regulations and 95% are used to store petroleum products. There are some exceptions from the definition, including farm and residential tanks of 1,100 gallons or less storing fuel for noncommercial purposes; septic tanks; wastewater collection systems; and storage tanks located in an enclosed underground area (basement). Even though excluded by the EPA, state or local laws may cover these types of tanks.

EPA regulations require UST owners to provide certain safety precautions, including corrosion protection and leak detection by monthly monitoring or inventory control. Owners must also provide tank tightness testing plus spill and overflow devices. Compliance was phased in over five years for USTs installed after December 1988, having all requirements in place upon installation. Qualified contractors must install new tanks according to code and tank owners must provide the EPA with certification of proper installation. The same is true for tank removal. Since October 1990, owners and operators of USTs must demonstrate responsibility for corrective actions and be able to compensate for injury or property damage from $500,000 to $4 million, depending on the number of tanks owned.

Discovery of an underground tank by a landowner or a prospective buyer can affect the value of that property. The first task is to find out what it contains and what condition it is in. Some abandoned tanks have been filled with sand, gravel, or other inert material. If the tank contains a liquid, it is necessary to find out what it is so that it can be properly disposed of, and to determine whether or not the tank has leaked or is leaking. A professional may be needed to perform a tank tightness test. If a hazardous substance is involved, a report to the EPA may be necessary.

The Federal Facility Compliance Act of 1992 amended RCRA to make it clear that all federal agencies are subject to all substantive and procedural requirements of federal, state, and local solid waste as well as hazardous waste and underground storage tank laws in the same manner as any private party, although the U.S. president may exempt a facility under certain circumstances.

The scale of leaking underground tanks has reached the point at which it is being called the "new asbestos problem" in terms of its potential gravity to public health and cost of remediation. The concern is so great that the EPA, in consultation with all 50 states, developed new guidance in response to the American Recovery and Reinvestment Act of 2009 (ARRA). This program guidance will assist the EPA's Regional Underground Storage Tank (UST) programs to negotiate and approve state Leaking Underground Storage Tank (LUST) Recovery Act assistance agreements and help states work with their EPA regional grants management offices to expeditiously award funding to states.

UST Effect on Loans

Discovery of an underground tank always raises a warning flag until it can be determined what the tank contains and what condition it is in. Insofar as lenders are concerned, the presence of underground tanks must be reported in an environmental site assessment, which would become a loan application requirement. The assessment examines the possible presence of contamination surrounding the tank or tanks. If tanks are found, the assessment would call for further testing of the soil around and below the tanks.

By 2015, many lenders have added guidance to determine if a dry cleaning operation was on a property due to recent findings that dry cleaning plants pose a recurring problem, as even the latest equipment has failed to prevent spills.

ELECTROMAGNETIC FORCES

Most environmental concerns are real and should always be considered when dealing with the question of land development and what may be built upon it. Yet there is no doubt that some people profit from environmental scares. Whether electromagnetic force is mostly a scare tactic or a real concern is not clear. Even so, enough reputable people are reporting that it is a carcinogen that it is necessary for anyone involved with real estate to know what it is.

Electromagnetic forces (EMFs) are silent and invisible. They exist anywhere electrons zip through transmission lines or the innards of appliances or even electric blankets. They are nearly impossible to avoid altogether. Thus far, no clear relationship has been established between the strength of an electromagnetic field and the incidence of cancer, particularly leukemia. In November 1996, the National Research Council, after three years of examining more than 500 studies, stated, "The current body of evidence does not show that exposure to these fields presents a human-health hazard." A comprehensive World Health Organization EMF health-risk assessment was published in June 2007 titled, "Environmental Health Criteria monograph, Extremely Low Frequency Fields." Its main conclusions, quoted from the assessment, are as follows:

> *Scientific evidence suggesting that every day, chronic, low-intensity ELF magnetic field exposure poses a possible health risk is based on epidemiological studies demonstrating a consistent pattern of an increased risk of childhood leukemia. Uncertainties in the hazard assessment include the role of control selection bias and exposure misclassification. In addition, virtually all of the laboratory evidence and the mechanistic evidence fail to support a relationship between low-level ELF magnetic field exposure and changes in biological function or disease status. Thus, on balance, the evidence is not strong enough to be considered causal and therefore ELF magnetic fields remain classified as possibly carcinogenic [IARC classified ELF magnetic fields as possibly carcinogenic in 2001; see below].*
>
> *A number of other diseases have been investigated for possible association with ELF magnetic field exposure. These include other types of cancers in both children and adults, depression, suicide, reproductive dysfunction, developmental disorders, immunological modifications, neurological disease, and cardiovascular disease. The scientific evidence supporting a linkage between exposure to ELF magnetic fields and any of these diseases is weaker than for*

childhood leukemia and in some cases (for example, for cardiovascular disease or breast cancer) the evidence is sufficient to give confidence that magnetic fields do not cause the disease.[10]

When examining electromagnetic fields, it is important to know that their strength is sharply reduced by moving a short distance away from the source. For instance, 12 inches away from a can opener or hair dryer rather than 6 inches reduces the field strength by 75%.

Electromagnetic fields are measured in gausses, which is the CGS unit of magnetic induction. CGS means centimeter-gram-second. A centimeter is a unit of length, a gram is a unit of weight, and a second is a unit of time. For our purposes, magnetic fields are measured in milligausses. Following are examples of several different magnetic fields in milligausses at one foot from the source:

Ceiling fan	3
Dishwasher	10
Electric clothes dryer	2
Power saw	40
Washing machine	7

The federal government has researched problems with EMFs, but so far has issued no rules or regulations. Some states have released rules, primarily for power line construction and improvements. For real estate agents, it is a subject that must be given serious consideration. If EMF testing is required by a potential buyer, this can be done by going room-to-room and even to appliances with a small gauss meter.

WASTE PRODUCERS AND THEIR TOXIC IMPACT

Other specialty properties present their own unique environmental issues, such as gas stations, printers, auto repair shops, paint shops, furniture-refinishing facilities, and storm drains. States work with the EPA in the development of specific requirements for these types of specialty properties. Real estate professionals should know where to find these types of pollution-prevention work plans. An example is "A Guide on Hazardous Waste Management for Florida's Auto Repair and Paint and Body Shops,"

---

[10]"Electromagnetic fields and public health: Exposure to extremely low frequency fields," World Health Organization, June 2007, accessed February 11, 2015, http://www.who.int/peh-emf/publications/facts/fs322/en/

a 2009 report released by the state of Florida that can be found at http://www.dep.state.fl.us/waste/quick_topics/publications/shw/hazardous/business/Paint_and_Body8_09.pdf

ENERGY-EFFICIENT BUILDINGS

The secondary market recognizes the value of energy-efficient properties by offering easier loan qualification if such a building is the collateral. For residential properties meeting state code energy efficiency requirements, Freddie Mac does not use a maximum amount. The income-to-expense ratios may be extended due to energy efficiency; however, all mortgages are now subject to a maximum 45% debt-to-income ratio. Fannie Mae and FHA allow 2% stretches for their qualifying ratios (applies to fixed payment or "back-end" ratio) as discussed in Chapter 8. The premise is that these properties will have lower utility expenses, which allows homeowners more income with which to make mortgage and tax payments.

What is an energy-efficient building? The definition derives from the Comprehensive National Energy Policy Act, which became law in October 1992. It is a sweeping piece of legislation that, among other things, mandates energy-efficiency standards for residential, commercial, and industrial buildings. It is part of an accelerating trend of environmentalism that has led to a growing body of energy conservation programs.

The legislation requires states to establish minimum commercial building energy codes and consider minimum residential codes based on voluntary standards. There is a link between the availability of federal mortgage assistance for new residential buildings and compliance with Model Energy Code requirements. Some states have aggressively upgraded their building codes on energy efficiency, an example being California, which had approximately 50% more efficient residential housing efficiency standards than the national average after it updated its energy-efficiency standards in residential buildings by 20% in 2010. These updated building standards added roughly $2,170 to the cost of a new home being built in California.[11] Then in 2013, the California Energy Commission established a goal of tightening the energy code by another

---

[11] "Building Code Update: Summary Energy Building Standards Put California Businesses at Disadvantage," California Chamber of Commerce, report, 2012.

15% for commercial buildings and 25% for residential buildings, and those took effect in 2014.

Currently, the most stringent energy-efficiency code is that of the Council of American Building Officials (CABO), located in Leesburg, Virginia, and the Model Energy Code of 1992. In addition to establishing performance standards for heating, cooling, and ventilation components, the Model Energy Code defines performance standards for the building "envelope"—the barrier between the inside and outside of the building.

In 2005, President George W. Bush signed the Energy Policy Act of 2005 into law. It was designed to spur domestic energy production, increase efficiency, modernize the U.S. electricity grid and energy delivery system, and promote investment in effective energy alternatives such as increasing energy efficiency and conservation, ensuring adequate energy supplies and generation, renewing and expanding the energy infrastructure, encouraging investment in new energy technologies, and ensuring suitable deliberation of the effects of regulatory policies on energy supplies.

The American Recovery and Reinvestment Act passed in 2009 provides a number of energy-efficiency and alternative-energy-generation tax incentives for both small and large businesses as well as residential real estate owners, all with the intent of sustainability, reduced dependence on foreign oil, and the reduction of greenhouse gases.

CONCLUSIONS

Environmental problems escaped the nation's attention for so many years that it will take time to define the true extent of contamination. The rush to prevent further damage and begin restoration has resulted in steps taken that have not always been effective. However, various environmental laws are undergoing review, and further improvements can be expected. An assortment of regulatory agencies has been seeking cooperative procedures to reduce the overlap of requirements. However, as yet there is no movement toward consolidation of agencies; rather, the trend appears to be toward the creation of new oversight agencies charged with bringing greater uniformity when standards are in conflict.

The problems are new, and they are serious, and landowners are at the forefront of managing their resolution.

Questions for Discussion

1. Define an environmental site assessment.
2. Discuss Fannie Mae/Freddie Mac environmental requirements as stated in their mortgage instruments.
3. Explain the innocent landowner defense as defined by CERCLA.
4. What is an ASTM transaction screen?
5. Discuss the EPA's asbestos-managing plan for building owners. What threat is considered the "new asbestos"?
6. Where is lead most likely to be found in a household?
7. Identify the criteria for determining existence of wetlands.
8. What happens to land containing an endangered species habitat?
9. Discuss a landowner's rights in a regulatory taking of land.
10. Explain the key liability issue that owners, investors, and lenders might face if they, their employees, or the public are harmed by environment problems that they are responsible for creating or have been ordered to remove.

Multiple Choice Questions for Review

1. Many properties require an environmental assessment of several different hazards that might affect a piece of real estate. Which of the following is generally thought to be the most costly?
   a. loss of value of property
   b. cost of cleanup
   c. limitations on the property's use
   d. health problems for the owners

2. While not fully residential or fully commercial, Freddie Mac and Fannie Mae multifamily housing loans require which type of assessment?
   a. a Phase I Environmental Site Assessment
   b. both Phase I and Phase II Environmental Site Assessments
   c. a Fannie Mae or Freddie Mac Special Standard Assessment
   d. none of these

3. For which of the following studies is the purpose to ascertain if any prior use would indicate the presence of environmental contamination or hazardous substances, and if an adequate inquiry is made with proper records maintained and nothing of a hazardous nature is found, the buyer may be classed as an innocent landowner?
   a. Environmental Protection Special Standard Assessment Report
   b. Phase I Environmental Site Assessment
   c. Phase II Environmental Site Assessment
   d. ASTM 17-1277-92 Assessment Report

4. Transaction screens represent a reduced scope of work from the Phase I Assessment and are designed to aid in developing information about the environmental condition of commercial real estate. Use of the transaction screen is intended to constitute appropriate inquiry for the purposes of CERCLA's innocent landowner defense.
   a. true
   b. true, with some limitations
   c. false
   d. must be done by an environmental engineer if to be used as a defense

5. Of the following types of hazardous materials that can affect the value of real estate, which is being called the "new asbestos"—a problem caused by water from excessive humidity, leaks, condensation, or flooding, and a maintenance issue for the property owner?
   a. mold
   b. radon
   c. polychlorinated biphenyls (PCBs)
   d. leaking underground storage tanks

6. Which of the following substances was once considered a problem in major parts of the country, but through 30 years of education and cleanup efforts has ceased to be a hazardous material threat in most real estate?
   a. fiberglass
   b. lead paint
   c. radon gas
   d. underground storage tanks

7. Which of the following is one of the criteria set out by the Corps of Engineers that defines a "wetland"?
   a. Land must be underwater for at least six months of each year
   b. The land must contain a predominance of vegetation typically adapted for life in water-saturated soils
   c. Any land that is water inundated for a long enough period that amphibious life is dependent on it for reproduction
   d. All of the above

8. Which of the following would be a "taking" when land privately owned falls under the Endangered Species Act?
   a. The killing of any listed plant, animal, fish, or insect
   b. Any harm or harassment of an endangered species is prohibited under the ESA
   c. The commercial profiting from renting photographic visitations to protected areas that do not otherwise infringe on the provision of the ESA
   d. The overt modification, damaging, or destruction of habitat even though the species may not be present at the time

9. A property owner can expect to have which of the following rights if his or her land is to be taken over to meet the requirements of the Endangered Species Act?
   a. full compensation for partial loss of use
   b. compensation for delays in construction due to migration of protected species
   c. compensation for property taken under the right of eminent domain
   d. all of these

10. Which of the following risks from environmental hazards will real estate owners, investors, or possibly lenders face?
    a. They can limit the use of the contaminated property and thus its value.
    b. The EPA has the right to force expenditures for cleaning hazards up.
    c. They may negatively affect the health of the owners and their employees.
    d. Each of the answers is possible.

Information Resources

http://www.epa.gov/superfund/sites/query/queryhtm/nplfin.htm
  The best way to see if a piece of real property may be in or near a known Superfund site is by visiting the website above.

http://www.epa.gov/
  A good source of information on issues that impact real estate development's compliance with the various laws and regulations can be found at this EPA website.

http://www.sustainablecitiesinstitute.org/
  The concept of sustainability is becoming more important as the confluence of federal, state, and local laws concerning land use, energy conservation, and minimizing pollution affect long-term economic development. The Sustainable Cities Institute website is one of a few devoted to creating communications tools for interactive use.

http://www.dtsc.ca.gov/
  Most states have internal pollution control departments. The California Department of Toxic Substances Control can be accessed via the URL above.

http://www.envirobank.org/
  The URL above will take you to the website of the Environmental Bankers Association where you can read through their latest alerts to their members for interesting developments in environmental risk management for commercial real estate.

http://edrnet.com/assessing-flood-risk-commercial-real-estate/
  The URL above will take you to the website of the well-known environmental consulting firms that work with the property due diligence industry. You will find on this link a good look at the way to assess the flood risk in commercial real estate from an environmental view.

CHAPTER 15

TECHNOLOGY ADVANCES IN MORTGAGE LENDING

KEY TERMS AND PHRASES

automated underwriting
Automated Valuation Model (AVM)
Automated Valuation System (AVS)
collateral assessment
computerized loan origination (CLO)
Desktop Originator® (DO)
Desktop Underwriter® (DU)
EarlyCheck™
internet loan applications
loan origination system (LOS)
Loan Prospector®
manual underwriting
online real estate service
risk-based mortgage loan pricing
universal account

LEARNING OBJECTIVES

At the conclusion of this chapter, students will be able to:
- Describe the key supporting technology tools for residential loan origination.
- Understand the origins, uses, and evolution of automated credit scoring technologies and vendors.
- Describe how advanced data repositories and automated systems aided in the development of the subprime loan market, and enumerate the lessons learned from that overreliance on modeling.

- Explain the various ways that internet lending has changed the way lenders and borrowers approach the pricing, marketing, and closing of residential mortgage loans.
- Describe the various online real estate services.

INTRODUCTION

Advances in computer technology in the past 20 years have made it possible for financial institutions to organize and manage mortgage loan pools and their related cash flows into mortgage-backed securities. Innovative technologies have broadened the loan market by adding many newcomers. New software has been developed to analyze loan applications and give recommendations for loan approval, if justified. With this software, decisions on loan applications can be made with much greater speed. The new technology has brought greater depth to the analysis of the creditworthiness of borrowers, giving lenders more precision in loan analysis while allowing firms to operate more efficiently and improve their bottom lines. Technological access to increasingly larger databases has allowed the development of additional loan products. The rise of the subprime loan market was made possible in large part by the perceived ability to better understand how to pass on the risk in an originate-to-distribute model. Unfortunately, computer models did not capture all the true risks of the global economy. Warning signs were ignored. As a Lehman Brothers employee commented about a year before the firm went into bankruptcy, "Events that models predicted would happen only once in 10,000 years happened every day for three days."[1] The failure to use known economic history in the calibration of many models and the failure to heed the warning signs that a crisis was approaching will likely cause a shift away from the development of forward-looking customer acquisition technologies. The changeable nature and velocity of new regulation is breathtaking, and it will require that mortgage technology development dollars be dedicated to the upgrading and development of compliance databases.

COMPUTERIZED LOAN ORIGINATION (CLO)

One of the early applications of computer technology to mortgage lending was **computerized loan origination (CLO)**. Used as a method of transmitting

---

[1] Kaja Whitehouse, "One Quant Sees Shakeout for the Ages – 10,000 Years." *Wall Street Journal*, August 11, 2007.

information between computer terminals for analysis by human underwriters, this system was introduced nationally in 1986 by Citicorp, the New York bank company. Citibank's *Mortgage Power* software program was sold to loan originators across the country. Terminals were installed in the offices of companies whose employees had contact with home buyers, appraisers, lawyers, title companies, mortgage companies, and real estate agents.

Citibank expanded use of its *Mortgage Power* program through the late 1980s into over 3,000 terminals around the country, and in 1989 Citibank became the nation's largest originator of mortgage loans, largely because of the use of this system. However, Citibank has since withdrawn from its computer network, although the company remains very active in the mortgage market.

Almost from the origin of CLO, a controversy developed between the Mortgage Bankers Association (MBA) and the National Association of REALTORS® (NAR). The MBA saw an intrusion into its specialized field of mortgage loan origination, especially by real estate agents who had first contact with a potential buyer. The MBA's position was that the Real Estate Settlement Procedures Act (RESPA) prohibited a real estate agent from making a fee for a loan, which might be considered a kickback. At the very least, it argued, such action amounted to "steering" the buyer to one lender, which is also prohibited by RESPA.

But NAR felt that a real estate agent was allowed to earn a fee because CLO was a service provided to the buyer, which is allowed by RESPA. Furthermore, NAR wanted its members to offer a "one-stop-shopping" service to property buyers that would include assistance in arranging a mortgage loan.

A decision was sought from the Department of Housing and Urban Development (HUD), the monitor of RESPA. HUD looked beyond the immediate argument and saw advantages to computerized loan systems. They made mortgage money more available to potential home buyers and they could lower the cost of loan origination. Furthermore, they offered a less-biased system, as there was a minimum of human contact.

Nevertheless, it was not until June 1996 that HUD issued a final rule covering its earlier HUD Informal Opinion Number 13, issued February 14, 1995. An earlier rule that had allowed a CLO operator to charge any fee that seemed fair so long as it was disclosed and approved in writing by the borrower was eliminated. In its place, the final rule limited the CLO operator to charging a fee that was "reasonably related to the value of the services provided." Furthermore, a listing of only one lender (which was formerly permitted) was considered to furnish "no or nominal compensable services."

As the market evolved over the years, both mortgage brokers and real estate agents found that by working together, it was possible to increase their sales by allowing both parties to earn a portion of the origination fee. Real estate professionals and lenders must be aware of the specific guidance and additional information coming from HUD Informal Opinion Number 13 and a legal case against World Savings in 2004. These provided greater insights for real estate professionals and taught us that HUD will look at the specific facts of each case, including: (1) whether an arrangement or contract calls for certain work to be performed in order to earn a fee, (2) whether such work was actually performed, (3) whether the services are necessary for the transaction, and (4) whether they were duplicative of services performed by others. In the past, HUD generally would be satisfied that no §8 RESPA violation (no anti-kickback provision violation) had occurred if a real estate salesperson: (1) took information from the borrower and filled out the loan application, (2) performed at least five additional items on the *Loan Origination Services List* as itemized later, and (3) received a fee reasonably related to the market value of the services performed.

HUD has since expressed particular concern that lenders paying a fee for steering customers to that particular lender could be disguised as compensation for "counseling-type" activities. Therefore, if a salesperson relies on taking the application and performing only "counseling-type" services (Items [b], [c], [d], [j], and [k] on the Loan Origination Services List below) to justify a fee, HUD will also ask for proof that meaningful counseling, not steering, is provided. In this circumstance, HUD would be satisfied that no §8 RESPA violation had occurred if: (1) the counseling gives the borrower the opportunity to consider products from at least three different lenders, (2) the salesperson performing the counseling receives the same compensation regardless of which lender's product was ultimately selected, and (3) any payment made for "counseling-type" services is reasonably related to the services performed and not based on the amount of loan business referred to the lender.

According to HUD Informal Opinion Number 13, some or all of the following services are normally performed in the origination of a loan:

- taking information from a borrower and filling out an application;
- analyzing a borrower's income and debt and prequalifying him or her to determine the maximum mortgage he or she can afford;

- educating a borrower in the home-buying and financing process, advising him or her about the different types of loan products available, and demonstrating how closing costs and monthly payments would vary under each product;
- collecting financial information (tax returns, bank statements) and other related documents that are part of the application process;
- initiating/ordering verifications of employment and verifications of deposits;
- initiating/ordering requests for mortgage and other loan verifications;
- initiating/ordering appraisals;
- initiating/ordering inspections or engineering reports;
- providing disclosures (Truth-in-Lending, Loan Estimate, others) to a borrower;
- assisting a borrower in understanding/clearing credit problems;
- maintaining regular contact with the borrower, real estate agents, and the lender between application and closing to apprise them of the status of the application and to gather additional information needed;
- ordering legal documents;
- determining whether the property is located in a flood zone (or ordering such service); and/or
- participating in the loan closing.

Recent changes in disclosure requirements and the updated Loan Estimate form may limit these gains. More full disclosure of fees and yield spread premiums are now required by the Mortgage Disclosure Improvement Act (MDIA), enacted in July 2008, which must be disclosed on the Loan Estimate form. The regulator responsible for RESPA—the Consumer Financial Protection Bureau—now is responsible for lender compliance with the Loan Estimate disclosure form that deals with those requirements of the Truth-in-Lending Act as well as RESPA.

Real estate agents interested in utilizing a CLO system, now called **manual underwriting**, are generally resorting to intermediary companies that perform the loan services, via computer, of a loan broker or a mortgage company. By sending information on a potential borrower to the intermediary, the real estate agent is prompted if all necessary information has not been submitted. Furthermore, the intermediary has contacts with lenders and is able to place acceptable loans rather quickly. An origination fee split is negotiable between the intermediary and the agent, as both assist the borrower.

If there is an ownership interest of 1% or more between the parties involved with a CLO, it is considered a controlled business arrangement and must be disclosed to the consumer. Furthermore, there can be no required use of the affiliated company, and nothing of value may be given the affiliate other than a return on the ownership interest.

Larger mortgage companies either allow loan closing by agents using the mortgage company's name or buy loans from the agents. To pay the agents, mortgage companies often allow them to earn a portion of the interest rate that is charged. This is called a *yield spread premium* or a *service release premium*.

LOAN ORIGINATION SYSTEMS (LOS)

The **loan origination system (LOS)** has been developed over the years by several vendors specifically to support the loan application processing needs of banks, financial institutions, and the mortgage brokerage community. Loan origination systems employ workflow technology to control and monitor the various work steps involved in loan processing, and use digital imaging technology to reduce the delays and inefficiencies involved in handling paper documents. LOS allows the workflow tracking of each application from the time it is entered into the system through the various work steps of credit review and loan approval process. Most LOS will allow these work steps to be performed in different locations (generally through the "cloud") while maintaining control of the flow and making sure no required steps are being missed. More will follow on LOS since many are programmed to be fully and seamlessly integrated into the business process management software applications of banks, investment banks, and the government-sponsored agencies' automated underwriting systems.

In the past, traditional software licenses had to be purchased for each employee's computer on a single, multiuser license for a server-based application that all employees in a firm could access. With cloud computing, there has been a significant workload shift. Software applications are no longer loaded on local computers or network servers that require maintenance and support. The network of servers that run the internet and the software providers, such as Mortgagebot and Calyx, that make up the cloud handle them instead. The use of the cloud will reduce software and server utilization on the part of the bank, broker, or credit union. The only thing the user's computer needs is the cloud computing system's interface software, such as Mortgage Marvel or WebCaster, which can be accessed via a web browser. The cloud's network manages the process.

With the rapid pace of product modifications and compliance, many originators have developed their own business-process management systems that incorporate compliance tracking. Others are using third party-developed software solutions, such as Pegasystems' SmartBPM®, that enable originators to quickly comply with changes to Fannie Mae and Freddie Mac guidelines, thus avoiding the resulting buybacks that occur when mortgage documentation contains mistakes. Various product development enhancements to automate the lending process and avoid manual errors, lag time, and data entry will create a key competitive edge over the next few years. SaaS, cloud computing, and other hosted or outsourced tech arrangements will become popular in the near future, helping lenders manage a new load of risk management, loss mitigation, workout, and compliance responsibilities. Mortgage Builder Software, Inc., an LOS software provider based in Michigan, has introduced a SaaS-based LOS offering called Mortgage Builder®.

AUTOMATED UNDERWRITING SYSTEMS

More advanced use of the computer has been developed by larger lenders as more experience and better technology has become available. In 1995, both Freddie Mac and Fannie Mae introduced separate **automated underwriting** systems for use by their seller/servicers. Each has developed advanced software capable of analyzing a loan application and approving it for funding if qualifications are met. Other lenders produced their own systems to assist in analyzing loan applications.

At about the same time, the Federal Reserve Bank Board announced its own software system, called *Partners*, that tells a potential borrower if he or she qualifies for a mortgage loan. It is designed to help professionals assist low- and moderate-income borrowers, but is accessible to anyone seeking help.

A brief description of two automated underwriting systems, Freddie Mac's *Loan Prospector*® and Fannie Mae's *Desktop Underwriter*®, follows.

> ## Where Are We Now?
>
> Because of the dynamic secondary market, the services and capabilities offered by Fannie Mae change frequently. Visiting the Fannie Mae website often is highly recommended. Below are a few specific areas of interest.
>
> - **Fannie Mae's Monthly National Housing Survey**
>   http://www.fanniemae.com/portal/research-and-analysis/housing-survey.html
> - **"Americans' Housing Optimism Gains More Momentum amid Reported Income Growth; Supports Forecast of Pickup in Housing Activity This Year"**
>   http://www.fanniemae.com/portal/research-insights/surveys/monthly-may2015.html
> - **"HUD and Fannie Mae Annouce Expansion of Green Preservation PLUS that Pays for Energy-Efficient Upgrades in Affordable Apartments"**
>   http://fanniemae.com/portal/media/corporate-news/2014/6117.html
> - **The Fannie Mae Loan Lookup enables mortgage borrowers to quickly determine if Fannie Mae owns their loan.**
>   https://www.knowyouroptions.com/loanlookup
> - **Know Your Options: Avoid Foreclosure**
>   http://www.knowyouroptions.com/avoid-foreclosure
> - **What Lenders Don't Know About E-recording**
>   https://simplifile.com/whitepapers/what-lenders-dont-know-about-e-recording/

Freddie Mac's Loan Prospector®

Freddie Mac's automated underwriting system, called **Loan Prospector®**, was released nationally in February 1995. It is limited for use by Freddie Mac's seller/servicers, who are required to submit verification of the data submitted. The information submitted is that required by the Uniform Residential Loan Application (Freddie Mac Form 65). In earlier years, the initial charge for an analysis was $100; now it is just

$20. Verification of the applicant's employment, income, and assets is required.

If the loan-to-value ratio is greater than 80%, the application is forwarded to a private mortgage insurer chosen by the lender. All major mortgage insurers are represented on the Freddie Mac system.

Loan Prospector® is intended to provide lenders with a quick and easy way to streamline the document-gathering process for borrowers, with two documentation levels that define required borrower documentation needs and offer helpful underwriting reminders. Loan Prospector® benefits borrowers as it allows them to know exactly what they need to gather, and users have found it easier to process more loans with less work. When a loan is submitted to the site, one of the following recommendations will be returned on the Full Feedback Certificate: (1) Accept, or (2) Caution.

If the product is an Agency loan product, Freddie Mac offers reduced representations and warranties on eligible loans that receive an "Accept" recommendation. In addition to providing a "Credit Risk" recommendation of either Accept or Caution, Loan Prospector® computer software classifies the "accepted" applications into two classifications that drive documentation requirements for the loan applicant, as follows:

- **Streamlined Accept**—allows one to take advantage of fewer documentation requirements than traditionally underwritten loans for the Accept risk class. For example, salaried and hourly income borrowers will need just one pay stub showing year-to-date earnings for the most recent 30 days, one W-2, verbal verification, and one recent bank statement.
- **Standard**—requires Standard Guide documentation for higher-risk loans, including some Accept risk class loans, A-minus eligible loans, and Caution risk class loans. For this level, additional documentation must be collected; for example, two bank statements and two W-2s. Note, however, that one pay stub covering the most recent 30 days and verbal verification of employment are still required.

If the classification is Caution, which is true for about 30% of those applications submitted, it, too, is returned to the lender's underwriters. The most common reason for this return is that some serious issue has been found that may disallow Freddie Mac from purchasing the loan. The computer does not reject any loan, but sends those applications that do not meet approval/acceptance back to the lender for further human underwriting.

Credit Approval by Loan Prospector

A lender is allowed to choose among five approved credit reporting companies.[2] Credit reports are available that merge information from at least two of the three major databases. *Loan Prospector* also has the ability to access the credit card database to determine total credit available and the percentage of credit being used.

Collateral Assessments

Property evaluation is not called an "appraisal" by *Loan Prospector*; it is a **collateral assessment**. The program assesses whether or not the collateral is sufficient to secure the loan.

Freddie Mac's **Automated Valuation Model (AVM)** tool simplifies the mortgage process by streamlining the collateral valuation cycle. It is called Home Value Explorer® (HVE®). This system is replacing a service called *Gold Works* that, up until November 2008, linked a lender directly with the appraiser. For over 15 years, Freddie Mac has effectively employed AVMs internally for its own risk and portfolio management. AVMs have become an integral part of today's mortgage market, and AVM technology has advanced the world of automated valuation services from novelty to necessity.

In nationwide tests conducted by large wholesale lenders, HVE consistently performs at the top in the areas of coverage, accuracy, and reliability. HVE actually encompasses several models rolled into a single product for one low cost. Freddie Mac believes that lenders will benefit from its unique proprietary algorithm that blends multiple model estimates returned by the repeat sales model and the hedonic model.

Today, AVMs are efficient, effective, and essential tools for staying competitive. AVMs expedite processes, lower costs, and minimize risk. When choosing an AVM, it is important to consider coverage, vendor reputation, current technology, accuracy, and price. Freddie Mac claims to have a dedicated team of modeling experts that will continue to improve and enhance the HVE tool.

---

[2]"List of Approved Credit Reporting Companies for Loan Prospector®," Freddie Mac, accessed on February 7, 2015, http://www.loanprospector.com/about/crc.html.

Where Are We Now?

Visiting the Freddie Mac website frequently is essential in a rapidly changing market. Some of the resources found on the website include the following:

Media Room

Find the latest news releases, corporate facts, select officer biographies, speeches and statements, economic and housing research commentary, industry reports and publications, the results of Freddie Mac's weekly PrimaryMortgage Market Survey®, and subscriptions to a variety of email alerts and RSS feeds.

- corporate facts
- executive perspectives
- speeches and statements
- economic and housing research
- industry reports and publications
- PrimaryMortgage Market Survey®
- news release archives
- subscription center
- RSS feeds

Investor Relations

Find information on Freddie Mac's common and preferred stock, corporate financials, corporate governance, corporate responsibility, securities trading, investor news, investor events, and additional investor resources such as investor presentations, credit ratings, and analyst coverage.

- FRE stock information
- corporate financials
- corporate governance
- Section 16 filings, director and executive officer ownership reporting
- investor news releases
- investor resources
- investor relations contact information

Fannie Mae's Desktop Underwriter®

In April 1995, Fannie Mae released two programs to its seller/servicers. The basic program, called **Desktop Underwriter® (DU)**, uses artificial intelligence and information from Fannie Mae's seller/servicer guide to properly analyze a loan application.

A second program, called **Desktop Originator® (DO)**, is designed to allow an agent or a mortgage broker to take an application in a potential borrower's home with a laptop computer, relaying the information to the lender who is the seller/servicer.

Information on the loan and the applicant must come from the same form as used by Freddie Mac, the Uniform Residential Loan Application (Fannie Mae Form 1003, Freddie Mac Form 65). The lender must verify the information and then submit it to Fannie Mae through its *Desktop Underwriter®*, after which a response can be provided within one minute or less on "approved" applicants. The lender is responsible for notifying the broker or agent who originated the loan, who in turn notifies the applicant. Over the past 10 years, DU has further enabled other business channels, including retail, wholesale, correspondent, internet/call center, and point of sale, by allowing Loan Origination System (LOS) vendors to offer direct access to Desktop Originator® and/or Desktop Underwriter®. Some of these vendors, such as Point®, a Calyx Software LOS product, and Destiny Loan Origination System, an Integra Software Systems LOS product, could be found at the following website at the time of the publication of this text: https://www.fanniemae.com/singlefamily/authorized-los-integration-vendors.

While Fannie Mae is seeking better and faster ways to handle its appraisals, the company still uses many of the traditional methods. Still, the streamlined property valuation and reporting options available through DU can save borrowers time and money and can help lenders more efficiently manage the property valuation process.

It is expected that in the near term DU will have tie-ins with automated closing and documentation systems that meet the electronic signature and recording requirements established under the various electronic signature Acts passed in the late 1990s and early 2000s. In April 2011, Oklahoma Governor Mary Fallin signed into law a bill that permits digital signatures on real estate contracts. Oklahoma had been the last state that did not have a mechanism for a virtual closing in place. Industry trade associations have already introduced SMART Doc® Framework (Ver. 1). The following terms make up the acronym:

- **s**ecurable
- **m**anageable
- **a**chievable
- **r**etrievable
- **t**ransferable

The ideal electronic document requirements include descriptive information in the form of metadata with a visual representation of that embedded data linked into the visual representation so that electronic signatures seem a natural part of the process. The system would need tamper-evident security and provide an audit trail of any changes. Figure 15-1 below illustrates how such a system might be configured.

Fannie Mae's DU-based **Automated Valuation System (AVS)** utilizes the data entered, at which point the system will recommend one of the following documentation levels for each eligible one-unit property loan with a valid property address:

- appraisal with interior and exterior property inspection
- appraisal with exterior-only property inspection
- an exterior-only property inspection (no appraisal required)

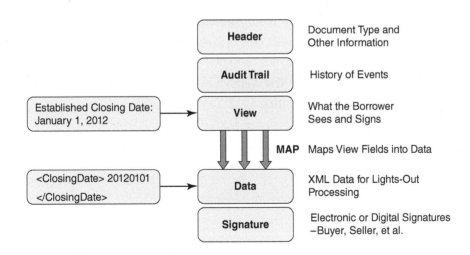

FIGURE 15-1 Smart doc® Framework

Source: © 2021 Mbition LLC

Lenders continue to manage the property appraisal process for loans submitted through DU, including selecting the appraiser, ordering the appraisal, and reviewing the appraisal report. As a result, lenders are responsible for the traditional warranties to Fannie Mae regarding the selection of the appraiser and the quality of the appraisal. As for credit reporting, studies are seeking other ways of satisfying lender requirements, particularly in regard to property evaluations. One study uses pictures taken from satellites to determine if a building actually exists on specific property. Some firms currently use available GPS location support for many applications. For example, Environmental Systems Research Institute, Inc.'s ARCGIS Call software provides a front-end solution for anyone to use. ARCGIS ties the location to actual, current tax data found in county tax offices that can be accessed by a computer program such as the Fannie Mae AVM system.

Fannie Mae's **EarlyCheck™** service assists lenders in identifying and correcting potential eligibility and/or data issues as early in their processes as possible. The goal is to help lenders identify potential problems prior to loan delivery.

Prior to a loan closing, lenders have the following two EarlyCheck™ access options:

- **a service that can be directly integrated with a lender's LOS** (This option is a Desktop Underwriter® (DU®)–like integration solution (i.e., it takes a 1003 flat file or MISMO[3] AUS 2.3.1 file as input and returns viewable results and/or a result data file).); or
- **a web-based user interface.** This option enables a user to import loan data in a 1003 flat file format (which can be exported from most loan origination systems) or the MISMO AUS 2.3.1 file format, run the checks, and view the results.

MORTGAGES ON THE INTERNET

The use of computers in mortgage lending has expanded so that borrowers can negotiate loans on the internet. Most active mortgage loan companies

---

[3]MISMO stands for Mortgage Industry Standards Maintenance Organization, Inc., a leading technology standards development body for the residential and commercial real estate finance industries, and a wholly owned subsidiary of the Mortgage Bankers Association. The MISMO standards are grounded in an open process to develop, promote, and maintain voluntary electronic commerce procedures and standards that allow mortgage lenders, investors in real estate and mortgages, servicers, industry vendors, borrowers, and other parties to exchange real estate finance-related information and eMortgages more securely, efficiently, and economically.

and financial institutions have websites that offer mortgage loans directly to consumers who qualify, but there are a few caveats.

There are several reasons for the growing interest in **internet loan applications**. Many applicants live in rural areas and want to avoid traveling long distances to branch offices in metropolitan areas. Even though the usual time-consuming verifications are still required, people who are pressed for time look to the internet to expedite the loan process. Another lure is anonymity. People with tarnished credit histories do not have to face a skeptical loan officer. Even people with good credit records sometimes feel more comfortable with impersonal vending devices than face-to-face encounters. Studies show that consumers shop for the best available price and terms, and that even the most sophisticated borrowers often find it difficult to effectively shop for mortgages.[4]

Mortgages negotiated through the internet may have lower origination fees, perhaps three-eighths of a point compared to 1 to 1.5 points with regular mortgage brokers. But the other fees and interest rates are about the same as regular mortgages. There is also a problem in not having a real person with whom to talk through financial needs. Because anonymity works both ways, the internet has its share of shady operators who can take advantage of unwary borrowers. However, there is no denying the growth in internet mortgage originations. The top 22 mortgage lenders in all loan production in 1999 only reported a little over 13,000 online mortgages for a total of $4.7 billion in mortgage production.[5] The top online originator in the first quarter of 2010 originated double the number of mortgages originated by the top 22 online lenders in all of 1999.[6] Some of the more innovative firms, such as CUNA Mutual Group, are using a product called "Smartphone Loan Technology." These firms originated over $1 billion in loans via mobile devices between launch of technology in 2012 and the end of 2013.[7] *Inside Mortgage Finance* reported that Quicken Loans Inc., one of the largest nonbank mortgage lenders, made $96 billion of loans in 2016. In the last quarter of 2018, the nonbank lender Quicken Loans surpassed Wells Fargo as the leading mortgage lender in the United States, with two of the top five being online-only lenders.

---

[4]William Apgar and Ren S. Essene, *Understanding Mortgage Market Behavior: Creating Good Mortgage Options for All Americans* (Cambridge: Joint Center for Housing Studies, Harvard University, 2007), iv.
[5]Michael LaCour-Little, "The Evolving Role of Technology in Mortgage Finance," *Journal of Housing Research* 11, no. 2 (2000): 197.
[6]*National Mortgage News Quarterly Data Report, Q1* (Arlington, VA: SourceMedia, 2010).
[7]Jess Noelck, "CUNA Mutual Group's Smartphone Loan Technology Reaches Major Milestone" CUNA Mutual Group, August 22, 2013, accessed February 9, 2015, http://www.cunamutual.com/portal/server.pt?open=512&objID=902&PageID=951486&mode=2

Online mortgage originators fall into three general categories:

1. **direct lenders** (They are those mortgage loan originators that actually fund the loan. They exist at the national, state, and local levels. Bank of America is an example of a national lender. Southside Bancshares, Inc., in Tyler, Texas, is an example of a state lender. Local mortgage loan originators can function as online mortgage lenders just by having a website with an application form on it.);
2. **mortgage brokers** (In the past, the advantage of using a mortgage broker was that it gave customers access to a wider availability of lender programs and loan options. Most brokers have a basic online mortgage application website from which they can take mortgage loan applications.); and
3. **lead generators.** (Also referred to as referral websites, these tend to specialize in generating leads from borrowers and then passing those leads along to one of the direct lenders, rather than making loans themselves. They are considered the most effective tool used by both direct lenders and mortgage brokers.)

It has become easy for loan originators of any size to have some basic online loan origination presence. Software applications such as PG Mortgage Software are available to individual mortgage brokers who want an individualized basic online presence. This software combines features, such as LOS-application tracking, that are compatible with Calyx Point and Fannie Mae LOS, with the ability to export application forms to these well-known programs and work with them offline. Moreover, the software has site security with SSL Certification. Some of the other service providers, with software or other consulting services to help set up online mortgage origination capabilities, include the following:

- Byte Mortgage Origination Software (http://www.bytesoftware.com)
- Ellie Mae's – Encompass (https://www.elliemae.com/encompass/encompass-overview)
- Mortgage Builders Software (http://www.mortgagebuilder.com/)
- RK New York Web Design (http://www.rknewyorkwebdesign.com/mortgage-web-site-design)
- Lead Press (http://leadpress.com/)
- Kaleidico's Mortgage Web in a Box (http://www.kaleidico.com/mortgage-website)

- Calyx Software's WebCaster (http://www.calyxsoftware.com/products/webcaster/)
- Lender Home Page (http://www.lenderhomepage.com/)
- vLender (https://www.vlender.com/)

ONLINE REAL ESTATE SERVICE

Many companies offer an **online real estate service** that allows consumers access to information on a full range of services. In 1998, software giant Microsoft stepped into this arena. Microsoft offers consumers a service that gives them the opportunity to search for homes, find builders, compare mortgage products, and apply for loans. In other words, the service gives consumers access to information that had previously been the special province of real estate agents and mortgage brokers. Over the years, real estate professionals have created products that allow individual real estate brokers the ability to create the image of a broad-market online real estate service. One such vendor is DwellAgent.com, which offers features such as self-publishing, attractive and effective listing websites (at the level of individual property if desired), a primary website, a blog, and other features.

Companies offering these services deny any intention to replace existing agents. All the service expects to provide is information on what is available and a comparison of prices. To close any deal, the consumer must contact an agent in that business. Technology brings rapid changes that create better and more information along with faster response times. The following websites offer an idea of just how diverse the information offered on the internet is:

- **www.bytesoftware.com** — Byte Software, founded in 1985, is located in Kirkland, Washington. The company is a wholly owned subsidiary of CBCInnovis. Byte Software's flagship product is BytePro Standard, a comprehensive loan origination software package that allows a loan originator to prequalify, originate, process, and close loans. Byte offers six expansion versions of its mortgage LOS system to meet the needs of larger and more demanding technology platforms, including the internet and security packages.
- **www.calyxsoftware.com** — Calyx was founded in 1991 in San Jose, California, and is most well-known for its Point loan origination platform. According to a 2010 study conducted by Access Mortgage

Research & Consulting, 72.5% of mortgage brokers reported using Calyx Point. Loan origination systems (LOS) like those developed by Calyx are also utilized by community banks, credit unions, and mortgage bankers, and can be used with DU and DO along with several other vendors mentioned earlier in the chapter.

- **www.fiserv.com/resources/easylender-mortgage-brochure.aspx** — EasyLender® Mortgage from Fiserv is a scalable LOS designed for community banks and mid-tier credit unions that runs under the latest Microsoft® Windows® operating systems. EasyLender® supports originations for mortgage and home equity loans with a loan origination and processing software providing comprehensive lending automation from application through closing.

- **www.elliemae.com/encompass/encompass-overview** — Encompass® is an end-to-end solution, provided using on-demand software that functions as the core operating system for mortgage originators and spans customer relationship management, loan origination, and business management. Rather than loading an LOS software onto their server or laptop, users of Encompass® connect to the web to use Encompass® and pay by the "drink." Encompass® is a software offering of Ellie Mae, a provider of on-demand automation solutions for the mortgage industry. An American Bankers Association (ABA) *Real Estate Lending Survey Report* listed Encompass as the most-used LOS by banks in 2014.[8] Ellie Mae was founded in 1997 and is based in Pleasanton, California.

- **www.ditech.com** — Ditech was founded in 1995 to address the needs of customers for faster, easier access to mortgage loans. GMAC Mortgage, a major financial services company and one of America's leading mortgage loan originators, acquired all the assets of Ditech Funding Corporation in 1999. This marked the beginning of significant growth for Ditech, enabling the company to invest further in its products, technology, and customer service, and set the stage for Ditech's emergence, and current status, as one of the larger online mortgage loan originators.

- **www.eloan.com** — Founded in Palo Alto, California, as an online mortgage brokerage firm, E-Loan, Inc., now known as E-LOAN,

---

[8]Debbie Whiteside, *21st Annual ABA Real Estate Lending Survey Report* (Washington, DC: American Bankers Association, 2014), 6.

is a wholly owned subsidiary of Banco Popular North America. It offers prequalification and preapproval for home equity loans, as well as first mortgages and refinancing. The site has a link that helps users compare values of different homes in a given neighborhood. It even has a feature that allows the user to hold out for a particular interest rate and to receive an email when the rate becomes available. There are actually awards for website media interactivity. E-Loan earned the top spot for three different categories of these awards in 2013.

- **www.hsh.com** — Offered by the financial publishing company HSH Associates of Butler, New Jersey, the site surveys 2,500 lenders across the country and provides updates daily. It does not make loans and accepts only limited consumer advertising (it makes the bulk of its revenues from lead generation), which makes it an excellent source of objective data on interest rates and terms.

- **www.dh.com/lending/mortgage-lending/mortgagebotlos** — A wholly owned subsidiary of Davis + Henderson Corporation, a leading provider of integrated solutions to customers in the financial services industry based in Toronto, Canada. A dominant player in the United States, its products are very popular in the community banking and credit union sectors. Its Powersite Suite of programs provides affordable, easy-to-use, and secure technology solutions developed to be fully integrated with most LOS software. This product is competitive because it can be deployed with surprising speed. Since it is completely internet-based, there is no software or hardware to install or maintain. In 2007, Mortgagebot introduced its Mortgage Marvel, an internet-based solution for smaller lenders who want to expand past their traditional base but may not have the expertise or funding to develop an internet-based site that will appeal to customers beyond those in their traditional customer base. Mortgagebot was ranked third in its category of "Top Loan Origination Systems" In the 2014 ABA *Real Estate Lending Survey Report,* moving it ahead of Calyx Point, which was in 5th place in the survey.

- **www.mortgagebuilder.com** — Mortgage Builder, headquartered in Southfield, Michigan, has been providing a fully integrated server-based application for a wide base of possible needs in the mortgage finance business for 12 years. Mortgage Builder is an end-to-end lending solution for retail and wholesale mortgage production channels, delivering prequalification tools, processing, underwriting, closing, post-closing, final document tracking, secondary marketing, warehousing, delivery, interim servicing, and construction loan tracking. Pricing and product eligibility, electronic document management, and electronic loan delivery functionality for the GSEs are built in and available on demand, while compliant loan documents are provided at no additional cost. Third-party originator web portals such as FHA Connect, as well as consumer-facing virtual tools, are also available, thus enhancing flexibility.

- **www.phhmortgage.com** — PHH Mortgage is located in Mount Laurel, New Jersey, and is a wholly owned subsidiary of PHH Corporation. PHH Corporation is among the top five residential mortgage originators, but its online business consists of the firm's own retail online mortgage operations. PHH is also the leading provider of private label mortgage outsourcing to companies that want to have an online loan origination presence without the cost of the technology development, staff training, recruiting, and other barriers to entry for many smaller lenders.

- **www.provident.com** — Provident Funding Associates, L.P., is the largest private mortgage company in the United States and one of the top five direct online lenders for the past three years. Provident Funding has developed their own proprietary online mortgage origination software platform and it is recommended for viewing since Provident is so successful.

- **www.rcanalytics.com** — Real Capital Analytics, Inc. is a global research firm founded in 2000 based in New York City. The firm's proprietary research is focused exclusively on the investment market for commercial real estate. Real Capital Analytics offers in-depth, comprehensive and current information of activity in the industry by collecting transactional information for property sales and financings. RCA then interprets data such as capitalization rates, market trends, pricing, and sales volume. RCA also quantifies the market forces and identifies the trends that affect the pricing and liquidity of commercial real estate around the world. The firm publishes a series of *Capital Trend* reports and offers an online service that provides current transactional and troubled asset information on all markets globally.

USING COMPUTERIZED INFORMATION IN THE FUTURE

As technology advances, indications are that mortgage loans will move to a **risk-based mortgage loan pricing** system where lenders assess borrowing costs loan by loan. This will be possible with computerized loan evaluation systems capable of forecasting the default risk dictated by each applicant.

In addition, secondary-market companies are able to adjust the guarantee fees charged to lenders to more accurately reflect the risks represented by the individual mortgages within a loan pool that an originator wants to sell. As lenders pay varying guarantee fees, market forces may prompt them to pass the distinctions on to borrowers in the form of similarly varying mortgage fees. The final and full implementation of the Qualified Residential Mortgages (QRM) Rule defines which loans are exempt from the risk retention requirements of the Dodd-Frank Wall Street Reform and Consumer Protection Act. Since sound and responsible underwriting plays such an important part in making sure a loan is originated to avoid risk retention requirements, good underwriting will have to have the following general characteristics:

- regular periodic payments that are substantially equal;
- no negative amortization, interest only, or balloon features;
- a maximum loan term of 30 years;
- total points and fees that do not exceed 3% of the total loan amount, or the applicable amounts specified for small loans up to $100,000;
- payments underwritten using the maximum interest rate that may apply during the first five years after the date on which the first regular periodic payment is due;
- consideration and verification of the consumer's income and assets, including employment status if relied upon, and current debt obligations, mortgage-related obligations, alimony and child support; and
- total DTI (debt-to-income) ratio that does not exceed 43%.

This means that the ongoing adoption of automated underwriting systems and their integration with LOS and compliance systems will provide the lending industry the ability to measure risk more quickly and accurately than ever before. Fannie Mae recently released DU Version 9.2 that reflected lower maximum LTV, CLTV, and HCLTV ratios for fixed-rate cash-out refinance transactions secured by a one-unit primary residence. Those transactions are subject to a maximum LTV/CLTV/HCLTV ratio of 80%, instead of 85%. Desktop Underwriter Release Notes issued in January 2018 are an example of controlling risk levels.

For years, the country's main residential market, sometimes referred to as the *prime market*, has relied primarily on average cost pricing. Every mortgage interest rate includes a premium to cover the risk of default, with all prime borrowers paying the same interest rate. With risk-based pricing, the alignment of risk and reward is more closely met by giving lower interest rates to less risky borrowers. Fannie Mae has instituted the Loan-Level Price Adjustment (LLPA) Matrix and Adverse Market Delivery Charge (AMD), which mandate that higher interest rates and/or higher minimum mortgage insurance coverage will be assessed based on certain eligibility or other loan features, such as credit score, loan purpose, occupancy, number of units, product type, and loan-to-value ratio. A website listed at the end of the chapter allows access to the most current matrix approved for use by Fannie Mae.

It is possible that future mechanically determined, more-accurate risk assessment may lead to a **universal account** that could make mortgages obsolete. The idea would be a combination of loans, such as a car loan, a personal loan, or a mortgage loan, into one loan account. Multiline financial institutions, such as commercial firms and stock brokerages, are already moving in this general direction, recognizing the value of cross-selling products, a concept that is key to giving this futuristic financial instrument its universal applicability. The financial supermarket entered into by many financial services firms may become more of a reality due to current and future advances in internet delivery systems.

Questions for Discussion

1. What is HUD's position on computerized loan origination?
2. Explain what is meant by *manual underwriting* and *automated underwriting*.
3. Describe the principal features of Freddie Mac's Loan Prospector.
4. What does Fannie Mae offer in terms of automated underwriting?
5. What is a Loan Origination System?

6. Why did the Mortgage Bankers Association object to the use of computerized loan origination?
7. Explain the three categories of internet mortgage originators and how they differ in approach.
8. Describe the kinds of people who may want to arrange mortgage loans through the internet.
9. Describe the dominant online mortgage originators and real estate online offerings, and list the key online players today.
10. Describe risk-based pricing as it applies to mortgage loans.

Multiple Choice Questions for Review

1. All of the following government-sponsored enterprises (GSEs) encourage the use of computerized loan origination systems EXCEPT:
   a. GNMA
   b. Fannie Mae
   c. Freddie Mac
   d. FHA

2. True or false? Automated underwriting on systems such as Desktop Underwriter and Loan Prospector has replaced manual underwriting.
   a. true
   b. false

3. When using Freddie Mac's Loan Prospector, a property valuation is referred to as a/an:
   a. AVS
   b. appraisal
   c. collateral assessment
   d. none of these

4. What value-added software tool has Fannie Mae added to its Desktop Underwriting system to help avoid and correct eligibility errors?
   a. Automated Valuation System
   b. Calyx Webcaster interface
   c. EarlyCheck
   d. SmartDoc

5. Risk-based pricing:
   a. lenders assess borrowing costs loan by loan.
   b. will be possible because loan evaluation systems can forecast risk
   c. both a and b
   d. cannot be used as technology advances

6. An Alt-A loan is:
   a. riskier than a subprime loan, but less risky than a prime loan
   b. less risky than both a subprime and prime loan
   c. riskier than a prime loan, but less risky than a subprime loan
   d. a higher risk than subprime and prime loans

7. Of the three categories of internet loan originators, which is considered the most effective in terms of bringing in mortgage loan prospects?
   a. direct lenders
   b. mortgage brokers
   c. lead generators
   d. webcasters

8. The primary reasons that consumers use the internet for mortgage loans include all the following EXCEPT:
   a. anonymity
   b. getting the best interest rates available
   c. avoiding travel and the need to take time off from work
   d. expediting the loan process

9. The key online mortgage originators are which of the following?
   a. banks
   b. mortgage brokers
   c. independent mortgage banks
   d. insurance companies

10. The recent financial crisis has taught us which of the following related to risk-based pricing?
    a. Higher interest rates on loans to riskier borrowers can compensate for liquidity risk.
    b. The data models can more accurately predict within a narrow range of probability the extremes of market downturns.
    c. There are multiple unresolved problems in which risk-based pricing has been rendered less useful.
    d. The recent financial crisis has taught us none of these.

Additional Online Resources

http://www.pega.com/insights/resources/new-tools-new-rules-mortgage
   Information on using Pegasystems's SmartBPM® and Solution Frameworks to deliver quality control, including a feature enabling one to review improvement in order to stop the origination or purchase of broken loans, can be found at the website above.

http://www.pria.us/
   The Property Records Industry Association provides a forum for the identification, research, discussion, development, drafting, and implementation of national standards, best practices, and new technology solutions to promote the integrity of the public records system.

http://www.spers.org/

The Standards and Procedures for Electronic Records and Signatures (SPeRS) is an eCommerce initiative sponsored by the Electronic Financial Services Council (EFSC). SPeRS creates voluntary, industry-wide guidelines for the electronic execution of signatures, record retention, printing, delivery, and presentation of information.

https://www.fanniemae.com/singlefamily/technology-integration?taskId=task-97

Fannie Mae maintains a listing of the LOS vendors that have integration capabilities with its Desktop Underwriter® and Desktop Originator® systems at the webpage above.

https://www.fanniemae.com/content/pricing/llpa-matrix.pdf

Fannie Mae's "Risk-Based Pricing Matrix," called Loan-Level Price Adjustment (LLPA) Matrix and Adverse Market Delivery Charge (AMDC), contains risk-based price adjustments based on certain eligibility or other loan features, such as credit score, loan purpose, occupancy, number of units, and product type. The special feature codes (SFCs) that are required when delivering loans with these features are listed next to the applicable LLPAs at the website above for the most current LLPA and AMDC Matrix.

ANSWER KEY FOR MULTIPLE CHOICE QUESTIONS

Chapter 1

1. b
2. b
3. a
4. c
5. d
6. c
7. b
8. d
9. b
10. d

Chapter 2

1. b
2. d
3. c
4. c
5. b
6. d
7. c
8. d
9. c
10. c

Chapter 3

1. b
2. c
3. b
4. c
5. b
6. c
7. c
8. b
9. b
10. c

Chapter 4

1. c
2. b
3. c
4. d
5. d
6. b
7. c
8. a
9. c
10. c

Chapter 5

1. c
2. c
3. c
4. c
5. b
6. d
7. a
8. d
9. c
10. d

Chapter 6

1. b
2. c
3. b
4. d
5. d
6. b
7. c
8. b
9. c
10. b

Chapter 7

1. b
2. c
3. b
4. d
5. c
6. d
7. c
8. d
9. d
10. c

Chapter 8

1. b
2. d
3. c
4. a
5. c
6. b
7. d
8. c
9. a
10. d

Chapter 9

1. b
2. d
3. b
4. d
5. d
6. b
7. d
8. c
9. b
10. b

Chapter 10

1. b
2. b
3. c
4. d
5. c
6. a.
7. b.
8. c
9. d
10. b

Chapter 11

1. c
2. c
3. d
4. c
5. c
6. c
7. b
8. c
9. d
10. c

Chapter 12

1. a
2. d
3. c
4. b
5. a
6. c
7. a
8. c
9. b
10. b

Chapter 13

1. c
2. b
3. b
4. c
5. c
6. b
7. c
8. c
9. c
10. c

Chapter 14

1. b
2. a
3. b
4. c
5. d
6. b
7. b
8. c
9. c
10. e

Chapter 15

1. a
2. b
3. c
4. c
5. c
6. c
7. c
8. b
9. a
10. c

APPENDIX

Uniform Residential Loan Application	666
Uniform Residential Loan Application (effective July 2019)	671
Request for Verification of Deposit	679
Request for Verification of Employment	681
Sample FHA Gift Letter	683
Sample General Mortgage Company Disclosure Notice	684
Lead Poisoning Notice	689
Disclosure of Notice on Lead-Based Paint and or Lead-Based Paint Hazards	691
Uniform Residential Appraisal Report	692
Deed of Trust	698
Specific Closing Instructions	720
Credit Report	726
Closing Disclosure	732

666 Appendix

Uniform Residential Loan Application

This application is designed to be completed by the applicant(s) with the Lender's assistance. Applicants should complete this form as "Borrower" or "Co-Borrower," as applicable. Co-Borrower information must also be provided (and the appropriate box checked) when ☐ the income or assets of a person other than the Borrower (including the Borrower's spouse) will be used as a basis for loan qualification or ☐ the income or assets of the Borrower's spouse or other person who has community property rights pursuant to state law will not be used as a basis for loan qualification, but his or her liabilities must be considered because the spouse or other person has community property rights pursuant to applicable law and Borrower resides in a community property state, the security property is located in a community property state, or the Borrower is relying on other property located in a community property state as a basis for repayment of the loan.

If this is an application for joint credit, Borrower and Co-Borrower each agree that we intend to apply for joint credit (sign below):

_____ _____
Borrower   Co-Borrower

I. TYPE OF MORTGAGE AND TERMS OF LOAN

Mortgage Applied for:	☐ VA ☐ FHA	☐ Conventional ☐ USDA/Rural Housing Service	☐ Other (explain):	Agency Case Number	Lender Case Number
Amount $	Interest Rate %	No. of Months	Amortization Type:	☐ Fixed Rate ☐ GPM	☐ Other (explain): ☐ ARM (type):

II. PROPERTY INFORMATION AND PURPOSE OF LOAN

Subject Property Address (street, city, state & ZIP)				No. of Units
Legal Description of Subject Property (attach description if necessary)				Year Built

Purpose of Loan	☐ Purchase ☐ Refinance	☐ Construction ☐ Construction-Permanent	☐ Other (explain):	Property will be: ☐ Primary Residence ☐ Secondary Residence ☐ Investment

Complete this line if construction or construction-permanent loan.

Year Lot Acquired	Original Cost $	Amount Existing Liens $	(a) Present Value of Lot $	(b) Cost of Improvements $	Total (a + b) $

Complete this line if this is a refinance loan.

Year Acquired	Original Cost $	Amount Existing Liens $	Purpose of Refinance	Describe Improvements Cost: $	☐ made ☐ to be made

Title will be held in what Name(s)	Manner in which Title will be held	Estate will be held in: ☐ Fee Simple ☐ Leasehold (show expiration date)

Source of Down Payment, Settlement Charges, and/or Subordinate Financing (explain)

III. BORROWER INFORMATION

Borrower			Co-Borrower		
Borrower's Name (include Jr. or Sr. if applicable)			Co-Borrower's Name (include Jr. or Sr. if applicable)		
Social Security Number	Home Phone (incl. area code)	DOB (mm/dd/yyyy) Yrs. School	Social Security Number	Home Phone (incl. area code)	DOB (mm/dd/yyyy) Yrs. School
☐ Married ☐ Unmarried (include ☐ Separated single, divorced, widowed)	Dependents (not listed by Co-Borrower) no. ages		☐ Married ☐ Unmarried (include ☐ Separated single, divorced, widowed)	Dependents (not listed by Borrower) no. ages	
Present Address (street, city, state, ZIP)	☐ Own ☐ Rent ____ No. Yrs.		Present Address (street, city, state, ZIP)	☐ Own ☐ Rent ____ No. Yrs.	
Mailing Address, if different from Present Address			Mailing Address, if different from Present Address		

If residing at present address for less than two years, complete the following:

Former Address (street, city, state, ZIP)	☐ Own ☐ Rent ____ No. Yrs.	Former Address (street, city, state, ZIP)	☐ Own ☐ Rent ____ No. Yrs.

IV. EMPLOYMENT INFORMATION

Borrower			Co-Borrower		
Name & Address of Employer	☐ Self Employed	Yrs. on this job	Name & Address of Employer	☐ Self Employed	Yrs. on this job
		Yrs. employed in this line of work/profession			Yrs. employed in this line of work/profession
Position/Title/Type of Business	Business Phone (incl. area code)		Position/Title/Type of Business	Business Phone (incl. area code)	

If employed in current position for less than two years or if currently employed in more than one position, complete the following:

Uniform Residential Loan Application
Freddie Mac Form 65   7/05 (rev.6/09)

Fannie Mae Form 1003   7/05 (rev.6/09)

Appendix

IV. EMPLOYMENT INFORMATION (cont'd)

Borrower			Co-Borrower		
Name & Address of Employer	☐ Self Employed	Dates (from – to)	Name & Address of Employer	☐ Self Employed	Dates (from – to)
		Monthly Income $			Monthly Income $
Position/Title/Type of Business	Business Phone (incl. area code)		Position/Title/Type of Business	Business Phone (incl. area code)	
Name & Address of Employer	☐ Self Employed	Dates (from – to)	Name & Address of Employer	☐ Self Employed	Dates (from – to)
		Monthly Income $			Monthly Income $
Position/Title/Type of Business	Business Phone (incl. area code)		Position/Title/Type of Business	Business Phone (incl. area code)	

V. MONTHLY INCOME AND COMBINED HOUSING EXPENSE INFORMATION

Gross Monthly Income	Borrower	Co-Borrower	Total	Combined Monthly Housing Expense	Present	Proposed
Base Empl. Income*	$	$	$	Rent	$	
Overtime				First Mortgage (P&I)		$
Bonuses				Other Financing (P&I)		
Commissions				Hazard Insurance		
Dividends/Interest				Real Estate Taxes		
Net Rental Income				Mortgage Insurance		
Other (before completing, see the notice in "describe other income," below)				Homeowner Assn. Dues		
				Other:		
Total	$	$	$	Total	$	$

* Self Employed Borrower(s) may be required to provide additional documentation such as tax returns and financial statements.

Describe Other Income

Notice: Alimony, child support, or separate maintenance income need not be revealed if the Borrower (B) or Co-Borrower (C) does not choose to have it considered for repaying this loan.

B/C		Monthly Amount
		$

VI. ASSETS AND LIABILITIES

This Statement and any applicable supporting schedules may be completed jointly by both married and unmarried Co-Borrowers if their assets and liabilities are sufficiently joined so that the Statement can be meaningfully and fairly presented on a combined basis; otherwise, separate Statements and Schedules are required. If the Co-Borrower section was completed about a non-applicant spouse or other person, this Statement and supporting schedules must be completed about that spouse or other person also.

Completed ☐ Jointly ☐ Not Jointly

ASSETS Description	Cash or Market Value	Liabilities and Pledged Assets. List the creditor's name, address, and account number for all outstanding debts, including automobile loans, revolving charge accounts, real estate loans, alimony, child support, stock pledges, etc. Use continuation sheet, if necessary. Indicate by (*) those liabilities, which will be satisfied upon sale of real estate owned or upon refinancing of the subject property.		
Cash deposit toward purchase held by:	$			
List checking and savings accounts below		LIABILITIES	Monthly Payment & Months Left to Pay	Unpaid Balance
Name and address of Bank, S&L, or Credit Union		Name and address of Company	$ Payment/Months	$
Acct. no.	$	Acct. no.		
Name and address of Bank, S&L, or Credit Union		Name and address of Company	$ Payment/Months	$
Acct. no.	$	Acct. no.		
Name and address of Bank, S&L, or Credit Union		Name and address of Company	$ Payment/Months	$
Acct. no.	$	Acct. no.		

Uniform Residential Loan Application
Freddie Mac Form 65 7/05 (rev. 6/09)

Fannie Mae Form 1003 7/05 (rev.6/09)

Appendix

VI. ASSETS AND LIABILITIES (cont'd)

Name and address of Bank, S&L, or Credit Union		Name and address of Company	$ Payment/Months	$
Acct. no.	$	Acct. no.		
Stocks & Bonds (Company name/ number & description)	$	Name and address of Company	$ Payment/Months	$
		Acct. no.		
Life insurance net cash value	$	Name and address of Company	$ Payment/Months	$
Face amount: $				
Subtotal Liquid Assets	$			
Real estate owned (enter market value from schedule of real estate owned)	$			
Vested interest in retirement fund	$			
Net worth of business(es) owned (attach financial statement)	$	Acct. no.		
Automobiles owned (make and year)	$	Alimony/Child Support/Separate Maintenance Payments Owed to:	$	
Other Assets (itemize)	$	Job-Related Expense (child care, union dues, etc.)	$	
		Total Monthly Payments	$	
Total Assets a.	$	Net Worth (a minus b) ▶ $	**Total Liabilities b.**	$

Schedule of Real Estate Owned (If additional properties are owned, use continuation sheet.)

Property Address (enter S if sold, PS if pending sale or R if rental being held for income) ▼	Type of Property	Present Market Value	Amount of Mortgages & Liens	Gross Rental Income	Mortgage Payments	Insurance, Maintenance, Taxes & Misc.	Net Rental Income
		$	$	$	$	$	$
	Totals	$	$	$	$	$	$

List any additional names under which credit has previously been received and indicate appropriate creditor name(s) and account number(s):

Alternate Name	Creditor Name	Account Number

VII. DETAILS OF TRANSACTION

a.	Purchase price	$
b.	Alterations, improvements, repairs	
c.	Land (if acquired separately)	
d.	Refinance (incl. debts to be paid off)	
e.	Estimated prepaid items	
f.	Estimated closing costs	
g.	PMI, MIP, Funding Fee	
h.	Discount (if Borrower will pay)	
i.	Total costs (add items a through h)	

VIII. DECLARATIONS

If you answer "Yes" to any questions a through i, please use continuation sheet for explanation.

	Borrower		Co-Borrower	
	Yes	No	Yes	No
a. Are there any outstanding judgments against you?	☐	☐	☐	☐
b. Have you been declared bankrupt within the past 7 years?	☐	☐	☐	☐
c. Have you had property foreclosed upon or given title or deed in lieu thereof in the last 7 years?	☐	☐	☐	☐
d. Are you a party to a lawsuit?	☐	☐	☐	☐
e. Have you directly or indirectly been obligated on any loan which resulted in foreclosure, transfer of title in lieu of foreclosure, or judgment? (This would include such loans as home mortgage loans, SBA loans, home improvement loans, educational loans, manufactured (mobile) home loans, any mortgage, financial obligation, bond, or loan guarantee. If "Yes," provide details, including date, name, and address of Lender, FHA or VA case number, if any, and reasons for the action.)	☐	☐	☐	☐

Uniform Residential Loan Application

VII. DETAILS OF TRANSACTION		VIII. DECLARATIONS					
		If you answer "Yes" to any questions a through i, please use continuation sheet for explanation.	Borrower		Co-Borrower		
			Yes	No	Yes	No	
j. Subordinate financing		f. Are you presently delinquent or in default on any Federal debt or any other loan, mortgage, financial obligation, bond, or loan guarantee?	☐	☐	☐	☐	
k. Borrower's closing costs paid by Seller		g. Are you obligated to pay alimony, child support, or separate maintenance?	☐	☐	☐	☐	
		h. Is any part of the down payment borrowed?	☐	☐	☐	☐	
l. Other Credits (explain)		i. Are you a co-maker or endorser on a note?	☐	☐	☐	☐	
m. Loan amount (exclude PMI, MIP, Funding Fee financed)		j. Are you a U.S. citizen?	☐	☐	☐	☐	
		k. Are you a permanent resident alien?	☐	☐	☐	☐	
n. PMI, MIP, Funding Fee financed		l. **Do you intend to occupy the property as your primary residence?** If Yes," complete question m below.	☐	☐	☐	☐	
o. Loan amount (add m & n)							
p. Cash from/to Borrower (subtract j, k, l & o from i)		m. Have you had an ownership interest in a property in the last three years? (1) What type of property did you own—principal residence (PR), second home (SH), or investment property (IP)? (2) How did you hold title to the home— by yourself (S), jointly with your spouse (SP), or jointly with another person (O)?	☐	☐	☐	☐	

IX. ACKNOWLEDGEMENT AND AGREEMENT

Each of the undersigned specifically represents to Lender and to Lender's actual or potential agents, brokers, processors, attorneys, insurers, servicers, successors and assigns and agrees and acknowledges that: (1) the information provided in this application is true and correct as of the date set forth opposite my signature and that any intentional or negligent misrepresentation of this information contained in this application may result in civil liability, including monetary damages, to any person who may suffer any loss due to reliance upon any misrepresentation that I have made on this application, and/or in criminal penalties including, but not limited to, fine or imprisonment or both under the provisions of Title 18, United States Code, Sec. 1001, et seq.; (2) the loan requested pursuant to this application (the "Loan") will be secured by a mortgage or deed of trust on the property described in this application; (3) the property will not be used for any illegal or prohibited purpose or use; (4) all statements made in this application are made for the purpose of obtaining a residential mortgage loan; (5) the property will be occupied as indicated in this application; (6) the Lender, its servicers, successors or assigns may retain the original and/or an electronic record of this application, whether or not the Loan is approved; (7) the Lender and its agents, brokers, insurers, servicers, successors, and assigns may continuously rely on the information contained in the application, and I am obligated to amend and/or supplement the information provided in this application if any of the material facts that I have represented herein should change prior to closing of the Loan; (8) in the event that my payments on the Loan become delinquent, the Lender, its servicers, successors or assigns may, in addition to any other rights and remedies that it may have relating to such delinquency, report my name and account information to one or more consumer reporting agencies; (9) ownership of the Loan and/or administration of the Loan account may be transferred with such notice as may be required by law; (10) neither Lender nor its agents, brokers, insurers, servicers, successors or assigns has made any representation or warranty, express or implied, to me regarding the property or the condition or value of the property; and (11) my transmission of this application as an "electronic record" containing my "electronic signature," as those terms are defined in applicable federal and/or state laws (excluding audio and video recordings), or my facsimile transmission of this application containing a facsimile of my signature, shall be as effective, enforceable and valid as if a paper version of this application were delivered containing my original written signature.

<u>Acknowledgement</u>. Each of the undersigned hereby acknowledges that any owner of the Loan, its servicers, successors and assigns, may verify or reverify any information contained in this application or obtain any information or data relating to the Loan, for any legitimate business purpose through any source, including a source named in this application or a consumer reporting agency.

Borrower's Signature X	Date	Co-Borrower's Signature X	Date

X. INFORMATION FOR GOVERNMENT MONITORING PURPOSES

The following information is requested by the Federal Government for certain types of loans related to a dwelling in order to monitor the lender's compliance with equal credit opportunity, fair housing and home mortgage disclosure laws. You are not required to furnish this information, but are encouraged to do so. The law provides that a lender may not discriminate either on the basis of this information, or on whether you choose to furnish it. If you furnish the information, please provide both ethnicity and race. For race, you may check more than one designation. If you do not furnish ethnicity, race, or sex, under Federal regulations, this lender is required to note the information on the basis of visual observation and surname if you have made this application in person. If you do not wish to furnish the information, please check the box below. (Lender must review the above material to assure that the disclosures satisfy all requirements to which the lender is subject under applicable state law for the particular type of loan applied for.)

BORROWER	☐ I do not wish to furnish this information		CO-BORROWER	☐ I do not wish to furnish this information	
Ethnicity:	☐ Hispanic or Latino	☐ Not Hispanic or Latino	**Ethnicity:**	☐ Hispanic or Latino	☐ Not Hispanic or Latino
Race:	☐ American Indian or Alaska Native ☐ Native Hawaiian or Other Pacific Islander	☐ Asian ☐ Black or African American ☐ White	**Race:**	☐ American Indian or Alaska Native ☐ Native Hawaiian or Other Pacific Islander	☐ Asian ☐ Black or African American ☐ White
Sex:	☐ Female ☐ Male		**Sex:**	☐ Female ☐ Male	

To be Completed by Loan Originator:
This information was provided:
☐ In a face-to-face interview
☐ In a telephone interview
☐ By the applicant and submitted by fax or mail
☐ By the applicant and submitted via e-mail or the Internet

Loan Originator's Signature X		Date
Loan Originator's Name (print or type)	Loan Originator Identifier	Loan Originator's Phone Number (including area code)
Loan Origination Company's Name	Loan Origination Company Identifier	Loan Origination Company's Address

Uniform Residential Loan Application
Freddie Mac Form 65 7/05 (rev.6/09)

670   Appendix

CONTINUATION SHEET/RESIDENTIAL LOAN APPLICATION

Use this continuation sheet if you need more space to complete the Residential Loan Application. Mark **B** f or Borrower or **C** for Co-Borrower.	Borrower:	Agency Case Number:
	Co-Borrower:	Lender Case Number:

I/We fully understand that it is a Federal crime punishable by fine or imprisonment, or both, to knowingly make any false statements concerning any of the above facts as applicable under the provisions of Title 18, United States Code, Section 1001, et seq.

Borrower's Signature X	Date	Co-Borrower's Signature X	Date

Uniform Residential Loan Application
Freddie Mac Form 65   7/05 (rev.6/09)   Fannie Mae Form 1003   7/05 (rev.6/09)

Source: www.efanniemae.com

Appendix 671

*To be completed by the **Lender:***
Lender Loan No./Universal Loan Identifier _____ Agency Case No. _____

Uniform Residential Loan Application

Verify and complete the information on this application. If you are applying for this loan with others, each additional Borrower must provide information as directed by your Lender.

Section 1: Borrower Information. This section asks about your personal information and your income from employment and other sources, such as retirement, that you want considered to qualify for this loan.

1a. Personal Information

Name *(First, Middle, Last, Suffix)* _____

Alternate Names – *List any names by which you are known or any names under which credit was previously received (First, Middle, Last, Suffix)*

Social Security Number _____ – ____ – _____
(or Individual Taxpayer Identification Number)

Date of Birth *(mm/dd/yyyy)*
____/____/_____

Citizenship
○ U.S. Citizen
○ Permanent Resident Alien
○ Non-Permanent Resident Alien

Type of Credit
○ I am applying for **individual credit.**
○ I am applying for **joint credit.** Total Number of Borrowers: _____
  Each Borrower intends to apply for joint credit. *Your initials:* _____

List Name(s) of Other Borrower(s) Applying for this Loan
(First, Middle, Last, Suffix)

Marital Status
○ Married
○ Separated
○ Unmarried
 (Single, Divorced, Widowed, Civil Union, Domestic Partnership, Registered Reciprocal Beneficiary Relationship)

Dependents *(not listed by another Borrower)*
Number _____
Ages _____

Contact Information
Home Phone (____) ____ – _____
Cell Phone (____) ____ – _____
Work Phone (____) ____ – _____ Ext. _____
Email _____

Current Address
Street _____ Unit # _____
City _____ State _____ ZIP _____ Country _____
How Long at Current Address? ____ Years ____ Months **Housing** ○ No primary housing expense ○ Own ○ Rent ($ _____ /month)

If at Current Address for LESS than 2 years, list Former Address ☐ *Does not apply*
Street _____ Unit # _____
City _____ State _____ ZIP _____ Country _____
How Long at Former Address? ____ Years ____ Months **Housing** ○ No primary housing expense ○ Own ○ Rent ($ _____ /month)

Mailing Address – *if different from Current Address* ☐ *Does not apply*
Street _____ Unit # _____
City _____ State _____ ZIP _____ Country _____

Military Service – Did you (or your deceased spouse) ever serve, or are you currently serving, in the United States Armed Forces? ○ NO ○ YES
If YES, check all that apply: ☐ Currently serving on active duty with projected expiration date of service/tour ____ / _____ *(mm/yyyy)*
☐ Currently retired, discharged, or separated from service
☐ Only period of service was as a non-activated member of the Reserve or National Guard
☐ Surviving spouse

Language Preference – **Your loan transaction is likely to be conducted in English.** This question requests information to see if communications are available to assist you in your preferred language. Please be aware that communications may NOT be available in your preferred language.

Optional – Mark the language you would prefer, if available:
○ English ○ Chinese ○ Korean ○ Spanish ○ Tagalog ○ Vietnamese ○ Other: _____ ○ I do not wish to respond

Your answer will NOT negatively affect your mortgage application. Your answer does not mean the Lender or Other Loan Participants agree to communicate or provide documents in your preferred language. However, it may let them assist you or direct you to persons who can assist you.

Language assistance and resources may be available through housing counseling agencies approved by the U.S. Department of Housing and Urban Development. To find a housing counseling agency, contact one of the following Federal government agencies:

- U.S. Department of Housing and Urban Development (HUD) at (800) 569-4287 or www.hud.gov/counseling.
- Consumer Financial Protection Bureau (CFPB) at (855) 411-2372 or www.consumerfinance.gov/find-a-housing-counselor.

Uniform Residential Loan Application
Freddie Mac Form 65 • Fannie Mae Form 1003
Effective 07/2019

1b. Current Employment/Self Employment and Income   ☐ Does not apply

Employer or Business Name _____ Phone (___) ___ – _____
Street _____
City _____ State _____ ZIP _____

Position or Title _____
Start Date ____ / _____ (mm/yyyy)
How long in this line of work? _____ Years _____ Months

Check if this statement applies:
☐ I am employed by a family member, property seller, real estate agent, or other party to the transaction.

☐ Check if you are the Business Owner or Self-Employed
○ I have an ownership share of less than 25%.
○ I have an ownership share of 25% or more.

Monthly Income (or Loss)
$ _____

Gross Monthly Income
Base $_____ /month
Overtime $_____ /month
Bonus $_____ /month
Commission $_____ /month
Military Entitlements $_____ /month
Other $_____ /month
TOTAL $_____ **/month**

1c. IF APPLICABLE, Complete Information for Additional Employment/Self Employment and Income   ☐ Does not apply

Employer or Business Name _____ Phone (___) ___ – _____
Street _____
City _____ State _____ ZIP _____

Position or Title _____
Start Date ____ / _____ (mm/yyyy)
How long in this line of work? _____ Years _____ Months

Check if this statement applies:
☐ I am employed by a family member, property seller, real estate agent, or other party to the transaction.

☐ Check if you are the Business Owner or Self-Employed
○ I have an ownership share of less than 25%.
○ I have an ownership share of 25% or more.

Monthly Income (or Loss)
$ _____

Gross Monthly Income
Base $_____ /month
Overtime $_____ /month
Bonus $_____ /month
Commission $_____ /month
Military Entitlements $_____ /month
Other $_____ /month
TOTAL $_____ **/month**

1d. IF APPLICABLE, Complete Information for Previous Employment/Self Employment and Income   ☐ Does not apply

Provide at least 2 years of current and previous employment and income.

Employer or Business Name _____
Street _____
City _____ State _____ ZIP _____
Position or Title _____
Start Date ____ / _____ (mm/yyyy)   **End Date** ____ / _____ (mm/yyyy)

☐ Check if you were the Business Owner or Self-Employed

Previous Gross Monthly Income
$ _____

1e. Income from Other Sources   ☐ Does not apply

Include income from other sources below. Under Income Source, choose from the sources listed here:

- Alimony
- Automobile Allowance
- Boarder Income
- Capital Gains
- Child Support
- Disability
- Foster Care
- Housing or Parsonage
- Interest and Dividends
- Mortgage Credit Certificate
- Mortgage Differential Payments
- Notes Receivable
- Public Assistance
- Retirement (e.g., Pension, IRA)
- Royalty Payments
- Separate Maintenance
- Social Security
- Trust
- Unemployment Benefits
- VA Compensation
- Other

NOTE: Reveal alimony, child support, separate maintenance, or other income ONLY IF you want it considered in determining your qualification for this loan.

Income Source – use list above	**Monthly Income**
	$
	$
	$
Provide TOTAL Amount Here	$

Borrower Name: _____
Uniform Residential Loan Application
Freddie Mac Form 65 • Fannie Mae Form 1003
Effective 07/2019

Appendix 673

Section 2: Financial Information — Assets and Liabilities.
This section asks about things you own that are worth money and that you want considered to qualify for this loan. It then asks about your liabilities (or debts) that you pay each month, such as credit cards, alimony, or other expenses.

2a. Assets – Bank Accounts, Retirement, and Other Accounts You Have

Include all accounts below. Under Account Type, choose from the types listed here:
- Checking
- Savings
- Money Market
- Certificate of Deposit
- Mutual Fund
- Stocks
- Stock Options
- Bonds
- Retirement (e.g., 401k, IRA)
- Bridge Loan Proceeds
- Individual Development Account
- Trust Account
- Cash Value of Life Insurance *(used for the transaction)*

Account Type – use list above	Financial Institution	Account Number	Cash or Market Value
			$
			$
			$
			$
			$
		Provide TOTAL Amount Here	$

2b. Other Assets You Have ☐ Does not apply

Include all other assets below. Under Asset Type, choose from the types listed here:
- Earnest Money
- Proceeds from Sale of Non-Real Estate Asset
- Proceeds from Real Estate Property to be sold on or before closing
- Sweat Equity
- Employer Assistance
- Rent Credit
- Secured Borrowed Funds
- Trade Equity
- Unsecured Borrowed Funds
- Other

Asset Type – use list above	Cash or Market Value
	$
	$
	$
Provide TOTAL Amount Here	$

2c. Liabilities – Credit Cards, Other Debts, and Leases that You Owe ☐ Does not apply

List all liabilities below (except real estate) and include deferred payments. Under Account Type, choose from the types listed here:
- Revolving (e.g., credit cards)
- Installment (e.g., car, student, personal loans)
- Open 30-Day (balance paid monthly)
- Lease (not real estate)
- Other

Account Type – use list above	Company Name	Account Number	Unpaid Balance	To be paid off at or before closing	Monthly Payment
			$	☐	$
			$	☐	$
			$	☐	$
			$	☐	$
			$	☐	$

2d. Other Liabilities and Expenses ☐ Does not apply

Include all other liabilities and expenses below. Choose from the types listed here:
- Alimony
- Child Support
- Separate Maintenance
- Job Related Expenses
- Other

	Monthly Payment
	$
	$
	$

Borrower Name: _____
Uniform Residential Loan Application
Freddie Mac Form 65 • Fannie Mae Form 1003
Effective 07/2019

Section 3: Financial Information — Real Estate.
This section asks you to list all properties you currently own and what you owe on them. ☐ *I do not own any real estate*

3a. Property You Own   If you are refinancing, list the property you are refinancing FIRST.

Address
Street _____ Unit # _____ City _____ State _____ ZIP _____

Property Value	Status: Sold, Pending Sale, or Retained	Monthly Insurance, Taxes, Association Dues, etc. if not included in Monthly Mortgage Payment	For Investment Property Only	
			Monthly Rental Income	For LENDER to calculate: Net Monthly Rental Income
$		$	$	$

Mortgage Loans on this Property ☐ *Does not apply*

Creditor Name	Account Number	Monthly Mortgage Payment	Unpaid Balance	To be paid off at or before closing	Type: FHA, VA, Conventional, USDA-RD, Other	Credit Limit (if applicable)
		$	$	☐		$
		$	$	☐		$

3b. IF APPLICABLE, Complete Information for Additional Property   ☐ *Does not apply*

Address
Street _____ Unit # _____ City _____ State _____ ZIP _____

Property Value	Status: Sold, Pending Sale, or Retained	Monthly Insurance, Taxes, Association Dues, etc. if not included in Monthly Mortgage Payment	For Investment Property Only	
			Monthly Rental Income	For LENDER to calculate: Net Monthly Rental Income
$		$	$	$

Mortgage Loans on this Property ☐ *Does not apply*

Creditor Name	Account Number	Monthly Mortgage Payment	Unpaid Balance	To be paid off at or before closing	Type: FHA, VA, Conventional, USDA-RD, Other	Credit Limit (if applicable)
		$	$	☐		$
		$	$	☐		$

3c. IF APPLICABLE, Complete Information for Additional Property   ☐ *Does not apply*

Address
Street _____ Unit # _____ City _____ State _____ ZIP _____

Property Value	Status: Sold, Pending Sale, or Retained	Monthly Insurance, Taxes, Association Dues, etc. if not included in Monthly Mortgage Payment	For Investment Property Only	
			Monthly Rental Income	For LENDER to calculate: Net Monthly Rental Income
$		$	$	$

Mortgage Loans on this Property ☐ *Does not apply*

Creditor Name	Account Number	Monthly Mortgage Payment	Unpaid Balance	To be paid off at or before closing	Type: FHA, VA, Conventional, USDA-RD, Other	Credit Limit (if applicable)
		$	$	☐		$
		$	$	☐		$

Borrower Name: _____

Uniform Residential Loan Application
Freddie Mac Form 65 • Fannie Mae Form 1003
Effective 07/2019

Appendix   675

Section 4: Loan and Property Information.
This section asks about the loan's purpose and the property you want to purchase or refinance.

4a. Loan and Property Information

Loan Amount $ _____   **Loan Purpose** ○ Purchase   ○ Refinance   ○ Other *(specify)* _____

Property Address Street _____ Unit # _____

City _____ State _____ ZIP _____

County _____ Number of Units _____ **Property Value** $ _____

Occupancy   ○ Primary Residence   ○ Second Home   ○ Investment Property   ○ FHA Secondary Residence

1. **Mixed-Use Property.** If you will occupy the property, will you set aside space within the property to operate your own business? *(e.g., daycare facility, medical office, beauty/barber shop)*   ○ NO   ○ YES
2. **Manufactured Home.** Is the property a manufactured home? *(e.g., a factory built dwelling built on a permanent chassis)*   ○ NO   ○ YES

4b. Other New Mortgage Loans on the Property You are Buying or Refinancing   ☐ *Does not apply*

Creditor Name	Lien Type	Monthly Payment	Loan Amount/ Amount to be Drawn	Credit Limit *(if applicable)*
	○ First Lien ○ Subordinate Lien	$	$	$
	○ First Lien ○ Subordinate Lien	$	$	$

4c. Rental Income on the Property You Want to Purchase   For Purchase Only   ☐ *Does not apply*

Complete if the property is a 2-4 Unit Primary Residence or an Investment Property	Amount
Expected Monthly Rental Income	$
For LENDER to calculate: Expected Net Monthly Rental Income	$

4d. Gifts or Grants You Have Been Given or Will Receive for this Loan   ☐ *Does not apply*

Include all gifts and grants below. Under Source, choose from the sources listed here:
- Relative
- Unmarried Partner
- Employer
- Religious Nonprofit
- Community Nonprofit
- Federal Agency
- State Agency
- Local Agency
- Other

Asset Type: Cash Gift, Gift of Equity, Grant	Deposited/Not Deposited	**Source** – *use list above*	Cash or Market Value
	○ Deposited ○ Not Deposited		$
	○ Deposited ○ Not Deposited		$

Borrower Name: _____
Uniform Residential Loan Application
Freddie Mac Form 65 • Fannie Mae Form 1003
Effective 07/2019

Section 5: Declarations.
This section asks you specific questions about the property, your funding, and your past financial history.

5a. About this Property and Your Money for this Loan

A. Will you occupy the property as your primary residence?	○ NO ○ YES
If YES, have you had an ownership interest in another property in the last three years?	○ NO ○ YES
If YES, complete (1) and (2) below:	
(1) What type of property did you own: primary residence (PR), FHA secondary residence (SR), second home (SH), or investment property (IP)?	_____
(2) How did you hold title to the property: by yourself (S), jointly with your spouse (SP), or jointly with another person (O)?	_____
B. If this is a Purchase Transaction: Do you have a family relationship or business affiliation with the seller of the property?	○ NO ○ YES
C. Are you borrowing any money for this real estate transaction (*e.g., money for your closing costs or down payment*) or obtaining any money from another party, such as the seller or realtor, that you have not disclosed on this loan application?	○ NO ○ YES
If YES, what is the amount of this money?	$ _____
D. 1. Have you or will you be applying for a mortgage loan on another property (not the property securing this loan) on or before closing this transaction that is not disclosed on this loan application?	○ NO ○ YES
2. Have you or will you be applying for any new credit (*e.g., installment loan, credit card, etc.*) on or before closing this loan that is not disclosed on this application?	○ NO ○ YES
E. Will this property be subject to a lien that could take priority over the first mortgage lien, such as a clean energy lien paid through your property taxes (*e.g., the Property Assessed Clean Energy Program*)?	○ NO ○ YES

5b. About Your Finances

F. Are you a co-signer or guarantor on any debt or loan that is not disclosed on this application?	○ NO ○ YES
G. Are there any outstanding judgments against you?	○ NO ○ YES
H. Are you currently delinquent or in default on a federal debt?	○ NO ○ YES
I. Are you a party to a lawsuit in which you potentially have any personal financial liability?	○ NO ○ YES
J. Have you conveyed title to any property in lieu of foreclosure in the past 7 years?	○ NO ○ YES
K. Within the past 7 years, have you completed a pre-foreclosure sale or short sale, whereby the property was sold to a third party and the Lender agreed to accept less than the outstanding mortgage balance due?	○ NO ○ YES
L. Have you had property foreclosed upon in the last 7 years?	○ NO ○ YES
M. Have you declared bankruptcy within the past 7 years? If YES, identify the type(s) of bankruptcy: ☐ Chapter 7 ☐ Chapter 11 ☐ Chapter 12 ☐ Chapter 13	○ NO ○ YES

Borrower Name: _____

Uniform Residential Loan Application
Freddie Mac Form 65 • Fannie Mae Form 1003
Effective 07/2019

Section 6: Acknowledgments and Agreements. This section tells you about your legal obligations when you sign this application.

Acknowledgments and Agreements

I agree to, acknowledge, and represent the following statements to:
- The Lender (this includes the Lender's agents, service providers and any of their successors and assigns); AND
- Other Loan Participants (this includes any actual or potential owners of a loan resulting from this application (the "Loan"), or acquirers of any beneficial or other interest in the Loan, any mortgage insurer, guarantor, any servicers or service providers of the Loan, and any of their successors and assigns).

By signing below, I agree to, acknowledge, and represent the following statements about:

(1) The Complete Information for this Application
- The information I have provided in this application is true, accurate, and complete as of the date I signed this application.
- If the information I submitted changes or I have new information before closing of the Loan, I must change and supplement this application or any real estate sales contract, including providing any updated/supplemented real estate sales contract.
- For purchase transactions: The terms and conditions of any real estate sales contract signed by me in connection with this application are true, accurate, and complete to the best of my knowledge and belief. I have not entered into any other agreement, written or oral, in connection with this real estate transaction.
- The Lender and Other Loan Participants may rely on the information contained in the application before and after closing of the Loan.
- Any intentional or negligent misrepresentation of information may result in the imposition of:
   (a) civil liability on me, including monetary damages, if a person suffers any loss because the person relied on any misrepresentation that I have made on this application, and/or
   (b) criminal penalties on me including, but not limited to, fine or imprisonment or both under the provisions of federal law (18 U.S.C. §§ 1001 *et seq.*).

(2) The Property's Security
- The Loan I have applied for in this application will be secured by a mortgage or deed of trust which provides the Lender a security interest in the property described in this application.

(3) The Property's Appraisal, Value, and Condition
- Any appraisal or value of the property obtained by the Lender is for use by the Lender and Other Loan Participants.
- The Lender and Other Loan Participants have not made any representation or warranty, express or implied, to me about the property, its condition, or its value.

(4) Electronic Records and Signatures
- The Lender and Other Loan Participants may keep any paper record and/or electronic record of this application, whether or not the Loan is approved.
- If this application is created as (or converted into) an "electronic application", I consent to the use of "electronic records" and "electronic signatures" as the terms are defined in and governed by applicable federal and/or state electronic transactions laws.
- I intend to sign and have signed this application either using my: (a) electronic signature; or (b) a written signature and agree that if a paper version of this application is converted into an electronic application, the application will be an electronic record, and the representation of my written signature on this application will be my binding electronic signature.
- I agree that the application, if delivered or transmitted to the Lender or Other Loan Participants as an electronic record with my electronic signature, will be as effective and enforceable as a paper application signed by me in writing.

(5) Delinquency
- The Lender and Other Loan Participants may report information about my account to credit bureaus. Late payments, missed payments, or other defaults on my account may be reflected in my credit report and will likely affect my credit score.
- If I have trouble making my payments I understand that I may contact a HUD-approved housing counseling organization for advice about actions I can take to meet my mortgage obligations.

(6) Use and Sharing of Information
I understand and acknowledge that the Lender and Other Loan Participants can obtain, use, and share the loan application, a consumer credit report, and related documentation for purposes permitted by applicable laws.

Borrower Signature _____ Date *(mm/dd/yyyy)* ____/____/____

Borrower Signature _____ Date *(mm/dd/yyyy)* ____/____/____

Uniform Residential Loan Application
Freddie Mac Form 65 • Fannie Mae Form 1003
Effective 07/2019

Section 7: Demographic Information. This section asks about your ethnicity, sex, and race.

Demographic Information of Borrower

The purpose of collecting this information is to help ensure that all applicants are treated fairly and that the housing needs of communities and neighborhoods are being fulfilled. For residential mortgage lending, Federal law requires that we ask applicants for their demographic information (ethnicity, sex, and race) in order to monitor our compliance with equal credit opportunity, fair housing, and home mortgage disclosure laws. You are not required to provide this information, but are encouraged to do so. You may select one or more designations for "Ethnicity" and one or more designations for "Race." **The law provides that we may not discriminate** on the basis of this information, or on whether you choose to provide it. However, if you choose not to provide the information and you have made this application in person, Federal regulations require us to note your ethnicity, sex, and race on the basis of visual observation or surname. The law also provides that we may not discriminate on the basis of age or marital status information you provide in this application. If you do not wish to provide some or all of this information, please check below.

Ethnicity: *Check one or more*
☐ Hispanic or Latino
  ☐ Mexican ☐ Puerto Rican ☐ Cuban
  ☐ Other Hispanic or Latino – *Print origin:*
  _____
  For example: Argentinean, Colombian, Dominican, Nicaraguan, Salvadoran, Spaniard, and so on.
☐ Not Hispanic or Latino
☐ I do not wish to provide this information

Sex
☐ Female
☐ Male
☐ I do not wish to provide this information

Race: *Check one or more*
☐ American Indian or Alaska Native – *Print name of enrolled or principal tribe:* _____
☐ Asian
  ☐ Asian Indian ☐ Chinese ☐ Filipino
  ☐ Japanese ☐ Korean ☐ Vietnamese
  ☐ Other Asian – *Print race:* _____
  For example: Hmong, Laotian, Thai, Pakistani, Cambodian, and so on.
☐ Black or African American
☐ Native Hawaiian or Other Pacific Islander
  ☐ Native Hawaiian ☐ Guamanian or Chamorro ☐ Samoan
  ☐ Other Pacific Islander – *Print race:*
  _____
  For example: Fijian, Tongan, and so on.
☐ White
☐ I do not wish to provide this information

To Be Completed by Financial Institution (*for application taken in person*):

Was the ethnicity of the Borrower collected on the basis of visual observation or surname? ○ NO ○ YES
Was the sex of the Borrower collected on the basis of visual observation or surname? ○ NO ○ YES
Was the race of the Borrower collected on the basis of visual observation or surname? ○ NO ○ YES

The Demographic Information was provided through:

○ Face-to-Face Interview (*includes Electronic Media w/ Video Component*) ○ Telephone Interview ○ Fax or Mail ○ Email or Internet

Section 8: Loan Originator Information.

Loan Originator Information

Loan Originator Organization Name _____
Address _____
Loan Originator Organization NMLSR ID# _____ State License ID# _____
Loan Originator Name _____
Loan Originator NMLSR ID# _____ State License ID# _____
Email _____ Phone (_____) _____ – _____

Signature _____ Date (*mm/dd/yyyy*) _____ / _____ / _____

Borrower Name: _____
Uniform Residential Loan Application
Freddie Mac Form 65 • Fannie Mae Form 1003
Effective 07/2019

Source: www.efanniemae.com

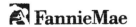

Request for Verification of Deposit

Privacy Act Notice: This information is to be used by the agency collecting it or its assignees in determining whether you qualify as a prospective mortgagor under its program. It will not be disclosed outside the agency except as required and permitted by law. You do not have to provide this information, but if you do not your application for approval as a prospective mortgagor or borrower may be delayed or rejected. The information requested in this form is authorized by Title 38, USC, Chapter 37 (If VA); by 12 USC, Section 1701 et.seq. (If HUD/FHA); by 42 USC, Section 1452b (if HUD/CPD); and Title 42 USC, 1471 et.seq. or 7 USC, 1921 et.seq. (If USDA/FmHA).

Instructions: Lender — Complete Items 1 through 8. Have applicant(s) complete Item 9. Forward directly to depository named in Item 1.
Depository — Please complete Items 10 through 18 and return DIRECTLY to lender named in Item 2.
The form is to be transmitted directly to the lender and is not to be transmitted through the applicant(s) or any other party.

Part I — Request

1. To (Name and address of depository)

2. From (Name and address of lender)

I certify that this verification has been sent directly to the bank or depository and has not passed through the hands of the applicant or any other party.

3. Signature of lender

4. Title

5. Date

6. Lender's No. (Optional)

7. Information To Be Verified

Type of Account	Account in Name of	Account Number	Balance
			$
			$
			$

To Depository: I/We have applied for a mortgage loan and stated in my financial statement that the balance on deposit with you is as shown above. You are authorized to verify this information and to supply the lender identified above with the information requested in Items 10 through 13. Your response is solely a matter of courtesy for which no responsibility is attached to your institution or any of your officers.

8. Name and Address of Applicant(s)

9. Signature of Applicant(s)

To Be Completed by Depository
Part II — Verification of Depository

10. Deposit Accounts of Applicant(s)

Type of Account	Account Number	Current Balance	Average Balance For Previous Two Months	Date Opened
		$	$	
		$	$	
		$	$	

11. Loans Outstanding To Applicant(s)

Loan Number	Date of Loan	Original Amount	Current Balance	Installments (Monthly/Quarterly)		Secured By	Number of Late Payments
		$	$	$	per		
		$	$	$	per		
		$	$	$	per		

12. Please include any additional information which may be of assistance in determination of credit worthiness. (Please include information on loans paid-in-full in Item 11 above.)

13. If the name(s) on the account(s) differ from those listed in Item 7, please supply the name(s) on the account(s) as reflected by your records.

Part III — Authorized Signature
Federal statutes provide severe penalties for any fraud, intentional misrepresentation, or criminal connivance or conspiracy purposed to influence the issuance of any guaranty or insurance by the VA Secretary, the U.S.D.A., FmHA/FHA Commissioner, or the HUD/CPD Assistant Secretary.

14. Signature of Depository Representative

15. Title (Please print or type)

16. Date

17. Please print or type name signed in item 14

18. Phone No.

Fannie Mae
Form 1006   July 96

Instructions

Verification of Deposit

The lender uses this form for applications for conventional first or second mortgages to verify the cash deposits that the applicant listed on the loan application.

Copies

Original only.

Printing Instructions

This for must be printed on letter size paper, using portrait format. When printing this form, you must use the "shrink to fit" option in the Adobe Acrobat print dialogue box.

Instructions

The applicant must sign this form to authorize his or her depository to release the requested information. Separate forms should be sent to each depository named in the loan application. However, rather than having the applicant sign multiple forms, the lender may have the applicant sign a borower's signature authorization form, which gives the lender blanket authorization to request the information it needs to evaluate the applicant's creditworthiness. When the lender uses this type of blanket authorization, it must attach a copy of the authorization form to each Form 1006 it sends to the depository institutions in which the applicant has accounts.

For First Mortgages

The lender must send the request directly to the depositories. We will not permit the borrower to hand-carry the verification form. The lender must receive the completed form directly from the depositories. The completed form should not be passed through the applicant or any other party.

For Second Mortgages

The borrower may hand-carry the verification to the depositories. The depositories will then be required to mail this form directly to the lender.

The lender retains the original form in its mortgage file.

Instructions Page

Source: www.efanniemae.com

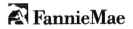

Request for Verification of Employment

Privacy Act Notice: This information is to be used by the agency collecting it or its assignees in determining whether you qualify as a prospective mortgagor under its program. It will not be disclosed outside the agency except as required and permitted by law. You do not have to provide this information, but if you do not your application for approval as a prospective mortgagor or borrower may be delayed or rejected. The information requested in this form is authorized by Title 38, USC, Chapter 37 (if VA); by 12 USC, Section 1701 et. seq. (if HUD/FHA); by 42 USC, Section 1452b (if HUD/CPD); and Title 42 USC, 1471 et. seq., or 7 USC, 1921 et. seq. (if USDA/FmHA).

Instructions: Lender — Complete items 1 through 7. Have applicant complete item 8. Forward directly to employer named in item 1.
Employer — Please complete either Part II or Part III as applicable. Complete Part IV and return directly to lender named in item 2.
The form is to be transmitted directly to the lender and is not to be transmitted through the applicant or any other party.

Part I — Request

1. To (Name and address of employer)
2. From (Name and address of lender)

I certify that this verification has been sent directly to the employer and has not passed through the hands of the applicant or any other interested party.

3. Signature of Lender
4. Title
5. Date
6. Lender's Number (Optional)

I have applied for a mortgage loan and stated that I am now or was formerly employed by you. My signature below authorizes verification of this information.

7. Name and Address of Applicant (include employee or badge number)
8. Signature of Applicant

Part II — Verification of Present Employment

9. Applicant's Date of Employment
10. Present Position
11. Probability of Continued Employment

12A. Current **Gross Base Pay** (Enter Amount and Check Period)
☐ Annual ☐ Hourly
☐ Monthly ☐ Other (Specify)
$ _____ ☐ Weekly

13. For Military Personnel Only

	Pay Grade	
Type		Monthly Amount
Base Pay		$
Rations		$
Flight or Hazard		$
Clothing		$
Quarters		$
Pro Pay		$
Overseas or Combat		$
Variable Housing Allowance		$

14. If Overtime or Bonus is Applicable, Is Its Continuance Likely?
Overtime ☐ Yes ☐ No
Bonus ☐ Yes ☐ No

15. If paid hourly — average hours per week

16. Date of applicant's next pay increase

17. Projected amount of next pay increase

18. Date of applicant's last pay increase

19. Amount of last pay increase

12B. Gross Earnings

Type	Year To Date	Past Year	Past Year
Base Pay	Thru _____ $	$	$
Overtime	$	$	$
Commissions	$	$	$
Bonus	$	$	$
Total	$ 0.00	$ 0.00	$ 0.00

20. Remarks (If employee was off work for any length of time, please indicate time period and reason)

Part III — Verification of Previous Employment

21. Date Hired
22. Date Terminated
23. Salary/Wage at Termination Per (Year) (Month) (Week)
Base _____ Overtime _____ Commissions _____ Bonus _____
24. Reason for Leaving
25. Position Held

Part IV — Authorized Signature

Federal statutes provide severe penalties for any fraud, intentional misrepresentation, or criminal connivance or conspiracy purposed to influence the issuance of any guaranty or insurance by the VA Secretary, the U.S.D.A., FmHA/FHA Commissioner, or the HUD/CPD Assistant Secretary.

26. Signature of Employer
27. Title (Please print or type)
28. Date
29. Print or type name signed in Item 26
30. Phone No.

Fannie Mae
Form 1005 July 96

Instructions

Verification of Employment

The lender uses this form for applications for conventional first or second mortgages to verify the applicant's past and present employment status.

Copies
Original only.

Printing Instructions
This form must be printed on letter size paper, using portrait format.

Instructions
The applicant must sign this form to authorize his or her employer(s) to release the requested information. Separate forms should be sent to each firm that employed the applicant in the past two years. However, rather than having an applicant sign multiple forms, the lender may have the applicant sign a borrower's signature authorization form, which gives the lender blanket authorization to request the information it needs to evaluate the applicant's creditworthiness. When the lender uses this type of blanket authorization, it must attach a copy of the authorization form to each Form 1005 it sends to the applicant's employer(s).

For First Mortgages:
The lender must send the request directly to the employers. We will not permit the borrower to hand-carry the verification form. The lender must receive the completed form back directly from the employers. The completed form should not be passed through the applicant or any other party.

For Second Mortgages:
The borrower may hand-carry the verification to the employer. The employer will then be required to mail this form directly to the lender.

The lender retains the original form in its mortgage file.

Instructions Page

Source: www.efanniemae.com

SAMPLE - FHA Gift Letter

I, _____, hereby certify that I/We given/will give a gift of
    DONOR NAME

$_____ to _____, my _____,
  GIFT AMOUNT   RECIPIENT NAME   RELATIONSHIP

on _____ to be applied toward the purchase of the above property.
      DATE

I/We certify that this is a bona fide gift and that there is no obligation, expressed or implied, to repay this sum in cash or other services of any kind now or in the future.

I/We understand that this gift will require documentation, including proof that I/we have given the gift from the account listed below, and proof that the funds have been received by the applicant or the applicant's attorney prior to settlement.

THE LENDER may confirm that the funds came from the account listed below:

Name of Depository or other Source: _____

           Address of Same: _____

                                     _____

            Account Number: _____

I/We Certify that the funds given to the homebuyer were not made available to the donor from any person or entity with an interest in the sale of the property including the seller, real estate agent or broker, builder, loan officer, or any entity associated with them.

_____   _____
SIGNATURE OF DONOR   TELEPHONE NUMBER

_____
DONOR ADDRESS

_____   _____
    SIGNATURE OF RECIPIENT   SIGNATURE OF RECIPIENT

NECESSARY DOCUMENTATION FOR ALL FHA/VA LOANS:
Verification that gift funds were deposited into applicant's bank account (bank statement, interim printout) or attorney trust account (escrow letter)
    (1)   Donor's withdrawal slip or cancelled check (or other <u>conclusive evidence</u> funds came from donor's account)
WE ARE AWARE OF THE FOLLOWING:
I/We fully understand that it is a Federal crime punishable by fine or imprisonment, or both, to knowingly make any false statements when applying for this mortgage, as applicable under the provision of Title 18, United States Code, Section 1014 and Section 1010.

SAMPLE "GENERAL MORTGAGE COMPANY DISCLOSURE" NOTICE   Page 1 of 5

Applicant(s) Name: _____

Subject Property Address: _____

Affidavit of Occupancy
Applicant(s) hereby certify and acknowledge that, upon taking title to the real property described above, their occupancy status will be as follows:

_____ Primary Residence - Occupied by Applicant(s) within 30 days of closing.

_____ Secondary Residence - To be occupied by Applicant(s) at least 15 days yearly, as second home (vacation, etc.), while maintaining principal residence elsewhere. [Please check this box if you plan to establish it as your primary residence at a future date (e.g., retirement)].

_____ Investment Property - Not owner occupied. Purchased as an investment to be held or rented.

The Applicant(s) acknowledge it is a federal crime punishable by fine or imprisonment, or both, to knowingly make any false statement concerning this loan application as applicable under the provisions of Title 18, United States Code, Section 1014.

Anti-Coercion Statement
The insurance laws of this state provide that the lender may not require the applicant to take insurance through any particular insurance agent or company to protect the mortgaged property. The applicant, subjected to the rules adopted by the Insurance Commissioner, has the right to have the insurance placed with an insurance agent or company of his choice, provided the company meets the requirement of the lender. The lender has the right to designate reasonable financial requirements as to the company and the adequacy of the coverage.
I have read the foregoing statement, or the rules of the Insurance Commissioner relative hereto, and understand my rights and privileges and those of the lender relative to the placing of such insurance.

Fair Credit Reporting Act
An investigation will be made as to the credit standing of all individuals seeking credit in this application. The nature and scope of any investigation will be furnished to you upon written request made within a reasonable period of time. In the event of credit denial due to an unfavorable consumer report, you will be advised of the identity of the Consumer Reporting Agency making such report and of your right to request within sixty (60) days the reason for the adverse action, pursuant to provisions of section 615(b) of the Fair Credit Reporting Act.

REQUIRED USE DISCLOSURE
The following list contains Information about some of the settlement service providers that we select and require you to use. In each case, the estimate of the cost of the settlement service provider's service given is based on our experience of the amount charged by the settlement service provider in the last twelve months.

A. Credit Reporting Companies
Credit Scoring Company
9876 Joyous Shinning Ave., Suite 600
Van Nuys, CA 91406
(800) 555-1212

B. Flood Insurance Map Review
C. Tax Service
D. Review Appraiser The above service providers are selected from a list that the final lender controls.
E. Appraiser: The appraiser for your loan is selected from a list we control.

F. Private Mortgage Insurance Companies
The final lender selects the private Mortgage Insurance Company for your loan from a list of controlled and approved by the Federal National Mortgage Association (ENMA) or the Federal Home Loan Mortgage Corporate EoE (FHLMC). The premium schedules charged by all companies are regulated by the State Insurance Commissioner's Office.

CALIFORNIA CREDIT SCORE NOTICE*
In connection with your application for a home loan, the lender must disclose to you the score that a credit bureau distributed to users and the lender used in connection with your home loan, and the key factors affecting your credit scores.
The credit score is a computer-generated summary calculated at the time of the request and based on information a credit bureau or lender has on file. The scores are based on data about your credit history and payment patterns. Credit scores are important because they are used to assist the lender in determining whether you will obtain a loan. They may also be used to determine what interest rate you may be offered on the mortgage. Credit scores can change over time, depending on your conduct, how your credit history and payment patterns change, and how credit scoring technologies change.
Because the score is based on information in your credit history, it is very important that you review the credit-related information that is being furnished to make sure it is accurate. Credit records may vary from one company to another.
If you have questions about your credit score or the credit information that is furnished to you, contact the credit bureau at the address and telephone number provided with this notice, or contact the lender, if the lender developed or generated the credit score. The credit bureau plays no part in the decision to take any action on the loan application and is unable to provide you with specific reasons for the decision on a loan application. If you have questions concerning the terms of the loan, contact the lender.
The credit score will be provided by the following: Credit Scoring Company, 9876 Joyous Shinning Ave., Suite 600, Van Nuys, CA 91406
Information about credit scores can be obtained on the Internet at www.myfico.com or by calling the Fair Isaac and Company credit score help line at 1-800-777-2066

Your Credit score(s) is: _____

X _____   X _____
Borrower signature   Date   Co-Borrower signature   Date

GENERAL MORTGAGE COMPANY DISCLOSURE NOTICE

MORTGAGE BROKER FEE DISCLOSURE _____

General Mortgage Company Representative   Date

You have applied to a mortgage broker for a residential mortgage loan. The mortgage broker will submit your application for a residential mortgage loan to a participating lender with which it from time to time contracts upon such terms and conditions as you may request or a lender may require. The lenders have asked that this form be furnished to you to clarify the rote of mortgage brokers. This form supplements other disclosures or agreements required by law that you should receive from the mortgage broker concerning your application.

Section 1. Nature Of Relationship: In connection with this mortgage loan:
* - The mortgage broker may be acting as an independent contractor and not your agent. If you are unsure of the nature of your relationship, please ask the mortgage broker for clarification.
*- The mortgage broker has separate independent contractor agreements -with various
*- While the mortgage broker seeks to assist you in meeting your financial needs, it does not distribute the products of all lenders or in the market and cannot guarantee the lowest price or best terms available in the market.

Section 2. The Broker's Compensation: The lenders whose loan products are distributed by the mortgage broker generally provide their loan products to the mortgage -broker at a wholesale rate.
*- The retail price a mortgage broker offers you - your interest rate, total points and fees - -will include the broker's compensation.
*- In some cases the mortgage broker may be paid all of its compensation by either you or the lender.
*- Alternatively, the mortgage broker may be paid a portion of its compensation by both you and the lender. For example, in some cases, if you would rather pay a lower interest rate, you may pay higher up4ront points and fees.
* Also, in some cases, if you would rather pay less up-front, you may wish to have some or all of your fees paid directly by the lender, which will result in a higher interest rate and higher monthly loan payments then you would otherwise be required to pay.
* The mortgage broker also may be paid by the lender based on (I) the value of the Mortgage Loan or related servicing rights in the market place or (ii) other services, goods or facilities performed or provided by the mortgage broker to the lender.

You may work with the mortgage broker to select the method in which it receives its compensation depending on your financial needs, subject to the lender's loan program requirements and credit underwriting guidelines.

The amount of fees and charges that you pay in connection with your loan will be estimated on your Good Faith Estimate. The final amount will be disclosed on your HUD-1 or HUD-I A Settlement Statement.
By signing below, applicant(s) acknowledge that you have read and understand this document. By your signature, you also acknowledge that you have received a copy of this document.

Acknowledgment of Mortgage Loan Applicant(s)
I/We have read and understood the disclosure; and understand that the disclosure is a required part of the mortgage application as evidenced by my/our signature(s) below. I/We also acknowledge that I/We have received a copy of this document.

THE HOUSING FINANCIAL DISCRIMINATION ACT OF 1977 FAIR LENDING NOTICE

It is illegal to discriminate in the provisions of or in the availability of financial assistance because of the consideration of:
1. Trends, characteristics or conditions in the neighborhood or geographic area surrounding a housing accommodation, unless the financial institution can demonstrate in the particular case that such consideration is required to avoid an unsafe and unsound business practice; or
2. Race, color, religion, sex, marital status, national origin or ancestry. It is illegal to consider the racial, ethnic, religious or national origin composition of a neighborhood or geographic area surrounding a housing accommodation or whether or not such composition is undergoing change, or is expected to undergo change, in appraising a housing accommodation or
in determining whether or not, or under what terms and conditions, to provide financial assistance. These provisions govern financial assistance for the purpose of the purchase, construction, rehabilitation or refinancing of a one-to-four unit family residence occupied by the owner and for the purpose of the home improvement of any one-to-four unit family residence. If you have any questions about your rights, or if you wish to file a complaint, contact the management of this financial institution or the agency noted below:
DEPARTMENT OF REAL ESTATE - 111 S. NARROW St, ROOM 789, LOS ANGELES, CA 90011
DEPARTMENT OF REAL ESTATE - 666 FERRY ST., ROOM 3456, SAN FRANCISCO, CA 94007

NOTICE OF RIGHT TO RECEIVE COPY OF APPRAISAL REPORT

You have the right to receive a copy of the appraisal report to be obtained in connection with the loan for which you are applying, provided that you have paid for the appraisal. We must receive your written request no later than 30 days after we notify you about the action taken on your application or you withdraw your application. If you would like a copy of the appraisal report, contact:
GENERAL MORTGAGE COMPANY, P.O. BOX 1234, SANTA MONICA, CA 90408

EQUAL CREDIT OPPORTUNITY ACT

The Federal Equal Credit Opportunity Act prohibits creditors from discriminating against credit applicants on the basis of race, color, religion, national origin, sex, marital status, age (provided the applicant has the capacity to enter into a binding contract); because all or part of the applicant's income derives from any public assistance program; or because the applicant has in good faith exercised any right under the Consumer Credit Protection Act. The Federal Agency that GENERAL MORTGAGE COMPANY is required to disclose to you that you need not disclose income from alimony, child support or separate maintenance payment if you choose not to do so. Having made this disclosure to you, we are permitted to inquire if any of the income shown on your application is derived from such a source and to consider the likelihood of consistent payment as we do with any income on which you are relying to qualify for the loan for which you are applying. Administers compliance with this law concerning this company is the: FEDERAL TRADE COMMISSION, PENNSYLVANIA AND 6TH STREET N.W., WASHINGTON, DC 20580

X _____   X _____
Borrower signature   Date   Co-Borrower signature   Date

GENERAL MORTGAGE COMPANY DISCLOSURE NOTICE

SERVICING DISCLOSURE STATEMENT

NOTICE TO MORTGAGE LOAN APPLICANTS: THE RIGHT TO COLLECT YOUR MORTGAGE LOAN PAYMENTS MAY BE TRANSFERRED. FEDERAL LAW GIVES YOU CERTAIN RELATED RIGHTS. IF YOUR LOAN IS MADE, SAVE THIS STATEMENT WITH YOUR LOAN DOCUMENTS. SIGN THE ACKNOWLEDGMENT AT THE END OF THIS STATEMENT ONLY IF YOU UNDERSTAND ITS CONTENTS.

Because you are applying for a mortgage loan covered by the Real Estate Settlement Procedures Act (RESPA) (1 2 U.S.C. Section 2601 et seq.) you have certain rights under that Federal law. This statement tells you about those rights. It also tells you what the chances are that the servicing for this loan may be transferred to a different loan servicer. "Servicing" refers to collecting your principal, interest and escrow account payments, if any. If your loan servicer changes, there are certain procedures that must be followed. This statement generally explains those procedures.

Transfer practices and requirements: If the servicing of your loan is assigned, sold, or transferred to a new servicer, you must be given written notice of that transfer. The present loan servicer must send you notice in writing of the assignment, sale or transfer of the servicing not less than 15 days before the effective date of the transfer. The new loan servicer must also send you notice within 15 days after the effective date of the transfer. The present servicer and the new servicer may combine this information in one notice, so long as the notice is sent to you 15 days before the effective date of transfer. The 15 days period is not applicable if a notice of prospective transfer is provided to you at settlement. The law allows a delay in the time (not more than 30 days after a transfer)
for servicers to notify you, upon the occurrence of certain business emergencies.

Notices must contain certain information. They must contain the effective date of the transfer of the servicing of your loan to the new servicer, and the name, address, and toll-free or collect call telephone number of the new servicer, and toll-free or collect call telephone numbers of a person or department for both your present servicer and your new servicer to answer your questions. During the 60 day period following the effective date of the transfer of the loan servicing, a loan payment received by your old servicer before its due date may not be treated by the new loan servicer as late, and a late fee may not be imposed on you.

Complaint Resolution: Section 6 of RESPA (12 U.S.C. Section 2605) gives you certain consumer rights, whether or not your loan servicing is transferred. If you send a "qualified written request" to your servicer, then your servicer must provide you with a written acknowledgment within 20 Business Days of receipt of your request. A "qualified written request" is a written correspondence, other than notice on a payment coupon or other payment medium supplied by the servicer, which includes your name and account number, and the information regarding your request. Not later than 60 Business Days after receiving your request, your servicer must make any appropriate corrections to your account, or must provide you with a written clarification regarding any dispute. During this 60 Business Day period, your servicer may not provide information to a consumer reporting agency concerning any overdue payment related to such period or qualified written request. A Business Day is any day in which the offices of the business entity are open to the public for carrying on substantially all of its business functions.

Damages and Costs: Section 6 of RESPA also provides for damages and costs for individuals or classes of individuals in circumstances where servicers are shown to have violated the requirements of that Section.

Servicing Transfer Estimates: We will not service your loan. We do not service mortgage loans and we have not serviced mortgage loans in the past three years. We presently intend to assign, sell or transfer the servicing of your mortgage loan. You will be informed about your servicer. This is only our best estimate and it is not binding. Business conditions or other circumstances may affect our future transferring decisions. This information does not include assignments, sales or transfers to affiliates or subsidiaries.

Acknowledgment of Mortgage Loan Applicant(s)
I/We have read and understood the disclosure; and understand that the disclosure is a required part of the mortgage application as evidenced by my/our signature(s) below. I/We also acknowledge that I/We have received a copy of this document.

CALIFORNIA ADDENDUM TO LOAN APPLICATION*

As a result of California's Community property laws*, can anyone, other than you, claim an interest in the property that will secure repayment of the loan?

_____ YES   _____ NO

If yes, who may be able to claim the interest? _____

California law presumes all real property acquired during either a marriage or Registered Domestic Partnership, except as acquired by gift, descent, or devise, to be community property. Therefore, the lender will require that either spouses, or registered domestic partners, sign the security instrument, in order to ensure that is fully enforceable.

This Addendum has been prepared in response to the California Domestic Partner Rights and Responsibilities Act of 2003, effective January1, 2005. The act provides that registered domestic partners shall have equal status under all California laws, administrative regulations, court rules, government policies, common law, or any other provisions or sources of law as are granted to and imposed upon spouses.

You should consult an attorney for specific legal advice regarding homestead rights and for specific legal advice regarding benefits, protections and responsibilities under the California domestic Partners Rights and Responsibilities Act of 2003.

X_____   X_____
Borrower signature   Date   Co-Borrower signature   Date

GENERAL MORTGAGE COMPANY DISCLOSURE NOTICE

PRIVACY POLICY DISCLOSURE (Protection of the Privacy of Personal Non-Public Information)

Respecting and protecting customer privacy is vital to our business. By explaining our Privacy Policy to you, we trust that you will better understand how we keep our customer information private and secure while using it to serve you better. Keeping customer information secure is a top priority, and we are disclosing our policies to help you understand how we handle the personal information about you that we collect and disclose. This notice explains how you can limit our disclosing of personal information about you. The provisions of this notice will apply to former customers as well as current customers unless we state otherwise.

The Privacy Policy explains the Following:
Protecting the confidentiality of our customer information. - Who is covered by the Privacy Policy. - How we gather information. - The types of information we share, why, and with whom. - Opting Out - how to instruct us not to share certain information about you or not to contact you.

Protecting the Confidentiality of Customer Information:
We take our responsibility to protect the privacy and confidentiality of customer information very seriously. We maintain physical, electronic, and procedural safeguards that comply with federal standards to store and secure information about you from unauthorized access, alteration, and destruction. Our control policies, for example, authorize access to customer information only by individuals who need access to do their work. From time to time, we enter into agreements with other companies to provide services to us or make products and services available to you. Under these agreements, the companies may receive information about you but they must safeguard this information, and they may not use it for any other purposes.

Who is Covered by the Privacy Policy:
We provide our Privacy Policy to customers when they conduct business with our company. If we change our privacy policies to permit us to share additional information we have about you, as described below, or to permit disclosures to additional types of parties, you will be notified in advance. This Privacy Policy applies to consumers who are current customers or former customers.

How We Gather Information:
As part of providing you with financial products or services, we may obtain information about you from the following sources:
Applications, forms, and other information that you provide to us, whether in writing, in person, by telephone, electronically, or by any other means. This information may include your name, address, employment information, income, and credit references;
Your transaction with us, our affiliates, or others. This information may include your account balances, payment history, and account usage;
Consumer reporting agencies. This information may include account information and information about your credit worthiness; Public sources. This information may include real estate records, employment records, telephone numbers, etc.

Information We Share:
We may disclose information we have about you as permitted by law. We are required to or we may provide information about you to third-parties without your consent, as permitted by law, such as:
To regulatory authorities and law enforcement officials. - To protect against or prevent actual or potential fraud, unauthorized transactions, claims, or other liability. - To report account activity to credit bureaus. - To consumer reporting agencies. - To respond to a subpoena or court order, judicial process or regulatory authorities. - In connection with a proposed or actual sale, merger, or transfer of all or a portion of a business or an operating unit, etc.
In addition, we may provide information about you to our service providers to help us process your applications or service your accounts. Our service providers may include billing service providers, mail and telephone service companies, lenders, investors, title and escrow companies, appraisal companies, etc.
We may also provide information about you to our service providers to help us perform marketing services. This information provided to these service providers may include the categories of information described above under "How We Gather Information" limited to only that which we deem appropriate for these service providers to carry out their functions.
We do not provide non-public information about you to any company whose products and services are being marketed unless you authorize us to do so. These companies are not allowed to use this information for purposes beyond your specific authorization.

Opting Out
We also may share information about you within our corporate family of office(s). We may share all of the categories of information we gather about you, including identification information (such as your name and address), credit reports (such as your credit history), application information (such as your income or credit references), your account transactions and experiences with us (such as your payment history), and information from other third parties (such as your employment history).
By sharing this information we can better understand your financial needs. We can then send you notification of new products and special promotional offers that you may not otherwise know about. For example, if you originally obtained a mortgage loan with us, we would know that you are a homeowner and may be interested in hearing how a home equity loan may be a better option than an auto loan to finance the purchase of a new car.
You may prohibit the sharing of application and third-party credit-related information within our company or any third-party company at any time. If you would like to limit disclosures of personal information about you as described in this notice, just check the appropriate box or boxes to indicate your privacy choices.

_____ Please do not share personal information about me with non-affiliated third-parties.

_____ Please do not share personal information about me with any of your affiliates except as necessary to effect, administer, process, service or enforce a transaction requested or authorized by myself.

_____ Please do not contact me with offers of products or services by mail.

_____ Please do not contact me with offers of products or services by telephone.

Note for Joint Accounts: Your Opt Out choices will also apply to other individuals who are joint account holders. If these individuals have separate accounts, your Opt Out will not apply to those separate accounts.

X _____   X _____
Borrower signature   Date   Co-Borrower signature   Date

"GENERAL MORTGAGE COMPANY" DISCLOSURE NOTICE

IDENTITY STATEMENT AND DISCLOSURE (Patriot Act Disclosure)

The USA Patriot Act requires all financial institutions to obtain, verify and record information that identifies every customer. Completion of this documentation is required in order to comply with the USA Patriot Act. A completed copy of this information must be retained with the loan file.

Name of Applicant: _____	Name of Applicant: _____
Social Security #: _____	Social Security #: _____
Date of Birth: _____	Date of Birth: _____
Present Address: _____	Present Address: _____
Primary Identification: _____	Primary Identification: _____
Issuing Government/State: _____	Issuing Government/State: _____
Document ID Number: _____	Document ID Number: _____
Issue Date: _____	Issue Date: _____
Expiration Date: _____	Expiration Date: _____
Secondary Identification: _____	Secondary Identification: _____
Issuing Government/State: _____	Issuing Government/State: _____
Document ID Number: _____	Document ID Number: _____
Issue Date: _____	Issue Date: _____
Expiration Date: _____	Expiration Date: _____

BORROWERS' CERTIFICATION AND AUTHORIZATION

The Undersigned certify the following:

1. I/We have applied for a mortgage loan from GENERAL MORTGAGE COMPANY. In applying for the loan, I/We completed a loan application containing various information on the purpose of the loan, the amount and source of the down payment, employment and income information, and the assets and liabilities. I/We certify that all of the information is true and complete. I/We made no misrepresentations in the application or other documents, nor did I/We omit any pertinent information.

2. I/We understand and agree that GENERAL MORTGAGE COMPANY reserves the right to change the mortgage loan review processes to a full documentation program. This may include verifying the information provided on the application with the employer and/or the financial institution.

3. I/We fully understand that it is a Federal crime punishable by fine or imprisonment, or both, to knowingly make any false statements when applying for this mortgage, as applicable under the provisions of Title 18, United States Code, Section 1014.

4. You are hereby authorized to release any information required by GENERAL MORTGAGE COMPANY to complete the processing of the loan request. Necessary credit information may include employment verification, savings deposits, checking accounts, consumer credit balances, payments and history including mortgage payment records and balances. A photographic or carbon copy of this authorization (being a photographic or carbon copy of the signature(s) of the undersigned) may be deemed to be the equivalent of the original and may be used as a duplicate original. Your prompt reply will help expedite my real estate transaction.

X _____   X _____
Borrower signature   Date   Co-Borrower signature   Date

* Many states have disclosures or notices that are required in addition to those mandated by Federal mortgage origination laws. Those required by the state of California have been used for illustration purposes in this sample general disclosure notice for mortgage applicants that is for a fictitious mortgage lender referred to as "General Mortgage Company"

Source: General Mortgage Company, San Diego, CA

U.S. Department of Housing and Urban Development

NOTICE TO PURCHASERS OF HOUSING CONSTRUCTED BEFORE 1978.

WATCH OUT FOR LEAD-BASED PAINT POISONING!

If the home you intend to purchase was built before 1978, it may contain lead-based paint. About three out of every four pre-1978 buildings have lead-based paint.

> **YOU NEED TO READ THIS NOTICE ABOUT LEAD**

WHAT IT LEAD POISONING?

Lead poisoning means having high concentrations of lead in the body.
LEAD CAN:

- Cause major health problems, especially in children under 7 years old.
- Damage a child's brain, nervous system, kidneys, hearing, or coordination.
- Affect learning.
- Cause behavior problems, blindness, and even death.
- Cause problems in pregnancy and affect a baby's normal development.

WHO GETS LEAD POISONING?

Anyone can get it, but children under 7 are at the greatest risk, because their bodies are not fully grown and are easily damaged. The risk is worse if the child:

- Lives in an older home (built/constructed before 1978, and even more so before 1960).
- Does not eat regular meals (an empty stomach accepts lead more easily).
- Does not eat enough foods with iron or calcium.
- Has parents who work in lead-related jobs.
- Has played in the same places as brothers, sisters, and friends who have been lead poisoned. (Lead poison cannot be spread from person to person. It comes from contact with lead).

Women of childbearing age are also at risk, because lead poisoning can cause miscarriages, premature births, and the poison can be passed onto their unborn babies.

WHERE DOES IT COME FROM?

The lead hazards that children most often touch are lead dust, leaded soil, loose chips and chewable surfaces painted with lead-based paint. A child may be harmed when it puts into its mouth; toys, pacifiers, or hands that have leaded soil or lead dust on them. Lead also comes from:

- Moving parts of windows and doors that can make lead dust and chips.
- Lead-based paint on windows, doors, wood trim, walls and cabinets in kitchens and bathrooms, on porches, stairs, railings, fire escapes and lamp posts.
- Soil next to exterior of buildings that have been painted with lead-based paint and leaded gasoline dust in soil near busy streets.
- Drinking water (pipes and solder).
- Parents who may bring lead dust home from work on skin, clothes, and hair.
- Colored newsprint and car batteries.
- Highly glazed pottery and cookware from other countries.
- Removing old paint when refinishing furniture.

In recent years some uses of lead in products that could cause lead poisoning have been reduced or banned. This is true for lead in gasoline, lead in solder used in water pipes, and lead in paint. Still, a great deal of lead remains in and around older homes, and lead-based paint and accompanying lead dust are seen as the major sources.

HOW DO I KNOW IF MY CHILD IS AFFECTED?

Is your child:

- cranky?
- vomiting?
- tired?
- unwilling to eat or play?
- complaining of stomach aches or headaches?
- unable to concentrate?
- hyperactive?
- playing with children who have these symptoms?

These can be signs of lead poisoning. However, your children might not show these signs and yet be poisoned; only your clinic or Doctor can test for sure.

WHAT CAN I DO ABOUT IT?

Your child should first be tested for lead in the blood between six months and one year old. Ask the clinic or your doctor to do it during a regular checkup. Your doctor will tell you how often you should have your child tested after that. A small amount of lead in the blood may not make your child seem very sick, but it can affect how well he or she can learn. If your child does have high amounts of lead in the blood, you should seek treatment and have your home tested for lead-based paint and lead dust.

HOW DO I KNOW IF MY HOME HAS LEAD-BASED PAINT?

The HUD inspection does not determine whether a home actually has lead-based paint. It only identifies whether there is defective paint in a home that might have lead-based paint. Therefore, the only way you can know for sure is to have the home tested by a qualified firm or laboratory. Both the interior and exterior should be tested. You should contact your local health or environmental office for help.

WHAT DO I DO IF MY HOME DOES HAVE LEAD?

Do not try to get rid of lead-based paint yourself, you could make things worse for you and your family. If your home contains lead-based paint, contact a company that specializes in lead-based paint abatement. Have professionals do the job correctly and safely. This may cost thousands of dollars, depending on the amount of lead-based paint and lead dust found in your home, but it will also protect you and your children from the effects of lead poisoning. In the meantime, there are things you can do immediately to protect your child:

- Keep your child away from paint chips and dust.
- Wet-mop floors and wipe down surfaces often, especially where floors and walls meet.
- Be sure to clean the space where the window sash rests on the sill. Keeping the floor clear of paint chips, dust and dirt is easy and very important. Do not sweep or vacuum lead-based paint chips or lead dust with an ordinary vacuum cleaner. Lead dust is so fine it will pass through a vacuum cleaner bag and spread into the air you breathe.
- Make sure your children wash their hands frequently and always before eating.
- Wash toys, teething rings, and pacifiers frequently.

WILL HUD INSURE A MORTGAGE LOAN ON A HOME WITH LEAD-BASED PAINT?

HUD will insure a mortgage on a house even if it has lead-based paint. If you purchase a property with lead-based paint, HUD will not remove it. You will have to pay for the cost of removal yourself.

ACKNOWLEDGEMENT

I acknowledge that I have received and read a copy of this Notice before signing the sales contract to purchase my property.

_____ _____ _____ _____
Signature   Date   Signature   Date

_____ _____ _____ _____
Signature   Date   Signature   Date

Source: HUD.gov

Disclosure of Information on Lead-Based Paint and/or Lead-Based Paint Hazards

Lead Warning Statement

Every purchaser of any interest in residential real property on which a residential dwelling was built prior to 1978 is notified that such property may present exposure to lead from lead-based paint that may place young children at risk of developing lead poisoning. Lead poisoning in young children may produce permanent neurological damage, including learning disabilities, reduced intelligence quotient, behavioral problems, and impaired memory. Lead poisoning also poses a particular risk to pregnant women. The seller of any interest in residential real property is required to provide the buyer with any information on lead-based paint hazards from risk assessments or inspections in the seller's possession and notify the buyer of any known lead-based paint hazards. A risk assessment or inspection for possible lead-based paint hazards is recommended prior to purchase.

Seller's Disclosure

(a) Presence of lead-based paint and/or lead-based paint hazards (check (i) or (ii) below):

  (i) _____ Known lead-based paint and/or lead-based paint hazards are present in the housing (explain).

  _____

  (ii) _____ Seller has no knowledge of lead-based paint and/or lead-based paint hazards in the housing.

(b) Records and reports available to the seller (check (i) or (ii) below):

  (i) _____ Seller has provided the purchaser with all available records and reports pertaining to lead-based paint and/or lead-based paint hazards in the housing (list documents below).

  _____

  (ii) _____ Seller has no reports or records pertaining to lead-based paint and/or lead-based paint hazards in the housing.

Purchaser's Acknowledgment (initial)

(c) _____ Purchaser has received copies of all information listed above.

(d) _____ Purchaser has received the pamphlet *Protect Your Family from Lead in Your Home*.

(e) Purchaser has (check (i) or (ii) below):

  (i) _____ received a 10-day opportunity (or mutually agreed upon period) to conduct a risk assessment or inspection for the presence of lead-based paint and/or lead-based paint hazards; or

  (ii) _____ waived the opportunity to conduct a risk assessment or inspection for the presence of lead-based paint and/or lead-based paint hazards.

Agent's Acknowledgment (initial)

(f) _____ Agent has informed the seller of the seller's obligations under 42 U.S.C. 4852(d) and is aware of his/her responsibility to ensure compliance.

Certification of Accuracy

The following parties have reviewed the information above and certify, to the best of their knowledge, that the information they have provided is true and accurate.

Seller	Date	Seller	Date
Purchaser	Date	Purchaser	Date
Agent	Date	Agent	Date

Source: HUD.gov

Appendix

Uniform Residential Appraisal Report File

The purpose of this summary appraisal report is to provide the lender/client with an accurate, and adequately supported, opinion of the market value of the subject property.

SUBJECT

Property Address		City		State	Zip Code
Borrower		Owner of Public Record		County	

Legal Description
Assessor's Parcel #   Tax Year   R.E. Taxes $
Neighborhood Name   Map Reference   Census Tract
Occupant ☐ Owner ☐ Tenant ☐ Vacant   Special Assessments $ ☐ PUD   HOA $ ☐ per year ☐ per month
Property Rights Appraised ☐ Fee Simple ☐ Leasehold ☐ Other (describe)
Assignment Type ☐ Purchase Transaction ☐ Refinance Transaction ☐ Other (describe)
Lender/Client   Address
Is the subject property currently offered for sale or has it been offered for sale in the twelve months prior to the effective date of this appraisal? ☐ Yes ☐ No
Report data source(s) used, offering price(s), and date(s).

CONTRACT

I ☐ did ☐ did not analyze the contract for sale for the subject purchase transaction. Explain the results of the analysis of the contract for sale or why the analysis was not performed.

Contract Price $ Date of Contract   Is the property seller the owner of public record? ☐ Yes ☐ No Data Source(s)
Is there any financial assistance (loan charges, sale concessions, gift or downpayment assistance, etc.) to be paid by any party on behalf of the borrower? ☐ Yes ☐ No
If Yes, report the total dollar amount and describe the items to be paid.

NEIGHBORHOOD

Note: Race and the racial composition of the neighborhood are not appraisal factors.

Neighborhood Characteristics	One-Unit Housing Trends	One-Unit Housing	Present Land Use %
Location ☐ Urban ☐ Suburban ☐ Rural	Property Values ☐ Increasing ☐ Stable ☐ Declining	PRICE AGE	One-Unit %
Built-Up ☐ Over 75% ☐ 25-75% ☐ Under 25%	Demand/Supply ☐ Shortage ☐ In Balance ☐ Over Supply	$ (000) (yrs)	2-4 Unit %
Growth ☐ Rapid ☐ Stable ☐ Slow	Marketing Time ☐ Under 3 mths ☐ 3-6 mths ☐ Over 6 mths	Low	Multi-Family %
Neighborhood Boundaries		High	Commercial %
		Pred.	Other %

Neighborhood Description

Market Conditions (including support for the above conclusions)

SITE

Dimensions   Area   Shape   View
Specific Zoning Classification   Zoning Description
Zoning Compliance ☐ Legal ☐ Legal Nonconforming (Grandfathered Use) ☐ No Zoning ☐ Illegal (describe)
Is the highest and best use of the subject property as improved (or as proposed per plans and specifications) the present use? ☐ Yes ☐ No If No, describe

Utilities	Public	Other (describe)		Public	Other (describe)	Off-site Improvements—Type	Public	Private
Electricity	☐		Water	☐		Street	☐	☐
Gas	☐		Sanitary Sewer	☐		Alley	☐	☐

FEMA Special Flood Hazard Area ☐ Yes ☐ No FEMA Flood Zone   FEMA Map #   FEMA Map Date
Are the utilities and off-site improvements typical for the market area? ☐ Yes ☐ No If No, describe
Are there any adverse site conditions or external factors (easements, encroachments, environmental conditions, land uses, etc.)? ☐ Yes ☐ No If Yes, describe

IMPROVEMENTS

General Description	Foundation	Exterior Description materials/condition	Interior materials/condition
Units ☐ One ☐ One with Accessory Unit	☐ Concrete Slab ☐ Crawl Space	Foundation Walls	Floors
# of Stories	☐ Full Basement ☐ Partial Basement	Exterior Walls	Walls
Type ☐ Det. ☐ Att. ☐ S-Det./End Unit	Basement Area sq. ft.	Roof Surface	Trim/Finish
☐ Existing ☐ Proposed ☐ Under Const.	Basement Finish %	Gutters & Downspouts	Bath Floor
Design (Style)	☐ Outside Entry/Exit ☐ Sump Pump	Window Type	Bath Wainscot
Year Built	Evidence of ☐ Infestation	Storm Sash/Insulated	Car Storage ☐ None
Effective Age (Yrs)	☐ Dampness ☐ Settlement	Screens	☐ Driveway # of Cars
Attic ☐ None	Heating ☐ FWA ☐ HWBB ☐ Radiant	Amenities ☐ Woodstove(s) #	Driveway Surface
☐ Drop Stair ☐ Stairs	☐ Other Fuel	☐ Fireplace(s) # ☐ Fence	☐ Garage # of Cars
☐ Floor ☐ Scuttle	Cooling ☐ Central Air Conditioning	☐ Patio/Deck ☐ Porch	☐ Carport # of Cars
☐ Finished ☐ Heated	☐ Individual ☐ Other	☐ Pool ☐ Other	☐ Att. ☐ Det. ☐ Built-in

Appliances ☐ Refrigerator ☐ Range/Oven ☐ Dishwasher ☐ Disposal ☐ Microwave ☐ Washer/Dryer ☐ Other (describe)
Finished area **above** grade contains: Rooms   Bedrooms   Bath(s)   Square Feet of Gross Living Area Above Grade
Additional features (special energy efficient items, etc.).

Describe the condition of the property (including needed repairs, deterioration, renovations, remodeling, etc.).

Are there any physical deficiencies or adverse conditions that affect the livability, soundness, or structural integrity of the property? ☐ Yes ☐ No If Yes, describe

Does the property generally conform to the neighborhood (functional utility, style, condition, use, construction, etc.)? ☐ Yes ☐ No If No, describe

Freddie Mac Form 70 March 2005   Fannie Mae Form 1004 March 2005

Uniform Residential Appraisal Report

File #

There are _____ comparable properties currently offered for sale in the subject neighborhood ranging in price from $_____ to $_____.
There are _____ comparable sales in the subject neighborhood within the past twelve months ranging in sale price from $_____ to $_____.

FEATURE	SUBJECT	COMPARABLE SALE # 1		COMPARABLE SALE # 2		COMPARABLE SALE # 3	
Address							
Proximity to Subject							
Sale Price	$		$		$		$
Sale Price/Gross Liv. Area	$ sq. ft.	$ sq. ft.		$ sq. ft.		$ sq. ft.	
Data Source(s)							
Verification Source(s)							
VALUE ADJUSTMENTS	DESCRIPTION	DESCRIPTION	+(-) $ Adjustment	DESCRIPTION	+(-) $ Adjustment	DESCRIPTION	+(-) $ Adjustment
Sale or Financing Concessions							
Date of Sale/Time							
Location							
Leasehold/Fee Simple							
Site							
View							
Design (Style)							
Quality of Construction							
Actual Age							
Condition							
Above Grade Room Count	Total Bdrms. Baths	Total Bdrms. Baths		Total Bdrms. Baths		Total Bdrms. Baths	
Gross Living Area	sq. ft.	sq. ft.		sq. ft.		sq. ft.	
Basement & Finished Rooms Below Grade							
Functional Utility							
Heating/Cooling							
Energy Efficient Items							
Garage/Carport							
Porch/Patio/Deck							
Net Adjustment (Total)		☐ + ☐ -	$	☐ + ☐ -	$	☐ + ☐ -	$
Adjusted Sale Price of Comparables		Net Adj. % Gross Adj. %	$	Net Adj. % Gross Adj. %	$	Net Adj. % Gross Adj. %	$

I ☐ did ☐ did not research the sale or transfer history of the subject property and comparable sales. If not, explain

My research ☐ did ☐ did not reveal any prior sales or transfers of the subject property for the three years prior to the effective date of this appraisal.
Data source(s)
My research ☐ did ☐ did not reveal any prior sales or transfers of the comparable sales for the year prior to the date of sale of the comparable sale.
Data source(s)
Report the results of the research and analysis of the prior sale or transfer history of the subject property and comparable sales (report additional prior sales on page 3).

ITEM	SUBJECT	COMPARABLE SALE # 1	COMPARABLE SALE # 2	COMPARABLE SALE # 3
Date of Prior Sale/Transfer				
Price of Prior Sale/Transfer				
Data Source(s)				
Effective Date of Data Source(s)				

Analysis of prior sale or transfer history of the subject property and comparable sales

Summary of Sales Comparison Approach

Indicated Value by Sales Comparison Approach $

Indicated Value by: Sales Comparison Approach $ Cost Approach (if developed) $ Income Approach (if developed) $

This appraisal is made ☐ "as is", ☐ subject to completion per plans and specifications on the basis of a hypothetical condition that the improvements have been completed, ☐ subject to the following repairs or alterations on the basis of a hypothetical condition that the repairs or alterations have been completed, or ☐ subject to the following required inspection based on the extraordinary assumption that the condition or deficiency does not require alteration or repair:

Based on a complete visual inspection of the interior and exterior areas of the subject property, defined scope of work, statement of assumptions and limiting conditions, and appraiser's certification, my (our) opinion of the market value, as defined, of the real property that is the subject of this report is
$_____, as of _____, which is the date of inspection and the effective date of this appraisal.

Freddie Mac Form 70 March 2005   Fannie Mae Form 1004 March 2005

Uniform Residential Appraisal Report   File

ADDITIONAL COMMENTS

COST APPROACH TO VALUE (not required by Fannie Mae)

Provide adequate information for the lender/client to replicate the below cost figures and calculations.

Support for the opinion of site value (summary of comparable land sales or other methods for estimating site value)

ESTIMATED ☐ REPRODUCTION OR ☐ REPLACEMENT COST NEW	OPINION OF SITE VALUE .... = $
Source of cost data	Dwelling Sq. Ft. @ $ .... = $
Quality rating from cost service Effective date of cost data	Sq. Ft. @ $ .... = $
Comments on Cost Approach (gross living area calculations, depreciation, etc.)	
	Garage/Carport Sq. Ft. @ $ .... = $
	Total Estimate of Cost-New .... = $
	Less Physical Functional External
	Depreciation =$( )
	Depreciated Cost of Improvements... = $
	"As-is" Value of Site Improvements... = $
Estimated Remaining Economic Life (HUD and VA only) Years	Indicated Value By Cost Approach .... = $

INCOME APPROACH TO VALUE (not required by Fannie Mae)

Estimated Monthly Market Rent $ X Gross Rent Multiplier   = $ Indicated Value by Income Approach

Summary of Income Approach (including support for market rent and GRM)

PROJECT INFORMATION FOR PUDs (if applicable)

Is the developer/builder in control of the Homeowners' Association (HOA)? ☐ Yes ☐ No   Unit type(s) ☐ Detached ☐ Attached

Provide the following information for PUDs ONLY if the developer/builder is in control of the HOA and the subject property is an attached dwelling unit.

Legal name of project

Total number of phases   Total number of units   Total number of units sold

Total number of units rented   Total number of units for sale   Data source(s)

Was the project created by the conversion of an existing building(s) into a PUD? ☐ Yes ☐ No   If Yes, date of conversion

Does the project contain any multi-dwelling units? ☐ Yes ☐ No   Data source(s)

Are the units, common elements, and recreation facilities complete? ☐ Yes ☐ No   If No, describe the status of completion.

Are the common elements leased to or by the Homeowners' Association? ☐ Yes ☐ No   If Yes, describe the rental terms and options.

Describe common elements and recreational facilities

Freddie Mac Form 70   March 2005   Fannie Mae Form 1004   March 2005

Uniform Residential Appraisal Report

File #

This report form is designed to report an appraisal of a one-unit property or a one-unit property with an accessory unit; including a unit in a planned unit development (PUD). This report form is not designed to report an appraisal of a manufactured home or a unit in a condominium or cooperative project.

This appraisal report is subject to the following scope of work, intended use, intended user, definition of market value, statement of assumptions and limiting conditions, and certifications. Modifications, additions, or deletions to the intended use, intended user, definition of market value, or assumptions and limiting conditions are not permitted. The appraiser may expand the scope of work to include any additional research or analysis necessary based on the complexity of this appraisal assignment. Modifications or deletions to the certifications are also not permitted. However, additional certifications that do not constitute material alterations to this appraisal report, such as those required by law or those related to the appraiser's continuing education or membership in an appraisal organization, are permitted.

SCOPE OF WORK: The scope of work for this appraisal is defined by the complexity of this appraisal assignment and the reporting requirements of this appraisal report form, including the following definition of market value, statement of assumptions and limiting conditions, and certifications. The appraiser must, at a minimum: (1) perform a complete visual inspection of the interior and exterior areas of the subject property, (2) inspect the neighborhood, (3) inspect each of the comparable sales from at least the street, (4) research, verify, and analyze data from reliable public and/or private sources, and (5) report his or her analysis, opinions, and conclusions in this appraisal report.

INTENDED USE: The intended use of this appraisal report is for the lender/client to evaluate the property that is the subject of this appraisal for a mortgage finance transaction.

INTENDED USER: The intended user of this appraisal report is the lender/client.

DEFINITION OF MARKET VALUE: The most probable price which a property should bring in a competitive and open market under all conditions requisite to a fair sale, the buyer and seller, each acting prudently, knowledgeably and assuming the price is not affected by undue stimulus. Implicit in this definition is the consummation of a sale as of a specified date and the passing of title from seller to buyer under conditions whereby: (1) buyer and seller are typically motivated; (2) both parties are well informed or well advised, and each acting in what he or she considers his or her own best interest; (3) a reasonable time is allowed for exposure in the open market; (4) payment is made in terms of cash in U. S. dollars or in terms of financial arrangements comparable thereto; and (5) the price represents the normal consideration for the property sold unaffected by special or creative financing or sales concessions* granted by anyone associated with the sale.

*Adjustments to the comparables must be made for special or creative financing or sales concessions. No adjustments are necessary for those costs which are normally paid by sellers as a result of tradition or law in a market area; these costs are readily identifiable since the seller pays these costs in virtually all sales transactions. Special or creative financing adjustments can be made to the comparable property by comparisons to financing terms offered by a third party institutional lender that is not already involved in the property or transaction. Any adjustment should not be calculated on a mechanical dollar for dollar cost of the financing or concession but the dollar amount of any adjustment should approximate the market's reaction to the financing or concessions based on the appraiser's judgment.

STATEMENT OF ASSUMPTIONS AND LIMITING CONDITIONS: The appraiser's certification in this report is subject to the following assumptions and limiting conditions:

1. The appraiser will not be responsible for matters of a legal nature that affect either the property being appraised or the title to it, except for information that he or she became aware of during the research involved in performing this appraisal. The appraiser assumes that the title is good and marketable and will not render any opinions about the title.

2. The appraiser has provided a sketch in this appraisal report to show the approximate dimensions of the improvements. The sketch is included only to assist the reader in visualizing the property and understanding the appraiser's determination of its size.

3. The appraiser has examined the available flood maps that are provided by the Federal Emergency Management Agency (or other data sources) and has noted in this appraisal report whether any portion of the subject site is located in an identified Special Flood Hazard Area. Because the appraiser is not a surveyor, he or she makes no guarantees, express or implied, regarding this determination.

4. The appraiser will not give testimony or appear in court because he or she made an appraisal of the property in question, unless specific arrangements to do so have been made beforehand, or as otherwise required by law.

5. The appraiser has noted in this appraisal report any adverse conditions (such as needed repairs, deterioration, the presence of hazardous wastes, toxic substances, etc.) observed during the inspection of the subject property or that he or she became aware of during the research involved in performing this appraisal. Unless otherwise stated in this appraisal report, the appraiser has no knowledge of any hidden or unapparent physical deficiencies or adverse conditions of the property (such as, but not limited to, needed repairs, deterioration, the presence of hazardous wastes, toxic substances, adverse environmental conditions, etc.) that would make the property less valuable, and has assumed that there are no such conditions and makes no guarantees or warranties, express or implied. The appraiser will not be responsible for any such conditions that do exist or for any engineering or testing that might be required to discover whether such conditions exist. Because the appraiser is not an expert in the field of environmental hazards, this appraisal report must not be considered as an environmental assessment of the property.

6. The appraiser has based his or her appraisal report and valuation conclusion for an appraisal that is subject to satisfactory completion, repairs, or alterations on the assumption that the completion, repairs, or alterations of the subject property will be performed in a professional manner.

Uniform Residential Appraisal Report

File #

APPRAISER'S CERTIFICATION: The Appraiser certifies and agrees that:

1. I have, at a minimum, developed and reported this appraisal in accordance with the scope of work requirements stated in this appraisal report.

2. I performed a complete visual inspection of the interior and exterior areas of the subject property. I reported the condition of the improvements in factual, specific terms. I identified and reported the physical deficiencies that could affect the livability, soundness, or structural integrity of the property.

3. I performed this appraisal in accordance with the requirements of the Uniform Standards of Professional Appraisal Practice that were adopted and promulgated by the Appraisal Standards Board of The Appraisal Foundation and that were in place at the time this appraisal report was prepared.

4. I developed my opinion of the market value of the real property that is the subject of this report based on the sales comparison approach to value. I have adequate comparable market data to develop a reliable sales comparison approach for this appraisal assignment. I further certify that I considered the cost and income approaches to value but did not develop them, unless otherwise indicated in this report.

5. I researched, verified, analyzed, and reported on any current agreement for sale for the subject property, any offering for sale of the subject property in the twelve months prior to the effective date of this appraisal, and the prior sales of the subject property for a minimum of three years prior to the effective date of this appraisal, unless otherwise indicated in this report.

6. I researched, verified, analyzed, and reported on the prior sales of the comparable sales for a minimum of one year prior to the date of sale of the comparable sale, unless otherwise indicated in this report.

7. I selected and used comparable sales that are locationally, physically, and functionally the most similar to the subject property.

8. I have not used comparable sales that were the result of combining a land sale with the contract purchase price of a home that has been built or will be built on the land.

9. I have reported adjustments to the comparable sales that reflect the market's reaction to the differences between the subject property and the comparable sales.

10. I verified, from a disinterested source, all information in this report that was provided by parties who have a financial interest in the sale or financing of the subject property.

11. I have knowledge and experience in appraising this type of property in this market area.

12. I am aware of, and have access to, the necessary and appropriate public and private data sources, such as multiple listing services, tax assessment records, public land records and other such data sources for the area in which the property is located.

13. I obtained the information, estimates, and opinions furnished by other parties and expressed in this appraisal report from reliable sources that I believe to be true and correct.

14. I have taken into consideration the factors that have an impact on value with respect to the subject neighborhood, subject property, and the proximity of the subject property to adverse influences in the development of my opinion of market value. I have noted in this appraisal report any adverse conditions (such as, but not limited to, needed repairs, deterioration, the presence of hazardous wastes, toxic substances, adverse environmental conditions, etc.) observed during the inspection of the subject property or that I became aware of during the research involved in performing this appraisal. I have considered these adverse conditions in my analysis of the property value, and have reported on the effect of the conditions on the value and marketability of the subject property.

15. I have not knowingly withheld any significant information from this appraisal report and, to the best of my knowledge, all statements and information in this appraisal report are true and correct.

16. I stated in this appraisal report my own personal, unbiased, and professional analysis, opinions, and conclusions, which are subject only to the assumptions and limiting conditions in this appraisal report.

17. I have no present or prospective interest in the property that is the subject of this report, and I have no present or prospective personal interest or bias with respect to the participants in the transaction. I did not base, either partially or completely, my analysis and/or opinion of market value in this appraisal report on the race, color, religion, sex, age, marital status, handicap, familial status, or national origin of either the prospective owners or occupants of the subject property or of the present owners or occupants of the properties in the vicinity of the subject property or on any other basis prohibited by law.

18. My employment and/or compensation for performing this appraisal or any future or anticipated appraisals was not conditioned on any agreement or understanding, written or otherwise, that I would report (or present analysis supporting) a predetermined specific value, a predetermined minimum value, a range or direction in value, a value that favors the cause of any party, or the attainment of a specific result or occurrence of a specific subsequent event (such as approval of a pending mortgage loan application).

19. I personally prepared all conclusions and opinions about the real estate that were set forth in this appraisal report. If I relied on significant real property appraisal assistance from any individual or individuals in the performance of this appraisal or the preparation of this appraisal report, I have named such individual(s) and disclosed the specific tasks performed in this appraisal report. I certify that any individual so named is qualified to perform the tasks. I have not authorized anyone to make a change to any item in this appraisal report; therefore, any change made to this appraisal is unauthorized and I will take no responsibility for it.

20. I identified the lender/client in this appraisal report who is the individual, organization, or agent for the organization that ordered and will receive this appraisal report.

Uniform Residential Appraisal Report   File

21. The lender/client may disclose or distribute this appraisal report to: the borrower; another lender at the request of the borrower; the mortgagee or its successors and assigns; mortgage insurers; government sponsored enterprises; other secondary market participants; data collection or reporting services; professional appraisal organizations; any department, agency, or instrumentality of the United States; and any state, the District of Columbia, or other jurisdictions; without having to obtain the appraiser's or supervisory appraiser's (if applicable) consent. Such consent must be obtained before this appraisal report may be disclosed or distributed to any other party (including, but not limited to, the public through advertising, public relations, news, sales, or other media).

22. I am aware that any disclosure or distribution of this appraisal report by me or the lender/client may be subject to certain laws and regulations. Further, I am also subject to the provisions of the Uniform Standards of Professional Appraisal Practice that pertain to disclosure or distribution by me.

23. The borrower, another lender at the request of the borrower, the mortgagee or its successors and assigns, mortgage insurers, government sponsored enterprises, and other secondary market participants may rely on this appraisal report as part of any mortgage finance transaction that involves any one or more of these parties.

24. If this appraisal report was transmitted as an "electronic record" containing my "electronic signature," as those terms are defined in applicable federal and/or state laws (excluding audio and video recordings), or a facsimile transmission of this appraisal report containing a copy or representation of my signature, the appraisal report shall be as effective, enforceable and valid as if a paper version of this appraisal report were delivered containing my original hand written signature.

25. Any intentional or negligent misrepresentation(s) contained in this appraisal report may result in civil liability and/or criminal penalties including, but not limited to, fine or imprisonment or both under the provisions of Title 18, United States Code, Section 1001, et seq., or similar state laws.

SUPERVISORY APPRAISER'S CERTIFICATION: The Supervisory Appraiser certifies and agrees that:

1. I directly supervised the appraiser for this appraisal assignment, have read the appraisal report, and agree with the appraiser's analysis, opinions, statements, conclusions, and the appraiser's certification.

2. I accept full responsibility for the contents of this appraisal report including, but not limited to, the appraiser's analysis, opinions, statements, conclusions, and the appraiser's certification.

3. The appraiser identified in this appraisal report is either a sub-contractor or an employee of the supervisory appraiser (or the appraisal firm), is qualified to perform this appraisal, and is acceptable to perform this appraisal under the applicable state law.

4. This appraisal report complies with the Uniform Standards of Professional Appraisal Practice that were adopted and promulgated by the Appraisal Standards Board of The Appraisal Foundation and that were in place at the time this appraisal report was prepared.

5. If this appraisal report was transmitted as an "electronic record" containing my "electronic signature," as those terms are defined in applicable federal and/or state laws (excluding audio and video recordings), or a facsimile transmission of this appraisal report containing a copy or representation of my signature, the appraisal report shall be as effective, enforceable and valid as if a paper version of this appraisal report were delivered containing my original hand written signature.

APPRAISER

Signature _____
Name _____
Company Name _____
Company Address _____
_____
Telephone Number _____
Email Address _____
Date of Signature and Report _____
Effective Date of Appraisal _____
State Certification # _____
or State License # _____
or Other (describe) _____ State # ____
State _____
Expiration Date of Certification or License ____

ADDRESS OF PROPERTY APPRAISED
_____
_____

APPRAISED VALUE OF SUBJECT PROPERTY $ _____
LENDER/CLIENT
Name _____
Company Name _____
Company Address _____
_____
Email Address _____

SUPERVISORY APPRAISER (ONLY IF REQUIRED)

Signature _____
Name _____
Company Name _____
Company Address _____
_____
Telephone Number _____
Email Address _____
Date of Signature _____
State Certification # _____
or State License # _____
State _____
Expiration Date of Certification or License ____

SUBJECT PROPERTY
☐ Did not inspect subject property
☐ Did inspect exterior of subject property from street
   Date of Inspection _____
☐ Did inspect interior and exterior of subject property
   Date of Inspection _____

COMPARABLE SALES
☐ Did not inspect exterior of comparable sales from street
☐ Did inspect exterior of comparable sales from street
   Date of Inspection _____

Freddie Mac Form 70   March 2005   Fannie Mae Form 1004   March 2005

Source: www.efanniemae.com

123 Milam Street, Suite 200

Houston, Texas 77056

_____ [Space Above This Line For Recording Data] _____

DEED OF TRUST

DEFINITIONS

Words used in multiple sections of this document are defined below and other words are defined in Sections 3, 11, 13, 18, 20 and 21. Certain rules regarding the usage of words used in this document are also provided in Section 16.

(A) "**Security Instrument**" means this document, which is dated _____September 11th , 2015, together with all Riders to this document.
(B) "**Borrower**" is **JOHN DOE AND SPOUSE, JANE DOE** . Borrower is the grantor under this Security Instrument.
(C) "**Lender**" is ___GENERAL MORTGAGE COMPANY_____. Lender is a ___LIMITED LIABILITY CORPORATION__ organized and existing under the laws of _____THE STATE OF TEXAS_____. Lender's address is __123 Milam Street, Suite 200, Houston, Texas, 77056_____. Lender is the beneficiary under this Security Instrument.
(D) "**Trustee**" is _____Ura Hogg_____.
Trustee's address is ___987 Milam Street Houston, Texas 77056_____.
(E) "**Note**" means the promissory note signed by Borrower and dated _September 11th, 2015,___. The Note states that Borrower owes Lender ___Three Hundred Thousand AND NO/100ths__ Dollars (U.S. $ _300,000.00_____) plus interest. Borrower has promised to pay this debt in regular Periodic Payments and to pay the debt in full not later than __October 1st, 2045_____.

(F) "**Property**" means the property that is described below under the heading "Transfer of Rights in the Property."
(G) "**Loan**" means the debt evidenced by the Note, plus interest, any prepayment charges and late charges due under the Note, and all sums due under this Security Instrument, plus interest.

(H) "Riders" means all Riders to this Security Instrument that are executed by Borrower. The following Riders are to be executed by Borrower [check box as applicable]:

☐ Adjustable Rate Rider   ☐ Condominium Rider   ☐ Second Home Rider

☐ Balloon Rider   ☐ Planned Unit Development Rider   ☐ Other(s) [specify]

☐ 1-4 Family Rider   ☐ Biweekly Payment Rider

(I) "Applicable Law" means all controlling applicable federal, state and local statutes, regulations, ordinances and administrative rules and orders (that have the effect of law) as well as all applicable final, non-appealable judicial opinions.

(J) "Community Association Dues, Fees, and Assessments" means all dues, fees, assessments, and other charges that are imposed on Borrower or the Property by a condominium association, homeowners association or similar organization.

(K) "Electronic Funds Transfer" means any transfer of funds, other than a transaction originated by check, draft, or similar paper instrument, which is initiated through an electronic terminal, telephonic instrument, computer, or magnetic tape so as to order, instruct, or authorize a financial institution to debit or credit an account. Such term includes, but is not limited to, point-of-sale transfers, automated teller machine transactions, transfers initiated by telephone, wire transfers, and automated clearinghouse transfers.

(L) "Escrow Items" means those items that are described in Section 3.

(M) "Miscellaneous Proceeds" means any compensation, settlement, award of damages, or proceeds paid by any third party (other than insurance proceeds paid under the coverages described in Section 5) for: (i) damage to, or destruction of, the Property; (ii) condemnation or other taking of all or any part of the Property; (iii) conveyance in lieu of condemnation; or (iv) misrepresentations of, or omissions as to, the value and/or condition of the Property.

(N) "Mortgage Insurance" means insurance protecting Lender against the nonpayment of, or default on, the Loan.

(O) "Periodic Payment" means the regularly scheduled amount due for (i) principal and interest under the Note, plus (ii) any amounts under Section 3 of this Security Instrument.

(P) "RESPA" means the Real Estate Settlement Procedures Act (12 U.S.C. §2601 et seq.) and its implementing regulation, Regulation X (24 C.F.R. Part 3500), as they might be amended from time to time, or any additional or successor legislation or regulation that governs the same subject matter. As used in this Security Instrument, "RESPA" refers to all requirements and restrictions that are imposed in regard to a "federally related mortgage loan" even if the Loan does not qualify as a "federally related mortgage loan" under RESPA.

(Q) "Successor in Interest of Borrower" means any party that has taken title to the Property, whether or not that party has assumed Borrower's obligations under the Note and/or this Security Instrument.

TRANSFER OF RIGHTS IN THE PROPERTY

This Security Instrument secures to Lender: (i) the repayment of the Loan, and all renewals, extensions and modifications of the Note; and (ii) the performance of Borrower's covenants and agreements under this Security Instrument and the Note. For this purpose, Borrower irrevocably grants and conveys to Trustee, in trust, with power of sale, the following described property located in the _____County_____ of _____Harris_____:

[Type of Recording Jurisdiction]   [Name of Recording Jurisdiction]

LOT ONE (1) BLOCK FOUR (4) SECTION FIVE (5), SUGARHILL, SUBDIVISION

which currently has the address of _____1333 SUGAR LANE_____

[Street]

_____HOUSTON_____, Texas _____77333_____ ("Property Address"):

[City]   [Zip Code]

TOGETHER WITH all the improvements now or hereafter erected on the property, and all easements, appurtenances, and fixtures now or hereafter a part of the property. All replacements and additions shall also be covered by this Security Instrument. All of the foregoing is referred to in this Security Instrument as the "Property."

BORROWER COVENANTS that Borrower is lawfully seised of the estate hereby conveyed and has the right to grant and convey the Property and that the Property is unencumbered, except for encumbrances of record. Borrower warrants and will defend generally the title to the Property against all claims and demands, subject to any encumbrances of record.

THIS SECURITY INSTRUMENT combines uniform covenants for national use and non-uniform covenants with limited variations by jurisdiction to constitute a uniform security instrument covering real property.

UNIFORM COVENANTS. Borrower and Lender covenant and agree as follows:

1. Payment of Principal, Interest, Escrow Items, Prepayment Charges, and Late Charges. Borrower shall pay when due the principal of, and interest on, the debt evidenced by the Note and any prepayment charges and late charges due under the Note. Borrower shall also pay funds for Escrow Items pursuant to Section 3. Payments due under the Note and this Security Instrument shall be made in U.S. currency. However, if any check or other instrument received by Lender as payment under the Note or this Security Instrument is returned to Lender unpaid, Lender may require that any or all subsequent payments due under the Note and this Security Instrument be made in one or more of the following forms, as selected by Lender: (a) cash; (b) money order; (c) certified check, bank check, treasurer's check or cashier's check, provided any such check is drawn upon an institution whose deposits are insured by a federal agency, instrumentality, or entity; or (d) Electronic Funds Transfer.

Payments are deemed received by Lender when received at the location designated in the Note or at such other location as may be designated by Lender in accordance with the notice provisions in Section 15. Lender may return any payment or partial payment if the payment or partial payments are insufficient to bring the Loan current. Lender may accept any payment or partial payment insufficient to bring the Loan current, without waiver of any rights hereunder or prejudice to its rights to refuse such payment or partial payments in the future, but Lender is not obligated to apply such payments at the time such payments are accepted. If each Periodic Payment is applied as of its scheduled due date, then Lender need not pay interest on unapplied funds. Lender may hold such unapplied funds until Borrower makes payment to bring the Loan current. If Borrower does not do so within a reasonable period of time, Lender shall either apply such funds or return them to Borrower. If not applied earlier, such funds will be applied to the outstanding principal balance under the Note immediately prior to foreclosure. No offset or claim which Borrower might have now or in the future against Lender shall relieve Borrower from making payments due under the Note and this Security Instrument or performing the covenants and agreements secured by this Security Instrument.

2. Application of Payments or Proceeds. Except as otherwise described in this Section 2, all payments accepted and applied by Lender shall be applied in the following order of priority: (a) interest due under the Note; (b) principal due under the Note; (c) amounts due under Section 3. Such payments shall be applied to each Periodic Payment in the order in which it became due. Any remaining amounts shall be applied first to late charges, second to any other amounts due under this Security Instrument, and then to reduce the principal balance of the Note.

If Lender receives a payment from Borrower for a delinquent Periodic Payment which includes a sufficient amount to pay any late charge due, the payment may be applied to the delinquent payment and the late charge. If more than one Periodic Payment is outstanding, Lender may apply any payment received from Borrower to the repayment of the Periodic Payments if, and to the extent that, each payment can be paid in full. To the extent that any excess exists after the payment is applied to the full payment of one or more Periodic Payments, such excess may be applied to any late charges due. Voluntary prepayments shall be applied first to any prepayment charges and then as described in the Note.

Any application of payments, insurance proceeds, or Miscellaneous Proceeds to principal due under the Note shall not extend or postpone the due date, or change the amount, of the Periodic Payments.

3. Funds for Escrow Items. Borrower shall pay to Lender on the day Periodic Payments are due under the Note, until the Note is paid in full, a sum (the "Funds") to provide for payment of amounts due for: (a) taxes and assessments and other items which can attain priority over this Security Instrument as a lien or encumbrance on the Property; (b) leasehold payments or ground rents on the Property, if any; (c) premiums for any and all insurance required by Lender under Section 5; and (d) Mortgage Insurance premiums, if any, or any sums payable by Borrower to Lender in lieu of the payment of Mortgage Insurance premiums in accordance with the provisions of Section 10. These items are called "Escrow Items." At origination or at any time during the term of the Loan, Lender may require that Community Association Dues, Fees, and Assessments, if any, be escrowed by Borrower, and such dues, fees and assessments shall be an Escrow Item. Borrower shall promptly furnish to Lender all notices of amounts to be paid under this Section. Borrower shall pay Lender the Funds for Escrow Items unless Lender waives Borrower's obligation to pay the Funds for any or all Escrow Items. Lender may waive Borrower's obligation to pay to Lender Funds for any or all Escrow Items at any time. Any such waiver may only be in writing. In the event of such waiver, Borrower shall pay directly, when and where payable, the amounts due for any Escrow Items for which payment of Funds has been waived by Lender and, if Lender requires, shall furnish to Lender receipts evidencing such payment within such time period as Lender may require. Borrower's obligation to make such payments and to provide receipts shall for all purposes be deemed to be a covenant and agreement contained in this Security Instrument, as the phrase "covenant and agreement" is used in Section 9. If Borrower is obligated to pay Escrow Items directly, pursuant to a waiver, and Borrower fails to pay the amount due for an Escrow Item, Lender may exercise its rights under Section 9 and pay such amount and Borrower shall then be obligated under Section 9 to repay to Lender any such amount. Lender may revoke the waiver as to any or all Escrow Items at any time by a notice given in accordance with Section 15 and, upon such revocation, Borrower shall pay to Lender all Funds, and in such amounts, that are then required under this Section 3.

Lender may, at any time, collect and hold Funds in an amount (a) sufficient to permit Lender to apply the Funds at the time specified under RESPA, and (b) not to exceed the maximum amount a lender can require under RESPA. Lender shall estimate the amount of Funds due on the basis of current data and reasonable estimates of expenditures of future Escrow Items or otherwise in accordance with Applicable Law.

The Funds shall be held in an institution whose deposits are insured by a federal agency, instrumentality, or entity (including Lender, if Lender is an institution whose deposits are so insured) or in any Federal Home Loan Bank. Lender shall apply the Funds to pay the Escrow Items no later than the time specified under RESPA. Lender shall not charge Borrower for holding and applying the Funds, annually analyzing the escrow account, or verifying the Escrow Items, unless Lender pays Borrower interest on the Funds and Applicable Law permits Lender to make such a charge. Unless an agreement is made in writing or Applicable Law requires interest to be paid on the Funds, Lender shall not be required to pay Borrower any interest or earnings on the Funds. Borrower and Lender can agree in writing, however, that interest shall be paid on the Funds. Lender shall give to Borrower, without charge, an annual accounting of the Funds as required by RESPA.

If there is a surplus of Funds held in escrow, as defined under RESPA, Lender shall account to Borrower for the excess funds in accordance with RESPA. If there is a shortage of Funds held in escrow, as defined under RESPA, Lender shall notify Borrower as required by RESPA, and Borrower shall pay to Lender the amount necessary to make up the shortage in accordance with RESPA, but in no more than 12 monthly payments. If there is a deficiency of Funds held in escrow, as defined under RESPA, Lender shall notify Borrower as required by RESPA, and Borrower shall pay to Lender the amount necessary to make up the deficiency in accordance with RESPA, but in no more than 12 monthly payments.

Upon payment in full of all sums secured by this Security Instrument, Lender shall promptly refund to Borrower any Funds held by Lender.

4. Charges; Liens. Borrower shall pay all taxes, assessments, charges, fines, and impositions attributable to the Property which can attain priority over this Security Instrument, leasehold payments or ground rents on the Property, if any, and Community Association Dues, Fees, and Assessments, if any. To the extent that these items are Escrow Items, Borrower shall pay them in the manner provided in Section 3.

Borrower shall promptly discharge any lien which has priority over this Security Instrument unless Borrower: (a) agrees in writing to the payment of the obligation secured by the lien in a manner acceptable to Lender, but only so long as Borrower is performing such agreement; (b) contests the lien in good faith by, or defends against enforcement of the lien in, legal proceedings which in Lender's opinion operate to prevent the enforcement of the lien while those proceedings are pending, but only until such proceedings are concluded; or (c) secures from the holder of the lien an agreement satisfactory to Lender subordinating the lien to this Security Instrument. If Lender determines that any part of the Property is subject to a lien which can attain priority over this Security Instrument, Lender may give Borrower a notice identifying the lien. Within 10 days of the date on which that notice is given, Borrower shall satisfy the lien or take one or more of the actions set forth above in this Section 4.

Lender may require Borrower to pay a one-time charge for a real estate tax verification and/or reporting service used by Lender in connection with this Loan.

5. Property Insurance. Borrower shall keep the improvements now existing or hereafter erected on the Property insured against loss by fire, hazards included within the term "extended coverage," and any other hazards including, but not limited to, earthquakes and floods, for which Lender requires insurance. This insurance shall be maintained in the amounts (including deductible levels) and for the periods that Lender requires. What Lender requires pursuant to the preceding sentences can change during the term of the Loan. The insurance carrier providing the insurance shall be chosen by Borrower subject to Lender's right to disapprove Borrower's choice, which right shall not be exercised unreasonably. Lender may require Borrower to pay, in connection with this Loan, either: (a) a one-time charge for flood zone determination, certification and tracking services; or (b) a one-time charge for flood zone determination and certification services and subsequent charges each time remappings or similar changes occur which reasonably might affect such determination or certification. Borrower shall also be responsible for the payment of any fees imposed by the Federal Emergency Management Agency in connection with the review of any flood zone determination resulting from an objection by Borrower.

If Borrower fails to maintain any of the coverages described above, Lender may obtain insurance coverage, at Lender's option and Borrower's expense. Lender is under no obligation to purchase any particular type or amount of coverage. Therefore, such coverage shall cover Lender, but might or might not protect Borrower, Borrower's equity in the Property, or the contents of the Property, against any risk, hazard or liability and might provide greater or lesser coverage than was previously in effect. Borrower acknowledges that the cost of the insurance coverage so obtained might significantly exceed the cost of insurance that Borrower could have obtained. Any amounts disbursed by Lender under this Section 5 shall become additional debt of Borrower secured by this Security Instrument. These amounts shall bear interest at the Note rate from the date of disbursement and shall be payable, with such interest, upon notice from Lender to Borrower requesting payment.

All insurance policies required by Lender and renewals of such policies shall be subject to Lender's right to disapprove such policies, shall include a standard mortgage clause, and shall name Lender as mortgagee and/or as an additional loss payee. Lender shall have the right to hold the policies and renewal certificates. If Lender requires, Borrower shall promptly give to Lender all receipts of paid premiums and renewal notices. If Borrower obtains any form of insurance coverage, not otherwise required by Lender, for damage to, or destruction of, the Property, such policy shall include a standard mortgage clause and shall name Lender as mortgagee and/or as an additional loss payee.

In the event of loss, Borrower shall give prompt notice to the insurance carrier and Lender. Lender may make proof of loss if not made promptly by Borrower. Unless Lender and Borrower otherwise agree in writing, any insurance proceeds, whether or not the underlying insurance was required by Lender, shall be applied to restoration or repair of the Property, if the restoration or repair is economically feasible and Lender's security is not lessened. During such repair and restoration period, Lender shall have the right to hold such insurance proceeds until Lender has had an opportunity to inspect such Property to ensure the work has been completed to Lender's satisfaction, provided that such inspection shall be undertaken promptly. Lender may disburse proceeds for the repairs and restoration in a single payment or in a series of progress payments as the work is completed. Unless an agreement is made in writing or Applicable Law requires interest to be paid on such insurance proceeds, Lender shall not be required to pay Borrower any interest or earnings on such proceeds. Fees for public adjusters, or other third parties, retained by Borrower shall not be paid out of the insurance proceeds and shall be the sole obligation of Borrower. If the restoration or repair is not economically feasible or Lender's security would be lessened, the insurance proceeds shall be applied to the sums secured by this Security Instrument, whether or not then due, with the excess, if any, paid to Borrower. Such insurance proceeds shall be applied in the order provided for in Section 2.

If Borrower abandons the Property, Lender may file, negotiate and settle any available insurance claim and related matters. If Borrower does not respond within 30 days to a notice from Lender that the insurance carrier has offered to settle a claim, then Lender may negotiate and settle the claim. The 30-day period will begin when the notice is given. In either event, or if Lender acquires the Property under Section 22 or otherwise, Borrower hereby assigns to Lender (a) Borrower's rights to any insurance proceeds in an amount not to exceed the amounts unpaid under the Note or this Security Instrument, and (b) any other of Borrower's rights (other than the right to any refund of unearned premiums paid by Borrower) under all insurance policies covering the Property, insofar as such rights are applicable to the coverage of the Property. Lender may use the insurance proceeds either to repair or restore the Property or to pay amounts unpaid under the Note or this Security Instrument, whether or not then due.

6. Occupancy. Borrower shall occupy, establish, and use the Property as Borrower's principal residence within 60 days after the execution of this Security Instrument and shall continue to occupy the Property as Borrower's principal residence for at least one year after the date of occupancy, unless Lender otherwise agrees in writing, which consent shall not be unreasonably withheld, or unless extenuating circumstances exist which are beyond Borrower's control.

7. Preservation, Maintenance and Protection of the Property; Inspections. Borrower shall not destroy, damage or impair the Property, allow the Property to deteriorate or commit waste on the Property. Whether or not Borrower is residing in the Property, Borrower shall maintain the Property in order to prevent the Property from deteriorating or decreasing in value due to its condition. Unless it is determined pursuant to Section 5 that repair or restoration is not economically feasible, Borrower shall promptly repair the Property if damaged to avoid further deterioration or damage. If insurance or condemnation proceeds are paid in connection with damage to, or the taking of, the Property, Borrower shall be responsible for repairing or restoring the Property only if Lender has released proceeds for such purposes. Lender may disburse proceeds for the repairs and restoration in a single payment or in a series of progress payments as the work is completed. If the insurance or condemnation proceeds are not sufficient to repair or restore the Property, Borrower is not relieved of Borrower's obligation for the completion of such repair or restoration.

Lender or its agent may make reasonable entries upon and inspections of the Property. If it has reasonable cause, Lender may inspect the interior of the improvements on the Property. Lender shall give Borrower notice at the time of or prior to such an interior inspection specifying such reasonable cause.

8. Borrower's Loan Application. Borrower shall be in default if, during the Loan application process, Borrower or any persons or entities acting at the direction of Borrower or with Borrower's knowledge or consent gave materially false, misleading, or inaccurate information or statements to Lender (or failed to provide Lender with material information) in connection with the Loan. Material representations include, but are not limited to, representations concerning Borrower's occupancy of the Property as Borrower's principal residence.

9. Protection of Lender's Interest in the Property and Rights Under this Security Instrument. If (a) Borrower fails to perform the covenants and agreements contained in this Security Instrument, (b) there is a legal proceeding that might significantly affect Lender's interest in the Property and/or rights under this Security Instrument (such as a proceeding in bankruptcy, probate, for condemnation or forfeiture, for enforcement of a lien which may attain priority over this Security Instrument or to enforce laws or regulations), or (c) Borrower has abandoned the Property, then Lender may do and pay for whatever is reasonable or appropriate to protect Lender's interest in the Property and rights under this Security Instrument, including protecting and/or assessing the value of the Property, and securing and/or repairing the Property. Lender's actions can include, but are not limited to: (a) paying any sums secured by a lien which has priority over this Security Instrument; (b) appearing in court; and (c) paying reasonable attorneys' fees to protect its interest in the Property and/or rights under this Security Instrument, including its secured position in a bankruptcy proceeding. Securing the Property includes, but is not limited to, entering the Property to make repairs, change locks, replace or board up doors and windows, drain water from pipes, eliminate building or other code violations or dangerous conditions, and have utilities turned on or off. Although Lender may take action under this Section 9, Lender does not have to do so and is not under any duty or obligation to do so. It is agreed that Lender incurs no liability for not taking any or all actions authorized under this Section 9.

Any amounts disbursed by Lender under this Section 9 shall become additional debt of Borrower secured by this Security Instrument. These amounts shall bear interest at the Note rate from the date of disbursement and shall be payable, with such interest, upon notice from Lender to Borrower requesting payment.

If this Security Instrument is on a leasehold, Borrower shall comply with all the provisions of the lease. If Borrower acquires fee title to the Property, the leasehold and the fee title shall not merge unless Lender agrees to the merger in writing.

10. Mortgage Insurance. If Lender required Mortgage Insurance as a condition of making the Loan, Borrower shall pay the premiums required to maintain the Mortgage Insurance in effect. If, for any reason, the Mortgage Insurance coverage required by Lender ceases to be available from the mortgage insurer that previously provided such insurance and Borrower was required to make separately designated payments toward the premiums for Mortgage Insurance, Borrower shall pay the premiums required to obtain coverage substantially equivalent to the Mortgage Insurance previously in effect, at a cost substantially equivalent to the cost to Borrower of the Mortgage Insurance previously in effect, from an alternate mortgage insurer selected by Lender. If substantially equivalent Mortgage Insurance coverage is not available, Borrower shall continue to pay to Lender the amount of the separately designated payments that were due when the insurance coverage ceased to be in effect. Lender will accept, use and retain these payments as a non-refundable loss reserve in lieu of Mortgage Insurance. Such loss reserve shall be non-refundable, notwithstanding the fact that the Loan is ultimately paid in full, and Lender shall not be required to pay Borrower any interest or earnings on such loss reserve. Lender can no longer require loss reserve payments if Mortgage Insurance coverage (in the amount and for the period that Lender requires) provided by an insurer selected by Lender again becomes available, is obtained, and Lender requires separately designated payments toward the premiums for Mortgage Insurance. If Lender required Mortgage Insurance as a condition of making the Loan and Borrower was required to make separately designated payments toward the premiums for Mortgage Insurance, Borrower shall pay the premiums required to maintain Mortgage Insurance in effect, or to provide a non-refundable loss reserve, until Lender's requirement for Mortgage Insurance ends in accordance with any written agreement between Borrower and Lender providing for such termination or until termination is required by Applicable Law. Nothing in this Section 10 affects Borrower's obligation to pay interest at the rate provided in the Note.

Mortgage Insurance reimburses Lender (or any entity that purchases the Note) for certain losses it may incur if Borrower does not repay the Loan as agreed. Borrower is not a party to the Mortgage Insurance.

Mortgage insurers evaluate their total risk on all such insurance in force from time to time, and may enter into agreements with other parties that share or modify their risk, or reduce losses. These agreements are on terms and conditions that are satisfactory to the mortgage insurer and the other party (or parties) to these agreements. These agreements may require the mortgage insurer to make payments using any source of funds that the mortgage insurer may have available (which may include funds obtained from Mortgage Insurance premiums).

As a result of these agreements, Lender, any purchaser of the Note, another insurer, any reinsurer, any other entity, or any affiliate of any of the foregoing, may receive (directly or indirectly) amounts that derive from (or might be characterized as) a portion of Borrower's payments for Mortgage Insurance, in exchange for sharing or modifying the mortgage insurer's risk, or reducing losses. If such agreement provides that an affiliate of Lender takes a share of the insurer's risk in exchange for a share of the premiums paid to the insurer, the arrangement is often termed "captive reinsurance." Further:

(a) Any such agreements will not affect the amounts that Borrower has agreed to pay for Mortgage Insurance, or any other terms of the Loan. Such agreements will not increase the amount Borrower will owe for Mortgage Insurance, and they will not entitle Borrower to any refund.

(b) Any such agreements will not affect the rights Borrower has – if any – with respect to the Mortgage Insurance under the Homeowners Protection Act of 1998 or any other law. These rights may include the right to receive certain disclosures, to request and obtain cancellation of the Mortgage Insurance, to have the Mortgage Insurance terminated automatically, and/or to receive a refund of any Mortgage Insurance premiums that were unearned at the time of such cancellation or termination.

11. Assignment of Miscellaneous Proceeds; Forfeiture. All Miscellaneous Proceeds are hereby assigned to and shall be paid to Lender.

If the Property is damaged, such Miscellaneous Proceeds shall be applied to restoration or repair of the Property, if the restoration or repair is economically feasible and Lender's security is not lessened. During such repair and restoration period, Lender shall have the right to hold such Miscellaneous Proceeds until Lender has had an opportunity to inspect such Property to ensure the work has been completed to Lender's satisfaction, provided that such inspection shall be undertaken promptly. Lender may pay for the repairs and restoration in a single disbursement or in a series of progress payments as the work is completed. Unless an agreement is made in writing or Applicable Law requires interest to be paid on such Miscellaneous Proceeds, Lender shall not be required to pay Borrower any interest or earnings on such Miscellaneous Proceeds. If the restoration or repair is not economically feasible or Lender's security would be lessened, the Miscellaneous Proceeds shall be applied to the sums secured by this Security Instrument, whether or not then due, with the excess, if any, paid to Borrower. Such Miscellaneous Proceeds shall be applied in the order provided for in Section 2.

In the event of a total taking, destruction, or loss in value of the Property, the Miscellaneous Proceeds shall be applied to the sums secured by this Security Instrument, whether or not then due, with the excess, if any, paid to Borrower.

In the event of a partial taking, destruction, or loss in value of the Property in which the fair market value of the Property immediately before the partial taking, destruction, or loss in value is equal to or greater than the amount of the sums secured by this Security Instrument immediately before the partial taking, destruction, or loss in value, unless Borrower and Lender otherwise agree in writing, the sums secured by this Security Instrument shall be reduced by the amount of the Miscellaneous Proceeds multiplied by the following fraction: (a) the total amount of the sums secured immediately before the partial taking, destruction, or loss in value divided by (b) the fair market value of the Property immediately before the partial taking, destruction, or loss in value. Any balance shall be paid to Borrower.

In the event of a partial taking, destruction, or loss in value of the Property in which the fair market value of the Property immediately before the partial taking, destruction, or loss in value is less than the amount of the sums secured immediately before the partial taking, destruction, or loss in value, unless Borrower and Lender otherwise agree in writing, the Miscellaneous Proceeds shall be applied to the sums secured by this Security Instrument whether or not the sums are then due.

If the Property is abandoned by Borrower, or if, after notice by Lender to Borrower that the Opposing Party (as defined in the next sentence) offers to make an award to settle a claim for damages, Borrower fails to respond to Lender within 30 days after the date the notice is given, Lender is authorized to collect and apply the Miscellaneous Proceeds either to restoration or repair of the Property or to the sums secured by this Security Instrument, whether or not then due. "Opposing Party" means the third party that owes Borrower Miscellaneous Proceeds or the party against whom Borrower has a right of action in regard to Miscellaneous Proceeds.

Borrower shall be in default if any action or proceeding, whether civil or criminal, is begun that, in Lender's judgment, could result in forfeiture of the Property or other material impairment of Lender's interest in the Property or rights under this Security Instrument. Borrower can cure such a default and, if acceleration has occurred, reinstate as provided in Section 19, by causing the action or proceeding to be dismissed with a ruling that, in Lender's judgment, precludes forfeiture of the Property or other material impairment of Lender's interest in the Property or rights under this Security Instrument. The proceeds of any award or claim for damages that are attributable to the impairment of Lender's interest in the Property are hereby assigned and shall be paid to Lender.

All Miscellaneous Proceeds that are not applied to restoration or repair of the Property shall be applied in the order provided for in Section 2.

12. Borrower Not Released; Forbearance by Lender Not a Waiver. Extension of the time for payment or modification of amortization of the sums secured by this Security Instrument granted by Lender to Borrower or any Successor in Interest of Borrower shall not operate to release the liability of Borrower or any Successors in Interest of Borrower. Lender shall not be required to commence proceedings against any Successor in Interest of Borrower or to refuse to extend time for payment or otherwise modify amortization of the sums secured by this Security Instrument by reason of any demand made by the original Borrower or any Successors in Interest of Borrower. Any forbearance by Lender in exercising any right or remedy including, without limitation, Lender's acceptance of payments from third persons, entities or Successors in Interest of Borrower or in amounts less than the amount then due, shall not be a waiver of or preclude the exercise of any right or remedy.

13. Joint and Several Liability; Co-signers; Successors and Assigns Bound. Borrower covenants and agrees that Borrower's obligations and liability shall be joint and several. However, any Borrower who co-signs this Security Instrument but does not execute the Note (a "co-signer"): (a) is co-signing this Security Instrument only to mortgage, grant and convey the co-signer's interest in the Property under the terms of this Security Instrument; (b) is not personally obligated to pay the sums secured by this Security Instrument; and (c) agrees that Lender and any other Borrower can agree to extend, modify, forbear or make any accommodations with regard to the terms of this Security Instrument or the Note without the co-signer's consent.

Subject to the provisions of Section 18, any Successor in Interest of Borrower who assumes Borrower's obligations under this Security Instrument in writing, and is approved by Lender, shall obtain all of Borrower's rights and benefits under this Security Instrument. Borrower shall not be released from Borrower's obligations and liability under this Security Instrument unless Lender agrees to such release in writing. The covenants and agreements of this Security Instrument shall bind (except as provided in Section 20) and benefit the successors and assigns of Lender.

14. Loan Charges. Lender may charge Borrower fees for services performed in connection with Borrower's default, for the purpose of protecting Lender's interest in the Property and rights under this Security Instrument, including, but not limited to, attorneys' fees, property inspection and valuation fees. In regard to any other fees, the absence of express authority in this Security Instrument to charge a specific fee to Borrower shall not be construed as a prohibition on the charging of such fee. Lender may not charge fees that are expressly prohibited by this Security Instrument or by Applicable Law.

If the Loan is subject to a law that sets maximum loan charges, and that law is finally interpreted so that the interest or other loan charges collected or to be collected in connection with the Loan exceed the permitted limits, then: (a) any such loan charge shall be reduced by the amount necessary to reduce the charge to the permitted limit; and (b) any sums already collected from Borrower which exceeded permitted limits will be refunded to Borrower. Lender may choose to make this refund by reducing the principal owed under the Note or by making a direct payment to Borrower. If a refund reduces principal, the reduction will be treated as a partial prepayment without any prepayment charge (whether or not a prepayment charge is provided for under the Note). Borrower's acceptance of any such refund made by direct payment to Borrower will constitute a waiver of any right of action Borrower might have arising out of such overcharge.

15. Notices. All notices given by Borrower or Lender in connection with this Security Instrument must be in writing. Any notice to Borrower in connection with this Security Instrument shall be deemed to have been given to Borrower when mailed by first class mail or when actually delivered to Borrower's notice address if sent by other means. Notice to any one Borrower shall constitute notice to all Borrowers unless Applicable Law expressly requires otherwise. The notice address shall be the Property Address unless Borrower has designated a substitute notice address by notice to Lender. Borrower shall promptly notify Lender of Borrower's change of address. If Lender specifies a procedure for reporting Borrower's change of address, then Borrower shall only report a change of address through that specified procedure. There may be only one designated notice address under this Security Instrument at any one time. Any notice to Lender shall be given by delivering it or by mailing it by first class mail to Lender's address stated herein unless Lender has designated another address by notice to Borrower. Any notice in connection with this Security Instrument shall not be deemed to have been given to Lender until actually received by Lender. If any notice required by this Security Instrument is also required under Applicable Law, the Applicable Law requirement will satisfy the corresponding requirement under this Security Instrument.

16. Governing Law; Severability; Rules of Construction. This Security Instrument shall be governed by federal law and the law of the jurisdiction in which the Property is located. All rights and obligations contained in this Security Instrument are subject to any requirements and limitations of Applicable Law. Applicable Law might explicitly or implicitly allow the parties to agree by contract or it might be silent, but such silence shall not be construed as a prohibition against agreement by contract. In the event that any provision or clause of this Security Instrument or the Note conflicts with Applicable Law, such conflict shall not affect other provisions of this Security Instrument or the Note which can be given effect without the conflicting provision.

As used in this Security Instrument: (a) words of the masculine gender shall mean and include corresponding neuter words or words of the feminine gender; (b) words in the singular shall mean and include the plural and vice versa; and (c) the word "may" gives sole discretion without any obligation to take any action.

17. Borrower's Copy. Borrower shall be given one copy of the Note and of this Security Instrument.

18. Transfer of the Property or a Beneficial Interest in Borrower. As used in this Section 18, "Interest in the Property" means any legal or beneficial interest in the Property, including, but not limited to, those beneficial interests transferred in a bond for deed, contract for deed, installment sales contract or escrow agreement, the intent of which is the transfer of title by Borrower at a future date to a purchaser.

If all or any part of the Property or any Interest in the Property is sold or transferred (or if Borrower is not a natural person and a beneficial interest in Borrower is sold or transferred) without Lender's prior written consent, Lender may require immediate payment in full of all sums secured by this Security Instrument. However, this option shall not be exercised by Lender if such exercise is prohibited by Applicable Law.

If Lender exercises this option, Lender shall give Borrower notice of acceleration. The notice shall provide a period of not less than 30 days from the date the notice is given in accordance with Section 15 within which Borrower must pay all sums secured by this Security Instrument. If Borrower fails to pay these sums prior to the expiration of this period, Lender may invoke any remedies permitted by this Security Instrument without further notice or demand on Borrower.

19. Borrower's Right to Reinstate After Acceleration. If Borrower meets certain conditions, Borrower shall have the right to have enforcement of this Security Instrument discontinued at any time prior to the earliest of: (a) five days before sale of the Property pursuant to any power of sale contained in this Security Instrument; (b) such other period as Applicable Law might specify for the termination of Borrower's right to reinstate; or (c) entry of a judgment enforcing this Security Instrument. Those conditions are that Borrower: (a) pays Lender all sums which then would be due under this Security Instrument and the Note as if no acceleration had occurred; (b) cures any default of any other covenants or agreements; (c) pays all expenses incurred in enforcing this Security Instrument, including, but not limited to, reasonable attorneys' fees, property inspection and valuation fees, and other fees incurred for the purpose of protecting Lender's interest in the Property and rights under this Security Instrument; and (d) takes such action as Lender may reasonably require to assure that Lender's interest in the Property and rights under this Security Instrument, and Borrower's obligation to pay the sums secured by this Security Instrument, shall continue unchanged. Lender may require that Borrower pay such reinstatement sums and expenses in one or more of the following forms, as selected by Lender: (a) cash; (b) money order; (c) certified check, bank check, treasurer's check, or cashier's check, provided any such check is drawn upon an institution whose deposits are insured by a federal agency, instrumentality, or entity; or (d) Electronic Funds Transfer. Upon reinstatement by Borrower, this Security Instrument and obligations secured hereby shall remain fully effective as if no acceleration had occurred. However, this right to reinstate shall not apply in the case of acceleration under Section 18.

20. Sale of Note; Change of Loan Servicer; Notice of Grievance. The Note or a partial interest in the Note (together with this Security Instrument) can be sold one or more times without prior notice to Borrower. A sale might result in a change in the entity (known as the "Loan Servicer") that collects Periodic Payments due under the Note and this Security Instrument and performs other mortgage loan servicing obligations under the Note, this Security Instrument, and Applicable Law. There also might be one or more changes of the Loan Servicer unrelated to a sale of the Note. If there is a change of the Loan Servicer, Borrower will be given written notice of the change which will state the name and address of the new Loan Servicer, the address to which payments should be made and any other information RESPA requires in connection with a notice of transfer of servicing. If the Note is sold and thereafter the Loan is serviced by a Loan Servicer other than the purchaser of the Note, the mortgage loan servicing obligations to Borrower will remain with the Loan Servicer or be transferred to a successor Loan Servicer and are not assumed by the Note purchaser unless otherwise provided by the Note purchaser.

Neither Borrower nor Lender may commence, join, or be joined to any judicial action (as either an individual litigant or the member of a class) that arises from the other party's actions pursuant to this Security Instrument or that alleges that the other party has breached any provision of, or any duty owed by reason of, this Security Instrument, until such Borrower or Lender has notified the other party (with such notice given in compliance with the requirements of Section 15) of such alleged breach and afforded the other party hereto a reasonable period after the giving of such notice to take corrective action. If Applicable Law provides a time period which must elapse before certain action can be taken, that time period will be deemed to be reasonable for purposes of this paragraph. The notice of acceleration and opportunity to cure given to Borrower pursuant to Section 22 and the notice of acceleration given to Borrower pursuant to Section 18 shall be deemed to satisfy the notice and opportunity to take corrective action provisions of this Section 20.

21. Hazardous Substances. As used in this Section 21: (a) "Hazardous Substances" are those substances defined as toxic or hazardous substances, pollutants, or wastes by Environmental Law and the following substances: gasoline, kerosene, other flammable or toxic petroleum products, toxic pesticides and herbicides, volatile solvents, materials containing asbestos or formaldehyde, and radioactive materials; (b) "Environmental Law" means federal laws and laws of the jurisdiction where the Property is located that relate to health, safety or environmental protection; (c) "Environmental Cleanup" includes any response action, remedial action, or removal action, as defined in Environmental Law; and (d) an "Environmental Condition" means a condition that can cause, contribute to, or otherwise trigger an Environmental Cleanup.

Borrower shall not cause or permit the presence, use, disposal, storage, or release of any Hazardous Substances, or threaten to release any Hazardous Substances, on or in the Property. Borrower shall not do, nor allow anyone else to do, anything affecting the Property (a) that is in violation of any Environmental Law, (b) which creates an Environmental Condition, or (c) which, due to the presence, use, or release of a Hazardous Substance, creates a condition that adversely affects the value of the Property. The preceding two sentences shall not apply to the presence, use, or storage on the Property of small quantities of Hazardous Substances that are generally recognized to be appropriate to normal residential uses and to maintenance of the Property (including, but not limited to, hazardous substances in consumer products).

Borrower shall promptly give Lender written notice of (a) any investigation, claim, demand, lawsuit, or other action by any governmental or regulatory agency or private party involving the

Property and any Hazardous Substance or Environmental Law of which Borrower has actual knowledge, (b) any Environmental Condition, including but not limited to, any spilling, leaking, discharge, release, or threat of release of any Hazardous Substance, and (c) any condition caused by the presence, use, or release of a Hazardous Substance which adversely affects the value of the Property. If Borrower learns, or is notified by any governmental or regulatory authority, or any private party, that any removal or other remediation of any Hazardous Substance affecting the Property is necessary, Borrower shall promptly take all necessary remedial actions in accordance with Environmental Law. Nothing herein shall create any obligation on Lender for an Environmental Cleanup.

NON-UNIFORM COVENANTS. Borrower and Lender further covenant and agree as follows:

22. Acceleration; Remedies. Lender shall give notice to Borrower prior to acceleration following Borrower's breach of any covenant or agreement in this Security Instrument (but not prior to acceleration under Section 18 unless Applicable Law provides otherwise). The notice shall specify: (a) the default; (b) the action required to cure the default; (c) a date, not less than 30 days from the date the notice is given to Borrower, by which the default must be cured; and (d) that failure to cure the default on or before the date specified in the notice will result in acceleration of the sums secured by this Security Instrument and sale of the Property. The notice shall further inform Borrower of the right to reinstate after acceleration and the right to bring a court action to assert the nonexistence of a default or any other defense of Borrower to acceleration and sale. If the default is not cured on or before the date specified in the notice, Lender at its option may require immediate payment in full of all sums secured by this Security Instrument without further demand and may invoke the power of sale and any other remedies permitted by Applicable Law. Lender shall be entitled to collect all expenses incurred in pursuing the remedies provided in this Section 22, including, but not limited to, reasonable attorneys' fees and costs of title evidence. For the purposes of this Section 22, the term "Lender" includes any holder of the Note who is entitled to receive payments under the Note.

If Lender invokes the power of sale, Lender or Trustee shall give notice of the time, place and terms of sale by posting and filing the notice at least 21 days prior to sale as provided by Applicable Law. Lender shall mail a copy of the notice to Borrower in the manner prescribed by Applicable Law. Sale shall be made at public vendue. The sale must begin at the time stated in the notice of sale or not later than three hours after that time and between the hours of 10 a.m. and 4 p.m. on the first Tuesday of the month. Borrower authorizes Trustee to sell the Property to the highest bidder for cash in one or more parcels and in any order Trustee determines. Lender or its designee may purchase the Property at any sale.

Trustee shall deliver to the purchaser Trustee's deed conveying indefeasible title to the Property with covenants of general warranty from Borrower. Borrower covenants and agrees to defend generally the purchaser's title to the Property against all claims and demands. The recitals in the Trustee's deed shall be prima facie evidence of the truth of the statements made therein. Trustee shall apply the proceeds of the sale in the following order: (a) to all expenses of the sale, including, but not limited to, reasonable Trustee's and attorneys' fees; (b) to all sums secured by this Security Instrument; and (c) any excess to the person or persons legally entitled to it.

If the Property is sold pursuant to this Section 22, Borrower or any person holding possession of the Property through Borrower shall immediately surrender possession of the Property to the purchaser at that sale. If possession is not surrendered, Borrower or such person shall be a tenant at sufferance and may be removed by writ of possession or other court proceeding.

23. Release. Upon payment of all sums secured by this Security Instrument, Lender shall provide a release of this Security Instrument to Borrower or Borrower's designated agent in accordance with Applicable Law. Borrower shall pay any recordation costs. Lender may charge Borrower a fee for releasing this Security Instrument, but only if the fee is paid to a third party for services rendered and the charging of the fee is permitted under Applicable Law.

24. Substitute Trustee; Trustee Liability. All rights, remedies and duties of Trustee under this Security Instrument may be exercised or performed by one or more trustees acting alone or together. Lender, at its option and with or without cause, may from time to time, by power of attorney or otherwise, remove or substitute any trustee, add one or more trustees, or appoint a successor trustee to any Trustee without the necessity of any formality other than a designation by Lender in writing. Without any further act or conveyance of the Property the substitute, additional or successor trustee shall become vested with the title, rights, remedies, powers and duties conferred upon Trustee herein and by Applicable Law.

Trustee shall not be liable if acting upon any notice, request, consent, demand, statement or other document believed by Trustee to be correct. Trustee shall not be liable for any act or omission unless such act or omission is willful.

25. Subrogation. Any of the proceeds of the Note used to take up outstanding liens against all or any part of the Property have been advanced by Lender at Borrower's request and upon Borrower's representation that such amounts are due and are secured by valid liens against the Property. Lender shall be subrogated to any and all rights, superior titles, liens and equities owned or claimed by any owner or holder of any outstanding liens and debts, regardless of whether said liens or debts are acquired by Lender by assignment or are released by the holder thereof upon payment.

26. Partial Invalidity. In the event any portion of the sums intended to be secured by this Security Instrument cannot be lawfully secured hereby, payments in reduction of such sums shall be applied first to those portions not secured hereby.

27. Purchase Money; Owelty of Partition; Renewal and Extension of Liens Against Homestead Property; Acknowledgment of Cash Advanced Against Non-Homestead Property. Check box as applicable:
    ☑   **Purchase Money.**

The funds advanced to Borrower under the Note were used to pay all or part of the purchase price of the Property. The Note also is primarily secured by the vendor's lien retained in the deed of even date with this Security Instrument conveying the Property to Borrower, which vendor's lien has been assigned to Lender, this Security Instrument being additional security for such vendor's lien.

☐ **Owelty of Partition.**

The Note represents funds advanced by Lender at the special instance and request of Borrower for the purpose of acquiring the entire fee simple title to the Property and the existence of an owelty of partition imposed against the entirety of the Property by a court order or by a written agreement of the parties to the partition to secure the payment of the Note is expressly acknowledged, confessed and granted.

☐ **Renewal and Extension of Liens Against Homestead Property.**

The Note is in renewal and extension, but not in extinguishment, of the indebtedness described on the attached Renewal and Extension Exhibit which is incorporated by reference. Lender is expressly subrogated to all rights, liens and remedies securing the original holder of a note evidencing Borrower's indebtedness and the original liens securing the indebtedness are renewed and extended to the date of maturity of the Note in renewal and extension of the indebtedness.

☐   **Acknowledgment of Cash Advanced Against Non-Homestead Property.**

The Note represents funds advanced to Borrower on this day at Borrower's request and Borrower acknowledges receipt of such funds. Borrower states that Borrower does not now and does not intend ever to reside on, use in any manner, or claim the Property secured by this Security Instrument as a business or residential homestead. Borrower disclaims all homestead rights, interests and exemptions related to the Property.

28. Loan Not a Home Equity Loan. The Loan evidenced by the Note is not an extension of credit as defined by Section 50(a)(6) or Section 50(a)(7), Article XVI, of the Texas Constitution. If the Property is used as Borrower's residence, then Borrower agrees that Borrower will receive no cash from the Loan evidenced by the Note and that any advances not necessary to purchase the Property, extinguish an owelty lien, complete construction, or renew and extend a prior lien against the Property, will be used to reduce the balance evidenced by the Note or such Loan will be modified to evidence the correct Loan balance, at Lender's option. Borrower agrees to execute any documentation necessary to comply with this Section 28.

BY SIGNING BELOW, Borrower accepts and agrees to the terms and covenants contained in this Security Instrument and in any Rider executed by Borrower and recorded with it.

Witnesses:

_____   _____(Seal)
                                                                        JOHN DOE - Borrower

_____   _____(Seal)
                                                                        JANE DOE - Borrower

_____ [Space Below This Line For Acknowledgment] _____

NOTE

_____September 11th, 2015_____   _____Houston_____, _____Texas_____
            [Date]   [City]   [State]

_____1333 Sugar Lane, Houston, Texas 77333_____
                        [Property Address]

1. **BORROWER'S PROMISE TO PAY**

   In return for a loan that I have received, I promise to pay U.S. $ __300,000.00__ (this amount is called "Principal"), plus interest, to the order of the Lender. The Lender is __GENERAL MORTGAGE COMPANY__. I will make all payments under this Note in the form of cash, check, or money order.

   I understand that the Lender may transfer this Note. The Lender or anyone who takes this Note by transfer and who is entitled to receive payments under this Note is called the "Note Holder."

2. **INTEREST**

   Interest will be charged on unpaid principal until the full amount of Principal has been paid. I will pay interest at a yearly rate of __4.5__ %.

   The interest rate required by this Section 2 is the rate I will pay both before and after any default described in Section 6(B) of this Note.

3. **PAYMENTS**

   (A) Time and Place of Payments

   I will pay principal and interest by making a payment every month.

   I will make my monthly payment on the __1ST__ day of each month beginning on __November 1st, 2015__. I will make these payments every month until I have paid all of the principal and interest and any other charges described below that I may owe under this Note. Each monthly payment will be applied as of its scheduled due date and will be applied to interest before Principal. If, on __October 1st, 2045__, I still owe amounts under this Note, I will pay those amounts in full on that date, which is called the "Maturity Date."

   I will make my monthly payments at __123 Milam Street, Suite 200, Houston, Texas 77056__ or at a different place if required by the Note Holder.

   (B) Amount of Monthly Payments

   My monthly payment will be in the amount of U.S. $ 1,520.06

   MULTISTATE FIXED RATE NOTE—Single Family—Fannie Mae/Freddie Mac UNIFORM INSTRUMENT   Form 3200   1/01 *(page 1 of 4 pages)*

4. **BORROWER'S RIGHT TO PREPAY**

   I have the right to make payments of Principal at any time before they are due. A payment of Principal only is known as a "Prepayment." When I make a Prepayment, I will tell the Note Holder in writing that I am doing so. I may not designate a payment as a Prepayment if I have not made all the monthly payments due under the Note.

   I may make a full Prepayment or partial Prepayments without paying a Prepayment charge. The Note Holder will use my Prepayments to reduce the amount of Principal that I owe under this Note. However, the Note Holder may apply my Prepayment to the accrued and unpaid interest on the Prepayment amount, before applying my Prepayment to reduce the Principal amount of the Note. If I make a partial Prepayment, there will be no changes in the due date or in the amount of my monthly payment unless the Note Holder agrees in writing to those changes.

5. **LOAN CHARGES**

   If a law, which applies to this loan and which sets maximum loan charges, is finally interpreted so that the interest or other loan charges collected or to be collected in connection with this loan exceed the permitted limits, then: (a) any such loan charge shall be reduced by the amount necessary to reduce the charge to the permitted limit; and (b) any sums already collected from me which exceeded permitted limits will be refunded to me. The Note Holder may choose to make this refund by reducing the Principal I owe under this Note or by making a direct payment to me. If a refund reduces Principal, the reduction will be treated as a partial Prepayment.

6. BORROWER'S FAILURE TO PAY AS REQUIRED

(A) Late Charge for Overdue Payments

If the Note Holder has not received the full amount of any monthly payment by the end of ___10___ calendar days after the date it is due, I will pay a late charge to the Note Holder. The amount of the charge will be _5_ % of my overdue payment of principal and interest. I will pay this late charge promptly but only once on each late payment.

(B) Default

If I do not pay the full amount of each monthly payment on the date it is due, I will be in default.

(C) Notice of Default

If I am in default, the Note Holder may send me a written notice telling me that if I do not pay the overdue amount by a certain date, the Note Holder may require me to pay immediately the full amount of Principal which has not been paid and all the interest that I owe on that amount. That date must be at least 30 days after the date on which the notice is mailed to me or delivered by other means.

(D) No Waiver By Note Holder

Even if, at a time when I am in default, the Note Holder does not require me to pay immediately in full as described above, the Note Holder will still have the right to do so if I am in default at a later time.

(E) Payment of Note Holder's Costs and Expenses

If the Note Holder has required me to pay immediately in full as described above, the Note Holder will have the right to be paid back by me for all of its costs and expenses in enforcing this Note to the extent not prohibited by applicable law. Those expenses include, for example, reasonable attorneys' fees.

7. GIVING OF NOTICES

Unless applicable law requires a different method, any notice that must be given to me under this Note will be given by delivering it or by mailing it by first class mail to me at the Property Address above or at a different address if I give the Note Holder a notice of my different address.

Any notice that must be given to the Note Holder under this Note will be given by delivering it or by mailing it by first class mail to the Note Holder at the address stated in Section 3(A) above or at a different address if I am given a notice of that different address.

8. OBLIGATIONS OF PERSONS UNDER THIS NOTE

If more than one person signs this Note, each person is fully and personally obligated to keep all of the promises made in this Note, including the promise to pay the full amount owed. Any person who is a guarantor, surety, or endorser of this Note is also obligated to do these things. Any person who takes over these obligations, including the obligations of a guarantor, surety or endorser of this Note, is also obligated to keep all of the promises made in this Note. The Note Holder may enforce its rights under this Note against each person individually or against all of us together. This means that any one of us may be required to pay all of the amounts owed under this Note.

9. WAIVERS

I and any other person who has obligations under this Note waive the rights of Presentment and Notice of Dishonor. "Presentment" means the right to require the Note Holder to demand payment of amounts due. "Notice of Dishonor" means the right to require the Note Holder to give notice to other persons that amounts due have not been paid.

10. UNIFORM SECURED NOTE

This Note is a uniform instrument with limited variations in some jurisdictions. In addition to the protections given to the Note Holder under this Note, a Mortgage, Deed of Trust, or Security Deed (the "Security Instrument"), dated the same date as this Note, protects the Note Holder from possible losses which might result if I do not keep the promises which I make in this Note. That Security Instrument describes how and under what conditions I may be required to make immediate payment in full of all amounts I owe under this Note. Some of those conditions are described as follows:

If all or any part of the Property or any Interest in the Property is sold or transferred (or if Borrower is not a natural person and a beneficial interest in Borrower is sold or transferred) without Lender's prior written consent, Lender may require immediate payment in full of all sums secured by this Security Instrument. However, this option shall not be exercised by Lender if such exercise is prohibited by Applicable Law.

If Lender exercises this option, Lender shall give Borrower notice of acceleration. The notice shall provide a period of not less than 30 days from the date the notice is given in accordance with Section 15 within which Borrower must pay all sums secured by this Security Instrument.

If Borrower fails to pay these sums prior to the expiration of this period, Lender may invoke any remedies permitted by this Security Instrument without further notice or demand on Borrower.

WITNESS THE HAND(S) AND SEAL(S) OF THE UNDERSIGNED.

_____(Seal)

JOHN DOE - Borrower

_____(Seal)

JANE DOE - Borrower

_____(Seal)

- Borrower

[Sign Original Only]

Appendix

Specific Closing Instructions v.2.2

SPECIFIC CLOSING INSTRUCTIONS

These Specific Closing Instructions are to be read in conjunction with the General Closing Instructions, which are incorporated by reference and may be found at www.mbaa.org/gci.htm. If any provisions in these Specific Closing Instructions conflict with the provisions in the General Closing Instructions, the Specific Closing Instructions shall control.

FILE/CASE NUMBER: DATE & TIME:

SETTLEMENT AGENT CONTACT INFORMATION

Settlement Agent Name: Phone Number:

Company Name: Fax Number:

Mailing Address: Email:

LENDER CONTACT INFORMATION

Instructions: If settlement is not completed within ___ hours after receipt of funds, Settlement Agent must notify the Lender's Contact Person immediately and return Lender's funds and Closing Documents to Lender immediately unless otherwise indicated.

Contact Name: Phone Number:

Lender Name: Fax Number:

Mailing Address: Email:

MORTGAGE BROKER CONTACT INFORMATION

Contact Name: Phone Number:

Mortgage Broker Name: Fax Number:

Mailing Address: Email:

BORROWER INFORMATION

Borrower Name: Phone Number:

Borrower Type: Fax Number:

Mailing Address: Email:

Power of Attorney Information:

Borrower Name: Phone Number:

Borrower Type: Fax Number:

Mailing Address: Email:

Power of Attorney Information:

SELLER INFORMATION

Seller Name: Phone Number:

Mailing Address: Fax Number:

     Email:

PROPERTY INFORMATION

Property Address: Property County:

Property Type: Sales Price: Down Payment:

Appraised Value: LTV:

Appendix 721

Specific Closing Instructions v.2.2

CLOSING DOCUMENT INFORMATION

Closing Document Expiration Date: Interest Rate Expiration Date:

Other Document Specific Information:

LOAN INFORMATION

Loan Purpose: Closing Date:

Vesting to Read:

Loan Number: MERS Number: Loan Amount:

Loan Type: Anticipated Disbursement Date: Funding/Settlement Date:

APR: Initial Payment Amount: Term/Amortization:

First Payment Date: Last Payment Date: Maturity Date:

Index: Margin: Interest Change Date:

Lifetime Rate Cap: Lifetime Rate Floor: Periodic Rate Cap:

REQUIRED DOCUMENTATION

Instructions: The following documents are necessary to complete the above-referenced loan transaction. Within [   ] hours after settlement, Settlement Agent must return to Lender the following documents, other than those to be presented for recording. [Settlement Agent must [use the enclosed envelope or label provided, and] send package to Lender by: [Regular Mail/Overnight/Expedite Delivery (If Lender is to pay for overnight delivery bill to [Carrier] [Account Number]]]. Settlement Agent must submit for recording, immediately upon obtaining signatures and receiving funds, the original Mortgage/Deed of Trust, Riders and/or Assignments.

Deed of Trust	Borrower's Certification	Credit Agreement
Legal Exhibit A	Initial Escrow Acct. Disc. Statement	Fair Lending Notice
Hazard Insurance Requirements	Notice of Right to Cancel	Patriot Act
4506		
	This list should be populated based on the loan package. Additional information may appear such as an annotation of who signs which document and references to the General Closing Instructions may be added, ex. Instructions for Notice of Right to Cancel.	*Overflow to appear on Attachment*

TITLE INSURANCE

Instructions: Settlement Agent shall not disburse Lender's funds until the following conditions are met:
1) Mortgagee's title insurance policy must insure that Lender's security instrument constitutes a valid [1st/2 nd] lien on the borrower's estate or interest identified in the title insurance commitment, title report or binder, dated [date], subject to the following exceptions:

2) The following endorsements must be incorporated into the final title insurance policy:

3) Insured Lender must appear as: [Insured Lender]
3) Secondary Financing in the amount of [amount] has been approved:
4) Title Policy Coverage Amount:
5) Survey Required: [Yes/No]
6) Other Conditions:

HAZARD INSURANCE

Loss payee/mortgagee clause to read:

Flood: Deductible:
Hazard: Deductible:
Other: Deductible:

Appendix

Specific Closing Instructions v.2.2

LOAN FEES, CHARGES, RESERVES & PAYOFFS

Instructions: The final HUD Settlement Statement must be completed at settlement and must accurately reflect all receipts and disbursements indicated in these closing instructions and any amended closing instructions subsequent hereto. If any changes to fees occur, Settlement Agent may not fund loan without Lender's prior written approval. Fax a certified copy of the final HUD-1 Settlement Statement to [_____], Attention: [____].
(may be laid out without lines for programming concerns – also add column/mark to indicate *fees deducted* from wire)

HUD #	Fee/Charge	POC	POC By	Bal. Due	Paid By	Paid To
	Blank Page *With No Data*					

B = Borrower, R= Broker, L = Lender, I = Investor, S = Service Provider, T = Title Company, O = Other
D = Deducted from Wire

Appendix 723

Specific Closing Instructions v.2.2

LOAN FEES, CHARGES, RESERVES & PAYOFFS

Instructions: The final HUD Settlement Statement must be completed at settlement and must accurately reflect all receipts and disbursements indicated in these closing instructions and any amended closing instructions subsequent hereto. If any changes to fees occur, Settlement Agent may not fund loan without Lender's prior written approval. Fax a certified copy of the final HUD-1 Settlement Statement to [_____], Attention: [_____].
This Is A REPEAT OF PAGE 3 with SAMPLE DATA –organized by fee type rather than line number – from copy of HUD.

HUD #	Fee/Charge	POC	POC By	Bal. Due	Paid By	Paid To
	Lender Fees					
801.	Loan Origination Fee			$605.00	B	L
802.	Loan Discount 1 %			$720.00	S	L
809.	Document Prep Fee			$150.00	S	L
	Total			**$1,475.0**		
	Broker Fees					
810.	Yield Spread Premium - 1.625%	$1,170.00	L			
815.	Automated Underwriting			$45.00	B	R
	Total			**$45.00**		
	Service Provider Fees					
804.	Credit Report Fee to Credit Report Service			$ 9.50	B	S
804.	Credit Report Fee to Credit Report Service			$25.00	R	S
814.	Courier Fee to Quick Courier			$40.00	B	S
				$74.50		
900.	**Items Required By Lender To Be Paid In Advance**					
901.	Interest from 12/25/11 to 01/01/12 @ $13.06851/day			$ 91.48	B	L
903.	Hazard Insurance to Good Insurance Co.			$ 580.00	B	L
	Total			**$671.48**		
1000.	Reserves Deposited with Lender					
1001.	Hazard Insurance 3 months @ $48.33 per month			$ 144.99	B	L
1004.	County Property - Taxes 4 mos. @ $101.77 per			$407.08	B	L
1009.	Aggregate Adjustment			-$ 48.33	B	L
	Total			**$503.74**		
1100.	**Title Charges**					
1101.	Settlement or Closing fee to Jane's Title Company			$255.00	S	T
1102.	Title Search			$140.00	S	T
1108.	Title Insurance			$600.00	B	T
	Total			**$995.00**		
1200.	**Government Recording and Transfer Charges**					
1201.	Recording Fees – Harris County			$ 86.00	B	O
1203.	State Tax Stamps			$ 56.35	B	O
	Total			**$142.35**		
	Payoffs					
	Lien Payoff #1			$1,777.77	S	O
	Lien Payoff #2			$ 585.00	S	O
	Total			**$ 2,362.77**		

B = Borrower, R= Broker, L = Lender, I = Investor, S = Service Provider, T = Title Company, O = Other

Specific Closing Instructions v.2.2

CONDITIONS TO BE SATISFIED PRIOR TO DISBURSEMENT OF LOAN PROCEEDS

Settlement Agent must obtain satisfactory evidence that all taxes are paid through settlement or Settlement Agent must otherwise notify Lender of procedures to assure timely payment. [Lender is to be at no expense in this transaction.]

Additional Funding Instructions:

Attachments: The following documents are attached:
___ Attachment to Specific Closing Instructions (Overflow Page)
___ Construction Addendum (outside scope of closing instruction project)
___ Government Loan Addendum (outside scope of closing instruction project)
___ Texas Loan Addendum (outside scope

Appendix

Attachment to Specific Closing Instructions

This is an "overflow" page for the excess data that doesn't fit into the allotted space. Additional information for Borrower, Seller, Required Documents, Loan Fees and Charges, Conditions, etc...

Appendix

Prepared By:
Daidalos Credit Group
599 Telhaven Dr.
Oxford, FL 34484
352-782-0000

Prepared For:
ABC Mortgage Company
456 Front Street
AnyTown, USA 00000

Report ID: 54323
Customer Code: B1234
Requested By: mjd

Ordered	Released	Reissued	Repositories Requested
6/06/2016	6/11/2016		TransUnion, Experian, Equifax

Applicant

Name	Social Security Number
Richard Chaney	123-45-6789

Current Address: 123 Darling Springs, Apt 667, Dallas, TX 75243

TransUnion	Experian	Equifax
FICO Risk Score, Classic (04)	Fair Isaac	Beacon 5.0
712	**717**	**722**
Credit Assure™	Credit Assure™	Credit Assure™
+2	**+22**	**OK**
We found opportunities to raise your credit score by 2 points with the default settings.	We found opportunities to raise your credit score by 22 points with the default settings.	We did not find opportunities to raise your credit score with the default settings.

Co-Applicant

Name	Social Security Number
Jane Chaney	987-65-4321

Current Address: 123 Darling Springs, Apt 667, Dallas, TX 75243

TransUnion	Experian	Equifax
FICO Risk Score, Classic (04)	Fair Isaac	Beacon 5.0
605	**611**	**620**
Credit Assure™	Credit Assure™	Credit Assure™
+4	**+10**	**OK**
We found opportunities to raise your credit score by 4 points with the default settings.	We found opportunities to raise your credit score by 10 points with the default settings.	We did not find opportunities to raise your credit score with the default settings.

This product is based on information derived from credit reports produced by the major credit reporting agencies by Cutie Expert Systems LLC and does not represent that Cutie Expert Systems Credit Scores are the same or similar to credit scores produced by other companies. Cutie Expert Systems is not associated with Fair Isaac Corporation. Score changes predicted by Cutie Expert System products are estimates and not guaranteed. Cutie Expert Systems LLC is responsible for inaccurate results due to incorrect, missing or outdated credit report information. It is intended for use as a demonstration of a fictional credit report for learning purposes.

Printed and Delivered by Experian Inc.

Fraud Messages

Date	Reported On	Comment
05/06/2015	05/07/2015	Authorized User Alert: 4% of Satisfactory Open Revolving Accounts are Authorized User Accounts *

Credit Summary

Account Type	Number of Accounts	Open Accounts	Accounts Currently Past Due	Past Due	Payment	Balance	Accounts	30 Days	60 Days	90+ Days
							Historical Late Payments			
Mortgage	1	1	0	$0	$679	$234,231	0	0	0	0
Installment	5	0	0	$0	$0	$0	1	5	5	0
Revolving/Credit Line	28	25	0	$0	$491	$16,742	2	3	1	0
Totals	33	25	0	$0	$491	$16,742	3	8	6	0

Number of Public Records: 0
Number of Collections/Charge-offs: 0
Bankruptcy: No
Available Credit: $86,186
Revolving/Credit Line Used: 16%
Number of Inquiries: 8
Number of Authorized User Accounts: 2

Late Payment History

1 Current	4 90-119 Days Late	8 Repossession
2 30-59 Days Late	5 120-149 Days Late	9 Charged Off / Collection
3 60-89 Days Late	6 150+ Days Late	X No Data Available

Trade	Type	2012 M J J A S O N D	2013 J F M A M J J A S O N D	2014 J F M A M J J A S O N D	2015 J F M A M J J A S O N D	2016 J F M A
AHM (1112)	Inst	3 3 X X X X X X X	X X X X 1 X X X X X X X	X X X X X X X X X X X X	X X X X X X X X X X X X	X X X X
FST USA BK B (0931)	Rev	1 1 2 2 3 1 1 1	1 1 1 1 1 1 1 1			

Merge(3)

Page 1 of 8

Prepared By:
Daidalos Credit Group
599 Telhaven Dr.
Oxford, FL 34484
352-782-0000

Prepared For:
ABC Mortgage Company
456 Front Street
AnyTown, USA 00000

Report ID: 54323
Customer Code: B1234
Requested By: mjd

Ordered	Released	Reissued	Repositories Requested
06/06/2016	06/11/2016		TransUnion, Experian, Equifax

Applicant / Co-Applicant

	Applicant	Co-Applicant
Name	Richard Chaney	Jane Chaney
Social Security Number	123-45-6789	987-65-4321
Age	62	23
Dependants	3	1
Marital Status	Married	Married
Current Address	123 Darling Springs, Apt 667, Dallas, TX 75243	123 Darling Springs, Apt 667, Dallas, TX 75243
Former Address		
Employer	Brown & Root, 123 Main, Dallas, TX 75222	Texas Metropolitian Exercise Inc., 154 Main, Dallas, TX 75222
Former Employer		

Repository Files

Name	Social Security Number	Repository	Score(s)	Pulled	File ID
Richard Chaney	123-45-6789	TransUnion	712	06/06/2016	TUC-A1
Richard Chaney	123-45-6789	Experian	717	06/06/2016	EXP-A1
Richard Chaney	123-45-6789	Equifax	722	06/06/2016	EQX-A1

Credit Score Information

Score	Name	Repository	Model	Developed By	Range	Calculated	Reported On
712	Richard Chaney	TransUnion	FICO Risk Score, Classic (04)	Fair Isaac	250-900	06/07/2016	TUC-A1

Factors (018, 030, 012, 010)
- Number of accounts with delinquency
- Time since most recent account opening is too short
- Length of time revolving accounts have been established
- Proportion of balances to credit limits is too high on bank revolving or other revolving accounts
- Score value was adversely affected by credit inquiries present in the credit file.

Score	Name	Repository	Model	Developed By	Range	Calculated	Reported On
717	Richard Chaney	Experian	Fair Isaac	Fair Isaac	300-850	06/07/2016	EXP-A1

Factors (18, 10, 08, 05)
- Number of accounts delinquent.
- Proportion of balance to high credit on bank revolving or all revolving accounts.
- Number of recent inquiries.
- Number of accounts with balances.

Score	Name	Repository	Model	Developed By	Range	Calculated	Reported On
722	Richard Chaney	Equifax	Beacon 5.0	Fair Isaac	300-850	06/07/2016	EQX-A1

Factors (30, 18, 23, 5)
- Time since most recent account opening is too short
- Number of accounts with delinquency
- Number of bank or national revolving accounts with balances
- Too many accounts with balances
- Score value was adversely affected by credit inquiries present in the credit file.

Credit History

Summary

Number of Accounts	Number of Open Accounts	Number of Delinquent Accounts	Credit Limit	High Credit	Past Due	Payment	Balance
5	4	0	$285,000	$266,485	$0	$1,395	$250,479

VISA	ECOA	Opened	Last Activity	Closed	Reported	Credit Limit	High Credit			
512 Main Street Fairfield, CT 06878	Individual	06/2004	05/02/2016		06/06/2016	$20,000	$16,800			
	Account Type	Collateral	Terms	Reported On		Manner of Payment		Past Due	Payment (Est.)	Balance
	Revolving	Credit Card		TUC-A1, EXP-A1, EQX-A1		Current (R01)		$0	$222	$6,800
Account Number 345678	Months Reviewed 48	30-59 Days Late 2 Times		60-89 Days Late 0 Times		90-119 Days Late 0 Times				
		120-149 Days Late 0 Times		150+ Days Late 0 Times						

Appendix

				Merge(3)				Page 2 of 8
Applicant **Richard Chaney**		Applicant's SSN **123-45-6789**	Co-Applicant **Jane Lynch**		Co-Applicant's SSN **987-65-4321**	Loan Number **66613666**		Report ID **54323**
				Credit History (continued)				

	ECOA Individual	Opened 11/2008	Last Activity 5/05/2016	Closed	Reported 06/06/2016	Credit Limit	High Credit $195,000			
ABC Mortgage Co. 5001 N. MacArthur Blvd. Irving, Texas 75038	Account Type Open	Collateral Secured	Terms	Reported On TUC-A1, EXP-A1, EQX-A1		Manner of Payment Current (O01)		Past Due $0	Payment (Min.) $1808	Balance $158.555
Account Number 1234567	Months Reviewed 1	30-59 Days Late 0 Times		60-89 Days Late 0 Times		90-119 Days Late 0 Times				
		120-149 Days Late 0 Times		150+ Days Late 0 Times						

	ECOA Joint	Opened 01/2008	Last Activity 5/31/2016	Closed	Reported 06/06/2016	Credit Limit	High Credit $18,213			
Lexis Finance USA 180 Main Street Fairfield, CT 06824	Account Type Installment	Collateral Secured	Terms	Reported On TUC-A1, EXP-A1, EQX-A1		Manner of Payment Current (R01)		Past Due $0	Payment (Min.) $269	Balance $8,999
Account Number 906DC85215	Months Reviewed 12	30-59 Days Late 0 Times		60-89 Days Late 0 Times		90-119 Days Late 0 Times				
		120-149 Days Late 0 Times		150+ Days Late 0 Times						

	ECOA Individual	Opened 06/11/2012	Last Activity 5/07/2016	Closed	Reported	Credit Limit $11,000	High Credit			
Volvo Texas 3496 Hollis Turnpike Austin, TX 75209	Account Type Installment	Collateral Secured	Terms	Reported On TUC-A1, EXP-A1, EQX-A1		Manner of Payment Current (R01)		Past Due $0	Payment (Min.) $259	Balance $15,555
Account Number 133BB85269	Months Reviewed 21	30-59 Days Late 0 Times		60-89 Days Late 0 Times		90-119 Days Late 0 Times				
		120-149 Days Late 0 Times		150+ Days Late 0 Times						

	ECOA Individual	Opened 01/2003	Last Activity 02/22/2012	Closed	Reported	Credit Limit $3,600	High Credit $1,817			
GEMB/WALMART POB 103027 Roswell, GA 30076 877-294-7880	Account Type Revolving	Collateral Charge Account	Terms	Reported On TUC-A1, EXP-A1, EQX-A1		Manner of Payment Current (R01)		Past Due $0	Payment (Min.) $0	Balance $0
Account Number 714331456132	Months Reviewed 48	30-59 Days Late 0 Times		60-89 Days Late 0 Times		90-119 Days Late 0 Times				
		120-149 Days Late 0 Times		150+ Days Late 0 Times						

Merge(3)

Page 1 of 8

Prepared By:
Daidalos Credit Group
599 Telhaven Dr.
Oxford, FL 34484
352-782-0000

Prepared For:
ABC Mortgage Company
456 Front Street
AnyTown, USA 00000

Report ID: 54323
Customer Code: B1234
Requested By: mjd

Ordered	Released	Reissued	Repositories Requested
06/06/2016	06/11/2016		TransUnion, Experian, Equifax

Applicant

Name	Social Security Number	Age	Dependants	Marital Status
Richard Chaney	123-45-6789	62	3	M

Current Address: 123 Darling Springs, Apt 667, Dallas, TX 75243
Former Address:
Employer: Brown & Root, 123 Main, Dallas, TX 75222
Former Employer:

Co-Applicant

Name	Social Security Number	Age	Dependants	Marital Status
Jane Chaney	987-65-4321	23	1	M

Current Address: 123 Darling Springs, Apt 667, Dallas, TX 75243
Former Address:
Employer: Texas Metropolitan Exercise Inc., 154 Main, Dallas, TX 75222
Former Employer:

Repository Files

Name	Social Security Number	Repository	Score(s)	Pulled	File ID
Jane Chaney	987-65-4321	TransUnion	605	06/06/2016	TUC-A1
Jane Chaney	987-65-4321	Experian	611	06/06/2016	EXP-A1
Jane Chaney	987-65-4321	Equifax	620	06/06/2016	EQX-A1

Credit Score Information

Score	Name	Repository	Model	Developed By	Range	Calculated	Reported On
605	Jane Chaney	TransUnion	FICO Risk Score, Classic (04)	Fair Isaac	250-900	06/07/2016	TUC-A1

Factors (018, 030, 012, 010)
- Number of accounts with delinquency
- Time since most recent account opening is too short
- Length of time revolving accounts have been established
- Proportion of balances to credit limits is too high on bank revolving or other revolving accounts
- Score value was adversely affected by credit inquiries present in the credit file.

Score	Name	Repository	Model	Developed By	Range	Calculated	Reported On
611	Jane Chaney	Experian	Fair Isaac	Fair Isaac	300-850	06/07/2016	EXP-A1

Factors (18, 10, 08, 05)
- Number of accounts delinquent.
- Proportion of balance to high credit on bank revolving or all revolving accounts.
- Number of recent inquiries.
- Number of accounts with balances.

Score	Name	Repository	Model	Developed By	Range	Calculated	Reported On
620	Jane Chaney	Equifax	Beacon 5.0	Fair Isaac	300-850	06/07/2016	EQX-A1

Factors (30, 18, 23, 5)
- Time since most recent account opening is too short
- Number of accounts with delinquency
- Number of bank or national revolving accounts with balances
- Too many accounts with balances
- Score value was adversely affected by credit inquiries present in the credit file.

Credit History

Summary

Number of Accounts	Number of Open Accounts	Number of Delinquent Accounts	Credit Limit	High Credit	Past Due	Payment	Balance
7	5	0	$285,000	$266,485	$0	$1,456	$261,790

Macy's/Foley's	ECOA	Opened	Last Activity	Closed	Reported	Credit Limit	High Credit			
512 Main Street Fairfield, CT 06878	Individual	06/2004	05/02/2016		06/06/2016	$14,500	$5,883			
	Account Type Revolving	Collateral Credit Card	Terms	Reported On TUC-A1, EXP-A1, EQX-A1	Manner of Payment Current (R01)			Past Due	Payment (Est.)	Balance
Account Number 906DC85215	Months Reviewed 48	30-59 Days Late 0 Times		60-89 Days Late 0 Times		90-119 Days Late 0 Times		$0	$180	$2,490
		120-149 Days Late 0 Times		150+ Days Late 0 Times						

Appendix

Merge(3) — Page 2 of 8

Applicant: Richard Chaney **Applicant's SSN:** 123-45-6789 **Co-Applicant:** Jane Chaney **Co-Applicant's SSN:** 987-65-4321 **Loan Number:** 66613666 **Report ID:** 54323

Credit History (continued)

Creditor / Address / Account #	ECOA	Opened	Last Activity	Closed	Reported	Credit Limit	High Credit	Past Due	Payment (Min.)	Balance
Real Finance 170 Georgetown Ave. Oft City, Grand Cayman BWI Account Number: 11	Individual Account Type: Open Months Reviewed: 37	11/2008 Collateral: Open	05/02/2016 Terms		06/06/2016		$11,000	$0	$99.99	$777
Manner of Payment: Current (O01) — Reported On: TUC-A1, EXP-A1, EQX-A1 30-59 Days Late: 8 Times 60-89 Days Late: 8 Times 90-119 Days Late: 3 Times 120-149 Days Late: 3 Times 150+ Days Late: 1 Times										
Lexis Finance USA 180 Main Street Fairfield, CT 06824 Account Number: 906DC85215	Joint Account Type: Installment Months Reviewed: 12	01/2008 Collateral: Secured	05/31/2016 Terms		06/06/2016		$18,213	$0	$269	$8,999
Manner of Payment: Current (R01) — Reported On: TUC-A1, EXP-A1, EQX-A1 30-59 Days Late: 0 60-89: 0 90-119: 0 120-149: 0 150+: 0										
Chase Auto Fin. 3496 Hollis Turnpike Long Island, NY 10087 Account Number: 1247950	Individual Account Type: Installment Months Reviewed: 21	03/2007 Collateral: Secured	05/07/2016 Terms		06/07/2016	$11,000		$0	$266	$3,666
Manner of Payment: Current (R01) — Reported On: TUC-A1, EXP-A1, EQX-A1 30-59: 0 60-89: 0 90-119: 0 120-149: 0 150+: 0										
GEMB/WALMART POB 103027 Roswell, GA 30076 877-294-7880 Account Number: 714331456132	Individual Account Type: Revolving Months Reviewed: 48	01/2003 Collateral: Charge Account	02/22/2015 Terms			$3,600	$1,817	$0	$0	$0
Manner of Payment: Current (R01) — Reported On: TUC-A1, EXP-A1, EQX-A1 30-59: 0 60-89: 0 90-119: 0 120-149: 0 150+: 0										
MACYS Account Number: 521320409	Individual Account Type: Revolving Months Reviewed: 1	04/2003 Collateral: Revolving Charge Account	05/22/2016 Terms		06/06/2016	$1,500	$521	$0	$10	$37
Manner of Payment: Current (R01) — Reported On: EXP-A1 30-59: 0 60-89: 0 90-119: 0 120-149: 0 150+: 0 Comment: CURR ACCT										
MANDEES 401 Hackensack Ave Hackensack, NJ 07601 201-489-2111 Account Number: 21117679	Individual Account Type: Revolving Months Reviewed: 43	10/2000 Collateral: Charge Account	03/22/2010 Terms	Paid	06/07/2016	$200	$61	$0		$0
Manner of Payment: Current (R01) — Reported On: TUC-A1, EXP-A1 30-59: 0 60-89: 0 90-119: 0 120-149: 0 150+: 0										
MCYDSNB Account Number: 523155269	Individual Account Type: Revolving Months Reviewed: 1	12/2000 Collateral: Revolving Charge Account	01/21/2010 Terms	3/31/2010	06/07/2016	$1,750	$560	$0		$0
Manner of Payment: Current (R01) — Reported On: EXP-A1, EQX-A1 30-59: 2 Times 60-89: 0 90-119: 0 120-149: 0 150+: 0 Comment: CURR ACCT										

Public Records

THE REPORTING BUREAU CERTIFIES THAT: public records have been checked for judgements, foreclosures, bankruptcies, tax liens, and other legal actions involving the subject(s) were obtained directly through the repositories used, or by direct searches, or a public records search firm other than the repository, or by all methods with the following results:
PUBLIC RECORDS LEARNED: NONE

Inquiries

Date	Name	Subscriber Code	Reported On	ECOA
3/31/2014	CIBMS P.O. Box 26776 West Haven, CT 06516 203-931-2020	Z 419063	TUC-A1	Individual
02/22/2013	CBD 530 Riverside Dr Salisbury, MD 21801 410-742-9551	Z 49997	TUC-A1	Participant
07/12/2011	CBOFDELMAR	243ZB00420	EQX-A1	
03/07/2009	CREDIT PLUS 530 Riverside Dr Salisbury, MD 21801 301-742-9551	1971155	EXP-A1	
11/19/2008	FIRST USA,NA 201 N Walnut St Fl 6 Wilmington, DE 19801 800-622-6528	1203600	EXP-A1	
05/10/2008	CBD 530 Riverside Dr Salisbury, MD 21801 410-742-9551	Z 49997	TUC-A1	Participant
05/10/2008	CBOFDELMAR	243ZB00420	EQX-A1	
05/10/2008	CREDIT PLUS 530 Riverside Dr Salisbury, MD 21801 301-742-9551	1971155	EXP-A1	

Fraud Messages

OFAC Statement: In compliance with section 326 of the Patriot Act, your credit provider has checked the applicant(s) name(s) supplied by the borrower against the Office of Foreign Asset Control (OFAC) data base maintained by the Department of the Treasury. Any messages returned by your credit provider are located in this section of this credit report.

Date	Reported On	Comment
05/07/2016	Applicant	OFAC (UltraAMPS) clear. SDN list published on 03/25/2009.
05/07/2016	Applicant	Input SSN Mismatch: SSN 123-00-3333 matches what the repositories have on file.
05/07/2016	EXP	THIS REPORT HAS BEEN SUBMITTED TO THE EXPERIAN OFAC NAME MATCHING SERVICE.
05/07/2016	EXP-A1	FACTA: ADDRESS DISCREPANCY - POSSIBLE ADDRESS MISMATCH DETECTED ON PREVIOUS, 2ND PREVIOUS ADDRESS
05/07/2016		Authorized User Alert: 4% of Satisfactory Open Revolving Accounts are Authorized User Accounts *

Merge(3)

Applicant	Applicant's SSN	Co-Applicant	Co-Applicant's SSN	Loan Number	Report ID
Richard Chaney	123-45-6789	Jane Chaney	987-65-4321	66613666	54323

Repository Files Returned (continued)

File ID	Name	Current Address	Current Employer
Experian / EXP-A1 Pulled 06/07/2016	Richard Chaney Social Security Number 123-45-6789 Age / DOB 62/1953	123 Darling Springs, Apt 667 Dallas, TX 75243 Former Address	Brown & Root Former Employer

File ID	Name	Current Address	Current Employer
Equifax / EQX-A1 Pulled 06/06/2016 Infile Date 06/07/2016	Jane Chaney Social Security Number 987-65-4321 Age / DOB 23/1993	123 Darling Springs, Apt 667 Dallas, TX 75243 Former Address	Texas Metropolitian Exercise

Credit Repositories

TransUnion	Experian	Equifax
P. O. Box 1000	P. O. Box 2002	P. O. Box 105851
Chester, PA 19022	Allen, TX 75013	Atlanta, GA 30348
800-888-4213	888-397-3742	800-685-1111
www.transunion.com/direct	www.experian.com	www.equifax.com

Credit Bureau certifies that this Merged Mortgage Credit Report (MMCR) meets the guidelines as set forth by the Consumer Data Industry Association (CDIA). This report contains information supplied by the repositories listed on the report and may also contain duplicate information.

This completed Credit Report includes all applicable Legislative Cost Recovery Fees from the respective credit repositories associated with the federal Fair and Accurate Credit Transactions Act of 2003 (FACT Act).

This report can be viewed on the web by visiting http://view.ampslink.com.
Report ID: 54323
Password: 286fbcec

End of Report

Closing Disclosure

This form is a statement of final loan terms and closing costs. Compare this document with your Loan Estimate.

Closing Information
- Date Issued: 2/15/2016
- Closing Date: 3/03/2016
- Disbursement Date: 3/04/2016
- Settlement Agent: Good Luck Charlie
- File #: 0076403294
- Property: 777 Gadzooks Drive, Anytown, USA 00000
- Sale Price: $300,000

Transaction Information
- Borrower: Joe Borrower, 123 Front Street, Anytown, USA 000000
- Seller: A William Aviles, 333 Front St, Anytown, USA 00000
- Lender: ABC Mortgage Company

Loan Information
- Loan Term: 30 years
- Purpose: Purchase
- Product: Fixed Rate
- Loan Type: ☐ Conventional ☒ FHA ☐ VA ☐ _____
- Loan ID #: 7654321
- MIC #:

Loan Terms

		Can this amount increase after closing?
Loan Amount	$294.566	NO
Interest Rate	5.00%	NO
Monthly Principal & Interest *See Projected Payments below for your Estimated Total Monthly Payment*	$1,581.29	NO

		Does the loan have these features?
Prepayment Penalty		YES • As high as $3,240 if you pay off the loan during the first 2 years
Balloon Payment		NO

Projected Payments

Payment Calculation	Years 1-7	Years 8-30
Principal & Interest	$1,581.29	$1,581.29
Mortgage Insurance	+ 132.69	+ 132.69
Estimated Escrow *Amount can increase over time*	+ 216.67	+ 216.67
Estimated Total Monthly Payment	**$1,930.67**	**$1,930.67**

Estimated Taxes, Insurance & Assessments *Amount can increase over time* *See page 4 for details*	$216.67 a month	This estimate includes ☒ Property Taxes ☒ Homeowner's Insurance ☒ Other: Homeowner's Association Dues *See Escrow Account on page 4 for details. You must pay for other property costs separately.*	In escrow? YES YES NO

Costs at Closing

Closing Costs	$12,450	Includes $5,073 in Loan Costs + $7,377 in Other Costs - $0 in Lender Credits. *See page 2 for details.*
Cash to Close	$14,398	Includes Closing Costs. See Calculation Cash to Close on *Page 2 for details.*

Closing Cost Details

Loan Costs	Borrower-Paid At Closing	Borrower-Paid Before Closing	Seller-Paid At Closing	Seller-Paid Before Closing	Paid by Others
A. Origination Charges	**$3,145**				
1% of Loan Amount (Points)	2,895				
Application Fee	250				
07					
08					
B. Services Borrower Cannot Shop For	**$378**				
Appraisal Fee	250				
Credit Report Fee	40				
Flood Determination Fee	12				
Flood Monitoring Fee					
Tax Monitoring Fee					
Tax Status Research Fee	76				
10					
C. Services Borrower Can Shop For	**$1,195**				
Pest Inspection Fee	45				
Survey Fee	225				
Title - Insurance Binder					
Title – Lender's Title Policy	925				
Settlement Agent Fee					
Title - Title Search					
D. TOTAL LOAN COSTS (Borrower-Paid)	**$4,718**				
Loan Costs Subtotals (A + B + C)					
Other Costs					
E. Taxes and Other Government Fees	**$1,418**				
Recording Fees and Other Taxes	50				
Transfer Taxes	1,368				
F. Prepaids	**$4,718**				
Homeowner's Insurance Premium (1 year)	600				
Mortgage Insurance Premium (12 months)	3,040				
Prepaid Interest ($39.59 per day for 23 days @ 5.00%)	+911				
Property Taxes (1 months)	167				
G. Initial Escrow Payment at Closing	**$516**				
Homeowner's Insurance $50.00 per month for 1 mo.	50				
Mortgage Insurance $132.69 per month for 1 Mo.	133				
Property Taxes $166.67 per month for 2 mo.	333				
H. Other	**$725**				
Title – Owner's Title Policy (Optional)	725				
I. TOTAL OTHER COSTS (E + F + G + H)	**$7,377**				
TOTAL CLOSING COSTS	**$12,450**				
D + I	$12,450				

CLOSING DISCLOSURE

Calculating Cash to Close

Use this table to see what has changed from your Loan Estimate.

	Loan Estimate	Final	Did this change?
Total Closing Costs (J)	$12,450	$12,450	NO
Closing Costs Paid Before Closing	0	0	NO
Closing Costs Financed (Paid from your Loan Amount)	-3,040	-3,040	NO
Down Payment/Funds from Borrower	2,000	2,000	NO
Deposit	-$500	-$500	NO
Funds for Borrower			NO
Seller Credits			NO
Adjustments and Other Credits			NO
Cash to Close	$10,910	$10,910	

Summaries of Transactions

Use this table to see a summary of your transaction.

BORROWER'S TRANSACTION

K. Due from Borrower at Closing		$310,910
01 Sale Price of Property		$300,000
02 Sale Price of Any Personal Property Included in Sale		
03 Closing Costs Paid at Closing (J)		$10,910
04		
Adjustments		
05		
06		
07		
Adjustments for Items Paid by Seller in Advance		
08 City/Town Taxes	to	
09 County Taxes	to	
10 Assessments	to	
11 HOA Dues		
12		
13		
14		
15		

L. Paid Already by or on Behalf of Borrower at Closing		$500
01 Deposit		$294,566
02 Loan Amount		
03 Existing Loan(s) Assumed or Taken Subject to		
04		
05 Seller Credit		
Other Credits		
06 Rebate from Epsilon Title Co.		
07		
Adjustments		$4,934
08		
09		
10		
11		
Adjustments for Items Unpaid by Seller		
12 City/Town Taxes 1/1/13 to 4/14/13		
13 County Taxes	to	
14 Assessments	to	
15		
16		
17		

CALCULATION

Total Due from Borrower at Closing (K)	$310,910
Total Paid Already by or on Behalf of Borrower at Closing (L)	$300,000
Cash to Close [X] From [ ] To Borrower	$10,910

SELLER'S TRANSACTION

M. Due to Seller at Closing		$300,000
01 Sale Price of Property		$300,000
02 Sale Price of Any Personal Property Included in Sale		
03		
04		
05		
06		
07		
08		
Adjustments for Items Paid by Seller in Advance		
09 City/Town Taxes	to	
10 County Taxes	to	
11 Assessments	to	
12 HOA Dues		
13		
14		
15		
16		

N. Due from Seller at Closing		
01 Excess Deposit		
02 Closing Costs Paid at Closing (J)		
03 Existing Loan(s) Assumed or Taken Subject to		
04 Payoff of First Mortgage Loan		$157,297
05 Payoff of Second Mortgage Loan		
06		
07		
08 Seller Credit		
09		
10		
11		
12		
13		
Adjustments for Items Unpaid by Seller		
14 City/Town Taxes 1/1/13 to 4/14/13		
15 County Taxes	to	
16 Assessments	to	
17		
18		
19		

CALCULATION

Total Due to Seller at Closing (M)	$300,000
Total Due from Seller at Closing (N)	$157,297
Cash [ ] From [X] To Seller	$142,703

CLOSING DISCLOSURE

Additional Information About This Loan

Loan Disclosures

Assumption
If you sell or transfer this property to another person, your lender
- ☐ will allow, under certain conditions, this person to assume this loan on the original terms.
- ☒ will not allow assumption of this loan on the original terms.

Demand Feature
Your loan
- ☐ has a demand feature, which permits your lender to require early repayment of the loan. You should review your note for details.
- ☒ does not have a demand feature.

Late Payment
If your payment is more than 15 days late, your lender will charge a late fee of 5% of the monthly principal and interest payment.

Negative Amortization (Increase in Loan Amount)
Under your loan terms, you
- ☐ are scheduled to make monthly payments that do not pay all of the interest due that month. As a result, your loan amount will increase (negatively amortize), and your loan amount will likely become larger than your original loan amount. Increases in your loan amount lower the equity you have in this property.
- ☐ may have monthly payments that do not pay all of the interest due that month. If you do, your loan amount will increase (negatively amortize), and, as a result, your loan amount may become larger than your original loan amount. Increases in your loan amount lower the equity you have in this property.
- ☒ do not have a negative amortization feature.

Partial Payments
Your lender
- ☒ may accept payments that are less than the full amount due (partial payments) and apply them to your loan.
- ☐ may hold them in a separate account until you pay the rest of the payment, and then apply the full payment to your loan.
- ☐ does not accept any partial payments.
If this loan is sold, your new lender may have a different policy.

Security Interest
You are granting a security interest in
456 Somewhere Ave., Anytown, ST 12345

You may lose this property if you do not make your payments or satisfy other obligations for this loan.

Escrow Account
For now, your loan
- ☒ will have an escrow account (also called an "impound" or "trust" account) to pay the property costs listed below. Without an escrow account, you would pay them directly, possibly in one or two large payments a year. Your lender may be liable for penalties and interest for failing to make a payment.

Escrow		
Escrowed Property Costs over Year 1	$2,000.04	Estimated total amount over year 1 for your escrowed property costs: Homeowner's Insurance Property Taxes
Non-Escrowed Property Costs over Year 1	$0.00	Estimated total amount over year 1 for your non-escrowed property costs: Homeowner's Association Dues You may have other property costs.
Initial Escrow Payment	$466.00	A cushion for the escrow account you pay at closing. See Section G on page 2.
Monthly Escrow Payment	$216.67	The amount included in your total monthly payment.

- ☐ will not have an escrow account because ☐ you declined it ☐ your lender does not offer one. You must directly pay your property costs, such as taxes and homeowner's insurance. Contact your lender to ask if your loan can have an escrow account.

No Escrow		
Estimated Property Costs over Year 1		Estimated total amount over year 1. You must pay these costs directly, possibly in one or two large payments a year.
Escrow Waiver Fee		

In the future,
Your property costs may change and, as a result, your escrow payment may change. You may be able to cancel your escrow account, but if you do, you must pay your property costs directly. If you fail to pay your property taxes, your state or local government may (1) impose fines and penalties or (2) place a tax lien on this property. If you fail to pay any of your property costs, your lender may (1) add the amounts to your loan balance, (2) add an escrow account to your loan, or (3) require you to pay for property insurance that the lender buys on your behalf, which likely would cost more and provide fewer benefits than what you could buy on your own.

Loan Calculations

Total of Payments. Total you will have paid after you make all payments of principal, interest, mortgage insurance, and loan costs, as scheduled.	$569,264.40
Finance Charge. The dollar amount the loan will cost you.	$274,698.40
Amount Financed. The loan amount available after paying your upfront finance charge.	$294.566
Annual Percentage Rate (APR). Your costs over the loan term expressed as a rate. This is not your interest rate.	5.1875%
Total Interest Percentage (TIP). The total amount of interest that you will pay over the loan term as a percentage of your loan amount.	93.33%

Questions? If you have questions about the loan terms or costs on this form, use the contact information below. To get more information or make a complaint, contact the Consumer Financial Protection Bureau at www.consumerfinance.gov/mortgage-closing

Other Disclosures

Appraisal
If the property was appraised for your loan, your lender is required to give you a copy at no additional cost at least 3 days before closing. If you have not yet received it, please contact your lender at the information listed below.

Contract Details
See your note and security instrument for information about
- what happens if you fail to make your payments,
- what is a default on the loan,
- situations in which your lender can require early repayment of the loan, and
- the rules for making payments before they are due.

Liability after Foreclosure
If your lender forecloses on this property and the foreclosure does not cover the amount of unpaid balance on this loan,
- [X] state law may protect you from liability for the unpaid balance. If you refinance or take on any additional debt on this property, you may lose this protection and have to pay any debt remaining even after foreclosure. You may want to consult a lawyer for more information.
- [ ] state law does not protect you from liability for the unpaid balance.

Refinance
Refinancing this loan will depend on your future financial situation, the property value, and market conditions. You may not be able to refinance this loan.

Tax Deductions
If you borrow more than this property is worth, the interest on the loan amount above this property's fair market value is not deductible from your federal income taxes. You should consult a tax advisor for more information.

Contact Information

	Lender	Mortgage Broker	Real Estate Broker (B)	Real Estate Broker (S)	Settlement Agent
Name	ABC Mortgage Co.		Omega Real Estate Broker Inc.	Alpha Real Estate Broker Co.	Epsilon Title Co.
Address	456 Front Street, Anytown, USA 00000		789 Local Lane Sometown, ST 12345	987 Suburb Ct. Someplace, ST 12340	123 Commerce Pl. Somecity, ST 12344
NMLS ID	789123				
ST License ID	321987		Z765416	Z61456	Z61616
Contact	Grace Smith		Samuel Green	Joseph Cain	Sarah Arnold
Contact NMLS ID	789123				
Contact ST License ID	321987		P16415	P51461	PT1234
Email	G.Smith@abcmtg.com		sam@omegare.biz	joe@alphare.biz	sarah@epsilontitle.com
Phone	512-556-5555		123-555-1717	321-555-7171	987-555-4321

Confirm Receipt

By signing, you are only confirming that you have received this form. You do not have to accept this loan because you have signed or received this form.

_____ _____ _____ _____
Applicant Signature   Date   Co-Applicant Signature   Date

CLOSING DISCLOSURE

GLOSSARY

The following terms are those most frequently used in real estate financing and are considered essential in understanding the material presented in this text.

203(B) home mortgage insurance As with all HUD/FHA programs, the property to be acquired and used as collateral for the loan must meet applicable standards. While there are no special requirements for the individual borrower under 203(b), he or she must have an acceptable FHA new minimum credit score and demonstrate an ability to make the required investment as well as to handle the monthly mortgage payments.

203(k) rehabilitation home mortgage insurance This program combines a purchase money mortgage with a construction loan. It targets the restoration of rundown houses as a practical means of adding to the country's housing stock.

abstract The recorded history of a land title. A compilation of all instruments affecting the title to a tract of land.

acceleration clause A clause in a mortgage instrument that permits the lender to declare the entire balance due and payable in the event of a default on the mortgage terms.

acknowledgment For real estate purposes, a signature witnessed or notarized in a manner that allows an instrument to be recorded.

acquisition cost The lesser of the purchase price or the appraised value.

ad valorem tax Property tax ("according to value" tax) that becomes a specific lien on real property on the date the tax is assessed by an authorized taxing authority.

adjustable-rate mortgage (ARM) A mortgage design that permits the lender to adjust the interest rate at periodic intervals, with the amount of change generally tied to changes in an independent published index of interest rates or yields.

affordable housing program Generally provides grants and subsidized loans to support affordable rental housing and home ownership opportunities.

agricorporate farm loans Loans for farm businesses that are similar to special-purpose property loans.

alienation The act of transferring rights in real property. Sometimes used to identify the clause in a mortgage that allows the lender to declare the balance due and payable if the mortgaged property is transferred to another.

allodial System of land ownership, in which ownership of land by individuals was absolute.

The landowner had few limitations or restrictions on the right to use or dispose of land.

American Recovery and Reinvestment Act (ARRA) Legislation signed into law on February 17, 2009, that changed the Federal Housing Administration (FHA) single-family loan limits and included a temporary expansion of the Homeowner's Assistance Program benefits for private home sale losses of both military and civilian Defense Department personnel.

amortization The systematic and continuous payment of an obligation through installments until such time as that debt has been paid off in full.

anchor tenant A major tenant that is crucial to the successful operation of a shopping center. The big merchant attracts shoppers that benefit the smaller merchants.

annual percentage rate (APR) The cost of credit expressed as a percentage of the net amount borrowed, calculated as required by Regulation Z implementing the Truth-in-Lending Act.

annual premium One of two types of FHA mortgage insurance premiums. Annual premiums are paid monthly and typically called mortgage insurance premiums (MIP).

annual return Represents the money earned on an investment, or the combination of interest earned over the life of the loan plus the discount taken at loan origination.

apartment Units leased as places of residence.

apartment building Multifamily building containing units leased as places of residence.

apparent age How old a building seems, according to the professional opinion of an appraiser.

application fee A nonrefundable fee charged by loan originators at the time an application is taken.

appraisal An estimate of property value by a qualified person.

appraisal principles Principles that guide professional thinking in evaluating property. These include: supply and demand, substitution, highest and best use, contribution, conformity, anticipation, and arm's length transaction.

appreciation An increase in value. In real estate, appreciation is considered the passive increase in property value resulting from population growth, scarcity, and/or the decreasing value of money.

asbestos A mineral fiber found in rocks; it can cause illness if inhaled.

assessed value Property value as determined by a taxing authority.

assessment A levy against a property owner for purposes of taxation; that is, the property owner pays a share of community improvements and maintenance according to the valuation of the property.

assets Real and personal property that may be chargeable with the debts of the owner.

assignment of mortgage Transfer by the lender (mortgagee) of the mortgage obligation.

assumption agreement A contract, by deed or other agreement, through which a buyer acquires title to property and undertakes the obligations of an existing mortgage.

assured income Certain income, such as wages or salary.

ASTM International (ASTM) Formally known as American Society for Testing and Materials. An international standards organization that develops and publishes voluntary consensus technical standards for a wide range of materials, products, systems, and services. They have created standards for environmental assessment.

audited statement A statement prepared by a CPA, in which the information has been prepared in accordance with accepted accounting practices and the numbers used have been verified by the preparer.

automated underwriting Advanced software capable of analyzing a loan application and approving it for funding if qualifications are met.

Automated Valuation Model (AVM) Freddie Mac's tool simplifing the mortgage process by streamlining the collateral valuation cycle.

Automated Valuation System (AVS) Fannie Mae's DU-based tool that utilizes the data entered to recommend a documentation level for each eligible one-unit property loan with a valid property address.

balance sheet A financial statement that itemizes personal or company assets and liabilities, with the difference between the two being net worth.

balloon payment A debt repayment plan wherein the installments are less than those required for full amortization of the loan, with the balance due in a lump sum at maturity. Technically, a final payment greater than two monthly payments.

basis point A unit of measure amounting to one-hundredth of 1%.

basket provision Regulations applicable to financial institutions that permit a small percentage of total assets to be held in otherwise unauthorized investments.

beneficiary The lender, or mortgagee, in a deed of trust transaction. The lender benefits from the note.

biweekly payment plan A loan repayment plan that calls for 26 half-monthly payments per year, which retires the loan earlier, thus reducing total interest costs.

blanket mortgage A mortgage that is secured by more than one parcel of real estate as collateral.

blind pool A syndicate organized to acquire property, the nature of which is not known or disclosed to the participants at the time of solicitation.

bond A debt instrument. A type of security that guarantees at maturity payment of the face value plus interest to the holder. It is usually secured by a pledge of property or a commitment of income, such as a tax revenue bond.

borrower A person or company using another's money or property; a borrower has both a legal and moral obligation to repay the loan.

bridge loan A short-term loan to cover the period between the termination of one loan and the beginning of another. Also called *interim loan*.

broker An intermediary between buyer and seller, or between lender and borrower, usually acting as agent for one or more parties, who arranges loans or buys or sells property on behalf of a principal in return for a fee or commission.

broker's price opinion A common way of estimating the value of a property.

Brownfields Program Program initiated by the EPA to remove about 25,000 sites from the federal Superfund program. This reduction in liability brought dormant sites back to useful life, improving former eyesores and making good use of well-located tracts.

build-to-suit Procedure in which the lessor agrees to construct a building to certain tenant specifications in return for a lease commitment from the prospective tenant. Also called *build-to-let*.

buydown mortgage A mortgage repayment design offering lower initial monthly payments achieved through the prepayment of a portion of the interest cost. The prepayment of interest is usually limited to the first few years and is normally paid by a seller to help attract buyers by allowing easier borrower qualification.

call provision A provision in a mortgage instrument that allows the mortgagee to accelerate full payment of the debt on a certain date or the occurrence of specified conditions.

capitalization A mathematical process for conversion of an income stream into a property valuation as used for an appraisal.

caps Limits placed on interest rate changes.

cash flow The amount of cash received over a period of time from an income property.

certificate of reasonable value (CRV) An estimate of property value prepared in accordance with requirements of the Department of Veterans Affairs. A VA appraisal.

Certified Public Accountant (CPA) The highest professional designation in accounting. A qualification that may be granted by each state. The requirements vary somewhat among the states, but all demand completion of educational courses, some experience in the field working for another CPA, and the passing of exhaustive qualification tests.

chain of title The sequence of ownership interests in a tract of land.

chattel An article of property that can be moved; personal property.

chattel mortgage An obsolete term defined as a mortgage secured by personal property. Under the Uniform Commercial Code, chattel mortgages have been replaced by security agreements.

closer The individual responsible for making final settlement of a property transaction and disbursement of the consideration.

closing The consummation of a real estate transaction wherein certain rights of ownership are transferred in exchange for the monetary and other considerations agreed upon. Also called *loan closing*.

closing costs Expenses of a property sale that must be paid in addition to the purchase price.

Closing Disclosure CFPB disclosure form that replaces the HUD-1 Settlement Statement. Borrowers must receive the Closing Disclosure at least three days prior to signing their final loan documents. If corrections are required to a Closing Disclosure that has been issued, an additional three-day waiting period may be triggered.

closing instructions These detail such items as the correct legal name for the mortgage instruments, the name of the trustee if a deed of trust is involved, and the terms of the mortgage note. Any special requirements to be included in the mortgage or deed of trust (that is, if the mortgage company is not submitting its own forms, or standardized documents, for a note and mortgage) are itemized.

cloud on title A defect in the chain of title to property that obstructs, or prevents, good delivery.

collateral Any asset acceptable as security for a loan.

collateral assessment Property evaluation assessing whether or not the collateral is sufficient to secure the loan.

collateralized debt obligation (CDO) Similar to a collateralized mortgage obligation except that it may have other asset classes besides single-family residential mortgages (such as credit card receivables, automobile loans, and second mortgages). The cash flows from the underlying mortgages or other collateral in the case of a CDO are applied first to pay interest and then to retire bonds.

collateralized mortgage obligation (CMO) A mortgage-backed security variation that segments cash flows from an underlying block of loans so as to retire different classes of bonds in a sequence based on the bonds' maturity.

commercial loan An imprecise term generally applied to an obligation collateralized by real property other than that used as a residence.

commercial paper A simple promise to pay that is unsecured (a corporate IOU).

commitment As applied to mortgage loans, a promise of loanable funds.

commitment fee Money paid in return for the pledge of a future loan.

common area That part of condominium property owned jointly by all unit owners.

common center A shopping center that offers all the services found in the neighborhood center plus an anchor tenant, such as a general merchandise store, an apparel store, a furniture outlet, a professional service, or some recreational facility.

community property Property owned equally by spouses.

Community Reinvestment Act (CRA) Passed in the late 1970s, the purpose of this Act is to ensure that regulated depository institutions serve the needs of their communities. It requires regulated institutions to publicize their lending services in their own communities and encourage participation in local lending assistance programs.

compensating balance A minimum balance held on deposit in accordance with a loan agreement.

compound interest Interest paid on accrued interest as well as on principal.

Comprehensive Environmental Response, Compensation, and Liability Act of 1980 (CERCLA) Legislation passed after the discovery of massive health problems near Love Canal that set up a $1.6 billion Hazardous Waste Trust Fund, which became known as Superfund. CERCLA provided a federal regulatory mechanism to identify, investigate, evaluate, and clean up inactive and abandoned waste sites throughout the United States. It authorized states and private parties to take appropriate action to clean up contaminated sites and seek reimbursement from the responsible parties.

comptroller of the currency Section 312 of the Dodd-Frank Act mandated the merger of OTS with the Office of the Comptroller of the Currency (OCC), the Federal Deposit Insurance Corp. (FDIC), the Federal Reserve Board, and the Consumer Financial Protection Bureau (CFPB) as of July 21, 2011.

computerized loan origination (CLO) Initiation of a mortgage loan through a terminal linked to a lender's computer. Subject to HUD limitations, the method allows real estate agents to assist in loan origination.

conditional sale An agreement granting possession of property to a buyer while title is retained by the seller until all required payments have been made.

condominium A unit in a multifamily structure or office building wherein the owner holds title to the unit plus an undivided common interest in the common elements with the other owners.

conduit A conduit makes or purchases loans from third-party correspondents under standardized terms, underwriting, and documents and then, when sufficient volume has been obtained, pools the loans for sale to investors in the CMBS market.

conforming loan A loan written on uniform documents as required by Fannie Mae and Freddie Mac if purchased by them. The loans are subject to limitations in size and kind set by the agencies and Congress.

consideration The cash, services, or token given in exchange for property or services.

constant payment A fixed payment amount, covering the interest due and a partial reduction of principal. Usually calculated in a manner that repays the loan within its term.

constant rate Also called *constant*, it is that percentage of the initial loan amount that must be paid periodically to repay the loan within the specified term.

construction loan A type of mortgage loan to finance construction, which is funded by the lender to the builder at periodic intervals as work progresses.

Consumer Financial Protection Bureau (CFPB) Independent Bureau of the Federal Reserve System under the Treasury Department that received rulemaking authority for more than a dozen federal consumer financial protection laws with the passage of the Dodd-Frank Act.

contingent liability The responsibility assumed by a third party who accepts liability for an obligation upon the failure of an initial obliger to perform as agreed.

contract for deed An agreement to sell property wherein possession is granted to the buyer while title remains with the seller for conveyance after payment has been made. Also called *land contract*.

contract of sale An agreement between a buyer and a seller of real property to deliver good title in return for a consideration.

conventional loan A loan that is not underwritten by a federal agency.

conveyance The written instrument by which an interest in real property is transferred from one party to another.

cooperative Ownership of real estate by a corporation or trust wherein the shareholders are also the tenants through leasehold agreement.

cost approach An approach to evaluation of property based on the property's reproduction cost.

cost-of-living expenses Necessary costs include food, clothing, transportation, personal and medical care, and other consumption items.

cost recovery period The time period over which tax deductions may be taken on a depreciable asset. Terminology stems from 1981 Tax Act that replaced *useful life* and *salvage value* as determinants of depreciation rates.

covenant An agreement between two or more parties that pledges the parties to perform, or not perform, certain specified acts.

creative financing A generalized term applied to many kinds of unconventional and innovative mortgage repayment plans.

Credit Alert Interactive Voice Response System (CAIVRS) System introduced by HUD in 1987 to collect and furnish credit data from its own files for lenders' and borrowers' use.

creditor One who lends something of value to another.

credit market An interesting feature of credit markets is the position of federal borrowing. Since there are no legal limits on what the government can pay for its money, it is capable of driving all other demands for credit out of the market.

credit report A report giving the credit history on an individual or company; it reveals previous debt payment experience as well as other identifying data.

credit scoring A method of giving a default probability number based on an individual's credit record.

credit union May be chartered by any group of people who can show a common bond. The bond has generally been that of a labor union, a company's employees, or a trade association. Most are relatively small and often managed by nonprofessional personnel. Their primary lending consists of small loans to their members for such purposes as buying a car or furniture.

curable depreciation Deterioration in property that can be corrected at a reasonable cost.

debenture bond An unsecured pledge to repay a debt.

debt An obligation to be repaid by a borrower to a lender.

debtor One who owes something of value to another.

debt service A term normally associated with commercial loans; it means the periodic payment of principal and interest.

deed A written instrument, which is signed, sealed, and delivered by the seller, transferring real property to another owner.

deed of trust A type of mortgage that conditionally conveys real property to a third party for holding in trust for the benefit of a lender as security for repayment of a loan.

deed restriction A clause in a deed that restricts the use of the land being conveyed.

default The failure to perform on an obligation as agreed in a contract.

deficiency judgment An unsecured money judgment against the debtor for the balance due that may be obtained in foreclosure if the collateral securing the note proves insufficient to cover the indebtedness.

delinquency A loan payment that is overdue but within the grace period allowed before actual default is declared.

Department of Housing and Urban Development (HUD) Government department that executes housing policies. The Federal Housing Administration (FHA) is part of HUD.

Department of Veterans Affairs (VA) Elevated to cabinet rank in 1989, this agency has home loan underwriting programs that have helped many people to buy and/or rehabilitate their homes. Though the VA is not in the business of making direct loans, they do offer financial assistance when disposing of repossessed properties.

depreciation The loss in value to property due to wear and tear, obsolescence, or economic factors. To offset depreciation loss, tax laws permit recovery of the cost of an investment through annual deductions from taxable income.

Desktop Originator® Fannie Mae program designed to allow an agent or a mortgage broker to take an application in a potential borrower's home with a laptop computer, relaying the information to the lender who is the seller/servicer.

Desktop Underwriter® Fannie Mae program that uses artificial intelligence and information from Fannie Mae's seller/servicer guide to properly analyze a loan application.

development loan Money loaned for the purpose of improving land by the building of streets and utilities so as to create lots suitable for sale or use in building homes.

disbursement procedures Information the lender gives the borrower about how the funds will be disbursed.

discount The difference between the amount paid for a note and the nominal or face value of that note. The reduction in the amount paid is normally measured in points as a percentage of the note amount.

discount analysis Method of analysis that takes each year's future cash flow and reduces it to its present worth.

discount rate The interest rate charged by the Federal Reserve Bank for loans made to regulated savings institutions, credit unions, and commercial banks.

disintermediation The withdrawal of deposits from savings account held by intermediaries, such as savings institutions or commercial banks, generally for reinvestment in higher yielding investments.

disposition The right of a landowner to sell, lease, give away, mortgage, or otherwise dispose of his or her land.

dollar limit A limitation on the amount of any single loan as a percentage of the lender's total assets and limits on the amount that can be loaned to any one individual.

down payment assistance programs Programs that offer down payment assistance for low-income, first-time home buyers and finance the development of multifamily, affordable rental housing.

due-on-sale clause A mortgage clause that calls for the payoff of a loan in the event of a sale or conveyance of the collateral prior to maturity of the loan.

EarlyCheck™ Fannie Mae service that assists lenders in identifying and correcting potential eligibility and/or data issues as early in their processes as possible.

earnest money A cash payment delivered to the seller of real property, or to an escrow agent for the transaction, as evidence of good faith to bind the purchase.

eCommitting™ A system Fannie Mae developed to allow approved conventional mortgage lenders more time to focus on growing their business. eCommitONE™ is an easy-to-use, web-based application that provides automated pricing information and best efforts committing processes.

economic obsolescence A loss of property value, normally incurable, resulting from factors outside the property itself, such as social, economic, or environmental forces.

Economic Stimulus Act of 2008 (ESA) Sets limits otherwise established for 2010 under Section 203(b), as amended by the Housing and Economic Recovery Act of 2008 (HERA), which are in turn based on 65% of the national conforming loan limits (used by Fannie Mae and Freddie Mac for one-unit homes in the continental United States). HERA stipulated that the national conforming loan limits be established using a house price index chosen by the Federal Housing Finance Agency (FHFA).

effective income This includes gross income from all sources, but does not include any income that HUD/FHA deems unacceptable, like a bonus, an unusually large commission, money reimbursed for travel expenses, or any repayment of principal on a capital investment.

effective interest Lower-than-market interest rates a seller could offer to a buyer during the early years of a mortgage by paying a lender part of the interest cost up front.

electromagnetic forces (EMFs) Silent, invisible electric currents that exist anywhere electrons zip through transmission lines or the innards of appliances.

eligibility Having the right qualifications to obtain a loan through satisfying the appropriate conditions.

eminent domain The right of state or federal governments, agencies of governments, or companies designated by governments, to take private property for a necessary public purpose with just compensation paid to the owner.

encroachment Any physical intrusion upon the property rights of another.

encumbrance A claim against land, such as a lien or easement. Anything that affects or limits the fee simple title to, or value of, property; for example, a mortgage.

Endangered Species Act Legislation passed in 1973 that was limited to the protection of endangered species on federal land. Since then, regulators have focused on controlling land usage, including private land, if it might contain an endangered species' habitat.

endorsement A method of credit enhancement sometimes used to expand automobile dealerships or recreational facilities is a manufacturer's endorsement of the obligation. This means that the manufacturer agrees to accept a contingent responsibility for repayment of the mortgage obligation on the special-purpose building.

entitlement Having a right to something. For VA loans, first eligibility must be met, and then the amount of entitlement determined.

environmental consulting Profession in which experts make specific environmental assessments. A growing profession for appraisers.

Environmental Protection Agency (EPA) A federal agency created in 1970 by consolidating various federal pollution control agencies. Its original authority has been substantially increased by adding responsibilities for the administration of subsequent environmental legislation.

environmental site assessment A recent requirement for loan qualification in which a professional assesses a property's potential for environmental problems for which the property owner could be liable.

Equal Credit Opportunity Act (ECOA) Federal legislation passed in 1974 to ensure the fair and impartial granting of credit by various financial institutions.

equitable title The right held by a purchaser under a contract for deed (and other similar agreements) to eventually obtain absolute ownership to property when legal title is held in the seller's or another's name.

equity The ownership interest—that portion of a property's value beyond any liability therein.

escalation The right of a lender to increase the rate of interest in a loan agreement.

escrow The process by which money and/or documents are held by a disinterested third party until all conditions of these escrow instructions, as prepared by the parties involved, have been satisfied, at which time delivery of the items can be made to the proper parties.

execute The act of signing a legal instrument by the involved parties, usually witnessed or notarized, so that it may be recorded.

Fair and Accurate Credit Transactions Act (FACT) Passed in 2003, the Act significantly amended the Fair Credit Reporting Act. The FACT sought to protect consumers from inaccurate credit information that might be reported by credit reporting agencies.

Fair Credit Reporting Act (FCRA) A federal law intended to protect the public from the reporting of inaccurate credit information by giving individuals the right to inspect information in their own file.

Fair Housing Act Federal legislation passed in 1968 with subsequent amendments that prohibits certain kinds of discrimination in the sale or rental of most residential property.

Fair Housing Amendments Act of 1988 Extended the prohibitions against discrimination in the 1968 Fair Housing Act to all residential real estate transactions and represents the only amendment to the Act to date. Prior law considers unlawful any discrimination in housing because of race, color, religion, gender, or national origin. The new amendment added two new categories for protection against discrimination: disability and familial status.

fair market value The highest monetary price or its equivalent available in a competitive market as determined by negotiation between an informed, willing, and capable buyer and an informed and willing seller. Also called *market value*.

family-resident farm loan Loan for farms where the farmer resides. Based on the three legs of any good mortgage loan: a creditworthy borrower, a property of sufficient value to provide good collateral, and the ability of the property and the borrower to produce an income, assuring repayment of the loan.

Fannie Mae Popular nickname for the Federal National Mortgage Association, a quasi-governmental agency that plays a major role in the secondary mortgage market.

farm and ranch loans Loans made for farms and ranches. Not classified as commercial loans, they require a very specialized knowledge of the borrower and the property pledged. Most of these loans are analyzed in the local area. There are few national guidelines, as each local area presents its own distinctive soil, weather, crops, and markets.

Farm Credit Administration (FCA) An independent federal agency that supervises, examines, and coordinates the Farm Credit System (FCS).

Farm Credit System (FCS) An elaborate cooperative (or borrower-owned) network of farm lending banks under the supervision, examination, and coordination of the Farm Credit Administration (FCA). Composed of five regional farm credit districts (reduced to four in 2011) owned by over a million American farmers and 5,000 of their marketing and business services cooperatives, the FCS makes long-term mortgage loans and short-term production or crop loans through different organizations.

feasibility study An analysis and evaluation of a building project to determine if it is feasible within the projected budget and will be profitable.

Federal Deposit Insurance Corporation (FDIC) An independent arm of the U.S. Treasury that insures deposits in banks and savings institutions.

federal funds rate An interest rate charged between banks for short-term loans that facilitate compliance with federal liquidity requirements. It is a rate used periodically by the Federal Reserve Bank as a guide in setting monetary policy.

Federal Housing Administration (FHA) A federal agency created in 1934, now a part of HUD, that insures high loan-to-value ratio residential loans.

Federal Reserve Bank System A central banking system created in 1913 to manage the nation's monetary system and serve as a national bank for its member institutions.

Federal Trade Commission's Privacy Rule The Privacy Rule requires that mortgage brokers, as well as depository institutions, provide an initial privacy notice as soon as the customer relationship is established.

fee simple A legal term designating the highest interest in land that includes all the rights of ownership.

feudal The feudal system of land ownership primarily granted the right to occupy and use land owned by a social superior.

FHA loan A loan insured by the Insuring Office of the Department of Housing and Urban Development; a Federal Housing Administration commitment.

FHA new minimum credit scores In 2011, the FHA tightened credit standards, incorporating minimum credit scores into the underwriting process and increasing mortgage insurance premiums. The effect is that borrowers with credit scores below 500 are not eligible.

finance fee The charge made by a lender for preparing and processing a loan package. Also known as *origination fee*.

Financial Institutions Reform, Recovery, and Enforcement Act (FIRREA) The 1989 Act dissolved the FSLIC and reorganized the deposit insurance system. A new Deposit Insurance Fund (DIF) was created, administered by the FDIC.

first mortgage A mortgage on property that is superior in right to any other mortgage because of its prior time of recording.

fixture Personal property so affixed to the land as to become a part of the realty.

forbearance Refraining from taking legal action, even though a mortgage may be in default.

foreclosure Legal action to bar a mortgagor's claims to property after default has occurred.

formal assumption With this type of assumption, the property is not conveyed to a new buyer until that person's creditworthiness has been approved by the FHA or its agent. With a creditworthy buyer assuming the loan, the seller may obtain a full release of liability from the FHA.

formaldehyde gas A colorless, toxic, and water-soluble gas that has a strong, pungent, pickle-like smell. It can be emitted by a number of household materials such as urea-formaldehyde foam insulation, formaldehyde-based adhesives used in pressed wood, particle board, plywood, shelves, cabinets, and office furniture. It can also be found in some draperies and carpeting. The gas can cause health problems ranging from minor eye, nose, and throat irritation to such serious effects as nasal cancer.

forward commitment A promise by a lender (meaning a purchaser of loans or an investor) to have certain funds available for qualifying loans submitted to that lender over a limited period of time, such as 30 days to six months.

Fraud Enforcement and Recovery Act of 2009 (FERA) Expanded the federal government's ability to prosecute mortgage fraud, securities and commodities fraud, and other types of fraud related to federal assistance and relief programs such as the Troubled Asset Relief Program (TARP).

functional obsolescence A loss in value of an improvement, resulting from poor or inadequate design or possibly from age.

funding fee A fee paid for a loan. Used to identify the fee paid to the VA for issuing its guaranty. Also may be applied to an additional fee paid for funding a conventional loan, typically a commercial loan, at closing.

future purchase contract A large continuing contract a distributor offers a supplier for its product that provides the supplier a proven source of cash flow to induce a lender's favorable decision on a loan.

gift letter A letter or statement given to a lender or government agency stating that money advanced to assist the purchase of real property is a gift and there is no obligation to repay.

Ginnie Mae Popular nickname for the Government National Mortgage Association, an agency under HUD authorized from time to time to subsidize housing assistance programs and to issue guarantees for approved pools of FHA, VA, and certain rural housing loans as a credit enhancement procedure.

grace period An agreed-upon time after an obligation becomes past due within which a party can perform without being considered in default.

graduated-payment mortgage A repayment plan popularized by the FHA, but also approved as a conventional loan, that offers early-year monthly payments substantially lower than those of a constant-level plan, permitting easier qualification for a borrower. Payment amounts increase annually at a predetermined rate until reaching a level that fully amortizes the loan within its term.

gross income The total money derived from an operating property over a given period of time.

growing equity mortgage (GEM) Method that can be used to shorten a loan term, thus reducing interest costs. Many variations may be found, but the basic pattern is to make certain increases in the payment amount each year. Then, the entire amount of the increase is applied to repayment of the principal. Also called a *graduated equity mortgage product*.

guarantee *(verb)* The act of pledging by a third party to assure performance of another.

guaranty *(noun)* A pledge by a third party to assume the obligation of another. Also applied to the government-assured portion of a VA loan.

hard-money mortgage Any mortgage loan funded in cash rather than given to finance the acquisition of real property.

hazard insurance The insurance covering physical damage to property.

hazardous materials Designation by the Environmental Protection Agency of which materials are dangerous enough to mandate cleanup wherever a concentration of such materials is found.

Home Affordable Foreclosure Alternatives Program (HAFA) Program targeting borrowers who have a mortgage payment that is unaffordable and borrowers who are interested in transitioning to more affordable housing. The typical borrower is eligible for a short sale or deed in lieu of foreclosure through HAFA.

Home Affordable Modification Program (HAMP) FHA initiative intended to help borrowers lower their monthly mortgage payment to 31% of their verified monthly gross (pretax) income to make their going-forward mortgage payments more affordable.

Home Affordable Refinance Program (HARP) FHA initiative intended to help borrowers who are current on their mortgages and have been unable to obtain a traditional refinance because the value of their homes has declined.

Home Equity Conversion Mortgage (HECM) FHA's reverse annuity mortgage.

home equity loan A loan in which the borrower pledges the property to secure a revolving line of credit. A home equity credit line stays in place for years, giving the borrower more flexibility in financing. Interest is paid only on the portion of the credit that is used, just like a credit card account. Generally, the interest rate on the loan is adjusted periodically and floats without a maximum ceiling other than usury limits.

homeowners association Association of homeowners for a neighborhood, group of condominiums, or planned unit developments. The purpose is to agree on how to maintain common areas and improve the homes or property.

homestead A tract of land owned and occupied as the family home. Also a legal life estate in land created in differing ways by state laws devised to protect the possession and enjoyment of the owner against the claims of certain creditors.

housing expense This includes the mortgage payment of principal, interest, real estate taxes, and hazard insurance, plus flood insurance if applicable. (In conventional loans, this payment is often identified simply as PITI.) The housing expense also includes the FHA annual premium charge and homeowners association or condo fees if applicable.

Housing Finance Agency Innovation Fund for the Hardest-Hit Housing Markets (HHF) Program established by the U.S. Treasury Department in early 2010 to provide at least $7.6 billion in targeted aid to states hit hard by the economic crisis. This program continues to be coordinated with various state housing finance agencies to develop innovative programs to stabilize the local housing markets and help borrowers avoid foreclosure.

HUD The Department of Housing and Urban Development.

hypothecation A pledge of property without delivering possession; for example, a mortgage.

immediate commitment This means that the loans do exist and can be delivered without delay.

impound account Money held for payment of an obligation due at some future time. Also known as an *escrow account*.

income Money or other benefit received from the investment of labor or capital.

income approach Method of estimating property value by examining the actual return per dollar invested.

income property Real estate capable of producing net revenue.

income ratio method Method of qualifying the loan applicant introduced by the VA in 1986. The income ratio method (used in conjunction with the residual method) uses some different measures—one being that the applicant's income is gross income (i.e., income taxes and Social Security taxes are not a recognized deduction).

index rate The rate to which the interest rate on an adjustable-rate mortgage is tied.

innocent landowner defense A valid defense for the landowner against future cleanup liability should contamination occur later through no fault of the landowner. The landowner must make an appropriate inquiry into the previous ownership and usage of the property before taking title to ascertain if any prior use would indicate the presence of environmental contamination or hazardous substances. If an adequate inquiry is made with proper records maintained and nothing of a hazardous nature is found, the buyer may be classed as an innocent landowner.

installment note A promissory note providing for repayment of the principal in two or more payments.

instrument A legal document in writing.

interest Payment for the use of money.

interest-only mortgage A mortgage feature that allows monthly payments of the interest only with the principal balance due in full at maturity.

interest rate indicators Treasury bill rate, prime rate, Fannie Mae/Freddie Mac–Administered Yield Requirements, and U.S. Treasury security rates all provide clues about the direction of the real estate mortgage business.

interim loan A loan made with the expectation of repayment from the proceeds of another loan. Most often used in reference to a construction loan. Also called *interim financing*.

internet loan application Increasingly popular way to shop for mortgages. This is becoming popular for applicants living in rural areas, people who are pressed for time, people with tarnished credit histories, people who feel more comfortable with impersonal vending devices than face-to-face encounters, and consumers who want to easily compare available prices and terms.

judicial foreclosure Type of foreclosure normally used when a regular mortgage is the security instrument. A default is handled by filing the required notices to the debtor, followed by a suit in court to foreclose the mortgage claim. If the court agrees with the claim, it can order that the property be sold to satisfy the debt. The sale is handled through a public auction, usually called a sheriff's sale.

junior mortgage A mortgage of lesser than first-lien priority.

kickback Any arrangement in which a fee is charged, or accepted, when no services have actually been performed.

land contract Another term used to indicate a contract for deed.

land development loan Loan made for land development.

land leases When land is leased for development.

land loan Money loaned for the purchase of raw land.

land survey An accurate measurement of the property, not a legal description of it.

late charge A fee added to an installment as a penalty for failure to make a timely payment.

Leadership in Energy and Environmental Design (LEED) An internationally recognized green building certification system. LEED is the leading third-party verification of construction designed and built using strategies aimed at increasing performance, reducing waste, and improving quality of life.

lead poisoning Harmful ingestion of lead. Most threatening to children in their formative years. Its symptoms are wide-ranging and can easily go undiagnosed and even unnoticed.

leasehold An estate in real property limited as to time, obtained and held with the consent of and by the payment of a consideration to the owner.

leverage The capacity to borrow an amount greater than the equity in property. The larger the loan in relation to the equity, the greater the leverage.

liabilities Amounts due from other depository institutions and cash items in the process of collection. These are referred to as liabilities since they are owed by the depository institution to their depositors.

LIBOR The London Interbank Offered Rate is a daily reference rate based on the interest rates at which banks borrow unsecured funds from other banks in the London wholesale money market (or interbank lending market).

lien A legal claim or attachment, filed on record, against property as security for payment of an obligation.

lien theory With this method, the borrower retains legal title to the property and grants a lien to the lender as security for repayment of a loan.

life insurance companies Not considered depository institutions; they are fully regulated by the various states that charter them. Their primary interest in using their substantial investment funds is to provide the highest yield possible commensurate with the safety of their policyholders' money.

like-kind exchange A swap of one business or investment asset for another. These transactions fall under Internal Revenue Code 1031, and an owner will have little or no tax payable at the time of the exchange.

liquidity The extent to which assets held in other forms can be easily and quickly converted into cash.

limited partnership A form of business organization, recognized in all states, that provides for one or more general partners who are responsible for the management and are personally liable for the partnership's obligations.

loan A granting of the use of money in return for the payment of interest.

loan application The basis for analysis of a borrower.

Loan Estimate A preliminary listing of the anticipated closing costs as required by the Real Estate Settlement Procedures Act.

loan modification A permanent change in the repayment amount of interest rate, often for the purpose of reducing monthly payment.

loan origination system (LOS) Systems employing workflow technology to control and monitor the various work steps involved in loan processing and using digital imaging technology to reduce the delays and inefficiencies involved in handling paper documents.

loan originator A person or company seeking mortgage loan contracts or customers.

loan pool A block of loans held in trust and pledged as security for the issuance of a guarantee certificate, which is called a mortgage-backed security.

Loan Prospector® Freddie Mac's automated underwriting system.

loan-to-value ratio (LTVR) The ratio between the amount of a loan and the value of property pledged.

loan servicing Includes the record-keeping section that maintains customers' or borrowers' accounts.

loan status report A report on the current status of an existing loan prepared by the mortgagee for the mortgagor; a statement, usually in letter form, citing the remaining balance due on the loan, the monthly payments required, the reserve held in the escrow account, and the requirements and cost of a loan payoff. Also called *mortgagor's information letter*, *mortgagee's report*, or *prequalification form*.

lock-in clause A clause in a promissory note that restricts prepayment.

maker The person who executes a promissory note.

manual underwriting Manual process (as opposed to an automated process) of evaluating the borrower's ability to repay a loan. The lender assigns a person to review the borrower's application and supporting documents.

marginal property Property capable of making only a very low economic return.

maturity The date that final payment is due on a loan.

mechanics' lien A claim for payment for services rendered or materials furnished to a property owner and filed on record in the county where the property is located. Also known as *mechanics' and materialmen's lien*, or *M&M lien*.

merchantable title A salable title that is reasonably free from risk of litigation over defects and that would be accepted by a well-informed and prudent person. Also known as *marketable title*.

mini warehouse One-story structure partitioned into small rental spaces.

monetary system The policies used in a country to control the flow of money and the monetary supply.

mortgage A conditional conveyance of property held as security for a debt.

mortgage-backed securities A type of asset-backed security that is secured by a mortgage or collection of mortgages.

mortgage banker They originate the mortgage loan, fund the loan at closing, and service the loan as it is paid off.

mortgage broker They structure loans and place them with funding sources.

mortgage debt outstanding The mortgage share of the U.S market, which normally commands 20–25% of the total credit available each year.

Mortgage Disclosure Investment Act (MDIA) Requires that any yield spread premium be fully disclosed on the newly revised Loan Estimate disclosure form, pointing out this fee that was often hidden from consumers in the past.

mortgagee A lender of money and the receiver of the security in the form of a mortgage. *(Memory note:* Lender and mortgagee both have two E's.*)*

mortgage loan originators (MLO) Institutions or individuals that work with a borrower to complete a mortgage transaction.

mortgage note A description of the debt and a promise to pay; the instrument that is secured by the mortgage.

mortgage payment A term normally used to distinguish the monthly payment on a home loan, including principal and interest plus one-twelfth of the annual property tax and insurance premium. Also known as PITI.

mortgage pool A specific block of mortgage loans held in trust as collateral for the issuance of a mortgage-backed security.

mortgage portfolio The aggregate of mortgage loans held as an investment.

mortgage release A disclaimer of further liability on the mortgage note granted by the lender. When used with a deed of trust, it is a *deed of reconveyance*.

mortgaging out Securing a loan upon completion of a project that is sufficient to cover all costs; a 100% loan.

mortgagor The borrower of money and the grantor of a mortgage as security. *(Memory note:* Borrower and mortgagor both have two O's.)

multifamily mortgage A government term designating an apartment or any property with more than four dwelling units.

Mutual Mortgage Insurance Fund A fund established by the National Housing Act into which all FHA mortgage insurance premiums and other specified revenues of the FHA are paid and from which claims are met.

mutual savings bank A nearly obsolete term designating a state-chartered savings bank owned by its own depositors. As many shift to stockholder-owned institutions, the word *mutual* is being dropped from its name.

National Mortgage Licensing System (NMLS) Created to provide a uniform mortgage application for state mortgage regulatory agencies; a nationwide repository of licensed mortgage loan origination professionals; and a minimum education, experience, and testing requirement under the SAFE Mortgage Licensing Act of 2008 (SAFE).

negative amortization A periodic increase in the principal balance due on a mortgage loan, usually resulting from unpaid interest added to the principal.

negative cash flow When cash expenditures to maintain an investment exceed the cash income derived therefrom.

negotiable instrument Any written instrument that may be legally transferred to another by endorsement or delivery, such as a check or promissory note.

neighborhood center A shopping center in a large corner area with a strip of two or more stores. Merchandise offered is mostly daily essentials such as food, drugs, hardware, and other everyday services.

net income That portion of gross income remaining after the payment of all expenses.

net lease Lease type in which the tenant pays all maintenance and operating costs, plus all insurance and taxes on the building. In such a lease, management expenses are held to a bare minimum.

net operating income That portion of gross income remaining after the payment of all expenses.

net yield The one factor for loans of similar type, size, and quality that the potential purchaser is interested in when a mortgage loan is offered for sale.

nominal interest rate The stated, or named, interest rate in a note or contract; the nominal interest rate may differ from the true or effective rate.

nonrecourse loan A loan on which the borrower is not held personally liable.

note A unilateral instrument containing a promise to pay a sum of money at a specified time; the evidence of a debt.

office buildings Buildings acquired or constructed for their own occupancy or for lease to others.

Office of Thrift Supervision (OTS) Held federal regulatory authority for savings associations until the rechartering of savings associations as banks. Section 312 of the Dodd-Frank Act mandated the merger of OTS with the OCC, the FDIC, the Federal Reserve Board, and the CFPB. The OTS ceased to exist on October 19, 2011.

office/warehouse A variation of the general warehouse that combines an office facility in front and larger warehouse-type space in the rear.

online real estate service Service many companies offer that allows consumers access to information on a full range of services. This gives consumers the opportunity to search for homes, find builders, compare mortgage products, and apply for loans.

open-end mortgage An expandable mortgage containing a clause that permits additional money to be advanced by the lender and secured by the same collateral pledge.

open-market operations A tool the Fed can use to influence the economy. If the Fed decides the economy needs slowing down, it can issue an order—through a limited group of approved investment bankers who must be qualified and capable—to sell some of the Fed's supply of government bonds. Alternatively, if the Fed decides it is necessary to speed up the economy, it can buy government bonds, thus increasing the cash available to banks.

operating statement Summarizes a company's revenues and expenses over the entire reporting period. Also known as a P&L statement, statement of earnings, income statement, or statement of income.

option The right to purchase or lease a piece of property at a certain price without the obligation to buy or lease for a designated period of time.

originate-to-distribute model The originate-to-distribute model is based on the development of securities products that allowed lenders who make mortgages initially to no longer have any significant retained exposure to losses for loans they originated.

origination fee The amount charged for services performed by the company handling the initial application and processing of a loan. Normally paid at the time of closing.

package mortgage A mortgage pledge that includes both real and personal property.

partial release clause A mortgage clause that allows the release of certain parcels of land from the blanket mortgage. Commonly used by land developers selling lots to home builders.

participation loan A loan funded by more than one lender and serviced by one of them.

pass-through security A bond, certificate, or other form of security collateralized by a block of mortgage loans. Monthly payments on the mortgage loans are "passed through" a trustee to the holders of the securities.

pension funds Have become investors in mortgage loans through purchasing mortgage-backed securities. A few pension groups offer home loan programs as primary lenders.

percentage guideline method Considers an applicant's monthly liabilities in two separate categories and measures each amount against the applicant's effective income. The two categories and limits applied are: housing expense should not exceed 31% of the applicant's effective income; and housing expense plus other recurring charges are identified and should not exceed 43% of effective income.

percentage lease Lease for space at percentage rates based on the nature of the tenant's business, rather than as a flat percentage for the entire center.

permanent loan A mortgage loan granted for a term of 20 to 40 years, based on the economic life of a property.

personal property A possession; any item of value that is not real estate.

Phase I assessment An environmental due diligence assessment to ascertain if any prior use would indicate the presence of environmental contamination or hazardous substances.

Phase II assessment Assessment type that is required if a Phase I assessment turns up indications of actual or potential contamination. The purpose is to target those areas believed to be contaminated, and includes the collection and chemical analysis of soil samples, surface, and groundwater samples as well as other relevant investigations and analyses. Sampling must be undertaken pursuant to EPA or state regulatory procedures, or both.

Phase III assessment Assessment type that calls for a definition of the extent of contamination, determining the remedial action necessary, and the implementation of the most appropriate cleanup procedures.

piggyback loan A residential mortgage financing option where a property is purchased using more than one mortgage from two or more mortgagees.

PITI An acronym used to identify the components of a mortgage payment: principal, interest, taxes, and insurance.

planned unit development (PUD) A comprehensive land development plan employed primarily in the more efficient planning of residential areas.

pledged-account mortgage (PAM) A mortgage repayment plan that features lower initial monthly payments similar to a graduated-payment design. With a PAM, the borrower deposits a portion of the down payment in an escrow account with the lender and allows the lender to withdraw enough money from the account to supplement the borrower's monthly payments. The result is a constant-level, fully amortized payment applied to the loan each month.

point A unit of measure of finance charges, including but not limited to a loan discount, that amounts to 1% of a loan. One point is 1% of the subject loan.

pooler A corporation, such as investment banker Salomon Smith Barney, Inc., that buys loans to create these pools.

possession Occupancy; the highest form of notice.

preliminary title report Furnished by the title company to both the real estate agent and the mortgage company, this provides confirmation of the correct legal description, and includes the names of the owners of the property as filed in the county records, any restrictions or liens on the property, any judgments against the owners of record, and a listing of any requirements the title company may have to perfect title before issuance of a title insurance policy.

prepaid items Includes property taxes, insurance premiums (including the FHA mortgage insurance premium), and possibly subdivision maintenance fees, most of which must be placed in an escrow account with the lender.

prepayment penalty An amount disclosed in the terms of a note requiring an additional fee to be paid the lender if all or part of a loan is paid prior to maturity.

primary market The market where loans are originated; the primary market is composed of borrowers and lenders.

prime rate A base interest rate, determined independently by banks, that generally is charged the bank's most creditworthy customers.

principal The amount of the mortgage debt. Also identifies a party to a transaction.

principal, interest, taxes, and insurance (PITI) Also known as *housing expense*. These expenses include the mortgage payment of principal, interest, real estate taxes, and hazard insurance, plus flood insurance if applicable.

Privacy Act Legislation passed in 1974 that established fair information practices that govern the collection, maintenance, use, and dissemination of information about individuals that is maintained in systems of records by federal agencies.

private mortgage conduits Entities that pool mortgages and other loans.

private mortgage insurance (PMI) Insurance against default on repayment of a mortgage loan, as offered by private insurance carriers.

production-related income Pay that is not assured, such as commissions, bonuses, and in some cases, piecework pay.

profit and loss statement (P&L) A statement of income and expense.

pro forma statement A financial statement that includes projected balance sheets, income statements, and statements of cash flows.

promissory note A written promise to pay someone a given amount of money at a specified time.

property appraisal Provides information that has several uses in financing real estate. It is used as an important measure of the loan amount.

purchase money mortgage A mortgage taken by the seller as all or part of the purchase consideration. Also identifies a mortgage wherein the proceeds of the loan are used to purchase the property.

qualified buyer A buyer who has demonstrated the financial capacity and creditworthiness required to afford the asking price.

radon A colorless, odorless, naturally occurring gas produced from the decay of uranium and other radioactive materials.

rate index A regulator-approved index not under the control of the lender, to which any change in the interest rate of adjustable-rate mortgages must be tied.

raw land Land in its unused, natural state.

real estate Land and that attached thereto, including minerals and resources inherent to the land, and any manufactured improvements so affixed as to become a part of the land. Also known as *realty*.

Real Estate Investment Trusts (REITs) An entity structured as a corporation, trust, or association that owns, operates, or finances income-producing real estate. For an entity to qualify as a REIT, it must meet certain regulatory guidelines.

Real Estate Mortgage Investment Conduit (REMIC) A tax device that allows cash flows from an underlying block of mortgages to be passed through to security holders without being subject to income taxes at that level. Thus, the interest income is taxed only to the security holder, not to the trustee or agent handling the pass-through of cash.

Real Estate Settlement Procedures Act (RESPA) A federal consumer protection statute, originally enacted in 1974 (updated several times since). RESPA is enforced by the Consumer Financial Protection Bureau coordinating with Department of Housing and Urban Development (HUD), the Federal Reserve Bank, and the Federal Deposit Insurance Corporation. Its purposes are to help consumers become better shoppers for settlement services and to eliminate kickbacks and referral fees that unnecessarily increase the costs of certain settlement services.

real property In addition to the land and that attached thereto, real property includes the interests, benefits, and rights inherent in the ownership of real estate.

realty funds Funds organized by persons or companies wishing to raise equity money for real estate projects, such as the purchase of raw land, a construction project, or the purchase of existing income properties.

recording Filing a legal instrument in the public records of a county.

recourse note A debt instrument allowing recovery against both the property and the borrower, or endorser, personally.

redemption Right of borrowers who felt they had been unjustly deprived of their property to appeal to an official to seek a hearing for their grievances and to petition for a chance to redeem the land with a late payment of the obligation.

redemption period A specific time period given to borrowers in foreclosure during which they can buy back, or "redeem," their property.

red flags Signs that raise concerns about the loan quality during the settlement process.

redlining Practice of specifying areas or neighborhoods within a city as acceptable or unacceptable for making loans. From drawing lines on city maps to guiding loan officers, such identification has been interpreted as leading to possible discrimination in violation of the Fair Housing Act.

refinancing Obtaining a loan for the purpose of repaying an existing loan.

regional center A shopping center that offers a full range of merchandise and services.

regulated lenders Those depository institutions and life insurance companies that are subject to various government regulatory agencies.

release clause Provision within a mortgage contract that allows for freeing of part of a property from claim by the creditor after a proportional amount of the mortgage has been paid.

release of liability A selling veteran is entitled to be released from liability for a VA loan if the following conditions are met: the loan must be current; the purchaser/assumptor must qualify from the standpoint of income and be an acceptable credit risk; and the purchaser must agree to assume the veteran's obligations on the loan.

religious facility financing Church or other financing of buildings for the use of religious organizations that requires the authorized officials of the organization to meet some unique prequalification requirements.

remaining useful life The appraiser's judgment of how many years a property will continue to be useful, which is used as an underwriting guideline for a conventional loan.

residual method One of two VA methods of qualifying an applicant's income. It starts with the applicant's gross monthly income. Then, mandatory deductions start with the applicant's monthly tax liabilities, continue with shelter expenses and other fixed obligations, and result in what the applicant has left. What remains after the applicable mandatory obligations have been deducted is called residual income.

Resolution Trust Corporation (RTC) Created by FIRREA in 1989, the RTC was given the authority to take the necessary steps to sell or liquidate failing thrifts.

responsible parties Those deemed responsible by the Environmental Protection Agency for the costs of cleanup of hazardous materials.

retail store building A freestanding building containing retail stores, which can be an interesting investment for individuals as well as large companies.

reverse annuity mortgage A mortgage designed to use the equity value of a home as collateral for a loan funded in installments intended primarily to supplement living costs. Also called a *reverse mortgage* and may be insured by the FHA.

right of rescission Some mortgage features will cause a loan transaction to be rescindable. A consumer must be given a notice explaining that the creditor has a security interest in the consumer's home, that the consumer may rescind, how the consumer may rescind, the effects of rescission, and the date the rescission period expires. This most frequently occurs as a requirement of the Truth-in-Lending Act for cash-out refinance mortgages.

risk-based mortgage pricing System where lenders assess borrowing costs loan by loan.

Rural Housing Service (RHS) An agency of the U.S. Department of Agriculture (USDA) that offers a wide range of programs under the USDA's Rural Mission.

SAFE Act The new federal law gave states one year to pass legislation requiring the licensure of mortgage loan originators according to national standards and the participation of state agencies in the Nationwide Mortgage Licensing System and Registry (NMLS).

savings banks Originated during the early years of the United States when most people traded in cash and needed a place to deposit their surplus for safekeeping.

SEC requirements The Securities and Exchange Commission (SEC) was created during the Depression years of the 1930s. It is charged with correcting possible abuses in the sale of securities to the general public, as well as overseeing market activities, including the sale of mortgage bonds and advance payments on real estate.

secondary financing Negotiation of a second mortgage, or a junior mortgage, to assist in the acquisition of property.

secondary market A market for the purchase and sale of existing mortgages.

secured creditor exemption Exemption that permits lenders to make mortgage loans without being included as a responsible party should toxic waste cleanup become a problem.

security As used in finance, an instrument evidencing ownership (stock) or debt (bond) in a corporate entity.

security instrument All states with community property statutes that give special protection for both parties to a marriage require some security instrument that gives a creditor the right to have the security property sold to satisfy the debt if the debtor fails to pay the debt according to the terms of the agreement.

security interest A generic term for the property rights of a lender or creditor whose right to collect a debt is secured by property.

seller/servicer Loan originators who are approved to sell loans to Fannie Mae or Freddie Mac and who also service the loans for them.

servicing (loan servicing) The work involved with handling mortgage payments; it comprises the collection of payments, remittance of principal and interest to the note holder, accounting for escrow funds with proper disbursement, and follow-up on delinquencies.

servicing fee The charge made for handling the loan after it has been funded. Services involve collecting and accounting for periodic loan payments, handling the escrow portion of the payments, and following up on delinquent accounts.

settlement agent The person or company selected to bring together the instruments of conveyance, mortgages, promissory notes, and, of course, the monetary consideration to be exchanged between the buyer and seller of real estate.

settlement procedure The steps taken to finance the funding of a loan agreement and a property transfer. Also called *loan closing*.

shared appreciation mortgage (SAM) Alternative mortgage method in which a portion of the collateral's appreciation is accepted as "contingent interest."

shared equity mortgage Alternative mortgage method in which a lender or other investor subordinated to the mortgagee holds a claim, a lien, on that portion of the property value that represents an increase from the time of loan origination in return for their consideration in making the loan or for contributing to the down payment. But this claim or lien falls short of title to the property.

shopping center A building containing retail stores. The development and leasing of shopping centers is a specialized business.

shorter-term loans Loans that reduce the interest paid by making the term shorter and the payments higher.

simple assumption With this type of assumption, property may be sold and the loan assumed without notification to the FHA or its agent (the mortgage lender). However, with this method, the seller remains fully liable to the FHA and the lender for repayment of the loan, regardless of the buyer's assumed obligation.

simple interest Interest computed on the principal only.

special-purpose buildings Buildings that offer a specific kind of service and are more difficult to convert to any other usage. Examples of special-purpose buildings include fast-food restaurants, bowling lanes, service stations, recreational structures, theaters, and automobile dealerships.

spot loan Money loaned on individual houses in various neighborhoods, as contrasted with new houses in a single development.

statutory redemption State laws that permit a mortgagor a limited time after foreclosure to pay off the debt and reclaim the mortgaged property.

straight note One that calls for payment of the interest only at periodic intervals and the principal balance due in full at maturity.

strict foreclosure After appropriate notice is given to a delinquent borrower and proper papers are filed in court, the court establishes a specific time period during which the entire defaulted debt must be paid. If full payment is not made within the time period, the borrower's redemption rights are waived and the court awards full legal title to the lender. There can be no deficiency judgment claimed under strict foreclosure.

"subject to" mortgage Taking title to mortgaged property that is subject to an existing mortgage without accepting the obligation on same.

subordination To make a claim to real property inferior to that of another by specific agreement.

subprime loans Loans made to persons who do not have a top-grade credit record as is required to qualify for a regular mortgage loan.

Superfund A $1.6 billion hazardous waste trust fund set up by the Comprehensive Environmental Response, Compensation, and Liability Act of 1980 (CERCLA).

supplier financing A tool sometimes used by a supplier to gain an advantage in a competitive market. Such assistance may be obtained through extended terms that allow later payment or through a direct loan by the supplier.

survey The measurement and description of land by a registered surveyor.

sweat equity An ownership interest in property earned by the performance of manual labor on that property.

syndication A group of individuals or companies joined together in pursuit of a limited investment purpose.

takeout commitment Many builders will arrange with a lending institution a takeout commitment for mortgage money that can be used by the home buyer to provide permanent financing to the buyer and take out (pay off) the construction lender or builder if he or she is using their own sources of funding.

takeout loan A type of loan commitment; a promise to make a loan at a future specified time. Most commonly used to designate a higher-cost, shorter-term backup commitment as a support for construction financing until a suitable permanent loan can be secured.

tax-exempt bond A type of security sold by states and municipalities paying interest that is not subject to federal income taxes.

teaser-rate mortgage An adjustable-rate mortgage with an initial rate well below existing market rates.

term The time limit within which a loan must be repaid in full.

term lease A short-term lease that may or may not be in writing.

term loan A loan that requires interest-only payments until maturity.

time deposit Money held on deposit that is not subject to demand withdrawal.

title The right to ownership in land.

title commitment The title company's promise to issue a title insurance policy for the property after closing.

title insurance Protection against adverse claims to ownership arising from defects in the chain of title.

title theory In a title theory state, the lender will hold title to the property in the name of the borrower through a deed of trust; generally foreclosure occurs through a nonjudicial proceeding.

Torrens certificate A certificate issued by a public authority in the few states that recognize the Torrens system, which establishes an indefeasible title for the registered owner of the land.

toxic waste sites Properties containing hazardous materials that could endanger people's lives.

tract loan An individual mortgage loan negotiated for houses of similar character located in a new development.

transaction screen One method developed by the ASTM that sets standards for an appropriate inquiry into a property's environmental condition. It comprises a series of about 23 questions (using Fannie Mae Form 4340) that examines a property's history. The screen requires answers from owners, occupants, and the preparer of the report, and may be sufficient for small commercial transactions.

trustee One who holds property in trust for another to secure performance of an obligation. Also identifies the third party holding a conditional title to property held as collateral under a deed-of-trust mortgage.

trustor One who borrows money under the terms of a deed of trust mortgage.

Truth-in-Lending Act (TILA) A federal law that became effective in July 1969 as a part of the Consumer Credit Protection Act. It is implemented by the Federal Reserve Board's Regulation Z. The purpose of the law is to require lenders to give meaningful information to borrowers on the cost of consumer credit, which includes credit extended in real estate transactions.

underground storage tank (UST) Any tank that has 10% or more of its volume below ground and contains either petroleum or hazardous substances.

underwriter The person or company taking responsibility for rating risks and approving mortgage loans. Also used to identify those who provide credit enhancement for mortgage loans, such as Fannie Mae and Freddie Mac.

underwriting The process of analyzing and approving a loan.

Uniform Collateral Data Portal® A single portal for the electronic submission of appraisal data files. Lenders are required to use UCDP® to submit electronic appraisal data files that conform to all GSE requirements, including the Uniform Appraisal Dataset (UAD) when applicable, before the delivery date of the mortgage to either Fannie Mae or Freddie Mac.

unit That part of a property intended for any type of independent use that has an exit to a public street or corridor.

universal account Potential future system that would combine all of a person's loans into one account.

unsecured loan A loan made without the benefit of a pledge of collateral.

up-front mortgage insurance premium (UFMIP) Mortgage insurance premium that is paid up front.

usury Interest paid or accepted in excess of that permitted by state law.

VA loan A loan made by private lenders that is partially guaranteed by the Department of Veterans Affairs.

variable-rate mortgage A nearly obsolete term for a mortgage that allows the periodic adjustment of the interest rate during the term of the loan. More commonly called *adjustable-rate mortgage*.

vendor's lien A lien securing the loan by a seller that is used to purchase the property.

Wall Street Reform and Consumer Protection Act Passed in 2010, also known as the Dodd-Frank Act, this law made changes in the American financial regulatory environment of all federal financial regulatory agencies and virtually every segment of the financial services industry. It focused on the systemic risk that existed in the financial industry that seemed more obvious after the 2007 financial crisis.

warehouse building Another type of income property that is preferred by many investors because of its relatively low maintenance and management requirements.

warehousing The practice, mostly by mortgage companies, of pledging mortgage notes to a commercial bank for cash used to fund originated mortgage loans; a line of credit.

wetlands Water-saturated land areas that cannot be disturbed without a permit from the Corps of Engineers.

whole loan A term used in the secondary market to indicate that the full amount of a loan is available for sale with no portion or participation retained by the seller.

willingness to pay Sometimes called *credit character*, this factor judges creditworthiness from an applicant's previous record of meeting obligations.

wraparound mortgage A junior mortgage that acknowledges and includes an existing mortgage loan in its principal amount due and in its payment conditions. Payment is made to the holder of the wrap or his or her agent, who in turn makes payment on the existing mortgage. The purpose is to gain some advantages in lower interest cost on an existing loan, to hold the mortgage priority of an existing loan, and to retain an element of control over the loan payments.

yield The total money earned on a loan for the term of the loan, as computed on an annual percentage basis. Also known as *rate of return*.

yield spread premium The additional spread added when some lenders charge a higher-than-market interest rate (rather than charging discount points) to add additional profits.

INDEX

1Malaysia Development Berhad (1MDB), money laundering risks, 73
2MP. *See* Second Lien Modification Program
80-20-0 loan, 318
80-20 loan, 318

A

AAI. *See* "all appropriate inquiries"
AARMR. *See* American Association of Residential Mortgage Regulators
Aaron v. The Trump Organization, 554
AARP. *See* American Association of Retired Persons
AASHE. *See* Association for the Advancement of Sustainability in Higher Education
ability to pay, 58–63
A borrower, 295
A- borrower, 295
abstract of title
    attorney opinion, 459–460
    defining, 460
abstract search, 144
acceleration clause, 254
"accepted" applications, computer software classification, 643

Access Mortgage Research & Consulting, 651–652
"according to value" tax, 263
accounts payable aging reports, 545
accounts receivable reports, 545
accrued interest, 311–312
acquisition cost, 352
ACRES database, usage, 613
active duty service personnel, 372
additional advances, 477
add-on factor (AOF), 583
adjustable-rate mortgage (ARM), 277, 287–288
    introduction, 307
    loan, 223
    option ARM, Washington Mutual development, 309–310
    "pay-option ARMs," 310
    product offerings, evolution, 309–310
    setting, 284
    support, 308
    VA usage, 382
adjustable-rate note, 302
adjustable-rate plans, aspects, 308–309
Administrative Procedures Act (APA), 90, 101–103
ADR. *See* alternative dispute resolution
ad valorem tax ("according to value" tax), 263, 298

Adverse Market Delivery (AMD) Charge, 656
Aegon Hypotheken, 231
Aegon Levensverzekering, 231
Aegon N.V., 231
affordable housing goals, FNMA/FHLMC requirements, 36–37
affordable housing loans, 111–113, 395
    support, 112
agencies, 110
agency ratings methodologies, flaws (SIV financing market exposure), 38
AgFirst Farm Credit Bank, 117
AgriBank, 117
agricorporate farm loans, 587
agricultural lending, 115–118
Alcohol and Tobacco Tax and Trade Bureau (TTB), 72
alienation clause, 255
alimony, 60
"all appropriate inquiries" (AAI), 604, 608
allodial, 4
Ally Financial, 288
"also known as," term (usage), 531–532
alternative dispute resolution (ADR) methods, 103
AMC. *See* Appraisal Management Company

AMD. *See* Adverse Market Delivery
amenities, building offering, 519
American Association of Residential Mortgage Regulators (AARMR), 210
American Association of Retired Persons (AARP), 202
American Bankers Association (ABA), *Real Estate Lending Survey Report*, 652, 653
American Home Mortgage Servicing, Inc., 83
American Recovery and Reinvestment Act (ARRA), 114, 347, 378–379
    passage, 631
    response, 627
American Society for Testing of Materials (ASTM)
    ASTM-named Phase I assessment, 609
    E 1527-05 standards, 609
    E1527-13 Standard, basis, 595–596, 609
    methods, 609–610
    non-scope considerations, 609–610
    Standards, 608
    transaction screen, 609
American Society of Appraisers, 502
American Society of Farm Managers and Rural Appraisers, 502
AMFI. *See* average medium family income
amortization, 286
    impact, 315
    negative amortization, 294, 309–310, 312, 333

anchor tenant, 574–575
annual assessments, 143
annual MIP calculation, practice exercise, 357–358
annual percentage rate (APR), 93, 95
    excess, 501
annual premium, 355, 357
annual return, 162
anticipation (appraisal principle), 504
Anti-Fraud Provisions, 554
AOF. *See* add-on factor
Aozora Bank, Ltd., 230
APA. *See* Adminstrative Procedures Act
apartment
    construction, proposal, 571
    dwellers, accessibility (improvement), 569
    unit, purchase steps, 527–528
apartment buildings, 569–573
    income/expenses, analysis, 571–572
    location, 569
    management, 570
    physical facilities, 569–570
    term leases, 572–573
apparent age, 522
application fee, 217
Appraisal Management Company (AMC), usage, 499–500
Appraisal Qualifications Board (AQB)
    education criteria, 497
    USPAP conformity, 500
"Appraisal Report" (USPAP), 506
appraisal reports, 505, 506–508
    appraisal date/purpose, 507
    appraiser certification/qualifications, 508

    background data, 507
    forms, 448t
    property description, 506
    qualifying conditions, 507
    standard form, 506
    value approaches, 507
    value estimate, 508
appraisals, 548, 647
    associations, 502–503
    date/purpose, 507
    defining, 495
    feasibility study, 549–550
    federal/state certification, 496–497
    fees, 137
    FHA definition, 446
    FIRREA standards, 128
    fraud, 329
    initiating/ordering, 639
    making, 407
    principles, 503
    problems, 293–294
    scope, 408, 409
    standards, 500–501
    types, 504–508
appraised value, determination, 495–496
appraisers
    selection, 499–500
    standards, 497–499
    trainee, 498
Appraisers Association of America, Inc., 502
appraising, principles, 503–504
AQB. *See* Appraisal Qualifications Board
ARCGIS Call software, 648
ARGUS Developer, 544
ARGUS Property Budget, 544
ARGUS Valuation-DCF, 544

arm's length transaction (appraisal principle), 504
ARRA. *See* American Recovery and Reinvestment Act
articles of incorporation, 546
artificial intelligence (AI), usage, 39
asbestos, 614
    friable asbestos, 616
    impact, 597
    loose asbestos, 615
    problem, 627
    usage, 615–616
Ashley Stewart Holdings, bankruptcy, 566
asking price, sales prices (relationship), 511
Assessment, Cleanup, and Revolving Loan Fund, 613
assets, 63
    lender examination, 63
associated companies, 6–7
Association for the Advancement of Sustainability in Higher Education (AASHE), founding, 606
assumption, 254–256
    creditworthy buyers, 387–388
    formal assumption, 344–346
    rules, change, 344
    simple assumption, 344
    VA loan assumption, 386–388
assumption fee, 138
assured income, 58
attorneys, fees, 139
audited financial statements, CPA preparation, 541
audited statement, 411
    CPA preparation, 547
authorities, 110

"Authorization to Withhold Sale Price," completion, 512
automated loan underwriting, 220
Automated Underwriter System (AUS), 449
    findings, usage, 449–450
automated underwriting
    defining, 220–221
    systems, 641–648
Automated Valuation Model (AVM), 644
Automated Valuation System (AVS), usage, 647
automatic loan processing, qualification, 384
automatic transfer service (ATS) accounts, 54
automatic underwriting, 57
average clauses, 261
average medium family income (AMFI), 114
Average Prime Offer Rate (APOR), 501
AVM. *See* Automated Valuation Model
AVS. *See* Automated Valuation System

B

back-end ratio, 402
"back-end" ratio, 630
background data, usage, 507
balance sheet, 541
balloon
    adjusted rate, allowance, 316
    amortization, impact, 315
balloon payment, 315, 320
    note, 315
Banco Popular North America, 653
Bank Deregulation Act, 197

bankers, environmental risk insurance, 611
Bank Holding Company Act, 68
Banking Act (1933), 74–75
Bank of America, 83, 166, 482
    settlement, 484
Bank of Tokyo-Mitsubishi UFJ, Ltd., 230
Bankruptcy Abuse Prevention and Consumer Protection Act (BAPCA), 479
banks
    capital injections, 76–77
    statements, copies (usage), 440
banks for cooperatives, 116
BAPCA. *See* Bankruptcy Abuse Prevention and Consumer Protection Act
"bare-wall" leases, 581
barter system, impact, 44
base lines, 532–533
basis points, 165
    spread, 231
B borrower, 295
bedrooms, number, 517–518
beneficiary, 479
benevolent associations, funds, 230
BEP. *See* Bureau of Engraving and Printing
BIF, 76, 85
Biggert-Waters Flood Insurance Reform Act (FIRA), 262–263
bill of sale, 250
biological pollutants, 614
biweekly payment mortgage product, 322
biweekly payment plan, 322
Blackstone Group, 232
blanket mortgage, 250
blind pool, 18

blocks, division, 531–532
bond money, 184–185
bonds, 224
    categories, 225
    coupon interest rate, example, 226–227
    funding source, 589
bonus, 59
"Bootstrap" Homebuilder Loan Program, 114
borrowed money, compensation, 30–31
borrowers
    analysis, 57, 351
    corporation status, 546
    creditworthiness, analysis, 636
    FICO scores, 37
    financial evaluation, 57–58
    foreclosure, 23
    home-buying/financing process education, 639
    income qualification, 398–399
    payment ability/willingness, 494
    personal endorsement, 558
    personal income, 538
    protection, 302
    qualification, 395, 398
    rating, 402
    types, 295–296
    VA qualification, 403–406
bounds, 532
BPO. *See* broker price opinion
bridge loan, 248
brokerage-type service, 109
broker price opinion (BPO), usage, 529–530
Brownfields Program, 611–614
    EPA initiation, 612
builder-contractor entity, lease, 582

builder-investor, preleased office space, 581
building materials, usage, 519
"Building Owners' Guides" (EPA), 615–616
building societies, 83–84
build-to-lease, 14
build-to-let, 14
build-to-suit, 14
Bulletin 2017-18 (Office of the Comptroller of the Currency), 8–9
Bunning-Bereuter-Blumenauer Flood Insurance Reform Act, 262
Bureau of Engraving and Printing (BEP), currency printing, 70
bureau scores, 419
Bush, George W., 75, 178, 301, 631
business
    business owner-occupied buildings, 580
    business-process management systems, 641
    risk, 538
    tax returns, 545
business cycle duration, NBER study, 26
buydown mortgage, 312–314
    buyer inducement, 314
    cost, example, 313
    period, span, 313
buyer, creditworthiness approval, 345
Byte Mortgage Origination Software, 650
BytePro Standard, 651
Byte Software, 651
bytesoftware.com, 651

C

CABO. *See* Council of American Building Officials
CAIVRS. *See* Credit Alert Interactive Voice Response System
California, Homeowner Bill of Rights, 458
Calyx, 640, 646
    WebCaster, 641, 651
Calyx Point, 650
calyxsoftware.com, 651–652
Canadian rollover, 288
capability, credit, collateral (three Cs), 58
"capacity to influence," 603
capitalization method, 515
Capital Purchase Program, 78
caps, 288, 307–309
Carrington Mortgage Services, LLC, 219
cash flow
    passage, 168
    pro forma cash flow statements, 543–544
    projections, 544
    residual (addition), present worth (example), 517t
cash reserve requirements, setting, 47
casualty insurance companies, 200
C borrower, 295–296
CBRA. *See* Coastal Barrier Resources Act
Central Bank of Norway, 230
Century 21, 289
CERCLA. *See* Comprehensive Environmental Response, Compensation, and Liability Act of 1980

certificate of deposit (CD) rates, federal discount rate (impact), 53f
certificate of reasonable value (CRV), 7, 377, 403, 408–409
Certified General Real Property Appraiser, qualification, 497
Certified Public Accountant (CPA)
    audited financial statements preparation, 541
    qualification, 547
Certified Residential Real Property Appraiser, role, 497
CFPB. See Consumer Financial Protection Bureau
changed circumstance, 97
Chapter 7 bankruptcy, filing, 479
Chapter 13 bankruptcy, filing, 479
chattel mortgage, 250
check society, 80
child support, 60
Cisneros, Henry, 370
Citibank, *Mortgage Power*, 637
Citigroup, 83, 482
city/county property taxes, 142
Civil War, monetary policy, 45
claim without conveyance, 470
Class Z bonds, 190
cleanup costs, liability, 601–603
Clean Water Act, 620
    compliance, 622
    jurisdiction control, 624
    support, 621–622
Clean Water Act: A Summary of the Law, 621–622
ClearSpring Loan Services, 83
climate change, discussion, 624–625
Clinton, Bill, 92
CLO. See computerized loan origination

closing costs, 348. See also lender
    amount, requirement, 353
Closing Disclosure, 97–98
    form, design, 135–136
    lender usage, 457
    red flags, 328–329
Closing Disclosure Settlement Statement, 129f–133f
closing fees, 143
Closing Instructions, 147, 148f–152f
closing settlement, 152–153
Closing Statement, 127–153
cloud
    computing, 640–641
    usage, 640
CMBSs. See commercial mortgage-backed securities
Coastal Barrier Resources Act (CBRA), 354
CoBank, 117
co-borrower's income, 59
coin/currency, production, 70
coinsurance clauses, 260
Coldwater Creek Inc., bankruptcy, 567
collateral, 3. See also capability, credit, collateral
    assessment, 449, 644
    property service, 312
    qualification, 406–409
collateralized debt obligations (CDOs), 182
collateralized mortgage obligations (CMOs), 169, 182, 225
    purpose, 190
Collateral Underwriter (CU), usage, 514
Colonia Self-Help Centers (TDHCA), 114
combustion by-products, 614

commercial banks, 196–199
    regulation, 199
commercial building energy codes, establishment, 630
commercial condominiums, 526–527
commercial loan application, 410–412
    information, requirement, 540–546
commercial loans, 253–254, 397–398, 409–412
    agreement, 412
    applicant, creditworthiness (determination), 411
    environmental assessments, 596–597
    funding, 205
    information sources, 539
    qualification, example, 411
    residential loans, distinction, 538
    review, 411
    term, usage, 538
commercial mortgage-backed securities (CMBSs), 191
    ascendance, 297
    commercial mortgage loan placement, 561
commercial paper, 38, 227–228
Commercial Paper Funding Facility (CPFF), 227
commercial property investments, initial presentation, 547
commercial real estate
    investment, growth, 19
    investment/lending, liquidity risks, 549–550
    lead-based paint remediation, 596–597

loans, study, 566–567
risks, 538
values, decline, 571–572
commission, 59
commitment method
construction, 6
purchase, 6
common areas, 524
common bond, 202
requirement, 203
community centers, 575
community needs
meeting, 91
serving, financial institutions (impact), 106
community-oriented programs, 112
Community Reinvestment Act (CRA), 55, 90–91
FIRREA amendment, 91–93
grading, 92
categories, 92
ratings, 93
comparable, term (usage), 511
compensation, tax crackdown, 486
competition analysis, 550
competitive market, 228
competitive method, 5
complete appraisal, 505
compliance
grades, 111
role, 55–56
Comprehensive Environmental Response, Compensation, and Liability Act of 1980 (CERCLA), 600–601, 604
case law, authority, 605
liability defenses, 609
liability limitation, 609–610
requirements, 608

Comprehensive National Energy Policy Act, 630
computerized information, usage, 655–656
computerized loan origination (CLO), 290, 636–640
condominiums, 524–527
commercial condominiums, 526–527
defining, 361
loan, endorsement, 526
projects, problems, 526
property qualification, 526
conduit lenders, 225
Conference of State Bank Supervisors (CSBS), 210
Confidential Remarks, code entry, 512
conforming loans, 257–259, 269, 332
parameters, 215
qualification, 332–335
conformity (appraisal principle), 504
constant-level payment, example, 311
construction
commitment method, 6
disbursement, 556
existing construction, 407
lender, risk, 555–556
lending, 555
impact, 560–561
money, sources, 558
proposed construction, 406
construction loans, 198, 247, 555–561
contract basis, 558–559
costs payment, assurance, 556–557
definition, 556–558

disbursement risks, lender minimization, 557
draw requests, mistakes, 561
income property usage, 560–561
plans, completion, 557
residential property usage, 558–560
speculative basis, 559
takeout commitment, 559–560
time-interval method, 556
consumer, borrower categories, 279
consumer compliance protection, 57
Consumer Credit Protection Act, 93
Consumer Financial Protection Bureau (CFPB), 11, 80
agencies, 104
enforcement, 96, 554
establishment, 105
fines, 484
Regulation X, 122
RESPA, administration/ enforcement, 123
responsibility, 639
TILA amendment implementation, 501
Consumer Handbook on Adjustable-Rate Mortgages, 302
contract for deed, 245–246
transaction, buyer risks, 245
usage, 246
contraction/recession, ending, 26
contract rate, 304
contribution (appraisal principle), 504
conventional lending, 589

conventional loans
    qualification, 332–335
    refinancing, 291–294
conventional mortgages,
    refinancing, 403
conventional qualifying housing
    ratios, example, 334–335
cooperative apartments, 527–528
Cooper Industries v. Aviall, 603
corporate, borrower categories,
    279
corporate borrowing resolution,
    546
corporate IOU, 38
corporations, financing, 32
correspondent basis, 215–216
Corzine, John, 175
cost approach, usage, 508–510
cost of living expenses, 404–405
cost recovery actions, defenses,
    603
costs disclosure, borrower right,
    134–135
Council of American Building
    Officials (CABO), energy-
    efficiency code, 631
counseling, 458
"counseling-type" services,
    payment, 638
covered accounts, 67
CPFF. *See* Commercial Paper
    Funding Facility
CRA. *See* Community
    Reinvestment Act
Cranston-Gonzalez National
    Affordable Housing Act, 220
credit. *See* capability, credit,
    collateral
    advancement, Federal Reserve
        Bank authority, 52–53
    information, 66

Loan Prospector approval, 644
    markets, 280–281
    offering, types, 91
    overdraft lines, 56
    policy, instruments, 57–69
    records, keepers, 65
    reporting problems, 69
Credit Alert Interactive Voice
    Response System (CAIVRS),
    471–472
    expansion, 485
credit card accounts, records, 65
credit demand, 279–281
    comparison, 280, 280t
creditors, 67
credit reports, 65–69, 418–420
    fee, 138
    submission, 138
Credit Risk recommendation, 643
credit score
    case study/workshop, 465
    factors, 395
    requirements, 402–403
credit scoring, 57–58, 69
    usage, 420
credit unions, 202–204
    authority, increase, 203
    regulation, 203–204
creditworthiness approval, 345
crowd funding, 231–232
CRV. *See* certificate of
    reasonable value
CSBS. *See* Conference of State
    Bank Supervisors
CUNA Mutual Group, 649
current real estate appraisal, 546
current rent roll, 545

D

Davis + Henderson
    Corporation, 653

D borrower, 296
dead pledge, 243
dead space, usage, 582
dead transaction, contract, 245
debenture bonds, 225
    sale, 166
debt
    forgiveness, 24
    maximum debt ratio,
        determination, 400
    monetization, 71
    recovered amount, absence,
        299
debt coverage ratio (DCR)
    method, LTV method
        (comparison), 550–551
    requirements, 231
debt relief, 486
    income consideration, 23–24
debt service, 542, 572
    deduction, 542–543
debt service coverage ratio, 206
debt-to-income (DTI) ratios, 655
    computation, 400, 402
deed. *See* contract for deed
    transaction, contract, 245
    warranty deed, 461
deed in lieu of foreclosure,
    249–250
deed of trust (trust deed)
    beneficiary, 479
    lien placement, 259
    notes, relationship, 241–242
deed to secure debt, 257
default insurance, obligations, 23
default mortgage insurance,
    standard, 8
defaults, 30, 470–472
    impact, 470–471
    reporting, 471–472
    VA default, 472

deficiency judgment, 484–486
    obtaining, 259
deficit spending levels, impact, 50
delinquencies
    impact, 470–471
    occurrence, 213
    rates, 572
delivery slip, importance, 463
demand deposits, 48, 54
de minimis exemption, 7
Department of Housing and Urban Development (HUD), 209, 340
    affordable housing goals, 36–37
    appraisals, value determination, 407
    assumption rules, change, 344
    borrower income qualification, 398–399
    CFPB coordination, 96
    Credit Alert Interactive Voice Response System (CAIVRS), 471–472
    credit score requirements, 402–403
    floor/ceiling limits, 364t
    GNMA assignment, 172
    HUD-1, 127–153
        settlement statement, 128, 135–136
    HUD-approved prepurchase counseling, 342
    HUD-insured commitments, secondary financing, 349
    Informal Opinion Number 13, 638
    Loan Origination Services List, 638
    pressure, application, 35
    program details, 360
    purpose, 346
    qualification procedures, 369
    rule, 6–7
    terminology, 352–354
    "Your home loan toolkit," 121–122
Department of Housing and Urban Development Act, passage, 90
Department of the Treasury
    employees/structure, 70
    operations, 70
Department of Veterans Affairs (VA), 340, 371
    appraisal, scope, 409
    ARMs, 382
    borrower qualification, 403–406
    case study, 389–390
    cost-of-living figures, 332
    default/foreclosure, 472
    entitlement, 386
        restoration, 377–379
        value, 377
    entitlement increments, 386t
    form 26-1843, 403
    funding fee, 380–382, 381t
    guarantee calculation, example, 375
    Home Affordable Modifcation Program (VA-HAMP), 473
    income ratio method, 331–332
    Lender Appraisal Processing Program, 403
    manufactured home loans, 384–385
    negotiated interest rate/discount, 382
    owner-occupied residence, 374
    qualification, requirements, 409
    requirements/procedures, 383–384
    sliding scale guaranty, 374, 376t
    Tier 1 (partial entitlements), 376–377
        limit, 377
    VA-supported loans, 164
    workshop, 389–390
Department of Veterans Affairs (VA) loans
    application, analysis, 385
    assumption, 386–388
    default/foreclosure, 380
    guaranty program, 371–385
    origination, 109
    programs, 386–388
    servicing, 384
    term, 384
Departure Provision (USPAP), 505
deposit advance products, 56
deposit insurance, 74
    funds, reorganization, 75–76
Deposit Insurance Fund (DIF), creation, 75
depository institutions
    cash reserve requirements, setting, 47
    reserve requirements, 81–82
Depository Institutions Deregulation Act, impact, 81, 203
Depository Institutions Deregulation and Monetary Control Act (DIDMCA), 84
depreciation, 509–510
designated service providers, 123, 127

Desktop Originator (DO). *See* Federal National Mortgage Association
Desktop Underwriter (DU). *See* Federal National Mortgage Association
   Qualitative Analysis Appraisal Report, 448
   Release Notes, 656
Destiny Loan Origination System, 646
Deutsche Bank, settlement, 483
development corporations, 110–111
development loan, limitation, 552–553
dh.com, 653
DIDMCA. *See* Depository Institutions Deregulation and Monetary Control Act
Dietz, Robert, 25
dioxin, waste, 600
direct endorsement, 369
   eligibility, 362
Direct Endorsement Program, HUD establishment, 369
direct lenders, 650
direct loan, 21, 198
direct-loan programs, 201
disability protection, 300
Disaster Mitigation Act (2000), passage, 262
disaster-prone areas, 521
disbursement procedures, 147
discarded commercial chemical products (P-list) (U-list), 601
disclosure
   provision, 639
   requirements, 303
discount, 31
   defining, 163–165

discount analysis, 515
   method, 515–516
discounted cash flow analysis, 206
discounted sale and leaseback (DSL), 15–16
discounted sale-leasebacks, 15–17
discount fee, payment, 524
discount rate of interest. *See* interest
discrimination, Fair Housing Act violation, 520
distressed assets, purchase, 76–77
ditech.com, 652
Ditech Funding Corporation, 652
dividends, 61
DO. *See* Federal National Mortgage Association
documents
   preparation, 138
   priority, 266–267
   releases, 267
   uniform loan documentation, GSE-conforming loans (impact), 268–269
Dodd-Frank Act. *See* Wall Street Reform and Consumer Financial Protection Act of 2010
Dots LLC, bankruptcy, 566
down payment, 348
   calculation, 352–353, 366–367
Down Payment Assistance Program, 114
down payment assistance programs, adoption, 110–111
down payment simplification, 341
draw requests, mistakes, 561
Drywall Safety Act of 2012, 610

DSL. *See* discounted sale and leaseback
DTI. *See* debt-to-income
DU. *See* Federal National Mortgage Association
due diligence
   completion, 546–547
   focus, 567
due-on-sale clause
   provisions, 245
   trigger, 251
due-on-sale provisions, enforcement, 255
DwellAgent.com, 651
dwelling units, 517

E

EarlyCheck service, 648
easements, 146
ECOA. *See* Equal Credit Opportunity Act
eCommitONE, 283–284
eCommitting, 283
Economic Growth, Regulatory Relief, and Consumer Protection Act, 93
   passage, 105–106
   Section 109, 98
economic influences, 494
Economic Stimulus Act of 2008 (ESA), 352
economy
   Fed influence, 46–47
   impact, 29–40
EEH. *See* Energy Efficient Homes
effective income, 399
electromagnetic forces (EMFs), 628–629
   gauss measurement, 629
   regulations, 598

electronic appraisal data file, submission, 512
Eleventh District cost of funds, 304
eligibility measures, 361
elliemae.com, 652
Ellie Mae's Encompass, 650
E-LOAN, 652
eloan.com, 652–653
Emergency Economic Stabilization Act (2008), 75, 76–77, 486
employment fraud, 329
Encompass (software), 652
encumbrances, 240–241, 268
    placement, 254
endangered species, 622–626
    harm/harassment, prohibition, 623
    protection, 623
Endangered Species Act, 598
    impact, 622–623
    mitigation, rulings (impact), 624–625
    net effect, 623–624
endorsement, 568
endowment funds, management, 229
energy design, leadership, 606–607
energy-efficient buildings, 630–631
Energy Efficient Homes (EEH), 402
Energy Policy Act (2005), 631
Enforcement Council (EPA), 606
entitlement, 386
    increments, 386t
    restoration, 377–379
environmental assessments, 594–596

commercial loan environmental assessment, 596–597
    standards, 606
environmental audit, 546
Environmental Bankers Association, 611
environmental cleanup liens, searches, 605
environmental conditions, appraiser comment (FHLMC requirement), 597
environmental consultants/consulting, 610
environmental contamination, discovery, 595
environmental design, leadership, 606–607
environmental due diligence assessment, 604
"Environmental Health Criteria monograph, Extremely Low Frequency Fields," 628
environmental issues, 599
    importance, 567
environmental problems, 598–599
Environmental Protection Agency (EPA), 595, 600–601
    "Building Owners' Guides," 615–616
    Enforcement Council, 606
    "Final Rule," 604
    policy statement, statutory exemption (contrast), 595
    web site features, 625
environmental risk insurance, 611
environmental savings, 607
environmental site assessment, 594

Environmental Site Assessment (ESA), 595
Equal Credit Opportunity Act (ECOA), 45, 61, 127, 395–397
    compliance, 209
    enactment, 64
    requirements, compliance, 67
Equifax, information, 66, 419
equipment bonds, 225
equitable title, 245
equity interests, sale, 17–19
ESA. *See* Economic Stimulus Act of 2008; Environmental Site Assessment
escrow account, initial deposit, 141–143
escrow closing, 119
escrow company, 119
escrow cushion, limitation, 260
estoppel, 244
excess residual income, 406
excess residual ratio, 406
existing construction, 407
expedited assessment, 449
expenses
    analysis, 571–574
    display, 543
    shopping centers, 576–577
Experian, information, 66, 419
extended terms, 21
Exterior-Only Inspection Individual Condominium Unit Appraisal, 513
Exterior-Only Inspection Individual Cooperative Interest Appraisal Report, 513
Exterior-Only Inspection Residential Appraisal Report, 513

exterior-only property inspection, 647
external obsolescence, 509–510

F

Fair and Accurate Credit Transactions Act (FACT)
  passage, 66–67
  requirements, compliance, 67
Fair Credit Reporting Act (FCRA), 65, 66–68
Fair Housing Act, 300
  violation, 520
Fair Housing Amendments Act of 1988, 300
fair housing requirements, 300
Fair, Isaac, and Company (FICO), 418
Fallin, Mary, 646
family income, eligibility, 60
family-resident farm loans, 586–587
farm and ranch loans, 586–589
  agricorporate farm loans, 587
  family-resident farm loans, 586–587
  ranch loans, 587–588
  religious facility financing, 588–589
Farm Credit Administration (FCA), 116
  examination/supervision, 211
  regulations, 100
  supervision, 179
Farm Credit Bank of Texas, 117
Farm Credit System (FCS), 116–117
Farmer Mac I Program, 180
Farmer Mac II Program, 180
Farmer Mac III Program, 180

Farmers Home Administration (FmHA), 115
farm loan, term, 586
Farm Mortgage Bankers Association, 207
F borrower, 296
FCRA. *See* Fair Credit Reporting Act
FDIC. *See* Federal Deposit Insurance Corporation
feasibility study, 549–550
federal agency, 66–68
Federal Agricultural Mortgage Corporation (Farmer Mac), 34, 179–180
Federal Bailout Legislation, H.R. 1424, 265, 299–300
Federal Deposit Insurance Corporation (FDIC), 74–82, 96, 197, 199, 209
  establishment/creation, 74–75
  Financial Institution Letter 492015, 297
federal discount rate, change (impact), 53f
Federal Emergency Management Agency (FEMA), 262
  flood hazard determination, reliance, 521
  flood maps, 354
Federal Enterprise Regulatory Reform Act (2003), 176
Federal Equal Credit Opportunity Act, 59
Federal Facility Compliance Act (1992), 627
Federal Financial Institutions Examination Council (FFIEC)
  FIRREA establishment, 496

federal funds rate, change, 52
Federal Home Loan Bank Board (FHLBB)
  authority, 80–81
  design, 288
  establishment, 83–84
  loan writing approval, 290–291
Federal Home Loan Bank (FHLB) System, 82–86
Federal Home Loan Mortgage Corporation (FHLMC) (Freddie Mac), 161, 174–176
  Automated Valuation Model (AVM), 644
  creation, 586
  FHLMC 65, 397
  FHLMC-administered yield requirements, 283–284
  Form 70, 500–501
  limits, 9
  Loan Prospector, 221, 350, 641, 642–644
  money earning, 176
  oversight, 107
  Phase I Environmental Site Assessment, 595–596
  powers, 34
  rehabilitation, 35
  Uniform Residential Appraisal Report, sample items, 523
  website features, 645
Federal Housing Administration (FHA), 342–351
  appraisals, value determination, 407
  assumption rules, change, 344
  benchmark guidelines, excess, 359t

borrower income qualification, 398–399
BPO usage, 530
case study, 388–389
connection, appraiser selection, 499–500
creation, 33
credit score requirements, 402–403
FHA-approved lenders, impact, 500
FHA Connect, 654
FHA-insured commitments, secondary financing, 349
FHA-insured loan program, 352–355
FHA-insured loans, loan-to-value (LTV) ratio requirements, 402
"FHA Spot Approval," 525
FHA-supported loans, 164
floor/ceiling limits, 364t
forbearance rules, 478
Home Affordable Modification Program (HA-HAMP), 473
HUD, relationship, 34
market share, growth, 35
maximum national loan limit ceiling, 347
minimum national loan limit floor, 347
Mortgagee Letter 1996-26, 498
mortgage insurance premiums, 355–358
mortgage loans, 11
mortgages, standards, 498–499
new minimum credit scores, 360, 402
program details, 360
programs, implementation, 207
purpose, 342, 346
qualification, 361
procedures, 369
Refinance for Borrowers with Negative Equity (FHA Short Refinance), 473, 474
Section 203(b), 353
terminology, 352–354
workshop, 388
Federal Housing Administration (FHA) loans
assumption, 343–346
categories, 344–345
limits, 347–348
origination, 109
usage, 360–368
Federal Housing Enterprises Financial Safety and Soundness Act (FHEFSSA), 177–178
Federal Housing Finance Agency (FHFA), 10, 107, 178
The Appraisal Foundation, meeting, 513–514
oversight, 34
Federal Housing Finance Board (FHFB), 80, 107, 178
OFHEO staff combination, 34
federal intermediate credit banks, 116
federal land
banks, 116
endangered species protection, 623
federal legislation, impact, 90
federal lien, impact, 264
federally chartered credit unions, authorization, 203
federally related, term (usage), 496
Federal Manufactured Home Requirements, HUD imposition, 528
Federal National Mortgage Association (FNMA) (Fannie Mae), 161, 176–179
community-oriented programs, 112
conversion, 177
creation, 33, 166–167
Desktop Originator (DO), 646
Desktop Underwriter (DU), 221, 350, 641, 646–648
FNMA-administered yield requirements, 283–284
Form 65, 127
Form 1003, 127, 397, 646
Form 1004, 128, 500–501, 506
Form 1004B, 128
Form 1004MC, 128
Form 1005, 443–445
Form 1006, 439–442
Form 1025/1073, 449
Form 1032, 449
Form 2000, 449
Form 2055/2065/2075, 450
high-cost area loan limits, 9–10
limits, 9
OFHEO oversight, 177–178
oversight, 107
Phase I Environmental Site Assessment, 595–596
powers, 34
privatization, 33
purchase requirements, 164
REALTOR Programs, 115
rehabilitation, 35
Uniform Residential Appraisal Report, sample items, 523
website features, 642

Federal Open Market
  Committee (FOMC)
  developments, 54
  impact, 35
  Policy Normalization
    Principles and Plans, 54
Federal Reserve Act, 52–53
Federal Reserve Bank, 96
  consumer compliance laws,
    55
  creation, 196
  intervention, 279
  market stabilization, 34–35
  responsibility, 56
Federal Reserve Bank Board
  chairman selection, 45
  money amount control, 50
  money circulation
    responsibility, 69–70
  Partners, 641
Federal Reserve Bank of New
  York, MBS purchases, 35
Federal Reserve Bank System,
  45–55, 197
Federal Reserve, Board of
  Governors (consent), 70
Federal Reserve Board,
  Regulation Z, 93
Federal Reserve System, 44–57
  funding, 105
  lending authority, Dodd-
    Frank Act (impact), 53
  monetary policies, 281
  political accommodation,
    71
  Regulation Q, 84, 160
  structure/operations, flow
    chart, 46f
Federal Savings and Loan
  Insurance Corporation
  (FSLIC)

  deposit insurance, 74
  management, 75
  problems, 80–81
federal savings bank, operation,
  81
federal supervisory agencies, 91
federal tax claims, 264–265,
  299–300
Federal Trade Commission
  (FTC), 209
  Privacy Rule, 68
  Red Flag Rules, 67
*Federal Wetlands Determination
  Manual*, 621
fee, encumbering, 268
fee title, encumbrance, 13
FERA. *See* Fraud Enforcement
  and Recovery Act of 2009
feudal system, 4
feudal, term (usage), 4
FHEFSSA. *See* Federal Housing
  Enterprises Financial Safety
  and Soundness Act
FHFA. *See* Federal Housing
  Finance Agency
FHFB. *See* Federal Housing
  Finance Board
FHLB. *See* Federal Home Loan
  Bank
FHL Banks, overseeing, 85
FHLBB. *See* Federal Home Loan
  Bank Board
FHLMC. *See* Federal Home
  Loan Mortgage Corporation
FICO. *See* Fair, Isaac, and
  Company
Field, R. William, 616
Fifth Amendment, impact,
  625–626
"Final Rule" (EPA), 604
finance charge, 95

finance companies, 289
Financial Crimes Enforcement
  Network (FinCEN), 73
financial information
  collection, 639
  supply, 547–548
Financial Institutions Reform,
  Recovery, and Enforcement
  Act (FIRREA), 75, 84, 111, 496
  appraisal standards, 128
  compliance, 501
  impact, 91–92
  reporting requirements,
    expansion, 106–107
financial leverage, use/overuse,
  549
financial market instruments, 32
financial risk, 538
Financial Services
  Modernization Act, 92
Financial Services Regulatory
  Relief Act, passage, 54
financial statements,
  preparation, 547–548
financing
  background, 4–5
  wetlands, effect, 622
FIRA. *See* Biggert-Waters Flood
  Insurance Reform Act
FIRREA. *See* Financial
  Institutions Reform, Recovery,
  and Enforcement Act
first mortgage, delivery, 557
first-time home buyer, HUD-
  approved prepurchase
  counseling, 342
First-Time Homebuyer
  Program, 114
fiserv.com, 652
fixed-interest, constant-level
  plans, 277, 286–287

fixed operating expenses, 571
fixed payment, 400–401
   ratio, 402
fixed-rate mortgage (FRM)
   credit, source, 276
   repayment schedule, 286–287
fixed-rate note, 302
F-list (nonspecific source wastes), 600–601
Flood Disaster Protection Act, passage, 520–521
flood insurance, 261–263
   FHA requirements, 354–355
   "forced placement," 521
Flood Insurance Notice, lender provision, 458
Flood Insurance Reform Priorities Act, 262
flood-prone areas, 520–521
forbearance, 478
foreclosures, 22–23, 30, 168, 380
   action, high-priority claim, 263
   avoidance, 355
   capital gains/losses, 487–488
   deed in lieu of foreclosure, 249–250
   friendly foreclosure, 346
   Home Affordable Foreclosure Alternatives (HAFA), 474
   loan default, relationship, 470
   mortgagor redemption rights, 480–482
   PMI obligations, 417
   procedure, steps, 481
   proceeding, 248
   reporting, 471–472
   sale, 484
   status, 482–484
   tax impacts, 486–488
   types, 478–484
   VA foreclosure, 472

foreign lenders, 230–232
Form 65 (FNMA), 127
Form 1003 (FNMA), 127, 397, 646
Form 1004 (FNMA), 128, 500–501, 506
Form 1004B (FNMA), 128
Form 1004MC (FNMA), 128
Form 1006 (FNMA), 439
Form 1025/1073, 449
Form 1032, 449
Form 2000, 449
Form 2055/2065/2075, 450
formal assumption, 344–346
formaldehyde gas, 614–615
   testing, 615
Form RD 410-4, 118
forward commitment, 215
foundations, 230
Franklin American Mortgage Company, FHA/VA loan origination, 109
fraternal associations, funds, 230
Fraud Enforcement and Recovery Act of 2009 (FERA), 214
fraud for profit, 329
friable asbestos, 616
friendly foreclosure, 346
FRM. *See* fixed-rate mortgage
FSLIC. *See* Federal Savings and Loan Insurance Corporation
full service, meaning, 207
functional obsolescence, 509
funding fee, 380–382, 381t
   payment, exemption, 381
funds
   borrowing, collateral, 29–30
   cost, 303
   disbursement, 153
future land value, impacts, 598

future purchase contract, 568–569

G

gap loan, 248
Garn-St. Germain Act of 1982, 54
GE Capital, 288
GEM. *See* growing equity mortgage
general warehouse, 584–585
"gentrification," 520
GFE. *See* Good Faith Estimate
gift loan fraud, 330
global warming, discussion, 624–625
GMAC Mortgage, 652
GM Financial, 288
gold bonds, 109
Goldman Sachs, 166
Good Faith Estimate (GFE), 118–127
   lender usage, 457
   usage, 123
Good Faith Estimate (2010), replacement, 96–97
goods/services, trading (barter system), 44
government
   borrower categories, 279
   government-guaranteed loans, participation, 92
   government-insured loans, participation, 92
   guarantee, 173, 175
   limits, 268–269
   survey, 532–533
government bonds, 225
government employees, security, 62
government loan programs, 115–116

Government National Mortgage
 Association (GNMA)
 (Ginnie Mae), 161, 172–174
    assignment, 172
    certificate, 173
    issuer criteria, 174
    loan underwriting
      limitations, 34
Government Pension
 Fund Global of Norway
 (Norges Bank Investment
 Management), 230
government recording, 145–146
government-sponsored
 enterprises (GSEs), 11,
 172–181
    failure, risk (reduction),
      177–178
    FHFA oversight, 34
    GSE-conforming loans,
      impact, 268–269
    knowledge, 181
    market leadership
      domination, 161
    private ownership, 38
    requirements, enhancement,
      107
government-subsidized loans,
 participation, 92
Graduated-Payment Mortgages
 (GPMs), 277, 311–312, 360,
 363–367
    factors, 367t
graduated-payment program, 322
Gramlich, Edward, 8
Gramm-Leach-Bliley Act, 55
    signing, 92
Great Depression, 26, 33
    Banking Act (1933),
      enactment, 74–75
    monetary policy, 45

mortgage loan function, 160
recovery, 39
Great Recession, 26, 219
    market intervention, 77
    monetary policy, 45
    reforms, 76–78
    warehouse lines of credit,
      decrease, 214
green buildings
    savings, 607
    value, 608
green home improvements,
 significance, 612–613
Greenspan, Alan, 8
gross income, 404
gross monthly income, 403
gross rate, 164
ground lease, 12
growing equity mortgage
 (GEM), 322
guarantee calculation, example,
 375
"Guide on Hazardous Waste
 Management for Florida's
 Auto Repair and Paint and
 Body Shops," 629–630

H

HAFA. *See* Home Affordable
 Foreclosure Alternatives
Hagel, Chuck, 176
HAMP. *See* Home Affordable
 Modification Program
Hatteras Financial Corp., 223
hazard insurance, 140, 260
    adequacy, 521
    minimum requirement,
      260–261
    premium, 354
    proceeds, disbursement, 261
    purchase, 141

hazardous materials, 600
hazardous waste
    areas, real property concern,
      519
    records, review, 605
Hazardous Waste Trust Fund
 (Superfund), 600
    bankers, environmental risk
      insurance, 611
    cost recovery actions,
      defenses, 603
    lender liability, 603
    liabilities, private insurance,
      611
    minimum quantity
      requirement, absence, 602
    pollution insurance, 611
    responsible parties, 602–603
    Section 107(a), 602
    secured creditor exemption,
      603
Health Care and Education
 Reconciliation Act (2010), 325
health, improvement, 607
HECM. *See* Home Equity
 Conversion Mortgage
HERA. *See* Housing and
 Economic Recovery Act
HHF. *See* Housing Finance
 Agency Innovation Fund
 for the Hardest-Hit Housing
 Markets
Higher Education Opportunity
 Act, passage, 92
Higher-Priced Mortgage Loans
 (HPML) Appraisal Rule, 501
highest and best use (appraisal
 principle), 504
high-grade securities, investors,
 168
high-quality yields, search, 71

High Volatility Commercial Real Estate (HVCRE) Exposures, 613
historical information, reviews, 605
HMDA. *See* Home Mortgage Disclosure Act
HOEPA. *See* Home Ownership and Equity Protection Act
Homart Development Company, 575
Home Affordable Foreclosure Alternatives (HAFA) Program, 474, 476–477
Home Affordable Modification Program (HAMP), 473, 474–475
Home Affordable Refinance Program (HARP), 373, 473, 475
home builder, 289
  commitments, 5–7
home buyer education programs, 25
home equity
  line of credit, 317–318, 323
  loans, 323
  revolving loans, 323–324
Home Equity Conversion Mortgage (HECM), 327, 357, 465
  loans, 342–343
  program, 327–328
home improvement loan insurance (Title 1), 360, 367–368
HOME Investment Partnerships Program, 114
home loans
  environmental assessments, 594–596
  market, 82

Home Loan Toolkit, 96
Home Mortgage Disclosure Act (HMDA), 91, 106–107
home mortgage lending, federal regulation, 106–107
Homeowner's Assistance Program, 378
homeowners association, impact, 525
Home Ownership and Equity Protection Act (HOEPA), 458
home ownership loans, 117–118
Home Possible, 112
home purchase mortgage, 328
HomeReady, 112
Honda Financial Services, 288
Honoring America's Veterans and Caring for Camp Lejeune Families Act of 2012 ("Honoring Veterans Act"), 381
Hooker Chemical Company, chemical waste dumping, 600
hot checks, Fed writing, 50–51
hourly wages, 59
house
  apparent age, 522
  construction, tax assessment, 142–143
housing
  expense, 399
  resort housing, 523–524
Housing and Community Development Act, passage, 36–37
Housing and Economic Recovery Act (HERA), 103–104, 107, 178, 269, 341, 360
Housing Finance Agency Innovation Fund for the Hardest-Hit Housing Markets (HHF), 473, 474, 476

Housing Finance Corporation, 114–115
HPML. *See* Higher-Priced Mortgage Loans
hsh.com, 653
HVCRE. *See* High Volatility Commercial Real Estate
hypothecation, 30

I

Ichigo Real Estate Investment Corporation, 230
Identity Theft Deterrence Act (ITDA), 68
ILSFDA. *See* Interstate Land Sales Full Disclosure Act
immediate commitment, 215
Important Notice to Reverse Mortgage Loan Applicant disclosures, 458
income
  analysis, 571–574
  approach, usage, 514–517
  capitalization, 515
  consideration, 23–24
  effective income, 399
  fraud, 329
  income from children, 60
  measurement, 549
  properties, construction loans, 560–561
  qualification, residual method, 403–406
  ratio, 331–332
  residual income, 399, 401
  shopping centers, 576–577
  stability, 61
  stabilized income property, 583
  statement, 541
  stream, 515
  types, 58–61

income ratio method (VA), 331–332
indemnification clause, 417–418
indemnity, 23
index
  application, 304–307
  characteristics, 310
  historical record, 304, 305t–306t
  movement, rate basis, 306–307
  usage, 303–304
index plus margin, rate basis, 305
Individual Condominium Unit Appraisal Report, 513
Individual Cooperative Interest Appraisal Report, 513
individual retirement accounts (IRAs), balances, 48
indoor air pollution, 614–617
  asbestos, usage, 614, 615–616
  biological pollutants, 614
  combustion by-products, 614
  formaldehyde gas, 614–616
  laws, 598
  radon gas, 614, 616–617
  tobacco smoke, 614
  volatile organic compounds, 614
indoor environment, health (improvement), 607
Industrial Revolution, advent, 4–5
information
  financial information, supply, 547–548
  release, authorization, 546
  requirement, 540–546
  requirements (RESPA requirement), 121
  sources, 539

ING Group, 288
Inhofe, James, 596
Initial Escrow Statement, usage, 457
innocent landowner defense, 604–610
Inside Mortgage Finance, 649
installment loans, 56
installment obligation, 254
insurance, 545
insured commitment, 363
  calculation (Section 245), 365–366
insured loan, 412
insured name, 412
interest, 61, 278–288
  charge, 139
  costs, TILA requirements, 209
  discount rate, 51–53
  per diem interest, 353–354
  prime rate, 52
Interest on Lawyers' Trust Accounts (IOLTAs), 76
interest-only mortgage, 316–317
  LIBOR, relationship, 317
interest-only note, 316–317
interest-only payment, calculation, 310
interest rate
  APR, contrast, 95
  environment, creation, 36
  fluctuation, risk, 170
  indicators, 281–285
  movements, signaling, 47
  quoting, 164
interest rate reduction refinancing loans (IRRRLs), 382–383
interests, sale, 17–18
interim loan, 247–248
interlocking documents, 256

internal revenue, assessment/collection, 70
Internal Revenue Code 1031, 19
International Association of Assessing Officers, 503
International Monetary Fund (IMF), Treasury Department involvement, 72–73
Internet
  loan applications, 649
  mortgages, 648–651
  usage, 289–290
Interstate Land Sales Full Disclosure Act (ILSFDA), 554–555
Invesco Morgage Capital, Inc., 223
investment
  bankers, 289
  policies, 200
  portfolio statements, usage, 440
  risk, 228
investors
  due diligence, 530
  financing, restrictions (exceptions), 347
  mortgagors, elimination, 346
IOLTAs. *See* Interest on Lawyers' Trust Accounts
IRRRLs. *See* interest rate reduction refinancing loans
ITDA. *See* Identity Theft Deterrence Act
ITT, purchase, 222

J

job-hopping, 62
job time, length, 61–62
joint, term (usage), 601
JPMorgan Chase, 83, 166, 482
  Bear Stearns and Company, merger, 225

Leverage Ratio MRQ, 178–179
settlement, 483
judicial foreclosure, 478–479
jumbo loans, 296–297
junior mortgage, 248–249

K

Kaleidico, Mortgage Web in a Box, 650
Keogh accounts, balance, 48
kickbacks, 134–135
consideration, 637
elimination, 96
K-list (source-specific wastes), 601

L

land
land-sale-leaseback, function, 16
leases, 12
sale, absence, 12
survey, 530
Torrens system, 462–463
value, variation, 510
land development loans, 552–555
land loan, 551
landlord, 4
landownership, 3–4
growth, 4–5
restriction, 4
land purchase loans, 551–552
LaQuinta Inns, purchase, 222
lead
handling, 619–620
"point of use" treatment device, usage, 620
presence, 620
property value impact, 619
testing, 618

lead-based paint
hazards, 597
remediation, 596–597
rule, 619
Leadership in Energy and Environmental Design (LEED), 577, 606–607
Lead Exposure Reduction Amendments Act of 2013, 597
lead generators, 650
lead poisoning, 617–620
damage, 618
inhalation/ingestion, 618
rules, 598
sources, 618
Lead Press, 650
Leaking Underground Storage Tank (LUST) Recovery Act assistance agreements, 627
leaseback, sale (relationship), 14–15
leased land, financing development, 12–17
leasehold, 12
interest, creation, 566
leasing, cost (reduction), 12
LEED. *See* Leadership in Energy and Environmental Design
legal documents, ordering, 639
lendable funds, raising, 287
Lender Appraisal Processing Program (VA), 403
Lender Home Page, 651
lender notices, 457–458
provision, RESPA requirement, 457
lenders
advance payments, 139–140
closing costs, 464–465
community, defining, 91

delinquency/default, impact, 470–471
direct lenders, 650
forms, provision, 457–458
inspection fee, 138
liability, 603
management agreement, usage, 525
nonsupervised lender, 384
reserves, deposit, 140–141
supervised lender, 383
lenders, title insurance, 143–145
policy, 462
Lender's Title Policy, 144
lending
policies, 197–199
practices, discrimination (avoidance), 92
Leverage Ratio MRQ, 178–179
liabilities, 62–63
release, 379–380
liability release, obtaining, 471
LIBOR. *See* London Interbank Offered Rate
Licensed Residential Real Property Appraiser (LRRPA)
applicants, course completion, 498
qualification, 497–498
liens, 240–241
placement, 259
vendor's lien, 249
lien theory, 240
title theory, contrast, 257
life insurance companies, 199–201
regulation, 201
"life of the loan" cap, 308
lifetime of mortgage cap, 288
like-kind exchanges (Internal Revenue Code 1031), 19
limited appraisal, 505

limited partnership, 17
liquidity
  issues, addressing, 105
  requirement, 174
  risk, 538–539, 549–550
LLPA. *See* Loan-Level Price Adjustment
loan
  ability-to-repay requirements, 11
  acquisition group, impact, 213–214
  agreement, 30, 412
  amount, maximum, 231
  analysis, 494–495
  closing, participation, 639
  construction loans, 247, 555–561
  coverage volume, MGIC increase, 413
  criteria, 416
  discount, 137
  documentation, standardization, 127–128
  documents, 598
  dollar amount, 9–12
  Endangered Species Act, net effect, 623–624
  farm/ranch loans, 586–589
  guaranty entitlement, 386
  insured loan, 412
  life, interest rate change, 308
  maximum amounts, 529
  minimum loan limits, 10–12
  modification, 477
  mortgage company funding, 214–216
  nonrecourse loan, 487–488
  origination, 344–345
    services, 638–639
  originator awareness, 521

payable item, 136–139
payment, property sale (impact), 378
poolers, 173, 216
pools, 182–184
  assembly, 183–184
portfolio, management, 172
price, 162
program. *See* Federal Housing Administration.
purchase policies, constraints, 35
purchasers, 166–171
qualification guidelines, comparison, 477–478
quality, standard, 8
restructuring, 293
sources, analysis, 78–79
status, report, 120
syndications/participations, 561
types, 288–290
UST effect, 627
verifications, requests (initiating/ordering), 639
loan applications, 397–398
  analysis, 349–351
  computerized analysis, 350
  initiation, 539–547
  taking, 64
loan default, 380
  foreclosure, relationship, 470
Loan Estimate, 118–127, 639
  lender usage, 457
  preliminary information, 120
  revision, 97
Loan-Level Price Adjustment (LLPA) Matrix, 656
Loan Modification Agreement, sample, 478
loan origination, 198–199
  fee, 136

Loan Origination Services List (HUD), 638
loan origination system (LOS), 640–641, 646, 648, 652
  LOS-application tracking, 650
loan originators, 31–32
  application fee, 217
  income dependability, 217
loan pricing
  standard, 7–8
  usage, 162–163
Loan Prospector. *See* Federal Home Loan Mortgage Corporation
loan servicing, 213–214
  disclosure notice, 219–220
loan terms
  changes, 477
  maximum, 655
loan-to-value limit, 197
  variable loan-to-value limits, elimination, 341
loan-to-value loan, 264, 286
  offering, 298
loan-to-value (LTV) method, DCR method (comparison), 550–551
loan-to-value ratio (LTV), 7–9, 197, 206, 290–291
  levels, variation, 524
  loans, creation, 39
  usage, 37
loan-to-value (LTV) ratio requirements, 402
loan-to-value ratios (LTVRs), 57
local government programs, 110–111
local programs, 110–113
location
  analysis, 550
  apartment buildings, 569

lock-in provisions, 253–254
London Interbank Offered Rate (LIBOR), 285, 304
   interest-only mortgages, relationship, 317
loose asbestos, 615
LOS. *See* loan origination system
lot and block description, 244
lots, division, 531–532
Love Canal, chemical waste dumping, 599–600
low-balance home equity lines of credit, 530
low income, definition, 111
low-ratio properties, 406
LRRPA. *See* Licensed Residential Real Property Appraiser
LUST. *See* Leaking Underground Storage Tank

M

M1 (money category), 49
M2 (money category), 49
M3 (money category), 49–50
MAI appraiser, 548
"make-or-break" factor, 570
Making Home Affordable Program (MH), commencement, 72
"Making Home Affordable" programs, 473–478
management
   agreement, usage, 525
   risk, 539
manual underwriting, 57, 639–640
Manufactured Home Appraisal Report, 513

manufactured home loans, 384–385
manufactured homes
   conversion, 529
   HUD definition, 384–385
manufacturing housing, 528–530
margin
   addition, requirement, 305
   generation, 168–169
market
   analysis, 550
   conditions, impact, 540
   intervention, 77
Market Conditions Addendum (Form 1004MC), 128
market value, 407
   definition, revision, 512
maximum debt ratio, determination, 400
MDIA. *See* Mortgage Disclosure Improvement Act
meridians, 532–533
metes, 532
Military Annual Percentage Rate (MAPR), 56
Military Lending Act (MLA), updates, 56
minimum credit scores, 403
minimum loan limits, 10–12
mini warehouses, 585
MIP. *See* mortgage insurance premium
MISMO. *See* Mortgage Industry Standards Maintenance Organization
mitigation banking, 622
Mizuho Bank, Ltd., 230
MLOs. *See* Mortgage loan originators
MLS. *See* Multiple Listing Services

MMI. *See* Mutual Mortgage Insurance
mobile homes, 528–530
Model Energy Code (1992), 631
Model State Act, endorsement, 101
Model Toxics Control Act (MTCA), 604–605
moderate income, definition, 111
Monetary Control Act, 54
monetary policies, 46–47
monetary system
   Fed usage, 46–47
   usage, 44–45
money
   categories, 49–50
   circulation, Federal Reserve Bank Board responsibility, 69–70
   defining, 44–57
   definition, 48–50
   loan willingness, 33
   printing, 71
   value symbol, 44
   walking money, 553
money, borrowing, 71
   reason, 278–279
money-market deposit accounts, 76
money market funds, 279
money supply, 45, 47, 279
   increase, 50–51
   management, 50–51
monthly mortgage payments, calculation, 366–367
Morgan Stanley, 166, 216
mortgage, 30, 242–243. *See also* Internet
   bankers, 204, 207
   brokers, 204–206, 650
   buydown mortgage, 312–314
   cap, lifetime, 288

claim, 268
collections, 77
conveyance-type instrument, 243
counseling notice, 458
covenants, 254
credit, market, 202
crisis, development, 35–37
first mortgage, delivery, 557
form, 258
fraud, 328–330
grant of title, 239
growing equity mortgage (GEM), 322
GSE purchase, 318
impact, 320–323
instrument, 243, 255–256
interest rate, increase, 307–308
lender, qualifications, 208
lending, 108–110
limits, 363, 365
negotiation, 649
note, 217
   relationship, 242–244
notice of mortgage counseling, requirement, 458
obligation, reworking, 23
parties, 243
payment, 542
pledged-account mortgage, 314–315
pools, usage, 287
procedures, 265–269
regular mortgage, 241
release clauses, usage, 248
servicing, transfer note, 99
term mortgage, 316–317
two-step mortgage, 316
variations, 241

verifications, request (initiating/ordering), 639
mortgage-backed bonds, 225
mortgage-backed securities (MBSs), 185–190, 226
   acceptance, 171
   attraction, 170–171
   development, 160
   issuance, 166
   offering, 169
   purchase, 35, 76–77
   sale, 216
   usage, 279
Mortgage Bankers Association (MBA), 207
   controversy, 637
   survey, 33
mortgage bonds, 225
   sale, 20
Mortgagebot, 640, 653
mortgagebuilder.com, 653–654
Mortgage Builder Software, Inc., 641
Mortgage Builders Software, 650
mortgage companies
   funding process, 214–216
   income, 216–219
   operations, 213–214
   term, usage, 108–109
mortgage debt
   analysis, 78
   categories, 78t
   lender ownership, 79t
   outstanding, 202
Mortgage Debt Relief Act of 2007, 24
Mortgage Disclosure Improvement Act (MDIA), 134, 218, 324, 639
mortgagee, 3
   Closing Instructions, 148f–152f

mortgagee errors and omissions policy, 174
Mortgage Electronic Registration Systems (MERSCORP, Inc.), 483
Mortgagee Letter
   1996-26, 498
   2013-04, 356, 357
   2013-05, 351
   2015-01, 357
mortgagee's information letter, 120
mortgagee's report, 120
Mortgage Forgiveness Debt Relief Act (2007), 265
Mortgage Guaranty Insurance Co. (MGIC), 291
   loan coverage volume, increase, 413
Mortgage Industry Standards Maintenance Organization (MISMO) AUS 2.3.1, 648
mortgage insurance application fees, 138
Mortgage Insurance for Disaster Victims, 403
mortgage insurance premium (MIP), 139–140, 355
   annual MIP, increase, 356
   payments, cancellation, 341
   reserve requirement, 141
mortgage lending
   instruments, special provisions, 252–256
   tax impacts, 298–302
mortgage lending activities, 5
   description, 2–3
Mortgage Letter 2014-25, impact, 348
mortgage loan
   approval, "go/no-go" determinants, 517

borrower categories, 279
contract rate, 255
cost comparison, example, 321t
market, 31–32
officers, licensing, 209–212
origination process, requirements, 68–69
pools, creation, 167–168
repayment, 552
sale, 161–171
structuring, requirements, 22
third-party mortgage loan servicing operation, 219
underwriting, 495
mortgage loan originators (MLOs), 204, 211
operation, 100
Mortgage Marvel, 641, 653
Mortgage Partnership Finance Program (MPF), 85–86
mortgage payment, 333
amount, 309
mortgage pools, 79
federal underwriting, 171–172
Mortgage Power (Citibank), 637
mortgage-product features/offerings, 277
mortgage repayment
design, introduction, 316
plans, usage, 276–277
mortgage revenue bonds (MRBs), 114
Mortgage Web in a Box (Kaleidico), 650
mortgagor's information letter, 120
MPF. *See* Mortgage Partnership Finance Program
MRBs. *See* mortgage revenue bonds

MTCA. *See* Model Toxics Control Act
multifamily loans, seller/services FNMA requirement, 597–598
multifamily MBS, decline, 572
Multiple Listing Services (MLS)
data, usage, 512
special code, usage, 511–512
multiple-occupancy building, economic advantages, 527
municipal bonds, 225
private use, tax exemption, 184
mutual funds, 279
Mutual Mortgage Insurance (MMI) fund, 356
Mutual Mortgage Insurance Fund, 90
MZM (money category), 50

N

NAMB. *See* National Association of Mortgage Brokers
NAR. *See* National Association of REALTORS
National Appraisal Institute, building value analysis, 608
National Assn. of Home Builders v. Defenders of Wildlife, 624
National Association of Home Builders, 25
National Association of Independent Fee Appraisers, 503
National Association of Mortgage Brokers (NAMB), 204–205
National Association of Real Estate Appraisers, 503

National Association of REALTORS (NAR)
controversy, 637
member information, 597
study, 5
surveys, 232
National Bank Act, 196
national banks, supervision, 70
National Bureau of Economic Research, business cycle duration study, 26
National Conference of Commissioners on Uniform State Laws, 101
National Credit Union Administration, 197
charters, 203–204
National Credit Union Insurance Fund, 197
National Credit Union Share Insurance Fund, setup, 74
National Emission Standards for Hazardous Air Pollution (NESHAP), 616
National Flood Insurance Act (1994), 521
National Flood Insurance Program (NFIP), 261–262, 520
National Flood Insurance Program Act, 262
National Flood Insurance Reform Act, 261
National Guard, 372, 374
National Housing Act (1934), 90, 276, 342
National Mortgage Licensing System (NMLS), 7, 204
establishment, 208
licensing/compliance rules, 211

minimum qualifications, 210
registration, 212
Nationwide Mortgage Licensing System and Registry (NMLS), state agency participation, 100
"Nationwide Permit 29," filing, 622
negative amortization, 294, 309, 312, 333
　occurrence, 310
negotiable instrument, 32
negotiated interest rate/discount, 382
neighborhood centers, 575
neighborhoods (property location), 519–520
NESHAP. *See* National Emission Standards for Hazardous Air Pollution
net basis rate, 164
net lease, 574, 585
net operating income (NOI), 542–543
　determination, 205–206
　financials, types, 206
net rentable area (NRA), example, 583
net transaction accounts, 54
net useable area (NUA), 583
net yield, 162
new money, advancement (absence), 95
new space absorption rates, decrease, 27
NFIP. *See* National Flood Insurance Program
NINJA loans. *See* "no income, no job, and (no) assets" loans
NMLS. *See* National Mortgage Licensing System and Registry

no-bid procedure, 380
"no income, no job, and (no) assets" loans (NINJA loans), 277
nominal rate, 313
nonbank lenders, 288
non-exchange-traded REITs, filings, 224
nonexpedited assessment, 449
noninterest-bearing transaction account, 76
nonjudicial foreclosure, 479
nonrecourse loan, 487–488
nonrecourse note, 259
nonrefundable application fee, 217
nonspecific source wastes (F-list), 600–601
non-spouse co-ownership, 379
nonsupervised lender, 384
Norman Conquest, 4
notary fee, 138–139
notes
　deed of trust, relationship, 241–242
　mortgage, relationship, 242–244
Notice of the Right to Rescind, usage, 457
NOW accounts, 54, 76
NRA. *See* net rentable area
NUA. *See* net useable area

O

OCC. *See* Office of the Comptroller of the Currency
occupancy fraud, 330
Ocwen Financial Corporation, settlement, 484
OEC. *See* owner's extended coverage
office buildings, 580–583

　business owner-occupied buildings, 580
　lease, 581–583
　preleased office space, 581
　rent calculations, example, 583
　speculative office buildings, 581–582
Office of Consumer Affairs and Regulatory Functions, 122
Office of Federal Housing Enterprise Oversight (OFHEO), 107
　FHFB staff combination, 34
　FNMA, oversight, 177–178
Office of Interstate Land Sales, responsibility, 553–554
Office of Tax Policy, 73
Office of the Comptroller of the Currency (OCC), 79, 197
　bank review, 92
　Bulletin 2017-18, 8–9
　Policies and Procedures Manual (PPM) issuance, 93
Office of Thrift Supervision (OTS), 79, 197, 302
　existence, cessation, 80
office/warehouses, 585
"Oil Belt" recession, 28
"one-stop-shopping" service, offer, 637
One-year Treasury securities, 304
one-year Treasury security rate, example, 305
　usage, 307
online mortgage originators, categories, 650
online real estate service, 651–654
open-ended checking account, 70

open-end mortgage, 246–247
open market operations, 47, 51
Open Market Trading Desk (the Desk), 35
operating expenses, 576–577
operating history, profitability, 573
operating margin, 285
operating statement, 543
operations-and-maintenance (O&M) plans, 595–596
opportunity cost, 322–323
option ARM
   loan type, 311
   Washington Mutual development, 309–310
originate-to-distribute model, 182
origination fee, 217–218
   mortgage company split, 218
originators
   business-process management systems, 641
   online mortgage originators, categories, 650
"other tangible property," 301
OTS. *See* Office of Thrift Supervision
overhead expenses, reduction, 582
overtime wages, 59
owners
   owner-occupant applicants, Section 245 (impact), 364
   owner-occupied buildings, 578–579, 581
   owner-occupied buildings, space lease, 582–583
   owner-occupied property, 522
   personal endorsement, 558
owner's extended coverage (OEC) policy, usage, 464
ownership
   feudal right, 4
   separation, 12
owners, title insurance, 145
   policy, 461

P

package mortgage, 250
"paid in full" note, 267
paper, sale, 20
partial release clause, 248
participation agreement, 296–297
participation certificates (PCs), 175
participation loan, 296–297
Partners, 641
part-time employment, 61
pass-through securities, 216
pass-through special-purpose entities, framework (usage), 222
Patriot Act, information collection, 68
paved streets, importance, 518
payment abatements agreement, 312–313
"pay-option ARMs," 310
PCs. *See* participation certificates
Peer Capital Advisors, dead space usage, 582
Pegasystems, SmartBPM, 641
pension funds, 279, 290
pension programs, 201–202
penson income, 60
percentage guideline method, 399–402
   summary, 477t
percentage guideline, monthly basis, 401

percentage leases, 577–578
percentage rent rates, 578
per diem interest, 353–354
period cap, 288
periodic interest rate change, 308
permits, obtaining, 546–547
personal financial statements, 545
personal income tax returns, 545
pest inspection, 146
PG Mortgage Software, 650
Phase I assessment, 596, 598, 604
   performing, 605
Phase I ESAs, 595–596
Phase II assessment, 605
Phase III assessment, 605
PHH Corporation, 654
phhmortgage.com, 654
physical characteristics, 517
physical deterioration, 509
physical facilities, 569–570
"pick-a-pay," 310
"pick-a-payment," 310
piggyback loan, 318
   advantages/disadvantages, 318–320
PITI. *See* Principal, Interest, Taxes, Insurance
P&L. *See* profit and loss statement
planned unit developments (PUDs), 360
pledged-account mortgage, 314–315
P-list (discarded commercial chemical products), 601
PMI. *See* private mortgage insurance (PMI)
PMI Insurance Company, 291
POA. *See* power of attorney
"point of use" treatment device, usage, 620

points, 165
    basis points, 165
    measurement, 31, 137
Policies and Procedures Manual (PPM), OCC issuance, 93
Policy Normalization Principles and Plans (FOMC), 54
"Policy Toward Owners of Residential Property at Superfund Sites" (EPA), 595
pollution insurance, 611
polychlorinated biphenyls (PCBs), waste, 600
pooler, 225
portfolio
    approach, 167
    purchase, 166–167
power of attorney (POA), obtaining (importance), 464
Powersite Suite, 653
PPIP. *See* public-private investment program
predatory lending, 294–296
preleased office space, 581
preleased space, 578, 579
preliminary title report, 120–121
pre-loan activities, conducting, 612
premium
    changes, 356–357
    charges, 415–416
    refund, 343
prepaid items, 353–354
prepayment penalty, 252–254
prepayment premium, 252
prequalification forom, 120
price, yield conversion, 164t
price/yield table, calculation, 163t
primary market, 31
    lenders, 288–290
    lenders, risks, 107

primary mortgage conduits, 182
prime market, 656
prime rate, 282
prime rate of interest. *See* interest
principal amount due, 244
principal balance, maximum, 269t
principal, borrowing, 258
Principal, Interest, Taxes, Insurance (PITI), 399, 404, 542
    defining, 330–331
    maximum PITI, explanation, 400
    workshop, 330–335
principals
    creditworthiness, 206
    résumés, 546
Privacy Rule (FTC), 68
private investment, attraction, 106
private lenders, 228–229
private MBSs
    emergence, 35
    market, recovery, 108
private mortgage insurance (PMI), 8, 290–291, 412–418
    coverage amount, offering, 414–415
    coverage, cancellation, 416
    history, 413
    indemnification clause, 417–418
    obligations, 417
    payment component, 319
    premiums, charges, 415–416
    property coverage, 415
    qualifying information, requirement, 414
    removal, requests, 530
    requirement, determination, 417

standardization, absence, 412–413
    term, 414
private mortgage insurance (PMI) companies, 414
    mortgage insurance application fee charge, 138
private property rights, 625–626
production-related income, 58
profit and loss statement (P&L), 410, 541–543
    detail, 542
pro forma cash flow statements, 543–544
pro forma statement preparations, 544
prohibited practices (RESPA requirement), 121
promissory certificates, issuance, 44
promissory note, 30
    form, 256
    standardization, 258
property
    acquisition, sale of interests, 18
    address, 647
    age, 521–522
    analysis, 351
    apparent age, 522
    appraisal, 495–504
    characteristics, 517–524
    condition/location/usage, 494
    conveyance, absence, 470
    coverage, 415
    description, 506
    "early warnings," 597
    evaluation, 548–551
    fair market valuation, 206
    fair market value, 487
    hypothecation, 240
    identification, 243–244

insurance, 260–261
loans, 197
location, 519–521
low-ratio properties, 406
operating statements, 540
physical characteristics, 517
purchase price, 16
qualification, 406–409
remaining useful life, 522
sale, 378
sale of interests, 17–18
transfer, 251
usage, 522–524
valuation, 646–647
example, 249, 252
property owners
debt load, 17
federal government assistance, 520
property rights
state law control, 239
transfer, 242
property taxes, 263–264, 354
ad valorem tax, 298
bill, 546
handling, 13
property value, 348, 4307
appraisal report forms, 448t
approaches, 508–517
comparison, 516
AUS findings, usage, 449–450
cost approach, 447
determination, methodologies, 447–449
income approach, 447
lead, impact, 619
market approach, 447
walking away, 485
property value, estimation
cost approach, usage, 508–510

income approach, usage, 514–517
sales comparison analysis, usage, 510–514
proper value, 407
proposed construction, 406
provident.com, 654
Provident Funding Associates, L.P., 654
Prudential Real Estate, 289
Public Law 104-105, 179
Public Law 111-229, passage, 355
public notice/comments, posting, 91
public-private investment program (PPIP), 223
public-sector investments, distribution, 106
PUDs. *See* planned unit developments
purchase
commitment method, 6
contract, 545
purchase money mortgage, 249–250
purchase price, repayment, 480

Q

QM. *See* Quality Mortgage
QRM. *See* Qualified Residential Mortgages
qualification, VA income ratio method, 331–335
qualified agricultural real estate loan, 179–180
Qualified Mortgages, guidance, 11
Qualified Residential Mortgages (QRM) Rule, 655

qualified tax advisor, consultation, 24
qualifying conditions, 507
qualifying military/service personnel, 372, 374
qualifying veterans, spouses (eligibility), 374
Qualitative Analysis Appraisal Report, 448
Quality Mortgage (QM) appraisal issues, 501–502

R

Radian Group, Inc., 112
radon gas, 614, 616–617
testing, 617
RAM. *See* reverse annuity mortgage
ranch loans, 587–588
Ranieri Partners, 219
rate index, 288
"rate swings," limit, 308
ratios, usage, 401–402
rcanalytics.com, 654
RCRA. *See* Resources Conservation and Recovery Act of 1976
Real Capital Analytics, 654
real estate
advance payments, 20
bonds, 224–225
brokerage firms, 289
current real estate appraisal, 546
history/development, 238
loans, limits, 197
syndicates, operation methods, 17–18
trusts, 221–224
underwater status, 571–572
values, forces, 450

real estate cycle, 25–26
  phases, 26–27
real estate finance, 2–5
  FHA contributions, 370–371
  principle, consistency, 3
Real Estate Investment Trusts
  (REITs), 221–224, 568
  non-exchange-traded REITs,
    filings, 224
  specialized REITs, growth,
    223–224
*Real Estate Lending Survey
  Report* (ABA), 652, 653
real estate market
  implications, 286
  transactions, traits, 73
Real Estate Mortgage
  Investment Conduit
  (REMIC), 182, 190–191, 225
Real Estate Settlement
  Procedures Act (RESPA), 90,
  96–100, 119, 637
  amendment, 165, 220
  CFPB administration/
    enforcement, 123
  changes, occurrence, 218
  details, 96–98
  disclosure requirements, 99
  impact, 209
  notice provision, 457
  practice prohibitions, 99
  purpose, 96
  requirements, 121–127
  special information booklet,
    121–122
  violations, 99, 638
real estate transactions
  impacts, 598–599
  SEC regulations, 19–20
real property
  loans, financing, 30–31

manufactured homes,
  conversion, 529
realty funds, 18–19
"reason to know" test, passage,
  608
recapture, term (usage), 514
recording, action, 266–267
redemption
  equity right, 481
  right, 239
Red Flag Rules (FTC), 67
red flags, 328–329
redlining, 520
reduced rate contribution
  clauses, 261
referral fees, elimination, 96
referral websites, 650
refinance boom, occurrence, 36
refinancing
  benefits, 292
  costs, 293
  location, 292
  rate reduction, 292
  term, usage, 291
regional center, 575
Registered Mortgage Loan
  Originator (RMLO), 211–212
*Registration Requirements with
  HUD*, 554
regular mortgage, 241
regulated lenders, 82–83
  classes, 83–86
  CRA grading, 92
Regulation B, 55
Regulation BB, 55
Regulation D, compliance, 18
Regulation G, 55
Regulation M, 55
Regulation Q (Fed), 84, 160
Regulation X (CFPB), 122
Regulation Z, 55, 501

Regulation Z (Federal Reserve
  Board), 93
Regulation Z (Truth-in-Lending
  Act), 94–95
regulatory gaps, addressing, 104
Rehabilitation Home Mortgage
  Insurance, 347, 362–363
Reilly, William, 616
RE InfoLink (REIL), 512
REITs. *See* Real Estate
  Investment Trusts
release clause, 553
religious associations, funds, 230
religious facility financing,
  588–589
remaining useful life, 522
REMIC. *See* Real Estate
  Mortgage Investment
  Conduit
rental rates, reduction, 582
REO listings, 530
repayment
  plan types, discussion, 277
  track record, 551
reporting requirements, levels
  (USPAP definitions), 505
representative basis, 215–216
Request for Verification of
  Deposit (FNMA Form 1006),
  439–442
Request for Verification of
  Employment (FNMA Form
  1005), 443–445
required net basis yield, 284
rescission, right, 95–96
reserve requirements, 53–55
  placement, 54–55
reserves, 140–141
Residential Appraisal Field
  Review Report, 449
residential ARM requirements, 302

residential loans, 296–297, 394, 522
　application, information requirement, 397
　Closing Disclosure Settlement Statement, 129f–133f
　commercial loans, distinction, 538
　participation packages, reasons, 297
residential mortgage-backed securities (RMBSs), 182, 310
　ascendance, 297
residential mortgage pool, assumption, 169
residential mortgages, offering, 92
residential properties
　construction loans, 558–560
　contract basis, 558–559
　speculative basis, 559
　usage categories, 522–524
residential real estate
　decline, 28
　markets, peaks, 27t
　prices, downturns, 473
residential sector, time lag, 28
residual guideline, 332
　method, monthly basis (example), 405
residual income, 399, 401, 403
　excess residual income, 406
residual method, 403–406
residual value, 514
Resolution Trust Corporation (RTC), role, 76
Resona Bank, Limited, 230
resort housing, 523–524
resort-type developments, discount fee payment, 524

Resources Conservation and Recovery Act of 1976 (RCRA), 626
　amendment, 627
RESPA. *See* Real Estate Settlement Procedures Act
responsible parties, 601
restraint on alienation, 255
restrictive report, 505
　letter form, 505–506
retail store buildings, 573–574
　income/expenses, analysis, 573
　net lease, 574
retirement account statements, usage, 440
retirement programs, 201–202
Revenue Ruling 59-60, factors, 505
reverse annuity mortgage (RAM), 325–327
Reverse Mortgage Worksheet Guide, usage, 458
right of rescission. *See* rescission
rights-of-way, 146
right to sell/due-on-sale clause, assumption, 254–256
risk
　analysis, 550
　level, 32
　management, 539
　passage, 170
　risk-based mortgage loan pricing system, 655
　types, 538–539
RiverTower, renovation, 232
RK New York Design, 650
RMLO. *See* Registered Mortgage Loan Originator
roadways, direct access, 573
rollover, 247
Rosengren, Eric, 232

Royal Bank of Canada, 610
Rural Development Agency loans (USDA), 173
Rural Development Housing and Community Facilities Programs, 117
Rural Development Services, 350
Rural Develpment Agency (USDA), 115
rural housing loans, 180
Rural Housing Service (RHS), 115, 117
Rural Mission (USDA), 115
rural, term (usage), 519

S

SAFE Act. *See* Secure and Fair Enforcement for Mortgage Licensing Act of 2008
"safe harbor" procedure, 624
SAIF. *See* Savings Association Insurance Fund
salary, 59
sale
　leaseback, relationship, 14–15
　short sale, 16, 530
sale-and-leaseback technique, 15
sale of equity interests. *See* equity interests
sale of interests. *See* interests
sales
　comparison analysis, usage, 510–514
　sales and servicing contract, 215
sales/brokers, commission, 136
sales price
　asking price, relationship, 511
　tax purposes, 487
SAM. *See* shared appreciation mortgage

Savings Association Insurance Fund (SAIF), 75–76, 85
SAIF-insured savings associations, reports, 303
savings associations, 83–85
regulatory authorities, 79–80
savings bank, 80–81, 83
savings institutions, 83
elimination, 84–85
SBA. *See* Small Business Administration
Schedule A, information review, 463–464
Schedule B-1, 464
Sears, Roebuck & Company, development business, 575
secondary financing, 349
secondary market, 31
environmental requirements, 597–599
expansion, 161
impact, 642
investors, sales, 31
loan documents, 598
participants, 171–172
procedures, usage, 162–165
reemergence, 277
yield requirements, 217
second job, 59
Second Lien Modification Program (2MP), 473, 474
second-mortgage market, 229
Section 203(b) (FHA), 353
home mortgage insurance, 360–362
qualification, 365
Section 203(b)(Veteran), 361–362
Section 203(k)
maximum mortgage calculation, basis, 363
rehabilitation home mortgage insurance, 347, 360, 362–363
Section 203(h), borrower usage, 403
Section 245, Graduated-Payment Mortgage (GPM), 360, 363–367
factors, 367t
Section 245, insured commitment (calculation), 365–366
Section 245, replayment plans, 365
Section 1031 like-kind exchanges, impact, 19
sections, 533
securable manageable achievable retrievable transferable (SMART), 647
Secure and Fair Enforcement for Mortgage Licensing Act of 2008 (SAFE Act), 7, 90, 100–101, 103–104, 197
passage, 208
requirements, 204
Secure and Fair Enforcement for Mortgage Licensing Act of 2008, interpretation, 15
secured creditor exemption, 603
Securities and Exchange Commission (SEC)
creation, 19–20
regulations. *See* real estate.
requirements, 20
securities market, 226–228
securitizing mortgages, 216
security instrument, 239
security interest, 3
Selected Reserves, 372, 374
Selene Finance LP, 219
self-employed persons, 60–61
seller-financed home mortgages, 21–22
seller-financed transaction, 22
wrap, fitting, 251
server-based application, 640–641
service mortgage loan, transfer right, 457
service release premium, 640
servicer, notice (usage), 457
Servicing Disclosure Notice, lender provision, 457
Servicing Disclosure Statement, 122
servicing fee, 218–219
settlement
agent, 119
charges, 146
costs, disclosure, 128, 134
fees, 143
practices/costs, 135–146
prohibited practices, 134–135
total settlement charges, 146
Settlement Statement, 127–153
several, term (usage), 601
severance pay, tax crackdown, 486
shared appreciation mortgage (SAM), 324–325
shared equity mortgage, 325
share draft accounts, 54
shelter expenses, 331, 404
sheriff's sale, 479
Shinsei Bank, Limited, 230
shopping centers, 574–580
anchor tenant, 574–575
classification, 575
financing, 578–580
income/expenses, 576–577
operating expenses, 576–577
owner-occupied buildings, 578–579

percentage leases, 577–578
preleased space, 578, 579
speculative projects, 578, 579–580
shorter-term loans, 320–321
shorter-term mortgage loans, 198
short sale, 16, 530
short-term borrowing, federal discount rate (impact), 53f
short-term lease, usage, 572
simple assumption, 344
single-family homes, delinquency rates, 572
single-family housing, 517
mortgage insurance programs (FHA), 356
single-family mortgages, requirements, 598
sliding scale guaranty, 374, 376t
Small Business Administration (SBA), 115
Small Business Jobs Act, 301
small-denomination bonds, sale, 109
Small Entity Compliance Guide, 502
small landowner, permit, 622
Small Residential Income Property Appraisal Report, 513
SMART. *See* securable manageable achievable retrievable transferable
SmartBPM (Pegasystems), 641
SMART Doc Framework (Ver. 1), 647, 647f
"Smartphone Loan Technology," 649
software programs, development, 57
source-specific wastes (K-list), 601

SouthSide Works, 613
space
lease, 582–583
unit, classification, 524
special-purpose buildings, 567–569
applicant earnings record, 568
endorsement, 568
future purchase contract, 568–569
Specification for Gypsum Board (C1396/C1396M-14A), 610
speculative builder-investor, tenant attraction, 581
speculative office buildings, 581–582
speculative projects, 578, 579–580
"Spot Approval" process, elimination, 525
square footage, basis, 518
SR 9-4, usage, 505
SSL Certification, 650
stabilized income property, 583
"stabilized income property," acquisition, 581
standard (application classification), 643
"standby" charges, 551
standby commitment. *See* takeout commitment
state-chartered institutions, operation, 81
state-designated entities, 110
"stated income" loans, 277
state government programs, 110–111
state-mandated notices, examples, 458
Statement of Limiting Conditions and Appraiser's

Certification (Form 1004B), 128
statement of operations, 541
state programs, 110–113
Statutory Exemptions, 554
statutory lien period, expiration, 558
stock
certificates, 224
sale, large-scale operation, 222
straight note, 316–317
streamlined accept (application classification), 643
stressed property owner, loss conditions, 16–17
strict foreclosure, 480
strict liability, 601
structural concerns, addressing, 104
structured investment vehicles (SIVs) financing market, impact, 38
subdivision maintenance fees, 354
"subject to" mortgage, 250–251
subordinated agreement lease, 13–14
subordinate finance instruments, 246–252
subordination, 267–268
subprime borrowers, 294
subprime lending, 294–296
subprime loan market, rise, 636
subprime loans, 294
subprime market, FNMA/FHLMC control, 37
subprime mortgages, 182
substitution (appraisal principle), 504
suburban, term (usage), 519

Sumitomo Mitsui Banking Corporation, 230
Superfund. *See* Hazardous Waste Trust Fund
Superfund Act, 594
supervised lender, 383
supplier
   direct loan, 21
   finance, 20–21
   loans, 21
supply and demand (appraisal principle), 503
supremacy, federal claim, 299
surveys, 146, 530–531, 546
   legal description, 531–533
swaps, impact, 170
sweat equity contribution, 408
syndication, 17–18

T

TAF. *See* The Appraisal Foundation
takeout commitment (standby commitment), 5, 559–560
taking, term (usage), 623
TAPA. *See* Texas Administrative Procedures Act
tariff laws, promulgation/enforcement, 70
TARP. *See* Troubled Asset Relief Program
tax(es)
   assessment, 263
   deductions, 301–302
   impacts, 486–488
   law, effect, 293
   liabilities, 404
   promulgation/enforcement, 70
   reserves, 542–543
   tax-deferred basis, 19
   tax-exempt bonds, 184–185

Tax Act (1993), 301
Tax Act (1986), revisions, 301
Tax Cuts and Jobs Act of 2017, 488
Tax Relief, Unemployment Insurance Reauthorization, and Job Creation Act of 2010 (Tax Relief of 2010), 301
teaser rate, 310
   proliferation, 317
temporary buydown mortgage, 312–313
temporary "Making Home Affordable" programs, 473–478
tenants
   anchor tenant, 574–575
   financial stability, 206
   tenant-occupied property, 522
Term Asset-Backed Securities Loan Facility (Federal Reserve), 223
term leases, 572–573
term loan, 316–317
term mortgage, 316–317
Test Methods for Chemical Analysis of Gypsum and Gypsum Products, 610
Texas Administrative Procedures Act (TAPA), 101
Texas Department of Housing and Community Affairs (TDHCA), 114
Texas Finance Code
   Chapter 156, *de minimis* exception, 7
   Chapter 343, 458
Texas Government Code, requirements/provisions, 101–103
Texas loan programs, 113–115
Texas Open Meetings Act, incorporation, 101

Texas Real Estate Commission (TREC), 101
Texas Real Estate Commission Standards & Enforcement Services Division (TREC SES), 103
Texas State Affordable Housing Corporation (TSAHC), 115
Texas Veterans Land Board, 110
Texas Veterans Land Fund, 113
The Appraisal Foundation (TAF), 497
   FHFA meeting, 513–514
The Appraisal Institute, 502
third-mortgage market, 229
third-party fees, usage, 499–500
third-party mortgage loan servicing operation, 219
Thompson, Elizabeth, 25
three Cs. *See* capability, credit, collateral
thrift institutions (thrifts), 83
   supervision, 70
Tier 1 (partial entitlements), 376–377
   limit, 377
TILA. *See* Truth-in-Lending Act
time deposits, 48, 83
time-interval method, 556
title
   abstract. *See* abstract of title.
   charges, 143
   commitment, 463–464
   equitable title, 245
   examination, 144
   protection, 459
   qualification, 459–463
   search, 144
   services, 143–145
Title 1 (home improvement loan insurance), 360, 367–368

Title 38, Section 3703(d), 312
title companies, 135, 229
title insurance, 461–462
   binder, 144
      fees, 144
   lenders, policy, 462
   payer, identification, 462
   protection, 144
title insurance owners
   policy, 461
   title insurance, 145
title theory, 240
   lien theory, contrast, 257
Title XI, impact, 496
tobacco smoke, 614
"Top Loan Origination Systems," 653
Torrens, Robert, 462
Torrens system, 462–463
total debt, repayment, 480
total interest cost, reduction, 277
   mortgages, impact, 320–323
"Total Open To Approved Lenders" (TOTAL), FHA introduction, 350–351
total settlement charges, 146
total transaction accounts, 54
township, section, 533f
toxic waste sites, 599–614
   first federal action, 600
   problem, discovery, 599–600
toxic waste sites, cleanup, 594
   laws, 598
   liability, exemption, 595
transaction screen, 609
   ESAs, 609
transfer charges, 145–146
Transunion, information, 66, 419
Treasury bill (T-bill) rate, 281
Treasury rate, history, 282–283

TREC. See Texas Real Estate Commission
TREC SES. See Texas Real Estate Commission Standards & Enforcement Services Division
TRID. See Truth in Lending/Real Estate Settlements Procedure Integrated Disclosure
triple net, 574
Troubled Asset Relief Program (TARP), 77
   capital, usage, 223
   financing, 223
trust. See deed of trust
   form, 259–265
trust income, 60
Truth-in-Lending
   disclosure, lender usage, 457
   regulation, 302
   rules, amendment, 3234
Truth-in-Lending Act (TILA), 45, 55, 90–, 93–96
   amendments, implementation, 501
   interest cost disclosure requirements, 209
   Regulation Z, 94–95
   requirements, 639
Truth in Lending/Real Estate Settlements Procedure Integrated Disclosure (TRID), 123
   sample, 124f–126f
   tolerance buckets, 98t
TTB. See Alcohol and Tobacco Tax and Trade Bureau
Two Harbors Investment Corp., 223
two-step mortgage, 316

U

UAD. See Uniform Appraisal Dataset
UCC. See Uniform Commercial Code
UCDP. See Uniform Collateral Data Portal
UFMIP. See up-front mortgage information premium
U-list (discarded commercial chemical products), 601
UMDP. See Uniform Mortgage Data Processing
underground storage tanks (USTs), 626–627
   handling, 598
   impact. See loan.
   owners, safety precautions, 626
underlying fee, 12
underwater property, 15–16, 571–572
Underwriter's Guide (HUD/FHA), 352, 369
underwriters, loan purchase policies (constraints), 35
underwriting, 494
   acquisition, 166
   due diligence, 297
   guidelines, 359t
   manual underwriting, 57, 639–640
   purchase, 167–171
   three Cs, 58
Uniform Appraisal Dataset (UAD)
   discussion, 514
   electronic appraisal data file submission, 512
   requirement, 499

Uniform Collateral Data Portal
(UCDP)
  FHFA development, 512
  introduction, 514
Uniform Commercial Code
(UCC)
  provisions, 250
  regulation, 528
Uniform Interagency Consumer
Compliance Rating System
(CC Rating System), 55
uniform loan documentation,
GSE-conforming loans
(impact), 268–269
Uniform Mortgage Data
Processing (UMDP) initiative,
514
Uniform Residential Appraisal
Report (URAR), 128, 420,
448, 499, 513
  examination, 446–456
  FNMA Form 1004/FHLMC
    Form 70 revision, 500–501
  sample, 451–456
  sample items, 523
Uniform Residential Loan
Application (URLA),
127–128
  acknowledgments/agreements
    (Section 6), 421
  borrower information
    (Section 1), 421–426
  declarations (Section 5), 421,
    431–433
  demographic information
    (Section 7), 421
  examination, 420–438
  financial information–assets/
    liabilities (Section 2), 421,
    427
  financial information–real
    estate (Section 3), 421,
    427–428
  loan and property
    information (Section 4),
    421, 429–431
  loan originator information
    (Section 8), 421
  requirements, 642–643
  sample, 434–438
  sections, 421
Uniform Standards of
Professional Appraisal
Practice (USPAP), 497, 498
  "Appraisal Report," 506
  change, 504
  compliance, 501
  Departure Provision, 505
  Standards Rule 2-2(a), 506
United States Department of
Agricultural Development,
117–118
United States Department of
Agriculture (USDA)
  Rural Development Agency,
    115
  Rural Mission, 115
United States Government,
fiscal policies, 281
United States, monetary system
(usage), 44–5
universal account, 656
unpaid intereset, accumulation,
311–312
unreported income, 59
unsubordinated ground lease,
13
up-front information,
requirement, 302–303
up-front mortgage information
premium (UFMIP), 341, 355
  partial refund, 343
  practice exercise, 357–358
up-front premiums, 357
  choice, 326–327
URAR. See Uniform Residential
Appraisal Report
urban, term (meaning), 519
urea-formaldehyde foam
  insulation, impact, 597
  popularity, 614
URLA. See Uniform Residential
Loan Application
usage concept, analysis, 550
U.S. credit markets, funds
(raising), 280t
U.S. geodetic survey, 532–533
U.S. Green Building Council
(USGBC), 606
U.S. Mint, 69–74
  coin production, 70
USPAP. See Uniform Standards
of Professional Appraisal
Practice
U.S. Treasury, 69–74
  security rates, 284
USTs. See underground storage
tanks
usury, 285–286
utilities
  adequacy, 518
  service, separation, 576
utility bonds, 225

V

VA. See Department of Veterans
Affairs
value
  approaches, 507
  determination, 407
  estimate, 495, 508
  estimation, act/process, 446
  market value, 407

Van De Mieroop, Marc, 2
VantageScore 2.0, 419
VantageScore 4.0, 419
variable loan-to-value limits, elimination, 341
variable-rate mortgage (VRM), 288
vendors, lien, 249
veteran
   compensation, 381
   eligibility, 372
   entitlement, substitution, 378
   home loan guarantee eligibility requirements, 373t
   liability, release, 379–380
   non-spouse co-ownership, 379
   rights, 378–379
   surviving spouse, death, 381
Veterans Home Improvement Program (VHIP), 113–114
Veterans Housing Act of 1970, 384–385
Veterans Housing Assistance Program (VHAP), 113
Veterans Land Board (VLB), 113
vLender, 651
volatile organic compounds (VOCs), 614
VRM. *See* variable-rate mortgage

W

waiting periods, basis, 97
wait periods, 97
walking money, 553
Wall Street investment banks, bailing out, 77
Wall Street Reform and Consumer Financial Protection Act of 2010 (Dodd-Frank Act), 39, 75, 90, 103, 277, 501
   impact, 53
   requirements, 209
   RESPA amendment, 165
   risk retention requirements, 655
   signing, 285–286
warehouse buildings, 583–585
   construction design, 584–585
   facility, usage, 584
   general warehouse, 584–585
   mini warehouses, 585
   net lease, 585
   office/warehouses, 585
warehouse lines of credit, 198, 214
warranty
   deed, 461, 545
   plan, 407
Washington Mutual, option ARM development, 309
Washington State, Model Toxics Control Act, 604–605
waste producers, impact, 629–630
water, lead (presence), 620
web-based user interface, 648
WebCaster (Calyx), 641, 651
Wells Fargo N.A., 83, 482
wetlands
   areas, protection, 598
   criteria, 621
   definition, 621
   effect, 622
   protection, 620–622
willingness to pay, 64
Woolley, Leonard, 2
worker productivity, 607
workforce productivity, increase, 47–48
work, type, 62
World Savings, legal case, 638
wraparound mortgage, 251

Y

yield, 32, 162
   adjustment, loan pricing (usage), 162–163
   conversion, 164t
   defining, 163–165
   Fannie Mae/Freddie Mac-administered yield requirements, 283–284
   net yield, 162
   required net basis yield, 284
yield spread premium (YSP), 217, 218, 640
Yturria, Frank, 624

Z

zero balance checking account, offering, 48
zoning
   requirements, 546–547
   restrictions, 596